JAPANESE INDUSTRIALIZATION

AND ITS SOCIAL CONSEQUENCES

Sponsored by
the Social Science Research Council

This volume is one of a series on Japanese society published by the University of California Press under a special arrangement with the Social Science Research Council. Each volume is based upon a conference attended by Japanese and foreign scholars; the purpose of each conference was to increase scholarly knowledge of Japanese society by enabling Japanese and foreign scholars to collaborate and to criticize each other's work. The conferences were sponsored by the Joint Committee on Japanese Studies of the American Council of Learned Societies and the Social Science Research Council, with funds provided by the Ford Foundation.

JAPANESE INDUSTRIALIZATION AND ITS SOCIAL CONSEQUENCES

Edited by
HUGH PATRICK
with the assistance of
LARRY MEISSNER

1976

UNIVERSITY OF CALIFORNIA PRESS
Berkeley · Los Angeles · London

University of California Press
Berkeley and Los Angeles, California

University of California Press, Ltd.
London, England

ISBN 0-520-03000-1
Library of Congress Catalog Card Number: 75-7199
Printed in the United States of America

Contents

Editors' Note

Japanese personal names are written in the Western order of given plus family name. Japanese government agencies are cited by their Japanese names to facilitate finding the sources in library card catalogs. All information contained in figures and tables has been included in the Index.

Contributors

JOHN W. BENNETT is Professor of Anthropology, Washington University, St. Louis.

TUVIA BLUMENTHAL is Associate Professor of Economics, Tel-Aviv University, Tel-Aviv.

MASAYOSHI CHŪBACHI is Professor of Economics, Keio University, Tokyo.

ROBERT E. COLE is Associate Professor of Sociology, University of Michigan, Ann Arbor.

HIROSHI HAZAMA is Professor of Sociology, Tokyo Kyoiku University, Tokyo.

SOLOMON B. LEVINE is Professor of Business and Economics, University of Wisconsin, Madison.

RYOSHIN MINAMI is Associate Professor of Economics, Economic Research Institute, Hitotsubashi University, Tokyo.

HIROSHI OHBUCHI is Professor of Economics, Chuo University, Tokyo.

AKIRA ONO is Professor of Economics, Seikei University, Tokyo.

HUGH PATRICK is Professor of Economics, Yale University, New Haven.

WILLIAM V. RAPP is with Morgan Guaranty Trust Company, Tokyo.

GARY R. SAXONHOUSE is Associate Professor of Economics, University of Michigan, Ann Arbor.

KOJI TAIRA is Professor of Economics and Labor and Industrial Relations, University of Illinois, Champaign.

KEN'ICHI TOMINAGA is Professor of Sociology, Tokyo University, Tokyo.

TSUNEHIKO WATANABE is Professor of Economics, Osaka University, Osaka.

KOZO YAMAMURA is Professor of Economics, University of Washington, Seattle.

YASUKICHI YASUBA is Professor, Center for Southeast Asian Studies, Kyoto University, Kyoto.

Preface

This volume is the result of a conference held 20-24 August 1973 at the University of Washington's Lake Wilderness conference center outside Seattle. The Conference on Japanese Industrialization and Its Social Consequences was one of a series of five international conferences planned under the auspices of the Joint Committee on Japanese Studies of the American Council of Learned Societies and the Social Science Research Council. Funds for the conference series were provided by the Ford Foundation in a grant to the Social Science Research Council in 1969.

The conference, and this volume, benefited from considerable lead time, extensive planning, and the cooperative efforts of a number of persons. The main work in determining specific themes, identifying potential paper-writers, and selecting other participants was done by the planning committee, consisting of John W. Bennett, Washington University; Solomon Levine, University of Wisconsin; Kazushi Ohkawa, Hitotsubashi University; Henry Rosovsky, Harvard University; Koji Taira, University of Illinois at Urbana-Champaign; Tsunehiko Watanabe, Osaka University; Kozo Yamamura, University of Washington; Yasukichi Yasuba, Kyoto University; and myself as chairman. The committee encouraged collaborative research where feasible and desirable; four of the twelve papers in this volume are the result of intensive collaborative efforts. The conference budget contained very limited funds for research support; these nonetheless were particularly helpful in making three papers possible. John Creighton Campbell of the Social Science Research Council aided substantially in these preparatory stages.

The participants in the conference were twenty-five economists, sociologists, and anthropologists from the United States, Japan, England, and Israel. They were John W. Bennett, Washington University; Tuvia Blumenthal, Tel-Aviv University; Martin Bronfenbrenner, Duke University; Masayoshi Chūbachi, Keio University; Robert E. Cole, University of Michigan; Ronald Dore, University of Sussex; Hiroshi Hazama, Tokyo Kyoiku University; Solomon Levine, University of Wisconsin; Ryoshin Minami, Hitotsubashi University; James Nakamura, Columbia University; Chie Nakane, Tokyo University; Hiroshi Ohbuchi, Chuo University; Kazushi Ohkawa, Hitotsubashi University (emeritus); Akira Ono, Seikei University; Hugh Patrick, Yale University; William V. Rapp, Morgan Guaranty Trust Company; Henry Rosovsky, Harvard University; Gary Saxonhouse, University of Michigan; David L. Sills, Social Science Research Council; Michio Sumiya, Tokyo

University; Koji Taira, University of Illinois at Urbana-Champaign; Ken'ichi Tominaga, Tokyo University; Tsunehiko Watanabe, Osaka University; Kozo Yamamura, University of Washington; and Yasukichi Yasuba, Kyoto University. Susan B. Hanley, University of Washington, capably and effectively took care of all local arrangements, as well as serving as a rapporteur. Larry Meissner, Yale University, was the main rapporteur; John Wisnom, University of Washington, assisted both in their responsibilities.

The original drafts of the twelve papers contained in this volume provided the foci for the conference discussions. Participants were expected to have read the papers in advance, so it was not necessary for authors to present them. Instead, two or three discussants presented prepared comments on each paper; the author was given the opportunity to reply; and a general discussion followed. The discussions were extraordinarily frank, direct, friendly, critical, and interdisciplinary. All participants—paper-writers and discussants—took an active role in making the conference a success. It was not a meeting in which most Japanese participants took one position and most American participants took another. Americans criticized Americans and Japanese; Japanese criticized Japanese and Americans. I believe the fine rapport was achieved both because of the high level of professionalism of the participants and because most of them already knew one another. Others have pointed to the virtually continuous Ping-Pong game outside meeting hours as both a highly integrative and competitive force.

The conference discussions subjected each paper to thorough analysis, which resulted in substantial revision by the authors for inclusion in this volume. To that has been added extensive editing, particularly by Larry Meissner who has done a job beyond the call of duty.

Louise Danishevsky has, as always, efficiently handled the retyping and duplication of edited manuscripts and a myriad of other small but essential details. To all who have contributed so much to make the conference a success and this volume possible, I offer my thanks.

HUGH PATRICK
Yale University

An Introductory Overview

HUGH PATRICK

Japanese economic development has been a source of fascination for foreigners and Japanese alike, not only in its purely economic context as well as its broader social, political, and cultural context but also for purposes of international comparison. Much research by economists has focused on establishing the general contours of Japan's process of economic growth in the aggregate. Even discussions of industrialization—particularly those in Western languages—have tended to be aggregative in nature. At the same time other social scientists have examined other features of the Japanese process of change, usually taking as given the concurrent process of economic development.

Substantive research seldom occurs in a vacuum. The topics deemed important, the questions asked, are inevitably influenced by perception of the states of knowledge and ignorance — by the results of earlier research. At the Conference on Japanese Industrialization and Its Social Consequences, held in August 1973, the intellectual antecedents of the participants have several major strands, reflecting the diversity of the group. Many American and some Japanese participants felt a linkage to certain of the earlier conferences on Japanese modernization, particularly the Conference on the State and Economic Enterprise in Japan, under William W. Lockwood's chairmanship, and the Conference on Social Change in Modern Japan under Ronald P. Dore's chairmanship, both held in 1963. In important respects the conference resulting in this book was also related, at least for the economists participating, to two international conferences on the macro features of the Japanese long-run growth experience held in Japan in 1966 and 1972 under the chairmanship of Kazushi Ohkawa.[1] One consequence of these results has been the realization of the need for future research to turn to more microeconomic issues, and especially to explore the interrelation between social and economic variables in order to understand the Japanese experience better.

This book is both ambitious and, in certain significant respects, limited. Its ambition lies in attempting to analyze the interrelationships among the broad themes, Japanese industrialization and its social consequences, and in bringing together at the conference specialists on Japan from anthropology, economics, and sociology to consider problems of common or overlapping interest.

---

[1]The results of these four conferences are published in Lockwood (1965), Dore (1967), Klein and Ohkawa (1968), and Ohkawa and Hayami (1973).

1

We recognized from the beginning this would be a pioneering effort, for it meant exploration of topics not yet well covered in the literature. More importantly, we recognized analysis of the feedback among aspects of industrialization and social change in Japan, as elsewhere, is complex and difficult at best. Nonetheless this is the first book in Western languages treating Japanese industrialization which provides extensive emphasis on the social dimensions. The limitation is that we certainly far from succeeded in fully integrating social and economic theory and data. We did not plan the conference with any preconceived, overreaching framework of comprehensive hypotheses, nor did we attempt to end up with any such framework. This was probably unavoidable in what was, after all, a major innovative effort to explore the effects of industrialization on social change. As such it was inevitable that only a few of the possible causal interrelationships and effects could be treated.

This book reflects certain other limits imposed by the conference planning committee. We attempted to cover the entire time period from early Meiji (which began in 1868) to the present. It should be remembered that we are considering an evolutionary, historical process of industrial development and social change; the Japan of 1975 is far different from the Japan of a century ago. Inevitably, the committee had to delimit the topics to be considered, and to some extent were constrained by the research interest and activities of possible paper-writers. Because considerable research at the macro level on Japanese industrialization has recently appeared in English,[2] the committee asked certain authors to prepare microeconomic studies of three selected industries and other authors to focus on selected aspects of the industrialization process itself. The range of possible social consequences of the industrialization process is extraordinarily wide; the committee had to select a few that seemed of major importance and amenable to treatment within the context of the conference. Perhaps the greatest delimitation was the decision to exclude from formal consideration the other side of the coin: the social *causes* of industrialization, as distinct from consequences. We leave this important theme to future research. Inevitably, social causes did creep into the discussions and the papers themselves, as in the theme of paternalism or examination of the role of female workers.

Each of the papers in this volume stands on its own as a significant new contribution in English to our understanding of Japan. At the same time there is substantial overlapping and interrelation of themes among most of the papers, as authors examine different facets of the same general problem. This provides much greater continuity and focus to this volume than occurs in some conference results. It also poses some problems of classification, for several alternative schemes are valid. The papers here are divided into three parts—those dealing with evolving sociological and economic aspects of Japanese as industrial workers, those treating specific industries and the issues and problems associated with various features of industrial firms by size, and

[2]See, in addition to the items cited in the previous footnote, Ohkawa and Rosovsky (1973).

those examining certain important social consequences of industrialization.

In the initial paper in this volume Hazama summarizes and generalizes from his extensive research published in Japanese on the evolution of life styles of industrial workers. Cole and Tominaga examine the changing occupational composition of Japanese workers, and consider the concept of occupation in Japan in terms both of the relatively low level of occupational consciousness and the importance of occupational position as providing information on such important aspects of stratification as a worker's economic status, political opinions, and educational career. Saxonhouse, in a paper which in certain respects is also an industry study, examines labor-force recruitment and technological diffusion in the prewar cotton-spinning industry.

In addition to cotton-spinning, two other industries of importance in Japan's historical industrialization process are examined. Blumenthal analyzes the growth of, technological induction in, and the role of government in the development of the shipbuilding industry. Yamamura examines the origins, growth, and continued evolution in function of the large, general trading firms (*sōgō shōsha*), one of the few uniquely Japanese economic institutions in modern industrial societies. Three papers compare aspects of the economies of scale and production in large and small firms, a theme that came up in many contexts throughout the conference. Rapp examines the evolving structure of export production and industrial development in terms of the changing shares of small and large firms in exports in a paper related to Yamamura's discussion. Yasuba traces and analyzes the emergence and widening of wage differentials by size of factory in a number of industries for the prewar and the postwar periods. The differential structure in wages has had profound implications for life style, income distribution, poverty, the nature of labor-management relations, and the like—as is apparent in a number of the other papers. Minami stresses the significance of electrification and particularly the development of small electric motors in enabling small firms to compete on relatively less disadvantageous terms with large firms, thereby narrowing productivity and wage differentials from what might have been the case otherwise (assuming small firms could have continued to exist, certainly true for some industries).

A major purpose of this volume is to break new ground in exploration of the social consequences of Japanese industrialization, which are many, varied, complex, and on the whole relatively unexplored, at least in publications in Western languages. Perhaps one of the most fundamental changes in Japan is summed up as demographic transition: Japanese population growth accelerated with initial industrialization, and then slowed, and the patterns of fertility and mortality have changed dramatically. Ohbuchi considers this transition, with particular emphasis on the socioeconomic forces bringing it about. He also evaluates critically the various estimates of population size and growth from early Meiji to the first population census in 1920. Ono and Watanabe examine changes in income distribution, particularly between rural and urban areas, as a consequence of the process of industrialization. This, too, is an area in which data are poor and not much research has been done on either the historical or the postwar period. Chūbachi and Taira examine the concept and facts of poverty, particularly urban poverty, over the course of Japanese industrialization—another important, relatively new area of research.

In treating the theme of social consequences, the planning committee was concerned that the conference incorporate consideration of major social costs of industrialization as well as benefits and other effects. We also thought it useful that, although most papers would focus on rather precise topics, one paper should be devoted to a broader assessment of the social effects of the industrialization process, building in part on the analyses of the other papers prepared for the conference. Bennett and Levine have prepared such a paper: they focus on the undesired consequences — social costs, absolute and relative deprivation — that have manifested themselves and become widely perceived as social problems. This has occurred mainly within the past decade. They examine the welfare gap, environmental problems, population density and urbanization, and conditions of work and leisure, particularly as they come to cut across classes, occupations, and geographical boundaries.

It is impossible to summarize succinctly yet adequately the main findings of these papers, or to convey the richness of evidence and analysis they embody. Nor is it the purpose of this introductory overview. Rather, in what follows I discourse on some of the major themes of the conference and of this volume, problems of methodology, and related matters.

APPROACH

The conference discussions fortunately did not bog down in disputes on methodology or terminology. Happily, the participants steered away from such vague and complex concepts as "modernization versus Westernization" and "modern versus traditional," although they did consider the concepts of "economic dualism" and "paternalism." The papers reflect these efforts at precision. While trying to isolate certain issues and utilize case studies fully, the participants struggled with the problem of recognizing that everything relating to the conference topic depends on everything else. This was true not only in an input-output sense—the use of electric motors by small enterprises depended on both electrification and a motor-producing industry, and shipbuilding and innovations in that industry depended on the availability and improved quality of steel, for instance—but also true of interdependence among a host of economic and social variables. Many of the consequences of industrialization have been unintended, or certainly not well understood when they first appeared. Who, for example, a hundred years ago would have anticipated the effects of industrialization and urbanization on fertility and mortality rates?

With regard to methodology, it may be noted that on the whole the approach of all authors is comparative, and a number of the papers explicitly incorporate comparative data. This is important and desirable, though it was not one of the major mandates of the planning committee. Fortunately, there were few assertions in the papers or at the conference that Japanese were either unique or just like Westerners. It was pointed out that surplus labor and wage differentials by size of firm are characteristic of certain other developing countries as well as Japan; what is impressive is that substantial wage and productivity differentials have persisted since the early phases of modern industrialization. On the other hand, the evolution of the general trading company in its prewar and contemporary roles is an institutional development not replicated elsewhere. The participants noted Japanese firms were particularly skilled at absorbing foreign technology, although all were puzzled as to how and why. The cotton-spinning case study provides important insights, as is discussed further on.

In retrospect, the conference discussions were dominated by two interrelated themes: the conditions of people as industrial workers (in contradistinction, say, to consumers or farmers), and differences between large enterprises and small. This was mainly the consequence of the topics selected for papers, the selection of authors, and particularly the choice of participants. It was clear throughout the conference that the most significant interfacing of knowledge, methodology, and interests among the participants from different social sciences had to do with workers—such issues as their life styles, occupation, mobility, distribution by sex, wage differentials, and the causes thereof. This volume is somewhat broader in its coverage, for other social consequences are emphasized as well as those affecting Japanese as industrial workers.

LARGE AND SMALL ENTERPRISES COMPARED

The participants noted how certain constellations of features seemed to characterize particular phenomena when data were not adequate to determine either essential features or the relative importance of various features. For example, large firms were described as having new and usually imported technologies, skilled male labor, more capital per worker, higher output per worker, higher wages, and a special life style—in comparison with small enterprises. Yet the cotton-spinning industry—quantitatively by far the most important of the early modern industries engaging in large-scale units of production—depended mainly on unskilled female labor, who had a very different life style. And, as Yasuba shows, very small firms could not coexist with large once cotton spinning was well established, by 1910 or so.

Large firms were also described as either more or less paternalistic than small, according to the definition used. Nakane stressed the involvement of close personal relationships in paternalism, with discretionary modes of behavior making it applicable mainly to small firms. Dore and Cole contrasted this kind of paternalism with the mangerial or institutional paternalism of large firms in which benefits are determined by impersonal rules rather than by personal relationships. Yasuba suggested large firms have to pay higher wages and fringe benefits to compensate for their *lack* of personal paternalism. Minami regarded this as one aspect of a fundamental behavioral difference between large and small (family-owned) enterprises: large firms can be characterized as attempting predominantly to maximize economic goals (profits, growth), whereas owners of small firms, especially those using unpaid family workers, do not behave as economic maximizers but as the urban equivalents of agricultural households concerned with total family income and average income-sharing rather than marginalist calculations. Most of the conference participants agreed with the propositions concerning large firms. The characterization of small firms remains in dispute, however—a manifestation of the economic dualism controversy between those who characterize Japan as having gone through a classical surplus-labor economy phase and those who reject that interpretation in favor of a neoclassicist historical model of abundant labor with low productivity and wages equal to labor's marginal product.

Minami's position reflects his synthesis of two quite different ways in which the participants, following the rather confused literature, used the concept of economic dualism. At one point in the conference all were asked to write down their definition of dualism, and these were circulated to clarify varying uses of the term. One use stressed the phenomenon of wage differentials by size of firm within the same industry. The other definition of dualism was the classical two-sector case, in which labor in the modern, manufacturing, large-enterprise sector is paid its marginal product because owners are profit maximizers, and (surplus) labor in the traditional, agricultural, small-scale sector receives more than its marginal product because owners behave according to some sharing, average, or institutional (constant institutional wage) principle different from profit maximizing. This second concept was in the background in most of the conference discussion, but is explicitly incorporated into the papers by Minami and by Ono and Watanabe. The latter associate the postwar narrowing of income differentials with the ending of the surplus labor phase of Japan's development.

The framing of dualism primarily in economic terms was, in retrospect, excessively narrow. As some at the conference stressed, dualism is a comprehensive, complex, social phenomenon: economic variables are important but not all-encompassing. And many of the costs and benefits of dualism are social, not simply economic. The emphasis on economic criteria reflects the greater research on Japanese dualism by economists than other social scientists. This remains one topic (among many) for which a more comprehensive and integrated approach is needed.

WAGE DIFFERENTIALS

The wage differential issue is important in understanding not only the historical process of development in Japan, but the continuing process in developing countries today, for it is a general phenomenon with significant implications for policy in resource allocation and income distribution. We all well understand some wage differentials are inevitable and desirable, for example, differentials arising from occupational differences in skill requirements and in attractiveness of work. These differentials are associated with evolving demands for different types of labor and with evolving supplies of such labor based on education and on-the-job training. One might also expect some regional differences in wages because of local labor markets, costs of moving, and differences in costs of living.

Dualism in wage differentials refers to contexts in which they remain—typically by size of firm or by sex—even after adjustments are made for differences in labor skills, abilities, regions, and types of work. Standard economic analysis indicates such dualism should not persist over time. If in fact it does, we need to consider both possible economic and noneconomic (social) causes of such dualism. Yasuba finds that even after standardization for sex, age, operating day, and rough occupational categories, wage differentials by size of firm do exist, that they started prior to World War I (earlier than previously thought), and that they widened within given industries and increased among industries by the 1930s.

The conference did not consider the explanations of wage differentials by sex, a topic on which little research on Japan has been done. Part of the problem is that men and women are usually in different occupational categories; relatively few occupations employ both male and female workers. My understanding is that sexist discrimination now occurs in Japan not so much in initially paying women lower wages than men for the same work as in preventing women from entering or being promoted into more highly skilled occupations, and in providing women lesser wage increments by seniority, lesser retirement benefits, and the like.

A further economic explanation of wage differentials lies in capital market imperfections, whereby differentials by size of firm in availability and cost of borrowed funds are greater than differences in degrees of risk of default and in transaction costs of loans. Several papers suggest large firms not only have been able to borrow funds at substantially lower interest rates than small firms, but also have greater access to funds. This makes it profitable for large firms to use relatively more capital and less labor than small firms. Two theoretical implications, supported by empirical evidence (some of which is in Yasuba's paper), are that the profit per unit of capital would be lower in large firms, and that output per worker would be greater in large firms. These capital market imperfections may result from a variety of possible causes: ignorance of actual risks, a high degree of risk aversion, governmental restrictions on interest rates and on the operations of financial institutions, non-profit-maximizing behavior by large financial institutions, and/or oligopolistic power of financial institutions. One analytical dilemma is that although capital market imperfections make it possible for large firms to have more capital and output per worker, there is no explanation of why management actually pays workers more. Clearly more than ability to pay has to be involved. Equally important, Yasuba provides data suggesting the rate of interest was not significantly higher for small firms in the early 1930s; this, however, may have been a temporary phenomenon. Certainly in the postwar period borrowing costs have been substantially higher for small firms than large.

A number of plausible causes of wage differentials by size of firm after adjustment for normal economic explanations were considered at the conference. Cole emphasized that forces which may have caused wage differentials initially do not necessarily explain their continuation, or their widening or narrowing. The participants also recognize the importance of distinguishing conceptually and empirically between issues concerning the existence of such dualism and issues concerning its degree, both in number of workers involved and in the size of wage differentials.

As causes of wage differentials, Dore and others emphasized institutional features that distinguish large firms from small. Dore pointed to (1) the practices by large firms of hiring workers directly from school, providing formal on-the-job training, and seniority wage increments; (2) to changes in labor legislation; and (3) in the postwar period to the rise of unions. Many economists, particularly Taira, have stressed that the development of permanent employment and seniority increments before World War I, which became more widespread among large firms in the 1920s and 1930s, were rational efforts by management to reduce costs of labor turnover and especially the loss of skilled workers. Moreover in the early postwar period of economic disruption, the newly strong union movement put great emphasis on job security, and to some extent wages according to need, which was related to seniority. Thus, these institutional patterns were deliberately created by profit-maximizing entrepreneurs; yet when firmly established, they have both taken on an independent character and have been absorbed into union goals. They are now institutions which have to be accepted more or less as givens by large enterprises. And they have had considerable social consequences, for example, on workers' life styles.

Another variable important in the explanation of wage differentials, according to the analysis and evidence presented by Yasuba, was the process of induction of foreign technology. Virtually all Japanese industries relied on foreign technology. Large firms, not small, typically imported foreign technology and adapted it to their specific organizations. Such technology often required skilled labor, which in part was trained on the job. Although some of the skills may have been general enough to be transferred if the worker moved to another firm, some were specific to the particular firm's technology; thus the worker was more productive in that firm than elsewhere. Moreover, the process of diffusion of technology to smaller firms, or indeed to other large firms, was relatively slow. A firm benefited from retaining skilled workers by paying higher wages, recouping the costs of training workers from that component of their higher productivity specific to the firm which accordingly did not have to be paid out in wages. This theory is supported by Yasuba's evidence that wage differentials were more predominant in industries undergoing rapid technological change. However, one would expect once an innovation has been diffused to all firms, the productivity differentials and wage differentials would disappear. Thus, to explain the persistence of wage differentials, either firm-specific differences in technology that benefit large firms must persist, or the flow of technology importation and innovation by large firms must be continuous.

This theory is also supported by Saxonhouse's evidence on the cotton-spinning industry, where technology was not firm-specific. The industry's technology was indeed foreign; virtually all spindles were imported until 1925 from one British company, which maintained a staff of engineers in Japan. The technology did not change rapidly, and it was relatively easy to learn. Moreover, Bōren, the Cotton-Spinners Trade Association (cartel), diffused innovations rapidly among all cotton-spinning firms through technical publications, exchange of engineers, and the like. Thus, there were no firm-specific technologies requiring firm-specific skills. A firm would not hesitate to hire a competent worker away from another firm. And what do we find? No system of permanent employment of production workers, low seniority increments (presumably reflecting the real learning-by-doing that occurred), apparently relatively small wage differentials by size of firm (mainly because, unlike other industries, no really small firms could survive), and continuing high turnover of each cohort of entering workers even after factory living conditions improved over the early years of this century (about half of the new entrants left the firm within six months). In other words, where there was no technological gap, wage differentials were not significant.

This is all very neat—except for the fact the cotton-spinners were female, typically young, and unmarried. One might argue that in Japan, even in the early stages of industrialization, women were not expected to work permanently or to become highly skilled. They were expected to work for a few years and then quit to marry. So perhaps the firm-size wage differential is a phenomenon that developed primarily for males. However, as Saxonhouse has shown, women left the cotton-spinning industry much too quickly and hence at too young an age simply for marriage; they continued in the labor force for awhile, being absorbed in other sectors. As permanent employment and seniority increments become increasingly institutionalized in the postwar period and as wages rise, female workers in large firms also benefit, although much less than their male counterparts. Nonetheless their higher rewards have substantially reduced the female turnover rate; unlike prewar, postwar females were more likely to leave textiles for reasons of marriage.

This example points to a major difficulty in analysis of wage differentials and of many other phenomena: there are a number of competing, plausible explanations. It is difficult to assess the relative importance of each because data—particularly for prewar years—are inadequate, and insufficient research has been done. Moreover, one has to be cautious in specifying the structure of causal relationships; there may well be synergistic interactions among various causal variables.

One might well ask: why and how have small firms been able to survive, much less thrive, over the full course of Japan's industrialization? Several papers shed light on the issue, though none examines it comprehensively for the full sweep of a century. Minami stresses the essentiality of the development of motive power—water wheels, steam engines, electric motors—for industrialization. Steam power came first; its economies of scale could have doomed small units of production. However, electric motors can be built with very small to very large capacities. As Minami shows, their introduction and diffusion, with spreading electrification, was virtually complete in small firms by 1930; it may not be an exaggeration to say this innovation saved many small industrial firms from extinction. Although not completely eliminating economies of scale—larger electric motors are cheaper per unit of horsepower than small—they reduced the productivity differentials to levels that could be compensated by wage differentials. Smaller firms, paying lower wages, hired less-skilled or less-able workers, and compensated them in part by personalistic paternalism. Also, small firms have continued to be an important component of Japan's industrial activity by specialization. Subcontracting has been one outstanding feature, but by no means the whole picture. Rapp points out small firms producing export goods specialized relatively more in export production than comparable large firms, though the relative share of large firms in exports has risen substantially, in large part due to changes in industrial composition. In certain industries, as Minami illustrates, economies of scale are not so important. And small firms have long produced many consumer goods for local markets, where transport costs are relatively high, product differentiation is possible, and/or luxury items are produced for a relatively small market.

The dichotomy between large and small firms, and their workers, is overly simplistic in several respects. In size, enterprises of course range from miniscule to gigantic. However, many of the differential features we have noted do change smoothly as the size of firm changes. More important, such dichotomizing may seem to imply greater homogeneity in, say, large enterprises than in fact has existed. This is demonstrated quite clearly in the industry studies and in Hazama's paper on the evolving life style of industrial (blue-collar) workers, all of which referred mainly to relatively large firms.

LIFE STYLES OF WORKERS

Hazama delineates three modal types of workers, and their respective life styles, in the early phase of industrialization: relatively skilled male workers in machinery and shipbuilding; female workers in textiles; and male workers in mining. The first category of workers emanated in considerable part from artisan occupations, with their life styles based on skills, high mobility, high consumption, and short time horizons. Gradually they evolved into large-enterprise-type workers: diligent, stable, more family-oriented, concerned with security, and with new patterns of consumption and use of leisure time. They learned their life styles largely from government workers and white-collar workers in large firms. Today their lives are built around their company, their union, and their family. This type of worker has not only increased in absolute number and as a proportion of the labor force, more importantly he appears as a model whose life style workers in smaller enterprises attempt to emulate. He is the pacesetter in Japanese life styles, patterns of consumption, tastes, and other forms of behavior and values. As Chūbachi and Taira put it, "Japan is as solidly a middle class society today as any country in the world."

One has been tempted in the past to disregard female industrial workers as an unimportant category, only temporarily employed, with no distinctive life style, analytically uninteresting. An unexpected feature of the conference and of this volume is the rehabilitation, as it were, of analysis of the role of women in Japan's industrialization. Cole and Tominaga emphasize that a high proportion of Japanese factory labor was female: over 50 percent until the early 1930s, according to the census of manufactures; somewhat less when workers in the very small firms excluded from the census are counted but nonetheless greater than the early industrial experience of other developed countries. Women have worked predominantly in textiles, and in the postwar period in electronics and other light and precision manufacturing. Before World War II they were usually recruited from rural villages. They have lived in company dormitories, with life styles dominated by the firm.

The history of the evolution of the female factory workers' life style has been one of gradual improvements in company-provided living facilities, reduction in work hours, and lessening of company restrictions on personal freedom. In Hazama's words for the prewar period, "the life style in the textile industry has been criticized as approximating that of a desert which drove female factory workers to satisfying their hunger and their sexual desires by having trysts with men." Management voiced great fear for their female workers' morality, concerned too that they would become pregnant. Bad living conditions no doubt accounted for the high rates at which girls ran away from their factory jobs. Saxonhouse found that the supposed improvements in living conditions made by large firms in the 1920s and 1930s did nothing to slow down the runaway rate. Certainly an important message of the prewar experience is that the paternalistic methods adopted by management did not succeed in motivating female workers, at least anywhere near to the extent previously assumed.

Apparently these problems in female worker life style have been less severe in postwar Japan. Two points are worth mentioning. First, differences between large and small firms in industries which predominantly hire female workers are less than in male-oriented industries. Second, the expectations of young, unmarried females in large enterprises appear not to have changed substantially, though it is difficult to know much about expectations. Most plan to marry (now an industrial worker, rather than a farmer – a reflection of where the men are), to quit work when they marry, and to adopt the life style of their husband's colleagues. Recently as the labor market has tightened, the number of married female workers in industry has increased; many are middle-aged workers whose children are in school or grown up and who have returned to employment in smaller firms.

Hazama's third category was exemplified by male workers in mining. In the early phase of industrialization they often were drifters, dropouts from society, hired under subcontracting arrangements with labor bosses, given to hedonism in consumption and use of leisure time. Eventually to some degree they evolved into, or more likely were replaced by, large-enterprise-type workers. As drifter types they fall out of Hazama's analysis. Presumably their refuge was low-wage, small firms. At worst they merged with the urban poor studied by Chūbachi and Taira.

Chūbachi and Taira note the special poverty problems of minority groups in Japan—*burakumin*, Koreans, Ainu, Okinawans—but focus mainly on the mainstream urban poor, especially in ghettos. The urban poor have a distinctive life style, though not necessarily a culture of poverty which is inescapable. Theirs is a poverty of the working poor; in developing countries the poor cannot afford not to work. The occupational characteristics of the very poor in Japan evolved over time in response to the changing demands of industrialization. Traditionally they were rickshaw pullers, day laborers, street vendors, scavengers. As some occupations died away, they increasingly became day laborers, especially in construction-related activities, and wage-earners, probably in miniscule units of production engaged in simple manufacturing. Their real standard of living rose slowly over time in the prewar period. With the ending of labor abundance and with ever-growing postwar prosperity, the mainstream urban poor are disappearing in terms both of income and status.

THREE INDUSTRIES COMPARED

The heterogeneity of large enterprises and their workers is not only in life styles. Case studies of the cotton-spinning industry, shipbuilding, and the general trading companies reveal significant similarities as well as differences. In all three industries large firms are predominant. The economic importance of these industries has been substantial over the course of Japanese development. In a sense, modern industrialization began with cotton spinning, which thrived until World War II; now cotton has been largely replaced by synthetics. Shipbuilding, with an equally long history, has emerged postwar as a major world competitor, producing half the world's merchant ships over the past decade. General trading companies not only have long been important, but their role is probably growing. All three industries have been significantly involved in foreign trade.

Yet there have also been major differences among these industries. Workers are mainly white collar in trading companies, male skilled blue collar in shipbuilding, and female semiskilled in cotton spinning. Life styles historically were different but, as we have seen, they have become increasingly homogeneous in many respects. All three industries relied initially on foreign sources of technology and know-how. This technology was largely embodied in imported machinery in cotton spinning, less so in shipbuilding, and even less so in trading. Reliance on foreign technology decreased sharply in cotton spinning in the 1920s, whereas it has continued to be important in shipbuilding, although perhaps domestic adaptation and improvement have had greater impact. In trading companies, the high reliance on foreign methods had declined by the beginning of the century. As already noted, the large general trading companies are one of the few unique features of the Japanese economy. Yamamura analyzes why this has been the historical case: the general trading companies constitute an information industry *par excellence*. Moreover, they exist in substantial part as a way to overcome the strong language barriers between Japanese and foreigners, a means of economizing on scarce language skills of both.

Most important, perhaps, have been industry-specific differences in the nature and degree of government support. On the whole, the cotton-spinning industry developed without special government assistance. In contrast, the shipbuilding industry has always relied heavily on government support— military orders before the war, direct subsidies, subsidies to Japanese shipping firms buying Japanese-built ships, subsidies in the form of low-interest export credits to foreign buyers. The trading companies are an intermediate case. They were subsidized heavily in the nineteenth century in order to reduce the share of foreign trading firms in Japan's trade. Since then they have perhaps been on their own. How long it took these industries to become competitive is of interest: within about fifteen years cotton-spinning firms were exporting substantially; it took shipbuilding some seventy years. In his paper, Rapp points out that this sequencing of industrial development according to product cycles for each industry has in fact been typical of Japan's general development, with the time lag from technology import to export competitiveness varying according to an industry's technical sophistication and capital requirements. At the same time this shift has brought about a greater role for large firms in total exports.

SOCIAL CONSEQUENCES

The social consequences of Japanese industrialization have been profound, but our understanding of them is tentative and far from conclusive. For example, a basic feature of the past century has been the tripling of Japan's population—essentially all of which has come to reside in urban areas. The extensive migration on a voluntary basis suggests many Japanese perceived they would, all in all, be better off living in cities. Both accelerated population growth and increased urbanization have been consequences of industrialization; in turn they have had further significant, complex social consequences. Bennett and Levine directly consider postwar urbanization; it also underlies Hazama's discussion of the evolution of workers' life styles, Cole and Tominaga's paper on changes in occupational structure, and Chūbachi and Taira's treatment of the urban poor—to cite a few examples.

Industrialization and urbanization were significant causes of the decline in fertility observed since 1920. Women married later. Gross reproduction rates were lower in industrial than in agricultural prefectures and declined more rapidly. These factors are probably also important in explaining the increases in fertility and in population growth rates during the Meiji era, though the data are too meager to test hypotheses. Ohbuchi makes readers aware of the current controversy over Meiji population statistics in appraising the relative merits of several different projections. These may have significant implications for our understanding of Meiji agricultural performance, for the controversy over agricultural growth rates has focused particularly on per capita measures. Ohbuchi also used cross-sectional regressions over time to test the effects of industrialization, urbanization, level of income, education, mortality, and housing on the decline in postwar fertility by age groups. He was able to explain about two-thirds of the differential fertility by regions for the 1950s, and somewhat less for the 1960s.

Industrialization was the means of increasing family income and hence level of living, providing the material resources for changes in life styles. Increases in income and consumption were moderate and with some setbacks until World War II. The war was disastrous; it took some seventeen years to restore living levels. However, rises in average levels tell nothing about changes in the distribution of income, what is happening to certain groups absolutely and relatively. It is possible that all the benefits of industrialization accrued to only a few, but that does not seem to be true in an absolute sense even for prewar Japan. It appears that the material living conditions of virtually all Japanese improved between early Meiji years and the mid-1930s. However, this is far from completely demonstrated; we need to know more about the rural poor and the poor among minorities. Ono and Watanabe demonstrate that rural-urban income differentials, low in 1905, widened substantially to 1930, and differentials widened also within the urban sector due to wage differentials. After World War II the distribution of income became significantly more nearly equal, a consequence of zaibatsu dissolution and land reform in inflationary circumstances and, in the last fifteen years, of the ending of abundant labor supplies with attendant sharp rises in wages, especially for relatively unskilled workers. Data on income distribution are abysmally poor for the prewar period, and poor even for the postwar period. Probably equally important have been the major changes in the distribution of wealth, though even less data are available. Owners of land and corporate stock have gained dramatically in comparison with holders of bonds, loans, and savings deposits.

In organizing the conference and this volume, we have been well aware that Japanese industrialization has engendered many social costs, but we did not attempt to provide a comprehensive accounting of them. Their estimation is empirically and conceptually difficult (as is also true of social benefits). What is one group's benefit may be another group's loss. Comparisons and weighting involve value judgments. For example, do we regard the increase in importance of nuclear families—a consequence of industrialization—as good or bad? Or how do we compare increases in absolute income with worsening in relative income distribution? Chūbachi and Taira, in examining urban poverty, concluded it was not caused by industrialization; indeed, industrialization has brought an end to the urban poor, as they are absorbed into middle-class life—though probably as the last and the least to benefit from industrial growth.

Bennett and Levine, as already noted, tackle the problem of social costs head-on in a comprehensive, detailed paper. They focus mainly on the postwar period, on the reasonable grounds that what is important is the widespread perception of such grievances both as social problems and as problems which are amenable to solution rather than inevitable by-products of essential industrialization. One might well ask why the whole set of relative deprivation or quality of life issues have come to the fore only in the past decade rather than earlier on in the course of industrialization—for Japan, for the United States, and for other industrialized countries as well. Clearly part of the answer lies in historical political and social systems as well as the nation's economic goals, perhaps especially for Japan. But other propositions probably hold. Quality of life issues become relatively more important the higher the level of income. Industrialization increases pollution, congestion, and other external diseconomics, perhaps exponentially rather than linearly. There are threshhold effects of many such disamenities; for instance, discomfort is low for low levels of pollution but rises sharply once a certain level of pollution is reached. Thus, prewar Japan had lower levels of industrialization and income, so the social costs were not only less but people were more willing to tolerate them. Moreover, it is perhaps only when such costs spread from a limited, usually disadvantaged, group to affect larger, and more powerful, segments of society that social costs come to be widely perceived as important issues about which something should be done. The distribution of social costs can be considered analagously to the distribution of income. Indeed I suspect there is a high correlation: those with relatively low incomes bear a relatively high share of social costs. Those more affluent can escape, albeit at secularly rising costs. All segments of the population therefore suffer from varying degrees of sacrifice relative to what they would have previously expected as the standard of life corresponding to their newly won higher incomes. A sense of malaise—what some Japanese call "new poverty"—thus has pervaded the Japan of the early 1970s. At the same time there has emerged the sense, reflected in citizen groups and other methods of organizing across class or occupational lines, that these deprivations can be overcome by government action derived from political activism.

FUTURE RESEARCH

Good research begets frustration, as well as temporary euphoria. It heightens awareness of unanswered questions, and the need for further research. This volume demonstrates that Western knowledge of the Japanese economy and society has come a long way from that of prewar years or even a decade ago. We have a much stronger core of knowledge from which to operate. And, thanks to the efforts of many Japanese scholars, we now have historical statistics for many economic and social variables that are probably superior to the data bases for any other countries except the United States and the United Kingdom.

The charge to the conference did not include a requirement to produce a list of new important topics for future research. Nor do I have the temerity, or comprehensive knowledge of all the social sciences, to do so. Yet clearly a number of concrete themes requiring major new research do emanate from this volume. The social and economic causes of population growth and its geographic distribution are far from well understood. Part of the reason has been the inevitable focus to date on national development rather than evolving regional variations. Ohbuchi demonstrates the importance of regional differences, as do Ono and Watanabe in demonstrating the importance of taking into account early wide differences in price levels in making real income (and by implication wage) comparisons. One suspects life styles embody important regional differences. Only the surface has been scratched in analysis of income and wealth distribution issues. And although perhaps the mainstream urban poor are being absorbed into middle-class Japanese life, how about the minorities, the rural poor, or other disadvantaged groups? Clearly too, we need to understand much better the evolving economic and social role of women.

At a different level, we are aware Japan, like all other later developing nations, has relied heavily for industrialization on the importation, adaptation, and diffusion of foreign technology. Japanese have done this particularly well. How? Why? The absorptive capacity, the adaptiveness, the perception of opportunities, of Japanese surely are not genetic. To what extent did it depend on preexisting social institutions and cultural values which were thus causes of industrialization? To what extent did it come about as part of the complex, interactive process of industrialization, as, for example, the effects of education, the desire for military emulation, and the like? This certainly is an area in which interdisciplinary research is essential.

Even matters on which considerable research has already been done require further investigation. The issues of wage differentials and of economic dualism are still not fully resolved. If regional variations are taken into account, do differentials by firm size finally disappear? How can we incorporate differences in the basic quality of workers—intelligence and motivation—and is it necessary to do so, or are they distributed randomly over firm size? More broadly, we should know more about how an industrial labor force was created, with the attendant requisite human skills. How important was general education, vocational training in schools or firms; how were workers socialized? And there is clearly a great deal more that we should know about a number of other industries important in Japan's industrialization process.

We have only begun, as evidenced in this volume, to analyze the complexities of the interrelationships between social and economic variables in Japan's modern development. We still need a good comprehensive conceptual framework for understanding causes of social and economic change. To understand Japan requires us to place the Japanese experience in perspective. This requires not only the usual historical approach but an explicitly comparative analysis with the evolving experience of other industrial societies.

I regard this volume as one, hopefully significant, step on this journey of discovery and understanding. I hope that others will find it a stimulus to engage in research on these issues.

REFERENCES

Dore, Ronald P., ed. 1967. *Aspects of Social Change in Modern Japan.* Princeton University Press.

Klein, Lawrence, and Kazushi Ohkawa, eds. 1968. *Economic Growth—The Japanese Experience since the Meiji Era.* Irwin.

Lockwood, William W., ed. 1965. *The State and Economic Enterprise in Japan.* Princeton University Press.

Ohkawa, Kazushi, and Yujiro Hayami, eds. 1973. *Economic Growth—The Japanese Experience since the Meiji Era: Proceedings of the Second Conference.* Japan Economic Research Center, Paper no. 19, 2 vols.

Ohkawa, Kazushi, and Henry Rosovsky. 1973. *Japanese Economic Growth— Trend Acceleration in the Twentieth Century.* Stanford University Press.

PART ONE

Formation of an Industrial Work Force

Historical Changes in the
Life Style of
Industrial Workers

Hiroshi Hazama

One of the key factors in industrialization is the development of an industrial labor force. There have been several approaches to this problem in analyzing the Japanese historical experience. One is from the standpoint of business history, focusing on managers and particularly entrepreneurs,[1] but this approach does not adequately account for the relationship between the industrial worker, typically blue-collar, and industrialization. Another approach has been to focus directly on the worker. There have been a number of such studies, but almost all have dealt with the exploitation of the worker by the capitalist, that is, with the low wages at which laborers were forced to work and thus the miserable life they had to endure. Although valuable in relation to social problems or the labor movement, they are not particularly helpful in clarifying the role of the worker in the process of industrialization.

In this paper, I describe the origins and life style of the worker, the central figure in the industrialization of Japan. I try to explore whether workers were sufficiently flexible in their life style to help promote industrialization by asking to what extent workers were willing to adapt to the requirements of a factory system and thus to the creation of an industrial labor market.

Several points about the approach require explanation. A major problem is how to define "life style." Because each person's life contains many subjective and specific elements, the life style of each worker is in some respects different from that of others. Nonetheless, individual life styles are substantially shaped by a society's common conditions, and hence have certain common characteristics. The emphasis here is on such aspects of the

This paper was ably translated by Kozo Yamamura and Susan Hanley. My thanks to them for their careful work and helpful criticism.
[1]The two best books in English are Hirschmeier (1964) and Marshall (1967).

external environment as a worker's family situation, affecting the supply side of labor, and the situation of an employer, affecting the demand for and working conditions of labor. For example, one model is the life style of female laborers in the textile industry—the *dekasegi* type—in terms of the special characteristics of both the farm families from which they come (the supply side) and the textile industry (the demand side). Such models are conceptualizations rather than statistical averages (Weber 1924), although a good deal of empirical research and data analysis helped in forming the models (Hazama 1959, 1963, 1964).

The life style of a worker can be separated into elements pertaining to work and those pertaining to leisure.[2] Each of these is examined in its material and nonmaterial (psychological) aspects. For example, tools, machinery, the work environment, and wages pertain to the material side of a worker's "working" life, whereas his home, furniture, and household expenses relate to the material side of his "leisure" life. The worker's feelings toward his occupation, toward work itself, and toward religion are part of the nonmaterial side of both his work and nonwork life, and in turn determine his general attitude toward life.

Industrialization brought about various changes in the life style of the worker. The introduction of new machinery, a new wage system, and a new system of working hours produced great changes in the working life of the laborer, which naturally influenced the nonwork aspects of his life style. These innovations first caused material changes and through them caused changes in his overall attitude toward life. Thus, life style can be seen as a dependent variable shaped by industrialization. But the question of whether to accept new machines and a new wage system, whether to adopt them enthusiastically or not, depends on the worker's overall attitude. An attitude of acceptance by workers will greatly affect the speed of industrialization.[3] Thus, life style is in some respects a dependent variable and in others an independent variable. In general, however, the material aspects of life style tend to be dependent on industrialization, whereas the nonmaterial aspects (the worker's attitude toward life) tend to be independent.

Comprehensive discussion of the process of industrialization must consider the development of both traditional and modern industry. Modern industry, which first appeared in the Meiji period, was born of technology imported from advanced Western nations. At the same time traditional industry continued to grow, and it continues to exist to this day, side by side with modern industry.

These sectors have differently influenced the way a person lives, thereby creating different life styles among workers. Traditional industry has

[2]In Japan there is an active search for research methods to analyze life style, but to date an effective method has not been developed. Representative of the pioneer studies are Chūbachi (1956) and Aoi (1971).

[3]For example, in England, where industrialization originated, "traditionalism" in the attitudes among farmers and laborers persisted, with the effect of slowing industrialization after the nineteenth century (Bendix 1956, part 1).

perpetuated a premodern life style, while modern industry has created a new style among factory workers. Although both must be considered, I focus here on the predominant life style of modern industrial workers.

For an underdeveloped country industrialization is achieved through borrowing foreign production techniques and management methods. For Japan, industrialization was Westernization. Although rationalization of production techniques and management methods based on science has a pervasive pattern knowing no national or ethnic boundaries, in reality the process is related to ethnic and cultural factors. Thus, by adopting industrial techniques and methods of management from the West, Japan changed not only the machines used in factories and the organization of these factories but also life patterns. By adopting a Western mode of life, the Japanese were able to smoothly industrialize, that is, Westernize. To give the simplest example, blue-collar workers during the Meiji period wore the traditional kimono at work, but by the Taishō period they worked in Western dress.

In this essay, in referring to the life pattern of workers I mean blue-collar workers, and in tracing historical changes I use the following periodization:

1. First phase of industrialization, from the Sino-Japanese war to World War I (1894-1913).

2. Second phase of industrialization, from World War I to the Japanese invasion of China (1914-1937).

3. Third phase of industrialization, from the San Francisco Peace Treaty to the present (1951-1974).

In addition to these three phases, there was also a period between the Meiji Restoration and the Sino-Japanese war which might be called the pre-industrialization phase, and a period between the Japanese invasion of China and the peace treaty which might be called a period of industrial stagnation or abnormal industrialization. These will not be dealt with here.

THE LIFE STYLE OF TOKUGAWA ARTISANS

Before discussing the life style of workers during industrialization, I first briefly describe the life style of artisans (*shokunin*) during the Tokugawa period. Artisans performed the function of industrial workers, and their labor habits and life style strongly influenced workers in both the traditional and modern sectors in the first phase, in part because workers initially moved freely from one sector to the other.

The typical life pattern of the Tokugawa artisan follows.

Skill as a determinant of labor conditions. In Tokugawa society, the social status of artisans was below that of farmers, but artisans nevertheless had pride in their skill. Differences in skill, seen in rankings such as *jō-daiku*, *chū-daiku*, and *ge-daiku* in carpentry, determined wages and working conditions, including the number of hours worked. Few restrictions—such as when to begin and end work—were placed by the *oyakata* ("bosses") on those of superior skill.

High mobility. Young artisans who had completed their apprenticeship under a specific oyakata left to work under various other oyakata to improve their skills. Those who wished to become oyakata themselves had to work under a single oyakata for a long period and achieved their goal either by inheriting or purchasing an oyakata's *kabu* (guild privileges) on recommendation of their own oyakata. However, the possibility of becoming an oyakata was small, and most artisans did not consider years under a single oyakata bearable. Instead, many artisans became journeymen in order to enjoy an easier life, selecting the oyakata under whom they worked to suit their mood and leaving at will. Thus, though their occupation remained the same throughout life, they were highly mobile.

This high mobility affected the daily pattern of work. Their working hours were theoretically 8 A.M. to 6 P.M. (the schedule of carpenters and masons in the Osaka region at the end of the eighteenth century). In reality, however, these hours were rarely observed. If an oyakata insisted on them, the artisans would immediately quit. By custom, one or two holidays were granted each month, on the first and the fifteenth, but these were not strictly adhered to. In short, the working rules governing artisans were generally lax.

Lack of planning in consumption. A well-known saying characterizes the consumption patterns of artisans: "Do not keep money overnight." Artisans were confident that as long as they had their skill, they could support themselves. When paid, they tended to spend all their money immediately and often did not work again until their money ran out. However, at times no work was to be had; then they had to borrow from loan sharks or to pawn household goods to maintain even a low standard of living. In general, a lack of planning typified the consumption pattern of artisans.

Leisure: sake and festivals. "Wine, women, and gambling" were the entertainments characteristic of this group. However, given their available leisure time and income, it is unlikely they could spend much on a regular basis, though as income depended on skill and not on seniority, some of the single, highly skilled artisans had the money to indulge in these activities. Leisure activities for the married were largely confined to drinking and going to the many festivals of temples and shrines. Some artisans (carpenters, for example) had their own rites centering on the protectors of their vocation and formed their own organizations, which provided opportunities for entertainment.

Quasi-parent-child relationships and quasi-sibling relationships. Young men who wanted to become artisans lived as apprentices in the home of an oyakata, receiving training from him and older apprentices. As in later factories using the same system, the oyakata, as a quasi-parent, concerned himself with all aspects of the daily lives of his apprentices, which meant apprentices also had to function as cleaners, babysitters, and general household helpers. Quasi-parent-child relationships (*oyabun-kobun*) were maintained even after apprentices became independent artisans, as were the quasi-sibling relationships (kyōdai-bun) established among fellow apprentices. These ties played a significant role in the life of an artisan, especially in terms of finding work, getting married, and rendering mutual assistance in time of need.

THREE TYPES OF WORKERS: FIRST PHASE OF INDUSTRIALIZATION

Japan's industrialization began with an aggressive policy by the Meiji government to promote industry. The heart of the policy was establishment of government factories in all areas of mining and manufacturing. These factories took the lead in transforming industry in the pre-industrialization period, serving as models of technology and organization, as well as sources of personnel, for private firms. One can say Japan's modern workers were born at government factories.

The number of workers at government-run factories was never very large; in 1894, they comprised only 2.9 percent of workers employed in the secondary sector. However in the machine industry they made up 43.3 percent of the total (Nōshōmushō 1897). Workers in government factories were very important, nonetheless, because they helped create a new life style which served as a model for workers in private industry as well.

Table 1
Daily Wages of Workers in 1885
(in sen)

	Male		Female
Carpenters	22.7	Weaving	7.5
Day laborers	15.7	Silk-spinning	11.3
Day farm labor	15.1	Day farm labor	9.7
Tokyo Munitions Factory*	52.0	Tomioka Textiles*	7.2
Yokosuka Shipbuilding*	31.0	Private factories	8.3
Private factories	17.3		

Source: Rōdōshō 1957, p. 13.
*Indicates government factories. Even though Tomioka Textiles was government operated, its capital was small. However, the number of hours worked was short.

The life of workers at government factories differed significantly from that of the artisans. The factory buildings, machinery, tools, and other aspects of the working environment were almost completely Western. Both office workers and blue-collar workers of some rank, such as supervisors, worked in Western clothes. The rules governing work were much stricter than those applied to artisans. For example, the times set for beginning, taking breaks, and stopping work were rigidly observed. Wages were higher than for artisans, because working conditions were different and highly skilled workers were needed (Table 1). Because foreign engineers and other workers were also employed, the number of hours worked per day was eight to nine, the same as in Western European countries. In many government factories Sundays were holidays, and those who were injured and the families of those who died in the line of duty received benefits, both consequences of employing foreigners. By 1875 a compensation system common to all government factories had been set up.

Because the government factories of early Meiji had a Westernized work environment and good labor conditions, children of former samurai and of village leaders who wanted to embark on new careers went to work in them. Also, because of the general attitude of "revere government officials and the public be humble," workers at government factories considered themselves part of an elite.[4] As industrialization continued, however, workers at government-owned factories declined in number. By 1890, the government factories had expanded in size, but outside control over their budgets had increased, which meant management could no longer provide preferential treatment to their workers. Labor conditions deteriorated, becoming more like those at private factories.

Table 2
The Daily Wages of Factory Workers in 1900, 1903, and 1906
(in sen)

Occupation	1900	1903	1906
Textile workers	25.0	27.0	31.0
Workers in rolling stock	45.0	51.0	53.0
Typesetters	35.0	41.0	49.0
Carpenters	81.3	85.0	97.5
Plasterers	89.0	88.8	95.8
Day laborers	45.2	52.5	47.5

Source: Rōdōshō 1957, p. 36.

During this period labor conditions prevailing at private factories were characterized by low wages and long hours. The work day was ten to twelve hours, excluding overtime. The wages of skilled workers, such as those in the rolling-stock or printing industries, were lower than those of artisans (masons, for example) and even below those of day laborers (Table 2). Given such poor conditions, factories could not expect to obtain skilled personnel. More than half of the factory workers at this time came from the lower classes in cities and villages. In large cities, such as Tokyo and Osaka, workers at the largest factories lived in slums (Yokoyama 1949, p. 30) and could be properly called "working poor." Their social status was lower than that of small shopowners and upper-class artisans such as carpenters and masons.

The life style of workers during the first phase of industrialization might best be analyzed by considering three characteristic types: (1) male workers

[4] A typical example is found in the diary of a woman who worked at Tomioka Textiles, established in 1873 (Wada 1931). Her attitude toward her work was based on her pride as the daughter of a samurai and in working for her country.

in heavy industry such as machinery, shipbuilding, and rolling stock; (2) female workers in the textile industries, including silk yarn, spinning, and weaving; and (3) male workers in the mining industry. Women in the textile industry represent the largest number of workers.

Artisan-Type Workers in Heavy Industry

Male workers in heavy industry, especially skilled workers such as black-smiths, lathe operators, and finishers, had a life style similar in many ways to artisans. Common characteristics were pride in skill, high mobility, and a lack of planning with regard to consumption. Differences, of course, did exist. Wages were paid either by the day or on a piecework basis, so when work was abundant, it was advantageous to skilled workers to do piecework. Basically these workers were skilled in the use of machines, in contrast to the handicraft skills of the artisans.

Another difference was in training. Although in theory there was an apprenticeship of three to five years in the factories, many workers, after learning a few skills, left in the middle of their apprenticeship to work in another factory as skilled workers. This occurred with increasing frequency after the Sino-Japanese war, when the pace of heavy industrialization was so rapid that opportunities for employment were numerous. Thus, once basic factory skills were acquired, further training could be taken lightly.[5] This meant workers would readily move to another factory offering higher wages and more opportunities for overtime.[6]

Heavy industry was developing through an increase in the number of small factories, so employers were mainly oyakata and small factory owners subcontracting work from the large factories.[7] These employers could not offer workers steady employment because of fluctuating economic condi-tions. The result was that, for example, 52.5 percent of workers in six privately owned factories in heavy industry in 1901 had worked less than one year at that factory (Nōshōmushō 1903, 2:11). In contrast to artisans, these heavy industry workers also changed their type of work. This was especially manifest among educated workers[8] and was the reason Japan could not get a corps of workers highly skilled at specialized tasks.

[5] According to a day laborer, there was a system of promotion based on improvement in skill, but gradually promotions came to be determined by bribing the foreman (Yamamoto 1921, pp. 49-54).

[6] "If higher wages are paid elsewhere or there is a place where one can do night work, and thus income will go up, the number of people who leave rises" (Nōshōmushō 1903, 3:272).

[7] "In factories which employed many workers, the hiring of workers, dismissal, the method by which wages were paid, etc., were all left to the foremen; the head of the factory had practically nothing to do with any of this" (Nōshōmushō 1897, p. 5).

[8] "Educated factory workers in Japan tended to be discontented with their jobs; they didn't like doing the same thing for a long time and liked to do a variety of jobs on the side" (Nōshōmushō 1903, 3:268).

Though heavy industry workers received high wages in comparison to other workers, they could not live on their basic wages alone and had to supplement their income with overtime. Often their children also worked, and wives did piecework at home. Their economic difficulties were compounded by the practice of paying wages monthly or semimonthly. In the West, blue-collar workers have been customarily paid on a weekly basis, which is helpful to workers who tend to lack planning in making expenditures. It is not simple to distribute one's expenditures over a month evenly. For many, the temptation was to indulge in luxuries when a large sum of money was at hand. Many a worker thus found he was short of cash by the middle of the month. This meant reliance on loansharks or pawnshops and purchase of daily needs on credit until the end of the month, often at inflated prices.

Table 3
Monthly Household Budget of Factory Workers in 1910
(Number in household: 4.1 persons)

Items	Amount in yen
Actual income	22.29
Income of head	17.83
Income of other members	4.46
Actual expenditures	22.15
Food	11.86
Housing	3.84
Clothing	1.70
Miscellaneous	4.89
Remainder	0.14
Proportion spent on food	53.5%

Source: Rōdōshō 1957, p. 56.

Under such conditions, the level of consumption of industrial workers was limited to essentials. According to a survey of household expenditures of workers at a large factory, expenditures on food amounted to 53.5 percent of total expenditures, and of that percentage, 56.8 percent was spent on staples, that is, rice and wheat (Table 3). Main foods other than grains were vegetables, fish, shellfish, and seaweed.

This group frequently worked more than twelve hours a day, leaving little leisure time. Entertainment consisted only in going to the public bath, drinking sake, and occasionally gambling, whoring, or going to popular plays (*yose*),[9] but even the last three were denied married workers. At small factories, festival days of local shrines or temples were holidays, but not at

[9]"They returned home, and after eating and drinking they read about half the paper and if they took a bath, it was past ten. If they didn't get up at five the next morning, they would be late to work; they could barely rest their bodies" (Nōshōmushō 1903, 3:175). "After returning home, they gambled,

large factories. In addition to monthly holidays, there were the traditional holidays consisting of five days at New Years, *Bon* (a midsummer festival), and national holidays established during the Meiji period.

Several workers' organizations appeared during this phase of industrialization, such as the Ironworkers Union (1897-99), organized along the lines of the American Federation of Labor. However, no more than three thousand workers joined these organizations, even counting members of the large Ironworkers Union. Most workers had virtually no direct contact with labor unions. Later, at the end of the Meiji period, workers in a few large factories belonged to mutual benefit groups within the factory, and these played a fairly significant role in their lives.

Because the factory apprentice system was not as strict as an artisan's apprenticeship in terms of specification of skills to be acquired or period of training, quasi-parent-child relationships existed only to a limited degree among workers. Though there were loose groups formed by workers from the same village, these were extremely weak because most workers coming from the country were from the lowest agricultural class. However, workers living in the same residential district tended to help each other in times of need.[10]

Dekasegi-Type Workers in the Textile Industry

During the first phase of industrialization, there were more female than male workers, and most were found in silk yarn, weaving, spinning, and other textile activities. In 1909, women comprised about 62 percent of all factory workers (Cole and Tominaga, this volume, Table 3). Though the characteristics of these female workers varied by the job performed, they can generally be described as follows: (1) age less than twenty;[11] (2) mostly unmarried; (3) intended to work only a short period before marrying; (4) frequently from distant farm villages; and (5) most living in dormitories. In short, most were temporary workers from agricultural villages, which fits the definition of dekasegi, a term used during the Tokugawa period.[12] Though female factory

---

went to the whorehouse, or went to entertainment halls; they wasted the wages which they earned daily" (Nōshōmushō 1903, 3:72).

[10]The official who was in charge of the survey of ironworkers wrote: "I felt the bonds of friendship among the poor living in tenements to be much stronger than those of ordinary people. This is because each has experienced difficulties of his own and thus has become considerate of others" (Nōshōmushō 1903, 3:140).

[11]In a survey of female workers in a textile factory in Osaka in 1900, 58.4 percent were under age twenty, and 24.9 percent were twenty to twenty-four (Nōshōmushō 1903, 1:7).

[12]The "dekasegi-type" workers discussed here are different from "dekasegi" (workers). Dekasegi refers to workers who engage in temporary work in addition to their regular jobs, as, for example, the farmer who is a construction laborer during his off season. His main occupation remains farming. In contrast, the dekasegi-type worker in the textile industry has a deep relationship with the farm family into which she was born, but her occupation is in the textile industry.

Table 4
Living Conditions of Spinning-Mill Workers in 1901
(six factories in Kansai)

Type of housing	Male		Female	
	Number	Percentage	Number	Percentage
Dormitories	18	0.3	10,693	50.4
Designated boarding houses	1,293	21.5	754	3.6
Company housing	1,521	25.2	2,741	12.9
Commuting from home	3,192	53.0	7,016	33.1
Total	6,024	100.0	21,205	100.0

Source: Nōshōmushō 1903, 2:94.

workers also came from the working classes in cities and fishing villages, they too worked only because their elders forced them in order to help the family finances.[13]

Females were usually recruited by professionals hired by factories. The contracts essentially were made with parents or brothers who guaranteed them. Until the end of the nineteenth century, parents or brothers received money advanced against wages to be earned so this was, in effect, a method of trading in human beings. The system gradually disappeared in the early twentieth century, but for a long time when a young woman became a factory worker the decision required a resolution similar to that of selling herself into prostitution, as the social status was nearly as low.

Many of the female workers thus recruited were housed in dormitories (Table 4) and lived entirely under the control of the factory. This fact is of crucial importance in understanding their life style. Though some women commuted or lived in company houses, the factory preferred they live in dormitories, because it eliminated absenteeism and made it easier to force them to work overtime.

Labor conditions were extremely bad. In the textile industry there were two shifts, which meant the standard number of hours worked per day was twelve. In the weaving and silk industries there were no shifts, and the number of hours worked per day far exceeded twelve. Wages were calculated either by the day or on a piecework basis. However, not only were wages low, but the factory had total control over when and how they were paid. In theory wages were to be paid monthly or semimonthly, but in reality women received on payday only an itemization of wages plus a small amount of

[13]"It goes without saying that applicants were from the lower classes in society, their level of life was extremely low, and their manners and customs were extremely vulgar; their occupations, too, generally belonged to the lowest categories. . . . Few of the applicants chose to become textile workers of their own will. Many came to work directed by their elders and in order to help the family finances. Thus the wages earned were used to supplement the family income" (Dai Nippon 1898, pp. 9 and 12).

Table 5
Reasons for Leaving the Factory Given by Workers in a
Certain Textile Factory in 1900

| | Workers living in dormitories | | Commuting workers | |
	Male	Female	Male	Female
Fired	--	400 (11.6%)	397 (21.2%)	292 (12.3%)
Left without notice	--	2800 (81.0%)	1475 (78.6%)	2046 (86.4%)
Illness	--	225 (6.5%)	5 (0.2%)	30 (1.3%)
Died	--	31 (0.9%)	--	--
Total	--	3456 (100.0%)	1877 (100.0%)	2368 (100.0%)

Source: Nōshōmushō 1903, 1:69.

spending money. According to the company managers, these young women wasted their money, and therefore their wages were saved for them by the factory. What they really meant was that if cash was paid out, the women tended to run away.

In addition to low wages and long hours of work, they also suffered from a foul environment. Factories were dusty, the air was dirty, and the dormitories were unsanitary. For example, in textile factories having two shifts, the same bedding was used by both groups. For this reason, disease, especially tuberculosis, spread widely, and many women went home because of ill health.

Basically, the women lacked independence. Meals provided by the factory dormitories were insufficient in quantity and inferior in quality,[14] so the women had to supplement their diet by buying additional food. The factory encouraged women to buy daily necessities at the factory shop to absorb what little cash they had and thus further inhibit running away. In addition to these expenditures, women had to send money to their families.

In the face of such conditions, most of those quitting did so by running away (Table 5). Companies took measures against this by limiting the cash women had on hand, by restricting the time spent off the factory grounds after work, and by insisting on chaperoning when women went out, even on holidays.[15] (This issue is discussed further in the essay in this volume by Saxonhouse.)

Free time after work, even had it not been supervised, could not be used constructively because the women were exhausted from long hours of work. That supplementary education provided after work by the factory had little

[14]"Rice was of low quality [Note: it was cheap imported rice called nankinmai], and it was cooked in a crude way so that it had a certain odor. ... Foods in addition to rice were mainly vegetables and dried foods, and several times a month small fish were customarily served. There were places where meat was also served every week" (Nōshōmushō 1903, 1:140-141).

[15]There was a song sung by female workers, "It is even harder to live in a dormitory than to live in a prison or be a bird in a cage."

effect is readily understandable. In fact, life in the textile industry has been criticized as approximating that of a desert,[16] which drove female factory workers to satisfy their hunger and their sexual desires by having trysts with men. Many, who were not fortunate enough to get married, followed a downhill path into prostitution. When women left home to work in a factory they always hoped to return as soon as possible to marry a farmer, but for many this was never realized. The reasons for this were the differences between work at the factory and on the farm, inability to readjust to the strict customs of agricultural households, and the fact that they were looked down on in their own villages. Thus, most either married factory workers or became barmaids and remained in the cities.[17]

Drop-Out Laborers in the Mining Industry

Miners comprised approximately 22 percent of the labor force in secondary industries during the first phase of industrialization. Their life style differed both from female workers in the textile industry and from artisan-type laborers in heavy industry. From the Tokugawa period on miners were down-and-outers from farm villages, drifters from the cities, and criminals; that is, they were all drop-outs from ordinary society. After the mid-Meiji period, miners did not come exclusively from these groups, but the down-and-out or drop-out atmosphere prevailed from long tradition.

Miners called themselves *gezainin*, a term suggesting they had committed some crime. In a well-known miners' song a line goes "We go down into the mine carrying the mining lamp from the age of seven or eight; this is punishment on our parents." It is noteworthy that such a sense of punishment or notion of crime was pervasive among miners. This attitude, combined with the fact they did dangerous, heavy work underground, basically determined the life style of miners.

The life of miners was closely connected to the *hamba* (or *naya*), mining camps, typically with barracks-like quarters. There were two types of miners: those hired directly by the mining company and those employed through subcontracting oyakata. Both types lived at the hamba, which was rented to them by the mining companies. Miners directly employed by mining companies found themselves supervised by the company, whereas the oyakata

---

[16]Percy Holden, an English social worker who ran a workhouse in the slums in the East End of London, "came to Japan and saw that at Japanese textile factories most of the workers had no religion and lived in the unfriendly atmosphere of dormitories. He likened it to living in a desert. Female textile workers not only lived in a desert of thoughts but also their physical environment was a kind of desert as well" (Yokoyama 1949, p. 175).

[17]The following estimates were made from the results of a survey of twenty-eight prefectures in 1910 on dekasegi-type female factory workers who had returned home. Nationwide there were 200,000 female workers on dekasegi, of whom 120,000 did not return. Of the 80,000 who returned home, 13,000 were afflicted with serious diseases, one quarter of whom were tuberculosis sufferers (Ishihara 1914, pp. 187-188).

supervised their recruits. For both groups life was as closely supervised twenty-four hours a day, with severe restrictions on freedom, as it was for women in dormitories.

Labor conditions were made worse by the middlemen—subcontracting oyakata in charge of the hamba. They frequently engaged in loansharking and many skimmed off part of the wages due the miners. At times, they sold food to unmarried miners at higher than market prices. Though hours of work, number of holidays, and methods of payment were set by regulation, they were ignored by both employer and employe. When employers wanted to force workers to work, they resorted to physical coercion, and when miners did not feel like working, they simply stopped work, even in the middle of the day. Collisions resulted, and the miners either submitted to a severe going-over by thugs hired by the employer or they ran away. Thus the mobility of miners was high, though it differed between metal mines and coal mines. According to a survey of miners in 1906, 45 percent of the miners in coal mines had worked less than a year compared with 17 percent in metal mines.[18]

Because of the low social status of miners and the dangerous work, their life style was characterized by self-abandonment and hedonism, both in terms of their consumption patterns and their use of leisure time. For example, when they received their wages, they gambled instead of going back to work and frequently wasted their wages within a few days. Many piled up debts. Their entertainment was similar to artisan-type workers—sake, women, and gambling—but for miners, fighting was added.[19]

There were a few nascent unionlike organizations, but the large majority of miners were not involved. However, quasi-parent-child and quasi-sibling relationships were essential parts of their lives. One type of the former centered on the hamba, a term referring to both the mining camps and the employment relationship between the oyakata and the miners under him. Another quasi-parent-child relationship was between senior (*tomoko*) and junior miners. This was how mining skills were passed on and also involved quasi-sibling ties between coworkers.[20] These relationships performed an important function in finding a job and providing other assistance in time of need. Miners felt an especially strong bond to each other because of their inferior social status and shared dangers. This bond provided them with a strong sense of belonging and proved a means of supporting morale.

[18]Nōshōmushō 1908, p. 22. The difference in percentages may be explained by a higher level of skill and a more cohesive social community in metal mines than in coal mines.

[19]"Because there wasn't anything to amuse me, I liked to fight with self-abandon. Often we fought against large numbers and that gave me an invigorating feeling" (Nagaoka 1971, 2:242).

[20]*Tomoko* existed mostly in metal mining, where a high degree of skill was necessary. Tomoko means "friend," but its use is limited to experienced miners who act as oyabun (boss/"father") to younger ones (kobun: protégé/"child").   (note continues)

INDUSTRIAL DEVELOPMENT AND IMPROVEMENT OF THE SOCIAL
STATUS OF LABORERS: SECOND PHASE OF INDUSTRIALIZATION

The Emergence of Enterprise-Type Workers

In the interwar period large industrial enterprises desiring to compete in international markets actively introduced the most advanced technology, replacing various techniques adopted during the Meiji period. The new level of mechanization required correspondingly skilled workers. Gradually, in mining and heavy industry indirect hiring through oyakata was replaced by direct employment by the enterprise itself. The efficiency of labor became a serious concern for large factories, which led them to tackle the problem of labor management. Labor movement activity was another reason for the increased interest in labor management.

Knowledge of labor-management techniques was sought from the advanced nations, especially the United States. Employers studied various systems, especially scientific management (the Taylor system), and gradually began to adopt them. Large factories thus Westernized their labor-management methods, just as they had Westernized the work environment during the first phase of industrialization. Furthermore, international pressure (especially that exerted through the ILO for an eight-hour working day and the prohibition of female workers on the midnight shift) and Japanese labor union demands constrained managers to improve conditions to a level approximating that of Western countries. Thus labor conditions were also moving in the direction of Westernization.

Westernization of the workers' life style proved to be part of the process of improving working conditions. Wages, which had risen in both nominal and real terms during the World War I boom, increased substantially more in real terms during the 1920s (Table 6). Also, compared to the previous period, working hours were reduced by one to two hours a day in every industry. In the machine industry nine hours became standard, and ten to eleven in the textile industry. Rest periods and holidays also increased. In contrast, the income and number of working hours for farmers and artisans did not improve correspondingly. Consequently, the relative social as well as economic position of factory workers improved. They were no longer the working poor, and the farmers' psychological resistance to sending their children to work in factories rapidly diminished. The majority of the

---

Hamba existed at both metal and coal mines. A major reason an employment relationship extended into a parent-child relationship was that many miners had a dark past, such as running away, often with a woman, and thus none of their relatives or neighbors wanted to have anything to do with them. They were unable to enter ordinary occupations and were usually poverty-stricken. Therefore, they were grateful to the oyakata (head of the hamba) who gave them work and provided them with food, clothing, and shelter, however humble the nature of these items.

Table 6
Long-Term Trends in Daily Wages
(in sen)

Year	Wages			Nominal wage index 1934-36, average = 100	Real wage index 1934-36, average = 100
	Male	Female	Average		
1882	27	16	19	14.2	36.5
1900	41	20	26	19.4	40.0
1910	60	30	41	30.6	53.1
1920	193	96	140	104.5	72.0
1930	194	92	142	106.0	101.5
1938	215	73	151	112.7	93.2

Source: LTES 8:243.

gainfully occupied population were farmers (53.0 percent in 1920), and farms remained the most important source of industrial labor (Table 7; also see Cole and Tominaga 1975, Table 6).

As heavy industry expanded, important changes occurred among workers. There was a rapid employment increase in the metal, machinery, and chemical industries (Table 8), and the workers were almost all males. As large factories characterize these industries (Table 9), there was a marked increase in the number of males employed in large factories in heavy industry. This was a new type, an enterprise worker. These workers were inseparably linked to the firm's internal labor markets resulting from lifetime employment systems which had developed gradually, mainly in the largest firms. This was the group benefiting most from improved working conditions and enjoying better living standards.

The managers of large enterprises during this period had two major goals: to train and retain superior skilled workers and to deal with the labor movement, that is, to retain on a long-term basis capable workers whose ideologies were moderate. Those considered most suitable were children from middle-level farm households, or a level close to it, with no occupational experience. In terms of capability, graduates of middle schools (that is, those with more than compulsory education) with good scholastic records were preferred. As large factories began to hire with emphasis on quality rather than quantity, they began to select their own workers rather than recruit them publicly or hire them through oyakata.[21]

[21]Blue-collar workers with experience were given preference, as in Europe and the United States. Traditionally there had been no special hiring season, but in the 1920s large factories started to hire in April, when new graduates first sought jobs. These inexperienced workers were selected by simple tests of skill or academic ability, interviews stressing character, and a check on family background and school performance. All candidates also had to

Table 7
Classification of Workers by Previous Work Experience
(in percent)

Type of factory	Agriculture	Fishing	Commerce	Mining	Other industries	Same industries	Other	Total
Dyeing and weaving	48.2	1.4	3.4	0.2	3.1	29.5	14.3	100.0
Machinery	23.9	1.6	4.7	0.9	11.1	37.0	20.7	100.0
Chemicals	40.0	1.8	6.7	0.8	6.8	21.5	22.5	100.0
Food and beverages	48.4	4.0	4.9	0.2	4.8	15.0	22.8	100.0
Miscellaneous	31.9	1.4	7.0	0.3	5.4	33.3	20.8	100.0
Special	42.0	3.5	8.1	6.9	8.9	11.8	18.9	100.0

Source: Nōshōmushō 1919.
Note: This survey was made in 1917 by the Ministry of Commerce and Labor on
newly established and enlarged factories. Even among workers whose previous jobs
were in industry or commerce, it is presumed many originally came from farm families.
Therefore, the percentage of workers whose origin is agricultural is much larger than
indicated.

Table 8
Changes in the Number of Factory Workers by Type of Industry
(in thousands)

	A 1920	B 1928	$\frac{B}{A}$ x 100
Spinning	854.6	998.2	116.8
Metal	75.3	121.7	161.6
Machinery	200.1	250.6	125.2
Ceramics	68.2	68.2	100.0
Chemicals	102.4	120.1	117.3
Lumber and wood products	42.9	56.6	131.9
Printing and bookbinding	34.5	54.2	157.1
Food processing	107.2	167.6	156.3
Electricity and gas	6.9	3.6	52.1
Other	62.2	90.1	144.9
Total	1554.7	1936.2	124.5

Source: Shōkōshō 1920, 1928.

The only companies that could adopt such strict hiring policies and employ
a sufficient number of workers were large enterprises which could provide
better labor conditions—not medium or small enterprises. Comparing wage
levels in heavy industry, in 1914 the wage level of factories employing over
1,000 workers was 1.5 times that of the smallest factories (Sumiya 1967, pp.
192-193; this evolving situation is discussed in more detail in Yasuba's essay
in this volume). Furthermore, large factories began to give a bonus at the end
of each quarter and to provide welfare facilities. The existence of such an
income differential became an important factor in assuring a stable supply of
labor for the large factories.

—————————
undergo a health check. The intention was to obtain workers easily trained
and resistant to unionization.

Table 9
Changes in the Composition of Labor in Major Industries
by Factory Size

		Small factory	Medium factory	Large factory
Spinning	1920	37.8	23.7	38.5
	1928	33.2	26.8	40.0
Machinery	1920	45.7	21.8	32.5
	1928	25.9	16.7	57.4
Metals	1920	47.0	19.5	33.5
	1928	47.2	16.5	36.3
Chemicals	1920	49.4	36.6	14.0
	1928	43.1	34.3	22.6
Food processing	1920	89.3	8.9	1.8
	1928	70.5	32.8	16.7
Miscellaneous	1920	77.1	17.5	5.4
	1928	70.5	19.1	10.4

Source: Shōkōshō 1920, 1928.
Note: Small: 5-99 employes. Medium: 100-499 employes. Large: over 500 employes.

In addition, to ensure workers would stay, large factories also adopted a policy of not dismissing anyone hired on a regular basis. This policy was then called *fukaiko-shugi*, or the no-dismissal policy, and is the origin of the present *shūshin koyō* system (lifetime employment). Under this policy, wages may be reduced during a recession, but workers will not be dismissed. Moreover, the seniority system is used in providing benefits to employes. Wage increases, bonuses, the amount of money received at retirement, and promotions are all determined according to seniority. Thus, it is advantageous to work a long time at the same factory, and workers employed under this system stopped moving from place to place as artisan types had been doing.[22] However, workers who did not have the benefits of such policies, namely temporary employes, still faced layoffs.

Increased income for workers in large enterprises changed their consumption patterns. The proportion of disposable income spent for food declined rapidly after 1917 for all Japanese, and by the late 1930s was around 50 percent (Table 10). For factory workers the share spent on food was even lower, leaving more for other purposes (Table 11; see also the comparisons in the essay by Chūbachi and Taira in this volume). However, it should be noted differentials between workers of the large enterprises and small enterprises

[22]Stable employment results in reduced labor mobility. According to a survey of machine factories employing over 100 workers in Osaka in 1921, the annual rate of dismissal was 2.8 percent and the rate of new hiring was 2.1 percent (Osaka-fu 1928, p. 124).

Table 10
Trends in the Composition of Personal
Consumption Expenditures in Prewar Japan
(in percent)

Item	1874-1883	1896-1906	1917-1926	1931-1940
Total	100.0	100.0	100.0	100.0
Food	67.5	63.7	58.9	49.5
Clothing	7.9	8.2	12.8	12.9
Housing	7.2	7.9	8.6	12.4
Heat and light	5.5	3.0	4.0	4.4
Health	3.8	3.8	3.7	5.7
Transportation	0.2	1.3	2.6	3.5
Correspondence	0.1	0.3	0.4	0.7
Social expenditures	5.8	7.7	3.4	2.9
Culture and entertainment, etc.	3.9	4.1	5.6	8.0

Source: LTES 6:5.

Table 11
Food and Beverage Expenditures of Salaried and
Factory Workers, 1926-27
(share of total expenditures, in percent)

	Salaried workers	Factory workers
Food and beverages	31.49	37.92
of which:		
Grain staples	11.09	15.23
Other basic items		
Fish	3.02	3.31
Meat	1.12	1.91
Dairy products	1.04	0.80
Vegetables and dried foods	4.51	5.29
Seasonings	2.78	3.20
Luxuries		
Sweets and fruit	2.91	2.43
Liquor	1.59	2.60
Beverages	0.52	0.47
Restaurant meals	2.91	2.68

Source: Naikaku Tōkei-kyoku 1926, 1927.

increased.[23] As the level of consumption rose, the consumption of meat, milk, and eggs began to rise slowly, though the most important nonstaple items continued to be vegetables and fish. It was also during this period that workers began to drink beer.

As income rose, hours worked each day declined, and holidays increased, various leisure-related problems began to appear. From the Taishō period on, facilities and activities described as *taishū* or *minshū* (popular, mass) appeared, such as taishū novels, theater, and dining halls. It is clear taishū referred to the workers, and these were for their leisure activities. This is a long way from the artisans' and miners' sake, women, and gambling.

Because of the shortened workday, workers began to have time to read newspapers and magazines, unlike earlier periods when after work there was only sufficient time to take a bath, drink sake, and rest. This difference also reflected a difference in the level of education.[24] Drinking and gambling, either individually or with other workers, gave way to going to movies or eating out with families. Spending leisure time with families was a new development.[25]

Large enterprises began to concern themselves with the leisure activities of their employes in order to prevent unionism and socialism from taking hold among workers. Large factories provided libraries, game rooms, and athletic facilities, including playing fields for their employes, so leisure time came to be spent under the eyes of the employers. Because similar facilities were inadequate outside the factories, workers tended to use company facilities.

Although workers did begin to organize unions to improve conditions and provide mutual assistance, the number organized never exceeded 8 percent of the labor force even at the height of such activities. In contrast, the employe

[23]With regard to the savings accumulated by workers, according to a survey made in Osaka in 1926, savings in large machine factories with over one thousand employes was 453.3 yen per worker. In contrast, for small-medium machine factories of fewer than a thousand, savings averaged only 53.72 yen (Osaka-fu 1928, p. 78). This reflected not only differences in income but differences in life style. Workers in large factories had begun to shape their lives with some time perspective.

[24]Part of this can be explained by mass communication. Distribution of newspapers increased phenomenally after 1922, as did the number of weeklies, monthlies, and popular books, and radios became common. Workers also received more formal education.

Distribution of Labor Force by Highest Level of School Completed

Year	Higher School	Middle School	Primary School	Unschooled
1905	0.2	0.9	41.6	57.3
1925	0.8	4.9	74.3	20.0
1935	1.6	9.2	82.1	7.1

Source: Mombushō 1963, p. 59.

[25]Two contemporary accounts are Osaka-fu (1923, p. 272) and Naimushō (1921, p. 156).

organizations (workers' councils), formed with the assistance of employers and based on the factory as a unit, enjoyed nearly 100 percent participation by regular employes. These organizations were originally established to provide mutual assistance among the workers, but expanded to counteract the labor union movement. They ensured a flow of information between employer and employe and provision of facilities for employes' "wholesome" leisure activities. Their role at large factories was important.

The ties of workers, especially those at large factories, to the farm families from which they had come remained important. This is closely related to the fact that large factories employed children of middle-level farm households. These workers continued to communicate with their families and sought assistance from them in times of unemployment, sickness, or accident. Such was not the case for workers from lower income farm households who, even had they wanted to depend on their families, would not have found it possible. Also, many workers cherished the idea of returning to their villages on retirement and thus maintained ties with home. At a time when social welfare programs had not yet been developed, mutual assistance based on blood relationships was extremely important.

The enterprise worker reflected the attitude toward life of the class into which he was born. First, in contrast to the unstable attitude manifested by the artisan-type worker, the enterprise worker showed the diligence associated with the farmer. Second, in contrast to the unplanned consumption pattern of the artisan-type workers, he exhibited a considerable degree of planning, both in terms of his personal life and how he spent his money.[26] This new type of worker still formed only a small percentage of factory workers, and even in the large factories there were many artisan and drop-out types.

The typical life style found among full-time workers at a large factory can be summarized as follows: the workers came from middle-class farm families and received an education of two years beyond compulsory schooling, having graduated from higher elementary school (*kōtō shōgakko*). On graduation, they joined a firm after being evaluated on their ability to work and their general attitude toward life. Once in the company, they received further technical training designed to make them topnotch skilled workers. Then they stayed within the same firm until retirement. The working conditions in the large factories were better than those in the small- to medium-sized firms, especially for long-term employes. The aim of the worker was to increase his income through promotions and raises within one specific company. Both the

[26]Traditional concepts valued highly by Japanese farmers, especially independent farmers up to the end of the Tokugawa period, are exemplified by two slogans: *kokku-benrei* (work hard and study hard) and *kinken-chochiku* (diligence and thrift). With regard to personal relations within the village, people valued cooperation—that is, "harmony." This attitude toward life influenced the workers who came from farm villages, creating a tendency to value "harmony" among members of the same factory.

patterns of consumption and the way leisure was spent became more and more bound up with the company, both directly and indirectly. The style of life that resulted can be termed the enterprise life style. This style reflected the new labor-management approach which envisioned ideal workers to be those who worked faithfully and industriously over many years in the same firm, for which they were compensated accordingly.

Changes in the Life Style of Other Workers

As the difference between labor conditions in large and small-medium enterprises increased, and as the distinction between the regularly and temporarily employed became established in large enterprises, various changes occurred affecting the three types of workers of the first phase of industrialization.

Among the artisan-type, male, skilled workers, two tendencies appeared: one was for them to move from large to medium and small companies, and the other was for them to work as temporary employes at large factories. Temporary workers in large numbers had jobs which were unstable but paid well. As technological change continued in the large companies, the skills of these artisan-type workers became outdated. They tended to move to places where their skills could still be used, and this led to the small-medium size companies employing older techniques. Also, the labor-management policies being adopted by large companies were not suited to their life style. Young men confident of their ability would shun the low wages but secured future of the regularly employed worker and choose instead to become temporary laborers. Their life style, like the traditional artisan type, was "fat and short." That is, they wanted to live with flair, often at risk to their health.

Women workers in the textile industries continued to be young, unmarried, from farm villages, still mostly living in dormitories, and basically wanting to work only a short period before marriage. Both their living and working conditions improved, though with differences in degree between large and small-medium companies. In large companies, the incidence of disease, especially tuberculosis, declined, and supervision was relaxed, allowing women freedom to go out after work and on holidays.

How the many young women living in dormitories away from their homes were to spend their leisure time was a problem for their employers. It was not a question of labor unionism but one of morality. The young women's work was so tedious and boring that it led to a heightened interest in sex as one of the few available pleasures, and thus to attracting male factory workers, who frequently abandoned the women when they became pregnant.

Thus employers took pains to establish educational and entertainment facilities within the factory and dormitory complexes. Courses designed to teach wifely skills such as sewing, etiquette, tea ceremony, and flower-arranging were included. This was partly to counter criticism that women from dormitories were not capable of becoming housewives. The factories, through these courses, functioned as surrogate mothers. Improvements in life style as well as in labor conditions made recruitment easier and helped reduce mobility. (See, however, Saxonhouse's conclusions on this point in his essay in this volume.)

With the expansion of the heavy and chemical industries, the number of female workers increased. These women were not dekasegi-type workers. In general, they were given the same treatment as temporary workers even in the largest firms. This meant they faced no restrictions from their employers outside of working hours, but it also meant they had no job security or paternalistic concern. Their own attitude, in turn, was merely to work temporarily in order to help with the family finances.

For the drop-out laborer in the mining industry, conditions improved, first in the largest enterprises. The collapse of the subcontracting system had significant effects, one of which was a change in the quality of miners, especially in large enterprises where there was a shift to enterprise workers. The quasi-parent and quasi-sibling relationships, which had deep roots among the drop-out types of the past, were gradually weakened. Instead, miners forged closer relationships with the companies. Drop-out workers continued to exist in many other occupations, where labor conditions were inferior and mechanization lagged. This category includes transporting and cleaning at factories and in mines, in stevedore activities at ports and harbors, and in the construction industry.

POSTWAR ECONOMIC GROWTH AND THE TRANSFORMATION OF LIFE STYLES: THIRD PHASE OF INDUSTRIALIZATION

Democratization and the Increase in Enterprise Workers

In the postwar phase, various changes affected the lives of workers. In terms of the industrial mix, both the textile and mining industries began to decline, and differentials in the scale of operations between large and small-medium enterprises widened significantly. But most important was the tide of democratization. Labor unions, especially those organized along enterprise lines by workers in the largest firms, were the most important element. A desire also emerged for equal treatment for workers as a whole. These two changes not only helped transform the life style of enterprise workers in large firms but also began to affect the workers in small-medium enterprises.

In general terms, rapid economic growth brought equally rapid improvement in labor conditions. Real wages, only one-third of the 1931-36 level immediately following the war, rapidly recovered, reaching the prewar level by 1952 (Table 12). The wage level steadily improved, with the real wage in the early 1970s over four times the prewar level. The number of hours worked per day was about nine in the manufacturing industry during the 1930s, but by 1971 it had declined to about eight. Consumption patterns also improved. In 1960 over 40 percent of disposable income was spent on food, but by 1970 it was 35 percent, approaching the levels of the United States and West Germany (Table 13).

Table 12
Comparison of Wages in the Manufacturing
Industry Before and After the War
(base year, 1931-36)

Year	Nominal wage	Consumer price index	Real wage
1931-36	1.0	1.0	100.0
1947	32.9	109.1	30.2
1949	157.1	236.9	66.3
1951	235.2	255.5	92.1
1953	307.0	286.2	107.3
1955	340.4	297.4	114.5

Source: JERC 1958, p. 282.

Table 13
An International Comparison of Consumption Patterns
(in percent)

Item	Japan		U.S.A.		West Germany	
	1960	1970	1960	1970	1960	1970
Total	100.0	100.0	100.0	100.0	100.0	100.0
Food	42.7	35.1	34.9	33.1	39.8	34.1
Clothing	11.2	9.0	8.6	8.3	11.8	11.8
Housing	10.5	10.6	14.3	14.7	7.1	11.2
Light and fuel	3.7	3.6	4.3	3.2	2.7	2.2
Household furnishings	4.5	6.2	7.1	8.2	13.8	11.1
Miscellaneous	27.4	36.1	30.8	32.5	24.7	29.6

Source: Nakayama 1972, p. 140.

As large firms employed a larger part of the labor force, the life style of enterprise workers became dominant, particularly as it·became the model for most workers, blue and white collar. Owing to pressure from unions, labor conditions in the largest enterprises were maintained at a higher level than that prevailing in small-medium enterprises, many of which had no labor unions. Wage demands reflected union desires to maintain the seniority system, and this combined with the permanent employment system to strengthen the seniority wage system. Thus when wage levels in the large enterprises are compared with those in small-medium enterprises, the difference in wages and bonuses is especially significant for middle-aged to older workers.[27]

[27]The *Moderu Chingin Chōsa*, published by the Tokyo Chamber of Commerce in 1968, surveyed male factory workers with at least a middle

Employment security was strengthened by union demands against dismissals. The permanent employment system had been developed by large enterprises before the war to retain skilled workers and to counteract the labor movement. For this reason, there was no explicit guarantee of employment security. In the postwar period labor unions were able to obtain guarantees of permanent employment even when employers were not in favor of it. Thus, except for the departure of workers on reaching retirement age and the hiring of new school graduates, there was a tendency for labor mobility to be limited to a firm's internal labor market.

Unions rarely displayed concern for general consumer welfare. Some cooperated with consumer unions and similar groups, but not with any real vigor. Instead unions demanded more direct material benefits for members, including such items as the discount sale of clothing, food, and other daily necessities, and presentations of money at the time of weddings, births, serious illness, and natural disasters affecting workers or their immediate families. Shorter working hours led to successful demands for athletic fields, gymnasiums, and recreation facilities.

The most important demand has been for expansion of company housing. Before the war, city factories provided company dormitories or housing only for white-collar workers, unmarried apprentices, and female workers. In contrast, after the war, blue collar male workers also began to benefit, especially because general housing conditions were bad. This meant that in terms of food, clothing, and shelter, the lives of workers in large enterprises and their families were completely encompassed by the company. As a consequence, large enterprises began to take on the characteristics of an autarchic community. The growth of large enterprises thus contributed to the creation of the epitome of what is called here the life style of enterprise workers.

As workers in large enterprises became increasingly tied to the enterprise, their ties with the communities where they lived decreased. Workers found facilities to meet their needs at their companies that they could not find in

---

school education in large enterprises employing over 1000, medium enterprises employing 300 to 500, and small enterprises employing under 100. Wages of workers in large enterprises are used as a base of 100:

Age	Medium-size enterprises	Small-size enterprises
15	101	100
35	98	97
45	96	85
55	97	84

That is, before age thirty, not only is the difference in wages between large and small-medium enterprises minor, there is even a tendency for their wages to exceed those of large enterprises. However, after thirty, the wage level of large enterprises is higher.

their local communities. As their interests focused on their company community, their concern with what happened in the local community was limited.

A major change in the postwar years in large enterprises has been the transformation of the life style of the blue-collar workers to a pattern similar to that of white-collar workers. This trend emerged during the war years and was accelerated after the war with the demand for equality among workers. In the prewar years, the distinction between blue- and white-collar workers existed not only in their work but also in consumption patterns and use of leisure. For example, before the war it was easy to distinguish blue- from white-collar workers by their clothing.

The postwar union movement, however, demanded differences in the working conditions of blue- and white-collar workers be abolished. Some companies even eliminated the difference in their general categorization, calling all employes *sha-in*, or company employes. The equalization of the wage scale, number of hours worked, clothing worn at the factory, and meals continued, and these changes invariably reduced distinctions between the consumption and leisure patterns of these two groups (Table 14). Today it is not possible to identify workers, either blue or white collar, by looking at the clothing they wear when they go to work. Similarly, today wives of all employes are termed *okusan*, in contrast to the prewar period when wives of blue-collar workers were less politely referred to as *okamisan*, and only white-collar wives were okusan.

Table 14
How Time Was Spent on a Typical Day, 1970

	Blue collar		*White collar*	
Sleep	7 hr.	51 min.	7 hr.	51 min.
Meals	1	29	1	26
Personal hygiene	1	04	1	08
Work	8	05	7	30
Study		01		02
Household duties	1	03	1	16
Commuting		55	1	14
Conversation		32		38
Rest		32		27
Leisure activities		24		34
Reading*		32		44
Radio**		37		26
Television**		40		17

Source: NHK 1970, p. 359
*Newspapers, magazines, books.
**Because people carried out other activities while listening to the radio or watching television, the total exceeds twenty-four hours.

Improvements in the standard of living of blue-collar workers in large enterprises led to the Westernization of their life style. Although the Westernization of labor conditions and labor management had already begun during the second phase of industrialization, only after the war were consumption patterns and the use of leisure Westernized. This change was not limited to employes of large companies; it was experienced by all Japanese. The kimono came to be worn by men only on holidays or special occasions such as weddings. Consumption of starch staples declined and that of meat and eggs rose. Concrete apartment buildings were constructed instead of the traditional Japanese house of "paper, bamboo, and earth." Japanese-style rooms with tatami and cushions were replaced with Western-style rooms equipped with chairs. Workers still spent their leisure time on sports and music, but sumo and judo, *naniwabushi* and other popular songs of the past were replaced by baseball and soccer, jazz and rock.

For today's enterprise workers the company, the enterprise union, and the family are the three foundations on which their lives are built. One could even say a company community is built on these three. If an employe is from the country, his relationship to his family there remains important. Though it is rare for workers to seek assistance from their families when unemployed or in other difficulties, they still want to maintain ties so as to be able to escape from highly mechanized life in the cities and spend vacations and holidays in the country. Affected by the postwar atmosphere of demands for equality, even many artisan types at small-medium enterprises have adopted this life style, though of course they cannot match the standard of living enjoyed by employes of large firms.

Although the textile industry has declined, other industries, such as electric appliances, precision machines, and assembly of radios, televisions, and cameras, employ large numbers of female workers. These women usually come from the country, are young, unmarried, and live in dormitories, and thus a dekasegi-type life style continues. Even so, it is much improved materially, and the social environment is far better and freer. The loosening of restrictions imposed by management and weaker ties with families have also contributed to this change. The number of young women making financial contributions to their families has dramatically declined.

Overall, the living standard of Japanese has improved, but this does not mean poverty has been eliminated. Among the poor, one finds the drop-out still living for the moment. During the Second World War and the strained conditions of the Occupation, many suffered physically and psychologically, and these persons often became drop-outs, engaging in simple physical labor. Most would fall under the category of day laborers.

Recent Changes Among Workers

First, with the attainment of prosperity large-enterprise employes are no longer satisfied with economic well-being alone. Especially the younger employes seem to feel their freedom is being sacrificed to the enterprise, and even their employers have begun to question the desirability of being concerned with all aspects of the lives of their employes and families. Whether the life style of enterprise employes will continue for long without change is doubtful.

Second, some young men are rejecting the idea of joining large enterprises because they do not want to enter such closed societies. Others leave after entering because they cannot bear that kind of life. They tend to move from place to place and even occupation to occupation, but it is doubtful whether they can continue this floating existence when they become middle-aged. What kind of workers these new young drop-outs will become and what kind of life style they will create are questions now being asked.

Third, an increasing number have become drop-outs from circumstances beyond their control. These are the older workers. Life expectancy has increased rapidly over the last fifty years to longer than that for Americans,[28] but the retirement age in large enterprises is fifty-five. Some firms are extending this to between fifty-eight and sixty, but how older workers earn their living after retiring, whether at fifty-five, fifty-eight, or even sixty is a problem. Old-age pensions are not large enough to live on. This means as long as it is physically possible, men must engage in some kind of work, and so the number of older persons seeking work is rapidly increasing.

There also is a recent, marked trend for more married women to work.[29] They can be divided into two categories: those intending to work long term, and those intending to work only for a short time or only part time. In contrast to usual custom, in this group husbands are more likely to help in the home. These women learn to use time efficiently and also begin to want to have and spend money of their own. When a wife and mother goes out to work either part or full time, the life style of the entire family changes.

Thus, the life styles of all Japanese workers, which had seemed to be converging on that of the enterprise worker, have recently begun to show signs of new diversity and change. Several factors contribute to this.

One is the growing shortage of labor. Until recently the labor market, in the war years, had an excess supply of labor. Now there is an acute shortage, especially of young workers. For the worker, this new external labor market means increased opportunities for job mobility, even among the largest firms. Such mobility holds within the possibility of creating a new life style for the worker.

Second is the decline in the population working in the primary industries, especially agriculture. Because the major source of Japanese labor has long been the farm, the life style, and especially the attitudes, of farmers have had an important impact on the life of workers. Even after taking factory jobs,

[28]According to an estimate made by the Institute of Population Problems, Ministry of Welfare, the life expectancy of Japanese in 1935 was 46.9 years for men and 49.6 for women. These figures had improved by 1970 to 69.3 and 74.7, respectively.

[29]Never-married women constituted 51.7 percent of female employes in 1970 (Sōrifu 1970).

workers of rural origin preserved ties with their families. However, the population in the primary industry has declined since the end of the war, especially since 1950.[30] Urban working families have become the main source of labor.

Third, the shortening of the work week has increased leisure time, and it is expected that in the future longer vacations, such as winter and summer vacations, will begin to materially affect life styles. For many years Japanese have placed absolute importance on their work to the neglect of their life outside work. Because of this, they are unaccustomed to spending leisure hours fruitfully.

Fourth, social welfare programs have been inadequate, so workers have been forced to rely on their employers and themselves. This was an important factor in the rise of the enterprise worker. However, as public programs develop, there will be less necessity for the worker to rely on the company.

The fifth change involves the rise in the level of education among workers and the growing diversity in their values. A survey in March 1973 showed 89.4 percent of middle school graduates and 32.2 percent of high school graduates were planning to continue their education. In the past, blue-collar workers have ended their education with middle school and lower level white-collar workers with high school. Only white-collar workers of the middle ranks and above went to college. However, because of a general rise in the level of education, the standard for blue-collar workers has become graduation from high school. This suggests increased convergence of the life styles of blue- and lower white-collar workers. In addition, Occupation educational reforms have strongly influenced young workers. They have been estranged from traditional values—designated "groupism"—and instead hold diverse individualistic values similar to those in the West. In the future these diverse values are expected to lead to equally diverse life styles.

CONCLUSION

In this essay I have examined changes in the life style of the blue-collar worker during industrialization in Japan. These workers can be divided into two major categories: the enterprise worker, found mainly among full-time male employes in large firms, and the dekasegi type, found among female employes in the textile industry.

Although the textile industry held the most important position among Japan's industries until 1930, after 1940 the heavy and chemical industries, using male labor, came to occupy this position. Consequently, the importance of the enterprise worker rose with industrialization and continues up to the present.

---

[30]According to the national census of 1950, 48.5 percent of the total population was employed in primary industries, but this percentage had fallen to 19.3 in 1970.

Although I have dealt specifically only with blue-collar workers, it should be recalled the life style of those designated enterprise workers originated with the male white-collar employes in government bureaus and large private firms. After 1910 it gradually spread among male blue-collar workers.

In short, the enterprise life style has been the pacesetter for virtually all workers. Even though only some 28.6 percent of male employes in 1973 worked for the large firms (over 500 employes) where the pattern originated, it has influenced not only workers in small-medium-sized firms, but also farmers and women workers (the latter apparently wish to marry enterprise workers). This life style has been attractive because it provides a secure life. Throughout the pre- and postwar periods, most workers received low wages and faced a high risk of unemployment. They understandably longed for a life which promised long-term security, even at the cost of some freedom and possibly higher income. In addition, it was attractive because it approximated a Western life style.

The enterprise life style is currently undergoing visible change. It is becoming less attractive to workers and has ceased to be a pacesetter. What life style, then, will the workers of Japan adopt in the future? One possibility is that life styles may come to approximate those in Western industrialized countries today. This, of course, will be a repeat of the way Japan, as a latecomer, is following the path of Western nations in industrializing.

In retrospect, we can see the life of the workers was Westernized in more or less the following order:

1. From the working aspects of life to the leisure-time aspects.
2. From the material aspects to the overall attitude toward life.
3. From workers in government enterprises to those in private enterprise.
4. From the workers in large enterprises to those in small- and medium-sized enterprises.
5. From the white-collar worker to the blue-collar worker.
6. From male workers to female workers.

It must be noted here that this process has made the working aspects of Japanese blue-collar life very similar to those of blue-collar workers in the West. Nonworking aspects, however, have followed the pattern of the middle-class white workers in Europe and the United States. More precisely, blue-collar workers in Japan tried to adopt the life style of Japanese white-collar workers, who in turn were patterning theirs after middle-class life in the West.

Looked at this way, the life style of Japanese workers gradually began to approximate that of workers in the West and this trend will undoubtedly continue. However, it should be remembered Japanese have also attempted to maintain certain aspects of their own traditional life style. Only when Japanese have lost self-confidence, during such periods as early Meiji and just after World War II, did they abandon their traditional life style and try to adopt a completely Western style of life. Renewed confidence, as during the second stage of industrialization, has led to active efforts to revive the traditional ways of life.

Today, when Japan has reached the level of the advanced Western nations, Japanese are again actively reexamining the value of traditional elements in their society. If opportunities to come into close contact with the West continue to increase as expected, the life style of the workers will be increasingly influenced by the West. But at the same time, the traditional life style too will be reexamined and preserved. And in an international perspective, as China and other countries in Asia and Africa succeed in developing, they will eventually have increasing impact on the life style of Japanese workers. Thus, I cannot agree with the view that the life style of Japanese workers will eventually become indistinguishable from that of Western workers.

REFERENCES

Aoi, Kazuo, et al., eds. 1971. *Seikatsu Kōzō no Riron.* Yūhikaku.

Bendix, Reinhart. 1956. *Work and Authority in Industry*, part 1. Wiley.

Chūbachi, Masayoshi. 1956. *Seikatsu Kōzō-ron.* Kogaku-sha.

Dai Nippon Bōseki Dōgyō Rengōkai [Greater Japan's Asosiciation of Textile Companies]. 1898. *Bōseki Shokkō Jijō Chōsa Gaiyō Hōkokusho.*

Hazama, Hiroshi. 1959. "Chin-Rōdōsha no Keisei to Kazoku." In *Ie-Sono Kōzō Bunseki*, edited by Yuzuru Okada and Sei'ichi Kitano. Sobunsha.

———. 1963. *Nihonteki Keiei no Keifu.* Nihon Nōritsu Kyōkai.

———. 1964. *Nihon Rōmu Kanrishi Kenkyū.* Diamond-sha.

Hirschmeier, Johannes. 1964. *The Origins of Entrepreneurship in Meiji Japan.* Harvard University Press.

Ishihara, Osamu. 1914. *Jokō to Kekkaku.* Cited in *Jokō to Kekkaku*, edited by Takashi Kagoyama. Kōseikan. 1970.

JERC [Japan Economic Research Center]. 1958. *A Compilation of Japanese Economic Statistics.* Nihon Hyōron Shinsha.

LTES [Estimates of Long-Term Economic Statistics of Japan]. Series edited by Kazushi Ohkawa, Miyohei Shinohara, and Mataji Umemura. 1965-. 14 vols. Tōyō Keizai Shinpōsha.

———. Vol. 6. *Personal Consumption Expenditures.* 1967. Miyohei Shinohara.

———. Vol. 8. *Prices.* 1967. Kazushi Ohkawa et al.

Marshall, Byron. 1967. *Capitalism and Nationalism in Prewar Japan.* Stanford University Press.

Mombushō [Ministry of Education]. 1963. *Nihon no Seichō to Kyōiku.* Teikoku Chihō Gyōsei Gakkai.

Nagaoka, Kakuzo. 1971. *Kōfu no Seikatsu.* Cited in *Kindai Minshū no Kiroku*, vol. 2, *Kōfu*, edited by Hidenobu Ueno. San'ichi Shobō.

Naikaku Tōkei-kyoku [Cabinet Statistics Bureau]. 1926, 1927. *Kakei Chōsa.*

Naimushō [Ministry of the Interior]. 1921. *Tōkyō-shi Kyōbashi-ku Tsukishima ni Okeru Jitchi Hōkoku*, vol. 1. Included in *A Survey of Tsukishima*, edited by Kōichi Sekiya. Kōseikan. 1970.

Nakayama Taro. 1972. *Ningen to Shakai to Rōdō.* Nihon Seisansei Honbu.

NHK Broadcasting Public Survey Center. 1971. *Nihonjin no Seikatsu Jikan.* Nihon Hōsō Shuppan Kyōkai.

Nōshōmushō [Ministry of Agriculture and Commerce]. 1897. *Kōjō oyobi Shokkō ni kansuru Tsūhei Ippan*.

    . 1903. *Shokkō Jijō*. Reprinted by Seikatsusha Reprints, 1947-48, 3 vols. All citations are to the reprint edition.

    . 1908. *Kōfu Taigū Jirei*.

    . 1919. *Survey on Factories and Factory Workers*.

Osaka-fu. 1923. *Yoka Seikatsu no Kenkyū*. Kōbundō.

    . 1928. *Honshi ni Okeru Kōjō Rōdōsha no Chochikukin*.

Rōdōshō [Ministry of Labor]. 1957. *Monthly Report on the Survey of Labor Statistics*, vol. 9, no. 9.

Shōkōshō [Ministry of Commerce and Industry]. 1920, 1928. *Kōjō Tōkei-hyō*.

Sōrifu [Office of the Prime Minister]. 1970. *Rōdōryoku Chōsa 1970*.

Sumiya, Mikio, et al. 1967. *Nihon Shihonshugi to Rōdō Mondai*. Tokyo Daigaku Shuppankai.

Wada, Hide. 1931. *Tomioka Nikki*. Kokin Shoin.

Weber, Max. 1924. "Die Objekitivität Sozialwissenschaftlicher und Sozialpolitischer Erkenntnis." In *Gesaminelte Aufsätze zur Wissenschaftslehre*. J. C. B. Mohr.

Yamamoto, Nobutoshi. 1921. *Rōdō Sannen*. Naigai Shuppan Kabushiki Gaisha.

Yokoyama, Gennosuke. 1949. *Nihon no Kasō Shakai*. Iwanami Bunko. Originally published in 1898.

Japan's Changing Occupational Structure and Its Significance

Robert E. Cole and Ken'ichi Tominaga

The activities governing production and allocation of goods and services are of central importance in satisfying the basic imperatives of any ongoing social system. The forms of such activities, however, vary directly with the level of industrialization of the particular society; indeed, their structure constitutes a major part of the operational definition of industrialization itself.

Japan began its drive toward industrialization later than most major European powers. Yet, when we look at the role of contemporary Japan in the world economy, it is clear she has caught up to the Western nations in some areas and is rapidly approaching them in others. It follows that many of the structural changes associated with industrialization took place in Japan much more rapidly than in Western Europe. We expect these shifts to be reflected in a rapidly changing occupational structure.

Occupational structure is defined broadly to include the number of ways economic performance roles are differentiated and organized (Moore 1966, p. 194). It is not possible to treat all the varied dimensions of occupational structure. Consequently, we focus on those aspects for which there are data (primarily occupational composition) and which appear controversial for theoretical or empirical reasons in either the Japanese or the Western sociological literature.

In the literature on industrial societies and the process of modernization, a primary concern has been that degree changes in economic structure (that is, industrialization) invariantly produce a common outcome in social structure. It is generally agreed among scholars that variation is greatest with such elements as the political order, which is the arena for permanent or unsolved strains and tensions. In contrast, occupational structure is considered one of those elements displaying less variability, and indeed its similarity is said to reflect the convergence of industrial societies (Feldman and Moore 1969, pp. 59-60). One concern of this essay is the extent to which the shifting occupational structure in Japan fits Western models of occupational structure.

Some observers of Japanese society (both Westerners and Japanese) assert that emphasis on occupation is a Western value inapplicable to Japan, thereby making the analysis we propose a useless exercise. To summarize this view, the primary orientation and loyalty of employes is said to be to the business firm and immediate superiors rather than to occupation (for example, Abegglen 1958, pp. 68-70; Nakane 1970, pp. 1-4, 16-19; Dore 1973). Motivation to work arises from company loyalty rather than commitment to occupation. Payment on the basis of age and length of service (*nenkō*), a basic characteristic of Japanese industrial relations, allegedly reflects the lack of occupational consciousness and serves to diminish it. Furthermore, given the rule of permanent employment, it is hardly possible for occupational labor markets and consequently occupational consciousness among employes to emerge. Insofar as occupations are defined as job characteristics transferable among employers (Reiss 1961, p. 10), the logic of this position is that occupations in the Western sense do not exist in Japan. There is a tendency to generalize the preceding perspectives to all Japanese employes over the long period of Japanese industrial history.[1]

Faced with this kind of argument, a variety of responses is possible. It seems probable that understanding of the role of occupation in Western societies is distorted. There are good reasons, for example, to think the distribution of rewards by the criteria of age and length of service is far more important in the United States than the formal existence of occupational wage structures would suggest (for example, Rees and Schultz 1970; Ryder 1965). The American ideology of merit reward conceals the actual operation of its reward systems. On a different level, American sociologists for the most part have taken occupational status as their primary measure of social stratification (Hatt 1961, pp. 239-258). This may reflect less its empirical importance than the intellectual history of American sociology and the relative measurability of occupational status in an era when measurability has been a prime consideration. Finally, recent research suggests the image of open occupational markets in America is quite at odds with reality (Doeringer and Piore 1971). To the extent the latter factors are operative, differences between Japan and the United States are exaggerated (though not absent). Later in the paper, we will return to this issue.

Moreover, the Western sociological literature on occupational change has been biased by its focus on intergenerational movement, with the primary question being the degree of openness of various social systems (Moore 1966, pp. 195-196). A consequence of this approach is lack of research on the demand side; occupational positions are taken as given, with the goal being to analyze mobility as a process of sorting individuals into these positions. In line with Moore's analysis (1966, pp. 194-212), this study attempts to redress the balance by providing a detailed examination of occupational demand over

---

[1]Taira (1962) and Cole (1971) among others have criticized the ease with which spatial and temporal boundaries have been extended in erecting the well-known construct of "traditional Japan."

time for the case of Japan.[2] Specifically, the present study examines the changing demand for occupational skills over the course of Japanese industrialization as measured in gross fashion by shifting occupational structure and composition.

EARLY STAGE OF INDUSTRIALIZATION

Japanese occupational statistics were systematically collected for the first time in the first national census in 1920. Before that, occupational data are only fragmentary. Moreover, in each subsequent census in the pre-World War II period, the occupational classification system was drastically altered. Consequently, it is difficult to grasp in any consistent fashion the changes in occupational structure before World War II. It is only after 1950 that the occupational classification system in Japan stabilized to permit ready comparisons over time.

The changing occupational classification system in the pre-World War II period reflects the fact that the conception of occupation was not well established at this time. Indeed, the classification used in the first census was totally fused (and therefore confused) with the industrial classification.[3] Of course, it is now well known that industrial classification concerns activities of establishments whereas occupation concerns activities of individuals. However, in the case of the first national census, individual respondents were asked to fill in the name of their occupation, but actually many filled in the

---

[2]Moore (1966, p. 195), while recognizing the need for such studies, contented himself with suggesting hypotheses based on cross-sectional data.

[3]The first occupational classification designed in Japan is that used in "Population Census in Kainokuni" [Kainokuni Genzai Ninbetsushirabe] in 1879. It contained the following seventeen major categories: (1) farming, (2) food processing, (3) garments, (4) building, (5) furniture, (6) textile, (7) hardware, (8) other manufacturing, (9) commerce, (10) communication and financial, (11) public utilities, (12) religion, (13) education, (14) medicine, (15) arts and sciences, (16) entertainment, and (17) other. A glance at these categories shows it to be really an industrial classification.

After the 1879 survey, the Statistical Bureau of the Prime Minister's Office studied classifications used by advanced Western countries. It also conducted several other surveys such as the Taiwan Population Census (1905), Kumamoto-shi Occupation Survey (1907), Tokyo Municipal Census (1908), and the Second Taiwan Population Census (1915). The occupational classification system used in the 1920 National Census was the result of experience from these various studies and surveys.

Notwithstanding, the occupational and industrial classifications remained confused in the 1920 census. The occupational classification system consisted of 10 major, 41 intermediate and 252 minor categories. The 10 major categories are (1) farming, (2) fisheries, (3) mining, (4) manufacturing, (5) commerce, (6) transportation, (7) government and independent business, (8) other, (9) family employes, and (10) no occupation. See *Explanatory Notes on the 1920 Census (Taishō 9-nen Kokuseichōsa Kijutsuhen)* pp. 89-94.

name of their industry.[4] From 1920 until 1950, changes in the occupational classification in each new census represented a gradual separation of occupational from industrial classifications.[5]

A clear conception of occupation was not formed prior to 1920 because Japanese society was basically still agrarian. Over half the gainfully employed were in agriculture until World War I. Agriculture was perceived in terms of a livelihood (*nariwai*), that is, as life itself, rather than as an occupation in the modern sense with functionally specific roles containing a differentiated set of duties. Engaging in agricultural work was, for the most part, not a conscious choice among alternatives by individuals. This was especially true for the oldest son, who as heir to the family farm was not expected to change occupations.

The situation was different for the smaller numbers of craftsmen and merchants living in cities, who had a long history of organization according to occupational interests, reflected in the guilds (*nakama*) of the Tokugawa period. Such organization presumes a significant degree of occupational consciousness (see Endo 1968, chap. 3). However, membership generally lacked the modern component of occupation insofar as parents tightly controlled the occupational choice of individuals through the apprenticeship system. Such apprenticeships commonly began at a very young age.

Demand for labor in specialized urban occupations was controlled by the guilds, one of whose main functions was to limit entry and thus monopolize opportunities for masters. This obviously was a major restriction on occupational choice from the demand side. One of the first acts of the new Meiji leaders was to decree freedom of choice of occupation and dissolve the already weakened guilds. Yet there was a time lag between the edict and the institutionalization of practices ensuring its implementation.

As we have no national data before 1920, it is impossible to deal systematically with occupational structure prior to this date. However, it is at least possible and indeed important to focus on two points: (1) the decline of agricultural population, and (2) the formation of the category of industrial workers.

[4]The *Taishō 9-nen Kokuseichōsa Kijutsuhen*, p. 95, states, "In the case of those who were employed in companies or other associations, if a person's regular work is independent (i.e., skilled or craft worker) and corresponds to any classification category, he was classified in that category; if not, he was classified according to the business of the company or association he belongs to." See also Odaka (1958, pp. 9-10).

[5]However, to the present day, this process is still not complete. The major occupational categories in use today were established in the 1950 census. The eleven major categories include "Workers in Mining and Quarrying Occupations." These categories reflect industrial characteristics with no effort made to distinguish the various skill levels. It should be noted by way of comparison that the confusion of occupational with industrial classifications has not been entirely eliminated in Western countries either. Thus, Hodge and Siegel (1966, p. 178) report the U.S. Bureau of the Census' detailed census occupational classification is infused with industrial characteristics.

According to the 1920 census, the agricultural and forestry labor force was 14.1 million, about 52 percent of the total labor force. This compares to the estimate of 17.3 million in 1872, about 81 percent of the total labor force. The question is how this decline took place. First, we need estimates of the number of agricultural and forestry workers for this period. For a long time, Hijikata's estimate (Hijikata 1929; Ohkawa 1957) has been the only one available and was widely cited. In recent years, better estimates have been constructed by Henmi and Minami as well as Umemura (Henmi 1956; Umemura 1968). Each is based on different methods and assumptions. At present, it is common to use the Umemura estimate from 1872 to 1920 and the census at five-year intervals thereafter, interpolating the Minami estimate to cover the years between.[6] The results of such a procedure appear in Table 1.

According to this table, the agricultural and forestry labor force was relatively constant in absolute terms between 1872 and 1914. To the extent the rural birth rate was above the replacement rate, the excess number migrated to urban areas. The percentage decline of agriculture is explained by the increase of the total gainfully employed, that is, the increment of total employment occurred in the nonagricultural sector. In contrast, the five years between 1914 and 1919, which were years of economic boom, represented for the first time in Japanese history rapid absolute declines in agricultural employment (excluding earlier temporary declines resulting from natural calamities). After 1919, the absolute decline continued but at a much more moderate pace.

Based on Simon Kuznets's analysis, Moore (1966) reports the percentage in agriculture in Japan fell from 85.0 in 1872 to 45.0 in 1936. Reporting on international comparisons, Moore cites a mean annual decline of 0.63 percentage points for Japan, the highest of any nation besides the USSR. Moore suggests the hypothesis late developers may experience more rapid shifts from agricultural to nonagricultural occupations. He derives this from the relatively rapid decline in Japan and the Soviet Union compared to France and the United States.

Some additional commentary on the Moore analysis is necessary in view of our earlier statements. The trend of decline in primary industry population

[6]Hijikata's estimate is the earliest study of this sort and was adopted by Ohkawa (1957, pp. 143, 245-246). Hijikata's procedure was to apply the parabola regression by least squares, and the result is that the number of farmers describes a parabolic curve peaking in the years 1895-97.

Henmi questioned Hijikata's parabolic assumption and chose a different method, based on statistics of the annual number of farm households. The result of Henmi's estimate is that before World War I, the agricultural population was almost constant (Minami 1970, chap. 9). Minami (1970) further extended Henmi's approach.

Umemura's method (1968) is based on estimating the gainfully occupied population from the population by age and sex, and then dividing this total into agricultural and nonagricultural sectors. The result is almost parallel to the trend reported by Henmi-Minami but is thought to be more accurate.

Table 1
Trend of Agricultural Population 1872-1936
(in thousands)

	Total gainfully employed population	Agricultural population			Total gainfully employed population	Agricultural population	
		Number	Percent			Number	Percent
1872	21,379	17,293	80.9	1905	25,022	16,258	65.0
1873	21,403	17,250	80.6	1906	25,108	16,286	64.9
1874	21,422	17,204	80.3	1907	25,256	16,241	64.3
1875	21,489	17,162	79.9	1908	25,363	16,189	63.8
1876	21,602	17,117	79.2	1909	25,419	16,026	63.0
1877	21,701	17,075	78.7	1910	25,522	15,987	62.6
1878	21,790	17,031	78.2	1911	25,671	16,115	62.8
1879	21,807	16,987	77.9	1912	25,846	16,114	62.3
1880	21,926	16,939	77.3	1913	26,043	16,015	61.5
1881	21,943	16,899	77.0	1914	26,197	16,068	61.3
1882	21,981	16,846	76.6	1915	26,397	15,279	57.9
1883	22,162	16,821	75.9	1916	26,638	15,096	56.7
1884	22,294	16,792	75.3	1917	26,868	15,169	56.5
1885	22,373	16,736	74.8	1918	26,932	14,219	52.8
1886	22,412	16,670	74.4	1919	27,025	14,119	52.2
1887	22,525	16,625	73.8	1920	27,210	14,100	51.8
1888	22,742	16,595	73.0		27,262	14,124	51.8
1889	22,950	16,556	72.1	1921	27,406	14,178	51.7
1890	23,114	16,502	71.4	1922	27,633	14,085	51.0
1891	23,232	16,505	71.0	1923	27,873	13,238	47.5
1892	23,411	16,473	70.4	1924	27,875	13,563	48.7
1893	23,499	16,415	69.9	1925	28,106	13,397	47.7
1894	23,661	16,395	69.3	1926	28,433	13,335	46.9
1895	23,821	16,393	68.8	1927	28,486	13,117	46.0
1896	23,905	16,448	68.8	1928	28,825	13,257	46.0
1897	24,101	16,403	68.1	1929	29,173	13,448	46.1
1898	24,171	16,416	67.9	1930	29,619	13,487	45.5
1899	24,309	16,452	67.7	1931	29,938	13,613	45.5
1900	24,436	16,423	67.2	1932	30,224	13,799	45.7
1901	24,543	16,380	66.7	1933	30,543	13,617	44.6
1902	24,685	16,395	66.4	1934	31,197	13,735	44.0
1903	24,833	16,323	65.7	1935	31,790	13,474	42.4
1904	24,953	16,289	65.3	1936	32,069	13,398	41.8

Source: Nakamura 1971, pp. 338-339. The original estimates are Umemura's (1968) until 1920, and the census with Minami's estimates interpolated thereafter. For 1920 both Umemura's and census estimates are presented; as can be seen, only a small gap exists between the two totals.

peaks in certain time periods: prewar there was a peak in 1914-19, and postwar in 1955-70. Prior to 1914, the rate of decline in absolute terms was generally slow. Thus, we suggest that in the early stage of industrialization, Japan was not necessarily characterized by a rapid decline of its primary industry population.

This, of course, is a comparative statement, and to demonstrate its validity we must examine the experience of other industrializing nations. Six countries, selected on availability of data, are compared in Table 2. We investigated the time interval involved as the primary sector population moved from 60 to 40 percent and then from 40 to 20 percent of the labor force. Compared to France and Italy, the rate of decline from 60 to 40 percent was quite high for Japan but about the same as the United States and Sweden. It is in the rate of decline from 40 to 20 percent that Japan experiences an especially high rate compared to most other advanced nations, though even here the rate of decline for Italy is roughly comparable. In both cases, rapid postwar economic growth seems responsible.

Table 2
International Comparison of the Rate of Decline in the Proportion
of Primary Industry Labor Force
(in percent)

	Year when percentage in the primary industry was:			Time interval between:	
	A	B	C	A to B	B to C
	60	40	20		
France	1833[a]	1924	1962	91	38
Germany	*	1895	1954	*	59
Italy	1870	1954	1968	84	14[b]
Sweden	1885	1921	1951	36	30
United States	1860	1896	1934	36	38
Japan	1915	1956	1970	41	14

Note: The choice of countries included in this table was limited by the availability of data. Data sources are Bairoch 1968. Where necessary, years are interpolated from this source (with two exceptions).
[a]The data source is Clark 1951.
[b]The year is extrapolated.
*No data.

Table 3
Composition of Employes in the Manufacturing Sector in 1909

	Male		Female		Total	
	Number	Percentage	Number	Percentage	Number	Percentage
Textile	72,231	(14.8)	414,277	(85.2)	486,508	(100.0)
Machinery	60,721	(95.1)	3,100	(4.9)	63,821	(100.0)
Chemical	51,805	(66.5)	26,078	(33.5)	77,883	(100.0)
Food and beverage	64,320	(72.4)	24,420	(27.6)	88,740	(100.0)
Other manufacturing	54,197	(68.0)	25,576	(32.0)	79,773	(100.0)
Total	303,274	(38.0)	493,451	(62.0)	796,725	(100.0)

Source: Nōshōmushō, *Kojo Tōkei-hyo*. In the original table, workers in electricity and gas were included as workers of a "special factory," but are excluded here because we are limiting our focus to manufacturing industries.

Next, we turn to the problem of the formation of the category of industrial workers, by which we mean employes in the manufacturing sector. It was not until about 1890 that important nongovernmental industrial enterprises emerged. Consequently, it was only after this period the demand for industrial labor could take on significant dimensions. The first reliable statistics on the number of industrial workers are in the first factory census, taken in 1909. The composition of workers in manufacturing, as shown in Table 3, reveals 52 percent of the total were women in the textile industry (especially *bōseki jokō*). As is well known, these female operatives commonly went to urban settings and worked for short periods (typically two or three years) before leaving the labor force, returning to their rural villages to marry farmers. Although Saxonhouse's research reported in this volume shows the average seniority of female operatives increased due to extended employment of a small core of employes, generally the majority of female operatives constituted an unstable and temporary social stratum. The formation of a working class, in the sense of individuals passing their entire occupational careers as industrial workers, still had not progressed very far by 1909.

Moore (1966, p. 199) notes the female labor force participation rate is more strongly affected by institutional variation than is the case with males. Thus generalization across societies presents more of a problem in the case of females. In Japan's case, two distinct patterns in female labor force participation are apparent, as summarized in Table 4.

First, for blue-collar workers the proportion of females was over half the total in the early stages of industrialization. The proportion of females among factory workers registers 62 percent in 1909 but declines rapidly thereafter to 33.8 in 1940, only to begin to rise again in the postwar period to 44.3 percent. One caution is necessary: by excluding many urban self-employed craftsmen from the factory statistics, the proportion of females is exaggerated in the earlier years. Notwithstanding, the decline in the proportion of females in the pre-World War II period reflects the reduction of importance of the textile industry in the entire economy, with the postwar rise being accounted for by other factors.

Second, with the exception of the post-World War II reversal, an opposite pattern exists in the case of white-collar employes. Males dominated the white-collar category in the early stages of industrialization, with females accounting for only 6.5 percent of clerical employes in 1930. The proportion of females shows a large increase to 15.1 percent in 1940 and then gradually increases to 25.2 in 1960, at which point it seems to stabilize temporarily.

We do not have sufficient data to test the universality of these patterns. However, Table 5 presents some relevant data. It seems the first pattern is not universal, although because we do not have comparable time periods, caution

Table 4
Transition in the Proportion of Female Workers
among All Clerical and Factory Employes

	Clerical employes	Manual employes
	(percentage who were women)	
1909	--	62.0
1920	--	53.0
1930	6.5	52.6
1940	15.1	33.8
1950	18.6	34.7
1955	22.2	35.6
1960	25.2	36.9
1965	25.2	44.3

Source: Nōshōmushō, Kojo Tōkei-hyō. No data are available for clerical workers in 1909 and 1920.

Table 5
International Comparison of Proportion of Female Workers
among All Factory Employes
(in percent)

France		United States		Belgium		Italy		India	
1866	42.7	1870	24.0	1890	24.6				
1881	38.3	1880	28.8	1900	23.9				
1901	31.5	1900	32.6	1920	25.0	1901	31.4	1911	17.4
1921	31.6	1920	24.2	1930	20.9	1911	46.2	1921	17.5

Source: See Saxonhouse, Table 2, this volume. Saxonhouse has adjusted the data to measure factory workers, thus excluding self-employed, family workers, white-collar employes, and managerial personnel. Consequently, the data are most comparable to the right-hand column in Table 4.

must be exercised. In none of the other four countries does the proportion of females among blue-collar workers approximate the high levels attained in Japan's early industrialization. Moreover, although the proportion declines rapidly in Japan, it tends to increase moderately in the United States, Italy, and Belgium in the latter part of the nineteenth century and then declines moderately after the turn of the century in the United States and after 1920 in Belgium. As for the second pattern, concerning the increase in the proportion of females among white-collar employes, cross-sectional comparative data supports the Japanese experience of a low but rising proportion of females in white-collar work as a common one.

How can we explain the unusually high proportion of females among blue-collar workers? One way is to ask the complementary questions, why were males not entering the urban labor force in larger numbers? What was responsible for the persistence of male employment in the agricultural sector? In this sense, the two problem areas we are investigating—the slow decline of the primary industry population in the early stage of industrialization, and the relatively slow process of formation of a permanent industrial worker stratum—are closely related. Indeed, they are two aspects of one common process. The nature of this process appears at odds with the conventional wisdom of rapid Japanese industrialization. Many of the characteristics associated with a modern occupational structure were not achieved until well into the twentieth century.

The leading role played by light industry, especially silk and cotton spinning, is the principal reason the core of the early industrial labor force was female. Such industries did not require the skilled labor of males and, as seen in Saxonhouse's research, employers were not willing to invest in increased training for females. Rosovsky (1961, pp. 98-104) concerns himself with why Japan's early industrialization was not in accord with the role of late developer as postulated by Gerschenkron. The essence of Gerschenkron's model can be summarized in the following proposition: when relatively backward countries want to catch up with advanced nations, they tend to concentrate on heavy industry as the basic element of industrialization as manifest in the advanced countries. The best available technology is borrowed, so it takes less time for the late developing country to reach the level of an advanced country.

Gerschenkron developed his model by generalizing from the pattern of industrialization in continental nations such as France, Germany, and Russia, which were relatively backward compared to Great Britain. In the case of Japan, however, contrary to Gerschenkron's generalization, light industry initially dominated, as it had in Great Britain.

How do we understand Japan's deviation from the Gerschenkron model? Rosovsky (1961, p. 103) argued the difference was that "Japan was capable of forming a disciplined and reliable labor force, suitable for factory work, more easily than many backward countries of continental Europe." However, we have already observed "forming a disciplined and reliable labor force" was not necessarily easily achieved in Meiji Japan, and much of the labor for Japan's early industrialization was supplied by unskilled, short-term workers, especially women. It is commonly pointed out Japan's potential labor force was more highly educated than was the case in the early stage of industrialization in Western Europe. Although this is true generally, it does not seem so relevant given an industrial labor force consisting primarily of younger female textile workers. This is not inconsistent with Saxonhouse's observation that education increased productivity even for young female textile workers. The formation of a disciplined and permanent working class was not achieved at least until the 1930s.

When we examine the matter from the viewpoint of rural families, we must note the lack of pressure to reduce employment at this time. This is because rice cultivation generally is labor intensive, and there were no significant labor-saving innovations prior to World War II.

Minami (1970), applying Lewis's (1954) model to Japan, asserts the pattern of movement from the agricultural to the industrial sector before World War II was based on "unlimited" labor supply; consequently, "disguised unemployment" was characteristic of the agricultural sector. Taira (1970), on the contrary, argues there were no periods in modern Japanese history fitting the Lewis model.

The assumption of "unlimited" labor supply was devised as an explanation for the low level of wages in the industrial sector in early stages of industrialization. In short, the logic of the Lewis model is focused on behavior in the industrial sector. However, if we shift our focus to the agricultural sector, there is reason to doubt the assertion "labor force in the noncapitalistic sector was overpopulated compared to the given technological level and the amount of land" (Minami 1968, p. 26). Even though the amount of land per worker was small, it seems that, unlike the situation after 1955, this condition fit the prevailing technological level of rice cultivation. Therefore, agricultural households could not afford to allow their work force, other than unmarried females, to flow out of the villages.

Minami's argument regarding the rural village as a pool of "disguised unemployment" is substantially a repetition of that part of Ōkōchi's thesis that "the Japanese rural village was a bottomless reservoir of surplus and unemployed population" (Ōkōchi 1952, p. 5). However, surplus is always a relative concept—relative to available opportunity. If urban employment opportunities were clearly advantageous compared with the benefits derived from remaining in agriculture, there would be a rush to these urban jobs. Actually, however, apart from a relatively short period of decline in the agricultural population in 1914-18, there was no such rush prior to World War II.

Many of the second and third sons who were surplus to the extent they had no accepted positions in terms of land and/or work in their native villages did flow out every year. As Vogel (1967) correctly points out, they were not expected to return once they migrated. But most of the heirs (oldest sons) of the farm household stayed in the villages. One of the reasons they stayed was the traditional norm to be successor of their paternal home. However, in view of the experiences after 1955 when many did leave, it is likely the prevailing wage level for factory employment before World War II failed to cancel the advantage of remaining to work the family land. On the other hand, females, who became spinning workers prior to marriage, represented those members of rural farm families not expected to serve as permanent members of the family labor force. In any case they would have left their homes on getting married.

In short, the source of recruitment to permanent factory employment was largely restricted to the portion of the male labor force in rural families other than heirs. This was a major factor in the slower formation of the industrial worker class in the early stage of industrialization compared to its rapid growth in the period after 1955.

DEVELOPMENT BETWEEN THE TWO WARS

The twenty years between the two world wars witnessed both Japan's drive toward industrial maturity and the process of militarization. Quite apart from the ethical questions involved, militarization did not serve as a major hindrance to further industrialization, and there is even reason to think it promoted industrialization. During this period Japan, in terms of conventional measures of occupational and industrial structure, became for the first time an industrial society.

Table 6 presents the occupational composition according to the 1920 and 1930 census. Unfortunately, the quality of the 1940 census data did not lend itself to ready comparison and consequently is not utilized by Kuroda. As may be seen in Table 6, the proportion of the labor force in agriculture and forestry drops to below 50 percent for the first time between 1920 and 1930. However, as shown in Table 1, although slight declines in the absolute number employed in agriculture do occur, the basic pattern of the

Table 6
Occupational Distribution in 1920 and 1930, Using 1950 Categories
(in thousand persons and percent)

	1920		1930	
Professional	1,007	(3.7)	1,253	(4.3)
Managers	430	(1.6)	519	,(1.8)
Clerical	1,814	(6.7)	2,187	(7.5)
Sales	2,005	(7.4)	3,032	(10.3)
Farmers	14,286	(53.0)	14,342	(48.9)
Mining	289	(1.1)	221	(0.8)
Transport and communication	286	(1.1)	329	(1.1)
Production process	5,434	(20.2)	6,236	(21.2)
Service	889	(3.3)	1,152	(3.9)
Unclassifiable	542	(2.0)	71	(0.2)
Total	26,966	(100.0)	29,341	(100.0)

Source: Kuroda 1960, p. 73. Kuroda bases his estimates on population census data. To present the data in the post-1950 occupational categories, he carried out considerable rearrangement of the census categories. Because of the error introduced by these procedures, the figures here should be regarded as rough estimates.

agricultural population holding a constant level and expelling those in excess of this level continued until after World War II.

To the extent the proportion of the labor force in agriculture does decrease, we see gains for such "modern" categories as production process workers, professional employes, and clerical employes. These increases, however, are rather modest: production process employes increase by 802,000 (14.8 percent), professionals by 246,000 (24.4 percent), and clerical employes by 373,000 (20.6 percent). The decidedly less "modern" sales category shows the most marked increase of 1,027,000 (51.5 percent), from 2,005,000 in 1920 to 3,032,000 in 1930. Apart from agriculture, the sales category contains the highest proportion of self-employed and family workers. Although the proportion of sales workers increased rapidly between 1920 and 1930, it declined between 1930 and 1940. The end of the stagnation period was 1930, followed by a recovery involving the gradual organization of the economy on a military basis.

Table 7 shows the increase of employes in manufacturing was very rapid from 1909 to 1920, almost doubling from 777,000 to over 1.5 million, but the rate declines between 1920 and 1930, with the total going only from 1.5 to 1.7 million. In short, the stagnation in the 1920s temporarily disrupted the formation of the working class. On the other hand, the agricultural labor force was almost constant between the years 1909 and 1930. As proposed by Sumiya (1964) and now widely accepted, this means we cannot accept the Ōkōchi hypothesis, based on the importance of dekasegi, that rural villages

Table 7
Transition in Composition and Size
of Manufacturing Employment: 1909-40

	1909	1920	1930	1940
Textile	486,508	854,623	903,399	974,454
Metal and machinery	63,821	265,137	252,450	1,726,768
Chemical and ceramic	7.7,883	171,504	178,994	544,722
Food and beverage	88,740	107,284	138,280	222,483
Other manufacturing	77,773	138,919	202,449	361,408
Total	776,725	1,537,467	1,675,572	3,829,835

Source: Nōshōmushō, Kōjō Tōkei-hyō. Notes are the same as in Table 2.

absorbed surplus labor during economic declines. Rather, the growth of the tertiary sector, especially the sales category, in the stagnant period suggests the self-employed category in urban areas, rather than rural villages, plays the role of absorbing redundant labor.

Movement toward the creation of a modern occupational structure was temporarily halted in the 1920s because of the economic slump. However, with the economic prosperity of the 1930s resulting from expanding production, including military procurement, rapid structural change again took place. As shown in Table 7, the total number of manufacturing employes increased 2.3 times from almost 1.7 million in 1930 to over 3.8 million in 1940. Among these, the relative share of the textile industry declined conspicuously from 53.9 to 25.4 percent; in contrast, those employed in the metal and machinery sector increased sevenfold from 252,000 in 1930 to 1.7 million in 1940, and those in the chemical and ceramic sector increased threefold from 179,000 in 1930 to 545,000 in 1940. Before 1930, females outnumbered males among manufacturing employes, and employes in light industry outnumbered those in heavy industry. Both of these situations were reversed during the 1930s. At this point Japan finally can be properly classified an "industrial society."

Even the fairly rapid economic growth in this decade, however, did not bring about a sharp decline in the absolute number of the agricultural population. An interesting exercise here is to examine the change in the size of agricultural population in the 1920 period, the first half of which was generally dominated by stagnation and the latter half by prosperity (see Table 1). These business cycles are not clearly reflected in changes in the size of the agricultural population. Of course, it is true the rate of outflow from the agricultural population was higher in the 1930s than in the 1920s; according to Minami's estimate the average outflow from 1921 to 1930 was 0.88 percent, whereas from 1931 to 1940 it was 1.7 percent (Minami 1970, p. 234). Yet if we consider this is also a period of transition from a skilled labor surplus to a shortage situation, the outflow from agriculture was rather small.[7] In any case, the economic prosperity and the emergent skilled labor shortage together were not strong enough to undermine the continuing pattern of constant agricultural population, and thus a "turning point" in Minami's sense was not realized in this period.

Large-scale increases in the white-collar category began to occur in the 1930s. Their rate of increase exceeds that of blue-collar workers, so the percentage of white-collar workers in the labor force rose from 18.1 in 1920 to 29.6 in 1940. It built on the spread of secondary and higher education.

The pre-World War II education system was divided into four levels: primary education (six years), secondary education (five years), the first half of higher education (three years), and the second half of higher education (three years). Among these, only primary education was compulsory, with the percentage of the appropriate age cohort attending school rising to almost 100 in the early 1900s. Table 8 presents the number of annual graduates and the proportion of graduates relative to the total appropriate age cohort for each year from 1905 to 1937, and for each of the three levels excluding primary education.

Secondary and higher education in Japan advanced conspicuously in the 1920s. Only 47,225 graduated from secondary schools (*chūgakkō* and *kōtō jogakkō*) in 1920, compared to 132,124 in 1930, an almost threefold increase. The share of the appropriate age cohort rose from 4.2 to 10.0 percent. New preparatory high schools (*kōtō gakkō*), professional schools (*semmon gakkō*), and colleges and universities were created, and the annual number of preparatory and professional school graduates rapidly expanded from 9,395 to 19,140, with college and university graduates increasing from 5,466 to 20,423. Ironically, this was a decade of depression and consequently of little growth in employment opportunities. The graduates were often confronted with the difficult task of finding jobs, and the term "though I graduated from a university . . ." was in fashion. However, they were gradually absorbed by the business recovery after 1930, with its rapid increase in white-collar employes. This major structural change in employment resulted in the first massive formation of a new urban middle class.

The full-scale formation of heavy industry with its creation of industrial employes as a distinct social class (see Hazama's article in this volume, for example) and the large-scale expansion of a new urban middle class were the most important aspects of changing occupational composition in the two decades 1920-40. The 1940s were a decade of war and defeat, with industrial development halted by wartime devastation. In this sense, the level of

---

[7]The stagnant period of early Showa, reflecting the worldwide depression, began to be replaced by recovery after 1932, the general background of which was an expansion of military production. In the recovery stage, unemployed skilled workers were first absorbed in 1932-33, and then unemployed unskilled workers and new school graduates were recruited into the production process after 1934. Thus by the end of 1936, the labor market became tight, and there developed great competition for skilled workers, thus increasing labor mobility between factories (see Shōwa Dōjinkai 1960, pp. 290-291).

Table 8
Educational Attainment: 1905-1937

| | Secondary education (Chūgakkō and Kōtō Jogakkō) | | Early higher education (Kōtō Gakkō and Senmon Gakkō) | | Advanced higher education (universities and colleges) | |
	Number of graduates	Percentage of cohort	Number of graduates	Percentage of cohort	Number of graduates	Percentage of cohort
1905	18,899	2.1	3,525	0.4	947	0.1
1906	20,556	2.2	3,738	0.4	1,229	0.1
1907	21,132	2.4	3,827	0.5	1,300	0.2
1908	22,174	2.7	4,018	0.5	1,698	0.2
1909	24,656	2.7	4,077	0.4	1,761	0.2
1910	26,933	2.9	4,281	0.5	2,035	0.3
1911	28,664	3.0	4,467	0.5	1,752	0.2
1912	30,170	3.1	4,831	0.5	1,945	0.2
1913	29,294	3.0	5,135	0.6	1,855	0.2
1914	33,668	3.3	5,174	0.6	2,582	0.3
1915	35,504	3.3	5,546	0.6	2,402	0.3
1916	36,915	3.5	5,592	0.6	2,971	0.3
1917	39,112	3.6	5,896	0.6	2,682	0.3
1918	42,139	3.8	6,368	0.6	2,655	0.3
1919	43,642	3.8	7,063	0.7	2,960	0.3
1920	47,225	4.2	9,395	0.9	5,466	0.6
1921	52,903	4.8	8,538	0.8	4,060	0.4
1922	59,044	5.3	8,357	0.7	9,838	1.0
1923	65,945	6.1	8,914	0.8	10,461	1.0
1924	75,339	6.0	9,851	0.9	12,849	1.1
1925	90,413	7.5	11,912	1.2	11,924	1.2
1926	104,295	8.3	15,797	1.6	13,630	1.3
1927	114,352	9.1	14,335	1.2	15,129	1.5
1928	122,449	9.5	16,513	1.4	16,784	1.6
1929	126,786	9.3	18,095	1.4	18,569	1.8
1930	132,124	10.0	19,140	1.6	20,423	1.9
1931	134,800	10.0	19,937	1.6	20,182	1.8
1932	134,389	10.2	20,732	1.6	20,360	1.7
1933	132,726	9.8	20,749	1.6	21,170	1.8
1934	129,180	9.8	21,623	1.6	21,659	1.7
1935	131,530	10.3	21,563	1.7	21,151	1.7
1936	139,800	11.2	21,072	1.6	21,063	1.7
1937	146,327	9.5	–	–	21,454	1.7

Source. Calculated from *Teikoku Tokei Nenkan*, annual volumes, 1905 to 1937.
Note: Age cohort distributions of population in the yearbook are given only for every five years. Thus most of the percentages of cohort are rough figures.

attainment in the 1930s was the peak of pre-World War II development in Japan.

It must be emphasized, however, that the degree of transformation of the occupational structure was not comparable to the level of industrialization attained. The creation of blue-collar workers and white-collar employes occurred while the number of farm households remained stable at 5.5 million. Although participation in secondary and higher education increased, the highest percentage of the appropriate age groups graduating did not exceed 11.2 percent in the secondary schools and 1.9 percent in the higher education categories.

It was only with the explosive economic growth after 1955 that these limiting factors were finally cast aside. A variety of institutional reforms was necessary for this to occur. These were carried out in such areas as land reform, family system reform, and labor legislation which were products of defeat and the subsequent Occupation. It seems clear the rapid economic growth after 1955 would not have been achieved if the prewar institutional structure had been kept intact.

DEVELOPMENT SINCE WORLD WAR II

The greater availability of data for the post-World War II period allows more detailed examination of some of the themes presented in our introduction. Where possible, time series data including the prewar period will be presented. However, even the postwar data displays large gaps because of the introduction of new series and the incompatibilities introduced by shifting definitions and categories. Furthermore, the lack of occupational consciousness in Japan manifests itself in a relative paucity of detailed occupational time series data collected by governmental agencies. The absence of such data, however, should not be interpreted to mean that occupation is unimportant. That would be to confuse the decision to create a particular measure with behavior itself.

Table 9

Composition of Persons with a Job by Industrial Sector (1930-71)
(in percent)

Year	Primary[a]	Secondary[b]	Tertiary[c]	Total gainfully employed[d]
1930[e]	49.4	20.4	30.2	29,341
1940	44.0	26.1	29.9	32,231
1950	48.3	21.9	29.8	35,626
1956	42.0	23.9	34.1	39,863
1959	37.5	26.1	36.4	41,330
1962	30.2	31.0	38.6	42,855
1965	26.2	32.2	41.5	44,779
1968	22.1	33.5	44.3	49,006
1971	17.4	35.5	47.1	50,630

Source: For prewar and 1950 data, Sōrifu 1954. For postwar data beginning in 1956, Sōrifu 1970, pp. 212-215. For 1971 data, Sōrifu 1972, p. 52.

[a]Includes agriculture, forestry and hunting, and fisheries and agriculture.

[b]Includes mining, construction, and manufacturing.

[c]Includes wholesale and retail trade, finance, insurance, real estate, transportation and communication, electricity, gas and water, services, and government officials.

[d]In thousands. Numbers are for both sexes combined.

[e]Differences between prewar and postwar censuses plus differences between the census (Sōrifu 1954) and the *Employment Status Survey* (Sōrifu 1970 and 1972) suggest some caution in making comparisons. Some notable differences are that the prewar census includes gainfully employed population regardless of age whereas the *Survey* and the postwar census limits its consideration to those fifteen years old and over (except the 1956 *Survey*, which refers to those fourteen years old and over). Furthermore, the *Survey* classified unemployed persons as persons without occupation, but the prewar census did not have any classification for unemployed (who, once engaged in work, are included in gainfully occupied population).

Table 10
Distribution of Male Labor Force: Percentage in Agriculture
(selected countries)

Country	Percentage (unless otherwise noted, in 1965)
United Kingdom	5 (1961)
West Germany	8
United States	8
Canada	12
Israel	13
JAPAN	14 (1971)
Switzerland	15
Sweden	18
Argentina	23
Italy	24
Norway	24
France	25 (1962)
Chile	34
Czechoslovakia	38
Portugal	48
Bolivia	53
Brazil	57
Mexico	59
Ghana	60
Philippines	67
Thailand	78
Ivory Coast	86 (1964)

Source: For all countries except Japan, Taylor and Hudson 1972, pp. 332-334. For Japan, Sorifu, *Kozo Kihon Chosa*, 1972 edition, pp. 54-55.

Adapting Moore (1966), we will deal with the following topics relating to the demand side of the labor market in order to lay out the essentials of changing occupational structure in the postwar period: sectoral relocation, occupational upgrading, and bureaucratization.

Sectoral Relocation

The rapid shift out of the agricultural sector that accompanied the high rate of economic growth in the postwar period has been noted. As apparent in Table 9, it was not until the postwar recovery was complete in the early 1950s that the proportion engaged in agriculture begins a marked decline. Specifically, the period from 1950 to 1956 marks the first time in the postwar period the prewar figure of 44.0 percent in agriculture is breached, with the proportion declining to 42.0 in 1956. Thereafter the decline accelerates, dropping 11.8 percentage points in the six years between 1956 and 1962.

An international comparison, including Japan, is provided in Table 10, which presents cross-sectional data on the percentage distribution of the male labor force in agriculture for selected countries. This percentage declines with the degree of economic modernization and indicates Japan has moved into the ranks of the more economically advanced nations.

Although the data in Table 9 refer to shifts in employment among industrial sectors, they may be interpreted as proxies for the shift out of agricultural occupations toward occupations in the secondary and tertiary sectors of the economy.[8] Furthermore, these shifts have roughly coincided with increased urbanization of the population.

A number of scholars propose that the link between those remaining in agriculture and urban migrants during the course of industrialization was especially strong. Based on such mechanisms as kin ties, dekasegi migration patterns (migrants who worked in the cities only to return to the countryside), and patron-client ties, emphasis by Western scholars has been on the resultant continuity in values and behavior between those in agriculture and the mobile urban migrants filling the occupational positions of an expanding industrial society (for example, Vogel 1967; Levine 1965). Although such an emphasis undoubtedly captures a significant part of the Japanese experience, one wonders just how much of the variance in behavior it accounts for. It would seem to be most applicable to the large numbers of temporarily employed females who constituted a majority of factory employment until just after the 1930s. However, with the gradual reduction of this group as the textile industry declined in relative importance, and with the increase in the proportion of both males and females who became both permanent urban residents and long-term employes (especially the males), a different picture presents itself. For these individuals the shift from agricultural to urban-located occupations was a monumental change, just as it has been for individuals in other industrializing nations.[9] True, the mediating mechanisms mentioned previously may be the critical variables which discriminate between the Japanese and Western experiences, but this should not obscure the profound impact of the shift from agricultural to nonagricultural occupations for those making a permanent move.

Thus far, the discussion has centered on the movement out of agricultural occupations without much commentary on destination. Clark (1951) describes movement out of agriculture based on his reading of the Western experience as a temporal sequence whereby the shift is accompanied by a corresponding growth of employment in the secondary sector. This, in turn,

[8]According to a cross-tabulation of 1960 employment data, 98.7 percent of those employed in primary industry were fishermen, farmers, hunters, and loggers and related workers (Emi 1969, p. 156).

[9]For a dramatic account of the early impact of such movement on Meiji youth and particularly the children of wealthy peasants, see Pyle (1969). He especially emphasizes the role of the new schools of higher learning established after the Meiji Restoration designed to prepare the young for occupations in an industrial society. They served as agents of social and cultural revolution.

is followed still later by a shift into the tertiary sector. As is now well known, however, in many contemporary nonindustrial nations, a different pattern occurs. Urbanization increases without a concomitant expansion in the manufacturing sector; consequently, there occur large-scale movements directly from agriculture into the service sector. Much of this growth of urban employment represents an increase in those engaged in marginal service activities.

The Japanese case, until recently, seemed to conform more to the pattern of the contemporary underdeveloped nations than to the Western experience as analyzed by Clark.[10] Existing data on the hundred-year period of Japanese industrialization suggest the tertiary sector has always exceeded the secondary sector in employment (caution is necessary, as the quality of the data is far from satisfactory). The historical labor surplus character of the Japanese economy led to an abundance of people being forced to eke out an existence in the low productivity sectors of urban areas. In the pre-World War II period, tertiary employment grew notably in periods of business slowdown and stagnation as it absorbed those unable to obtain industrial employment; conversely, employment growth in the tertiary sector was stagnant or declined in periods of rapid industrial growth.[11] Emi examined the relationship between employment in service industries and per capita income level. He found, using 1960 data, compared to other countries, Japan had higher service sector employment than expected from its per capita income level (Emi 1969, pp. 147-150).

Analysis of this issue must proceed also through a comparison of the character of service sector employment. Japan's tertiary sector as compared to the United States is characterized by a heavier weight in wholesale-retail trade and other miscellaneous services. In addition, government employment is quite low compared to the United States and has shown no tendency to increase. Emi (1969) accounts for these differences primarily in terms of variations in sex ratios, employer-employe status, and scale of industry.

Notable in recent years is the rapid growth of the tertiary sector and particularly the service component, suggesting a new situation of service employment increasing even in periods of rapid expansion.[12] That is, it no longer simply absorbs workers in times of business stagnation (Emi 1969, pp. 145-146). Examining 1965 through 1968, Emi reports that of the total increase in nonprimary sector employment, 39.6 percent was in the secondary sector, while the tertiary sector accounted for 60.4, with 50.6

[10]For a treatment of employment composition in the Japanese tertiary sector, trends over time, and international comparisons, see Emi (1969, pp. 133-157). Subsequent discussion of the service economy in Japan builds on his presentation.

[11]Our discussion of the growth patterns of the sales category of employment in the prewar period suggests these same conclusions.

[12]Fuchs (1968) distinguishes service industries from goods industries and thereby excludes from the former, transportation, communications and electricity, and gas and water. See Table 9, note 3.

percent of the total in the service component of the tertiary sector.

An examination of the occupational composition of this service component shows that 13 percent of all employed persons in service industries are professional and technical workers; moreover, if we limit our scope to the subcategory of services, the proportion of professional and technical workers rises to 33 percent (Sōrifu 1969, pp. 326-327).[13] The service industries then are hardly simply a receptacle for unskilled surplus labor; they also involve high levels of labor skills and technology. Interestingly enough, the distributions between these two types do not show any sharp shifts based on higher increases for those services representing higher skills. For example, the proportion of professionals in services in 1950 is reported as 40 percent of all service employes; the roughly comparable figure for 1965 noted here shows a decline to 33 (Sōrifu 1954, pp. 477-479). If we examine those employed in personal services (the largest component employing unskilled workers in the entire service category) as a proportion of the total employed in services, we find it declined only slightly from 32 percent in 1950 to 29 in 1965 (Sōrifu 1954, p. 188; 1965, p. 326). There is no indication those engaged in personal services had significantly upgraded skills in 1965 compared to 1950. Thus, we may infer that growth of unskilled service occupations has tended to keep pace with the growth of skilled service occupations.

V. R. Fuchs, in his analysis of employment trends in the postwar United States, details the emergence of the "service economy." This is an economy in which more than half of the employed population is not involved in the production of food, clothing, houses, cars, or other tangible goods (Fuchs 1968). The Japanese often refer to these developments as the growth of the information society or leisure industries (for example, Tominaga 1971, p. 69). The choice of these two terms suggests somewhat the contradiction referred to here, for the term "information society" implies the formation of large numbers of highly skilled individuals, whereas the term "leisure industries" implies the formation of large numbers of unskilled service employes. Both types have greatly increased in recent years.

Occupational Upgrading

By industrialization we generally refer not only to the shift out of agriculture but also to changes in the occupational composition of the nonagricultural labor force. Moore (1966, p. 206) refers to the upgrading that occurs with the shift from manual to nonmanual occupations. Despite an overlapping of the distributions, the latter are generally associated with higher incomes and higher educational standards. Even within these rough categories we would expect upgrading as, for example, unskilled jobs are replaced with processes requiring semiskilled workers.

[13]In service industries, we include wholesale and retail trade, finance, insurance and real estate, services, and government. The industrial category of services includes repair services, amusement and recreation services, medical and other health services, educational services, and miscellaneous services.

Table 11 reports the changing distribution of employment by occupation (see Table 6 for prewar comparisons). The most marked changes over the twenty-year period 1950-70 come in the decline of agricultural occupations (-28.5 percentage points) and the increases in the craftsman, production process, and laborers category (+9.6) and in clerical employes (+5.6). These overall trends, however, conceal some notable changes within the twenty-year period. In particular, the share of the craftsman, production process, and laborers category as a proportion of the labor force grew most rapidly between 1955 and 1960. It then slowed markedly, so that between 1960 and 1970 it no longer registered the largest change (excluding the decline in agricultural occupations).[14] The increase of 3.1 percentage points in the craftsman category was more than matched in the 1960-70 period by the increase of 3.6 for clerical workers. Moreover, the next two largest increases were registered in this period by the professional (1.6) and managerial (1.6)

Table 11
Employment by Major Occupational Categories
(in percent)

	1950	1955	1960	1965	1970
Professional	4.4	4.9	4.9	5.6	6.7
Managerial	1.8	2.1	2.3	3.0	3.9
Clerical	8.4	8.7	10.4	13.0	14.0
Sales	8.4	10.6	10.6	11.7	12.0
Agriculture, forestry,					
and fishing	47.7	40.5	32.6	24.5	19.2
Mining	1.2	0.9	0.8	0.5	0.3
Transportation and					
communication	1.7	2.2	3.3	4.4	4.5
Craftsman, production					
process, and laborers	22.1	24.1	28.6	30.1	31.7
Protective service	4.3	6.1	1.1	1.2	1.3
Service			5.4	6.0	6.5
Total	100	100	100	100	100
Bases for percentages[a]	35,625.8	39,343.6	43,679.3	47,609.9	52,026.3

Source: Data for 1960-70 adapted from Keizai Shingikai 1972, pp. 24-25. Data for 1950-55 computed from Rōdōshō 1966, p. 22.
[a]In thousands. Numbers are for both sexes combined.

[14]Although there has been a decline in the rate of percentage increase of the distribution accounted for by blue-collar workers, the rate of numerical increase has not displayed a clear downward trend. After peaking in the 1955-60 period with an increase of 3 million, it fell to 1.8 million from 1960-65 and then rose to 2.2 million in the 1965-70 period. Although the blue-collar category continues to grow rapidly, other categories now have higher increase rates.

categories. In short, those occupations requiring higher education and rewarded highly in status and income are growing most rapidly.[15]

We can grasp recent trends in the relationship between the growth of white-collar and blue-collar jobs by comparing the destination of new school graduates over time. In 1960, 26.8 percent of new school graduates were going into white-collar jobs and 41.2 percent into blue-collar jobs.[16] By 1970, however, 38.9 percent were entering white-collar jobs and only 35.9 percent were entering blue-collar occupations.

We can obtain a picture of Japan's relative standing with respect to the proportion of the labor force in white-collar jobs from Table 12. With the nations arranged in descending order of GDP per capita, we observe the not surprising general pattern of a rising proportion of the economically active population in white-collar occupations the higher the level of economic development.[17] Japan ranks high (seventh) among the nations in the proportion of economically active population in white-collar jobs.

The proportion of professionals in the labor force is probably subject to fewer errors and definitional differences than the white-collar percentage and therefore provides a more accurate ordering of nations (Moore 1966, p. 206). Examining the proportion of male professionals in the labor force, we again find a positive relationship between level of economic growth and percentage professional. Of interest is that Japan's relative position declines from seventh in column 2 to twelfth in column 4. Japan's high ranking for white-collar stems in great measure from the proportion of the labor force accounted for by clerical workers (13.8); among the countries compared in Table 12, only the United States (16.6) and Australia (14.7) had a higher proportion of the labor force in clerical work. Some classificatory problems may be involved here. The tradition is strong in many Japanese organizations to treat young recruits as untrained and gradually lead them through "stages of difficulty." In practice, this means many future managers and professionals are assigned initially to menial clerical jobs. Although this practice is present in other industrialized nations (for example, see Smigel's discussion of Wall Street lawyers in Hall 1969, pp. 105-106), its institutionalization in Japan leads to a significant number of male employes being classified as clerical in Japan who would be classified as managerial or professional in other nations.

This interpretation is supported by the observation that for an advanced industrial nation, Japan has an unusually high proportion of clerical employes who are male (50.7 in 1970 compared to 25.2 percent for the United States). In Japan, as in other industrial nations, the proportion of clerical employes

[15]These data are inadequate for the conclusions, insofar as they do not take into consideration the changing job content within occupational categories (for the United States economy, see Scoville 1969).

[16]The remainder ended up in sales and service and agricultural occupations. Source for this data is the Keizai Shingikai (1972, p. 19).

[17]Caution should be exercised in making conclusive statements, for the selection of nations for comparison is based primarily on the availability of recent data.

who are male varies inversely with the level of industrialization. Generally, a shortage of urban opportunities for educated males (who take the lead in acquiring education) results in males preempting many clerical jobs in the early industrial period. However, the shift away from this pattern, as females acquire more education and as structural changes open up new more desirable opportunities for males, has been slower in Japan than in other industrial nations.

Table 12
White-Collar and Male Professionals as a Proportion
of the Economically Active Population
(selected countries)

Country[a]	Date	Economically active[b] (both sexes)	Percentage white collar[c]	Economically active[d] (males)	Percentage professional[e] (males)
United States	1970	85,903	29.6	54,343	12.8
Canada	1971	8,267	36.7	5,832	11.5
Sweden	1965	3,441	27.0	2,283	13.9
Australia	1966	4,856	30.3	3,422	7.6
Denmark	1965	2,252	21.6	1,488	7.1
United Kingdom	1966	24,857	26.4	15,994	9.2
JAPAN	1970	52,759	24.3	32,176	6.8
Israel	1970	1,001	31.7	704	10.9
France	1962	19,829	20.2	13,165	7.8
Italy	1965	19,920	13.3	14,420	4.6
Germany (Fed. Rep.)	1961	26,821	22.6	16,890	8.0
Venezuela	1970	3,120	20.2	2,467	6.2
Spain	1970	12,732	12.4	na	na
Hungary	1970	5,001	22.4	2,946	10.2
Bulgaria	1965	4,268	15.9	2,390	8.6
Chile	1970	2,942	17.8	2,194	3.6
Mexico	1960	11,332	10.5	9,297	2.8
Iran	1966	7,584	5.5	6,584	2.3
Philippines	1965	11,491	9.6	7,590	2.3
Colombia	1964	5,134	11.1	4,102	2.6
China (Taiwan)	1966	4,598	13.9	3,576	5.3
Algeria	1966	2,565	7.7	2,455	2.8
Korea	1968	9,757	8.2	6,216	3.3
Pakistan	1968	41,906	3.5	na	na

Source: ILO 1971.

[a]Countries are arranged in descending order from the highest gross domestic product (GDP) per capita to the lowest. About half of the dates for which the GDP per capita was calculated are the same as the dates for the employment data. The others differ by no more than three years. We did not regard this divergence as large enough to notably change the rank ordering of countries. Source: United Nations 1971.

[b]In thousands.

[c]Includes professional, technical, and related workers, administrative, executive and managerial workers, and clerical workers.

[d]In thousands.

[e]Includes professional, technical, and related workers. Calculated as a percentage of total economically active males. The basis for this sex restriction lies in the differences in accounting for unpaid family labor (predominantly female in the agricultural sector) by various nations. By basing the data on males, this incomparability is reduced (see Taylor and Hudson 1972, p. 292).

Bureaucratization

Along with sectoral relocation and the upgrading of occupational composition that accompany economic development there occurs what sociologists label a bureaucratization of the labor force (Bendix 1963, pp. 211-244). We may describe this as occupational performance becoming characterized by routine procedures (see Bendix 1963, p. 211; Caplow 1954, p. 149; Taylor 1968, pp. 88-112). This suggests the systemic and impersonal aspects of bureaucratic organization both with respect to work content and treatment of employes.[18] The most straightforward measure of bureaucratization lies in the proportion of the labor force who are wage and salary earners. Unlike some of the measures implied by narrower definitions (for example, Caplow 1954, pp. 149-150), this has the virtue of being comparable between nations. As Moore (1966, p. 210) notes, the proportion of the labor force accounted for by wage and salary earners shows a long-term increase in "capitalist" countries and is nominally complete in socialist economies.

Table 13 presents the changing distribution of Japanese employment by employment status. The overall trends conform to what we would expect as the pace of economic development quickened between 1950 and 1970.

Table 13
Distribution of Persons with a Job by Employment Status
(in percent)

Year	Self-employed workers	Family workers[a]	Employes	Bases for percentages[b]
1950[c]	25.6	33.7	38.5	363.1
1955	25.1	31.4	43.5	409.0
1960	22.7	23.9	53.4	443.6
1961	21.9	23.0	55.1	449.8
1962	21.0	22.1	56.9	455.6
1963	20.7	21.1	58.2	459.5
1964	20.3	20.3	59.4	465.5
1965	19.9	19.3	60.8	473.0
1966	19.5	18.4	62.0	482.7
1967	19.7	17.9	62.4	492.0
1968	19.7	17.3	62.9	500.2
1969	19.7	16.7	63.5	504.0
1970	19.2	15.8	64.9	509.4

Source: Japan Productivity Center 1972, p. 102. Original source for 1955 to 1970 is the *Rōdō Chōsa Nenpō* (Rōdōshō). For 1950, the source is ILO 1954, p. 88.
[a]2.2 percent were classified as others.
[b]In hundred thousands. Numbers are for both sexes combined.
[c]Refers to unpaid family members of the self-employed, working for his business (Labor Force Survey definition).

[18]Some of the most commonly discussed attributes of bureaucracy are cited by Richard Hall as hierarchy of authority, division of labor, technically competent participants, procedural devices for work situations, rules governing

Employes as a proportion of total employed rose from 38.5 to 64.9 percent; in absolute terms the number more than doubled from 14.0 to 33.1 million. This growth was particularly marked by the rapid decline of family workers, from 33.7 percent of the employed to 15.8; in absolute terms the decline was from 12.2 to 8.1 million. Self-employed workers present a somewhat more ambiguous case. In relative terms, there was a modest decline from 25.6 to 19.2 percent. An examination of the actual numbers involved, however, shows a decline from a 1955 high of 10.3 million to a 1965 low of 9.4 million and then a gradual increase until 1969, at which point the total returned to about the 1961 level of 9.9 million.

The slowing down of the relative decline of the self-employed and actual increase in their absolute numbers is not an entirely surprising phenomenon. In the United States, from 1960 to 1970, the self-employed declined by some 814,000, but a closer look shows agriculture, manufacturing, mining, and construction experienced the sharpest declines; the service sector experienced an increase of almost 350,000.

A detailed examination of the structure of Japanese self-employment reveals some parallels and some differences (Sōrifu 1970, pp. 228-229; 1972, p. 60). As in the United States, self-employment in agriculture shows a steady decline in Japan (from 5.8 million in 1957 to 3.8 million in 1971), while significant growth in self-employment is recorded in the services (from 1.1 million in 1956 to 1.4 million in 1971). Significant differences are that overall self-employment continues to grow in Japan, and it shows surprising growth in the manufacturing sector, just the sector we might expect the self-employed to be gradually forced out of, as inability to take advantage of economies of scale put them in a less favorable competitive position. Self-employment in the manufacturing sector went from 814,000 in 1956 down to 786,000 in 1962 and then began a steady upward turn that had reached 1.4 million in 1971.

To grasp the locus of these increases, we can examine the growth of self-employment by manufacturing category in 1968-71 (Sōrifu 1969, p. 20; 1972, p. 52). Self-employment in manufacturing increased from 1.2 to 1.4 million in this period, with different categories recording increases and decreases; food and tobacco manufactures suffered the largest decrease, 13,000. Three of the fifteen manufacturing categories accounted for 84.3 percent of the 190,000 increase: textile mill products, 64.7 percent; electrical machinery and equipment, 11.6 percent; and fabricated metal products, 8.0 percent. Miscellaneous manufacturing industries account for an additional 11.6 percent of the increase. The increased number of self-employed in manufacturing created extremely small enterprises; of the aforementioned

---

behavior of positional incumbents, limited authority of office, differential rewards by office, impersonality of personal contact, administration separate from ownership, emphasis on written communication, and rational discipline. Among the scholars surveyed by Hall, agreement on a category as an attribute of bureaucracy was highest in order of this listing. The above is cited and discussed in Miller and Form (1964, pp. 10-11).

190,000 increase, 84 percent were one-person enterprises (Sōrifu 1969, p. 26; 1972, p. 60).

Females accounted for some 72 percent of the 183,000 increase in the four manufacturing categories reported above. The increase in the textile mill product cagegory was particularly striking: females accounted for 86 percent. The proportion of females among self-employed in manufacturing has risen steadily from some 20 percent in 1959 to 41 percent in 1971. This parallels the more modest growth in the proportion of females among self-employed in all industries, which went from 22 percent in 1959 to 30 percent in 1971. Most of this growth, however, has occurred in the agricultural sector as a consequence of the failure of young males to replace older male farmers leaving the labor force. The growth in the proportion of females among self-employed in the nonagricultural sector (not limited to just manufacturing) is still more modest, shifting from 27 percent in 1959 to 33 percent in 1971.

One approach to understanding the growth of self-employment in manufacturing is to consider motivation. Self-employed workers in manufacturing with at least one employe earn an average annual income of almost twice that of ordinary employes (¥1,557,000 for the self-employed compared to ¥793,000 for ordinary employes in 1971; Sōrifu 1972, pp. 113, 136). Although these averages conceal considerable variation, the point is that such large discrepancies in income are acknowledged in public opinion and become important incentives for self-employment. The discrepancies are widened still further by more lenient taxation of the self-employed.

This model of job creation is based on the supply of new entrepreneurs; unfortunately it does not fit very well with a model of job creation based on demand factors. Moreover, it presumes a suspiciously rosy picture of the upgrading of female employment status. On closer examination, we find 68 percent of the increase in self-employed of both sexes from 1968 to 1971 are home handicraft workers. This is even truer for females, where 78 percent are home handicraft workers. Home handicraft workers are defined as those doing piecework at their homes without the fixtures or the equipment of a shop or works. This category increased from 32 percent of all self-employed in manufacturing in 1968 to 37 percent in 1971 (overall it accounted for 13 percent of all self-employed in the nonagricultural sector of the economy). In short, there is a growing tendency of the self-employed in manufacturing to be home handicraft workers, as distinct from people who operate their own enterprises. What we see here is the maintenance if not expansion of an area of petty manufacturing production in which economies of scale are not applicable. This does not mean, however, that an expanded arena for self-reliant entrepreneurs is being established. Rather, there is a shift to relatively low paid people—often females—engaged in piecework and motivated in many cases by the desire to supplement family income.

We can get a better picture of Japan's relative standing among nations on this measure of bureaucratization by examining the proportion of the economically active population composed of salaried employes and wage earners. Japan, with 63.6 percent of its economically active population falling in this category, ranks quite low compared to other industrialized nations. The discrepancy is explained not so much by the high proportion of self-employed (19.0), but by the unusually high proportion of family workers (16.0). However, as seen in Table 14, the proportion of family workers among total employed is declining rapidly so the distribution of employment status is coming to resemble that of other industrialized nations.

As organizations increase in size and complexity, bureaucratization seems to increase (Miller and Form 1964, pp. 10-11). In particular, growing size seems to enhance possibilities for establishing and lengthening the hierarchy of authority, increasing division of labor, and growing impersonality with all the attendant consequences for organizational practices. Consequently, a

Table 14
Structure of Economically Active Population
(selected countries)

Country	Date	Percentage salaried employes and wage earners	Percentage employers and workers on own account	Family workers	Status unknown	Bases for percentage[a]
United Kingdom	1966	90.1	6.4	0.7	2.8	24,857
United States	1970	90.0	8.3	1.2	0.6	85,903
Canada	1971	86.1	10.5	2.3	1.1	8,627
Sweden	1965	85.1	11.2	3.8	–	3,450
Australia	1966	83.2	14.3	0.9	1.6	4,856
Germany (Fed. Rep.)	1970	82.9	10.4	6.7	–	27,011
Denmark	1970	80.3	14.6	5.1		2,390
Hungary	1970	78.0	2.4	0.8	18.8	5,001
France	1970	75.7	21.2[b]	–	3.0	21,332
Chile	1970	72.0	24.1	3.2	0.7	2,942
Israel	1970	70.8	21.7	3.7	3.8	1,001
Italy	1970	67.8	22.7	7.8	1.8	19,571
Spain	1970	64.9	23.3	11.8	–	12,732
Mexico	1960	64.1	34.2	1.0	0.7	11,332
JAPAN	1970	63.6	19.0	16.0	1.4	52,759
Algeria	1966	60.2	21.6	6.2	12.1	2,565
Venezuela	1961	60.1	33.7	4.5	1.8	2,351
Colombia	1964	57.3	33.2	8.2	1.4	5,134
China (Taiwan)	1966	49.4	26.9	16.4	7.2	4,598
Iran	1966	43.8	37.1	8.9	10.2	7,584
Korea (Rep. of)	1968	35.5	33.2	26.2	5.1	9,757
Philippines	1965	32.0	37.6	22.1	8.3	11,491
Pakistan	1968	30.3	48.5	19.9	1.2	41,906

Source: ILO 1971.
[a]In thousands, number are for both sexes combined.
[b]Includes family workers.

useful measure of bureaucratization capturing this dimension is the distribution of employment by size of firm.[19] Table 15 presents the distribution of employes in manufacturing industries by size of firm from 1956 to 1971. There is obviously no specific size at which we can with assurance call a firm bureaucratized. We presume, however, that for firms of one hundred or more employes the probability is high the work setting is bureaucratized.

The most remarkable change is the reduction of the proportion working for smaller firms, with those at firms of 1-9 employes going from 17.1 percent of all manufacturing employes in 1956 to 10.6 in 1971, and those at firms of 10-29 going from 19.3 percent in 1956 to 14.2 in 1971. The 30-99 employes category shows only minor changes in the same period. Almost all the losses of the smallest categories are thus accounted for by growth of the 100+ employe category, from 45.6 percent in 1956 to 58.2 in 1971. The decline of employes at presumably less bureaucratic firms is most notable in 1956-62. Indeed, there is a surprising growth in the 1-9 category after 1965, with a slowdown in the growth of the 100+ category in the same period.

We may conclude bureaucratization, as measured by proportion distribution of employes by size of firm, is proceeding as greater numbers of employes come to be located in larger corporate units; however, the pace of bureaucratization as measured by this variable appears to have slowed markedly in recent years (especially given the increased rate of economic growth that characterized 1965-71). This slowdown invites speculation as to whether some optimal level of bureaucratization has been reached.

On the other hand, we cannot assume the process of bureaucratization is absent in smaller firms. In the context of the strong links between large Japanese firms and small firms via subcontracting and financing arrangements, in recent years larger firms have exercised increasing control over operations

Table 15
Distribution of Employes in Manufacturing
by Size of Firm 1956-71 (Japan)
(in percent)

Year	Number of employes in firm				Bases for percentages[a]
	1-9	10-29	30-99	100+	
1956	17.1	19.3	17.9	45.6	5,783
1959	12.6	18.0	19.0	49.5	6,855
1962	9.5	15.1	18.3	56.6	9,041
1965	8.6	15.7	17.8	57.4	9,837
1968	10.6	14.4	17.5	57.1	10,750
1971	10.6	14.2	17.0	58.2	11,743

Source: Sōrifu 1970, pp. 234-35; 1972, pp. 62-63.
[a]In thousands. Numbers are for both sexes combined.

[19]Dore (1973) in his recent work suggests large Japanese firms are more highly bureaucratized than British firms of comparable size.

in subcontracting firms, in order to cut costs as well as standardize and raise product quality. Relative to the larger firms in manufacturing, there has been a marked increase in value added per employe in the smaller firms. This reflects both more rapidly increasing wages in the smaller firms and rapidly rising productivity. In the long run, the rise in the former could not be sustained without a corresponding rise in the latter. Whereas firms of fewer than ten workers had a value added per employe 32 percent that of firms with more than one hundred employes in 1956, the ratio rose to 63 percent by 1968 (OECD 1972, p. 56).

In an influential article, Kiyonari criticizes the myth of low productivity in the small and medium firms (1970, pp. 30-45). He discusses the sources of a rising productivity which include, in addition to the factors mentioned previously, the demand for specialized products and the appearance of research-intensive rather than capital-intensive industry.[20] We conclude the process of bureaucratization appears to be going on both in the relative shift of employment to larger firms and also as part of the internal reorganization of smaller firms.

In summary, bureaucratization as measured in gross fashion by the proportion of employes in the labor force and distribution by firm size has proceeded at a relatively rapid pace; it cannot help but have had important consequences for Japanese social structure. Well over a majority of the employed labor force now work in bureaucratic organizations where the practice of routine administration becomes the standard, and impersonality and formalization increase at the expense of the more personal and informal working conditions experienced by self-employed and family workers. The latter two categories as recently as 1955 constituted a majority of Japanese workers.

Western scholars have focused on the fact Japanese business firms retain more personal and informal practices which set them apart from Western firms. Our conclusions in no way contradict these observations. But in focusing on the comparison with Western nations, the profound consequences involved in the shift of a majority of the employed from family worker and self-employed status to employe status with all its important implications for the organization of individual behavior and work are obscured and often ignored. Although individuals may make the shift from family worker or a self-employed status to employe status in the course of their own work history, the shift is undoubtedly more common on an intergenerational basis.

There has been a strong tendency in the area studies tradition, in particular, to assume that because behavior is culturally distinctive, it must be of primary importance in determining the behavior of individual social factors. Instead, the association between these two should be seen as empirically problematic. A persistent focus on the elements of cultural and behavioral distinctiveness distorts the kinds of questions we ask and systematically

---

[20]For further analysis of the growing strength of small- and medium-size firms, see Nakamura (1964).

directs attention away from many important intellectual concerns. Whatever the differences from Western practice (and there *are* notable differences), the shift to employe status in Japan as elsewhere is of major importance for the individuals involved. To ignore this is to significantly distort the nature of the interaction of the individual and his work.

The Importance of Occupation for Individual Behavior

To detail changes in occupational structure at the aggregate level is not the same as demonstrating their impact on individual behavior. One view is that what is important for the individual is the size and prestige of his employer, with all the attendant consequences flowing from being at one rather than another size firm. Although we accept that the size and prestige of a firm have unusually significant consequences in Japan, we are not prepared to discount the role of occupational structure. Just what does it mean to say one's position in the occupational structure is relatively unimportant and what really counts is one's membership in this or that company? Does it mean social status and behavior do not derive from occupational achievement, contrary to Western experience where sociologists view it as the critical determinant? Data are available which permit us to examine these relationships. We will not examine the equally interesting question of how social status determines occupational achievement, as it is beyond the confines of this essay.

In some cases, it is clear individuals will be directly affected by the shifting distribution of occupations, for example, when occupational roles are made obsolete by technological innovation and sectoral shifts. Affected workers have to find new jobs, or perhaps they may even be forced to withdraw from the labor force. In many other cases, the impact of the changing occupational distribution is felt on an intergenerational basis as young family members respond to the new occupational opportunities. We have no data to evaluate the relative distribution of these consequences.

But whether the change in occupational and employment structure is felt on an intragenerational or intergenerational basis, it is through the growing bureaucratization of work that a lasting impact on occupational incumbents is achieved. Just the fact that the majority of Japanese workers are now employes rather than self-employed or family workers, in contrast to the early postwar period, is of major importance for individual values and behavior in both work and nonwork situations.

Although data are limited in this area, we can document in rough fashion the significance of occupational position for the organization of individual lives. First, we examine the educational stock associated with the attainment of given occupational positions. If individuals have to study significantly different lengths of time to prepare for given occupational positions, the nature of occupational attainment tells us a good deal about that person quite apart from the size and prestige of his employer.[21] Table 16 presents the

[21]A more careful testing of this proposition would involve consideration of the possibility there may be a clustering of occupations (or incumbents in

Table 16
Persons with a Job by Occupation and Level of Educational Attainment: 1968
(in percent)

	Persons completing school	Elementary school[a]	High school[b]	College[c]	Persons still attending school	Bases for percentage[d]
Professional and technical	98.9	11.4	29.2	58.2	1.2	3,032
Managers and officials	100.0	25.6	37.2	37.2	0.0	1,388
Clerical and related workers	99.2	17.2	63.5	18.4	0.8	7,507
Sales workers	99.4	45.5	43.5	10.4	0.6	6,045
Farmers, lumbermen, and fishermen	99.6	83.6	15.1	0.9	0.4	10,752
Workers in mining and quarrying	100.0	85.9	13.5	0.5	0.0	185
Workers in transportation and communication occupations	99.6	58.8	37.7	3.1	0.4	2,242
Craftsmen and production process workers	98.9	65.8	29.8	3.3	1.1	12,645
Laborers	98.5	77.9	19.0	1.6	1.5	2,079
Service workers	99.4	62.2	32.1	5.1	0.6	3,124
Total						49,006

Source: Sorifu 1970, pp. 558-559.
[a]Educational attainment refers to highest type of school completed.
[b]Includes senior high school graduates.
[c]Includes junior college, college, and university.
[d]In thousands. Numbers are for both sexes combined.

educational attainment of gainfully occupied persons of both sexes in 1968 by major occupational categories.

As expected, there are marked differences in educational attainment among major occupational categories. Only 16 percent of the large farmer, lumberman, and fisherman category attend school beyond the elementary level, and almost all who go beyond stop after completing high school. In the largest category, craftsman and production process workers, 65.8 percent stop after completing elementary school. This compares to only 17.2 percent of clerical workers stopping after elementary school; 63.5 percent complete high school and 18.4 percent college.

The educational level of the craftsman and production process category and that of clerical workers has risen markedly in recent years. This is clear from examining the educational attainment of the younger cohorts. Although only 29.8 percent of the total craftsman and production process category have completed high school, the percentage stands at 37.7 for twenty-five to thirty-four year old workers. In the case of clerical workers, 63.5 percent of the total category completing high school compares to 79.0 percent for the fifteen to twenty-four year old category.

occupations) at specific size firms. To the extent this is true, it confounds the relationship between size and occupation.

As expected, we find the highest levels of educational attainment among the professional and managerial categories. Only 11.4 of the professionals and 25.6 of the managerial categories stop their formal education on completing elementary school. Of the professionals, 29.2 percent and of the managers, 37.2 percent, stop after high school; 58.2 percent of the professionals and 37.2 percent of the managers complete college.

Examination of the younger cohorts of these two categories shows a pattern of rapidly rising education similar to that noted for craftsman and clerks. Particularly notable is the decline of the proportion ending their formal education at elementary school; the shift from high school to college is somewhat more modest because of the time lag between the current educational boom and the time it takes to attain professional and managerial occupational status.

It is common sense that there should be a marked variation in general educational attainment by occupational category. What is surprising is that so few of those who emphasize the importance of size and prestige of firm for individual behavior and values, as opposed to occupation, should fail to realize the implications of these different educational levels on work and nonwork behavior over the course of an individual's life. Just the differences in amount of time spent preparing for an occupational role suggests markedly different experiences as the individual passes through the life cycle. Moreover, the differing educational experiences probably result in significantly different values and behavior. We are not claiming changing occupational structure causes changes in educational requirements. The matter is more complicated, for increases in school enrollments often derive from changed government policies and heightened aspirations of citizens; educational requirements of occupations are often raised afterward in response to the improved quality of supply. But the point is that *at any given time* individuals understand roughly what the educational requirements are for general classes of occupations and make their decisions to seek specific amounts of education accordingly.

Moving further away from work-related behavior, we find some striking variation in political behavior by occupational category. Watanuki (1969, pp. 14-23) reports the probability individuals will vote, their support of political parties, their actual voting behavior, their channels of information about politics, their degree of social consciousness about various political issues as well as their consciousness of their own class position, all vary markedly by occupational category. In the same connection, Nishihira (1963, p. 74) examined a variety of determinants of political opinion. He found the strongest determinants were education, age, and occupation; the moderate determinates were sex, political party support, and the urban-rural differences; the weakest determinants were region and interest in elections. In short, occupation turned out to be one of the best predictors of political opinion among those variables considered. Unfortunately, he did not include size of firm.

A more direct, but still simple, measure of the impact of occupation on individual behavior and life experiences is to compare the distribution of earnings between and within occupational categories. The justification for focusing on earnings is that they are a critical determinant of standard of living as well as social status. If occupation is important, differences in mean income between occupational categories are expected to be significantly greater than differences within occupational cagegories. Using data on the distribution of income within and between major occupational categories, we conducted a simple analysis of variance, testing the null hypothesis that mean incomes of the eleven major occupational categories are equal.[22] An F test, based on the ratio of the between to the within estimate of variance, was carried out (see Table 17). We obtained an $F_{10,33561}=1048$, $p \leqslant 0.001$. Consequently, we are able to reject the null hypothesis and conclude that knowing the occupational category of an individual does, indeed, tell us something important about that individual's income. However, we want to be able to state to what degree knowledge of an individual's occupational category reduces uncertainty concerning his income position. For this purpose, we estimated ω^2 to be 0.238.[23] That is, an individual's occupational category explains 24 percent of the variance in incomes. Given the heterogeneity within the eleven occupational categories used, this suggests a moderately strong statistical association.

This discussion provides only a rough indicator of the importance of occupation. One may still ask whether size of firm is a more important predictor of income than occupation. Even in our consideration of education, we may ask whether educational resources can be converted into economic advantages through occupational achievement or through entering a large, prestigious firm. To test this, we need data permitting comparison of the relative impact on wages of occupation, education, size of firm, seniority, and

Table 17
One-Way Analysis of Variance of Mean Incomes by Occupational Category

	SS	D.F.	MS	F
Between	28,979,845	10	2,897,985	1,048
Within	92,765,651	33,561	2,764	
Total	121,747,500	33,571		

[22]Data are derived from Sōrifu (1972, pp. 152-153). The major occupational categories are the ten noted in Table 11, with the craftsman and production process category separated from the laborer category. Individuals were scored at the midpoint of the income categories. Values of 8 and 350 were used for the open-ended intervals. No corrections were made for continuity. I am indebted to Paul Siegel for supervising the data analysis, to Michael Flynn and Paul Siegel for suggesting interpretations, and to Terry Williams for carrying out the computations.

[23]Est. $\omega^2 = \dfrac{SS \text{ between} - (J-1) \, MS \text{ within}}{SS \text{ total} + MS \text{ within}}$. The percentage of explained variance is ω^2, just as r^2 is the percentage of explained variance in correlation analysis. J refers to sample size. For further discussion of ω^2, see Hays 1963, p. 382.

age. The best available data, on ninety-nine selected male occupations in the Basic Wage Structure Survey, permit only partial analysis (Rōdōshō 1968). The data present the mean total wages by occupation, size of firm, and age groups..They do not provide the variation in wages within these groups.[24] Consequently, we cannot calculate precisely how much of the interindividual variation in wages can be explained by such gross characteristics as occupation, age, and firm size. The ninety-nine detailed occupations used are overwhelmingly blue-collar; whatever conclusions we do reach apply to only a portion of the nonagricultural labor force, though certainly a significant portion.

Lacking the wage distributions within the groups, we attribute to each individual in a given group the mean wage of that group. That is, we attribute to the individual the mean total wage of the members of his age category working for firms of the same size at his specific occupation; it is not unreasonable to think of him as a representative individual. We can distinguish ninety-nine occupations, seven age categories (18-19, 20-24, 25-29, 30-34, 35-39, 40-49, 50-59) and three firm size classes (10-99, 100-999, 1000 or more). This provides 2079 (99 × 7 × 3) means for analysis. In the analysis each mean is weighted by the frequency of its observation. Because we not know the interindividual variance, we cannot calculate the ordinary statistics from the analysis of variance (that is, F ratios). But we can analyze the mean values by examining various decompositions of the variation in mean wages of occupation by age and by firm size groups. By comparing the proportion of variance explained by various combinations of variables, we can derive some indication of their relative importance, though we cannot thoroughly understand their overall importance.[25] Table 18 shows the results of five separate analyses of variance—the proportion of the total

Table 18
Decomposition of the Variation in Mean Wages
of Occupation by Age and Firm Size Groups

Variables in analysis of variance	Percentage of "total variance" explained
Occupation, age, firm size, interaction of age and size	92
Occupation, age, firm size	84
Occupation and age	82
Age, firm size, interaction of age and size	77
Occupation	27

[24]The wage data are for average monthly earnings (including overtime but not bonuses). I am indebted to Paul Siegel for supervising the data analysis and suggesting interpretations and to Walter Gruhn for carrying out the computations.

[25]This method suffers from all the defects for which Coleman (1966) was criticized (see Cain and Watts 1968, pp. 389-392).

variation in mean wages between occupations by firm size by age classes explained by various models. As may be seen in the table, 92 percent of the variance in mean total wages arises from differences in occupation, age, and firm size plus the interaction between age and size (as there are ninety-nine occupations, we cannot deal with the interaction involving occupations). Occupation, age, and size working additively account for 84 percent. In both of these statistics, age is the most important variable. Subtracting the 82 percent of variance attributable to occupation and age from the percentage of total variance explained by occupation, age, and firm size leaves a minimum of 2 percent of the variance explained by firm size; a maximum of 77 percent arises from firm size and age and their interaction.

If we subtract the 77 percent of total variance arising from age, firm size, and the interaction of age and firm size from the 92 percent arising from occupation, age, firm size, and the interaction of age and size, we arrive at an estimate of 15 percent as the minimum effect of occupation. A maximum estimate of the effect of occupation in determining differences in total mean wages (ignoring age and size) is the 27 percent explained by occupation alone.

In summary, we may conclude occupation accounts for 15 to 27 percent of the total variance in mean wages. Although age is clearly more important than occupation in determining mean wages, and firm size may also be, we cannot dismiss the importance of a variable that can account for as large a proportion of the variance as occupation. Moreover, by limiting the sample of occupations to primarily blue-collar jobs, we have omitted a good piece of the variance and thus the impact of occupation, for we lose the very important distinction between blue-collar and white-collar occupations.

INTERPRETATION

It is generally agreed that specific occupational consciousness is quite low in Japan relative to Western nations. Yet we should not exaggerate this difference, for there is substantial agreement on the prestige rankings accorded occupations in Japan and other industrial nations (for example, Hodge, Treiman, and Rossi 1966). Moreover, if we consider the broader consciousness associated with blue-collar versus white-collar rather than specific occupations, there is every indication this consciousness is well developed in Japan. Finally, we should not assume occupational consciousness to be invariant over time. Survey data suggest that with growing affluence and labor shortage the strong commitment of regular male employes to large firms is being reduced because of a greater concern with the work one is doing (Japan Research Center 1972).

Still, Japanese government officials often comment occupational statistics have no meaning in themselves but are collected only for statistical purposes. They compare this to European countries where occupational self-consciousness is high and is reinforced by collection of statistical data by occupation (for example, in many European countries, citizen identification cards contain an individual's occupational title, and telephone directories list occupational title following the individual listing). These data, in turn, appear to be used by individuals for comparative evaluation. In Japan, a formal education system which does not provide specialized occupational skills, the control by management in large firms of job training, and the absence of an explicitly occupationally based wage structure discourage occupational consciousness. In addition, the well-developed internal labor market in Japanese firms, based on the permanent employment system, seems to result in longer promotion ladders open to more workers than in Western countries (Koike 1973). Insofar as workers focus on achieving promotion aspirations as they move from job to job, their attachment to current occupational positions is reduced. This leads to a blurring of jurisdictional lines among closely related occupations. Japanese management officials also remark that workers change positions so often the collection of occupational data is almost impossible and serves no useful purpose.[26]

We, in contrast, have argued that the consequences of occupational locations and a changing occupational distribution are profound for the employed members of the labor force. How can we reconcile the seemingly different interpretations?

First, the view that occupation is unimportant is a corollary of the position that what is important to employes is enterprise loyalty, their organizational commitment. This latter proposition, although it has a very real basis, must be understood as the dominant management ideology that has pervaded much of Japanese industrialization in the twentieth century.[27] One must examine not only the sources of ideologies and the reasons for their acceptance (one of which, in this case, is dominant management power vis à vis workers) but their consequences as well. One of the major roles of management ideology is to legitimatize managerial authority. By emphasizing loyalty to the firm and implicitly rejecting the notion of employe organization by occupation, this ideology has been a significant basis of managerial strength.

The ideology contributes to a low level of occupational consciousness, including collective organization by occupational interests. At the level of craft, such organizations have, by all accounts, played a major role historically in such Western countries as England, Germany, and the United States (for example, Wolman 1924; Turner 1962). The forced draft character of pre-World War II Japanese industrialization led to large companies quickly breaking the hold of the then-existing weak craft organizations and assuming control over job entry and training. The Sōdōmei Federation of the prewar period was built predominantly on craft unions, but it failed to organize the

[26]The problems this low occupational consciousness can create for unknowing Western scholars is illustrated by the American economist who wanted to collect data on work duties through a survey. On his interview form was a simple question asking workers what their job was. The result was entirely unusable answers such as, "I work in the first press section."

[27]For a detailed treatment of the evolution of managerial ideologies in Japan, see Yoshino (1968, pp. 48-84), who draws heavily on the work of Hiroshi Hazama.

large firms effectively and never assumed the role in industrial relations comparable to that achieved by Western craft organizations. The absence of a strong craft tradition in the early stages of Japanese industrialization, particularly around the World War I period, according to some Japanese scholars, explains a good deal of contemporary industrial relations practices (for example, Koike 1973). It is not accidental that even today occupational consciousness is much stronger in the medium- and small-scale firms than in the larger firms as a consequence of the more developed labor markets and weaker management control over job training in the smaller firms.

In postwar Japan, the most recent Ministry of Labor survey examining union structure was conducted in 1965. Unions were classified as either enterprise, craft (*shokushubetsu kumiai*), general, or others. Of 51,457 unit unions, only 1.0 percent were classified as craft unions, and they represented only 0.7 percent of total union membership of over 9.5 million.[28] Even unions commonly classified as craft unions such as the train engineers, teachers, and airplane pilots, on closer examination can be understood, in part, as single "company" unions; it just happens their employers employ large numbers of those practicing a specific occupation. For example, although Dōryokusha organizes only train engineers and is thus a craft union, its membership is limited to employes of the Japanese National Railways; train engineers employed by the private railways have a separate union organization. The situation is the same for airline pilots. A powerful craft organization would have *all* the train engineers in the same union regardless of employer. Given that vocational training separate from the business firm was relatively more important in the early stages of industrialization than in the postwar period (in which on-the-job training has dominated), craft consciousness seems to have been stronger in the pre-World War II Japan than it is today.

To return to the central point, the weakness of horizontal organization by occupational interests is partially a consequence of strong management power as reflected in a management ideology built on existing traditional values and internalized by a wide segment of the population. Thus, vertical loyalties to one's organization and superiors represent societal ideals individuals are expected to maximize in their behavior. Insofar as the conscious interests of employes have been met in return for employes committing themselves to the large firm, any conflict between ideology and reality has been small.

---

[28]The concept of craft unions has increasingly lost its cutting edge in the West as the process of amalgamation and federation among allied crafts has proceeded (for example, Barbash 1956, p. 88). Nevertheless, despite the rise of industrial unions and the process of amalgamation, craft-like unions continue to play a significant, if diminished, role with respect to union policy and the character of industrial relations. Moreover, we cannot ignore the fact that craft consciousness shows a remarkable hardiness as manifested in the aggressive role played by the skilled trade departments in such powerful unions as the UAW (see Gitlow 1963, pp. 80-81).

Yet this management ideology has not eliminated occupation as an important basis of social stratification (although it has kept consciousness of the fact very low—thereby minimizing collective action). Notwithstanding the ideology, the data presented in this paper show an individual's occupation is a significant basis of stratification in contemporary Japanese society. There is no conflict in these views; we are just dealing with different levels of analysis. *What is surprising is that so many Western and Japanese scholars have interpreted the relative lack of occupational consciousness in Japan to mean there are no notable consequences for the individual of a particular occupational position.*

Perhaps the point becomes clearer if we consider an analogy: the ideology in America is that it is a classless society. There is a good deal of evidence to suggest the level of class consciousness is lower in the United States than in Western Europe. Classes may be conceived as artificially constructed statistical groups useful for the sociologist as analytical categories. People in a given income, educational, and occupational category commonly are found to behave in ways which distinguish them from other income, educational, and occupational categories. In addition to being statistical groups, however, the subjective aspect of class differences is not absent. Even though Americans seem reluctant to admit it or think about it, they are quite aware of the different life chances characterizing their own social circles and those available to others. These different life chances are manifested in a variety of external cues such as ways of dressing, extent and nature of church attendance, likelihood of attending college, and so on. In short, even though individuals may not express differences in terms of class, class (or whatever we want to call it) has a very real meaning in the United States. By knowing a person's social class, we significantly increase the probability of making accurate predictions about his behavior.[29] In a similar fashion, by knowing an individual's occupation in Japan, we know a good deal about his life chances, values, and behavior. This is true, despite both the low level of occupational consciousness and the low level of collective organization by occupation.[30]

We are not suggesting that knowing an individual's occupation in Japan tells us just as much about that person's life chances as in Western industrial

[29]For a summary of some of the literature on the consequences of class in America, see Blumberg (1972).

[30]Degler (1971, p. 179) presents an analogous argument for why blacks in Brazil have failed to organize to protect their interests. The dominant ideology in Brazil claims the absence of prejudice (which is, in fact, demonstrably present). The internalization of this ideology at least partially even by Negroes, prevents many Negroes from asserting their blackness in organizations. In short, the weakness of Negro organization is in part a function of the Brazilian attitude toward race and color. Needless to say, this situation serves the interests of the white elite who hold power. This does not mean race as a basis of social stratification is absent, only that it is not manifested in collective action by the disadvantaged group.

societies. For one thing, it appears we are talking about a broader and more diffuse concept of occupation in the case of Japan than in, say, the United States. Moreover, we are not suggesting that occupational differences are the only important variables influencing an individual's social position. Figure 1 presents a more balanced picture of the various factors influencing individual access to power, authority, and wealth in any industrial society. As a summary of Figure 1, we note the following: there is a variety of factors influencing an individual's access to power, authority, and wealth; occupational achievement is one important factor operating to influence one's access *independent* of the effects of occupational consciousness; and the emphasis on the size and prestige of one's firm as a variable which influences social stratification is not unique to Japan, but rather the nature of the organization with which one affiliates to earn a livelihood has a powerful influence on one's access to power, authority, and wealth in all industrial societies (though it may be more important for selected participants in Japan).

CONCLUSION

One goal of this paper is to provide the first relatively systematic treatment in English of changing occupational structure over the course of Japanese industrialization, set in comparative perspective. Paucity of data, particularly in the pre-World War II period, forces us to rely on gross measures of occupational composition. This first task is primarily descriptive, although we try to focus on the implications of our data for the analytical formulations of other scholars. Thus, for example, the data on the slow formation of a permanent Japanese labor force call into question Rosovsky's attempt to save Gerschenkron's late-developer model of development.

The data on changes in occupational structure confirm our expectation that we would find both significant underlying similarities with other industrial

Figure 1. Basis for individual social position in industrial society.

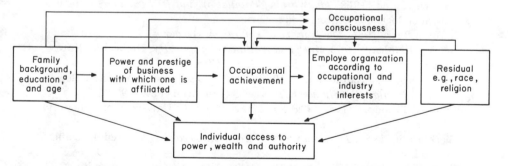

Note: Individual access to power, authority, and wealth is only one dimension of social stratification. It is not our intention to suggest that social stratification per se is an individual property nor to imply that we can simply aggregate individual scores on power, authority, and wealth and arrive at a meaningful understanding of social stratification.

[a]Level of educational achievement, prestige of school, and content of education.

societies in the transition of occupational structure as well as notable differences. In some cases, Japan's unique historical experience seems to shape these differences, whereas in others her late-developer status seems paramount. In still other cases our presentation is consistent with critiques of the alleged uniqueness of the Japanese experience (in showing, for example, the importance of the service sector as a receptacle for surplus labor as opposed to the dekasegi hypothesis).

In the light of the importance Western scholars, in particular, attach to company loyalty in Japan and the reported insignificance of occupational attachment, we believe it critical to analyze occupation. We conclude that a good deal of the confusion lies in the failure to distinguish between (1) the level of occupational consciousness in Japan, and (2) the consequences of occupational position for individual behavior and status. Based on a generalized formal education system, managerial control over job training, managerial ideologies of company loyalty, and traditional values, the level of occupational consciousness, particularly in large firms, has been quite low in Japan compared to western nations; this has been manifested in the lack of strong horizontal craft and professional organizations. Management ideology perpetuates the myth that the consequences of a specific occupational location are insignificant for the individual. The data suggest the contrary— that to know an individual's occupational position in Japan tells a good deal about such important aspects of stratification as his economic status, political opinions, and educational career.

We have no illusions that this paper constitutes a definitive statement on the impact of occupation in Japanese society. If it serves to stimulate research in this much neglected area in which so much is assumed and so little empirically documented, our goal will have been accomplished.

REFERENCES

Abegglen, James. 1958. *The Japanese Factory*. Free Press.

Bairoch, P., ed. 1968. *The Working Population and Its Structure*. L'Institut de Sociologie de l'Université libre (Brussels).

Barbash, Jack. 1956. *The Practice of Unionism*. Harper.

Bendix, Reinhard. 1963. *Work and Authority in Industry*. Harper and Row.

Blumberg, Paul. 1972. *The Impact of Social Class*. Crowell.

Cain, Glen, and Harold Watts. 1968. "The Controversy about the Coleman Report." *Journal of Human Resources* 3 (summer 1968):389-392.

Caplow, Theodore. 1954. *The Sociology of Work*. University of Minnesota Press.

Clark, Colin. 1951. *The Conditions of Economic Progress*, 2nd. ed. Macmillan (London).

Cole, Robert E. 1971. *Japanese Blue Collar*. University of California Press.

Coleman, James. 1966. *Equality of Educational Opportunity*. U.S. Dept. of Health, Education, and Welfare, Office of Education.

Degler, Carl. 1971. *Neither Black nor White: Slavery and Race Relations in Brazil and the United States*. Macmillan.

Doeringer, Peter B., and Michael J. Piore. 1971. *Internal Labor Markets and Manpower Analysis*. Heath.

Dore, Ronald. 1973. *British Factory-Japanese Factory*. University of California Press.

Emi, Kōichi. 1969. "Employment Structure in the Service Industries." *The Developing Economies* 7 (June 1969):133-157.

Endo, Motō. 1968. *Nihon Shokuninshi*. Yusankaku.

Feldman, Arnold, and Wilbert Moore. 1969. "Industrialization and Industrialism: Convergence and Differentiation." In *Comparative Perspectives on Industrial Society*, edited by William Faunce and William Form. Little, Brown.

Form, William, and Delbert Miller. 1964. *Industrial Sociology*. Harper and Row.

Fuchs, Victor. 1968. *The Service Economy*. National Bureau of Economic Research.

Gerschenkron, Alexander. 1962. *Economic Backwardness in Historical Perspective*. Harvard University Press.

Gitlow, Abraham. 1963. *Labor and Industrial Policy*, rev. ed. Irwin.

Hall, Richard. 1969. *Occupations and the Social Structure*. Prentice-Hall.

Hatt, Paul. 1961. "Occupation and Social Stratification." In *Occupation and Social Status*, edited by Albert J. Reiss, Jr. Free Press.

Hays, William. 1963. *Statistics*. Holt, Rinehart and Winston.

Henmi, Kenzō. 1956. "Nōgyō Yūgyō Jinkō no Suikei." In *Nihon no Keizai to Nōgyō*, edited by Sei'ichi Tobata and Kazushi Ohkawa. Iwanami Shoten.

Hijakata, Seibi. 1929. "Shokugyō betsu Jinkō no Hensen o Tsujite Mitaru Shitsugyō Mondai." *Shakaiseisaku Jihō* 108 (Sept. 1929).

Hodge, Robert, and Paul Siegel. 1956. "The Classification of Occupations: Some Problems of Social Interpretation." In *Proceedings of the American Statistical Association*, social statistics section.

Hodge, Robert, Donald Treiman, and Peter Rossi. 1966. "A Comparative Study of Occupational Prestige." In *Class, Status and Power*, 2nd ed., edited by Reinhard Bendix and Seymour Lipset. Free Press.

ILO [International Labour Office]. 1971. *Yearbook of Labour Statistics, 1971*.

Japan Productivity Center. 1972. *Katsuyō Rōdō Tōkei: Meiji 47*.

Japan Research Center. 1972. *Wakamono Ishiki Chōsa*.

Keizai Shingikai, Rōdōryoku Kenkyū Iinkai [Economic Council, Labor Force Research Subcommittee]. 1972. *Rōdōsha no Nōryoku Hakki no Mondai*.

Kiyonari, Tadao. 1970. "Reisai Kigyō Gekizō wa Gyakukō Genshō Ka?" *Keizai Hyōron*, March 1970, pp. 30-45.

Koike, Kazuo. 1973. "Who Regulates On-the-Job-Problems?" In *Industrialization and Manpower Policy in Asian Countries*, Proceedings of the 1973 Asian Regional Conference on Industrial Relations, edited by the Japan Institute of Labour.

Kuroda, Toshio. 1960. "Jinkō no Shokugyōteki Idō." In *Keizai Shutaisei Kōza*, edited by Hiromi Arisawa, Seiichi Tobata, and Ichiro Nakayama. Series in Economic Subjects, vol. 3. Chūōkōronsha.

Levine, Solomon. 1965. "Labor Markets and Collective Bargaining." In *The State and Economic Enterprise in Japan*, edited by William Lockwood. Princeton University Press.

Lewis, Arthur. 1954. "Economic Development with Unlimited Supplies of Labour." *Manchester School of Economic and Social Studies* 22 (May):139-191.

Miller, Delbert, and William Form. 1964. *Industrial Sociology*, 2nd edition. Harper International.

Minami, Ryōshin. 1966. "Nōringyō Shūgyōshasū no Suikei, 1872-1940." *Keizai Kenkyū* 17 (July 1966):275-278.

——. 1970. *Nihon Keizai no Tenkaiten*. Sōbunsha. [English edition: *The Turning Point in Economic Development: Japan's Experience*. Kinokuniya. 1973.]

Moore, Wilbert. 1966. "Changes in Occupational Structures." In *Social Structure and Mobility in Economic Development*, edited by Neil Smelser and Seymour Lipset. Aldine.

Nakamura, Hideichirō. 1964. *Chūken Kigyō Ron*. Keizai Shinpōsha.

Nakamura, Takafusa. 1971. *Senzenki Nihon Keizaiseichō no Bunseki*. Iwanami Shoten.

Nakane, Chie. 1970. *Japanese Society*. University of California Press.

Nishihira, Shigeki. 1963. *Nihonjin no Iken*. Seishin Shobo.

Odaka, Kunio. 1958. *Shokugyō to Kaisō*. Mainichi Shinbunsha.

OECD [Organization for Economic Cooperation and Development]. 1972. *OECD Economic Surveys: Japan*, 1972 edition.

Ohkawa, Kazushi. 1957. *The Growth Rate of the Japanese Economy since 1878*. Kinokuniya.

Ōkōchi, Kazuo. 1952. *Reimeiki no Nihon Rōdō Undō*. Iwanami Shoten.

Pyle, Kenneth. 1969. *The New Generation in Meiji Japan*. Stanford University Press.

Rees, Albert, and George Shultz. 1970. *Workers and Wages in an Urban Labor Market*. University of Chicago Press.

Reiss, Albert J., Jr. 1961. *Occupations and Social Status*. Free Press.

Rōdōshō [Ministry of Labor]. 1966. *Sengo Rōdō Keizaishi*. Labor Laws Association.

——. 1968. *Chingin Kōzō Kihon Tōkei Chōsa Hōkoku Shōwa 42*, vol. 5.

——. Annual. *Rōdō Chōsa Nenpō*.

Rosovsky, Henry. 1961. *Capital Formation in Japan, 1868-1940*. Free Press.

Ryder, Norman. 1965. "The Cohort as a Concept in the Study of Social Change." *American Sociological Review* 30 (Dec. 1965):843-861.

Scoville, James. 1969. *The Job Content of the U.S. Economy, 1940-1970*. McGraw-Hill.

Shōwa Dōjinkai. 1960. *Wagakuni Chingin Kōzō no Shiteki Kōsatsu*. Shiseido.

Sōrifu, Tōkei-kyoku [Office of the Prime Minister, Statistics Bureau]. 1920. *Taishō 9-nen Kokuseichōsa Kijutsuhen*.

——. 1954. *1950 Population Census of Japan*. Vol. 5, part 2: "All Japan: Labor Force Status, Occupation, Industry, Class of Worker."

——. 1969. *1965 Population Census of Japan*. Vol. 5, part 2: "Industry and Occupation."

——. 1966, 1969, 1972. *Shūgyō Kōzō Kihon Chōsa Hōkoku*. Triennially since 1956.

——. 1970. *Nihon no Shūgyō Kōzō, Shōwa 43, Shūgyō Kōzō Kihon Chōsa Kekka Kaisetsu*.

Sumiya, Mikio. 1964. *Nihon no Rōdō Mondai*. Tōdai Shuppankai.

Taira, Koji. 1962. "Characteristics of Japanese Labor Markets." *Economic Development and Cultural Change* 10 (Jan. 1962):150-168.

———. 1970. *Economic Development and the Labor Market in Japan.* Columbia University Press.

Taylor, Charles, and Michael Hudson. 1972. *World Handbook of Political and Social Indicators.* Yale University Press.

Taylor, Lee. 1968. *Occupational Sociology.* Oxford University Press.

Tominaga, Ken'ichi. 1969. "Trend Analysis of Social Stratification and Social Mobility in Contemporary Japan." *The Developing Economies* 7 (Dec. 1969):471-498.

———. 1971a. "Sangyōka to Rōdōsha." *Nihon Rōdōkyōkai Zasshi* 145 (April 1971):2-15.

———. 1971b. "Post-Industrial Society and Cultural Diversity." *Survey* 1 (winter 1971):68-77.

———. 1973. *Sangyōshakai no Dōtai.* Tōyō Keizai Shinpōsha.

Turner, Herbert Arthur. 1962. *Trade Union Growth, Structure, and Policy.* Allen and Unwin.

Umemura, Mataji. 1968. "Yūgyōsha-sū no Shinsuikei 1871-1920." *Keizai Kenkyū* 19 (Oct. 1968):322-329.

United Nations. 1971. *United Nations Statistics Yearbook, 1971.*

Vogel, Ezra. 1967. "Kinship Structure, Migration to the City, and Modernization." In *Aspects of Social Change in Modern Japan*, edited by Ronald Dore. Princeton University Press.

Watanuki, Joji. 1969. "Rōdōsha no Tōkyō Kōdō to Seito Shiji Taido." *Nihon Rōdō Kyōkai Zasshi* 11 (Jan. 1969):14-23.

Wolman, Leo. 1924. *The Growth of American Trade Unions.* National Bureau of Economic Research.

Yoshino, Michael Y. 1968. *Japan's Managerial System.* MIT Press.

Country Girls and Communication among Competitors in the Japanese Cotton-Spinning Industry

Gary R. Saxonhouse

It is hard to overemphasize the importance of studying Japan's textile industry. The development of this industry stands as the first Japanese instance of truly successful assimilation of modern manufacturing techniques. Because it was the first success, it was large long before other now-familiar Japanese industries were; hence the industry's presence dominates Meiji and Taishō manufacturing statistics (see Table 1). It was also the harbinger of what has now become a familiar Japanese developmental pattern: import substitution followed by worldwide export success. As late as 1890, Japan imported more cotton yarn than was produced domestically. By World War I and through the 1930s, Japan dominated world cotton-textile markets. In 1937, by weight, 37 percent of all cotton fabrics entering international trade was made in Japan. This was half again larger than the British share. Lancashire had been dethroned.

Despite all the elements in the cotton-textile industry success story which are familiar, its history is worthy of still further study precisely because it is a well-known tale of Japanese industrial success using what some now consider very un-Japanese modes of industrial organization. Great technological sophistication appears to have been present in an industry containing many relatively small-scale mills which were, for the most part, fostered neither by the great zaibatsu nor by the Japanese government. The sixty-plus spinning

Members of the following institutions gave me aid and comfort while I collected and interpreted some of the materials used in this paper: All-Japan Spinners Association, Hitotsubashi University, Howard and Bulloughs, Kanegafuchi Spinning Company, Keio University, Kyoto University, Osaka University, Platt Brothers, Toyo Spinning Company, and Yale University.

Table 1
Percentage Composition of Manufacturing Output
(current prices)

	Textiles	Food products	Chemicals	Machinery	Other
1874-85	26.47	36.17	18.06	2.56	16.74
1877-86	27.83	37.00	16.59	2.44	16.14
1882-91	33.08	36.82	13.53	2.15	14.42
1887-96	41.03	32.04	12.08	2.13	12.72
1892-1902	40.22	33.30	10.92	2.82	12.78
1897-1906	35.00	35.42	11.25	4.40	13.97
1902-11	32.57	35.23	11.60	6.00	14.60
1907-16	32.95	30.88	11.35	8.46	17.36
1912-21	34.79	22.93	10.66	13.54	18.08
1917-26	36.46	23.79	10.26	11.39	18.10

Source: Computed from data in LTES 10:140-141.

firms were organized into what appears to be the only pre-Pacific War instance of a successful cartel in a major Japanese industry. What is probably most unusual about this industry in the Japanese context is the composition of its labor force. In a nation which has made lifetime employment its ideal if not its practice, the cotton textile industry throughout its fifty-year journey to world dominance relied almost entirely on a labor force of women whose average (mean) entrant lived in a company dormitory and stayed at work no more than two years. It is this important phenomenon which will be studied in this paper.

The first section documents the high female labor force turnover in the cotton textile industry throughout the period prior to the Pacific War. It also shows that the firms' widely publicized welfare programs were ineffective in dissuading the modal recruit from leaving the industry within the first six months of employment. The second section tests the hypothesis that there was little benefit to the industry from a more experienced work force. This hypothesis is rejected. Econometric evidence indicates a more experienced labor force contributed to the more efficient production of cotton textiles. The final section then attempts a reconciliation of these findings. If an experienced labor force was of considerable benefit, why did high turnover persist? It is suggested the institutional structure of the industry was such that textile firms experienced considerable difficulty in recouping costs which might have been associated with upgrading their labor force.

Note that a special feature of this study is the attempt to make extensive use of a number of hitherto unused primary materials. The first and third sections of this paper rely heavily on unpublished documents from Kanegafuchi Bōseki (Kanegafuchi Spinning Company) and Platt Brothers of Oldham (English manufacturers of spinning equipment). The second section uses unusually helpful materials from Dai Nihon Bōseki Rengōkai which, although familiar to Japanese scholars, have been largely unknown to others.

JAPAN'S FACTORY LABOR FORCE: FEMALE AND TRANSIENT

In even the most cursory examination of Japanese labor force statistics for the period between 1890 and 1935, one is struck by the large proportion of females and the high turnover of the blue-collar labor force (see Tables 2 and

Table 2
Proportion of Women among Factory Workers
(in percent)

Japan		France		United States	
1909	62.0	1866	42.7	1870	24.0
1920	53.0	1881	38.3	1880	28.8
1930	52.6	1901	31.5	1900	32.6
		1921	31.6	1920	24.2

Belgium		India		Italy	
1890	24.6	1911	17.4	1901	37.4
1900	23.9	1921	17.5	1911	46.2
1920	25.0				
1930	20.9				

Sources and notes: Japanese data relate to factories containing five or more employes and are from Tsūsanshō 1961. French data include clerical workers and are from *Statistique générale de la France* (various issues). American data are from Alba Edwards, *Comparative Occupation Statistics for the United States, 1870-1940*, U.S. Government Printing Office, 1943. Belgium data are taken from *Recensement de l'industrie et du commerce* (various issues). Indian data relate to factories of twenty or more workers and are from *Census of India* (various issues). Italian data relate to factories of ten or more workers and are from *Censimento generale della popolozione* (various issues).

Table 3
Distribution of Workers by Length of Employment
(in percent)

	Japan		United States	
Length of employment	1900	1918	1913-14	1917-18
Up to 6 months	20.1	24.6	20.5	21.1
6 months to 1 year	24.0	19.4	8.3	12.6
1 to 3 years	33.8	32.6	23.2	23.8
3 to 5 years	12.3	11.7	15.0	8.8
5 or more years	9.8	11.7	32.9	27.8

Source: Taira 1970, and Brissenden and Frankel 1922.

3). Of course, factory labor force statistics are synthetic. Such statistics may mask very different national industrial differences. From an international standpoint, prior to the Pacific War, Japan's industrial structure was highly concentrated in textiles, and textile industries the world over made use of relatively unskilled female labor in greater proportion than other major industries.

Note, however, that industrial structure, by itself, does not explain the distinctive features of Japan's early modern manufacturing labor force. Even in an international comparison of the textile industry, the Japanese experience appears extreme (see Tables 4, 5 and 6).

Whether the comparison is made with Lowell, Massachusetts, in the mid-nineteenth century, Bombay in the late nineteenth century, or the

Table 4
Composition of Employes in the Manufacturing Sector in Japan
(in percent)

	1909	1915	1920	1925	1930
Textiles	60.8	59.9	55.5	52.3	47.7
Metals	2.3	2.9	4.7	5.4	5.3
Machinery	5.8	7.8	12.3	13.2	12.5
Chemicals	3.2	4.0	5.9	5.6	6.0
Food processing	11.1	8.2	6.5	9.5	8.1
Other	16.8	17.2	15.1	14.0	20.5

Source: Rōdō Tōkei Yōran (various issues).

Table 5
Females as a Percentage of the Cotton Textile Labor Force
(in percent)

Japan		United States		United Kingdom	
1909	83.0	1830	66.0	1835	55.1
1914	83.3	1850	63.0	1847	58.7
1920	80.0	1890	54.5	1867	61.3
1925	80.6	1910	48.3	1878	62.7
1930	80.6	1919	42.4	1895	62.3

India		France	
1884	22.5	1886	53.0
1894	25.9	1896	50.0
1909	22.1	1906	45.5
1924	21.6		
1934	18.9		

Sources: Japanese data, Tsūsanshō 1961; American data for 1830, Jackson and Shearman 1832; American data thereafter, U.S. Dept. of Labor 1926a. British data, Chapman 1904; India, Morris 1965; France, Forrester 1921.

Table 6
Length of Service in Cotton Textile Industries
(in percentage of total labor force)

	Japan 1897	Japan 1918	Lowell, Mass. 1845
Less than 1 year	46.2	50.3	25.0
From 1 to 2 years	23.3	18.4	13.0
From 2 to 3 years	13.3	11.1	11.0
From 3 to 4 years	7.7	} 9.3 {	11.0
From 4 to 5 years	4.7		9.0
Total less than 5 years	95.2	89.1	69.0
From 5 to 10 years	4.6	7.0	25.5
Greater than 10 years	0.2	3.9	15.5

	American South 1925	Bombay, India 1890	Bombay, India 1927-1928
Less than 1 year	27.3	--	--
From 1 to 2 years	13.2	--	--
From 2 to 3 years	12.7	--	--
From 3 to 4 years	9.6	--	--
From 4 to 5 years	6.4	--	--
Total less than 5 years	69.2	72.2	46.5
From 5 to 10 years	19.1	11.1	24.3
Greater than 10 years	11.7	16.7	29.2

Sources: Japanese data 1897, Bōren 1897; Japanese data 1918, *Kojo Kantoku Nenpo*, vol. 3; Lowell, Massachusetts data, Ware 1931; American South data, U.S. Department of Labor 1926*b*; Bombay data, Morris 1965.

American South in the 1920s, the Japanese textile industry's labor force is clearly the most female and the most transient. This phenomenon is more than a curiosum. Lowell girls (young girls living in company dormitories with no permanent commitment to the industry) were resurrected in Osaka, not as a short episode in the life of one geographic area in a still-young national industry, but rather as the integral force in the fifty-year drive of the Japanese cotton textile industry to world dominance.

Some aspects of this phenomenon, of course, have attracted the attention of Japanese scholars. In particular, there has been considerable discussion of the long lag in Japan between the onset of industrialization, the development of a permanent labor force, and the well-known failure of the number of Japanese farming households to decline during the course of prewar industrialization. By contrast with what is taken by some Japanese economists to be the experience of Western economies, the nexus between rural farming and factory work was broken only very slowly in Japan.[1]

[1]Much of the work in this area has been associated with Kazuo Okochi. See,

Unfortunately, the transient, female character of Japan's prewar manufacturing labor force has been studied too much from the decision-making perspective of the rural migrant and too little from the perspective of the manufacturing employer. There has been considerable analysis of why the head of a farm household might not migrate to the industrial sector, but too little work on the determinants of the opportunity set confronting this potential migrant (see, for example, Masui 1970). Why was the market valuation of such a migrant's potential contribution so low? It is not enough to say farm household heads specifically and male workers in general could not compete with unskilled, inexperienced teenage girls, for such competition did occur in other textile industries in other economies. The choice of the Japanese input mix among physical capital, skill, and raw labor may not have been simply the result of the obvious labor-supply considerations.

DIMENSIONS OF TEXTILE-WORKER TRANSIENCE

In light of a considerable literature on the successful evolution of the Japanese textile industry labor-management practices, it may seem odd to ask why the industry made so little effort to cut labor turnover and attract a more stable labor force. Typical accounts of this evolution do stress the high turnover and poor working conditions of the late nineteenth and very early twentieth century as documented in the well-known *Shokkō Jijō* and the subsequent and widely emulated attempts by Kanebō (Kanegafuchi Bōseki), Kurabō (Kurashiki Bōseki), Fujibō (Fuji Bōseki), and Tōyōbō (Tōyō Bōseki) to ameliorate these conditions.[2] On the strength of the evidence, which documents a dramatic rise in the average length of service of the typical cotton textile worker between 1900 and 1930, and the claims of the industry itself, it is usually assumed that the seemingly elaborate dormitory, hospital, recreational, educational, and nutritional programs undertaken by most firms in the industry were efficacious. (Compare Table 7 with Table 6.)

Although the average length of service statistics provide one kind of information, there is the danger such data may be dominated by the length and time path of the industry's development. An accurate test of whether worker behavior with respect to factory life did indeed change requires a different kind of data set. In this context, the labor force records kept by Kanebō are a godsend. For each month during the period 1903-15, each of the mills operated by Kanebō kept a record of the number of workers entering and leaving their employ. Departing workers were classified according to their length of service, whether they left with permission or ran

---

for example, Okochi (1950). Other examples of this research include Namiki (1956) and Kubo and Murakami (1964).

[2]This view is expressed in any of a number of company histories. See, for example, *Tōyō Bōseki*, pp. 217-248, and *Kurashiki*, pp. 221-265. Taira (1970b and 1972) has forcefully advanced this same view.

away, and if they left with permission, what reason was given.[3] With this raw data it is possible to establish the time path of departure for each month's entering cohort.

Casual inspection of these patterns of departure suggests little change throughout the period between 1897 and 1915. In 1897, according to a survey by the industry cartel, 44 percent of the recruits to Kanebō's Hyōgo mill (managed by Sanji Mutō) left within the first six months (see Bōren 1897, p. 17). Although Table 8 gives evidence of a moderate, if persistent, decline between 1903 and 1914 in the percentage of workers leaving within the first six months of their employ, the situation in 1914 is still worse than that reported in 1897!

Table 7
Length of Service in the Japanese Cotton Textile Industry
after the First World War
(in years)

	1927	1936
Less than one	18.3	29.5
One to two	19.8	20.5
Two to three	17.2	15.4
Three to four	11.9	} 14.9
Four to five	7.9	
Less than five (sum)	75.1	80.3
Five to ten	17.5	11.9
More than ten	7.4	7.8

Source: Rōdō Tōkei Jitchi Chōsa Hōkokusho.

Table 8
Percentage of September Entering Cohorts Leaving Hyōgo Mill's Employment
within First Six Months 1903-14

1903	63.4	1909	53.7
1904	73.2	1910	58.4
1905	64.1	1911	63.7
1906	62.1	1912	58.8
1907	64.8	1913	47.7
1908	62.3	1914	55.6

Source: Mutō, unpublished.

[3]These data are available among the papers of Sanji Mutō, long-time managing director of Kanebō and publicly a leading proponent of humane working conditions.

Equally interesting is the manner of worker departure. A large majority of all workers leaving Kanebō's mills between 1903 and 1915 left without the permission of the management, as shown in Table 9. Although it is not especially surprising extremely high rates of labor force instability persisted through the First World War for the industry as a whole, this finding for Kanebō's Hyōgo mill is clearly unexpected. By 1914 Kanebō was widely publicized as a humane leader among Japanese textile firms for its strenuous efforts to promote worker welfare.[4] Table 8 does not challenge Kanebō's ordinal position, but it certainly casts doubt on the quality of this leadership.

If Table 8 confirms continuing gross unhappiness on the part of workers with spinning-mill work, Table 9 suggests mill dormitories were hardly the prisons they have often been made out to be, as in the following representative observation:

When the girls get to the mill, however, they are usually housed in barracks inside the mill compound and are never allowed to see strangers or to go outside without a chaperone and then only on rare occasions such as public holidays. The close confinement and the grind of steady work at long hours soon wearies most of them of mill life, but they find they cannot get away until their contract is up; and even if they could, they rarely have enough money to return home. Frequently they attempt to escape, but are usually found and returned by the police [Clark 1914, p. 200].

This must be in error. Notwithstanding barbed wire, high walls, guarantee deposits, and company regulations, running away in defiance of contractual obligation seems to have been the typical means of employe separation during this period. Presumably this practice had at least the tacit acquiescence of the Kanebō management, for security measures almost certainly could have been improved.

Table 9
Percentage of Kanebō Workers Leaving
without Permission 1903-15

1903	63.4	1910	67.0
1904	59.1	1911	72.3
1905	71.6	1912	72.9
1906	75.1	1913	69.3
1907	77.4	1914	68.5
1908	73.8	1915	63.9
1909	68.9		

Source: Mutō, unpublished.

[4]For sympathetic accounts of Kanebō's welfare work, see Clark (1914) and Uno (1912). The evidence presented in this paper tends to confirm the changes reported by Hosoi (1925, p. 105) that Kanebō's welfare work was heavy on publicity and fundamentally flawed.

While Kanebō's highly publicized welfare work was ineffectual in terms of cutting labor turnover, it is still necessary to extend this finding to other firms and to the period after World War I. Figure 1 approximates the percentage departed of a representative cohort entering a Kanebō mill plotted against time. This graph confirms the skewed relationship between percentage departed and time, which was intimated by the data in the tables earlier presented. The skewedness of the relation suggests it would be worthwhile to fit a log normal distribution to the available cohort data.

$$y = \frac{1}{(\sqrt{2\pi})\,(\hat{\sigma}t)} e^{-\frac{(\log t - \hat{u})^2}{2\hat{\sigma}^2}} \tag{1}$$

$y \equiv \dfrac{\text{total departures from time zero to time } t}{\text{total cohort (total aggregate entrants)}}$

$t \equiv$ time

$\hat{\mu} \equiv -0.805956$ (the sample geometric mean)

$\hat{\sigma}^2 \equiv 3.0957862$ (the sample variance)

The following well-known relationship

$$r = e^{\mu + \frac{\sigma^2}{2}}, r \equiv \text{arithmetic mean}, \tag{2}$$

holds between the arithmetic mean and the geometric mean of a distribution. Equation 2 provides an estimate that the average (mean) worker left the spinning industry after two years of service.

Estimates from Equation 1 work well in prediction situations. Given the textile industry labor force at time t, distributed according to length of service, it should be possible, using Equation 1, to predict the entire industry labor force distribution subsequent to t, provided recruitment data are available. Letting t be 1918, I will make predictions on the average length of service of the textile industry labor force for the years 1924, 1927, 1930, and 1933, for which actual data are available.

The close correspondence of the predictions with the benchmarks, as shown in Table 10, has considerable significance. The behavior of the early twentieth-century Kanebō recruit is apparently representative of the industry experience throughout the entire pre-Pacific War period. The elaborate, widely publicized welfare programs in the textile industry had no discernable effect on the desire of the recruits to remain within the industry labor force either before or after the First World War. The doubling or tripling of the average length of service seems entirely attributable to the length and time

Figure 1.

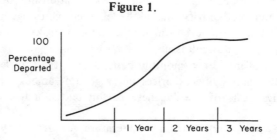

Table 10
Average Length of Service in Post-World War I
Japanese Cotton Textile Industry
(in months)

	Benchmark	Prediction
1924	33	36.2
1927	38	38.1
1930	46	44.8
1933	37	35.4

Sources: The recruitment and benchmark data are
taken from *Rodo Tokei Yoran, Kojo Kantoku Nenpo*,
and *Rodo Tokei Jitchi Chosa Hokokusho*.

path of the industry's development; gradually the firms accumulated a core of
workers who stayed much longer, thereby raising the average period worked
despite the unchanging rate at which the mean worker in any entering group
left.

WORKER EXPERIENCE AND PRODUCTIVITY

Cutting the rate of departure of newly recruited female workers was the
publicly stated objective of the paternalistic welfare practices of Japanese
cotton textile mills. In light of the evidence just presented, it seems these
mills failed in their efforts to retain a larger proportion of their new recruits.
By international standards the behavior of the cotton textile industry labor
force was extreme. Still, it is possible and necessary to ask whether the
persistence of this outwardly unstable situation was actually a case of
managerial failure. Although the ascription of such failure is not an
inappropriate function for the economic historian, the tradition of the last
fifteen years or so insists on careful attention to the decision-makers' range of
opportunities.[5]

   Indeed, in the midst of the great success story of the development of the
Japanese cotton textile industry one is most reluctant to attribute any such
failure. Initially it must be presumed that a rational assessment (explicit or
market-led) of the benefits and costs of developing a stable labor force led
cotton-mill owners to a decision against such a step. Some inquiry into the
structure of the relationships generating these benefits and costs is clearly in
order. As a first step in this inquiry the relationship between worker
experience and productivity should be clarified. Once again the rich data
available for the Japanese cotton textile industry make possible systematic
examination of this difficult issue.

   There are available, on a monthly basis, data at the firm level on output,
labor services, capital services, prices and wage rates, among other series, for a
full forty-five years of the Japanese cotton textile industry's history. In

[5]For a representative article from this literature, see McCloskey (1970).

addition, considerable information is available, mostly on an annual basis (but sometimes on a monthly basis) regarding the work experience of labor (such as was presented in the last section) and of management, the educational background of labor and management, the age profile of the capital stock, and the length of the working shift.[6]

In view of the rich data base, a fairly ambitious test of the relation between productivity and the length of service can be made. Assume first that some conventional production function defines the relationship between firm output and firm input in the Japanese cotton-spinning industry.[7]

$$Q = F(K,L) \tag{3}$$
$Q \equiv$ firm output, $K \equiv$ capital services, $L \equiv$ labor services.

A priori, it seems unlikely a simple relationship such as Equation 3 could successfully explain the complex variation in a data set combining cross-sections on factories for each of forty-five years. Assume, therefore, the parameters of the functional relationship (F) vary over time and that the movement of these parameters can be explained by Equation 4.

$$\theta_i = G_i\,(TT, WE, PE, FA, AC, LS) \quad i = 1, 2, .., 6 \tag{4}$$
$\theta_i \equiv i^{th}$ parameter of F

$TT \equiv$ higher technical school or university trained engineers per textile mill
$WE \equiv$ work experience of average member of labor force
$PE \equiv$ percentage of textile labor force with primary school education
$FA \equiv$ number of years average firm in operation
$AC \equiv$ average age of spindles in use
$LS \equiv$ length of shift

Taken together, Equations 3 and 4 represent a fairly general production relationship. Although the precise form of such a relationship cannot be easily posited, it seems reasonable to assume it can be approximated by the first- and second-order terms of a Taylor's series expansion. Thus an approximation of Equations 3 and 4 will be given by,

$$\log Q_{ft} = \alpha_0 + \alpha_K \log K_{ft} + \alpha_L \log L_{ft} + \sum_{j=3}^{8} \alpha_j \log X_{jt} \tag{5}$$
$$+ \tfrac{1}{2}\gamma_{KK}\,(\log K_{ft})^2 + \tfrac{1}{2}\gamma_{LL}\,(\log L_{ft})^2 + \gamma_{KL}\,\log K_{ft} \log L_{ft}$$
$$+ \left(\sum_{j=3}^{8} \gamma_{kj} \log X_{jt}\right) \log K_{ft} + \left(\sum_{j=3}^{8} \gamma_{Lj} \log X_{jt}\right) \log L_{ft}$$
$$+ \sum_{j=3}^{8} \sum_{k=3}^{8} \gamma_{jk} \log X_{jt} \log X_{kt}$$

[6]The source and quality of this data will be discussed in somewhat greater detail later in this study. A complete discussion is contained in Saxonhouse (1971).

The algebraic form given in Equation 5 is the increasingly well-known transcendental logarithmic production function.[8] This form is sufficiently general that using Equation 5 a variety of hypotheses can be tested about the specification of F and G, that is, about the nature of the specific relationships between output and the eight measured inputs, individually and collectively. This will aid in ascertaining the relationship between workers' experience and productivity.

The results of the generalized least squares estimation of Equation 5, presented in Table 11, suggest that of the eight independent variables listed here under Equations 3 and 4, workers' experience and five other variables have a statistically significant effect on output.[9]

Simple inspection shows that there are only six variables in Table 11 which have statistically significant first- or second-order coefficients. Direct testing on the statistical significance of the partial derivatives of output with respect to quantity of capital, quantity of labor, education of management, workers' experience, education of workers, and length of working shifts confirms that only these variables have a significant impact on productivity change.

TRANSIENCE AND TRAINING

The preceding findings, insofar as they do not relate to the issue at hand, will not be examined in detail here (see Saxonhouse 1971), but a few comments are in order. Substantial increases in Japanese cotton industry productivity are associated with substantial increases in the education of Japanese labor and management and even more closely associated with increases in the

---

[7]In a study on cotton textiles it may seem unusual that cotton is excluded from the production function. Preliminary empirical study has indicated raw cotton is so closely correlated with capital as to make the variables statistically indistinguishable. For a substantively similar treatment of the point, see David (1970).

[8]The Taylor's Series expansion and the conditions under which it is a good approximation to a functional form are discussed in chapter 17 of Allen (1938). A complete statement of this form and an interpretation of each of the parameters in (5) is provided in Christensen, Jorgenson, and Lau (1973).

[9]Efficient estimation of (5) is somewhat complicated. Equation 5 is an amalgam of two different kinds of data sets. Q, K, and L vary over firm and time, whereas the remaining independent variables vary only over time (this latter point will be formally examined later in this paper). Furthermore, the six independent variables in (4) surely will not exhaust the variance of θ. Thus, a number of time-varying stochastic terms enter multiplicatively into a number of the terms in (5). In consequence, the efficient estimation of the general relationship in (5) involves breaking down the estimation procedure into two steps which are tantamount to estimating forms of (3) and (4) successively. First, a time series of conventional cross-section production functions are estimated using generalized least squares. The resulting time series of production function parameter estimates are then regressed on the remaining independent variables. Such an approach will provide efficient

Table 11
Estimation of Cotton Industry Production Functions,
1891-1935

Parameter	Estimated coefficient	Standard error
αK	0.120748	0.434211×10^{-1}
αL	0.128439	0.572674×10^{-1}
αTT	0.847251×10^{-2}	0.261834×10^{-2}
αWE	0.808557×10^{-1}	0.183700×10^{-1}
αPE	0.317843×10^{-1}	0.527689×10^{-2}
αLS	$- 0.983217 \times 10^{-1}$	0.344485×10^{-1}
γKL	$- 0.633128 \times 10^{-1}$	0.268146×10^{-1}
γKPE	0.427162×10^{-2}	0.148535×10^{-2}
γKLS	$- 0.785737 \times 10^{-2}$	0.278422×10^{-2}
γLWE	0.979954×10^{-2}	0.308021×10^{-3}
γLLS	0.214944×10^{-2}	0.942156×10^{-3}
$\gamma TTPE$	$- 0.862485 \times 10^{-3}$	0.342810×10^{-3}
$\gamma WEWE$	$- 0.486612 \times 10^{-3}$	0.132859×10^{-3}
$\gamma WEPE$	0.228258×10^{-2}	0.971253×10^{-3}
$\gamma LSLS$	$- 0.350400 \times 10^{-3}$	0.938943×10^{-4}

Note: Lists only statistically significant results.

average length of service of the average worker and with the comparatively modest decline in the length of daily shifts.[10] A major part of this increase in Japanese productivity between 1890 and 1935 seems attributable to just those elements of the industry record which were earlier shown to be weakest from an international perspective. There is no inconsistency. It is quite reasonable that even a modest improvement from a very low level would

---

estimates of all parameters in (5). The estimation approach described here is discussed in more detail in Saxonhouse (1976 and *RES* forthcoming).

[10]The incidence of primary school education among female workers in the Japanese cotton industry increased dramatically during the period under study. In 1891, 26.1 percent of the labor force were at least primary school students. By 1935 this proportion had risen to 98 percent. Similarly in 1891 there was one formally trained engineer for every six plants in the industry. By 1935 the engineering depth of the industry was such that each firm had an average of five engineers for each of its plants. By contrast, shift length fell from eleven-plus hours to approximately eight and a half between 1891 and 1935. Finally, length of service of the average employe increased from a little more than one year in the 1890s to better than three years in the 1930s.

bring large benefits in productivity. Indeed, examination of the signs of the second-partial derivatives which result from the estimation performed here suggest, in the best tradition of the neoclassical production function, that net increase in productivity slows down as average experience increases and length of shifts declines. Furthermore, it is not unreasonable that shorter working hours, while greatly improving the productivity of workers at their jobs, might have no influence on their desire to remain at work.

A real problem for analysis, however, is posed by the clear and unmistakable influence of worker experience on productivity. Had no significant relationship been uncovered between productivity and worker experience, the results of the first section would be explicable: an experienced labor force in the Japanese industry did not evolve, because such a development would have had little effect on productivity. However, this easy avenue of explanation is now blocked.[11]

The Japanese cotton workers who remained in the industry did become more skilled and more productive. They were able to tend far many more ring frames than the recent recruit. They might move from being a piecer to being a first-class doffer. They might become head-girl in their section, or they might aspire to a job with rudimentary machinery repair responsibilities. In each of these positions and others, these experienced and especially productive workers were rewarded with extra remuneration. This extra

---

[11]As changes in the average length of service in the textile industry seem a phenomenon of the length and time path of the industry's development, it is legitimate to ask whether the econometric evidence presented speaks to the issue at hand. The statistically significant positive sign of the partial derivative of output with respect to worker experience may simply reflect the benefits which accrued to the industry from building up a core of overseers in the midst of a predominantly transient labor force. This is certainly a part of the story of this industry, but there is ample evidence cotton textile industries can derive substantial benefits in productivity from more experienced workers who are not overseers. In estimating (5), a measure of central tendency of workers' experience was used. In an effort to allow for an overseer effect, (5) is reestimated using a number of variables which reflect the distribution of this experience, specifically, by replacing the worker experience variable defined here with the following four variables: (1) proportion of work force with experience of six months to two years; (2) proportion of work force with two to four years' experience; (3) proportion of work force with four to seven years' experience; (4) proportion of work force with over seven years' experience. The net three additional variables which result from this substitution make it difficult to estimate (5). If instead it is assumed that in (3) and (4), F and G are linear in logarithms, then a form of (5) can be estimated which assumes

$$\gamma_{KK} = 0, \propto_{LL} = 0, \gamma_{LK} = 0, \text{ and } \sum_{j=3}^{8} \sum_{K=3}^{8} \gamma_{jk} = 0.$$

remuneration typically far exceeded the small special increment which most Japanese cotton-spinning firms paid to workers who stayed beyond the two- or three-year contract period.[12]

As it was clearly possible to earn higher wages within the industry, it seems appropriate first to study the issue of labor force transience from the perspective of the worker prior to examining the considerations of the employers. Workers did not desire to remain in this industry because the opportunities for higher wages did not become available without considerable cost. Other than those few who, because of natural skills and personality,

---

The work experience coefficients which result from this estimation are presented as follows:

Parameter	Estimated Coefficient	Standard Error
$\propto WE$(6m-2yrs)	0.250734×10^{-1}	0.934743×10^{-2}
$\propto WE$(2yrs-4yrs)	0.374827×10^{-1}	0.155492×10^{-1}
$\propto WE$(4yrs-7yrs)	0.310401×10^{-1}	0.132489×10^{-1}
$\propto WE$(>7yrs)	$* * * \equiv$ statistically insignificant	
γKWE(6m-2yrs)	$* * * \equiv$ statistically insignificant	
γKWE(2yrs-4yrs)	$* * * \equiv$ statistically insignificant	
γKWE(4yrs-7yrs)	$* * * \equiv$ statistically insignificant	
γKWE(>7yrs)	$* * * \equiv$ statistically insignificant	
γLWE(6m-2yrs)	$* * * \equiv$ statistically insignificant	
γLWE(2yrs-4yrs)	0.678136×10^{-3}	0.244310×10^{-3}
γLWE(4yrs-7yrs)	$* * * \equiv$ statistically insignificant	
γLWE(>7yrs)	0.510489×10^{-3}	0.215273×10^{-3}

These results suggest the earlier results reported on the coefficients of work experience in Table 11 do not simply reflect the augmentation of a core group of highly experienced supervisory workers. Accumulation of experience appears to confer substantial and rising benefits for the first seven years' experience.

[12]Data are available on wages cross-classified by mill function and length of service for two prewar Japanese cotton-spinning mills. Data for 1912 for Kanebō and Tōyō Mosurin have been examined for ring spinners with greater than three years of service. The following compares actual increments by year with service-related increments.

Years of service	4	5	6	7	8	9	10
Actual increments as a percent of service increments	147.1	274.0	666.7	250.0	356.8	317.6	216.2

effortlessly became model factory workers, most workers, if they wished to increase their earnings in the future, had to forego present income:[13] entering workers typically earned less than agricultural workers of comparable age, sex, and inexperience. Only the substantial recruitment bonus and the uncertain but not entirely negligible prospect of success as a factory worker kept inducing young farm girls for over fifty years to try their luck in the cotton-spinning mills.

Suppose most Japanese spinning-mill workers had not been forced to underwrite, through lower wages, the cost of their skill acquisition, how might the evolution of this industry have been different? The experience of the post-World War II period provides a clue as to what would have happened. After provision has been made for room and board costs, starting wages for newly recruited workers at the larger spinning firms during the 1950s were almost exactly comparable with what young women were receiving in the agricultural sector. And notwithstanding the higher initial level, the prospects for subsequent wage increases were almost as great in the 1950s as before the

[13]An analysis of the length-of-service-related wage data for Kanebō suggests after allowance has been made for room and board the daily wage paid newly recruited female ring-spinners varied from between 65 percent and 85 percent of the daily wage rate of female agricultural workers on annual contract throughout much of the prewar period. Female annual contract workers in agriculture were almost always young and unmarried and received room and board from the farm household for which they worked. Such work was a direct substitute for going to work in the spinning mills.

The lower wage does not mean it was necessarily financially disadvantageous to go to work in a spinning mill. Typically, a recruit's family received a substantial payment at the time the worker entered company service. For the year for which sample information is available, this payment averaged almost one month's wages. Thus, once the female worker was installed in the spinning mill she found she had a definite incentive to leave. Successfully running away and finding employ as a contract agricultural worker in most circumstances would leave herself and her family better off than remaining in the mill. The longer she remained in the mill the more the incentive to leave diminished; after two years of experience in the mill, remuneration in factory work was clearly superior to what could be earned in agriculture. Yet by this time more than 80 percent of any entering cohort had left. Even with superior remuneration, the strict discipline made work in a cotton-spinning mill an unattractive alternative for many. Although an experienced (five-plus years) female factory worker could earn considerably more than her counterpart in agriculture, this was not because their daily wage rates were very different. A cotton-factory worker could expect over three hundred days of work each year. An agricultural worker hired on a daily basis could expect no more than one hundred eighty days of work. Thus the differences in annual wage income are a poor measure of relative well-being. For this reason it is difficult to calculate the rate of return to a female factory worker's investment in herself.

war.[14] The explicit assumption by the cotton-spinning industry of the responsibility and cost of training its female workers was part of a broad change in industry policies in the early postwar period. The following remarks by a former president of Tōyōbō on this subject are instructive.

Of these employee training programs, we should like to make a brief study of the "Training-Within-Industry" system. Owing to the fact that the type of labor required by cotton spinning and weaving is mostly simple and does not require special skills, the systemic and extensive technical training of employees, such as is being conducted in the cotton industry today, is a relatively recent development. The training schools maintained in some spinning undertakings in the prewar days for the education of key technical staff were intended for only a minor fraction of the employees [Shindo 1961, p. 109].

The worker response to this change in industry training policies (together with the response to a deemphasis in piece-rate payment as a key component in wage determination) was remarkable. By 1957, the average length of service of a female worker in cotton spinning was sixty-three months (Sengō 1962, p. 468). In the prewar period this average was never more than forty-four months. If the log-normal distribution used here successfully to describe the time pattern of departure among an entering cohort in the prewar period is applied to postwar data, the average length of service is consistently and substantially underpredicted, as shown in Table 12. These results tend to underline the conclusion that there was a definite change in worker behavior in the 1950s in response to a change in cotton industry policies.

From these results it may be concluded that had the postwar labor policies been adopted by the industry in the prewar period, the extremely high rate of departure of new recruits from this industry would have been considerably lowered. Why did that not occur? Would the adoption of these policies have been profitable in the prewar context? The limited evidence available is most suggestive. Provided the average length of service went up by at least five months, the representative firm in 1912 would more than recover training costs through increased productivity in the very first year of operation of such a program. On the basis of the postwar evidence, such an increase in service would be a reasonable expectation. Moreover, the return to assuming training costs in any given year persists over time. Thus it would seem what

[14]The spinning-industry wage data used in the analysis here was prepared by Nihon Bōseki Kyōkai for publication in *Nihon Bōseki Rōdō Geppō*. Postwar estimates of the wages of annual contract workers have been prepared by Minami (1973, p. 298). Room and board costs for cotton-spinning workers used here are estimates of the Tōyōbō Keizai Kenkyūjo. In the 1950s the industry wage data cross-classified by length of service indicate an average increase of 37.3 percent during the first two years of service. The 1912 data used in the prewar analysis indicate increases in wages of some 45 percent during the first two years of service.

Table 12
Change in the Length of Service of
Cotton Spinners (in months)

	Actual	Predicted
1951	33	23
1953	47	33
1955	65	45
1957	60	43

Source: Recruitment and actual length of
service data from Nihon Bōseki Kyōkai.

was apparently profitable in the postwar period was also profitable in the prewar period.[15]

In assessing the profitability of the firm absorbing the costs of worker training, it was assumed trained workers had no choice but to remain at the firms which trained them. This assumption is reasonable provided the training which the worker received had no economic value elsewhere. If the skills acquired by the worker were equally valuable at another mill in the cotton industry or elsewhere, the individual mill owner would reap no direct benefit from his payment of training costs. There is every reason to believe that in the prewar period (and unlike the postwar period), relative to cotton textile industries in other countries, technical practice in Japan was unusually uniform. It follows that training received by a worker in one mill was quite likely equally valuable elsewhere in the industry. As a result the risk to the firm of an investment in training appears to have been relatively high, for the worker might readily move at higher wage (equal to the marginal product after training) to another firm. Japan's distinctive homogeneity of technical practice among its cotton-spinning mills apparently well explains the equally distinctive transience of its cotton textile labor force.

[15]The figure of five months has been derived by making explicit use of the production function estimated in Table 11. First, a supply function and a derived demand for labor function are obtained from the production function under the assumption firms maximize profits. It is assumed that for a time horizon of one year only the output and labor variables are under the mill manager's control. Using these functions and the 1912 average firm data, it is possible to calculate the benefits to a firm from any increase in the average length of service of the work force. For the purposes of the hypothetical calculation of these benefits, it is assumed trained workers had no choice but to remain at the firms which trained them if they remained in the industry at all. At the same time it is assumed firms, in an effort to retain as many trained workers as possible, paid workers in accordance with the value of their post-training marginal product. Thus, if firms recouped training costs at all it was done via producers' surplus. An increase in trained, experienced workers leads to a decline in wages paid such experienced workers and an

COMMUNICATION AMONG COMPETITORS

Was technical practice actually uniform? There is considerable evidence that information channels among the firms in the Japanese cotton industry were excellent, and that the transmission of best practice was very rapid. These channels were directly controlled by the industry cartel, Dainihon Bōseki Rengōkai (otherwise called Bōren, in English the All-Japan Cotton-Spinners Association). Bōren dominated the industry. Throughout most of its history its members controlled better than 97 percent of the industry spindleage. In periods of incipient oversupply, Bōren limited the capacity each firm could use for the spinning of yarn. Entry into the industry was relatively free, but on entry a new firm had almost no choice but to join Bōren. By agreement with Bōren, Japanese shippers would give rebates on raw cotton imports only to association members. Japanese cotton-spinners relied exclusively on imported raw cottons, as domestic cotton had proved unsuitable for the production of machinemade yarn.

In view of the frequent constraints put on the use of capacity by member firms, it was essential that Bōren have accurate records on production and inputs used. It was these records that were used in the econometric investigation performed earlier in this study. What is most interesting is the lack of any feeling of confidentiality regarding these data. The following information was published, broken down by firms, on a monthly basis in the association's journal throughout the period 1889 to 1937: (1) average number of spindles operated per day, (2) working days per month, (3) working hours per day, (4) yarn produced by count, (5) raw cotton consumed, (6) workers, male and female, (7) wages, male and female.[16]

---

adjustment in the amount of raw labor being used. These benefits must be matched against the costs of a change in labor force policies. These costs are assumed to be equal to the extra cost involved in paying inexperienced workers a wage equivalent to what they would have received had they been annual contract workers in the agricultural sector.

It will be noted the cost of recruitment does not enter these calculations. Under the system actually prevailing during the prewar period, recruitment costs were approximately equal to forfeited worker savings. During much of the prewar period most mills withheld and deposited from 3 to 10 percent of workers' wages in special savings accounts. These savings were returned to the workers only at the end of their contract period. As the contract period was usually two or three years, a high percentage of the workers forfeited their savings on leaving the mill. To the extent the incoming workers' rate of time preference was very high, this practice only served to exaggerate the already existing incentives for running away.

[16]These records were published on a monthly basis in *Rengō Bōseki Geppō*, nos. 1-26, *Bōshoku Geppō*, nos. 1-14, *Dai Nihon Bōseki Dōgyō Rengōkai Geppō*, nos. 112-122, *Dai Nihon Bōseki Rengōkai Geppō*, nos. 123-600. There is every reason to believe the mills accurately reported their data to Bōren. Yasuba (1965) in his study of prewar production statistics concludes the data available for the Japanese spinning industry appear to be entirely

Over and above even this detailed information, complete cost data for certain mills were occasionally published.[17] This tradition of publishing cost data may have gotten started in the early 1880s, when cotton-spinning firms periodically reported their cost information to Nōshōmushō (Kinukawa 1944, 3:154): "Received translation ... of article in Monthly Report. An account of our friend's experience ... reducing height of frames. No doubt this practice will go forward ... The Report is helpful" [Neill, Sept. 1892]. "Monthly Geppō [sic] discusses advantages of [domestically produced] hank cop reels. This will not be a market for Platt's" [Neill, Dec. 1892].

The printed word was not the paramount form of communication. If the Bōren-sponsored *Hompō Menshi Bōseki-shi* is to be believed, there is considerable evidence of direct firm-to-firm cooperation on technical matters; at least twenty instances are cited. For example, in 1885, the president of Miebō received advice from a colleague on mill design (Tōyō, pp. 54-55). Similarly, in 1893 Kishiwadabō received advice on willows from Amagasakibō.[18] It is helpful to quote a foreign observer: "Among the Japan mills there are no secrets, but the foreign visitor is regarded with suspicion. ... *Practice is uniform*" [Ainlie 1896, italics added].

Intensive communication among firms led to a not-surprising homogeneity of practice. Fully 87 percent of all 1,800,000 spindles in Japan in 1909 had been supplied by a single manufacturer, Platt Brothers of Oldham (Clark 1914, p. 213). Use of a single machinery supplier further increased the flow of technical information among firms. In advising firms as to the most appropriate design of machinery, Platt Brothers could draw on the whole range of Japanese experience.[19] This advice was not limited to mill design.

---

reliable. In an effort to independently confirm the reliability of the published data, they have been compared with the figures recorded in the unpublished private books of a number of spinning companies. This was done most comprehensively with the records of Kanebō. Private and public figures never differed by more than one percent.

[17]Between 1890 and 1897 articles containing detailed cost data were published in the *Bōren Geppō* on Miikebō, Miebō, Kanebō, Nagoyabō, Hiranobō, and Settsubō, among others. Between 1898 and 1907 similar articles were published on Tsushimabō, Miikebō, Wakayama Bōshoku, Takaokabō, and Settsubō, among others.

[18]Kinukawa (1944, 6:20). Other instances cited by Kinukawa of firm-to-firm technological assistance include Ōsakabō helping Ichikawabō (6:76), Tamashimabō helping Shodoshimabō (6:232), Kuwanabō receiving help from Owaribō (7:68). Ichinomiyabō received help from Nipponbō, Meijibō, and Miibō (1:121), Kuwaharabō from Settsubō (2:235), Okayama Bōsekijō from Himejibō and Shibutanibō (2:292), Ōsakabō from Kuwaharabō (2:390), Kishiwadabō from Senshūbō (6:62), Shimomurabō from Kuwaharabō and Tamashimabō (3:108), Miibō from Taiheibō (3:469), Jurabō from Shimomurabō (5:36), Kofubō from Ichikawabō (5:167), and Settsubō helping Takaokabō (5:20 and 5:36).

[19]For example, in a memorandum dated 30 October 1900, to Tōkyō Gasu, Platt Brothers discussed in detail the experience of Nipponbō.

Between the 1890s and 1910 many of the larger mills kept on Platt Brothers engineers and fitters as advisers. During their heyday before the First World War a small nucleus of representatives serviced the entire industry. Their important role in diffusing best practice, entirely unrecorded in Western annals, deserves recognition. Some of these foreign advisers were highly respected and maintained a long and continuous association with the Japanese industry. Best known in Japan was probably Henry Ainlie. As a young man in 1866 he drew the plans for Kagoshima Bōseki, the first cotton-spinning mill in Japan. Thirty-five years later, he was advising a well-established industry on improving the quality of its output through doubling and gassing. In the interim he had been closely associated with Ōsakabō, Kurabō, Nipponbō, and Amagasakibō, spending almost five years in all in Japan.

Still further evidence of the close technological relationship among firms in the industry may be seen in the switch from mule spinning machines to ring spinning machines. With the concurrence of Platt Brothers and following the English and Indian examples, the Japanese spinning industry began operations relying on mule spindles. Takeo Yamabe, the premier Japanese textile engineer, as late as 1886 after three years of experience with mules at Ōsakabō, could still recommend the purchase of a full complement of mules for Miebō. The following year as a result of some further experimentation with rings and mules and some discussion among themselves, it became clear to a number of Japanese textile men, Yamabe included, that given the Japanese yarn market the ring was the appropriate spinning machine for Japan.[20] With the exception of the mules imported for mills which were set up explicitly to spin fine yarns, importation of mules simply stopped after 1887. Ironically, the two largest mule mills, the aforementioned Ōsakabō and Miebō, were destroyed by fire not long after this switch in preference occurred, both to be replaced by large mills using rings.[21]

This experience was representative. Two years later T.W. Dohrenfield wrote Platt Brothers concerning the switch from the roller and clearer carding engine to the revolving flat carding engine: "Mr. Kikuchi of Hirano Spinning Mill is insistent [in his preference] for Flat Cards. ... R & C Cards will now be used only for waste spinning. ... *We can expect the entire industry will follow suit*" [Dohrenfield 1889, italics added]. After 1889, revolving flat carding engines were used exclusively by this industry.

Again, through mid-1889, all Japanese mills (twenty-odd in number) purchased hank-cop reelers from English machinery manufacturers. Though some seventy additional mills were built between mid-1889 and the outbreak of the First World War, only four used English-made hank-cop reelers.

[20]For a discussion of the relative virtues of the ring and the mule, see Taggart (1920, 3:331-333). Other material in this paragraph is based on Nōshōmushō (p. 24) and Tōyō Bōseki (pp. 59-60).

[21]Lest there be any suspicion on this point, the company history assures us these mills were not covered by fire insurance. *Tōyō Bōseki Nanajūnen-shi*, p. 38.

Japanese copies of this elementary piece of English textile machinery were developed in late 1888, and the Japanese spinners switched to domestic suppliers almost immediately thereafter (see Table 13).

The story of bundling press orders is similar. Through 1906 only eleven of ninety-seven mill orders failed to include bundling presses in their specifications. Though another forty mills were ordered between 1907 and 1916, there was only one additional bundling press ordered by Japanese spinners from English manufacturers. Again the coming of age of a domestically produced alternative played an important role in this dramatic shift in preference. During the decade before the First World War many new Japanese mills replaced power-driven English-made bundling presses with manually operated Japanese ones (see Table 14).[22]

Table 13
Percentage of Mill Orders Given English Manufacturers
which Included Hank-Cop Reels

1884	100	1892	0	1900	0
1885	No orders	1893	10	1901	0
1886	100	1894	0	1902	0
1887	100	1895	15	1903	0
1888	100	1896	8	1904	No orders
1889	40	1897	0	1905	0
1890	No orders	1898	0	1906	0
1891	No orders	1899	0	1907	0

Source: Orders for Platt Brothers and Howard & Bulloughs machinery placed respectively with Mitsui & Co. and Takata & Co.

Table 14
Percentage of Mill Orders Given English Manufacturers
which Included Bundling Presses

1884	100	1895	85	1906	80
1885	No orders	1896	88	1907	0
1886	100	1897	100	1908	0
1887	100	1898	100	1909	0
1888	100	1899	100	1910	0
1889	100	1900	100	1911	0
1890	No orders	1901	100	1912	4
1891	No orders	1902	100	1913	0
1892	66	1903	100	1914	0
1893	70	1904	No orders	1915	0
1894	89	1905	66	1916	0

Source: Same as Table 13.

[22]There is no evidence this preference for manually operated presses was anything more than an interlude. The preference certainly did not survive the

The preceding anecdotal evidence is most persuasive, but the need for additional and more systematic examination of the question of uniformity of firm practice remains. The production function estimation, the results of which were reported in Table 11, can easily be adjusted to make extensive use of firm and firm group dummies.

Recall that the six independent variables in Equation 4 are industrywide averages. The possibility of heterogeneity of practice among firms in the cotton industry can be introduced by allowing these inputs to vary among firms. While direct firm data on these variables are unavailable, some evidence on interfirm variation can be directly taken from the data set used in constructing Table 11. First, rewrite Equation 5 as follows:

$$\log Q_{ft} = \alpha_0 + \alpha_K \log K_{ft} + \alpha_L \log L_{ft} + \sum_{j=3}^{8} \log (1+d_f^j) X_{jt} \qquad (6)$$

$$+ \tfrac{1}{2}\gamma_{KK} (\log K_{ft})^2 + \tfrac{1}{2}\gamma_{22} (\log L_{ft})^2 + \gamma_{KL} \log K_{ft} \log L_{ft}$$

$$+ \sum_{j=3}^{8} \gamma_{Kj} \log (1+d_f^j) X_{jt} \log K_{ft} + \sum_{j+3}^{8} \gamma_{Lj} \log (1+d_f^j) X_{jt} \log L_{ft}$$

$$+ \sum_{j=3}^{8} \sum_{k=3}^{8} \gamma_{jk} \log (1+d_f^j) X_{jt} \log (1+d_f^k) X_{kt}$$

$$= \sum_{j=3}^{8} \log (1+d_f^j) + \sum_{j=3}^{8} \gamma_{Kj} \log (1+d_f^j) \log K_{ft} + \sum_{j=3}^{8} \gamma_{Lj} \log (1+d_f^j) \log L_{ft}$$

$$+ 2 \sum_{j=3}^{8} \sum_{k=3}^{8} \gamma_{jk} \log (1+d_f^j) \log X_{kt}$$

+ right-hand side terms in Equation 5.

Provided the expected values of the $(1+d_f^j)$ are equal to zero and the $(1+d_f^j)$ are independent of all the right-hand side variables in Equation 5, unbiased estimates of

$$\sum_{j=3}^{8} \log (1+d_f^j), \sum_{j=3}^{8} \gamma_{Kj} \log (1+d_f^j), \sum_{j=3}^{8} \gamma_{Lj} \log (1+d_f^j), \text{ and } \sum_{j=3}^{8} \sum_{k=3}^{8} \gamma_{jk} \log (1+d_f^j)$$

can be obtained by regressing time series of firm residuals from estimated Equation 5 on $\log K_{ft}$, $\log L_{ft}$, and the $\log X_{jt}$. The resulting sets of time series firm coefficient estimates can then be tested for homogeneity.

Would firm and firm group dummies make a significant contribution to the statistical analysis; Given equation (6), this means testing the following hypotheses.[23]

First World War. In contrast to these two examples, there are many instances where Japanese machinery manufacturers showed themselves technologically capable of producing looms or spinning machinery but were spurned on economic and quality grounds by the domestic cotton industry. Indeed, spinning machinery had been produced in Japan as early as the 1870s.

[23]Given what has preceded, good statistical practice might require the composite alternative to H_o, (note continues)

$$H_0: \sum_{j=3}^{8} \log (1+d_1^j) = \sum_{j=3}^{8} \log (1+d_2^j) = \ldots = \sum_{j=3}^{8} \log (1+d_{30}^j)$$

$$\sum_{j=3}^{8} \gamma_{Kj} \log (1+d_1^j) = \sum_{j=3}^{8} \gamma_{Kj} \log (1+d_2^j) = \ldots = \sum_{j=3}^{8} \gamma_{Kj} \log (1+d_{30}^j)$$

$$\sum_{j=3}^{8} \gamma_{Lj} \log (1+d_1^j) = \sum_{j=3}^{8} \gamma_{Lj} \log (1+d_2^j) = \ldots = \sum_{j=3}^{8} \gamma_{Lj} \log (1+d_{30}^j)$$

$$\sum_{j=3}^{8} \sum_{k=3}^{8} \gamma_{jk} \log (1+d_1^j) = \sum_{j=3}^{8} \sum_{k=3}^{8} \gamma_{jk} \log (1+d_2^j) = \ldots = \sum_{j=3}^{8} \sum_{k=3}^{8} \gamma_{jk} \log (1+d_{30}^j)$$

For testing these four hypotheses jointly, a statistic which is distributed as F with $(270, 1080)$ degrees of freedom is evaluated, giving

$$F = 0.87 < \text{critical region.}[24]$$

Clearly the same statistic does not fall into the critical region, and the null hypothesis cannot be rejected. The firm and firm group dummies taken together are statistically insignificant. In other words, the hypothesis that the technical and managerial practices of all firms were essentially the same cannot be rejected. Although it is possible this result should be interpreted as simply a rejection of the restrictive specification employed in generating the five dummies in the first place, it is reasonable to take it as supporting the hypothesis of substantially uniform technical and managerial practice among all the members of Bōren. In light of the other evidence presented here, this is certainly reasonable.

COMMUNICATION AND MONOPSONY

In Adam Smith's *Wealth of Nations*, it is alleged that when producers get together discussion will inevitably turn to the raising of prices. In Japanese cotton-industry history one might paraphrase this by saying whenever producers met the discussion inevitably turned to how the labor market could

---

$$H_A: \sum_{j=3}^{8} \log (1+d_1^j) \neq \sum_{j=3}^{8} \log (1+d_2^j) \neq \ldots \neq \sum_{j=3}^{8} \log (1+d_{30}^j), \text{ etc.}$$

be treated as the null hypothesis. In the absence of such an approach the design of the test may make the risk of mistakenly not rejecting the uniformity of practice hypothesis unacceptably high. Unfortunately given the state of mathematical statistics, taking a composite alternative and making it the null hypothesis is most difficult for the current purposes. Instead, uniformity of practice will be left as the null hypothesis, and the critical region will be expanded to guard against the dangers outlined here.

[24]Regardless of intuition, the addition of categorical variables does not always significantly improve the explanatory power of a regression on a time series of cross-sections. The addition of such variables in the analysis presented in Balestra and Nerlove (1966) is inconsequential for the explanatory power of the relations being examined.

be most advantageously segregated, that is, how labor mobility among firms could be minimized. This kind of cooperation was certainly as important as technical cooperation as a motivating force for the establishment of Bōren. If such activities actually were effective, individual firms would presumably have had much less difficulty in recouping any training outlays.

The trade association's monthly report during the industry's early years contains considerable discussion of labor piracy and the various steps Bōren and its constituent firms were taking to cope with labor force problems. For example, textile firms in Osaka formed a special alliance within Bōren to deal with unauthorized hiring of competitors' workers. Reports of the adjudication of complaints were published in the *Bōren Geppō*. How effective were these attempts, largely instituted in the 1880s and 1890s, to reduce competitiveness in the labor market? At least some contemporary observes thought they were ineffective.

Charges of enticement are frequently made. . . . Apparently, the Association's rules are ineffectual [Holt 1911].

In times when a mill is losing money for lack of help . . . rules and agreements are not always effective, especially as names are easily changed [Clark 1914, p. 200].

. . . to get a quick and easy supply of labor, the practice of abducting working girls from one factory to another was common in the pre-war period and to a great extent during the period of the industrial boom between 1917 and 1920. . . . The security of the labor force remains a problem [Harada 1928, p. 122].

Again the econometric estimation of the production function conducted earlier throws some light on the efficacy of Bōren activities in the labor market. With the aid of the results of that section, a time series of estimates of the output elasticity of labor can be examined. As is well known, if competition reigned in the Japanese textile industry labor market, this elasticity should conform to the shares of wages in output.[25] Let us test this by the following null hypothesis.

$$H_0 : \frac{\partial Q}{\partial L} \frac{L}{Q} = \left(\frac{WL}{Q}\right)_t \quad t = 1891, 1892, \ldots 1935 \tag{7}$$

This null hypothesis can be tested simultaneously using the following statistic:

[25]This, of course, assumes that the relevant production function is linear homogeneous or constant returns to scale. Actually the estimated production function exhibits mild economies of scale. This violation of the constant returns to scale assumption in no way qualifies the conclusions drawn in this section. In the presence of economies of scale, even if workers receive a share of output less than the output elasticity of labor, it does not necessarily signify the presence of exploitation. As I find that workers receive a share of output statistically indistinguishable from the output elasticity of labor even

$$\sum_{i=1}^{45} S_i = \chi^2_{45} \tag{8}$$

$$\sum_{i=1}^{45} S_i = 45.9742 < 59.8725 \equiv \text{critical value at } 0.05$$

$S_i \equiv$ appropriate S statistic for each year.

The hypothesis that the estimated output elasticity of labor is equal to the share of wages cannot be rejected. Apparently the labor market was competitive, and the presumption that textile firm cooperation to restrict the labor market was unsuccessful must remain.[26] Note the conclusion from Equation 8 is entirely consistent with Iemoto's (1951) pioneering work on the Japanese cotton-spinning industry production function.

CONCLUSION AND SUMMARY

A historian of the Japanese cotton textile industry must emphasize the persistent instability of the labor force and the close cooperation among the member firms of Dai Nihon Bōseki Rengōkai. From a comparative perspective, these features are striking. It is natural to imagine these industrial traits must be linked; this study has endeavored to demonstrate and analyze this linkage. The close cooperation among cotton textile firms led to a uniformity of practice which made an investment in training the labor force a relatively risky undertaking. In the process of constructing this link, the following has been uncovered:

1. Kanebō's worker welfare policies were not effective in reducing female labor turnover in the period prior to 1915.

2. The findings for Kanebō prior to 1915 are representative of the entire industry's experience between the 1890s and the 1930s.

3. A more experienced labor force has an unmistakable positive influence on cotton textile productivity. This finding is uncovered in the context of a research design which allows for the impact of management experience and training, worker education, age of the capital stock, and working conditions.

4. The beneficial experience indicated under 3 is acquired by most workers at a cost. In the prewar period this cost is borne by the workers themselves, in the form of initial wages lower than those of alternative employment opportunities.

5. Technological cooperation among firms in this industry was substantial. Among the important vehicles for the transmission of best practice were the

---

with the presence of economies of scale, my conclusions, if anything, are strengthened.

[26]That the share of the wage bill in output does not significantly differ from the output elasticity of labor also suggests the training which went on in the prewar period was quite likely worker financed; because workers received their full marginal product they had, through initial lower wages, to bear these training costs. This evidence bolsters the results of the previous section.

Bōren Geppō and the representatives of Platt Brothers of Oldham, England.

6. Taken together, it does not appear Japanese cotton textile firms differed significantly among themselves with respect to management experience and education, worker experience and education, age of capital, and working conditions *in a way that would have consequences for productivity*.

7. Despite considerable discussion and effort it does not appear the membership of Bōren succeeded in segregating the textile labor market sufficiently to obtain monopsony rents in the hiring of workers.

These results suggest further research is necessary into the nature of alternative training possibilities and institutional arrangements which might have allowed for external financing of the upgrading of the Japanese textile industry labor force. In particular, the change in training policies between the prewar and postwar period requires careful elaboration. Clarification and explication of this unusual and important instance of manufacturing assimilation will surely deepen and broaden an understanding of the process of industrialization and its social consequences.

REFERENCES

Ainlie, Henry. 1896. Letters to Platt Brothers.

Allen, R. G. D. 1938. *Mathematical Analysis for Economists*. Macmillan.

Balestra, Pietro, and Mark Nerlove. 1966. "Pooling Cross-Section and Time Series Data in the Estimation of a Dynamic Model: The Demand for Natural Gas." *Econometrica*, July 1966.

Bōren (Dainihon Bōseki Rengōkai). 1897. *Bōseki Shokkō Jijō Chōsa Gaiyō*.

Brissenden, Paul Frederick, and Emiel Frankel. 1922. *Labor Turnover in Industry*. Macmillan.

Chapman, Sidney J. 1904. *The Lancashire Cotton Industry*. Manchester.

Christensen, Laurits R., Dale W. Jorgenson, and Lawrence Lau. 1973. "Transcendental Logarithmic Production Frontiers." *Review of Economics and Statistics*, Feb. 1973.

Clark, W. A. Graham. 1914. *Cotton Goods in Japan*. U.S. Government Printing Office.

David, Paul. 1970. "Learning by Doing and Tariff Protection. A Reconsideration of the Case of the Ante-Bellum United States Cotton Textile Industry." *Journal of Economic History*, Sept. 1970.

Dohrenfield, T. W. 1889. Letter to Platt. Bound in Hiranobō mill plans.

Forrester, Robert Blair. 1921. *The French Cotton Industry*. University Press, London.

Harada, Shinichi. 1928. *Labor Conditions in Japan*. P. S. King.

Holt, H. 1911. Letter to Platt Brothers. Bound in Amagasakibō, Tsumori #2 plans.

Hosoi, Wakizo. 1925. *Jokō Aishi*.

Iemoto, Hidetaro. 1951. "*Douglas* Seisan Kansū ō Ikusei Suru Tachiba Kara." *Riron Keizai Gaku*, Jan. 1951.

Jackson, P. T., and E. B. Shearman. 1832. *Report on the Production and Manufacture of Cotton*. T. R. Marvin.

Kinukawa, Taichi. 1944. *Hompo Menshi Bōseki-shi*, vols. 3 and 6. Nihon Mengyō Kurabu.

Kubo, Machiko and Yasuke Murakami. 1964. "Wagakuni Nōson Kōzō ni Kansuru Khibunseki." In *Nijū Kōzō no Bunseki*, edited by Yoshio Tamanoi and Tadao Uchida. Tōyō Keizai Shinpōsha.

Kurashiki. *Kurashikikaiko Rokujūgonen*.

LTES [Estimates of Long-Term Economic Statistics of Japan]. Series edited by Kazushi Ohkawa, Miyohei Shinohara, and Mataji Umemura. 1965-. 14 vols. Tōyō Keizai Shinpōsha.

———. Vol. 10. *Mining and Manufacturing*. 1972. Miyohei Shinohara.

Masui, Yukio. 1970. "The Supply Price of Labor: Farm Family Workers." In *Agriculture and Economic Growth: Japan's Experience*, edited by Ohkawa Kazushi, Bruce Johnston, and Hiromitsu Kaneda. Princeton University Press.

McCloskey, Donald. 1970. "Did Victorian England Fail?" *Economic History Review*, Sept. 1970.

Minami, Ryōshin. 1973. *The Turning Point in Economic Development: Japan's Experience*. Kinokuniya.

Morris, Morris D. 1965. *The Emergence of an Industrial Labor Force in India*. University of California Press.

Mutō, Sanji. *Shihaininkai*. Unpublished.

Namiki, Masayoshi. 1956. "Nōka Jinkō no Idōkeitai to Shūgyōkōzō." In *Nōgyō ni okeru Senzai Shitsugyō*, edited by Seiichi Tohata. Nihon Hyōron Shinsha.

Neill, A. 1892. Letters to Platt Brothers.

Okochi, Kazuo. 1950. *Rōdō mondai*.

Saxonhouse, Gary R. 1971. "Productivity Change and Japanese Cotton Spinning, 1891-1935." Ph.D. dissertation, Yale University.

———. (1976) "Estimated Parameters as Dependent Variables." *American Economic Review*, March 1976.

———. (*QJE* forthcoming.) "Productivity Change and Labor Absorption in Japanese Cotton Spinning, 1891-1935." *Quarterly Journal of Economics*.

———. (*RES* forthcoming.) "Regressions on Samples Having Different Characteristics." *Review of Economics and Statistics*.

Sengō Bōseki. 1962. *Sengō Bōseki-shi*.

Shindo, Takejiro. 1961. *Labor in the Japanese Cotton Industry*. Japan Society for the Promotion of Science.

Taggart, W. Scott. 1921. *Cotton Spinning*. Macmillan.

Taira, Koji. 1970a. *Economic Development and the Labor Market in Japan*. Columbia University Press.

———. 1970b. "Factory Legislation and Management Modernization during Japan's Industrialization, 1868-1916." *Business History Review*, Spring 1970.

———. 1972. "The Characteristics of Japanese Labor Markets." *Economic Development and Cultural Change*, Jan. 1972.

Tōyō Bōseki. *Tōyō Bōseki Nanajūnen-shi*.

Tsūsanshō (Tsūshōsangyōshō) [Ministry of International Trade and Industry]. 1961. *Kōgyō Tōkei Gojūnen-shi*.

Uno, Riemon. 1912. *Shokkō jijō mondai shiryō*. Nihon Kyōiku Kai.

U.S. Department of Labor, Women's Bureau. 1926a. *Effects of Applied Research upon the Employment Opportunity of American Women*.
       . 1926b. *Lost Time and Labor Turnover in Cotton Mills*.
Ware, Caroline. 1931. *The Early New England Cotton Manufacture: A Study in Industrial Origins*. Harvard University Press.
Yasuba, Yasukichi. 1965. "Senzen no Nihon ni Okeru Kōgyō Tōkei no Shimpyōsei ni tsuite." *Osaku Daigaku Keizai Gaken*, Nov. 1965.

PART TWO

Industry Patterns and Problems of Scale

The Japanese
Shipbuilding Industry

Tuvia Blumenthal

Since 1956, the Japanese shipbuilding industry has ranked highest in the world in terms of tonnage. Moreover, in recent years Japan has accounted for about one half of total world production of ships, with the second-ranking country producing less than 10 percent (Table 1). Such a high concentration in the world market is surpassed by very few commodities, and by still fewer industrial products.

Japan's geographical position as an island country is certainly a favorable factor in the development of shipping and related industries, but this alone could hardly explain why and how Japan has reached its present standing. Furthermore, several factors were clearly detrimental to the development of a large shipbuilding industry, the foremost being Japan's poverty in iron ores used as raw materials by the industry. Not insignificant, however, is the historical setting in which the growth of the industry has taken place. During the long period of seclusion in the Tokugawa era, building ocean-going vessels was forbidden; in addition, the industry was badly damaged in World War II, so that the Japanese had to start over almost from scratch.

The purpose of this paper is to describe the path the industry has taken, and to try to explain how it reached its present position. However, the story of this industry seems to be instructive as well for understanding a much broader area—that of Japan's overall economic performance. I shall deal with this more general question in some detail.

This study was conducted during a one-year stay at the Institute of Economic Research, Kyoto University. I would like to thank the Institute for the facilities extended to me and to my devoted research assistant Michio Ohashi for his considerable contribution. I benefited from financial aid from the Japanese Society for the Promotion of Science, the Kansai Economic Research Center, the Social Science Research Council, and the Faculty of Social Science, Tel Aviv University. For valuable comments on an earlier draft I wish to thank Nathaniel Leff, Hugh Patrick, William Rapp, and Tsunehiko Watanabe.

Table 1
Ships Launched by Country, 1913-68
(in percentage of gross tons)

Year	World's total	Japan	England	Germany	Sweden	Other countries
1913	100.0	2.0	58.0	14.0	0.6	25.4
1921	100.0	5.2	35.4	11.7	1.5	46.2
1924	100.0	3.2	64.1	7.8	1.4	23.5
1927	100.0	1.9	54.6	12.9	3.0	27.6
1930	100.0	5.3	51.9	8.7	4.6	29.5
1933	100.0	15.4	27.3	8.8	12.7	35.8
1936	100.0	14.1	40.9	18.3	7.4	19.3
1939	100.0	13.1	25.3	12.1	8.5	41.0
1950	100.0	7.8	29.5	3.5	7.8	51.4
1953	100.0	10.9	25.8	16.1	9.5	37.7
1956	100.0	26.2	20.7	15.0	7.3	30.8
1959	100.0	19.7	15.7	13.7	9.8	41.1
1962	100.0	26.1	12.8	12.1	10.0	39.0
1965	100.0	43.9	8.8	8.4	9.6	29.3
1968	100.0	50.8	5.3	8.0	6.6	29.3

Source: 1913-30: League of Nations, Economic and Financial Section, *International Statistical Yearbook*. 1933-39: United Nations, *Statistical Yearbook*. 1950-68: Un'yūshō, *Kaiun Tōkei Nenpō*.

Note: Cargo ships are measured in gross tons, a measure of the ships' interior space (1 gross ton = 100 cubic feet). Warships are measured by displacement tons, the weight of water displaced when the ship is at its waterline. A rough comparison is 1 displacement ton equals 5 gross tons. A deadweight ton is the weight in metric or long tons required to bring a vessel to its waterline. (See Kaneko 1964, p. 154.)

It has long been contended that the static comparative advantage principle, as put forth by Ricardo, is of little value in shaping a development policy, as advantage prescribed by availability of natural resources alone is a poor criterion for determining the growth path of an economy. It can be conjectured that had Japan adhered only to this principle, it would probably still have a primarily agricultural economy and perhaps a large sector of light industry, but would not have its present remarkable body of heavy and chemical industries. Thus, the history of the shipbuilding industry shows how a comparative advantage is created—how the introduction of foreign technology, adapted and transformed to suit domestic conditions, is used to overcome the disadvantage of a lack of raw materials.

This process of creating a comparative advantage is closely related to the rise of infant industries protected by the government. Theoretically, these industries should be raised under the government's umbrella until they mature. However, such a two-stage development process of infancy and adolescence does not apply to the shipbuilding industry—nor, for that matter, to many others. In the greater part of the last hundred years, the industry has received government subsidies which have played a crucial role in overcoming obstacles scattered in its development path. In shipbuilding, the character of the Japanese economy as a "mixed economy" can be clearly seen. The government is pulling the economy in certain directions through the use of market mechanisms rather than by an overall planning system. Left to itself in a world of "free competition," the shipbuilding industry would have been crushed more than once by adverse conditions at home or abroad. It can be said that the course of the shipbuilding industry was characterized, on the whole, by quick adjustment to changing demand conditions and correct forecasting of future needs. Whether this should be attributed to sheer luck or to outstanding insight of the industry leaders is open to discussion but is irrelevant to the consequences. Except for one gross miscalculation during World War II, Japan was always quick to profit from wars and disturbances, regardless of whether she herself took a direct part in them. The shipbuilding industry is no exception to this rule: cornerstones in its development were the Russo-Japanese War, the First World War, the Korean War, and the 1956 and 1967 Middle East wars which closed the Suez Canal. It is not difficult to hypothesize a scenario in which the Japanese prognosis was wrong and the industry was defeated by world competition, but this did not usually happen.

Several features of the shipbuilding market have to be considered before evaluating the Japanese performance. Ships are large units, the end result of assembling a very large number of components. This means *inter alia* that the organizational aspect of production coordination is of utmost importance. Large cost reductions and productivity increases can be achieved by so-called nonembodied technological changes. Changes in the layout of the dock and in launching techniques, for example, were of great significance as major improvements. Another characteristic is that the product is nonhomogeneous, with each vessel having a different purpose and being fitted with different equipment. This leaves relatively little room for mass production techniques and standardization methods, though the Japanese have been the most successful in exploiting what room there is. It also prescribes a specific sequence of production and marketing. Although most other goods are first produced and stockpiled, then sold to consumers, ships are normally sold first and then built to specifications. But the Japanese sometimes changed this sequence—building ships before receiving orders and speculating the demand would be forthcoming.

This leads to the third feature of this market, the long production period. It takes, on average, about one year from the time the order is received until completion of the ship, a fact which is important in several respects. It creates a problem of financing construction, which is more severe for unordered ships, where the shipyard itself bears this burden. In addition, length of the construction period, as well as reliability of the prescribed delivery date, are important for determining competitive position in the world market.

A fourth characteristic is the instability of the market: the demand for civilian ships is a derived demand that depends on the amount of international trade and the movement of passengers by boat. As a consequence of the "acceleration principle," small changes in cargo and passenger volume cause large fluctuations in the demand for vessels. This is why stabilizing elements must be introduced for smooth functioning of the industry. These can come from a steady military demand, a rising demand from abroad, or support by the government. All three have played important roles in Japan.

If the large investments made in the shipbuilding industry reflected expectations of increased world trade, these expectations have certainly been fulfilled, especially in the period after World War II. The physical volume of international trade went up 2.0 percent per year during 1920-38, and 8.2 percent in the postwar period. In addition, there was an increase in the average distance of shipping (especially of oil) from 3215 miles in 1938 to 3625 in 1955. Emerging countries regarded a navy as well as a commercial fleet as one element of sovereignty. Companies—in particular, oil companies —were willing to own ships. The Japanese were also quick to spot the trends: they were ready to supply the increasing demand for tankers as well as ships for specific uses such as ore carriers and bulk carriers.

Before entering into the main subject of this study, I have to make one reservation. One problem inherent in a case study is that focusing attention on one industry takes it out of the whole industrial complex—and, in particular, its relations with close industries. In the present case the most important industries are iron and steel, as suppliers of raw materials, and the shipping industry as buyers. Although I shall refer to the role played by these two industries and their effect on shipbuilding, no detailed analysis will be performed; however, such an analysis should be attempted in the future.

The paper is composed of four sections. The first gives a description of the industry from its beginning in the late Tokugawa period until the end of World War II. The next deals with the industry in the postwar period. The third takes up the question of technological change, the role played by foreign technology, and its adaptation in Japan. The last provides a summary and conclusions, in which I relate the findings of this study to Japan's economic development in general.

THE SHIPBUILDING INDUSTRY IN THE PREWAR PERIOD

The seclusion policy of Tokugawa Japan specifically prohibited construction of ocean-going vessels. In the first half of the nineteenth century, several applications for permission to build ships were rejected by the bakufu.[1] Only after the government came to realize the importance of a navy were steps taken to establish a shipbuilding industry. The ban on the construction of large vessels was lifted in 1853. The following year, the bakufu sent notices to the clans around Edo, urging them to engage in the construction of vessels.

[1]In 1834 Nariaki Tokugawa, head of the Mito clan, asked the bakufu for permission to build a large vessel; this request was rejected, as was another request in 1838. For shipbuilding in this period, see Kobayashi (1966).

The central government and several clans (particularly those of Satsuma, Saga, and Mito) were active in this field. Dockyards were built by the government at Uraga[2] and by the Mito clan at Ishikawajima, and machinery was ordered from Holland. The first technology to be introduced came from the Dutch through a book, *Suijōsen Setsuryaku* [Short Explanation of Steamships], translated by the Satsuma clan in 1849; this was followed by Dutch engineers and equipment. However, it was under Russian supervision that the first foreign-style ship was built in Japan. In 1853, the Russian admiral Putiatin came to Japan to sign a trade treaty; while at anchor, his ship, the *Diana*, was badly hit by an earthquake. When it became clear the *Diana* could not be repaired, a new ship by the name of *Hetago* was constructed by the Russian crew and Japanese carpenters in four months. The blueprints and acquired skills were immediately put to use: sixteen sailing boats of the same type were built at Heta and Ishikawajima. This incident had an important impact, for the craftsmen who took part in the construction went to other dockyards and became key figures in later years (Takayanagi 1968, p. 43).

However, such haphazard technological borrowing could not be relied on, so the bakufu opened the Naval Training School in Nagasaki in 1855. A Dutch ship, the *Kankomaru*, was used for demonstration, and a Dutch crew was employed to teach Western shipping and shipbuilding techniques. Students were sent by the government and the clans. Subjects taught included navigation, artillery, and shipbuilding as well as basic studies such as arithmetic, geography, and the Dutch language.[3] This school was closed in 1859; the *Kankomaru*, together with two other Dutch ships which had arrived in the meantime, were sent to the Warship Training School at Edo.

France became a source of technological know-how when the Yokosuka Ironworks was established in 1864 under the supervision of François Leon Verney. Machines were imported from France, and a school was opened for ship engineers and mechanical workers. The school was closed for a short period during the Restoration, but reopened in 1880. Students graduated from this school became influential both in the navy and in private companies (Takayanagi 1968, p. 46).

Foreign technology was transmitted not only by foreign instructors and advisers but also by Japanese students who went abroad to study, which incidentally may have been the cheaper way.[4] It started with cursory visits of students at foreign ports where Japanese ships were being repaired; later, foreign studies were conducted on a more systematic basis. In 1863, fifteen students were sent to Holland on the recommendation of a committee set up

---

[2]This dockyard, used mainly for repairs, was built on a river. On the industry in this period, see Zōsen Kyōkai (1911).

[3]For a detailed account of the school curriculum, see Cornwall (1970, pp. 60-61).

[4]One reason for closing the Nagasaki school was its high cost. It was recommended that students be sent abroad instead (Cornwall 1970, p. 62).

by the bakufu to improve the military system. The original idea was to send them to the United States, but the American Civil War prevented this, so the destination was changed. Shipbuilding, casting, and the use of measuring machines were some of the skills acquired abroad and made use of when the students returned.

As a culmination of these efforts, a naval steamship, the *Chiyodagata*, was completed by the Japanese in 1866 without direct foreign assistance. It took four years; the 60-horsepower engine was produced in Nagasaki, and the body was constructed at Ishikawajima.

Although quantitative achievements up to the Meiji Restoration were relatively small, a modest start was made and a bridge was laid for the adoption of Western technology. The ability of the Japanese to learn quickly despite the language barrier and to reproduce new technology became apparent even at this early stage.[5]

Several factors favorable to the development of the shipbuilding industry emerged with the Restoration. The opening of the country to foreign trade, and the desire to see merchandise carried by Japanese vessels, called for the building of a marine fleet; in addition, the realization that political freedom could be secured only by strong armed forces gave high priority to a naval build-up. Against these factors stood several obstacles. Foremost were the lack of raw materials, the still embryonic state of the iron and steel industry, and the scarcity of skills. To overcome these, direct government intervention was needed to promote the fragile industrial structure.

One of the first acts of the new government was to abolish the ban on ownership of foreign vessels; Premier Declaration No. 968 in 1869 opened the way for Japanese shipping companies to import foreign-built ships. The dockyards constructed by the bakufu and the various clans were taken over by the government, and further investments were made in new docks and equipment. A few years later, however, a change in government policy took place under which shipyards were transferred to private hands on very favorable terms. In 1876, the Ishikawajima yard was sold to Hirano Tomizō; in 1881, the one in Nagasaki was bought by Iwasaki Yattarō (founder of Mitsubishi); and in 1887, the Hyōgō yard was sold to Kawasaki Shōzō.

The prices paid for these shipyards were fractions of the initial investment. The Nagasaki yard was sold for 459,000 yen, with payments spread over a period of fifty years, although the government had invested 1,130,000 yen. Likewise, the price for the Hyōgō dockyard was 188,000 yen with a similar payment arrangement, although the investment by the government had been 816,000 yen (Arisawa 1967). Through these transfers, a large subsidy was given the new companies, and the government was relieved of an expensive venture at a time when it was trying to curtail expenditures under the

[5]Arrow regards the transfer of knowledge as a coded message which has to be decoded, and points out that "in the first instance, a language itself is a code, and the sheer difficulty of translation perhaps can be underestimated" (Arrow 1969, p. 34).

balanced budget policy of Count Matsukata.[6] However, the government retained control over the Yokosuka dockyard, which was kept as a naval base. New shipyards were also established under private incentive. Foremost among them was the Osaka Ironworks, founded in 1881 by an Englishman named E. H. Hunter.

The name Osaka Ironworks illuminates an important contrast between the development of the shipbuilding industry in Japan and in Western countries. In the West, modern shipbuilding evolved after the emergence of the iron and steel industry; in Japan, the order was reversed with iron and steel being formed, to a large extent, as a subsidiary industry to shipbuilding (and, at the same time, as an armament industry).

The transfer of the dockyards to private hands did not, by any means, signify the end of government involvement in this area. The purpose of the government's activity was primarily to improve the quality of domestically built vessels, and only secondarily to encourage their production.[7] There had been a considerable increase in the import of good quality ships, mainly for the navy, as local production was mostly of now obsolete Yamato-type wooden boats. With Declaration No. 16, the government used its administrative power to prohibit the construction of Yamato-type boats in 1885. However, this attempt to promote Western-style shipbuilding was partially defeated by an increase in production of another low-quality type, known as Ainoko (crossbreed), a mixture of Japanese and Western types. The Ainoko-type was exempt from the regulations for inspection of vessels (decreed in 1884), which applied only to Western-style ships. Not until 1896, after the Sino-Japanese War, were the inspection regulations extended to all types of ships. This caused the gradual disappearance of the Ainoko-type and an increase in Western-type vessels.

Even at this early stage one of the important features of the Japanese approach to technological change can be seen—abolishing an old technology by introducing a new one. Instead of improving the existing technique of shipbuilding by blending the old with the new, the Japanese made a fresh start, clearly distinguishable as an import from the West.

The Sino-Japanese War of 1894-95 brought about a change in the attitude of the government toward the shipping industry—and, as a corollary, toward the shipbuilding industry as well. Before the war, both the navy and the

[6]The reason for the transfer is given by Lockwood as follows: "Later, as private initiative and experience developed, as the profits of government undertakings proved meager, and as the State needed funds for armament, it disposed of most of its industrial properties, often at bargain prices" (Lockwood 1954, p. 15).

[7]Atkinson and Stiglitz make a distinction between infant industries, on one hand, and infant techniques, on the other. When technological progress is localized, so that there are good prospects of developing one particular technique, "the government should be concerned not merely with the level of investment or output, but must make sure that firms are directed towards the right technique on long-run considerations" (1969, p. 575).

merchant fleet had been heavily dependent on imported vessels whose quality far surpassed that of the domestic ones; 80 percent of total Japanese tonnage during 1885-95 was imported, while the navy had about 60 percent of its tonnage made abroad during the same period. The locally produced vessels consisted mainly of boats for coastal shipping, whereas foreign ships carried the greater part of Japan's foreign trade. But after 1895 greater emphasis was put on development of ocean-going vessels and on more independence in shipping services. To achieve these goals, the government decided to use the carrot of economic subsidies rather than the stick of administrative controls.

There were basically two ways assistance could be provided to the industry. One was direct subsidy to the shipyards. The other was by subsidy to the shipping industry, with the double purpose of increasing demand for ships and helping the shipping companies themselves. There were long deliberations as to the proper method, even though subsidies to shipping companies had been paid before under different arrangements. Finally, two laws emerged in 1896: the law for the promotion of shipbuilding (Zōsen Shōrei Hō) and the law for the promotion of shipping (Kōkai Shōrei Hō). The first law applied to iron and steel ships of 700 tons or more, and the subsidy went up with the tonnage: vessels of 700 to 1000 tons got 15 yen per ton; those of over 1000 tons, 20 yen per ton. In addition, there was a payment of 5 yen per horsepower. The second law applied to ships of 1000 tons or more with speed of at least ten nautical miles per hour; the subsidy was 0.25 yen per mile of voyage.

However, it soon became clear the Shipping Promotion Law, while having the desired effect of increasing demand for ships, did not necessarily funnel this increased demand into domestic production, as the subsidy was paid for imported and domestic vessels alike. This loophole was partially closed in 1899, when the law was changed to provide imported ships with only half the subsidy. The two industries, shipping and shipbuilding, received very high priority from the government and a large share of all subsidy payments. The combined share of the two industries was about 75 percent of all government subsidies between 1897 and 1913, rising above 90 percent at the turn of the century and before the outbreak of World War I.

The end of the nineteenth century saw a marked increase in the number of shipyards, but Japanese shipbuilding technology was still very inferior to that of the West. Of sixty-three dockyards functioning in 1893, only four were suitable for the construction of iron vessels. A few years later, in 1898, a 6172-ton vessel, the *Hitachimaru*, was launched at the Mitsubishi-Nagasaki shipyard, but it was not until after the Russo-Japanese War (1904-05) that the navy was willing to rely on domestically produced ships rather than those imported from England. As seen in Table 2, the 1906-15 decade had a more than tenfold increase in the tonnage of domestically produced navy ships over the previous decade, and the percentage of imported naval ships went from almost 90 to less than 20 percent. The same trend can be seen in the total of all steamships: there was an absolute reduction of imported vessels, and the percentage of imported ships went down from about 70 to less than 40 percent.

One of the causes of this development lay in the protective policy taken by the government, imposing new tariffs on the imports of ships. In 1911 the tariff was increased from 5 to 15 percent, which was quite effective in curbing the import of foreign vessels (Hoshino 1966, p. 85).

Navy vessels were produced not only at the navy shipyards of Yokosuka, Kure, and Sasebo; large orders also were given to private companies, mainly Mitsubishi and Kawasaki. As a result, these companies carried out large expansions of their facilities. For example, Kawasaki constructed four additional docks, one of which was suitable for producing 7000-ton ships.

The economic boom Japan enjoyed in World War I was most apparent in its shipbuilding industry; Japan joined the front ranks in this field. Table 3 presents the growth of the industry between 1913 and 1918. There were fourfold increases in employes and paid-up capital; shipbuilding companies and shipyards multiplied tenfold. Compared with a mere 52,000 tons in

Table 2
Domestic and Imported Ships, 1874-1915

	1874-84	1885-95	1896-1905	1906-1915
	All steamships			
Domestic, tons	14,820	38,896	203,588	497,062
percentage	26.4	19.4	31.1	60.1
Imported, tons	41,253	162,114	450,437	330,485
percentage	73.6	80.6	68.9	38.9
	Navy warships			
Domestic, ships	7	15	21	58
tons	6,088	21,608	23,772	293,278
percentage of tonnage	34.9	41.5	11.4	80.8
Imported, ships	6	10	34	7
tons	11,355	30,484	183,917	69,711
percentage of tonnage	65.1	58.5	88.6	19.2

Source: Koyama 1943, pp. 107 and 128.

Table 3
Development of the Shipbuilding Industry, 1913-18

	1913	1918
Number of shipbuilding companies[a]	5	52
Paid-up capital (1000 yen)	23,150	109,554
Shipyards	6	57
Docks	17	157
Employes	26,139	107,260
Steamships constructed (gross tons)	51,525	626,695

Source: Teratani 1968, p. 55.
[a]Companies capable of producing ships of 1000 tons or more.

1913, ships launched in 1918 reached 627,000 tons. In 1917, the government abolished the Law for the Promotion of Shipbuilding, for the industry was no longer in need of protection—or so it was thought at the time.

During this period, Japanese-made ships first found their way into the international market: 300,000 tons of newly built ships and 100,000 tons of old ships were exported mainly to England (38.7 percent), France (24.6), and the United States (22.0) (Kaneko 1964, p. 155). Japan found itself in a typical sellers' market, where ships were being sold in spite of soaring prices.[8] The index of ships' prices in Japan went up from 100 in 1915 to 144 in 1916, 273 in 1917, and 459 in 1918 (LTES 8:158-159).

Instead of building to order, shipbuilding companies used mass production techniques to stockpile ships on the assumption demand would be forthcoming; thus, the vessels could be delivered on short notice. These ships were known as *shiiresen* (ships in stock) or *mikomisen* (ships built on expectation); in an industry characterized by differentiated products, this reversal of traditional procedure achieved considerable reduction in costs.

In 1917, when the United States put an embargo on the export of iron and steel, Japan's vulnerability to a reduction in the flow of raw materials became evident. Soon, however, the two countries realized an exchange of raw materials for finished products could benefit both; this took the form of a barter agreement to trade ships for iron and steel. Under the first agreement, signed in April 1918, one ton of steel was exchanged for one deadweight ton of ships. However, this was too favorable to the Japanese; a month later, a new agreement fixed the exchange rate at two tons of ships per ton of steel. Under these two agreements, forty-five ships with a total of 376,000 tons were built—one-third of the ships under the first agreement, and two-thirds under the second (Kawasaki 1959, p. 82).

As can be expected, the war prosperity was reflected in the profits of the shipbuilding companies. The records of the Ishikawajima Company show that net profits as a percentage of paid-in capital went from 15.4 percent in 1913 to 25.1 in 1916 and 89.2 in 1918 (Ishikawajima, p. 341).

At the end of World War I, Japan was the third-ranking shipbuilding country (after the United States and England), with 8.3 percent of world production (Kaneko 1964, p. 201). As Japan's share in 1913 was only about 2 percent, the boost given by the war is evident. However, this golden age of the shipbuilding industry came to an end soon after the war. The depression was worldwide: total production of ships dropped 77 percent, from a peak of 7.1 million gross tons in 1919 to 1.6 million gross tons in 1923 (Kaneko

---

[8]The British were at first unwilling to pay the high prices demanded by the Japanese. An article appeared in the London *Times* in November 1916, under the headline "Japanese ships for sale, prohibitive prices." The paper stated that although these ships could be received on short delivery, they were five times more expensive than in prewar days; it concluded that "at the price now being asked, British owners, badly as they need to replace their lost vessels, show no inclination to consider them" (Kawasaki 1959, p. 77).

1964, p. 201). Japan, however, was hit even more severely, as shown in Table 4. Its tonnage dropped 88.2 percent from 612,000 tons in 1919 to 72,000 tons in 1923, and Japan's share of the world market in 1927 had fallen back to the prewar level.

Faced with excess capacity, the industry was again aided by the government. This included cost reductions through exemption from tariffs on iron and steel, and a subsidy to logical steel producers for shipbuilding steel. To reduce foreign competition, custom duties were charged on imported vessels. The protective policy came to its logical conclusion in 1933 when imports of ships were all but prohibited. Financial aid was provided through low-interest loans for buyers of ships and an increase in loan funds at their disposal.

These measures, although mitigating to some extent the grave situation of shipbuilding companies, were not effective enough to reverse the trend. On top of the depression in the market for cargo ships, demand from the navy was severely cut by the Washington armament limitation agreement of 1921, which prescribed a fixed capital ship ratio of 5:5:3 among the navies of the United States, England, and Japan. Large orders for warships at both private and naval docks were canceled, and many workers were laid off. As seen in Table 5, the number of workers in companies producing large ships (of 1000 tons or more) went down from 82,000 in 1918 to 37,000 in 1925; after a small rise to 43,000 in 1929, it declined again to a trough of under 30,000 in 1931.

Shipbuilding companies, forced to adjust to the new conditions, found some refuge in other fields. On-land activities included production of

Table 4
Ships of Over 100 Tons Launched, 1912-39

Year	Number of ships	Gross tons (1000)	Year	Number of ships	Gross tons (1000)
1912	168	58	1926	26	52
1913	152	65	1927	19	42
1914	32	86	1928	37	104
1915	26	49	1929	40	164
1916	55	146	1930	37	151
1917	104	350	1931	42	84
1918	198	450	1932	44	54
1919	133	612	1933	30	74
1920	140	457	1934	155	152
1921	43	227	1935	177	146
1922	49	83	1936	180	295
1923	44	72	1937	180	451
1924	31	73	1938	146	442
1925	23	56	1939	121	324

Source: Kaneko 1964, pp. 200-201.

Table 5
Number of Workers in Shipbuilding Companies, 1918-44

Year	Number of workers (1000)	Year	Number of workers (1000)
1918	82.0	1932	30.5
1919	79.5	1933	34.0
1920	78.0	1934	44.0
1921	72.0	1935*	60.0
1922	54.0	1935*	63.9
1923	46.0	1936	88.9
1924	45.5	1937	95.5
1925	37.0	1938	111.5
1926	38.5	1939	132.3
1927	40.5	1940	130.3
1928	42.5	1941	142.6
1929	43.0	1942	185.6
1930	33.0	1943	264.4
1931	29.0	1944	333.7

Source: 1918-35: Tōyō Keizai 1950, 1:259. 1935-44: Tōyō Keizai 1950, 1:269.
Notes: 1918-35: workers in companies producing ships of 1000 tons or more. 1935-44: all workers (for 1935, both figures are given).

electrical machinery, boilers, chemical machinery, automobiles, and aircraft. This combination of marine and on-land activities is one of the characteristics of shipbuilding companies in both the prewar and postwar years.[9]

A temporary recovery in 1928-29 did not last long, and the industry lost more ground in 1932 when tonnage dropped to little more than 50,000 tons. It was again time for the government to come to the rescue of the shipbuilding companies; this time it responded with an imaginative and effective policy of scrap and build. This new measure had two goals: (1) to help the industry emerge from the depression; (2) to modernize the outdated shipping fleet. Starting in 1932, the policy was executed in three stages. As a result, 500,000 tons of ships (twenty-five years or older) were scrapped, and 300,000 tons of new vessels were constructed.[10] The new ships had superior engines and fuel consumption, and Japan came to possess the most up-to-date fleet in the world.

[9]During 1919-25, 85.3 percent of total production was in the construction and repair of ships, and 14.7 percent was devoted to on-land products. (Kaneko 1964, p. 241).
[10]One side effect of the scrap-and-build policy was to encourage the import of ships to receive the subsidy for scrapping them. This loophole was closed by an increase in tariffs on imported ships, which made the transaction unprofitable.

This policy, coupled with other measures taken by the government to promote the industry such as low-interest loans for purchase of ships, brought about recovery. Launched tonnage went from 54,000 tons in 1932 to 152,000 in 1934 and 451,000 in 1937. In December 1936, Japan declared the armament limitation regulations to be null and void, and started rapidly to increase its warship arsenal.

In 1937, Japan's share among shipbuilding countries increased from 1.9 a decade earlier to 21.2 percent, ranking second after the United Kingdom. This development was made possible by Japan's large unused capacity, which was idle during the depression and could be put back into use quickly, as well as new investments in both private and navy shipyards.

As a part of the change to a war economy, in 1941 the shipbuilding industry came under complete government control. After a short transition period, while ships in process were completed, the industry went into high gear to produce standardized ships. This standardization made it possible to use mass production methods, and production was allocated among shipyards. Six main types were prescribed, and the total production of ships from 1942 to 1945 exceeded that of the sixteen-year period 1926-41 (Arisawa 1967, 1:357).

Quantity came largely at the expense of quality. Toward the end of the war, the government put more emphasis on improving the latter; the lack of raw materials was an important reason for this change of policy (Kaneko 1964, p. 297). As seen in Table 6, the main increase in tonnage occurred (contrary to expectations) in cargo ships, whose volume increased sixfold between 1940 and 1944, whereas that of warships grew fourfold during the same period.

THE SHIPBUILDING INDUSTRY IN THE POSTWAR PERIOD

Dealing with Japan's economic growth in general and the development of any subsector of the economy in particular involves the following problem: Should the prewar and the postwar periods be regarded as a continuum, or as

Table 6
Ship Construction during World War II
(cargo ships in 1000 gross tons; warships in 1000 displacement tons)

Year	Cargo ships Number	Tonnage	Warships Number	Tonnage
1940	125	307.2	28	47.6
1941	112	241.1	39	88.6
1942	118	293.1	48	164.9
1943	294	800.5	84	109.2
1944	762	1,730.4	157	204.8
1945	215	565.3	75	108.6

Source: Tōyō Keizai 1950, 1:271.

qualitatively different? Have the same basic economic forces operated in both periods, or did the economy undergo some structural change between the two periods? This leads to the fundamental questions of what is structural change, and where are the boundaries between quantitative and qualitative changes, but they are questions beyond the scope of this essay.

The prewar/postwar question runs across many writings on the Japanese economy, including formal econometric models describing the economy's structure.[11] With respect to the shipbuilding industry, the answer to the question seems to be less ambiguous than in the case of other industries. Though a continuation does exist, great dissimilarities between the development of the industry in the two periods justify separate treatment. The differences lie mainly in three areas: (1) origin of demand; (2) production technology used; and (3) rate of growth of the industry.

Considering demand, there is a change from an industry producing only for the domestic market (with a short exception during World War I) to an industry whose outlet becomes more and more the foreign market. There was also a change in the sources of demand in the domestic market, the navy disappearing as a customer and all the demand being generated by the civilian sector. The change in technology was the introduction of the welding-block building technique, which revolutionized the whole production process. And concerning the rate of growth, compared to a 5 percent annual rate between the two world wars (including the long period of stagnation during the 1920s), the annual growth rate in the postwar period has been 18 percent. This is more than a quantitative change and signifies a transition from a slow-moving to a fast-growing industry. And although government assistance is present in both periods, there have been distinct differences in the nature and purpose of this intervention.

The development of the shipbuilding industry in this period is outlined in Table 7, which shows Japan's total production and the amount exported. Starting from scratch in the first postwar years, a level of 8.5 million gross tons was reached in 1968, accounting for half of total world production. Of this, about 60 percent was exported. Ships were Japan's largest single export product, accounting for 8.4 percent of her total exports.[12] As Table 7 indicates, growth had a strong cyclical pattern; there were years when production increased up to three times that of the preceding year. Japan is the only country that buys ships exclusively from its own production; it does not import any ships.

One factor in this growth process was postwar rehabilitation. However, the effect of this factor was short-lived, and other factors soon became dominant.

[11]Klein and Shinkai (1963, p. 2), in the introduction to their model, write: "To many observers it may appear self-evident that behavior and technology have radically changed as a result of the impact of World War II. There is often much that is basic in economic structure, transcending even the disruptive effects of a major catastrophe such as war."

[12]In 1968, ships accounted for 19 percent of all machinery exports (Tsūsanshō 1971, p. 442).

Table 7
Shipbuilding Production and Export, 1948-68
(gross tons)

Year[a]	Total production	Export	Export as percentage of total population
1948	163,308	840	0.5
1949	159,065	3,760	2.4
1950	227,014	76,060	33.5
1951	442,835	35,270	8.0
1952	503,916	23,500	4.7
1953	706,843	306,650	43.4
1954	412,325	110,889	26.9
1955	502,432	261,444	52.0
1956	1,529,420	1,118,990	73.2
1957	2,230,675	1,433,790	64.3
1958	2,284,666	1,350,970	59.1
1959	1,762,754	1,089,442	61.8
1960	1,807,151	935,389	51.8
1961	1,784,276	1,826,559	46.3
1962	2,154,224	857,243	39.8
1963	2,131,193	1,158,054	54.3
1964	4,078,712	2,251,326	55.2
1965	5,526,610	2,991,309	54.1
1966	6,396,183	3,777,298	59.1
1967	7,978,921	4,759,700	59.7
1968	8,481,444	5,109,887	60.2

Source: Sōrifu, Tōkei-kyoku.
[a]1948-53 refer to calendar years, 1954-68 to fiscal years (which began April 1). From 1964, the figures include steel boats of less than 100 tons.

As early as 1951, Japan regained its peak production level of the 1930s; in 1957 the wartime high of 1944 was surpassed. The next decade witnessed a fourfold increase in production, due mainly to new, postwar forces.

One question which has to be dealt with is whether the war itself had a stimulating or retarding effect on the technological progress of the industry. The direct damage suffered by the shipbuilding companies as a result of war activities was less than that suffered by other industries, notably shipping. When the war ended, fifty dockyards with a capacity of producing 800,000 tons were still operational (Arisawa 1967, 2:65). The rehabilitation of the industry could have been quick, were it not for the Occupation authorities' ban on the construction of ocean-going vessels and the need for permission to build ships of over 100 tons. Even without these administrative obstacles, the lack of raw materials made recovery difficult. Shipbuilding companies were using their workers to produce various items ranging from pots and pans to agricultural machines to small fishing boats. To make matters worse, the

Pauley report of 1946 proposed the removal of all shipbuilding equipment above a capacity of 150,000 tons as reparations, and twenty shipyards were selected for this purpose. Luckily for Japan, the aggravation of the cold war saved the industry from this fate, which would have pushed it back to the production level of the 1890s. Nevertheless, the two main sources of demand for ships—the Imperial Navy and the shipping companies—were in shambles, and only government action could reactivate the industry.

The mechanism through which the government helped the industry was "planned shipbuilding" (*keikaku zōsen*), which started in 1947 and has continued throughout the postwar period. Each year, the government decides how many ships are to be constructed with loans from the Japan Development Bank. These long-term, low-interest loans are divided among shipping companies according to prescribed criteria, and provide the shipbuilding industry with a stable source of demand.

The importance of the planned shipbuilding scheme can be seen from the following figures: It accounted for 85.2 percent of all ships constructed for the domestic market in 1950-54; the share went down to 39.7 percent in 1955-59, but rose again to 50.9 in 1960-64 and to 70.7 in 1965-69.[13] It should also be remembered that the emphasis was on high-quality, large ships.

Simultaneously, steps were taken to promote production for export. These included a favorable exchange rate for the industry under the multiple exchange rate system in effect before 1949 ($1 = ¥546), as well as the sugar link arrangement in 1954. According to the latter device, export proceeds could be used to import sugar, the price of which was high on the domestic market, thus giving the companies a premium of over 5 percent on the official exchange rate.

With the outbreak of the Korean War, the demand for Japan's ships increased. The number of contracts for ship construction went from 32 (for 51,000 gross tons) in 1950 to 233 (for 233,000 gross tons) in 1951 (Kaneko 1964, p. 392). Production for export reached 76,000 tons in 1950, one-third of total production.

This boom did not last long; with the end of hostilities, there was a drop in the demand from abroad. Contracted tonnage went down to 45,000 tons in 1952, and the share of export in total production fell to less than 5 percent. This worsening of the export markets, however, did not dictate the course of production, which continued to increase, due largely to measures taken by the government, to over half a million tons in 1952.

The next big spurt in production was again connected with exports; this was the tanker boom that started in 1956. The Japanese industry sensed increasing demand for petroleum would increase the need for carriers; when the Suez crisis closed the Suez Canal, the Japanese were ready to supply the demand for ever-larger oil carriers. A fourfold increase in exports (to over one million tons) made 1956 a turning point in the course of the industry's development, and brought total production to an all-time high of over one

---

[13]Calculated from Un'yūshō, *Shinzōsen*.

and a half million gross tons. Tankers, for both domestic use and export, continued to be an important part of shipbuilding, and consisted of about one-half of ships built for domestic use in the late 1950s. After a slight recession in the industry from 1958 to 1963, there was a revival in both the domestic and export markets, which brought about a steep rise in total production in later years. Domestic demand was affected by the government's planned shipbuilding program as well as by the close relationship between shipping and shipbuilding companies. Exports of ships benefited from extensive credit provided by the Japan Export-Import Bank, which during the period 1950-69 amounted to 59 percent of the total credit extended by the bank. This indicates the importance given by the government to this export item.

The high level of production was made possible by an increase in the capital stock, which took the form of imports of the most technologically advanced machinery and construction of new dockyards best suited for its use. If new technology is capital embodied, as I suppose it to be in the present case, then the introduction of new technology is related to the age of capital (Solow 1962). The age of capital is determined by two factors: the rate of replacement of old capital and the growth rate of the capital stock. When an industry is stable, the introduction of new technology is severely limited by the rate of depreciation and obsolescence. A firm will substitute a new machine for an old one only if the total cost of the new machine is less than the variable cost of the old one—that is, only if a very substantial reduction in cost is involved. This argument, taken from microeconomic textbooks, understates the problem, for the new techniques are highly interdependent and must be introduced simultaneously: new docks, for example, must be built for the new machinery. Thus, the growth of the Japanese shipbuilding industry was an accumulative process: an initial push by the government made the industry invest in new technology; this enabled it to compete with other countries still burdened with old and inferior production methods; and the growth of the industry called for new investments in even newer techniques. Growth sustained growth through the mechanism of capital embodiment.[14]

To understand this growth process, I shall look at the path taken by factors of production and factor proportions and make a comparison with prewar years—though lack of data, particularly capital estimates, makes such comparison difficult. Table 8 presents figures on capital, employment, and product, as well as their ratios for the industry as a whole in the postwar period. There are fluctuations in the number of employes in the early 1950s, with a trough in 1954 and a spurt during the 1956 tanker boom, but the number has been remarkably stable since then at the level of 140,000 to 150,000 workers. The capital series, on the other hand, shows a rapidly

[14]This model was used to explain the decline of the British steel industry, when the process worked in the opposite direction; lack of growth increased the age of capital (Temin 1966).

Table 8
Labor/Output, Capital/Output, and Capital/Labor Ratios, 1951-68

Year	Number of employes (thousands)	Fixed capital (billion ¥ in constant prices)	Output (thousand gross tons)	Labor/ output (employe/ ton)	Capital/ output (million ¥ ton)	Capital/ labor (million ¥/ employe)
	(1)	(2)	(3)	$(4) = \frac{(1)}{(3)}$	$(5) = \frac{(2)}{(3)}$	$(6) = \frac{(2)}{(1)}$
1951	120.4	13.4	442.8	0.272	30.3	0.111
1952	120.2	20.9	503.9	0.239	41.5	0.174
1953	113.5	30.7	706.8	0.161	43.4	0.271
1954	106.7	53.7	412.3	0.259	130.2	0.503
1955	118.1	63.4	502.4	0.235	126.2	0.537
1956	135.5	62.6	1529.4	0.089	40.9	0.462
1957	150.2	73.5	2230.7	0.067	32.9	0.489
1958	141.3	88.5	2012.1	0.070	44.0	0.626
1959	144.3	93.6	1827.3	0.079	51.2	0.649
1960	146.7	111.6	1758.5	0.083	63.5	0.761
1961	156.9	139.1	1897.6	0.083	73.3	0.887
1962	154.8	180.4	2181.7	0.071	82.7	1.165
1963	150.6	205.1	2266.0	0.066	90.5	1.362
1964	143.7	272.2	4078.7	0.035	66.7	1.894
1965	142.4	315.9	5526.6	0.026	57.2	2.218
1966	138.4	309.1	6396.2	0.022	48.3	2.233
1967	144.9	327.7	7998.9	0.018	41.0	2.262
1968	150.6	391.4	8481.4	0.018	46.1	2.599

Sources: Employes: 1951-62: Kaneko 1964, p. 497. 1963-68: Un'yūshō, Kaiun, 1969, p. 41. Capital: calculated using data from Mitsubishi Keizai Kenkyūsho (1951-70 annual editions) deflated by the implicit deflator of private gross domestic capital formation, excluding dwellings, taken from Keizai Kikaku-chō, Annual Report. Output: data for ships over 100 tons. 1950-57: Un'yūshō, Kaiun, 1958, p. 88. 1958-60: Un'yūshō, Kaiun, 1965, p. 34. 1961-68: Un'yūshō, Kaiun, 1969, p. 34.

increasing trend from 13.4 billion yen in 1951 to 391.4 billion yen in 1968 (both figures are in constant prices, with the index of investment goods as a deflator). This was a thirtyfold increase in the amount of capital. Output went through two depressions, in 1954 and 1958-60, but since then has shown a very high rate of growth.

As a consequence, the labor/output ratio shows a tremendous decrease throughout the period, from 0.272 employes per ton in 1951 to 0.018 employes per ton in 1968. In other words, one employe produced 3.7 gross tons of ships in 1951 and 55.6 tons in 1968. The capital/output ratio, although showing some fluctuations, was relatively stable except for the depression period of 1954-55 and the large investments at the beginning of the 1960s. The ratio of capital to labor in 1968 was twenty-four times larger than in 1951.

It is clear that during this period substantial capital deepening took place. This phenomenon resulted from the nature of the new technology introduced after the war—a technology highly dependent on automation, control systems, and organizational changes which made it possible to dispense with a large quantity of labor. It was also motivated by the labor shortage, which started to be felt at the beginning of the 1960s and resulted in considerable wage increases.

The scarcity of accurate data on capital for the prewar period prevents an overall comparison, but some inferences can be made on particular firms. Data for the Kawasaki Heavy Industries available for the period 1896-1956 show that whereas the capital/labor ratio fluctuated between two and five in the period before and during World War II, it spurted after the war to 16.8 in 1956.[15]

Thus we can say that the Japanese shipbuilding industry became relatively much more capital intensive in the postwar period, and achieved a high level of labor productivity. This brought the author of a study on the British shipbuilding industry to the conclusion that "Japanese yards do not employ many more men in new building than United Kingdom yards, yet the tonnage they produce may be four times as much" (Parkinson 1968, p. 5). These data also support the preceding argument explaining the development of the industry as a self-generating mechanism.

Other characteristics of the industry in the postwar period can be related to the prewar experience. As pointed out before, shipbuilding is not the only activity in which these companies engage; a considerable portion of their inputs are involved in other products. This multiproduct feature became even more pronounced after the war, when on-land activities included the manufacture of many types of machinery such as those for the production of iron and textiles, and the building of chemical plants and engines. As seen in Table 9, these activities constitute, on average, a larger proportion of output than do ships in the so-called major shipbuilding firms. In 1961, shipbuilding accounted for less than 40 percent of total production in the leading shipbuilding companies; the ratio varied from 25 percent in Mitsubishi to 88 percent in the Uraga Dockyard.

This structure has two marked advantages. First, it provides the companies with flexibility in the face of changing market conditions. It enables them to offset low profits in shipbuilding with high profits in other branches—and this, the companies claim, has been the case during this period. An estimate made by the Ministry of Transportation in the mid-1960s on the twelve largest firms in the industry put their profit rate on sales at 3 to 5 percent for shipbuilding, 15 percent for repairs, and 6 to 8 percent for on-land activities. Although the repair section is the most profitable, the on-land activities, due to their large share of the volume, provide the companies with most of their profits (Nihon Chōki 1968, p. 189).

The second advantage of this diversification is in the sphere of technological transfer; it enables the simultaneous use of technical skills in the production of different (though technically similar) products. The technological spillover

---

[15]Calculated from Kawasaki (1959). As a deflator of capital linking the prewar and postwar periods we used the index of investment goods' prices in LTES 8:134.

Table 9
Shares of Shipbuilding and On-Land Products in Major Companies (1961)
(in percent)

	Shipbuilding	On-land products
Mitsubishi Heavy Industries[a]	25.4	74.6
Hitachi Zōsen	62.9	37.1
Ishikawajima-Harima Heavy Industries	31.6	68.4
Kawasaki Heavy Industries	53.6	46.4
Mitsui Zōsen	64.3	35.7
Uraga Dockyard	88.3	11.7
Total	37.6	62.4

Source: Calculated from Kaneko 1964, p. 516.
[a]A sum of Mitsubishi Zōsen, Shin Mitsubishi Heavy Industries, and Mitsubishi Nihon Heavy Industries.

thus achieved, which in the usual production processes consists of an externality of the firm, is internalized here through horizontal integration and utilized by the same company.[16] There is also vertical integration, as the engines and boilers for the ships are produced by the shipbuilding companies.

Another aspect of the industrial structure lies in the concentration ratio. The shipbuilding industry has always had a high degree of concentration; a small number of large firms account for a very large share of the industry's output (Table 10). The three largest firms accounted for total output in 1915, but their share gradually and erratically declined thereafter until 1960, when it began to rise through merger. Similar patterns hold for the largest five and largest ten firms.

The present organizational structure of the industry was formulated during the 1960s, when several mergers took place. Ishikawajima-Harima merged with Kure Shipbuilding & Engineering and with Nagoya Shipbuilding; in 1963, the three Mitsubishi companies combined into one. As a result, five major companies emerged in the industry.[17] They produce the great majority of large ships; small- and medium-size firms are connected with them as subcontractors. The structure is highly effective; as evaluated in one study, "Japan's shipbuilding industry is one of the most perfectly reorganized and is best suited to today's demand of the worldwide shipping industry" (*The Oriental Economist*, September 1966, p. 533).

Another important feature of the Japanese industrial structure is the close relationship between shipbuilding and the iron and steel industry. It means shipyards can rely on getting the necessary supplies of materials when they are needed, and therefore do not have to hold large stocks. This is one advantage the Japanese industry has over its European competitors.

[16]On the importance of this factor, see Rosenberg (1963).
[17]The five companies are the Mitsubishi Heavy Industries, Ishikawajima-Harima Heavy Industries, Hitachi Shipbuilding & Engineering, Mitsui Shipbuilding and Engineering, and Kawasaki Dockyards.

Table 10
Shares of Largest Companies in
the Shipbuilding Industry

Year	Largest three	Largest five	Largest ten
1915	100.0	--	--
1919	60.5	79.7	94.2
1923	62.5	83.9	96.4
1926	58.7	82.6	99.0
1931	74.9	97.4	--
1934	75.7	86.7	--
1937	67.6	86.8	96.6
1940	57.2	73.5	90.8
1943	52.2	69.1	84.2
1950	39.1	61.8	94.1
1953	38.3	54.4	79.5
1955	41.5	60.2	81.4
1960	30.1	45.4	--
1962	39.5	56.0	81.7
1965	49.5	63.4	83.3

Source: 1915-1926: Kaneko 1964, pp. 149 and 190. 1931-1943: Tōyō Keizai 1950, 1:270-271. 1950-1955: Kōsei Torihiki Iinkai 1964, pp. 232-233. 1960: Nihon Sangyō 1963, p. 10. 1962: Arisawa and Nakayama 1965, p. 409. 1965: Katayama 1970, p. 270.

The rapid growth of Japan's shipbuilding industry was influenced by increased demand for ships resulting from the expansion of international trade, particularly the shipment of oil.[18] However, this factor should have worked in the same direction for all countries, and does not explain the large increase in Japan's share of the industry. As one study on the decline of the British shipbuilding industry put it, "It is Japan, and to a lesser extent Sweden and Norway, that have taken full advantage of the growing market for ships in the postwar period" (Parkinson 1968). How did the Japanese do it?

One of the favorite explanations of Japan's economic success maintains that because of her comparatively lower wages, Japan can offer lower prices than other countries. It is, however, not just wages but total costs that determine prices, so we must make an international comparison of costs. Although the scarcity of data does not allow a comprehensive analysis, even the existing fragmentary information available can shed some light on the issue.

Looking first at the cost structure of the industry, it turns out that a ship's cost consists of 70 percent for materials and only 30 percent for labor. This figure was derived from a study of British data for 1951. Material costs were 56.4 percent for steel plates, 35.3 for fabricated steel, 5.9 for pig iron, and

[18]During 1954-64, the world merchant fleet increased from 87 million to 140 million gross tons; oil tankers, from 24 to 50 million gross tons (OECD 1965, p. 14).

the remainder for brass, copper, lead, and aluminum (*Kaiun*, September 1957, p. 74). Wages, it turns out, account for a relatively small share of the total cost.

Table 11 presents data on shipbuilding costs in eleven countries. Japan stands out as having the highest material costs among all countries compared. In 1956 Japan's material costs were 62 percent higher than the United Kingdom, 57 percent higher than West Germany, and 17 percent higher than Sweden. This was somewhat compensated for by Japan's lower labor costs, less than half that of the United Kingdom. Still, total costs in 1956 were higher in Japan than in the United Kingdom and West Germany, although somewhat lower than in Sweden.

The figures for 1959, also presented in Table 11, indicate that this gap is closing with respect to both labor and material costs. Since the late 1950s relative wages in Japan have increased, but the Japanese steel industry has been able to supply shipbuilding with relatively cheap, high-quality construction materials. Thus, the wholesale price of iron and steel dropped by 19 percent between 1952 and 1968, whereas the price of all commodities increased by 8 percent during the same period (Kawahito 1972, p. 109). In this lay one of the reasons for Japan's comparative advantage. However, Japan's competitiveness in international markets was not the result of the cost factor alone. Important were nonprice features such as shorter delivery dates, made possible by meticulous planning of the production process.[19]

Table 11
International Comparison of Shipbuilding Costs, 1956 and 1959
(index, United Kingdom = 100)

	Material Costs 1956	Material Costs 1959	Labor Costs 1956	Labor Costs 1959	Total Costs 1956	Total Costs 1959
United Kingdom	100	100	100	100	100	100
Japan	162	115	44	55	127	97
West Germany	103	95	71	79	93	90
Sweden	138	113	149	169	141	141
Netherlands	116	102	66	70	101	92
U.S.A.	109	103	323	344	173	175
France	–	101	--	93	–	100
Italy	–	111	--	69	--	98
Norway	138	–	102	–	127	–
Denmark	121	–	119	–	120	--
Belgium	115	–	110	–	114	–

Source: 1956: *Kaiun*, September 1957, p. 77. 1959: Kaneko 1964, p. 427.

[19]For 1950-55, it was found the average construction period for a 32,000 deadweight ton tanker was 517 days in the United Kingdom, 269 days in West Germany, 204 days in Sweden, and 180 days in Japan. For a tanker of 10,000 deadweight tons, the difference was smaller, ranging from 281 days in the United Kingdom to 164 days in Japan (Kaneko 1964, p. 412).

However, the best planner cannot ensure delivery on time if the dockyards are plagued with strikes and disturbances, as are some of Japan's competitors. Due to her disciplined labor force and the unique structure of labor-management relations, Japan is relatively free of such problems. A detailed discussion of this aspect lies outside the scope of the present study; however, it should be mentioned that the hard core of the shipbuilding companies' labor force consists of permanent workers tied to a specific company through the system of lifelong employment, and who therefore regard the well-being of their company as in their own interest. In addition to the permanent workers, there are temporary workers who help the industry adjust to changing demand. The share of this type of worker goes up in boom periods, especially if the boom is unexpected. Thus, during the tanker boom of 1956-57, temporary workers constituted as much as 45 percent of the total labor force in the industry, but their share went down to 30 percent in 1958 (Katayama 1970, p. 207).

THE ROLE OF TECHNOLOGY

By now it is fairly well established that the growth experience of the Japanese economy has greatly benefited from the borrowing of foreign technology. During the first stage of her development, it was a reflection of Japan's late arrival to modern economic growth; however, the import of technology has continued to the present day. This mechanism for technological improvement has received relatively little attention by theoretical economists, compared to other processes of technological change such as learning-by-doing and research and development, although it is a major factor in explaining economic growth. Moreover, even though the factor has been widely acknowledged in the context of the Japanese economy, little is known about the way in which foreign technology was adopted and adapted to the specific needs of Japan. The shipbuilding industry provides one example of this process, and its record can give some insight into the manner borrowed technology has contributed to the economy as a whole. The construction of the *Hetago* in 1853 with foreign blueprints, which subsequently were dispersed throughout Japan as a model for other vessels, was a pointer to future developments.

At the beginning of the Meiji period, ships made of iron were already in use in Europe, yet the Japanese were still building and using wooden vessels. The Japanese did not buy iron ships from abroad for two reasons: they were expensive, and Japan lacked repair facilities for their maintenance. Neither did they build their own iron ships, because the need to import the iron materials made construction difficult, and attempts to use locally produced iron were not successful. An Englishman, William Lang, invited to build an iron ship at the Nagasaki Ironworks, found the iron unsuitable for the construction of ships; he ended up building a wooden vessel. The first iron vessels produced in Japan such as the *Nigatamaru* (completed in 1871) were nothing more than an assembly of parts imported from England. Further attempts produced ships made of both iron and wood. Finally, an all-iron vessel, the 496-ton *Asahimaru* with a 75-horsepower engine, was built in Kobe under the supervision of English engineers.

However, the iron age of shipbuilding did not last long, for superior steel vessels were being put into use. As seen in Table 12, this transition was rapid in the case of imports; as early as 1889, more than half of all imported ships were made of steel. In 1905, the ratio of steel ships went up to two-thirds, whereas the import of wooden vessels became negligible. Domestic production almost completely skipped the use of iron as raw material; the production of iron ships was below 7,000 tons per year during the 1898-1905 period. Although iron vessels remained at this low level, steel ships increased sevenfold—accounting for more than half of total production, while the share of wooden vessels went down.

Here is a concrete example of one of the advantages of latecomers in economic development: the ability to skip stages by adopting the most advanced techniques, rather than going through all the steps taken by the forerunners. This pattern is seen repeatedly in the shipbuilding industry as well as in Japan's economic development as a whole.

The change in building material was followed by a change in the size of ships. Up to 1897, there were only two Japanese-built vessels larger than 1000 tons. The obstacles to the construction of larger ships lay not only in the lack of technical knowledge, but also in the absence of suitable docks. In 1880, only two docks were available for repairing large ships—at Yokosuka,

Table 12
Steamships by Origin and Type, 1898-1905
(in thousand gross tons and percent)

Year	Domestic production			Imports		
	Steel	Iron	Wood	Steel	Iron	Wood
1898	18.7	6.6	73.7	194.5	168.5	2.2
	(18.9)	(6.7)	(74.4)	(53.3)	(46.1)	(0.6)
1899	33.4	5.7	66.0	219.1	159.3	1.5
	(31.8)	(5.4)	(62.8)	(57.7)	(41.9)	(0.4)
1900	42.8	6.1	72.8	221.1	173.5	2.0
	(35.2)	(5.0)	(59.8)	(55.8)	(43.7)	(0.5)
1901	66.5	6.4	78.9	228.3	179.6	2.5
	(43.8)	(4.2)	(52.0)	(55.6)	(43.8)	(0.6)
1902	76.3	5.4	82.8	241.9	180.7	2.6
	(46.4)	(3.3)	(50.3)	(56.9)	(42.5)	(0.6)
1903	102.4	6.8	85.6	258.6	164.7	23.5
	(52.6)	(3.5)	(43.9)	(57.9)	(36.9)	(5.2)
1904	105.4	6.8	94.7	354.6	209.3	3.4
	(50.9)	(3.3)	(45.8)	(62.5)	(36.9)	(0.6)
1905	124.3	6.8	102.4	430.7	245.9	3.4
	(53.2)	(2.9)	(43.9)	(63.3)	(36.2)	(0.5)

Source: Kaneko 1964, p. 154.

used mainly by the navy, and at Mitsubishi-Nagasaki. The enlargement of docks was a prerequisite to increasing the size of ships. The Mitsubishi-Nagasaki dock was enlarged twice (in 1895 and 1905) to reach 728 feet. At the same time, a dock with a capacity of 2500 tons was built at the Osaka Ironworks. The law for the promotion of shipbuilding was effective in increasing the demand for large vessels, and in 1898 the 6172-ton *Hitachimaru* was completed at the Mitsubishi-Nagasaki shipyard. This was a sister ship of one that had been built in England; all blueprints, as well as engineers and machinery (including a 150-ton crane) were brought to Japan. In this way, Japanese workers and management were trained in foreign techniques and acquired the necessary skills.

However, on-the-job training was only one device; it was complemented by more formal learning. Shipbuilding schools were started in the late Tokugawa period; instruction was given by foreigners at first. Thus, the Yokosuka school's first teaching staff was French, but became all Japanese in 1879. Shipbuilding was taught in universities, and in 1882 a shipbuilding department was established at Tokyo University, taking the place of the Yokosuka school. Between 1883 and 1907 there were 189 graduates who found employment with the navy and private companies (Takayanagi 1968, p. 52).

Machinery (sometimes including marine machinery) was taught in technical high schools; lower grade craftsmen were supplied by technical junior high schools. The Mitsubishi-Nagasaki shipyard established a school in 1899; the students were paid while studying, and joined the company as regular workers after finishing school. This emphasis on technical education, both formal and informal, was certainly an important factor in the industry's development.

Shortly before the Russo-Japanese War, construction of warships started; the first destroyer was completed in 1902. Two years later, production increased to twenty-five ships at both naval and private shipyards over a construction period of thirteen to fifteen months. Following the war, large battleships of more than 100,000 tons were built.

Among technological improvements in engines, the steam turbine was of major importance. This engine was developed in both the United States and England, and both versions were introduced into Japan. The Parsons steam turbine of England was adopted by Mitsubishi, which obtained the right to produce it in Japan; the Curtis turbine of America was used by the navy and Kawasaki. These two engines started a new way of introducing foreign technology—through contracts with foreign companies, under which patent rights were bought. This became a most important channel for technological transfer in subsequent periods. Other technical improvements which reduced costs and increased efficiency were the substitution of a water-tube boiler for the iron cyclical one, and a change in fuel from coal to a mixture of oil and coal. As a consequence, the engine's weight was reduced and a smaller engine could produce the same amount of energy (see, for example, Zōsen Kyōkai 1911, chap. 5).

Throughout the period before World War II, the steel plates which form the ship's body were joined by rivets. During the last years of the Meiji period, several improvements were introduced in this technique. In 1906, a

500-horsepower air compressor was imported by the Kawasaki Heavy Industry Company. In 1912, after two more compressors were brought in, a piping system was installed which made it possible to use the riveting machines in all parts of the dockyard. This was a major improvement over the water-powered machine which it replaced; the old system was limited to operation on land alone. Some idea of the work involved in riveting is given by the fact that a stock-boat of 9800 deadweight tons needed 650,000 heated rivets. A change from coal to coke as heating fuel took place at the beginning of the Taishō period, and a special factory for producing bolts was opened by Kawasaki in 1913. Some limited use was made of welding, which was to become the major technique after World War II, but only for fitting the ship and not in the building of the body itself. At the same time, large cranes made their first appearance in the dockyards and enabled the construction of larger vessels.

The major technological improvement after World War I was the introduction of the diesel engine through contracts with foreign firms. In 1920, the head of the planning section of Mitsui Bussan's shipbuilding department (later spun off as the Mitsui Shipbuilding Company) returned from a two-year tour of Europe and the United States. He reported that although the shipbuilding industry as a whole was in a recession, there was one exception in Denmark—where the Burmeister and Wain Company was doing good business in the production of diesel engines. The Mitsui Company began its study of the matter by sending several engineers abroad. In 1923, a 1600-horsepower engine was imported and installed in the newly built *Akashiroyama*. A conventional reciprocating engine was put into her sister ship, the *Akibayama*; the two were put on the Pacific line, where their performance was compared. The experiment showed the diesel engine was superior in performance and cheaper in cost. Consequently, a production and sales contract was signed with the B & W Company, an engine factory was established in 1927, and the Mitsui-B & W engine went into production (Mitsui 1968, p. 55).

Meanwhile, other Japanese companies entered into agreements with other diesel-engine producing firms: Mitsubishi with Sulzer of Switzerland, and Kawasaki with M.A.N. of Germany. The first engines were imported; within a few years, domestically produced diesel engines were developed and installed in Japanese-made ships.

The diesel engine quickly replaced the piston engine; in 1925, diesel engines were used in 65 percent of all ships launched throughout the world (Kaneko 1964, p. 178). In Japan, the percentage of ships moved by diesel engines rose from 24 percent in 1924 to 93 percent in 1931, but the diesel engine did not dominate the field for long; it soon faced severe competition from the turbine. An increase in the price of diesel fuel and improvements in the steam turbine reduced the diesel's share of installations to 50 percent in 1939. This percentage declined during World War II, and turbines rose to the 90 percent level near the end of the war. The development of the diesel engine, which made it possible to obtain high horsepower from a single shaft, reversed the trend again after the war, with diesel engines comprising more than one half in the early 1960s.

Introduction of the diesel engine gave Japanese companies an incentive for further research. For example, a cast metal research department was opened at the Mitsui Company in order to develop new qualities of steel and to check welding by the use of x-rays. The role played by Japanese research in the introduction of foreign technology was to develop minor improvements in imported techniques—and, of no less importance, to train people in the technology developed elsewhere. Thus, it was possible to learn about foreign techniques soon after their development, and to transfer them to Japan within a short time.

Although a fair amount of research was conducted during the war, no basic change in shipbuilding technology was made. Experiments with welding techniques had been undertaken as early as 1914, and in 1920 a 400-ton boat was built using this method, but welding was not utilized for actual construction—it had proved unreliable, as in the 1930s several ships broke apart during their trial voyages.

World War II created a large technological gap between Japan and the West. Whereas the war effort stimulated technological improvements in the West, it did not do so in Japan. Some obvious explanations were Japan's need to produce large quantities of standardized ships, and the labor shortage which made it necessary to use untrained workers in the shipyards—but there was probably more to it. The Japanese shipbuilding industry has always relied on imported technology, which it improved, adjusted, and applied to Japan's needs—but Japan has not yet shown a capability for originating major new technological changes on its own. When Japan was cut off from the technologically advanced countries during the war, she continued to utilize the old methods on a large scale but did not introduce new ones. Although research was going on in navy dockyards (for example, on the welding technique), it did not bear any tangible fruits. (For a further discussion of this argument, see Kaneko 1964, p. 466.) Thus, Japan found itself at a technological disadvantage.

After the war, shipbuilding engineers were sent abroad, much as in the Meiji period, to study and bring back the new technological achievements. Once the new ideas were introduced, Japan's ingenuity of application, extension, and improvement were again given their chance. It took Japan a relatively short time to gain a competitive position in world markets: in the mid-1950s, she again stood in the forefront with the best shipbuilding available.

In the early postwar years, technological imports came as machinery—import embodied technological borrowing. Later, this changed more to contracts for patent rights or know-how. Technological cooperation between Japanese and foreign firms became very important in the postwar period. From 1951 to 1967, for example, the Mitsui Shipbuilding and Engineering Company signed thirty long-term contracts (for periods of more than one year) and seventeen short-term contracts. In contrast, it had made only one major contract from its foundation in 1917 until 1950, with the B & W company for the diesel engine in 1926 (Mitsui 1968, pp. 592-593). The most important new techniques were those of electric welding, automatic cutting, and block building. The techniques had been known for some time, but there had been problems with their use.

Several technical problems had to be solved, primarily the development of a new type of steel. The use of inappropriate steel had plagued American shipbuilders; about 20 percent of American ships built during World War II were defective for this reason. The joint efforts of the Japanese steel and shipbuilding industries during 1951-52 succeeded in improving the quality of steel, making it possible to use automatic welding machines with thicker steel plates.[20] The most widely used of these machines, the Unionmelt, was imported from the United States.

The automatic welding method has several advantages over the labor-intensive riveting method. First, the steel input is reduced, because there is no need to overlap the plates or to use bolts. This substantially reduces the ship's weight. Second, the surface of the ship is smoother, reducing water resistance and increasing the efficiency of the engine. Third, welding is superior in assuring the watertightness of the ship. In addition, an important diseconomy of riveting—the deafening noise of drilling the holes for the bolts—disappeared from the dockyards.

A most important prerequisite to the welding method is the precise cutting of the steel plates. This could not be achieved by machine cutting; the problem was solved by automatic gas cutting, which marks the plates and cuts them automatically.[21]

A major revolution in shipbuilding technology was the introduction of the block-building method, in which the construction is done in two stages: first, individual blocks[22] are built; then those sections are assembled to make up the ship. The block method saves considerable construction time, for many blocks can be built simultaneously. It permits welding to be done under better conditions. It also increases the safety of the workers, because there is no need for a large number of workers to crowd together in a small area of the building berth. On the other hand, it requires a large yard for the simultaneous construction of blocks, large cranes for moving them, and a high degree of precision in putting the blocks together.

One corollary of the block-building method was a change in the fitting of the ship. When the ship was built as a single unit, fitting could be done only after construction was finished; under the block system, most of the fitting can be done at an earlier stage. Actually, 85 to 90 percent of the fitting is now carried out at the block stage, substantially reducing construction time (Kawasaki 1959, p. 295).

[20]In 1955, steel plates of 47 mm. could be welded (Kawasaki 1959, p. 286).

[21]In this method, the desired design is put into the automatic control system of the machine making the cutting.

[22]For a 260,000 gross ton tanker, 360 blocks, each weighing about 120 tons, are constructed.

Another important change in technology has been the building dock, which replaced the on-land building berth. There is no need to have the ship launched into the water, as it is assembled at sea level; after the ship is completed, the dock is filled with water—and the ship leaves under its own power. It is possible to start building blocks of a second ship before the first is finished, thus increasing the capacity of the shipyard.

The transition to the new technology of automatic cutting, welding, and block building involved difficult problems of coordination, quality control, shipyard layout, and employe training. Still, adaptation to the new techniques was rapid, as indicated by the transition within the Kawasaki shipyards. The ratio of gas cutting went up from 5 percent in 1944 to 40 in 1952 and 95 in 1956; welding increased from 21 to 85 and 95 percent, respectively, in the same period (Kawasaki 1959, p. 288).

This amounted to a total revolution in shipbuilding technology, and the various techniques were interdependent on each other. Welding of thick iron and steel plates could not be introduced without automatic cutting, nor could block building be efficient without a change in the layout of the shipyard. Many of these methods had been known since World War I, but could not be introduced sooner because of various obstacles. As different techniques were developed in different countries, the Japanese had the opportunity to choose and import the best available.

This highlights the process of technological borrowing in the context of the Japanese economy. First new machines are imported, embodying the new technological innovations; very soon, however, domestically produced machines replace them, with improvements and adjustments to fit Japan's needs.[23]

Instead of adapting the old dockyards, the Japanese use them for repairs and build new ones with sophisticated control devices and layouts appropriate for the new technologies.[24] These new technologies are adopted on a large scale, and old techniques are dropped immediately. This is possible because the new technologies have already undergone running-in periods in the countries which developed them; defects have been detected and eliminated, and the technologies have been proved successful through practical application.

SUMMARY AND CONCLUSIONS

Every student of the Japanese economy is faced with intriguing questions: How did the Japanese do it? Why is it that only Japan, of all Asian countries, has joined the club of leading economic powers? These questions can be asked

[23]The first automatic cutting machines of the Monopol and Citomat types were imported from Germany, but Japanese-made machines such as Remote-graph (produced by Kawasaki Heavy Industries) or Magni-graph (Mitsubishi Shipbuilding) soon replaced them. Similarly, welding machines have been produced in Japan since 1953.

[24]In 1964 the Mitsui Zōsen Company introduced electronic computers and

not only of the economy as a whole, but also with regard to specific industries. The shipbuilding industry is perhaps the most outstanding example. The
results of the foregoing study can shed some light on the more general questions of the process of Japan's economic growth.

Among the factors which explain the extraordinary growth of Japan's
shipbuilding industry are some common to all countries—such as the large
increase in the demand for ships that resulted from the expansion of world
trade. However, this cannot explain the increase in the relative share of Japan,
which now accounts for one-half of the world's production. We must look
into factors which were especially in Japan's favor: the transfer of foreign
technology and the role of the Japanese government.

A necessary condition for technological borrowing is a relatively inferior
technological level in the receiving country. Japan found itself in this position
in the period before World War II; her arrival on the economic scene was late,
and she lacked experience in shipbuilding because of the Tokugawa regime's
seclusion policy. A similar situation existed in the postwar period after Japan
had been cut off from the West during the war. However, this lack of
tradition and continuity was a blessing rather than an impediment, for it
enabled Japan to absorb the best technology of the time without being bound
to old production practices.

Both the government and the structure of the labor market made Japan's
adaptation process possible. The government's policy has always been to
promote high-quality ships, either by active assistance or by prohibiting the
production of low-quality boats. This trait has been evident since the Meiji
period, when production of the Yamato-type boat was prohibited, through
the present planned shipbuilding program. Moreover, the company-centered
structure of the labor force facilitated the introduction of new technology;
there were no pressure groups trying to prevent improvements, as there were
in the labor forces of other shipbuilding countries.

Technological borrowing is not synonymous with imitation. A choice must
be made on which technique is to be borrowed, and the new process must be
adapted to local conditions. The Japanese took full advantage of the fact that
several alternatives were open to them (for example, when choosing among
various types of engines); thus, they were able to skip stages which other
countries had to follow. World War II also enabled Japan to make a new start
with very different technologies—welding and blockbuilding—and spared her
the need to make costly adjustments in these new processes. Having
transferred the basic technology, she introduced minor improvements which
made the new technology even more productive.

At first, government assistance followed the infant industry pattern aimed
at putting the industry in a competitive position. This stage was thought to be
completed at the end of World War I. However, it soon became clear that the
government had to continue its promotion policy for two main reasons. One

---

a wireless system in which all loading in the shipyards was centrally
controlled by one man (Mitsui, p. 547).

was to ensure the high quality of the ships; the other was to ensure a continuous demand for the product. These two goals turned out to be complementary, as reflected in the scrap-and-build policy prior to World War II and the planned shipbuilding scheme in the postwar period. The success of these policies can be considered a major factor in promoting the shipbuilding industry to its present level.

REFERENCES

Arisawa, Hiromi. 1967. *Nihon Sangyō Hyakunen Shi.* 2 vols. Nihon Keizai Shimbunsha.

Arisawa, Hiromi, and Ichirō Nakayama. 1965. *Sangyō Yōgo no Kisō Chishiki.* Jiyū Kokuminsha.

Arrow, Kenneth J. 1969. "Classification Notes on the Production and Transmission of Technological Knowledge." *American Economic Review*, May 1969.

Atkinson, A. B., and Joseph E. Stiglitz. 1969. "A New View of Technological Change." *Economic Journal*, Sept. 1969.

Cornwall, Peter G. 1970. "The Meiji Navy: Training in an Age of Change." Ph.D. dissertation, University of Michigan.

Hoshino, Yoshirō. 1966. *Nihon no Gijutsu Kakushin.* Keisōshobo.

Ishikawajima Jūkōgyō Kabushiki Kaisha. 1961. *Ishikawajima Jūkōgyō Kabushiki Kaisha 108-nen Shi.*

Kaiun [The Shipping]. Published monthly by Nihon Kaiun Shūkaijo.

Kaneko, Eiichi, et al. 1964. *Zōsen.* Vol. 9: *Gendai Sangyō Hattatsu Shi.* Gendai Nihon Sangyō Hattatsu Shi Kenkyūkai.

Katayama, Makoto. 1970. *Nihon no Zōsengyō.* Nihon Kōgyō Shuppansha.

Katayama, Shin. 1970. *Nihon no Zōsen Kōgyō.* Nihon Kōgyō Shuppan Kabushiki Kaisha.

Kawahito, Kiyoshi. 1972. *The Japanese Steel Industry.* Praeger.

Kawasaki Jūkōgyō Kabushiki Kaisha. 1959. *Kawasaki Jūkōgyō Kabushiki Kaisha Shashi.*

Keizai Kikaku-chō [Economic Planning Agency]. *Annual Report on National Income Statistics.*

Klein, Lawrence R., and Yoichi Shinkai. 1963. "An Econometric Model of Japan, 1930-59." *International Economic Review*, Jan. 1963.

Kobayashi, Masa'aki. 1966. "Bakuhan'ei Zōsengyō no Tenkai." *Bulletin of the Japan Maritime Research Institute* 2 (Aug. 1966).

Kōsei Torihiki Iinkai [Fair Trade Commission]. 1964. *Nihon Sangyō Shūchū no Jittai.*

Koyama, Hirotake. 1943. "Nihon Gunji Kōgyō Hattatsu Shi." In *Nihon Sangyō Kikō Kenkyū*, edited by Hirotake Koyama et al.

League of Nations, Economic and Financial Section. *International Statistical Yearbook.*

Lockwood, William W. 1954. *The Economic Development of Japan.* Princeton University Press.

LTES [Estimates of Long-Term Economic Statistics of Japan]. Series edited by Kazushi Ohkawa, Miyohei Shinohara, and Mataji Umemura. 1965-.

14 vols. Tōyō Keizai Shinpōsha.
    . Vol. 8. *Prices*. 1967. Kazushi Ohkawa et al.
Mitsubishi Keizai Kenkyūsho. 1951-70. *Hompō Jigyō Seiseki Bunseki*.
    Annual.
Mitsui Zōsen KK. 1968. *Mitsui Zōsen KK Gojūnen-shi*.
Nihon Chōki Shinyō Sangyō Kenkyūsho. 1968. *Shinjidai ni Chōsen suru
    Nihon no Sangyō*. Mainichi Shinbunsha.
Nihon Sangyō Kikai Kōgyōkai. 1963. *Sangyō Kikai Kōgyō Keigyō Jittai
    Chōsahōkoku*.
OECD [Organization of Economic Cooperation and Development]. 1965.
    The Situation of the Shipbuilding Industry.
Parkinson, J. R. 1968. "The Financial Prospects of Shipbuilding after
    Geddes." *Journal of Industrial Economics* 17 (Nov. 1968).
Rosenberg, Nathan. 1963. "Technological Change in the Machine Tool
    Industry 1840-1910." *Journal of Economic History*, vol. 23, no. 4 (Dec.
    1963).
Solow, Robert M. 1962. "Technical Progress, Capital Formation, and
    Economic Growth." *American Economic Review*, May 1962.
Sōrifu. *Nihon Tōkei Nenkan*. Annual.
Sōrifu, Tōkei-kyoku. [Office of the Prime Minister, Statistics Bureau]. Nihon
    Sangyō Kikai Kōgyōkai. 1963. *Sangyō Kikai Kōgyō Kengyō Jittai
    Chōsahōkoku*.
Takayanagi, Satoru. 1968. "Zōsengyō ni okeru Gijutsu to Kei'ei." *Bulletin of
    the Japan Maritime Research Institute* 20 (Feb. 1968).
Temin, Peter. 1966. "The Relative Decline of the British Steel Industry
    1860-1913." In *Industrialization in Two Systems*, edited by Henry
    Rosovsky. Wiley.
Teratani, Takeaki. 1968. "Daiichiji Sekai Taisenki no Min'ei Zōsenshō."
    Bulletin of the Japan Maritime Research Institute 21 (March 1968).
Tōyō Keizai Shinpōsha. 1950. *Shōwa Sangyō Shi*. Vol. 1.
Tsūsanshō (Tsūshōsangyōshō) [Ministry of International Trade and In-
    dustry]. 1971. *Tsūshō Hakusho*.
United Nations, Statistical Office. *Statistical Yearbook*.
Un'yūshō [Ministry of Transportation]. *Shinzōsen Kōji Jittai*.
    . *Kaiun Tōkei Nenpō*.
Wolman, Leo. 1924. *The Growth of American Trade Unions*. National Bureau
    of Economic Research.
Yasuda, Saburo. 1971. *Shakai Idō no Kenkyū*. Tōdai Shuppankai.
Yoshino, Michael. 1968. *Japan's Managerial System*. MIT Press.
Zōsen Kyōkai. 1911. *Nihon Kinsei Zōsen Shi*. Kōdōkan.

General Trading Companies in Japan: Their Origins and Growth

Kozo Yamamura

Between 1 March and 30 September 1972 the ten largest general trading companies in Japan exported, imported, and traded among third parties and within Japan an amount exceeding 12 trillion yen or approximately 40 billion dollars each for exports and imports, or 51 percent of total exports and 75 percent of total imports for the same period. As seen in Table 1, the share of exports held by each of these "Big Ten" ranged between 1.8 and 9.9 percent of Japan's total exports and between 2.5 and 16.5 percent of total imports during the period. Because of the importance of international trade for the Japanese economy and the dominance of these companies in Japan's international trade, it is evident that the institution called the general trading company—"a phenomenon at present more or less unknown in other advanced countries" (*Economist* 1967, p. *xxv*)—plays a vital role in the continuing growth of the postwar Japanese economy.

Despite its obvious importance, however, our knowledge of this uniquely Japanese institution is limited to a nodding acquaintance, obtained mostly from journalistic descriptions. Although interest in these companies as Japanese-style conglomerates and as budding multinationals has grown, certain questions about them have not been answered. Why and how did general trading companies emerge and grow to be so large? Why do these companies exist in Japan and not elsewhere? And what exactly is a general trading company? The purpose of this chapter is to provide answers to these questions. Given the scope of the questions and the limits on length of this essay, emphasis will be placed on their international aspects. Thus, I shall not examine large general trading companies as members of zaibatsu or groups, as a force in domestic trade, or as shareholders in many subsidiaries.

To compensate for narrowness of focus, I will provide a historical perspective and an analytical framework useful in answering the questions posed here. Readers are forewarned that other questions will be raised in their minds as they read this essay. Some may be answered by the increasing

Table 1

The Big Ten General Trading Companies: Selected Data for 1 March-30 September 1972 (in 100 million yen, equals approx. 324,000 dollars; percentages are total Japanese exports and imports, respectively, for same period)

	Mitsubishi	Mitsui	Marubeni	C. Itoh	Sumitomo	Nissho-Iwai	Tomen	Kanematsu-Gosho	Ataka	Nichimen
Export	3,651	4,214	3,332	2,408	2,129	1,767	1,269	1,177	749	970
	8.6%	9.9%	7.8%	5.7%	5.0%	4.2%	3.0%	2.8%	1.8%	2.3%
Import	4,677	4,214	2,326	2,831	1,563	2,257	1,031	749	716	1,010
	16.5%	14.9%	8.2%	10.0%	5.5%	8.0%	3.6%	2.6%	2.5%	3.6%
Inter-third party*	1,121	1,344	739	1,182	865	1,001	634	358	380	700
Domestic	14,412	13,007	9,321	8,173	6,530	5,600	4,272	3,142	3,581	2,396
Total	23,861	22,779	15,718	14,595	11,087	10,646	7,208	5,426	5,426	5,076

Sources: Tōyō Keizai, 2 Dec. 1972, p. 91, and Sōrifu 1973.
*Trade conducted between two parties (usually but not necessarily of different nations) through the intermediation of a general trading company.

literature on the multinationals and the zaibatsu. Others, to be answered satisfactorily, require much further research.

The first section of this paper presents the basic analytical framework. It is followed by a discussion of the growth of three selected trading companies in four periods: 1859-86, preceding modern economic growth;[1] the 1887-1913 period of initial growth; 1914-40, including the First World War boom and the interwar years; and the post-1945 rapid economic recovery and growth. The companies are Mitsui Trading Company (Mitsui Bussan), C. Itoh Trading Company (Itoh Chū), and Iwai Trading Company (merged with the Nisshō Trading Company in 1968 to become Nisshō-Iwai). These giants ranked, in 1972, second, fourth, and sixth among the Big Ten and represent the major three discernible types of origins. Mitsui Trading represents former zaibatsu trading companies (Mitsubishi and Sumitomo), C. Itoh the companies which grew out of textile wholesalers (Nichimen, Tōmen, Marubeni, and Kanematsu Gōshō), and Iwai the companies which grew partly because they became designated wholesalers of the products of the major iron and steel companies (Ataka). This is the classification adopted by Japanese scholars.

ANALYTICAL FRAMEWORK

To examine the origins and to evaluate the raison d'être, growth, and recent transformations of general trading companies, it is crucial at the outset to identify analytical bases for what seem to be their three closely related major functions.

The first function is minimizing or reducing the risks inevitable in both domestic and international trade. The risks are fluctuation in demand and fluctuation in exchange rates. These are prohibitively costly for any single transaction to be insured against. Put simply, the trading companies reduce these risks by distributing them over many transactions. A decline in the demand for, and thus the price of, any single commodity can be offset by an increase in the demand for other commodities. The larger the number of commodities traded, the larger the number of transactions of a single commodity, and the more diversified sales are by geographic region and types of buyers, the more widely the risks involved can be distributed. It is general trading companies, in contradistinction to specialized trading companies, which are best able to benefit from these scale and diversification attributes.

A general trading company can minimize the risk of fluctuation in exchange rates because it can perform a role analogous to the institutional arrangement adopted by the banking industry to clear transactions. The net transfer of cash through clearing arrangements to settle interregional or interbank accounts is only a minute fraction of total transactions. Similarly, because a trading company deals both in importing and exporting, it is able both to buy

---

[1]The meaning of the phrase "modern economic growth" and the period designated for it in Japanese economic development follow Rosovsky's suggestions (1966, p. 113).

and sell in local currencies, thereby reducing transactions across currencies to a fraction of the total import and export business. This means that the volume of transactions exposed to the risks of fluctuation in exchange rates is substantially reduced through the activities of trading companies.

Another major function of trading companies is their ability to take advantage of economies of scale, which are extremely important in the production of transactions services. The output of these companies includes a number of services used as intermediate goods in the transfer of private property rights between economic units. Important services are information about market opportunities and economic intelligence in general, contract negotiations and enforcement, and obtaining transportation services. The costs of providing such outputs can be called "transaction costs." It is from the nature of information, negotiation, enforcement of contract, and of transportation—that is, from the transfer of goods from one owner to another—that these costs arise.

The theoretical conditions for economies of scale are met if the cost function can be approximated by a fixed initial cost and a constant or decreasing marginal cost (or even by an increasing marginal cost that is sufficiently small vis-à-vis a large initial fixed cost). All the products of these trading companies meet these theoretical conditions. The production of information about market opportunities (prices and the location of sellers and buyers) includes the costs of gathering and disseminating the information. The costs are fixed, as they are independent of the use to which the information is put. Though this fact alone argues for the existence of economies of scale, also important is the decline in search costs per unit of information when market size expands.

An increasing demand for transactions services will also reduce negotiation costs, for buyers and sellers become aware of their alternatives. With a growth in the demand for negotiation services, it becomes profitable to incur fixed costs involved in making new institutional arrangements that allow the use of new, lower cost contractual and enforcement procedures.

Transportation costs, characterized by a large fixed cost, can be reduced by various means. Even if trading companies themselves do not provide the transportation, they can coordinate shipping times and locations to reduce the cost per unit of goods transported. Transportation costs are also reduced because of facilities and arrangements made at ports of origin and destination. Such facilities and arrangements can also be characterized as having a large fixed cost and small marginal costs. Economies of scale also enable the trading companies to participate in the international forward exchange market to hedge the risks involved in exchange fluctuations at relatively less cost than for any single export manufacturer or import user dealing in a small number and quantity of goods.

Another factor is the productivity-increasing effect of what is known in the literature on technological change as learning by doing, that is, the productivity of a worker is increased because he does the same task many times within a given period or over a long period. Such increases in productivity, of course, are partially a function of economies of scale, because for a person to be able to do the same thing for a long period means he can specialize, and specialization is a function of volume of transactions, as Adam Smith pointed out two hundred years ago.[2] Learning by doing is typified by the increased command of foreign languages attained by veteran employes of trading companies.

The third function of the trading companies is to make efficient use of capital, a function based on their ability to reduce risks and to take advantage of economies of scale. By reducing risks (that is, reducing the variance of expected returns) in using capital, the trading companies are able to obtain capital (and create credit) which would not have been available to a single trader, or available only at a higher cost. The increased availability of capital to the transactions sector of the economy (international and domestic) in turn helps to even further reduce risks and to permit these companies to take advantage of greater economies of scale. That banks consider trading companies desirable customers can be explained in terms of their size and creditworthiness, but the latter, in the final analysis, rests on their ability to reduce the risks involved in transactions and to take advantage of economies of scale in using the capital made available to them. Thus, the trading companies can often function as providers or guarantors of credit, or can engage in trading with a variety of credit instruments rather than cash, in effect advancing credit to individual producers. The trading companies take on this function because bankers, for obvious reasons, prefer to deal with less risky trading companies than with individual producing companies. This is particularly true for smaller producers, where trading companies have superior information and are better able to screen applicants for credit and at lower costs than banks (Uchida 1971, pp. 131-141).

The foregoing discussion suggests that a general trading company can be defined as an economic organization whose functions consist of minimizing risks involved in transactions through its ability to distribute risks; reducing transaction costs through its ability to take advantage of economies of scale; and making efficient use of capital because of the two preceding abilities. Although some trade associations, banks, and other similar economic institutions perform some of these functions, they differ from the trading companies in the degree and scope of their ability to reduce risks and realize economies of scale, and thus to use capital more efficiently. Also, the main function of these institutions is, in most instances, more exclusive than that of the trading companies and can be more narrowly defined as, for example, banking services, exchange of information, or reducing transportation costs or negotiation costs, on an ad hoc basis.

[2]A good discussion of learning by doing with references and empirical testing (using Olympic swimmers) is Fellner (1969). The best article on the effects of market expansion (specialization, increasing returns, and technological change induced by an increase in economic activities) still is Allyn Young's classic (1928).

ORIGINS: 1859 TO 1887

With the help of the preceding framework, I shall now describe the origins and evaluate the growth of the general trading companies. In doing so, I touch on other institutional developments which also contributed to reducing the transactions costs involved in trade. I do this partly to place the relative importance of general trading companies in perspective, and partly because the description of other institutions has been neglected in the English literature on the early phase of Japanese economic growth.[3]

Between 1859 (when international trade began in Japan as a result of treaties signed with four Western powers the preceding year) and 1886 (when it first became evident domestic cotton was insufficient to meet the demand of the emerging cotton textile industry), trading practices between Japan and Western nations differed little from those between the Western nations and their colonies. In contrast to the American and English merchants who had accumulated both capital and experience, the Japanese were novices in international trade.

Japanese merchants were so unfamiliar with the basic skills needed in conducting international trade that they had to enlist the services of Chinese as interpreters and as general go-betweens. Few Japanese traders had any idea of the world price of the commodities in which they dealt. To compound their difficulties, most had only enough capital to conduct their trading from one transaction to the next. Rare indeed was the Japanese trader who could stock his goods over any length of time to take advantage of changing market conditions. The risks involved in the widely fluctuating relative value of monies was more than these traders could bear.

Japanese traders could hardly be blamed for their ignorance. Because of the nearly 250 years of *sakoku*, the closing of the nation from international trade enforced by the Tokugawa bakufu, they had little opportunity to acquire the necessary skills. What little trade was permitted with the Dutch and Chinese through Nagasaki was stringently controlled by the bakufu, and the practices adopted were scarcely useful in the newly opened free trade.[4] The opening of international trade put the Japanese merchants in a position quite akin to that of a master calligrapher who was suddenly required to type.

Neither the Tokugawa bakufu, which had been preoccupied with its own survival and intimidated by the black ships of the West, nor the Meiji government, which had yet to secure its footing and to free itself from the provisions of the unequal treaties, was able to provide much assistance to the

[3]The only exception is banking. See Patrick (1967) and Yamamura (1972).

[4]Several Japanese economic historians suggested to me the possible importance of the *tonya* (wholesalers) of the Tokugawa period as an institutional forerunner of general trading companies. This suggestion would have been investigated had I been concentrating on the role of the general trading companies in the domestic market. However, in the context of this paper, I chose not to pursue the suggestion, though I plan to do so in the future.

aspiring international traders of Japan. The bakufu's attempt to route exports through Japanese wholesalers was abandoned no sooner than it was instituted in the face of the Western objections, and the Meiji government's efforts to aid Japanese merchants in 1869 by means of the trade bureaus were short-lived more because of Western protest than because of the strong-arm tactics the government used in enlisting the participation of merchants.[5]

As the Meiji government became better established during the 1870s, it actively sought to encourage international trade in the following ways: by participating in international expositions (Vienna in 1873 and Philadelphia in 1876); requiring newly appointed consuls abroad to act as collectors for the minuscule amount of direct sales made by Japanese merchants overseas; providing subsidies to Japanese shipping firms during the mid-1870s; giving subsidies and assuming a part of the risks of newly established companies for international trade; helping to establish the first marine insurance company by means of a subsidy (Tokyo Marine Insurance Company, 1878); and establishing the Yokohama Specie Bank in 1880 for the purpose of providing banking services necessary for international transactions.[6]

Even by the mid-1880s, however, the effect of this government assistance was scarcely visible. The dominant method of international trade during this period was *shōkan bōeki*, international trade through Westerners' newly opened merchant houses at the port cities. The Japanese sellers (*urikomiya*) came to "sell into" (*urikomu*) the *shōkan* (merchant houses), and buyers (*hikitoriya*) came to "take in" (*hikitoru*) the goods these *shōkan* had to sell. To Japanese traders the foreign merchant houses were extensions of their countries.

Western merchants and the Chinese assistants fully exploited the relative naiveté and ignorance of Japanese traders. A hikitoriya of the period wrote, for example, "The heads of these shōkan gathered for lunch and decided on the prices among themselves. These prices apparently had no relationship to the prices in their countries but were determined solely by the demand-supply conditions in Japan. Japanese were always dancing to the tunes of Westerners." And "the shōkan refused to accept paper currency, while Japanese were paid in it" (Iwai 1964, pp. 111-112). An urikomiya noted that "the Chinese took, as a rule, a commission of one percent of the total value

[5]For a discussion of the origins and functions of the Trade Bureau and the eight *kawase kaisha* (bills of exchange companies), see Yamamura (1967, pp. 200-201).

[6]The establishment of the Yokohama Specie Bank was the outcome of nearly fifteen years of effort by the government to assist Japanese international traders. The bank was established to continue services performed by the only successful kawase kaisha (see preceding note) in Yokohama. The most significant service rendered by the kawase kaisha after 1870 was to cash checks issued to Japanese traders by foreign merchants. The Japanese traders, "unfamiliar with the nature of the checks," used them as money among themselves and "when they presented the checks to the bank (the Oriental Bank or the Chartered Mercantile Bank, both operated by the

of all sales. Japanese objected to this as the rate was considered high [for what the Chinese did for them]. Thus, the commission was abolished. But now a new charge of one percent was made for weighing the products" (Dainihon 1935, 1:121).

Reading through numerous such complaints, one can envision the helplessness and frustration experienced by the Japanese. The extent of the shōkan exploitation of the Japanese lack of knowledge and capital is well revealed in the following often-cited example of shōkan tactics. A shōkan buys a small quantity of silk yarn at high prices and announces that it is prepared to buy much more. On learning this, the urikomiya buys silk yarn from the producers to the limit of his capital. However, when he brings the yarn to the shōkan, he is told that the price has declined. Having tied up all of his capital, as well as borrowed capital in many instances, the urikomiya has no choice but to sell the yarn at the reduced prices which eliminates all of his profits, if not producing a loss (Matsui 1950, pp. 35-36).

Understandably, such tactics aroused many Japanese traders. Thus, the most victimized, the urikomiya of silk yarn, organized the Federation of Silk-Yarn Dealers in 1881 among twenty-seven dealers who handled about 93 percent of the silk yarn sold to the shōkan. The intent of the federation was to provide a warehousing service, to inspect the yarn (in order to eliminate the inspection fees charged) and most importantly to advance credit against the goods. The government and a few major banks were ready to provide the 5 million yen needed by the federation. However, the federation, which was the first important step taken by the Japanese international traders to compensate for their lack of experience and capital, had to be dissolved no sooner than it was established. The objection raised by the shōkan that it was against the treaty provision of free trade was not serious, but their ability to coerce Western shipping firms not to carry silk yarn channeled through the federation was fatal for the Japanese, who had no international shipping line of their own (Nakagawa 1967, pp. 15-16).[7]

Lacking institutional capabilities, human resources with the requisite skills, capital, and international shipping lines of their own, the Japanese international traders had to continue to use shōkan during this period. Within the

English), the bank frequently found reasons for not honoring the checks" (Abe 1972, p. 217). The reasons included presentation after the date specified on the checks; the original issuer had departed Japan; insufficient funds; or bankruptcy claimed by the makers of the checks. To avoid such losses, the kawase kaisha cashed these checks and paid Japanese traders with special bills denominated in dollars. That these bills were in dollars was not only convenient in doing business with foreigners but also helpful in reducing possible losses which could result by converting yen-denominated currency into foreign monies. For the services rendered Japanese traders by the kawase kaisha and later by the Yokohama Specie Bank, see Abe (1972, pp. 215-224) and Tsuda (1960, pp. 105-107).

[7]Using British consular reports, Grace Fox (1969, pp. 326-327) described the incident as follows: "In 1881 all silk transactions suffered from the

limitations imposed by the circumstances, individuals and firms attempted to conduct direct trading, circumventing the shōkan, but success was extremely limited. In fact, direct exports accounted for only 3.6 percent of total exports in 1877 and still only 12.5 percent (mostly to China) as late as 1887. Direct imports were even lower, by about one percentage point, for both years (Tsuda 1960, p. 112).

Rather than continue to describe the period in general terms and the data in the aggregate, I shall now turn to the three companies referred to earlier. These three also happen to be the first of the Big Ten, along with Mitsubishi, to enter international trade. The description of the efforts and trials of these early entrants not only tells us how they were established, but also offers a micro view of international trading in Japan before the mid-1880s. Nine companies were organized for international trade during this period. However, only Mitsui Bussan survives today.

Mitsui Bussan (Mitsui Trading Company)

Because of the financial assistance the House of Mitsui rendered cash-starved restoration forces and the struggling new government, Mitsui was given the lucrative privilege of acting as government treasury agent. This was extremely important in helping Mitsui replenish its depleted coffers as well as enabling it to establish twenty-seven branch offices across the nation which could also be used for domestic trading.

Thus, in 1874, the House of Mitsui established in Tokyo the Kokusangata Karihonten (Temporary Head Office for Domestic Trade). As the name of the head office indicated, its purpose was to coordinate domestic trade through the twenty-seven branch offices. The major products handled were rice, tea, and processed marine products, and business was conducted strictly on a commission basis. However, shortly after domestic trading began, the head office entered international trade, selling silk yarn and tea to the shōkan on a commission basis and acting as a forwarding agent of imported goods between Tokyo and Yokohama. Business, however, "could not be called good" (Shibagaki 1963, p. 53). The problem was that "though the Mitsui employees were masters of traditional trading, they were unable to make headway in a business of a new age. Thus, by the beginning of 1876, even [Mitsui's chief manager] Minomura was forced to think of closing out the venture" (Yasuoka 1960, p. 306).

---

formation of a new silk guild in Yokohama which tried to centralize the entire silk trade in that port and prohibited all outside sales on 15 September. British Consul Wilkinson told of the opposition of the foreign merchants, who boycotted the silk trade through this guild. There were no sales of silk in Yokohama for several months, until the outstanding issues were reconciled with the Japanese merchants. The guild was abolished in November 1881." Fox's book contains interesting observations which reveal how the British regarded the early efforts made by the Japanese in international trade.

At this critical point, Mitsui fortunately was offered Senshūsha by Kaoru Inoue.[8] This was a company organized in 1872 by Inoue and others, and managed by Takashi Masuda. It had been moderately successful, mostly on the strength of Inoue's political connections, which brought in lucrative procurement orders from the government for imported goods. Inoue was now returning to the government and wanted to sell the company to Mitsui, the principal source of his political funds. Mitsui jumped at the opportunity, as the company brought with it government contracts to buy imported woolen goods, guns, and fertilizer, and it had also been selling rice, tea, and silk abroad. On acquiring the company, and its political connections through Inoue, Mitsui organized the Mitsui Bussan Kaisha (the Mitsui Trading Company) in July 1876 by uniting the new acquisition and its own Temporary Head Office. Important also for the future of Mitsui Bussan was the fact Masuda, who had once worked for the largest American shōkan, came with the Senshūsha and was made the manager of Mitsui Bussan.

As soon as the Bussan came into being, Mitsui was given the right to market high-quality coal from the government-owned Miike mine. Perhaps an understanding had already existed between Mitsui and Inoue, or perhaps Inoue caused "the government officers' favorable consideration" to be given to Mitsui, as the first semiannual report of the Bussan acknowledged (Yasuoka 1960, pp. 315-316). In any event, selling coal in China through Shanghai immediately became an important and profitable business. Because of the rapidly increasing exports of coal, the Bussan established its first overseas office in Shanghai by the end of 1876. The office was small, manned only by a branch manager, three clerks, and three young boys, but it was a significant first step for the Bussan as an international trader. As with all business done by the Bussan, coal was sold on a commission basis, and the only capital the Bussan required was an agreement with the Mitsui Bank to be able to overdraw its account up to 50,000 yen.

The following year, 1877, was enormously profitable thanks to the Seinan War, a small-scale civil war fought in Kyūshū between die-hard elements of the former samurai led by Takamori Saigō and the conscripted forces of the Meiji government. The Bussan, which supplied nearly 60 percent of the provisions of the government forces, profited to the tune of 200,000 yen. On the strength of these profits, the Bussan opened a branch in Hong Kong in 1878 (to increase the sale of coal and other commodities) and an office in New York in 1879, the first outside Asia. The going was extremely difficult in these offices, for they had to do more than selling coal in a seller's market, as they did in Shanghai. Profitless, the New York office was closed in 1881, and the Hong Kong office eventually followed suit in 1886.

Business, however, continued to improve domestically and in Shanghai. Thus, in 1880, the Bussan was formally capitalized at 200,000 yen, provided

---

[8]Kaoru Inoue (1835-1915) was one of the leading political figures of the Meiji period and served as minister of foreign affairs, interior, and finance, and as a privy councilor.

by the House of Mitsui. Then in 1882, the Bussan had an opportunity to trade directly with English companies. This welcome development came through Takeo Yamabe, an engineer searching for machinery in London on behalf of the Osaka Textile Company, which was soon to begin operations. Yamabe, having decided to acquire machinery from Platt & Company and Hargreaves & Company, selected Mitsui to handle the transactions. His decision may have been due to Mitsui's established name, the known friendship between Eiichi Shibusawa (the major force behind the Osaka Textile Company) and the Bussan's manager Masuda, or to a desire by Yamabe, thinking to the future, to bypass the shōkan. Whatever his reasons, the Bussan now began business directly with London.

This transaction did not lead to others, as hoped, because of the still limited demand for such machinery in Japan during the early 1880s. Total imports of machinery from London by the Bussan never exceeded 30,000 yen per year before 1886. However, far more significant than the amount indicated was the experience the Bussan gained by doing business directly with Westerners, and in 1886 it managed to become the exclusive agent for Platt & Company in Japan. Few realized the importance of this agreement. After all, the cotton textile boom, heralding Japan's modern economic growth, was yet to come. No one foresaw that Bussan, a miniscule trading firm by international standards, and one still conducting its business strictly on a commission basis, was to grow into a large general trading company within a few decades, or that (as discussed in Saxonhouse's chapter in this volume) Platt & Company, selling through the Bussan, was to be the major source of cotton-spinning machinery for the next four decades.[9]

Chūbei Itoh and Bunsuke Iwai

Much more representative of Japanese international traders of this period are Chūbei Itoh and Bunsuke Iwai, whose names are now those of giant general trading companies.[10] Itoh, born in 1842, the son of a retailer of dry goods, began to accompany his brother on sales trips at age eleven in 1853, the year Perry came to Japan. By 1859, he was selling cloth in Kyoto and Osaka, and as he grew older, his sales trips grew to include Okayama and Hiroshima. In 1860, at eighteen, he became a part-time, small-scale wholesaler on the strength of his hard-earned nest egg. Undoubtedly an exceptional trader, he continued to prosper throughout the turbulent 1860s, and in 1872 he was successful enough to open a good-sized shop in Osaka. Ambitious and venturesome, Itoh succeeded in expanding his trade. By 1877, he employed seventeen persons and was one of the larger textile wholesaler-retailers in

---

[9]The data contained in the preceding three paragraphs were obtained from Togai (1972). Togai is one of the few persons who has had access to the records of the early years of the Mitsui Bussan. These records have not yet been released for public inspection.

[10]The sources for this section are Iwai (1964), Miyamoto (1963), Sakudō (1963), and Itoh (1969).

Osaka. His business grew enough by 1883 to justify opening a branch in Kyoto, and in 1884 his shop in Osaka was renamed the Itoh Honten (the Main Itoh Shop).

Though it is not clear when Itoh began to sell to shōkan in Kobe, in 1885 he and his nephew, Tetsujiro Sotoumi, organized the Itoh-Sotoumi Company in Kobe for the purpose of exporting, that is, selling to the shōkan. Though Itoh wished to sell his products abroad directly in order to gain larger profits and to avoid the disgraceful experience of dealing with the condescending Chinese and Westerners, he had no choice.

Iwai, also born in 1842, was the son of a part-time farmer and part-time pawnbroker. At age nine he was sent to work as an errand boy at a sundries shop in Osaka. When he left the shop at twenty-one to open a sundries shop of his own, he chose to specialize in the commodities then gaining popularity, imported products. At the beginning he bought indirectly through Japanese traders, as his trade was not even large enough to deal directly with the shōkan. His business of selling Western pottery, silk, oil products, woolens, glass, wine, matches, and papers grew slowly. In 1879 he almost lost the business when a bank failed—one which he had helped establish by contributing a small amount of money. By the mid-1880s, however, Iwai had grown to be one of the largest hikitoriya in Osaka, with sixteen or seventeen employes. By this time, he was large enough to do "the shōkan circuit" in Kobe on his own. He sold imported goods on a wholesale basis to merchants in western Honshū and Kyūshū, and his shop in Osaka retailed more than a hundred lines of imported products.

GROWTH: 1887 TO 1913

Led by the cotton textile industry, modern economic growth began in Japan during the mid-1880s. Growth, once initiated, proceeded at a rapid pace, and the Japanese economy on the eve of the First World War differed significantly from what it was in 1868. Paralleling the growth, changes in economic and legal institutions came thick and fast. The banks grew in number and in asset size, and the Bank of Japan, established in 1882, began to perform the functions of a central bank beginning in 1885, when the Matsukata policy brought an end to the post-Restoration inflation. The silver-backed Bank of Japan notes began to circulate at face value for the first time in January 1886.[11] (Gold-backed notes began to circulate similarly after 1900.)

Other changes significantly assisted the early growth of international trade. Stock exchanges, opened in 1878 both in Tokyo and Osaka, were ready to

[11]The branch offices of Mitsui Bussan in Hong Kong and Shanghai served as the first branch offices of the Bank of Japan in 1882 and 1883. The bank paid Mitsui 100,000 yen, a handsome amount by the standard of the period. Although the Bank of Japan undoubtedly benefited from the services rendered by these Mitsui offices, this arrangement more properly should be considered an example of the government's aid to struggling overseas branches of a trading company (Daiichi 1957, p. 413).

perform their intended functions after a trial run of a decade of trading government bonds. As the call money market emerged and various bills and notes began to be used in an increasing quantity from the mid-1880s, the first bill broker, Tokisaburō Moroi, began in 1899 to discount bills and act as an intermediary in the call money market. Soon Moroi had many competitors both in Tokyo and Osaka. The twice-delayed enactment and promulgation of commercial laws were finally carried out in 1896. These laws defined the privileges and responsibilities of an already large number of *kaisha* (companies) which had been organized on ad hoc charters. In 1900, insurance companies, which had been operating virtually unregulated, were covered by a general law governing their practices and privileges. The enactment of this law signaled the beginning of the end for the foreign insurance companies which had dominated the markets for fire and marine insurance since the beginning of the Meiji period.

Two other developments during the period affected the growth of international trade more directly. One was the rapid growth of shipbuilding and the expansion of shipping routes by Japanese companies. Benefiting from subsidies, low-cost loans, and other preferential considerations given by the government during the 1868-86 period, the Mitsubishi Shipbuilding Company was able to produce in 1887 a ship made of steel and equipped with a boiler. Though foreign-made ships had to be bought to wage both the Sino-Japanese and Russo-Japanese Wars, Japan was now capable of producing "black ships," and their number rose rapidly during this period (as discussed in Blumenthal's chapter in this volume). Shipping routes were rapidly expanded. Between 1886 and 1891, Nihon Yūsen Kaisha (NYK) and Osaka Shōsen Kaisha (OSK) opened regular services to six coastal cities of China and Korea, and in 1899, NYK began to serve the Kobe-Bombay route to facilitate importing raw cotton. The Sino-Japanese War accelerated the growth of ocean shipping. With the generous assistance provided under the Ocean-Shipping Promotions Act of 1896, NYK in 1897 began serving major ports in Europe, North America, and Australia.

The other development was the final elimination in 1911 of all the offending clauses in the unequal treaties initially signed in 1858. The process was a slow one. It was not until 1894—nearly fifteen years after Japan had first tried to eliminate extraterritoriality and obtain a most-favored nation clause—that England agreed to forgo the special privileges granted by the 1858 treaty. Others followed England in the course of the next five years. These renegotiations, however, did not grant Japan a most-favored nation clause, and on 104 products, most of which were industrial, Japan was still not free to set duties as she saw fit. It took the Russo-Japanese War and the ensuing changes in the international political power balance before the final success in 1911, ending fifty-three years of national humiliation.

Responding to and materially aiding the process of modern economic growth, the trading company as an institution took another significant step during this period. This change is most evident in the case of Mitsui Bussan, which transformed itself within the short span of twenty-seven years from a small commission agent to a worldwide company trading on its own account, that is, assuming risks. I shall now trace the growth of Mitsui Bussan, and the two traders with foreign merchants in Japan, Itoh and Iwai.

Mitsui Bussan

The initial stimulus for the growth of Mitsui Bussan came, as it did to the economy as a whole, from the cotton textile industry. The rapid growth of the industry—nearly a tenfold increase in the number of spindles and a fourteenfold increase in the output of cotton yarn between 1882 and 1890—meant rapid growth in the demand for raw cotton (Tōyō Menka 1960, pp. 10-12). By 1887, the amount of cotton produced domestically was no longer sufficient for Japan's needs or competitive in price, and a sharply increasing amount had to come from abroad to meet the voracious appetite of the textile industry. It was Mitsui Bussan which in short order established itself as the major importer of raw cotton.

Mitsui Bussan's cotton imports began in 1887 through its Shanghai office. But although imports of Chinese cotton were rising, it soon became evident that India would become the major supplier because her cotton was lower priced and of better quality (longer fiber).[12] Thus Mitsui sent a representative to Bombay in 1891 "on a tour of investigation" to determine the feasibility of importing raw cotton directly by short-circuiting the shōkan. Both the representative's report and the samples he sent were encouraging enough for the Bussan to send Yasunosuke Yasukawa to Bombay in 1892, where he opened a branch office the following year. Initially, the going was difficult, as Yasukawa later wrote: "Then, not a single Japanese lived in Bombay. Neither was there a Japanese consulate or a Japanese bank." Suffering from a "strange fever" which attacked him frequently, he had at the same time to deal with "sharp-trading" Indian brokers (Tōyō Menka 1960, p. 47).

Buying on its own account, and more and more from India, Mitsui Bussan by 1897 was importing nearly 17 million yen worth of cotton per year or 31.5 percent of the total cotton imports of Japan.[13] Because of Mitsui's dominance in the raw cotton market and because the prices Mitsui set closely reflected the world cotton market, the company began to "perform the role of a cotton exchange," an institutional arrangement which had not yet developed in Japan (Nakagawa 1967, p. 25). As demand for raw cotton continued to rise, Mitsui began in 1900 to buy cotton through its New York office (reopened in 1896). As in 1904 in Bombay, in 1912 the Bussan began to deal directly with United States producers, dispensing with native brokers. By the 1910-13 period, Mitsui averaged about 40 million yen in cotton

---

[12]The desirability of India as a source of raw cotton was reported by a delegation, consisting of a few officials of the Nōshōmu-shō (Ministry of Agriculture and Commerce) and several representatives of the major cotton textile firms, which visited India in 1899 (Tōyō Bōseki 1953, pp. 75-78).

[13]The trade statistics cited in this paragraph and the next are taken from Togai (undated, pp. 62 and 72).

imports, consistently accounting for at least a quarter of total cotton imports to Japan.

The rapid growth of the cotton textile industry was also responsible for helping Mitsui's growth as the major importer of spindles and other machines. In this, the Bussan's earlier experience in dealing in spindles and its exclusive dealership with Platt & Company of London was of crucial importance. Imports of spindles and other machines ranged between 25,000 and 46,000 yen annually during the 1885-87 period, but jumped to over 270,000 yen in 1888. In 1890 alone imports of machines—218,360 spindles being the major item—amounted to 284,000 yen. Imports of all types of machinery rose steadily, due in large part to the demand from the beginning of the twentieth century for machines and equipment for the rapidly growing railroads. By 1913 the total volume of all types of machinery imported by the Bussan exceeded 28 million yen, ten times the amount in 1890.

In contrast, Mitsui's success in exporting was slow in coming. Although coal and other products Mitsui had exported from the 1870s were still exported in increasing quantities, the total amount was still small. This, however, was soon changed by the cotton textile industry. As late as 1893, the best efforts of Mitsui's Shanghai and Hong Kong offices resulted in exports of only 30,000 yen worth of cotton yarn to China because of the inferior quality of Japanese goods compared with Indian products. Cotton goods were exported to "sell a brand name" rather than for immediate profits (Togai, undated, pp. 76-86). However, the picture suddenly began to improve, favored by a series of changes: elimination of export duties on cotton goods in 1894; the Sino-Japanese war; and the rapid improvement in the quality of Japanese goods. The total export of cotton goods to China increased, though from a very small base, nearly fortyfold between 1894 and 1899 (Tōyō Bōseki 1953, p. 86), and Mitsui aggressively shared in these increasing exports. The Bussan exported 165,000 yen worth of cotton goods in 1897 or 5.8 percent of the total exports of cotton goods from Japan, but by the 1910-13 period it was exporting around 10 million yen worth, nearly a third of total exported cotton goods (Tōyō Menka 1960, p. 54).

As the volume of trade rose, Mitsui Bussan continued to involve itself with ocean shipping. Its charter was amended in 1896 to include ocean shipping as one of its activities, and in 1898 it decided to go into a whole spectrum of operations related to transporting goods—ocean, coastal, and inland shipping, warehousing, and so forth. In 1903, a shipping division was established and assigned the task of dealing with ocean shipping. In 1910, when Mitsui Bussan was formally incorporated, the shipping division had nine ships of its own, twenty-eight leased for scheduled services, and over two hundred which the Bussan could call on if the need arose.[14]

From the early 1890s Mitsui Bussan had acted as an agent for insurance companies on an ad hoc basis for the benefit of its customers, and in 1898

[14]For Mitsui's role in the shipping industry during this period, see Kajinishi (1954, pp. 256-268).

amended its charter to become an agent for fire, life, and marine insurance. Mitsui was, in effect, selling insurance on a commission basis for major insurance companies, mostly to its own customers.

From Mitsui's incorporation in 1910, data useful for a more detailed analysis are available. Annual averages for the four-year period between 1910 and 1913 show that annual exports were around 123 million yen, imports 113 million yen, domestic trade 55 million yen, and inter-third-party trade 47 million yen. The total trade volume was 340 million yen. Including earnings from transportation and insurance agency business, Mitsui's total net profit was 5,275,000 yen. During this four years, Mitsui accounted for slightly over one-fifth of total Japanese exports and a little less than one-sixth of total imports (Togai 1968, pp. 82-83). Togai wrote of Mitsui Bussan around 1910:

About this time, Mitsui Bussan dealt in over 120 commodities. Through scores of its branch offices in Japan and abroad, it engaged in exports, imports, domestic trade, and inter-third-party trade. Not only was Mitsui building its foundation as a general trading company, it also was beginning to do a substantial amount of business in such subsidiary activities as transportation and insurance [1972, p. 3].

Behind the Bussan's growth was its constant effort to create what Masuda, head of the Bussan from its inception, called "the Mitsui international trade men." As early as 1891, the Bussan established a program to train young men in practical skills in international trade and Chinese. During the last decade of the nineteenth century, promising young men were sent to China to perfect their Chinese, and by 1902 an increasing number of university and commercial high school graduates were being sent to Australia, Canada, Bangkok, Saigon, Latin America, and Rangoon. Bussan became the first (in 1899) to dispense with Chinese compradores and was the only company to have a large number of men trained in practical skills and Western and Southeast Asian languages by the time of the Russo-Japanese War. Masuda's concern with the quality of "the Mitsui international trade men" is evident in the following speech he made in 1901:

The only way to become familiar with supply-demand conditions and with methods of dealing in various products, is to specialize in specific products. It is not possible to acquire all the necessary knowledge if one is to concern himself with many products. Ideally, the person dealing with a product should work with the product on long-term basis in order to learn all the intricacies related to the product and its market. It is also desirable that persons who become familiar with the culture and commercial customs of a specific country remain at the post as long as possible. Above all, however, the most important thing is to hire capable people after an extremely careful scrutiny [Noda 1967, p. 19].

C. Itoh and Company

The path followed by Itoh and Iwai was considerably different from that of Mitsui Bussan, with its increasingly large-scale trade and its backing by the Mitsui Bank. For Itoh, especially, late Meiji was still a thorny period spent in search of experience, a market, and profits.[15] As much as Itoh disliked the condescending attitude of the shōkan merchants, he had little choice but to use them, and he continued to buy textile goods from shōkan and to expand his domestic trade rapidly. He did establish a branch office in Shanghai in 1896, but it reported more losses than profits. But his business, on the whole, did well, and he increased the number of employes from twenty-nine in 1887 to one hundred by 1903, the year Itoh died a successful hikitoriya if not the bona fide international trader he had hoped to become.

Itoh's second son took over the business, and apparently he was no less capable than his father. With Japan's political position in Korea strengthened by the Russo-Japanese War, young Itoh sent two of his employes to Korea in 1905 in the hope of beginning direct exports rather than continuing to trade, as his father had done since 1898, through chōsenya, the shōkan specializing in Korean trade. Encouraged by the reports he received, Itoh established an independent export section in 1906 and opened a branch in Seoul in 1907. However, this branch reported continued difficulties because of "the low quality of Japanese products" (the quotes in this and the two following paragraphs are from Itoh 1969, pp. 53-54). Itoh also faced a graver problem in 1907 and into 1908: a huge loss incurred by the Shanghai office due to its inexperience in dealing with the volatile fluctuations in the value of silver, on which the Chinese currency remained based while the yen and major international currencies were based on gold. The crisis was overcome by cutting formal ties with the Shanghai office, which became an independent business to be salvaged by its employes.

Thanks, however, to rapidly increasing domestic business, C. Itoh & Company continued to grow despite the problems encountered in Seoul and in Shanghai. In March 1910, the younger Itoh, then twenty-three, left for England to "study at a university in London," but it is unlikely that he became seriously engaged in any type of structured study because he found "business was more interesting than study." Itoh learned that the intimidating shōkan in Japan were usually no more than agents of merchants in London and Manchester, and that shōkan were taking as much as 15 to 20 percent in commissions. He bought various woolen goods and other "high-class" textiles directly from wholesalers "at a savings of 20 percent" and sent them directly to his store in Japan. Sales were brisk because Itoh & Company could easily undersell other hikitoriya who were still paying high commissions. Also, Itoh found that a sixty-day note could be discounted at 2.5 to 2.75 percent with London banks once his company became known to them. Thus, he began to use credit from these banks rather than from the Yokohama Specie Bank or Japanese bill-brokers who charged 11 to 13 percent in discounting a similar note. Such savings also helped to reduce the cost of importing English goods to Japan.

The growth of Itoh & Company, however, was mainly due to its domestic trade. The total number of employes reached 375 by 1912. Itoh's trade with

[15]This section is based on Itoh (1969).

the English was still limited, and international trading as a whole was still in a precarious situation. The company history states of this period that "exporting had been in the red practically every year for ten years [since 1904]. The recession of 1907-08 was part of the reason, but inexperience, lack of knowledge, losses due to the fluctuating values of monies, and the rising cost of overseas operations all contributed to this. Different climates threatened the health of our employes abroad. The staff in the exporting section was severely tested."

Iwai and Company, Ltd.

Iwai, already one of the largest hikitoriya in Osaka by the mid-1880s, continued to expand his regular business into the 1890s.[16] At the same time, the range of Iwai's interests also expanded. In 1889 he invested in a crucibles manufacturing firm to help increase the sales of his imported oil, in 1891 in a firm to produce glass lampshades similar to those he was then buying from shōkan, and in 1893 in a firm to produce Western umbrellas. It is obvious his business was sufficiently profitable to provide him with the capital necessary for such investments.

Then, in 1897, on the suggestion of a friend who was already importing red phosphorus for matches directly through William Duff & Sons in London, Iwai began to import English and other Western European goods through this London merchant. This opportunity, however, was not purely a matter of good fortune. Duff & Sons had become willing to bypass shōkan if a creditworthy and sufficiently large importer could be found in Japan, and Iwai happened to fit the bill. Obtaining a direct pipeline to the West was important, but Iwai found he had to go to considerable lengths to be able to use the pipeline. He personally had to meet Korekiyo Takahashi, then vice-president of the Yokohama Specie Bank, before being permitted the use of trust receipts (implicit credit by the bank to cover imported goods), and he had to cope with the shōkan which understandably wished to dissuade Iwai from engaging in direct trade. One employe of Iwai recalled:

Since directly imported goods came marked *KB*, indicating our company, the shōkan could see immediately what was happening. They came to us saying that they would stop selling goods to us unless we discontinued direct trading. They were threatening us with a boycott. The shōkan told us that they had all decided to sell us goods at the prices at which we were buying directly from England. This, they told us, would eliminate all the details involved with the paperwork. Some even suggested that we might be made an exclusive agent of their goods. These were the threats and bribes which our president refused to listen to [Iwai, 1964, p. 120].[17]

[16]This section is based on Iwai (1964).

[17]The company's shipping mark *KB* stands for Kagaya Bunsuke. Kagaya is the name of the shop where Iwai first worked. It is a common Japanese practice to adopt the name of one's former employer when a tradesman opens a new shop of his own. Bunsuke was Iwai's first name.

The paperwork involved in direct trading was much more difficult than Iwai had initially anticipated. He had to employ a man who could read and write English, and the translations had to be typed. "But typewriters were scarce in those days, so the translations had to be copied first by a special copying-pencil and then duplicated by a special press which was cumbersome to operate. . . . Often employees worked all night so that bills of lading and other documents would reach Yokohama in time" (Iwai 1964, p. 160).

The direct trading with Duff & Sons was, however, worth all the effort. The English company sent original catalogs from England and elsewhere and charged only a 3 percent commission. As Iwai was one of the first to trade on this basis, his trade increased steadily. Once he had gained experience and established credit, Iwai began to trade directly with dealers in Germany and the United States. By the end of the century Iwai was importing medicine, fertilizer, galvanized sheets, steel plates, wire, gas pipes, woolen goods, cloth for umbrellas, paper, and a variety of other items. The list grew even longer during the first decade of the twentieth century.

Exporting was begun by Iwai in 1906, though the volume remained much smaller than imports throughout this period. Exports consisted of textile goods, matches, jute sacks, and sundry goods, and mostly went to India. In 1907 Iwai employes were dispatched on a short-term basis to India and Indonesia to sell Japanese goods as well as German pencils and English letter paper. Exports, unlike imports, were not profitable. In the thirteen semiannual reports between the first half of 1906 and the first half of 1912, exports showed losses in eight, whereas consistent and large profits were made by imports. The semiannual report for the first half of 1912 showed Iwai's trade amounted to 1,409,428 yen, with net profits of 40,853 yen (4,472 yen from exports and 36,381 yen from imports). Though Iwai was much smaller than Mitsui, which did 340 million yen of trading in 1913, by this year he was no longer a hikitoriya.

The results of the efforts of Japanese international traders, these three companies among them, can be seen in the data contained in Table 2. Though

Table 2
The Proportions of International Trade by Foreign and
by Japanese Traders
(in percent)

	Exports		Imports	
	Japanese	Foreigners	Japanese	Foreigners
1880	13.6	86.4	2.6	97.4
1887	13.0	87.0	11.9	88.1
1894	18.4	81.6	29.2	70.8
1900	37.1	62.9	39.4	60.6
1911 (Kobe)	51.5	48.5	63.8	36.2

Sources: 1880-1900: Tōyō Menka 1960, p. 5. 1911: Kajinishi 1954, p. 328.

the 1911 data are only for the port of Kobe, it is certain that the trend toward a change in the proportion of international trade carried out by foreign and by Japanese trading firms continued and, as shown by the Kobe data, probably at an accelerating pace until the beginning of the First World War, which even more rapidly reduced the foreigners' share.

GROWTH THROUGH DIFFICULTIES: 1914 TO 1940

The First World War literally transformed Japan from a fledgling industrial economy into one of the major industrialized nations in the world, and the economy, despite its share of woes, continued to grow during most of the 1920s and 30s. Japan's exports rose sharply during the First World War, when she took advantage of her industrial competitors' preoccupation with the war. Though trade slackened during the 1920s—the stagnant decade—it rose rapidly during the 1930s, especially with those nations then called the Yen Bloc.[18] By 1939, Japan's 5.6 million tons of ships were 8 percent of the world's total; Japan ranked third in merchant sea-power, behind only the United States and England, and her two major shipping lines (NYK and OSK) ranked third and fifth among world shipping lines (Tsuda 1960, p. 167). During this period, the growth of the trading companies was equally rapid. As a reflection of the condition of the economy itself, both C. Itoh & Company and Iwai & Company had to struggle for life during the 1920s, but they, along with Mitsui Bussan, were successful general trading companies by the late 1930s.

Mitsui Bussan

Mitsui Bussan, already established as a general trading company before 1914, took a great leap forward during the First World War boom as shown in Table 3. The annual average volume of trade during the 1914-20 period was

Table 3
The Growth of the Mitsui Bussan: Selected Data for 1914-40
(in million yen and percent)

Annual averages	Mitsui exports	Share of total exports	Mitsui imports	Share of total imports	Domestic trade	Inter-third party	Mitsui total
1914-20	298	(18.6)	268	(17.9)	271	398	1194
1921-27	258	(12.3)	239	(9.1)	253	262	1013
1928-30	275	(12.0)	262	(10.5)	425	260	1022
1931-36	287	(11.3)	250	(10.8)	521	290	1349
1937-40	455	(9.2)	549	(12.6)	1109	664	2777

Sources: Togai 1972, p. 11, Nihon Ginkō 1966, pp. 28-29 and 278-279.
Note: The figures are annual averages of the respective period. The figures in parentheses are percentages of total Japanese exports and imports respectively.

[18]An excellent paper dealing with the 1920s and 30s is Patrick (1971).

nearly triple the volume the company did in 1913. Even during the 1921-27 period, the Bussan's performance showed only a slight decline, and it rapidly improved throughout the 1930s. The decline in the Bussan's relative share of the trade during the late 1920s and 30s was due to increased competition by other trading companies. Also, after the mid-1930s when the proportion of trade with the Yen Bloc began to rise, the market share of new zaibatsu expanded rapidly in Manchuria, Formosa, and Korea, whereas Mitsui's trade with the West failed to increase given the political and economic circumstances of the 1931-40 period.[19] Despite the decline, Mitsui's 9.2 percent share in exports and 12.6 percent in imports during the 1937-40 period made the Bussan the largest international trader in Japan.

To finance such a volume, the Bussan required large resources; these were obtained by increasing its own capital, creating credit, and borrowing. The Bussan's own capital (the sum of paid-up capital, various reserves, cash on hand, and undistributed profits) rose from less than 37 million yen in 1914 to over 218 million yen in 1940, and its created credit (the sum of promissory notes outstanding and accounts payable) rose from 73 million yen to 469 million yen during the same period.[20] Its ability to create credit was partly due to the justified assumption that the Mitsui Bank stood behind the Bussan. In fact, the bank's official history acknowledges the bank actively aided the Bussan at the beginning and end of the First World War boom, even if it meant the bank had to adopt strong-arm tactics in collecting outstanding loans from others in order to make funds available to the Bussan (Mitsui Ginkō 1957, pp. 415-416).

The Bussan's network of international trade also expanded rapidly during this period, and by the early 1920s the company was able to boast of its corps of experienced and efficient Mitsui-men. The Bussan's branches and one-man posts increased to cover many parts of the world—"Japanese consulates followed the branch offices of the Mitsui Bussan"—so that on the eve of the Second World War, the Bussan had branches in fifty-nine cities around the globe along with a similar number of one-man posts. The total number of Mitsui-men stationed abroad was nearly 7000 (Kōsei 1955, p. 3).

The involvement of Mitsui Bussan in shipbuilding and other activities paralleled the growth of international trade. In 1917, the Bussan established a shipbuilding division which in 1937 became an independent company, Mitsui Shipbuilding K.K. The division averaged 5 to 10 million yen from the sale of

---

[19]The new zaibatsu, most emerging after the First World War, grew rapidly in the industries relating, directly or indirectly, to Japan's economic and military expansion into the Yen Bloc. Furukawa, Mori, Nissan, and several others are usually referred to as *shin-zaibatsu* (new zaibatsu).

[20]The sum of promissory notes and accounts payable were roughly the same as the sum of notes and accounts receivable during most of the interwar years. However, the latter began to gradually exceed the former during the second half of the 1930s, and in 1940 stood at 506 million yen. It seems that in times of rapid expansion of trade the Bussan's ability to "lend" in this fashion was important (Togai 1972, pp. 26-27).

ships during the 1920-37 period. After the First World War, Mitsui Bussan's shipping division mostly used ships built by its shipbuilding division. The shipping division's capacity was so great that 60 to 70 percent of the cargo it handled during the 1920-37 period was being carried for other firms. And as of 1937, the Bussan owned or effectively controlled nearly twenty companies, the largest of which was Taishō Marine Insurance Company, which acted as the marine insurance arm of Mitsui as well as of others.

An episode which took place during this period reveals the reasons for the Bussan's success: its size and its ability to take risks. In 1917, a branch manager gambled on the price of soybeans, and the result was a whopping loss of 30 million yen, an amount roughly equivalent to the paid-in capital of the Bussan at that time. This huge loss, which might have easily ruined most other trading companies was, however, covered by an equally large profit then being made by the shipbuilding and shipping divisions. An executive officer of the Bussan recalled the incident: "It was an extremely expensive tuition. But for the Bussan to grow and to become a worldwide trader, it was essential that each individual be able to use his talents fully, that is, that we give full responsibility and encourage initiative" (Noda 1967, pp. 125-126). What the executive failed to emphasize was the significance of the Bussan's size, which enabled it to pay such an expensive tuition.

C. Itoh & Company

The First World War boom was especially profitable for C. Itoh & Company. Its export division, which had been a consistent money-loser, became a huge profitmaker overnight. The company's domestic business also enjoyed enormous success as the price of textile products continued to rise. At the height of the boom, in 1918-19, the company reported a profit of 7 million yen on its paid-in capital of 10 million yen. On the strength of the boom, the company was divided: C. Itoh and Company (capitalized at 5 million yen), to conduct domestic business, and C. Itoh Trading Company (capitalized at 10 million yen), for specializing in international trade. By the end of 1919, the company had seven branches abroad: four in China and one each in Manila, Calcutta, and New York. The commodities it traded became quite diverse, including, along with textiles, numerous agricultural products, machinery, iron and steel products, and even automobiles.

However, because they were still relatively small and greatly dependent on textile products, the end of the boom nearly ruined both companies. Their joint accumulated deficit stood at 5 million yen for the accounting year 1919-20, and the losses continued to rise into the following year. In 1921, it was necessary to reorganize C. Itoh & Company; the new firm was named Marubeni Company. C. Itoh Trading spun off a new firm, Daidō Trading, which was made responsible for the Southeast Asian and the United States markets, which had become the least desirable of C. Itoh Trading's markets during these years. The total number of employes of these three companies in 1921 stood at 292 in contrast to the pre-reorganization high of 426.

The situation remained dismal for all three Itoh companies throughout most of the 1920s. C. Itoh Trading failed to declare any dividends until 1926; Daidō had constant difficulties in obtaining sufficient credit to conduct its business; and Marubeni's performance was poor until 1928. All in all "sluggish exports of cotton goods, the boycott of Japanese goods in China, that is, externally and internally undesirable conditions piled up, making the struggle to rebuild exceedingly difficult" (Itoh 1969, p. 89).

It was only after 1931 that the Itoh companies began to see a ray of hope. The Calcutta office, closed a decade earlier, was reopened in 1931, and then the new offices abroad were opened one by one: in 1932 in Sydney to import wool, and during 1933 and 1934 in Thailand and Indonesia to cope with the increasing trade with Southeast Asia. Daidō too began to show substantial profits, and C. Itoh Trading, now employing over five hundred, began to report steady profits and increased its capital to 12.5 million in 1937. Trading again was becoming more and more diversified, and C. Itoh could once more realistically hope to become a large general trading company.

Iwai & Company, Ltd.

Iwai, a successful importer and an unsuccessful exporter until 1913, abandoned its policy of trading through foreign agents in 1915 in order both to take advantage of the boom as well as to fill the gap left by foreign agents who could no longer serve Iwai because of the war. Iwai opened offices in New York, San Francisco, Singapore, London, and in several cities in China during the 1915-18 period. Profits from exports rose rapidly enough to permit Iwai to raise its capital to 5 million yen (from 2 million yen) in January 1918, and again to 10 million yen only six months later. During the boom Iwai exported all types of grain, green peas, potatoes, and other agricultural products.

Then, from June 1920 to November 1932, Iwai & Company suffered, as did the Itoh companies, a long period during which no dividends were declared, and small profits were interspersed with large losses. The company halved its capital to 5 million yen in 1930 and was "on the verge of bankruptcy" (Iwai 1964, p. 314). What saved the company were the profits earned as a designated wholesaler for major iron and steel companies. The biggest boon was being named in 1919 (along with Mitsui, Mitsubishi, and Ataka) a designed wholesaler for Yawata Seitetsujo, largest plant of Nihon Seitetsu, the semigovernmental, dominant producer of iron and steel. Yawata designated these trading companies exclusive agents for its goods to counter the declining trend in the price of its products. Iwai was selected because the company's business in metal products had been a relatively important part of its total trade. Modest profits were also earned by Iwai on earlier investments in companies producing celluloid, paint, caustic soda, and woolen goods, and from importing coal, iron ore, lumber, and tobacco from Southeast Asia.

Beginning in 1935, Iwai's trade with Korea, China, and Southeast Asian nations began to increase sharply. Profits from this trade had been rising since 1933, enough for Iwai to declare dividends, but it was only after 1935 that the company felt sufficiently sanguine to send its own trade missions to Latin

America, Africa, India, and Egypt. Profits continued to rise, and in 1937, like
Itoh, Iwai increased its capital to 12.5 million yen. By 1940, the company
was doing a total business of 247 million yen (54 million yen in imports, 25
million in exports, 27.5 million in domestic trade, and over 140 million in
intra-Yen Bloc trade, that is, among Korea, China, Taiwan, and Manchuria).
By this time the company had nine branch offices in China alone and one
each in Manila, Bombay, London, Sydney, Melbourne, and Buenos Aires. A
detailed listing of products traded by the company fills six pages of its
company history. There is no question that Iwai & Company, which adopted
a much less conservative policy in borrowing than did C. Itoh & Company
and did not divide its financial resources as Itoh had, grew throughout most
of the 1930s to become an important general trading company in Japan.

Postwar Dissolution and Growth

For Japan to be transformed from a defeated nation, subsisting with the aid
of the United States, into a prosperous industrial giant with a large trade
surplus required she be successful in the international market. Of the many
factors contributing to this success, there is little doubt general trading
companies played and continue to play a significant role. Given the historical
perspective already presented, one could have anticipated the course of
growth general trading companies followed and the means they adopted to
achieve the dominant positions they now occupy in Japan's international
trade and in the phenomenal postwar growth of the economy.

The initial policy adopted by the Supreme Command of Allied Powers
(SCAP) toward the general trading companies was harsh. All major companies
were dissolved, and in their place many small trading companies were created.
This was of little significance during the immediate postwar years when Japan
had virtually nothing to sell and no dollars with which to buy. When trading
was resumed in the summer of 1947, the "buyers," mostly American, came
to conduct their business in a fashion "very much reminiscent of the shōkan
trading" of the early Meiji era (Tsuda 1960, p. 205). International trade was
strictly regulated by SCAP, and exchange rates were set by commodity,
ranging from 600 yen to the dollar for sheet glass to 67 yen to the dollar for
pig iron. A uniform exchange rate of 360 yen to a dollar was set in April
1949, at which time trade regulations were somewhat relaxed. However,
international trade increased only slowly. In 1949 small trading companies,
the fragments of the large prewar companies, were competing for the
government's dollar allocation. Permission for trading company missions to
go abroad was granted in late 1949, but these missions had more hope than
dollars.

Then came the Korean War with its special war-demand boom. In 1951
special demand by U.N. forces accounted for 26.4 percent of the total dollars
available to Japan, and the figure rose to 36.8 and 38.2 during 1952 and 1953
(Hollerman 1966, pp. 135-136). Buoyed by the boom and the dollar, postwar
growth had begun. I shall now examine the revival and growth of Mitsui
Bussan, C. Itoh, and Iwai to gain insight into the reasons for the predominant
position they again came to occupy in Japan's international trade.

Mitsui Bussan

Mitsui Bussan, the largest prewar trading company and a zaibatsu firm, was dissolved by an order of SCAP, and seventeen new companies were created out of the Bussan's assets and personnel. The head office of Mitsui Bussan was renamed the Nittō Warehousing Company, and the largest among the trading companies created was called the Daiichi Bussan. However, as the economy began to show signs of growth and as it became possible to reestablish overseas networks, the chips of the former Mitsui Bussan began to reassemble themselves. Two direct factors contributing to this development were the end of SCAP rule and the general tightness of the capital market these trading companies faced as their need for funds rapidly increased.

Ignoring the absorption by a third chip of the two smallest companies created out of the former Bussan, the start of the regrouping dates from 1951. Nittō Warehousing Company absorbed two of the original seventeen before being renamed New Mitsui Bussan in 1952 (adoption of the prewar name having by then been made legal). Then in 1953 New Mitsui Bussan absorbed Muromachi Bussan (one of the original seventeen, which itself had absorbed two other splinters of the old Bussan). Daiichi Bussan absorbed the remainder of the original seventeen during the 1951-57 period, and when it merged with the New Mitsui Bussan in 1958, the process of reunification was complete. The newly unified trading company, not surprisingly, was named Mitsui Bussan (Arita 1972, pp. 58-62).

The motivation behind the reassembling was obvious. As the worldwide network of information and branch offices began to be rebuilt, and the shipping of goods to and from Japan increased—at times involving competition among the chips of the old Mitsui Bussan—cost savings to be had by mergers increased. Such savings plus prewar ties presaged reassembling, and the process was hastened by the severe 1954 recession following the end of the Korean War. Scores of smaller trading firms and many medium-sized firms which specialized in only a few commodities (chiefly textile products) went bankrupt. Safety could be had in pooling financial resources, diversifying commodities, and increasing scale.

Growth of the reassembled Mitsui Bussan was rapid. By 1970, the total volume of the Bussan's trade approached 2 trillion yen (about 6.8 billion dollars), of which exports accounted for about 16 percent, imports 23 percent, inter-third-party trade 3 percent, and domestic trade the remaining 58 percent. This huge volume of trading during the 1970-71 period was carried out on the Bussan's own capital of about 46 billion yen (paid-in capital amounted to only 22.16 billion yen), and an enormous amount of "others' capital" consisting of over 400 billion yen in promissory notes, 280 to 290 billion yen in accounts payable, and another 400 billion yen in long- and short-term loans. The ratio of "own" to "others' " capital was a mere 2.8 to 2.9 percent. In short Mitsui Bussan's trade grew on its ability to create credit and to borrow (Uchida 1971, pp. 131-141).

By 1972 Mitsui Bussan's outposts around the globe numbered 151: 98 direct branch offices, and 21 companies incorporated under the law of the host country with a total of 53 branch offices. These Mitsui offices were manned by 928 Japanese and 2067 nationals of the host countries. The "fine spider web of information," claimed by the Bussan to be the best in the world, is anchored by two giant Univac-1108 computers surrounded by a host of smaller computers, "message switching systems," and Teletypes (Togai 1971, pp. 99 and 103). The number of commodities traded by the Bussan is in the thousands—"from noodles to warships"—and many commodities are bought and sold both spot and in futures markets by experienced specialists. The Bussan's transportation division coordinates shipping schedules, and its insurance division makes certain that all necessary insurance is bought at the lowest possible cost. Coordinating teams and project groups are organized on an ad hoc or semipermanent basis to coordinate the Bussan's activities across divisions, commodity groups, and market areas and to investigate and develop new opportunities.

Beginning in the early 1960s and accelerating during the past several years, Mitsui Bussan, like others in the Big Ten, has acted as an increasingly active "organizer." The organizers, as the Japanese use the term, refer to those trading companies which seek new ventures, becoming the sole investor or a coinvestor, and bring it to profitable fruition. The organizers typically do much more. They develop detailed technical and marketing studies, attend to all necessary financial arrangements, assist in equipping and operating the venture, and make often long-term commitments to buy or sell the products or services which are to be produced. Uchida summarized these functions as financial, consulting, and information, that is, assistance in funding, establishing a going operation, and developing a market (1971, pp. 206-207).

The prewar Bussan also acted as an organizer but in a much more limited way. The prewar Bussan organized ventures using mostly its own capital, usually in Asia and only in cases where a ready market for the products clearly existed. In contrast the Bussan today organizes ventures all over the world either with coinvestors or for others, and in most instances markets must be developed. In a sense, by becoming an organizer Mitsui Bussan has become a creator of new economically useful information rather than merely gathering it.

To the extent that many of the ventures abroad are controlled by the Bussan—134 around the world as of 1972—the Bussan has become a multinational firm as well as a promoter of such firms. Through the 1960s total investment made by the Mitsui Bussan and firms organized by the Bussan was small relative to that made by their United States and West European counterparts. Bussan and Bussan-promoted companies abroad have been highly ethnocentric. Except for a few, most are still Japanese-dominated in management and ownership, but this is rapidly changing. In September 1972, Mitsui Bussan sent a directive to all employes abroad that Japanese-dominated and Japan-oriented practices be changed so that capital, personnel, and markets could in the near future be made more international. The Bussan has come a long way since 1876, when Rizaemon Minomura nearly abandoned Mitsui's international trade for lack of profits.

C. Itoh Trading Company

It was the Daiken Manufacturing, an entity created in 1944 by the merging of C. Itoh Trading, Marubeni, Daidō Trading, and Kureha Textiles (a subsidiary of C. Itoh), which faced the SCAP dissolution order.[21] SCAP divided the Daiken, hastily assembled for the war effort, into three parts: Kureha Textiles, C. Itoh Trading Company, and Marubeni. The latter two, unlike their predecessors, were made fully independent firms, each to engage both in domestic and international trade. (Marubeni merged with Takashimaya-Iida in 1955 to create Marubeni-Iida. See Table 1.)

C. Itoh Trading Company enjoyed a modest success during the 1949-50 period because its exports of textile goods were used to pay (at times on a barter basis) for imported grains. Nine-tenths of Itoh's business was in textile goods, the products most familiar to the company. By the beginning of 1950, the company had revived sufficiently to send its own trade missions to India, Pakistan, and the United States. However, it was the Korean War boom with the skyrocketing prices of cotton goods which helped Itoh's trading return to its prewar eminence. Profits from March to September 1951 were 656 million yen, sufficient to withstand a huge loss of 515 million yen over the next six months. Another reason Itoh was able to survive the blow was rapid diversification of its trade. The proportion of textile products decreased to 78 percent by the end of 1951, and it was further reduced to 68 percent by the end of 1952. Nontextile products traded in 1951 included petroleum, automobiles, machinery, and airplanes, for which demand was beginning to appear.

Thus, when the major recession of 1953-54 claimed 1013 wholesalers (mostly of textile products) and small- and medium-sized trading companies along with a few larger ones in Osaka, Itoh was sufficiently large and diversified to survive and to pick up the business left by the bankrupt firms. By 1954 the company had grown enough to win the exclusive dealership of Douglas Corporation for aircraft and parts and to obtain a 6 million dollar loan from an American bank for importing Mexican cotton. Itoh continued to grow from the mid-1950s, as did Japanese exports and the economy as a whole. Nowhere is the growth of C. Itoh more evident than in its ability to mobilize the capital necessary to conduct its rapidly increasing trade. While its internal (paid-in) capital increased from 150 million yen to 17.66 billion yen between 1949 and 1968, the company's short-term loans rose from 1.753 billion yen for the second half of 1949 to 93.603 billion yen by the second half of 1968. The promissory notes issued during the same period rose from 1.732 billion to 114.841 billion yen. Long-term loans increased steadily after 1955, reaching 68.586 billion yen by the second half of 1968. The total of "others'" capital thus rose from 3.485 billion yen to 276.780 billion yen during the nineteen-year period. By March 1970, promissory notes alone amounted to 252.512 billion yen.

[21]This section is based on Itoh (1969).

Itoh's network of information expanded around the world, branch offices
and subsidiaries were incorporated in various countries, and the company
performed the role of an organizer similar to that described for Mitsui Bussan.
C. Itoh Trading Company, which by 1972 had reduced its textile trade to
around 40 percent of its total trade of nearly 1.46 trillion yen, has also come
a long way since its founder in the 1880s made the rounds of the shōkan in
Kobe enduring the condescending attitudes of both the Chinese and
Westerners.

Iwai Trading Company

SCAP found Iwai's plan to divest itself of seven manufacturing subsidiaries
satisfactory, so the trading company itself was allowed to remain intact.
However, Iwai found the first few years extremely difficult. Unlike C. Itoh,
the company did not specialize in textile goods, the only major item of
international trade at the time. Instead, Iwai existed mostly on domestic
trade, and in 1949 about 80 percent of its still limited business was domestic.

Though the Korean boom was not as profitable for Iwai as it was for
C. Itoh, Iwai too found it "a merciful rain after a drought" (Iwai 1964, p.
459). Total sales in the December 1950-May 1951 period were more than
twice those of the preceding six months, standing at 22.9 billion yen. By
1951 the proportion of domestic trade had declined to 64 percent. Profits
during this six months were huge: 451 million yen, an amount not to be
surpassed until 1961. On the strength of the boom, Iwai reopened its New
York office in December 1950.

Because of its huge profits, the loss of 74 million yen incurred in the
December 1951-May 1952 period was not difficult to absorb, and the
company was able to ride out the recession of 1953-54 as well. Between 1950
and 1955, Iwai rapidly diversified, and the iron and steel and other metal
products which accounted for 65 percent of its total business in 1950 were
reduced to 46 percent by the end of 1954. New offices were opened in
Karachi and Bombay in 1952, London in 1954, and Sao Paulo, Rio de
Janeiro, Djakarta and Dusseldorf in 1955. From the mid-1950s, the growth of
Iwai Trading continued on a predictable course. Its capital rose to 3
billion yen in 1961, and the total sales for the December 1962-May 1963
period approached 80 billion yen.

However, Iwai's competitors by the early 1960s were much larger. C. Itoh's
capital in 1962 was six times as large as Iwai's, and its total sales were almost
twice as big. The Mitsubishi, Mitsui, and Marubeni-Iida trading companies
each had about three times the sales of Iwai. This gap continued to widen
during the mid-1960s for several reasons. Iwai's strength lay in importing
metal products, such as iron, steel, and machinery. Its imports during the
1960s were consistently between two and three times the amount of its
exports, and the company was also having difficulty in reducing the share of
metal products to less than 45 percent of its total business. This meant that
Iwai had to wage a battle against the general trend of the economy, that is,

Japan during this period was becoming an exporter of Iwai's specialties. These legacies of an import rather than export emphasis and heavy dependence on metal products dating from the interwar years were difficult to shed in the face of aggressive and larger competitors.

Once these signs of basic difficulties began to be recognized by others, especially the banks, Iwai began to experience increasing difficulties in meeting an ever-rising need for financial resources. Profits began to fall and discounts on its papers began to rise during 1967-68, and its overseas offices, smaller in number relative to the largest trading firms, were not increasing trade volume in contrast to the steep rises reported by the leading firms. Dominated by the Iwai family and relatively less imaginative, the weakness of the management of the company began to be openly discussed in the press.

Against this background, in December 1968, Iwai (then tenth largest among the major trading companies in total sales) merged with Nisshō Trading Company (then ranked seventh) on a 2:3 stock exchange basis, despite the fact the firms were capitalized at 62.8 and 70 million yen respectively. The newly merged firm, Nisshō-Iwai, became fifth in total sales among the trading companies (though it had fallen to sixth by 1972 because of the rapid growth of Sumitomo Trading). The statement issued on the merger noted that the increased financial resources and efficiency of two networks of international trade would help the merged company in coping with "an increasingly competitive international market, and increasingly complicated and seemingly less stable international monetary conditions" (Nisshō 1968, p. 587). Postmerger data testify that Nisshō-Iwai has become an entrenched member of the Big Ten, distinctly one of the majors.[22] Iwai Bunsuke, a hikitoriya born in 1842, could have scarcely imagined that his name could survive so long and so well alongside those of Mitsui and Mitsubishi, names he undoubtedly envied at one time.

CONCLUSION

In the hope that the preceding examination has provided basic answers to such questions as how these trading companies emerged and grew, I shall now ask why these companies came to be so dominant in Japan's international trade. Why are they found in Japan and not elsewhere? And how significant has the general trading company been during the past century of Japanese economic growth? At this stage of research, the answers are necessarily tentative.

After two centuries of self-imposed sakoku during which Japan remained unaffected by the international economy, she found in the late nineteenth century that her factor endowments and relative factor prices were sufficiently different from those of her potential trading partners to promise

[22]Total sales volume of the eleventh largest company is less than one-half of the tenth largest and volume from the twelfth on falls rapidly.

large economic gains from international trade.[23] However, as already
discussed, standing in the way of active foreign trade was a general lack of
experience and the absence of institutional arrangements and human
resources necessary for international transactions. Due to this lack, transactions costs were extremely high for Japanese aspiring to trade overseas.
Linguistic and cultural barriers and geographical isolation in a period of
limited communication facilities made the cost of information and contract
negotiations nearly prohibitive. Also, given Japan's geographical distance
from a majority of her potential traders and her still underdeveloped financial
and other institutions for providing insurance and other necessary services for
international trading, any would-be trader had to risk his capital for long
periods. This was a major deterrent, for the cost of capital itself was
extremely high and few had sufficient resources to assume the risks. Thus
Meiji Japan was faced with tantalizing opportunities for economic gains but
with virtual inability to realize them. Unlike many Western nations, Japan
lacked the experience of centuries of foreign trade which might have provided
her with sufficient capital to be mobilized for international trade and, more
importantly, would have provided a chance for development of the
knowledge, institutions, and human resources needed to reduce transaction
costs.

This was the background for the emergence of the forerunners of general
trading companies. Given the high costs of conducting business through
Western and Chinese traders, a more satisfactory solution had to be found.
This, in time, took the form of the institutional arrangement we have come to
call general trading companies. The solution was an effective one. It enabled
Japan, under economic and institutional constraints then imposed, to
conduct her international trade more efficiently. In some instances, trade
which would not have taken place was made possible (profitable) because of
the newly emerging institutions' abilities to reduce risks, to realize economies
of scale, and to make effective use of scarce capital.

Once established, the trading companies grew steadily, rising to occupy a
commanding position in Japan's international trade. By the first decade of
the twentieth century, Mitsui Bussan had become a general trading company
which dealt in more than 120 commodities through a number of branch
offices abroad. Others too, on a smaller scale, followed the footsteps of
Mitsui. Thanks largely to these trading companies, the Japanese were able to
conduct more than half of their own international trade by the eve of the
First World War. When the war came, placing Japan in a position to capture a
huge windfall, the trading companies were ready and able to seize the golden
opportunity. The number of commodities they dealt in rose sharply, the
network of branch offices abroad grew apace, and the suddenly increased
scale of their trading made them more willing and able to assume larger risks.
More and more foreigners were made aware that to penetrate the thick walls
of language and culture of the new industrial power in Asia, they needed

[23]A good empirical analysis of this point is found in Huber (1971).

these trading companies as their allies and that they were well worth the commissions charged.

Tracing their development from 1914 to 1940, it is clear that the ability of these companies to obtain and create credit perhaps was their principal source of strength and growth. As this review of the histories of three selected companies has not made this point explicitly, and the point is important in understanding the growth of these companies since 1945 as well, I shall examine this key factor more closely.

Beginning with the frenzied expansion of industrial capacity during the 1914-19 period, the interwar years saw, in rapid succession, the recession of the latter half of the 1920s; the bank panic of 1927, which made the largest banks even larger and smallest disappear; the untimely return to the gold standard, which had to be abandoned shortly afterward because of the Great Depression; and, finally, the renewed industrial expansion of an increasingly militaristic economy.[24]

By the late 1920s the spurts of rapid growth and a prolonged recession had produced what could perhaps be called a dual structure in the capital market. One segment of the economy, large and often zaibatsu-connected firms, obtained capital and credit from the largest banks both in good times and bad. In good times, the giant firms were the most favored customers, and in bad times, the largest banks could ill afford to withhold needed credit from firms in which they owned large blocks of stock. For another segment of the economy, consisting of many small and medium firms, the story was entirely different. In good times, they could obtain credit only after the needs of the largest firms had been met, and in bad times, they were the first to be sacrificed. In an economy in which well over half of capital is borrowed from banks rather than by issuing stock, the fate of many firms in this second category was always precarious. Thus, during the twenty-five years just described in a highly abbreviated fashion, many small and medium firms chose to, or were forced to, become subsidiary or "affiliated" firms of giant and mostly zaibatsu-related firms in order to have access to capital.[25]

For many manufacturers and distributors who produced for export or traded in imported goods, the credit advanced by the trading companies thus was crucial. Also, just as a zaibatsu firm was able to aid its affiliated firms including general trading companies, a large trading company could extend its blessings to manufacturers and distributors in the forms of loan guarantees, partial shareholding, dispatched executives, long-term contracts, and so forth.

[24]For a further discussion of the period see Patrick (1971) and Yamamura (1972 and 1973).

[25]These observations are elaborated in Yamamura (1972, pp. 192-197). It is well known that the financial control of the zaibatsu banks and the largest zaibatsu-related firms over even the largest nonzaibatsu firms expanded rapidly during the 1920s and into the 1930s. Many large banks during this period became "organ banks," that is, the banks which owned an increasing amount of stock in the largest firms.

And these blessings proved important to the banks when deciding whether or not to extend credit to these small and medium firms.

General instability of international exchange rates and the increasing scale of trading were, of course, also important factors enhancing the growth of the trading companies. To the extent such a dual structure was the combined product of Japan's rapid growth, relative capital scarcity, existence of the zaibatsu, and other factors, the growth of a phenomenon called the general trading company, seemingly unique to Japan, must also be seen as a product of the distinct path Japan chose to follow in her efforts to industrialize.

In evaluating the growth of general trading companies in post-1945 Japan, the phrase "trend acceleration," which Ohkawa and Rosovsky (1973) use to characterize the continuing economic growth during this century, can be appropriately applied. Once postwar growth was initiated, the demand for capital became even more intense than during the prewar years. Growth was more rapid and industries more capital intensive, and the dependence of industry and commerce on banks for funds continued to rise. If the prewar-type zaibatsu had been dissolved by SCAP, the new groupings of giant firms under the old zaibatsu banners again made a financial dual structure an undeniable fact of the postwar economy. The general trading companies' historical weapon, their ability to borrow and create credit, became and continues to be a crucial factor in their success. Thus, it is readily understandable why this ability was uppermost in the mind of a director of Mitsui Bussan when he attempted to describe the virtues of his company to potential foreign customers:

Because Japanese trading companies do such an enormous volume of business, they are proffered prime commercial rates. A trading company's intermediary role acts to the advantage of all parties in a transaction; banks favor large volume business which is impossible when dealing through individual manufacturers; traders utilize savings obtained from preferential interest rates to cut operating costs; clients under contract with trading companies obtain from them the needed funds or credits at rates they could never secure if they acted individually [Sueyuki 1964, p. 55].

Of course, the trading companies' ability to realize economies of scale and to distribute risks have reached new heights thanks to the rapidly increased volume of trading, sophisticated telecommunications and data processing, and to the accumulated knowledge and experience gained from a century of learning by doing.

However, as all the economically significant advantages realized by the general trading companies are functions of their size and not all companies could become large or even survive, one should also ask why a small number of international traders grew to become these large companies.

The answer is that they were the first entrants and were blessed with a combination of favorable factors. Mitsui Bussan had an established and respected name from the Tokugawa period, was appointed the fiscal agent of the Meiji government, was given the opportunity to acquire Inoue's Senshūsha, and had the backing of Mitsui Bank. Itoh grew rapidly as a domestic wholesaler of what were for many years the most important products (cotton textile goods) in Japan's international trade. Its success in the domestic market cushioned Itoh's early difficulties in the international market. Unlike many textile wholesalers who failed because of oversanguine management during booms, Itoh treaded the volatile markets of textile goods, both domestic and international, with caution and skill. Iwai succeeded by grafting onto his successful shōkan trade direct dealings with Duff & Sons. Acquiring the necessary skills to conduct direct trade before others, Iwai used his advantage well. Becoming a designated wholesaler of the iron and steel products of Yawata was also important in assuring the survival of Iwai during the difficult 1920s, but only secondarily so because the designation was based on the size and expertise which Iwai had already attained. In all three cases, as was true for other successful general trading companies, the fact they had imaginative and capable leaders was of paramount importance. Masuda's contribution to the growth of Mitsui Bussan was great, and many a trading company, not blessed with the talents of the Itoh and Iwai father-and-son teams, disappeared.

The preceding answer is not invalidated by the fact that the Sumitomo Trading Company was a postwar entrant which managed to become one of the Big Ten. Sumitomo, as a member of close-knit group, had access to sufficiently large amounts of capital and markets (mostly firms within the group) to make it possible to enter the field on a large scale, and thus to compete against established general trading companies.[26] That it took a Sumitomo company to be a successful later entrant and that no other firms succeeded in winning a niche among the Big Ten also speaks for the point being made here. All this, of course, is no more surprising than the growth and dominance achieved by the well-managed early entrants into the automobile or electric appliances industry in the United States. In these industries too, a few later entrants succeeded in overcoming initial capital requirements and other entry problems.

Although the answer is implicit in the foregoing, one needs to ask explicitly at this point why the general trading companies emerged in Japan and not elsewhere. Though a complete analysis requires lengthy research in comparative economic and business history, I shall hazard an abbreviated answer, restricting the meaning of "elsewhere" to the Western nations.

In the West, where economic growth came much more slowly and experience in international trade was accumulated over a longer time (or benefited by the experience of others, as the United States did), institutional arrangements required for international trade also developed gradually.

[26]The Sumitomo Trading Company was organized in 1952, but it grew rapidly for "one of the major goals of the Sumitomo group was to assist the growth of the trading company" (Suzuki 1966, p. 185). The annual average growth rate of the total sales volume of the company was 23 percent between 1960 and 1969 in comparison to 19.9 percent for the Mitsubishi Trading Company, the most rapidly growing among the established companies (Arita 1972, p. 116).

Capital and both demand and supply increased over generations. All this meant costs of capital and information were similarly reduced.[27] Unlike Japan, the need and desire to trade did not come overnight before sufficient capital had been accumulated and the human and institutional resources needed had come into being.

There was another significant difference between Japan and the Western nations. Because of the linguistic and cultural similarities and geographical proximity among the Western trading partners (and they traded among themselves more than with non-Westerners), the absolute costs of information, of negotiation, and of enforcement of contracts (thus, risks as well) were significantly lower than they were for Japan.[28]

Given the lower costs of capital and information—thus, the smaller risks—a Western exporter or importer could trade profitably even without the aid of an intermediary. To put it differently, in the West the price charged for intermediation (commissions) did not justify the savings such an intermediary provided. When the costs of capital and information are relatively low, the gains resulting from the reduction in risks by product diversification are correspondingly smaller. In comparison to individual would-be Japanese traders (manufacturers), the absolute size of the capital available to the Western traders (including manufacturers) is much larger, contributing to the latter's ability to risk the capital involved in any transaction. The absence of the Japanese-style dual structure in the capital market, and the existence of better developed capital markets in the West must also be considered significant factors accounting for the institutions which emerged to conduct international trade in that part of the world. These are general comparisons in a relative sense vis-à-vis Japan, and there are exceptions during some periods and in some of the Western nations. This is admittedly a less than satisfactory attempt to explain the absence of general trading companies in Western nations, but it must suffice until further research is conducted.

Finally, I come to the most important question: How significant has the general trading company been during the past century of Japanese economic growth? The answer to this question has been suggested here, but to make it explicit, in my judgment these general trading companies were no less significant than the banking institutions and the oft-discussed government pilot plants and subsidies. Not only did these companies make trade possible

[27]In contrast to England where the interest rate at the beginning of the Industrial Revolution was significantly below 10 percent (consols were earning 5 to 6 percent) interest rates in Meiji Japan ranged between 12 and 20 percent depending on the region and the nature of the loans (Yamamura and Lewis 1971).

[28]Though cultural and linguistic differences between Japan and her trading partners may still impose higher transactions costs on Japan relative to those imposed on Europe, the efficiency of the large Japanese general trading companies today may more than compensate for this disadvantage. A detailed empirical study clearly is called for to make such a comparison in the current setting.

or more profitable during the early phase of industrialization, but later they helped to increase international trade. In Japan's rapid growth, significant contributions were made by these companies in reduced transactions costs, stimulating industries to realize economies of scale and other advantages, and developing and using resources more efficiently.

Though thorough quantitative research is needed to prove the point, it is probable that the significance of the trading companies was further enhanced because their transaction services were provided competitively. This is to suggest that Japan had the best of two worlds: both competition and economies of scale with which to reduce transactions costs and use resources more efficiently. Beyond what economic theory suggests—the difficulties in maintaining profit-maximizing collusive activities for an industry with the cost and market characteristics of the trading companies—I should add a brief note in support of my assertion that the services of the largest trading companies were provided competitively.

Competition among the Trading Companies

Evidence of competition is abundant. During the prewar period fierce battles to maintain or establish markets, overall and in various products and regions, resulted in fluctuating market shares (including those of Mitsui, the unquestioned prewar leader). Perhaps the most eloquent evidence is the fact Mitsui was able to declare an average semiannual dividend of only 18.8 percent of par value of paid-in capital even during the 1914-20 First World War boom (Togai 1972, p. 5). In this period many firms in shipping, textiles, metal products, and several other industries were distributing, especially from 1915 to 1919, dividends from no less than 50 percent to well in excess of 100 percent. During the Meiji era, trading companies were still relatively small and were competing against foreign firms. Many new trading companies appeared during the First World War boom, and the older established companies had to compete fiercely to maintain their market share. During the prolonged recession from the mid-1920s to the early 1930s, the industry was also highly competitive. Several large companies failed, and the survivors had to scramble for a slowly growing market. The remainder of the 1930s was characterized by increased competition from the new zaibatsu in the Yen Bloc regions and by increasingly difficult international economic and political conditions. From the available evidence, it seems extremely difficult to characterize the profits and market behavior of these companies during the prewar years as either monopolistic or collusive.

Evidence of competition in the postwar period is also plentiful. Not only do the rankings of the Big Ten, measured by the total amount of trading, continue to change and growth rates of the firms differ significantly, but there is also quantitative evidence for constantly fluctuating market shares in many specific commodity and regional markets and a distinct negative trend in the ratio of gross profit to the total volume of trading conducted by these ten companies. When the author of an article entitled "Japanese Trading Companies: Volume not Profits" in *Forbes* (1972) expressed surprise at the low profit margins of the largest trading companies, he was clearly attesting to the competition which prevailed among them.

There are many examples indicative of the extent of competition among the Big Ten in the postwar period, and space permits giving only a few. The annual growth rate of total trading volume between 1960 and 1969 for each of the Big Ten ranged from 11 percent to 23 percent. The ratio of total trading in 1969 to that in 1960 for each of the Big Ten was as follows, listed in order of total trading volume in 1969: Mitsubishi, 5.03; Mitsui, 4.83; Marubeni-Iida, 3.53; C. Itoh, 3.77; Nisshō-Iwai, 4.52; Sumitomo, 6.65; Tōmen, 4.25; Michimen, 2.54; Kanematsu-Gōshō, 2.54; and Ataka, 4.55.

Changes in market shares in various product markets and the general instability of the mix of commodities in which each trading company dealt are clearly seen in Table 4, which shows the changes in the product mix handled by the four largest firms. The data are for March 1969 and March 1970, that is, for changes during only a one-year period.

The mean of the same four companies' gross profit ratios (gross profit divided by the total volume of amount traded) declined, with little variation among the four, from slightly less than 2.8 percent in 1956 to about 2.1 percent by 1962, and the ratio has remained at around 2.1 percent since then (the last data examined are for 1970). These calculations are based on the financial statements issued by the four firms between 1956 and 1970.

Also revealing are dividend rates (in percentages) declared semiannually. The rates, which closely correspond to returns on paid-in capital for each

Table 4
Changes in Market Shares 1969-70
(in percent)

		Textiles	Machinery	Metal products	Chemical products[d]	Foods	Others[d]
Mitsubishi	1969[a]	8.3	20.5	34.9	9.1	12.9	14.4
	1970[b]	8.0	18.2	39.2	8.5	12.5	13.6
	Growth[c]	27.3	18.5	50.0	25.0	29.4	26.3
Mitsui	1969[a]	8.0	18.4	35.2	12.8	12.8	12.8
	1970[b]	8.3	19.8	40.8	12.7	11.5	16.6
	Growth[c]	30.0	34.8	45.5	25.0	12.5	31.3
Marubeni-	1969[a]	25.0	19.3	28.4	8.0	11.4	10.2
Iida	1970[b]	21.9	19.3	30.7	7.0	10.5	10.5
	Growth[c]	13.6	29.4	40.0	14.3	20.0	33.3
C. Itoh	1969[a]	39.8	14.3	14.2	10.8	13.3	7.2
	1970[b]	35.7	14.3	17.0	11.6	13.4	8.0
	Growth[c]	21.2	33.3	58.3	44.4	36.4	50.0

Source: Computed from Arita 1972, p. 111.

[a]The proportion (percentage) of each of these product categories in the total traded volume in March 1969.

[b]The same as [a] for March 1970.

[c]The growth rate of each product category for each form during the March 1969-March 1970 period.

[d]For Mitsui and Mitsubishi, petroleum is included in others, and for Marubeni-Iida and C. Itoh, in chemicals.

general trading company, ranged between 14 and zero during the 1963-73 period. Although Mitsui tended to lead others with a relatively consistent 14 percent, the upper limit of other companies was 12 percent. For example, in March 1964, the highest was 14 percent and the lowest 10, with six companies declaring 12 percent. In March 1968, the range was between 14 and zero with a mode (five companies) of 12 percent. Nisshō (before the merger with Iwai) declared only 2 percent and Kanematsu-Gōshō, 8 percent. But these did better than Nichimen, which declared no dividend. And in March 1972, the rates ranged between 14 and 8 with a mode (five companies) of 12. Two declared 10 percent.[29]

It is evident that a careful, quantitative study is needed to support or reject the assertion made here in order to evaluate accurately the significance of these companies in Japan's international trade and industrialization and to appraise objectively the traditional Japanese scholarship which continues to be critical of the largest trading companies.

As the role of the trading companies is changing rapidly, no final assessment of these firms is possible. However, as of 1973, it is evident these international traders seem to have entered a new phase of development. As the costs of capital and of information have declined, and with both the Japanese economy and the position of Japan in the world economy changing rapidly, these trading companies have responded by becoming active organizers and are rapidly increasing their investments abroad. Since the end of the Second World War, Western enterprises have increasingly become multinational in order to make more efficient use of their capital, to reduce costs of information, and to minimize risks in the new setting of the postwar international market. At the same time, Japanese general trading companies, perhaps Japan's first knowledge industry and by now the largest and most sophisticated, are rapidly becoming organizers of multinationals both in competition and in cooperation with Western multinationals. The methods of conducting international trade in Japan and in the West are thus perhaps for the first time converging.

REFERENCES

Abe, Kenji. 1972. *Nihon Tsūka Keizai Shi no Kenkyū*. Kinokuniya Shoten.
Arita, Kyōsuke. 1972. *Sōgōshōsha*. Nihon Keizai Shinbunsha. First published in 1970. Page references are to 1972 reprinting.
Cheung, Steven N. S. 1969. "Transaction Costs, Risk Aversion, and the Choice of Contractual Arrangements." *Journal of Law and Economics*, 12 (April 1969).
Daiichi Ginkō. 1957. *Daiichi Ginkō Shi*. Vol. 1. Daiichi Ginkō.
Dainihon Sanshi-kai, ed. 1935. *Nihon Sanshigyō Shi*. Dainihon Sanshigyōkai.
Davis, Lance, and Douglass C. North. 1972. *Institutional Change and American Economic Growth*. Cambridge University Press.

[29]See the reports on these companies found in one of the weekly issues (usually appearing in February of each year) of *Tōyō Keizai*.

Demsetz, Harold. 1968. "The Cost of Transacting." *Quarterly Journal of Economics* 72 (Feb. 1968).

Economist. 1967. "The Rising Sun." May 27-June 3, 1967.

Fellner, William. 1969. "Specific Interpretations of Learning by Doing." *Journal of Economic Theory* 1 (Aug. 1969).

Forbes. 1972. "Japanese Trading Companies: Volume, not Profit." *Forbes* 109 (May 1, 1972).

Fox, Grace. 1969. *Britain and Japan, 1858-1883*. Oxford University Press.

Hattori, Shisō, ed. 1955. *Kindai Nihon Jimbutsu Keizai Shimpō Shi*. Tōyōkeizai.

Hollerman, Leon. 1966. *Japan's Dependence on the World Economy*. Princeton University Press.

Huber, Richard. 1971. "Effects on Prices of Japan's Entry into World Commerce after 1858." *Journal of Political Economy* 79 (May/June 1971).

Itoh Chū Shōji. 1969. *Itoh Chū Shōji 100-nen*. Itoh Chū Shōji.

Iwai Sangyō Kabushiki Kaisha. 1964. *Iwai Hyakunen Shi*. Iwai Sangyō Kabushiki Kaisha.

Kajinishi Mitsuhaya. 1954. *Nihon Shihonshugi Hattatsu Shi*. Yūhikaku.

Kōsei Torihiki Iinkai [Fair Trade Commission]. 1955. *Saihensei Katei ni aru Bōeki Shōsha no Kihon Dōkō*.

    . 1971. *Nihon no Kigyō-shūchū: Dai-kigyō ni yoru Shihon Shūchū, Kabushiki-shoyū, Gappei no Jittai*.

Matsui, Kiyoshi. 1950. *Nihon Bōeki-ron*. Yūhikaku.

Mitsui Ginkō [Mitsui Bank]. 1957. *Mitsui Ginkō 80-nen Shi*. Mitsui Ginkō.

Miyamoto, Mataji. 1963. "Meiji-ki ni okeru Bōeki Kaisha no Seiritsu Katei to Bōeki Shihon no Sangyō Ikusei: Iwai Shōten no Baai." *Osaka Daigaku Keizaigaku* 12 (March 1963).

Nakagawa, Keiichirō. 1967. "Nihon no Kōgyōka Katei ni okeru Soshikika Sareta Kigyōsha Katsudō." *Japan Business Review* 2 (Nov. 1967).

Nihon Ginkō [Bank of Japan]. 1966. *Hundred-Year Statistics of the Japanese Economy*.

Nisshō Kabushiki Kaisha. 1968. *Nisshō 40-nen no Ayumi*. Nisshō Kabushiki Kaisha.

Noda, Kazuo. 1966. *Nihon Kaisha Shi*. Bungei Shunjū.

    . 1967. *Zaibatsu*. Chūōkōron.

North, Douglass C., and Robert P. Thomas. 1970. "An Economic Theory of the Growth of the Western World." *Economic History Review* 23 (April 1970).

    . 1971. "The Rise and Fall of the Manorial System: A Theoretical Model." *Journal of Economic History* 31 (Dec. 1972).

Ogawa, Kunihara. 1972. "Meiji Seifu no Bōeki Seisaku to Yushutsu Kaisanbutsu." *Shakai Keizai Shigaku*, vol. 38, no. 1.

Ohkawa, Kazushi, and Henry Rosovsky. 1973. *Japanese Economic Growth: Trend Acceleration in the Twentieth Century*. Stanford University Press.

Patrick, Hugh. 1967. "Japan: 1868-1914." In *Banking in the Early Stages of Industrialization*, edited by Rondo Cameron. Oxford University Press.

    . 1971. "The Economic Muddle in the 1920s." In *Dilemmas of Growth in Prewar Japan*, edited by James W. Morley. Princeton University Press.

Rosovsky, Henry. 1966. "Japan's Transition to Economic Growth, 1868-1885." In *Industrialization in Two Systems*, edited by Henry Rosovsky. Wiley.

Sakudō, Yōtarō. 1963. "Bōeki Shōsha no Hatten to Kansaikei Kigyō no Keisei: Osaka KB Bōeki Shōsha no Keiei Shi-teki Kenkyū." *Osaka Daigaku Keizaigaku* 12 (March 1963).

Shibagaki, Kazuo. 1969. *Nihon Kinyūshihon Bunseki.* Tokyo University Press.

Sōrifu, Tōkei-kyoku [Office of the Prime Minister, Statistics Bureau]. 1973. *Monthly Statistics of Japan* 140 (Feb. 1973).

Sueyuki, Wakasugi. 1964. "How the Japanese Trading Companies Can Assist Banks and Businessmen." *Burrough's Clearing House* 48 (Sept. 1964).

Suzuki, Kenichi. 1966. *Sumitomo: Kigyō Gurūpu no Dōtai.* Chūōkōron.

Togai, Yoshio. Undated. "Nihon Mengyō-shōji no Mitsui Bussan to Mitsubishi Shōji." *Senshū Keieigaku Ronshū,* no. 3.

———. 1968. "Sōgōshōsha toshite no Mitsui Bussan Kaisha no Teichaku." *Japan Business History Review,* vol. 3, no. 1.

———. 1971. *Shin Mitsui Dokuhon.* Sawa Shoten.

———. 1972. "Sūkei kara mita Taishō-Shōwa-ki no Mitsui Bussan Kaisha." *Senshū Keieigaku Ronshū* 11 (March 1972).

Tōyō Bōseki Kabushiki Kaisha. 1953. *Tōyō Bōseki 70-nen Shi.* Tōyō Bōseki Kabushiki Kaisha.

Tōyō Keizai. 1972. [Weekly economic newsmagazine.] Tōyō Keizai Shimpōsha.

Tōyō Menka Kabushiki Kaisha. 1960. *Tōmen 40-nen Shi.* Tōyō Menka Kabushiki Kaisha.

Tsuda, Noboru. 1960. *Nihon Bōeki no Shiteki Kōsatsu.* Gaikoku Kawase Bōeki Kenkyūkai.

Uchida, Katsutoshi. 1971. *Sōgōshōsha.* Kōdansha.

Yamamura, Kozo. 1967. "The Role of the Samurai in the Development of Modern Banking in Japan." *Journal of Economic History* 27 (June 1967).

———. 1972. "Japan, 1868-1930: A Revised View." In *Banking and Economic Development,* edited by Rondo Cameron. Oxford University Press.

———. 1973. "Then Came the Great Depression: Japan's Interwar Years." In *The Great Depression Revisited,* edited by Herman van der Wee. Martinus Nijhoff.

Yamamura, Kozo, and K. Lewis. 1971. "Industrialization and Interregional Interest Rate Structure." *Explorations in Economic History* 8 (June 1971).

Yasuoka, Shigeaki. 1960. *Zaibatsu Keisei Shi no Kenkyū.* Minerva Shobō.

Young, Allyn. 1928. "Increasing Returns and Economic Progress." *Economic Journal,* Dec. 1928.

Firm Size and Japan's Export Structure:

A Microview of Japan's Changing

Export Competitiveness since Meiji

William V. Rapp

In this paper I explore some relationships among firm size, export development, and Japan's industrialization. The roles of large and small firms in Japan's economic development have been the subject of much research and discussion, yet little has been done to combine this with trade development, though trade is also a much analyzed aspect of Japan's economic evolution. These interrelationships appear to have important historical, theoretical, and policy implications.[1] More specifically, this paper chronologically traces and examines the dramatic change in the production structure of exports. It does this by analyzing the evolution of large export producers as a function of both industrial development and changing comparative advantage, with emphasis on the latter's relationship to "export concentration" and "export specialization." Although I do not discuss other countries, I believe Japan's current production and export structure in terms of firm size for her major export industries is probably similar to that of other advanced industrialized nations.

The paper's argument is that in Japan dominance of export production by large manufacturing firms has been systematically increasing over time and

The author would like to thank his wife, Diane Demont Rapp, for her invaluable help in gathering and preparing some of the data and editing the final manuscript. In addition, he wishes to acknowledge assistance from Kazuo Hayakawa, Gary Saxonhouse, and Hugh Patrick. Solomon Levine, Masu Uekusa, William Lockwood, Kozo Yamamura, C. Tate Ratcliffe, Yasukichi Yasuba, Kenzo Yukizawa, and Yoko Sazanami also supplied useful comments and advice. However, the author must accept full responsibility for the opinions and errors set forth in the paper. Keiko Takamatsu typed the final manuscript.

[1]A brief survey of the literature as well as discussions with various Japanese and American professors indicates little or no research on this subject for

that it is important to understand this trend. It is estimated 70 to 80 percent of current manufactured exports are produced by firms of over five hundred employes compared to about 50 percent of total shipments.[2] Yet historically the major proportion of Japan's exports have been produced in labor-intensive industries and by industries composed primarily of small firms.[3] For this reason, many Japanese policymakers are still concerned about the dependence of small- and medium-sized firms on export sales. This was indicated by the government's strong resistence in 1972 to a second revaluation, in the belief it would have a heavy impact on these firms. But in reality small- and medium-sized firms were much less affected than anticipated because, with the exception of a few firms and industries, exports account for less than 8 percent of their total production. As large firms produce most current exports, the effects of revaluation occurred more gradually than expected.

Large firms have greater financial, personnel, and material resources than small firms and can absorb the effects of export price changes while deciding whether to invest overseas, shift into new products or business, reduce prices, and so forth. Further, having once decided on a strategy, it is easier for them to follow through and implement it. At the same time, given exports' importance in their total sales (on average 15 to 20 percent), there is a definite corporate commitment to maintain overseas markets and to preserve previous marketing investment. As these firms have some control over price, output, and resource availability due to their relative size and market power, their decisions may differ somewhat from the perfectly competitive case and, particularly for foreign investment vis-à-vis price changes, will have a sizable impact on Japan's balance of payments in both the current and capital

---

Japan. Melvin and Warne (1973) and Pursell and Snape (1973) also state that the impact of firm size and industrial concentration on trade is a new theoretical and empirical research area for other countries as well.

[2]Based on calculations made later in this paper using data from Tsūsanshō 1973 and *Nihon Bōeki Geppō* (Okurashō). Also, in 1970 the two hundred leading export producers shipped about 60 percent of all exports, though accounting for less than 34 percent of total manufactured shipments and 0.03 percent of total manufacturing enterprises. Over 190 of these companies are among the top five hundred manufacturers ranked by sales, and all have over five hundred employes. (These rankings include only publicly held companies, so excluded are joint ventures and foreign-owned firms; however, this does not matter to the argument.) (*President Directory* 1971). The role of these two hundred firms is discussed in more detail later.

[3]In 1935, small manufacturing firms are estimated to have produced 65 percent of all manufactured exports and in 1956, 60 percent. Going back to 1868, rice, green tea, copper, and raw silk accounted for 95 percent of exports and in 1890, 60 percent. These products were produced primarily by small production units. For further discussion, see the sources of these data: Takahashi (1935, p. 80) and Tsūsanshō, *Chūshō Kigyō Hakusho* (1963-73 annual editions).

account. Their actions should thus be explicitly considered by the government in terms of increasing demand for social overhead and infrastructure investment as well as in terms of overall economic policy.

An additional development resulting from the decision to protect well-developed export markets, particularly through foreign investment, is the emergence of large Japanese multinational companies. Though the case for or against multinationals is neither clear-cut nor the concern of this paper, some observers hold multinationals can assert themselves independently of their home governments and can also exert greater competitive force in home markets.[4] As multinationals are already an important policy issue, a greater understanding of the role of large firms in Japan's export development is necessary. Some of the historical background for developing such an understanding is provided in this chapter.

The relative importance of an exporting industry is measured simply by taking the industry's share of total exports. To measure the comparative advantage of a given industry or group of firms relative to other industries or firms, I have computed their "export intensity." This is the ratio of an industry's share of total manufactured exports to its share of total manufacturing shipments. When the export intensity is greater than one, the industry is more export-oriented than Japanese industry as a whole, presumably because of comparative advantage. Thus, a ranking of export intensities provides a ranking of comparative advantage by industry; and over time, changes in the rankings represent changes in comparative advantage.

Concentration, both in terms of exports and total shipments, is also taken up. For my purposes, concentration is measured by share of firms with over five hundred employes in exports and total shipments.[5] The greater their share of exports and shipments, the greater the export or industry concentration. This definition is different than that used in concentration studies per se, but is appropriate for showing the changing role of large firms in exports, which is the purpose of this paper. The degree of concentration is computed by industry on the basis of available data, which become fairly complete after 1960 but are generally spotty for previous periods. Information on the textile industry is the most complete. Given these data, one can then evaluate the changing role of large firms in exports on the basis of changing comparative advantage and/or changes in concentration by industry. This is the main thrust of my inquiry.

[4]There is evidence on an intercountry basis that expanding market area contributes significantly to productivity increases and cost efficiency (Pryor 1972).

[5]Though perhaps over time this measure might seem inappropriate given expected changes in average firm size and in the distribution of firms having fewer than or more than five hundred employes, in reality this is not the case. From 1909 through the post-World War II period average firm size remains remarkably close to thirty employes, except during the 1920s when it rises to between thirty-five and forty. Further, the distribution of firms by size of plant employment also remains remarkably constant.   (note continues)

However, to explore the issue of firm size and export competitiveness more deeply, I also examine export specialization by firm size by industry. That is, even if large firms account for an increasing proportion of exports, this may be due primarily to differences between Japan's export product structure and her industrial product structure. Further, though it may be shown that large firms export absolutely more than small firms, do they export relatively more? Aggregate data suggests they do (18 versus 8 percent of sales), but a more detailed examination of this issue is required. In the paper, I therefore examine whether, among large firms that export, large firms export relatively more. In effect, this is an examination of export specialization by firm size for each industry. The results indicate export specialization in fact decreases as a function of increasing firm size.

JAPAN'S INDUSTRIALIZATION AND EVOLVING TRADE STRUCTURE

As has been examined in considerable detail elsewhere, Japan's trade development is a reflection of its industrial evolution.[6] As the economy has grown and incomes have risen (Table 1), wages and capital costs have altered so that traditional processed primary and labor-intensive industries such as food, handicrafts, and apparel have become relatively less competitive. At the same time, as incomes have risen, people have demanded more sophisticated products, and larger end-use demand has justified production of capital goods. Thus factor costs and demand changes have combined to shift industrial production from light, simple, labor-intensive products having a large initial domestic demand to more capital and technologically intensive goods.

Factories with over 500 employes as a percentage of all firms

Year:	1909	1925	1937	1949	1956	1964	1970
Percentage:	0.4	1.1	0.7	0.6	0.5	0.5	0.5

As this shows, only in the 1920s did the share deviate very much. Thus, I believe this consistency makes the over five-hundred employe basis a suitable, if arbitrary, cut-off. The Japanese government uses over three hundred employes to define a large firm.

Most of the industrial data for this study are taken from MITI's *Census of Manufactures* (Tsūsanshō, *Kōgyō*). Those data exclude establishments (plants) and firms of four or fewer employes; their contribution to exports is assumed to be negligible. Also, the data are collected at the level of individual plants (or "factories"). As larger firms may have several plants, the plant data used actually understate concentration and the general results given in this paper. For example, although data for 1968 indicate firms with over three hundred employes numbered 3384, they had 3946 plants, and accounted for 58.4 percent of total shipments compared to 50.6 percent on a plant basis. A similar argument is also made later with respect to treating wholly-owned subsidiaries as separate corporations.

[6]For example, see Rapp 1967a, Akamatsu 1962, Kojima 1973, and the works listed in Rapp 1967b, pp. 1-2.

Table 1
Japan
(1928-32 prices)

Year	Real per capita income (in dollars)	Wage interest ratio index	Industrial production as a percentage of GNP	Heavy industry as a percentage of industry[a]	Ratio of heavy industry as a percentage of exports compared to production
1890	57	37.1	9.8	12.1	–
1900	81	37.0	29.8	17.5	–
1910	88	67.3	23.1	31.9	–
1920	112	58.7	27.0	46.0	–
1930	192	110.7	28.6	50.0	0.2
1938	225	126.4	34.5	63.2	0.3
1948	128	40.9	30.8	56.0	0.7
1958	276	128.8	33.5	57.7	0.8
1968	750	241.1	38.0	71.0	1.0
By 1975[b]	1500	480.0		74.4	1.1

Sources: JERC 1972, Keizai Kikaku-chō 1970, Nihon Ginkō 1966, Rapp 1967a.
[a]Heavy industry includes machinery, metal, and chemical industries as opposed to food, textiles, apparel, miscellaneous manufacturing, and so forth.
[b]Estimated by author.

However, it takes time for industries to become internationally competitive once they have begun production. There typically is a lag between initial production and export competitiveness. For this reason, the proportion of industries such as food, textiles, pottery, and handicrafts in total exports during Japan's early years of development exceeded their proportion in total production. This became particularly noticeable in the 1920s and 30s as Japan's so-called heavy industries (steel, machinery, and chemicals) reached a stage where their proportion of production exceeded light industry's proportion of total production (Table 1).

Concommitant with this, it has been demonstrated historically that when Japanese industries first exported they were rather uncompetitive by international standards and exported to less-developed countries having few domestic producers, so that competition was only from other imports.[7] However, as Japanese firms have increased production and further lowered costs, export markets have shifted to the more advanced countries where markets are larger. Also, as particular Japanese industries have gained comparative advantage, more advanced countries such as the United States have lost it. That is, comparative advantage is a dynamic reflection of changes in industrial structure under conditions of economic growth and shifts in demand which produce differential growth rates and thus changes in relative production costs. Japan's relatively high investment rates and high growth

[7]The various points concerning the interaction of industrial and export development have been demonstrated in Rapp (1967a).

have of course accelerated this process, with the result that Japan has shifted its industrial structure and comparative advantage quite rapidly.[8] An extension of this industry-export development scenario for the purposes of this paper is the degree to which this shifting industrial structure and comparative advantage have meant a greater export role for large manufacturers.

PRE-WORLD WAR I (1870-1919)

In 1870, food, textiles, and apparel (mostly raw silk) accounted for over 90 percent of exports. This dropped to 84 percent in 1880, 78 in 1890, and 72 in 1900 (Table 2). This decline is mostly accounted for by a relative decrease in food exports, as rice and green tea became less important. In its early stages of economic development, Japan, like any less developed country, exported processed primary goods and imported manufactured products. By the 1909-19 period the industrial structure had shifted enough that processed primary goods were decreasing in importance compared to simple manufactured exports. Food and metal (mostly copper) exports maintained or lowered their share of exports compared to industry shipments, whereas textiles, ceramics, and miscellaneous manufactures increased their proportion.[9] Textiles especially dominated export production: 61.9, 64.8, and 69.9 percent respectively in 1909, 1914, and 1919, compared to 50.7, 48.1, and 51.0 percent of total shipments.

It is not possible to say anything about distribution of shipments according to firm size until 1929. One can, however, indicate the distribution of firms by industry as well as the employment distribution (Table 3), and, in addition, compute average firm size by industry according to employment and shipments (Table 4). These tables show that with the exception of textiles, export distribution was toward industries with a small proportion of large firms (over 499 employes) and little employment concentration. Similarly, again with the exception of textiles, industries with both a lower than average number of employes and average shipment size (Table 4) accounted for 24.4 and 16.8 percent of exports in 1909 and 1919 or 64.0 and 56.0 percent of nontextile exports respectively. (This compares to 18.6 percent in 1937 or 42.6 percent of nontextile exports.) Thus the scale of export industries other than textiles is smaller than that of textiles. Average firm-size weighted by exports falls below that for textiles alone (Table 4), and output per worker on this basis is less than the national average.

The data further show that the industries which maintained a high export intensity (share of exports exceeding that of total shipments) or increased their export intensity during the 1909-19 period were textiles, ceramics, and

[8]For a more detailed description of this process, see Abegglen and Rapp (1972).

[9]When an industry's share of total exports (Table 2) exceeds its share of total shipments, the industry's export orientation or emphasis (that is, "export intensity") is greater than 1.00.

miscellaneous manufactures, whereas metals and wood products declined sharply. Others remained relatively constant.

Industries increasing their share of total production were chemicals, metals, and machinery. Food, publishing, and miscellaneous manufactures lost share, and textiles, ceramics, and wood products were relatively unchanged. Thus, as might be expected, the leading exporters began to peak out in terms of domestic growth and found rising demand overseas. But the rapidly growing domestic sectors had not yet begun export expansion. The crossover effect seen in metals reflects the declining importance of copper exports on the one hand and the rising importance of domestic iron and steel production on the other. Processed raw materials such as wood, food, and copper were near the end of their product life cycle, with consumption becoming limited to domestic markets and exports beginning to fall. This pattern reflects the product and industry evolution described earlier.

The importance of large firms in these three groupings is different. Among the processed primary raw material industries food, lumber, and copper (most of metal in 1909), the number of firms with over five hundred employes is extremely small, less than 0.1 percent, whereas there is a very high proportion of small firms with under fifty employes. In addition, these small firms account for about 60 percent of total employment in these industries. The exports of these industries, therefore, were produced by small- and medium-sized firms with little or no export concentration.[10]

However, the second generation of export industries (textiles, ceramics, and miscellaneous manufacturers or the so-called light industries), whose export intensity rises in 1909-19, have a higher proportion of large firms than the raw material processors. In the case of ceramics and textiles this proportion rises. However, there is a difference in scale and the economic importance of firm size among these industries. Textile firms with over 499 persons employ a large proportion of the industry total (28.1 percent in 1909, rising to 37.6 percent in 1919). Ceramics and miscellaneous manufacturers do not (ceramics: 40.8 percent in 1909 and 15.8 percent in 1919; miscellaneous: 4.5 percent in 1909 and 5.3 percent in 1919). Certain ceramic industries such as glass, however, may be subject to economies of scale. This conclusion seems supported by the fact that after 1929 the proportion of total production accounted for by large firms exceeds their proportion in employment. This is

[10]Early production data by firm size are not available for silk reeling (raw silk, Japan's most important prewar processed raw material export). However, examination of postwar data shows no reeling plants with over 499 employes. Plants of fewer than 50 account for 80 percent of the firms and 13.7 percent of production. Plants with between 100 and 300 employes account for the bulk of production (68 percent). Given modernization between 1909 and 1964, an upgrading of optimal plant size is not surprising. Of course, there has probably been some substitution of capital for labor during the period as well. But the current absence of any really large firms indicates silk reeling in 1909 probably falls in a category similar to that of other processed raw materials.

Table 2
Distribution of Exports, Shipments, and Factories by Industry 1870-1937
(in percent, except export intensities are ratios)

Year		Food	Textiles and apparel	Lumber and wood	Publishing	Chemicals	Ceramics	Metals	Machinery	Miscellaneous
1870	Exports	41.4	51.4	–	–	5.0	–	1.4	–	0.7
1880	Exports	40.6	43.7	0.4	–	5.9	0.4	4.3	–	4.7
1890	Exports	25.0	42.9	1.6	0.2	7.4	2.9	12.8	0.2	7.1
1900	Exports	12.5	59.9	2.1	–	6.0	1.9	8.2	0.6	8.7
1909	Exports	12.5	61.9	2.5	0.2	5.4	2.3	7.1	1.1	6.9
	Shipments	18.5	50.7	2.6	2.0	10.1	3.3	4.2	5.4	3.2
	Intensity	0.7	1.2	1.0	0.1	0.5	0.7	1.7	0.2	2.2
	Factories	19.1	48.6	5.4	3.0	4.3	5.9	3.3	4.8	5.7
1914	Exports	11.3	64.8	2.7	0.1	5.1	2.0	6.4	1.0	6.5
	Shipments	16.1	48.1	2.7	2.1	12.0	2.8	5.4	8.1	2.8
	Intensity	0.7	1.3	1.0	0.05	0.4	0.7	1.2	0.1	2.3
	Factories	18.1	44.8	6.4	3.9	4.5	5.3	4.3	5.8	7.0
1919	Exports	7.5	69.9	1.7	0.1	6.2	2.6	5.1	1.9	4.9
	Shipments	10.8	51.0	2.9	1.2	10.5	3.2	8.2	10.3	1.9
	Intensity	0.7	1.4	0.6	0.08	0.6	0.8	0.6	0.2	2.6
	Factories	15.6	43.0	6.8	2.8	5.8	6.2	5.6	8.0	5.9
1921	Exports	6.7	73.7	1.8	0.2	5.3	3.3	2.9	2.2	3.9
	Shipments	16.1	46.5	3.6	1.9	10.2	3.0	6.0	10.4	2.3
	Intensity	0.4	1.6	0.5	0.1	0.5	1.1	0.5	0.2	1.7
	Factories	16.7	40.5	9.0	3.1	5.3	5.2	5.3	7.0	7.6

Table 2 (continued)

Year		Food	Textiles and apparel	Lumber and wood	Publishing	Chemicals	Ceramics	Metals	Machinery	Miscellaneous
1925	Exports	6.3	78.5	1.3	0.1	4.9	2.8	1.7	1.2	3.2
	Shipments	15.9	50.2	2.7	2.4	11.1	2.7	6.9	6.6	1.5
	Intensity	0.4	1.6	0.5	0.04	0.4	1.0	0.2	0.2	2.1
	Factories	20.6	37.8	7.4	4.3	5.3	5.2	6.2	8.3	4.8
1929	Exports	7.9	74.4	1.4	0.1	5.5	3.1	2.2	2.0	3.4
	Shipments	15.0	42.9	2.8	2.5	13.5	3.0	9.5	9.2	1.5
	Intensity	0.5	1.7	0.5	0.04	0.4	1.0	0.2	0.2	2.3
	Factories	20.0	36.2	8.3	4.3	5.4	5.9	6.4	8.8	4.5
1933	Exports	8.8	63.1	1.5	0.2	8.2	3.5	5.1	4.1	5.7
	Shipments	12.9	38.5	2.4	2.3	16.5	3.0	12.1	10.4	1.8
	Intensity	0.7	1.6	0.6	0.09	0.5	1.2	0.4	0.4	3.2
	Factories	18.0	34.9	8.7	4.3	5.7	5.3	7.8	10.9	4.5
1937	Exports	7.9	54.5	1.7	0.3	10.0	3.6	8.8	8.0	5.1
	Shipments	9.0	27.3	2.4	1.7	17.8	2.7	22.8	14.3	2.0
	Intensity	0.9	2.0	0.7	0.2	0.6	1.3	0.4	0.6	2.6
	Factories	15.7	31.5	9.7	3.7	5.5	5.3	9.6	13.8	5.4

Sources: Tsūsanshō Daijin Kambō 1961; Okurashō 1938; Oriental Economist 1935.
Notes: Production data by industry are not available for years before 1909. Intensity = export intensity (ratio of share of exports, first row, to share of shipments, second row).

Table 3

Distribution of Firms, Employment, and Shipments according to Firm Size by Industry
(in percent)

Year	Number of employes	Food share of			Textiles-apparel share of			Lumber-wood-share of		
		Firms	Employment	Shipments	Firms	Employment	Shipments	Firms	Employment	Shipments
1909	5-49	98.1	84.5	–	89.1	37.5	–	96.8	77.5	–
	over 499	0.03	1.5	–	0.8	28.1	–	–	–	–
1914	5-49	97.7	84.3	–	85.0	30.5	–	96.5	70.3	–
	over 499	0.07	3.0	–	1.1	31.3	–	0.1	3.5	–
1919	5-49	96.7	75.5	–	85.3	26.7	–	95.5	68.9	–
	over 499	0.06	2.6	–	1.4	37.6	–	–	2.6	–
1921	5-49	97.3	78.0	–	86.4	27.9	–	96.3	73.7	–
	over 499	0.01	0.9	–	1.3	36.6	–	–	–	–
1925	5-49	96.8	62.9	–	83.8	21.7	–	96.1	74.5	–
	over 499	0.3	17.0	–	1.9	44.7	–	–	0.9	–
1929	5-49	97.5	74.2	52.8	84.5	22.6	18.7	97.0	76.1	70.2
	over 499	0.05	2.6	3.4	1.7	40.6	47.2	–	–	–
1933	5-49	97.3	76.8	54.6	87.2	27.7	20.1	97.3	79.0	73.1
	over 499	0.04	2.2	3.9	1.3	32.2	47.4	–	–	–
1937	5-49	96.8	71.5	55.3	90.3	31.4	21.7	97.7	79.6	71.2
	over 499	0.03	3.0	4.8	1.1	34.6	48.9	–	–	–

Table 3 (continued)

Year	Number of employes	Publishing share of			Chemicals share of			Ceramics share of		
		Firms	Employment	Shipments	Firms	Employment	Shipments	Firms	Employment	Shipments
1909	5-49	91.6	56.0	–	93.1	49.1	–	94.9	58.5	–
	over 499	0.2	5.8	–	0.1	2.2	–	0.1	4.0	–
1914	5-49	90.9	52.6	–	87.6	39.5	–	93.5	53.1	–
	over 499	0.2	8.8	–	0.5	10.2	–	0.3	12.8	–
1919	5-49	89.9	50.8	–	84.7	33.5	–	91.0	43.4	–
	over 499	0.2	5.4	–	0.6	16.9	–	0.3	12.8	–
1921	5-49	90.7	51.8	–	87.0	38.7	–	92.5	47.3	–
	over 499	0.1	4.2	–	0.6	15.3	–	0.4	14.3	–
1925	5-49	91.8	51.2	–	85.7	33.0	–	91.2	42.5	–
	over 499	0.2	4.2	–	1.0	21.8	–	0.5	19.6	–
1929	5-49	93.2	55.8	34.4	85.9	31.6	26.7	92.6	44.2	22.3
	over 499	0.2	5.6	14.5	0.9	23.4	18.5	0.3	14.0	26.1
1933	5-49	94.5	58.8	36.2	85.5	28.8	22.9	92.2	46.5	23.7
	over 499	0.2	7.4	14.0	0.9	30.5	25.8	0.2	9.1	13.0
1937	5-49	95.3	61.4	32.4	85.7	20.4	18.4	91.6	41.6	21.2
	over 499	0.2	7.8	20.7	1.6	48.8	38.6	0.3	11.7	22.8

Table 3 (continued)

Year	Number of employes	Metals share of			Machinery share of			Miscellaneous share of		
		Firms	Employment	Shipments	Firms	Employment	Shipments	Firms	Employment	Shipments
1909	5-49	94.8	58.3	–	92.0	33.3	–	90.9	44.4	–
	over 499	–	–	–	0.7	35.9	–	0.2	4.5	–
1914	5-49	94.0	50.9	–	90.8	23.9	–	92.0	51.2	–
	over 499	0.4	15.6	–	1.1	51.5	–	0.1	3.9	–
1919	5-49	91.9	40.0	–	88.2	20.1	–	91.9	49.9	–
	over 499	0.7	27.7	–	1.4	55.5	–	0.2	5.3	–
1921	5-49	93.7	43.8	–	90.1	23.0	–	94.5	64.7	–
	over 499	0.5	26.4	–	1.3	53.0	–	–	0.5	–
1925	5-49	93.0	34.2	–	89.1	20.0	–	93.8	58.4	–
	over 499	0.6	39.1	–	1.6	56.8	–	0.1	2.5	–
1929	5-49	92.9	40.6	22.6	91.9	28.0	21.6	95.3	58.0	54.5
	over 499	0.4	21.1	28.4	0.9	45.6	44.6	0.2	15.5	9.8
1933	5-49	93.6	45.3	25.1	92.5	32.4	21.4	95.0	59.1	58.7
	over 499	0.5	23.8	42.1	0.8	40.6	44.1	0.1	9.9	8.4
1937	5-49	93.0	32.3	17.3	91.3	26.2	20.0	95.5	62.5	64.3
	over 499	0.7	37.0	60.3	0.9	49.0	51.3	0.1	9.5	4.2

Source: Tsūsanshō Daijin Kambō 1961.

Table 4
Average Number of Employes and Shipments per Firm by Industry 1909-1937
(shipments in thousand yen)

Year		Food	Textiles-apparel	Lumber-wood	Publishing	Chemicals	Ceramics	Metals	Machinery	Miscellaneous	Total manufacturing	Weighted by exports[a]
1909	Employes	12.7	33.1	14.0	22.8	22.2	21.2	19.1	33.0	22.1	25.6	26.8
	Shipments	24.0	25.9	12.2	16.8	58.3	13.9	31.7	28.2	14.2	24.8	24.2
1914	Employes	16.8	42.6	17.7	23.7	32.3	25.9	22.1	45.5	21.7	32.1	33.2
	Shipments	38.9	46.9	18.0	23.9	116.9	22.6	54.0	61.3	17.6	42.2	40.7
1919	Employes	18.4	52.7	20.9	29.2	46.3	32.2	35.6	66.4	25.8	41.4	42.4
	Shipments	109.2	186.9	67.7	65.0	283.3	81.6	220.9	204.2	49.9	157.6	153.8
1921	Employes	15.2	48.7	12.1	29.7	40.4	27.8	30.9	57.0	20.8	34.6	39.5
	Shipments	101.8	121.6	42.4	67.0	202.9	60.0	118.5	157.6	32.6	105.9	104.6
1925	Employes	19.4	58.2	16.6	28.6	44.9	24.3	36.6	62.9	21.3	40.9	46.3
	Shipments	109.1	188.6	51.4	78.5	297.3	73.2	156.6	113.2	42.6	141.8	153.6
1929	Employes	14.3	52.1	14.7	24.9	45.7	24.0	29.6	43.6	19.9	34.5	40.9
	Shipments	97.8	154.3	43.8	74.8	322.5	65.2	193.0	135.9	44.6	130.2	131.0
1933	Employes	13.0	40.8	12.8	21.1	47.7	23.1	26.7	36.7	18.7	29.4	31.7
	Shipments	79.0	121.5	31.1	59.6	317.5	63.1	170.4	105.7	43.4	110.1	104.0
1937	Employes	13.0	35.7	12.3	19.8	64.9	24.7	35.9	46.9	17.4	30.9	30.3
	Shipments	89.2	134.4	37.7	70.9	504.8	80.1	369.4	161.1	57.5	155.0	129.5

Sources: Tsūsanshō Daijin Kambō 1961, Oriental Economist 1935, Okurashō 1938.

[a] Weighting by exports is a measure of what total employment and the total number of firms would be if output were fixed but distributed according to export production, fixing average firm size and output per firm for each industry. From these new totals, I then calculate average firm size for industry as a whole. This procedure thus assumes neutrality between exports and firm size within industries.

not true for miscellaneous manufacturers, where workers in small firms (under 50) are more productive in terms of output per worker than in large firms. The indications are therefore that scale is not important in terms of production efficiency in miscellaneous manufacturing but is in textiles and some ceramic-related products. This conclusion is further supported by evidence presented later, on the current distribution by industry of the two hundred largest exporting firms.

The one common factor among these three industries, however, is their labor intensity relative to manufacturing as a whole. Output per worker for all Japanese industry is greater than output per worker for textiles, ceramics, and miscellaneous manufactures. This differs from some raw material and capital-intensive industries such as food, metals, and chemicals, where output per worker is higher than average. Thus the comparative advantage shift before and during World War I was from raw material processing, where large firms played a small production role, to more labor-intensive manufacturing industries where large firms played a greater but still not dominant role, and where production technology was labor intensive relative to other industries but still subject to economies of scale.

Because of the importance of scale in the textile industry and its large share of total exports, one can hypothesize that large firms played an important role in exports even at this time. This assumption is supported by unpublished data gathered by Saxonhouse breaking down cotton yarn exports according to individual spinning firms. Large spinners seem to have had an export advantage relative to small firms. That is, a few large firms accounted for all Japanese yarn exports:[11]

Year	1903	1906	1909	1912	1915
Number of firms	23	16	25	24	25

This situation compares with the total number of textile and related product producers (over four employes) of 15,574 in 1909 and 14,081 in 1914. These large spinners in turn exported:

Year	Million yen	Percentage of total exports	Percentage of total exports, excluding raw silk
1909	31.6	13.7	30.6
1914	78.6	22.3	42.1

[11]The data are gathered for all Japanese spinning mills. Firm production size is based on the number of rings. Exports are measured as the number of pounds of standard 16-count yarn. The exports of different counts have been standardized in terms of 16-count equivalents. Rank correlation coefficients for all years together for the two tests are $r = 0.65$ and -0.18. Correlation coefficients for actual firm size compared to actual export volume are

Total	1903	1906	1909	1912	1915
0.58	0.84	0.67	0.58	0.47	0.63

Thus, size might explain 40 to 50 percent of differences in export volume.

It therefore appears that spinning technology favored larger scale firms, which in turn increased their exports as Japan's comparative advantage in cotton spinning increased.

Analysis of the Saxonhouse data also indicates that among these large export spinning firms, the largest firms had an export advantage in terms of the total volume exported. Export volume is significantly correlated in terms of rank with production capacity (spindelage):

Year	1903	1906	1909	1912	1915
r rank coefficient	0.57	0.31	0.70	0.54	0.82

However, there is little or no significant relation between a firm's export specialization (exports as a percentage of production capacity) and its size. Though size is a factor in export performance and rank, it does not indicate export specialization rank. Given the following negative correlation, one can argue that among firms that are exporting, smaller firms have a higher degree of export specialization.

Year	1903	1906	1909	1912	1915
r rank coefficient	-0.20	-0.40	-0.12	-0.11	-0.15

This is the first indication of what shall be documented in greater detail for the post-World War II period: larger firms seem more likely to export, and larger firms as a group export a larger share of their production than small firms. But among firms that are exporting, smaller firms export relatively more of their production, though probably not absolutely more in terms of export volume.

Given the importance of large firms in this industry's exports, the preceding analysis indicates where scale is important, smaller firms are successful exporters only if they specialize in exports to a greater degree than larger firms. In this way they can meet the larger production orders, consistent quality, and increased technical requirements demanded by foreign buyers. These demands can be fairly easily met by large producers without sacrificing domestic sales. This is probably not true of smaller producers. The need for a minimum marketing scale may also be responsible for the traditional argument that trading firms standardize and organize the production of small firms for export. However, even from a trading company's viewpoint there may be a minimum size order related to its own volume of business. Data gathered by Yamamura and others suggest larger trading firms buy from larger producers. This is of course a way of minimizing their transactions costs, as Yamamura suggests in his chapter in this volume, and may be one of management's objectives. I shall return to this point about export specialization when examining certain post-World War II industries.

The preceding data on the spinning industry also suggest that for cotton textiles the role of small firms in early textile exports may have been overemphasized. Additional data on this point will be presented for the 1920s and 30s and for the 1960s. At the same time, the growing importance of large firms in export production during this early period is due primarily to Japan's

industrial development and shifts in comparative advantage, for example, the
development of the cotton-spinning industry.

Estimating the share of employment of all large firms (over five hundred
employes) in manufacturing as if output were distributed according to each
industry's export share indicates that in 1909 and 1919 their share of total
employment would have been 21.2 and 30.8 percent respectively.[12] This is
very close to their actual shares of 20.7 and 31.5 percent. However, on an
export weighted basis, the share of textile employment in total employment
in these two years would have been 71.4 and 71.6 percent, respectively,
compared to actual shares of 62.0 and 54.7 percent. Given the importance of
large firms in textile employment, one would thus expect export weighted
employment for large firms for all manufacturing substantially to exceed
their actual employment share. This did not occur, though, because compared
to actual employment shares the effect of an increasing textile share in
employment in the export weighted index was just about offset by the
continued export intensity of industries with a small proportion of large firms
(such as miscellaneous manufactures and ceramics) on the one hand, and the
increased production for domestic consumption of industries with a high
proportion of large firms (such as iron and steel products and machinery) on
the other. Nevertheless, the role of large firms in exports increased over the
period in pace with their greater role in domestic production, though the
source of that progress was different. In the one case, it was due to continued
importance of textile exports and in the other, due to development of
capital-intensive industry.

The primary reason for this increasing role for large firms in both domestic
production and exports seems to have been a shift in comparative advantage,
over the period, from industries where large firms accounted for a small
percentage of employment and production to those where their role was
greater. About 30 percent of the increased importance in exports of large
firms was due to changes in export share among major industry categories.
The remaining 70 percent was accounted for by large firms' increased share of
employment within export industries. But of this 70 percent, 65.8 percentage
points were due entirely to the increased percentage of large firms' share of
textile employment, which rose from 28.1 to 37.6 percent. As this
development reflects the growth of cotton textiles relative to raw silk, this
percentage is also the result of shifting comparative advantage. Thus, almost
95 percent of the increasing role of large firms in exports was due to changes
in comparative advantage.

At the same time, the Saxonhouse data indicate that large firms as a group
in cotton spinning exported absolutely and relatively more than small firms

[12]As in calculating average firm size weighted by exports (Table 4), this
calculation assumes output per worker and firm size distribution for each
industry remain constant while total industrial output is fixed. Output and
employment are then redistributed according to export shares. This calculation thus assumes neutrality between large and small firms in export
production within an industry and is designed only to indicate the effect of
changes in comparative advantage.

so that the shift in comparative advantage to cotton spinning increased large firms' role in total production as well. Therefore, even at this early period, the importance of large firms in exports, and conversely of exports to large firms, seems to have been of some increasing significance, though still in line with their role in industrial production as a whole.

INTERWAR PERIOD (1919-37)

Continuing the analysis into the 1920s and 30s leads to similar conclusions, though more changes occur during this period. Through 1925, development reflects a continuation of earlier trends. Textiles, ceramics, and miscellaneous manufactures continued to be the export-intensive industries with ratios of export share to shipment share exceeding 1.00. Textiles and ceramics increased both their export intensity and their export share during this period while miscellaneous manufactures' share declined. There is also a continued decline in the export importance of processed raw materials: food, lumber, and copper.[13] At the same time, the development of the metals, chemicals, and machinery industries slowed markedly in both total shipments and total exports. This was particularly true in the iron and steel and machinery industries built up during the war boom and reflected the Western economies' reassertion of their competitive strength in world markets (Table 2).

However, from 1925 to 1937, a distinct new shift in Japan's industrial structure can be seen. Metals, machinery, and chemicals increased their importance in total shipments from 24.6 percent in 1925 to 54.9 in 1937. At the same time their exports rose from 7.8 to 25.0 percent. Thus after 1925 they increased both their comparative advantage and export intensity, although by 1937 their export intensities still remained well below 1.00, that is, well below the national average (0.39, 0.56, and 0.46 respectively). Textiles, ceramics, and miscellaneous manufactures remained the most export-committed industries. Nevertheless, during this period Japan continued to shift her industrial structure from labor-intensive to more capital-and/or technology-intensive industries.

There seems to be no completely consistent statistical pattern to these new industries' structures during the period. There is only the very large percentage of output and employment accounted for by large firms in these industries compared to other Japanese industries, excepting textiles (Table 3). The chemical and metal industries have a high average level of output per employe compared to the average firm (Tables 4 and 5), but the machinery industry's output per worker is lower, indicating labor intensity. (Further, these high average output levels cannot be explained by high prices due to import protection and inefficiency, as these same differentials persist after World War II when the industries are efficient and tariffs are lower.) In 1925, the machinery industry's average shipments per firm were also below the national average.

[13]Through 1918 copper accounted for about 80 percent of total metal exports. From 1919 to 1921 this declined to 25 percent and by 1925 to about 7 percent.

Table 5
Exports and Productivity Ratios, 1929-1937

Food

Year	Productivity[a] Small firms	Large firms	Export share[b]	v/s[c]
1929	0.712	1.308	7.9	0.436
1933	0.711	1.773	8.8	0.443
1937	0.773	1.600	7.9	0.376

Publishing

Year	Small firms	Large firms	Export share	v/s
1929	0.616	2.589	0.1	0.473
1933	0.616	1.892	0.2	0.520
1937	0.528	2.654	0.3	0.472

Metals

Year	Small firms	Large firms	Export share	v/s
1929	0.557	1.346	2.2	0.354
1933	0.554	1.769	5.1	0.346
1937	0.536	1.630	8.8	0.271

Total

Year	Small firms	Large firms	Export share	v/s
1929	0.821	1.000	100.0	0.393
1933	0.738	1.072	100.0	0.403
1937	0.689	1.255	100.0	0.353

Textiles

Year	Productivity[a] Small firms	Large firms	Export share[b]	v/s[c]
1929	0.827	1.163	74.4	0.271
1933	0.726	1.472	63.5	0.271
1937	0.691	1.414	56.3	0.208

Chemicals

Year	Small firms	Large firms	Export share	v/s
1929	0.845	0.791	5.5	0.417
1933	0.795	0.845	7.7	0.449
1937	0.902	0.790	8.2	0.377

Machinery

Year	Small firms	Large firms	Export share	v/s
1929	0.771	0.978	2.0	0.674
1933	0.660	1.086	4.1	0.608
1937	0.763	1.047	8.0	0.553

Lumber and wood

Year	Productivity[a] Small firms	Large firms	Export share[b]	v/s[c]
1929	0.922	–	1.4	0.282
1933	0.925	–	1.5	0.298
1937	0.894	–	1.7	0.315

Ceramics

Year	Small firms	Large firms	Export share	v/s
1929	0.505	1.864	3.1	0.507
1933	0.510	1.429	3.5	0.616
1937	0.510	1.949	3.6	0.451

Miscellaneous

Year	Small firms	Large firms	Export share	v/s
1929	0.940	0.632	3.4	0.371
1933	0.993	0.848	5.7	0.363
1937	0.869	0.442	5.1	0.328

Sources: Same as Table 4.
[a]Industry productivity ratios are the output per employe for large and small firms compared to the average for each industry. A small firm is one with fewer than 50 employes, and a large firm has 500 or more.
[b]Industry's percentage of all industries' exports.
[c]Value added divided by shipments for each industry = v/s.

218

However, computing average value added per firm for each industry from data available from 1929 reveals these three industries were the only ones that exceeded the average for all industries. Thus, the shift in industrial structure was to industries with higher value added per firm and per employe, reflecting greater capital and technological intensity.[14] By 1937 this is uniformly reflected by higher-than-average output and employment per firm as well.

As expected, examining average value added per firm suggests the presence of advantages to large-scale production that explain the high proportion of employment and output accounted for by large firms.[15] But as large firms produce more output per worker than small firms in almost all industries (Table 5), except for lumber and miscellaneous manufactures, the presence of scale economies by themselves does not justify the greater importance of large firms in terms of employment and output for these industries. Rather, it is explained by the high average output per firm, which shows that the minimum firm size in these industries is larger than that of more labor-intensive industries. Fewer firms are associated with a given output, and large firms are more common.[16] The interrelation of production technology (minimum efficient plant size) and oligopoly was noted previously in the case of cotton spinning and seems to be repeating itself in these industries. This situation is very important in determining the increasing role of large firms in Japanese exports over time, for the shift in comparative advantage is toward industries with fewer and fewer production units.

Despite the increased export importance of chemical, metal, and machinery products and thus perhaps of large firms, the leading export-intensive industries throughout the 1925-37 period remain textiles, ceramics, and miscellaneous manufactures.[17] However, there is an appreciable decline, 24 percent, in textiles' share of total exports. This is accounted for mainly by a

[14]Food is the only other industry exceeding the average on a per employe basis, but it does not on a firm basis.

[15]Although data are not available for the prewar period on value added by firm size, examination of postwar data indicates that for many industries value added per unit of output for the very largest firms is less than the industry average. However, value added per unit of output in chemicals increases with scale, so that value added per worker in the very largest firms exceeds the industry average. Thus productivity in this industry is related to scale, as in other industries. The relation to scale is clear-cut for petroleum, rubber, and pulp and paper, which are included in chemicals in the prewar period but are treated separately after World War II.

[16]This fact is noted by Pryor (1972) in his international comparison as well.

[17]The dominance of a particular product group by small or large producers within an industry category presents a continuing aggregation problem. Thus, cotton spinners may be large producers, but specialty cotton textile producers are small. Within rubber products, three large producers manufacture all the tires, but rubber handicrafts (boots) are produced by small manufacturers. Similarly, blast furnace operators are quite large, but enamelware manufacturers are small. Thus, shifts in export emphasis within

decrease in raw silk exports from 39.3 percent of total exports in 1925 to 13.6 percent in 1937, along with increased exports of chemicals, metals, and machinery. This development continues the trend of phasing out processed primary goods and increasing manufactured goods as the economy matures. Cotton textiles thus became the dominant textile export industry, increasing the relative role of large firms in textile export production, as large firms dominated cotton textile production compared to raw silk spinning.

The role of large firms in exports seems very dependent on the composition of exports during this period. For example, within textiles two new products, rayon and wool, began to emerge during the late 1920s and early 30s. For rayon, because there is no appreciable difference in output per worker in small and large firms (Uyeda 1938, p. 122), almost no fabric seems to be woven in mills of over five hundred employes (only 2.0 percent in 1935). Thus as this industry increased its total production and later its export share, from 1.8 percent of textile exports in 1929 to 8.8 percent in 1937, the role of large firms in total textile employment fell (Table 3), offsetting the effect of declining raw silk production. However, due to higher productivity per worker in the large textile firms and growing demand for cotton exports, large textile firms maintained their share of total shipments during the period.

Similarly, although larger firms (over two hundred employes) dominated early production and exports of *mousselines de laines* and wool fabrics, as this industry developed, demand for mousselines fell, particularly export demand, from 78.3 percent of wool exports in 1925 to 9.7 percent in 1933 (Uyeda 1938, pp. 154-155). Also, small firms (under two hundred employes) increased their share of wool fabric production from nothing in 1925 to 58 percent in 1935 while improving their already high share of serge production (75 to 93 percent). This was due to widespread adoption of wool for kimono which stimulated increased output by smaller producers supplying domestic demand for narrow width fabrics. Concommitantly, large firms' share of wool fabric output decreased from 68 to 21 percent, while total wool production and exports were increasing in areas other than where large firms' comparative advantage lay. However, since the primary reason for small firms' increased output was increased domestic demand for narrow width kimono fabrics, it is apparent that a disproportionate amount of exports, which are mostly wide width, was produced by large firms. Though precise data are not available on this issue for wool, they are for cotton textiles; these data support the conclusion large textile firms during this period were more export oriented than small firms. This is examined in more detail shortly.

The importance of the changing composition of demand seems to be the primary determinant in changing the overall role of large firms in exports as a whole. The effect of diverse changes in demand for rayon yarn, rubber tires, bicycles, enamelware, or electric light bulbs illustrates this fact. Rayon yarn

industry categories can affect the actual importance of large firms in industry exports. I shall try to note some of these changes and their implications using data on prewar cotton, rayon, wool, rubber, bicycle, enamelware, and electric lamp industries supplied by Uyeda (1938).

and fiber are only produced by large firms (around two thousand employes). As their share of chemical exports rose from 0.1 percent in 1929 to 18.4 percent in 1937, the role of large firms in chemical exports increased. Tires are also only produced by the two to six firms with over five hundred employes. Thus, as tire output increased from 20 to 25 percent of rubber production between 1929 and 1935, so did the production share of large manufacturers (17.6 to 30.2 percent). On the other hand, there are no manufacturers of bicycles or enamelware employing over five hundred persons.

Thus, I conclude that the role of large firms in exports is dependent on technology and changing product demand. In certain industries such as rayon fiber, cotton spinning, cotton textiles, mousselines, and rubber tires, large producers dominate production and therefore exports. On the other hand, rubber boots, serges, rayon cloth, bicycles, and enamelware are produced by small firms, even though they may gather in communities and associations to rationalize production and to reduce purchasing and marketing costs. This fact illustrates one of the major issues involved in assessing the role of large firms in Japanese exports. That is, a large part of their role is defined by the nature of certain industries, and whether small or large firms are efficient producers. Shifts in domestic or export demand among products in the same industry or between industries change the role of large firms in production and export. The historical evidence seems to show that at any point in time the influence of these movements has been mixed. But in general they have favored large firms. Between 1925 and 1937 the intra-industry shift within textiles differed from the interindustry shift for all industries. On balance the overall movement toward heavy industry favored the large firm. Uyeda points out successive devaluations beginning in 1929 aided small firms and especially industries dominated by small firms. Thus, these industries were on the margin of Japan's comparative advantage, confirming that the effect of the product cycle movement toward newer industries favored large firms.

The effect of the devaluations in improving the competitiveness of small firms also raises the issue of whether within a given industry size is neutral with respect to export production. Do large firms have a higher share of an industry's exports than they do of its production? Even in an industry where small production units are economically efficient, the larger of these firms still may be more productive. In terms of output per worker (Tables 3 and 5) this seems to be the case. They may thus be more competitive and export-oriented as well.

Another related issue is whether, among exporting firms, the bigger firms specialize more. In cotton spinning the larger firms do export larger volume. However, among these large exporting firms, the smaller ones seem to export a larger share of their output.

These last two questions are particularly important for their policy and theoretical implications. Whereas the product cycle effect may be the primary reason for an overall increase in the export role of large firms, the effect of export demand or changes in currency rates on particular firms within a given industry will be equally or more sensitive to differences in export competitiveness or specialization among firms in this industry. If large minimum orders, quality standards, reliability, and so forth favor larger producers, they will be favored by export expansion. But if among these large producers, the smaller ones are particularly export specialized, they will be the most vulnerable to major swings in export demand or exchange rates. In effect they will bear the brunt of unfavorable product cycle demand trends.

Unfortunately, I do not have complete enough data for any industry during the interwar period to address both questions. However, we can look at the first for cotton textiles, where large firms appear to have had a definite export advantage. Cotton-spinning firms with over five hundred workers continued to monopolize cotton yarn production in the 1920s and 30s as they had in the pre-World War I period. In 1935, they accounted for over 90 percent of employment in this field. But the position of cotton yarn in total textile exports had declined by 1937 to 4.5 percent, from 22.3 percent in 1914, as production became more integrated and other textile exports increased.

Large firms maintained their export orientation and volume by producing and exporting cotton fabrics using continuous production techniques. They specialized in exports to the extent of 80 to 90 percent of their total fabric production, compared to 20 to 30 percent for specialty goods producers. Therefore, in 1929 large firms accounted for 61.6 percent of cotton cloth exports but only 35.2 percent of total output on a volume basis.[18] The reasons are (1) they had most of the wide-width power looms required to produce export cloth, whereas specialized weaving mills produced narrower cloth for the domestic market, often on handlooms; (2) the large manufacturers produced commodity items, such as shirtings and sheetings, which lent themselves to long production runs and economies of scale, although as demand shifted toward drills, flannel, crepe, and satin, they began to lose export and production share. Large firm share declined to 49.2 percent of cloth exports on a quantity basis by 1935 (41.8 percent on a value basis) and to 28.2 percent of production. Their export specialization and advantage in particular items, however, remained unchanged. Nevertheless, according to Uyeda, even among the specialty producers (the smaller firms), it was the larger of them who produced more exports. Again they could afford to invest in and could justify the use of the wide-width power looms. The very small firms were not really in the export business.

In summary, during the late 1920s and 30s, the net effect of various shifts in domestic and export demand within the labor-intensive industries seemed to be away from products whose production was dominated by large firms. Large firms' share of industry employment declined in textiles, ceramics, and miscellaneous manufactures from 40.6, 14.0, and 15.5 percent in 1929 to 34.6, 11.7, and 9.5 percent in 1937. In ceramics and miscellaneous manufactures, this was accompanied by a corresponding decline in output share and probably percentage of exports. In contrast, for textiles, substantial increases in worker productivity combined with increasing economies of scale appear to have enabled large firms to maintain their share of shipments (47.2

[18]Uyeda (1938, pp. 57-65) is the source of most data in this paragraph.

versus 48.9 percent) and probably of exports. However, as described here, during the early 1920s and especially around 1925, the share of large firms in cotton yarn, cotton textile, and wool fabric exports was obviously substantial and exceeded their share of total production. Thus there was some deterioration in the position of large textile firms during the 1930s compared to this earlier period. Though shipment data for all textiles by firm size is unavailable, their share of textile employment fell from 44.7 to 40.6 percent between 1925 and 1929.

At the same time, shifting comparative advantage between major industry groups toward chemicals, metals, and machinery favored a greater production and export role for large firms. Though as one would expect given the nature of this product cycle evolution, the effect on exports lagged somewhat in its effect on production. That is, weighting large firms' share of shipments for each industry by export share shows that firms with over five hundred employes would have accounted for 41.3 percent of exports in 1937 if they had only just maintained their share of shipments in export products. This was up from 39.1 percent in 1929. On the other hand, the share of large firms in total output was only 31.4 percent in 1929 but rose very rapidly to 42.8 percent in 1937. Japan's early development of a cotton textile industry resulted in increased importance of large firms in exports relative to industry as a whole. Then as newer, more concentrated industries developed, large firms' importance in domestic industry caught up. Subsequently, in the postwar period, as these new industries become more competitive, the importance of large firms in exports again outstripped their position in domestic output.

In terms of employment weight, the export index for large firms only rose from 30.8 percent of employment in 1919 to 32.0 percent of employment in 1937, while their actual share of total employment rose only slightly more, from 31.5 to 34.1 percent. But as relative productivity per worker in large firms, particularly in textiles, rose rapidly between 1929 and 1937, one could reasonably argue that in 1919 there was probably less difference between large firms' share of shipments and share of employment than there was in 1937. Indeed, in 1929, in terms of total industry output and employment, they were the same. On this basis, it would seem that 30 to 35 percent of exports in 1919 may have been an appropriate figure for large firms' export share. By 1937, or even 1929, this was more nearly 45 to 50 percent, for we know from Uyeda's data that large firms' export share in many key industries exceeded their share of shipments during this period. Although more detailed research is needed to establish a precise figure, it seems reasonable to conclude that the 35 percent 1935 export share for large firms hypothesized by some Japanese economists such as Takahashi is too low.

While small firms were still very important to total export production at this time, there seems little question changing comparative advantage during the interwar period, first in cotton textiles and later in chemicals, metals, and machinery, increased the export role of large firms substantially. In addition, one must now begin to question whether even the small export producers were the very small "cottage-type" often discussed by economic historians or were in fact medium-sized firms, the larger among the so-called small production units. I will address these issues in more detail for the postwar period.

POST-WORLD WAR II

In the initial postwar period, Japanese industrial and export development was comparable to that of the late 1920s and early 30s. Table 1 shows heavy industry did not regain its prewar significance until after 1958. Similarly, Table 6 reveals the major export-intensive industries in 1952 were textiles, apparel, ceramics, fabricated metals, measuring equipment, and miscellaneous manufactures.[19] Iron and steel seems export intensive, but after the Korean War fell to less than 1.00 in 1956 and 1960. With the exception of measuring equipment, these industries are the same ones that dominated the prewar period. Further, measuring and precision equipment such as cameras, although higher technology, are also labor intensive, as value added per worker is below the industrial average.

By 1960, several new industries had increased their share of exports and total shipments: transportation equipment, electrical machinery, iron and steel, and rubber. Transportation equipment, mostly ship exports, led this development, becoming an export-intensive industry in 1956, when the ratio of export to output share became greater than 1.00. Between 1960 and 1970, the new high-technology, more capital-intensive industries became fully export oriented. By 1970, the leading export-intensive industries were measuring equipment, transportation equipment, electrical machinery, machinery, iron and steel, and rubber. Together they accounted for 63.3 percent of exports compared to 43.2 percent of total shipments.[20]

Conversely, the share of industries which dominated exports in the prewar period and the early 1950s dropped sharply. Among these, only textiles, apparel, and miscellaneous manufactures remained export intensive in 1970. Even in these cases export fell as a share of industry output from 16.4, 19.8, and 26.1 percent respectively in 1952 to 12.2, 16.7, and 10.3 percent in 1970. Exports of traditional, labor-intensive industries have become less important relative to both their own production and exports as a whole.

The net effect of this shift is towards industries where large firms account for a greater share of total production (Table 7), continuing the trend already noted. A weighting of large firms' share of total shipments by exports shows an increase of 9.8 percent over the period. Further, whereas the actual share of large firms in total shipments is 38.8 and 42.9 in 1952 and 1970 respectively, on an export weighted basis it is 40.2 and 50.0 percent. However, we have already calculated that about 68 percent of 1970 exports were produced by firms (enterprise basis) of over 500 employes. The

[19]Data in this section are primarily taken or derived from Tsūsanshō statistical series (see list in References) and the *President Directory*.

[20]Including chemicals, nonferrous metals, and petroleum (similar industries, although not export intensive), the totals rise to 72.5 and 58.4 percent respectively.

additional 18 percent is thus accounted for partially by an export advantage larger firms appear to have over small firms due to their size and partly by the difference in large firms' share of shipments on a plant and enterprise basis. Calculating export share using plant data indicates large firms had 53.4 percent of exports in 1970. Thus of the 18 percent, only 3.4 percentage points seems due to export specialization by large firms. Changes in comparative advantage between industries or the increasing output share of large firms within industries on an enterprise basis seems to account for most of the rest. This result confirms the effect of the product cycle evolution lags predicted above during our analysis of the interwar period.

If a shift in export comparative advantage is not neutral between large and small firms, there should be a corresponding change in the share of output of large enterprises in each industry. That is, if large or small firms export a disproportionate part of their production, a relative increase or decrease in exports should increase or decrease their production share.

Of course an examination of changes in production share cannot be conclusively related to an increase or decrease in exports, as this could also be caused by a change in production composition within an industry as noted for the prewar period. However, the very large expansion in exports for certain industries is indicative of, as well as being further evidence for, the lack of neutrality between large and small firms in export production of a given product.

In the case of food, lumber, fabricated metals, and miscellaneous manufactures, the export share decline corresponded to an increase in the relative importance of large firms (Table 7). This confirms the importance of small exporters and producers in these industries. In the case of apparel, textiles, and ceramics the decline in export share accompanied a decrease in the weight of large firms in industry shipments. This result is not surprising for textiles but is for ceramics and apparel. However, examination of the 1970 census data shows that glass and pottery production are more highly concentrated than cement. (Firms of over five hundred employes account for 60.7 and 31.5 percent of their output respectively compared to 9.3 percent for cement.) Cement accounts for 45 percent of industry shipments but only 9.4 percent of exports.[21] Similarly, whereas more than 30 percent of apparel firms with over three hundred employes export, fewer than 25 percent of firms with under three hundred employes export. However, in attempting to compute apparel exports by large firms for 1968, it appears large firms may supply a smaller percentage of industry exports than they do industry shipments. Thus, a more detailed analysis for apparel may be required. In the case of textiles and ceramics, however, the evidence confirms the role of large firms in these industries' exports.

A breakdown by industry of the two hundred leading exporters, all relatively large firms, shows they are highly concentrated by industry, and

---

[21]Examination of the two hundred leading exporters confirms this. Of six companies listed for this industry, three are glass, two ceramic, and only one cement.

Table 6
Industries' Share of Exports, Shipments, Value Added, Employment, and Firms 1952-1970
(in percent, except export intensities)

Industry	1952 share of						1956 share of				1960 share of		
	Exports	Shipments	Intensity[a]	Value added	Employment	Firms	Exports	Shipments	Intensity	Employment	Exports	Shipments	Intensity[a]
Food	7.7	14.4	0.5	10.2	9.7	17.0	7.1	14.5	0.5	10.6	6.3	12.9	0.5
Textiles	31.1	18.9	1.6	14.8	20.3	17.2	25.7	15.6	1.6	18.9	22.9	11.1	2.1
Apparel	3.0	1.5	2.0	1.4	2.6	3.6	7.2	1.2	6.0	2.5	4.9	1.1	4.5
Lumber-wood	1.5	3.7	0.4	3.8	6.9	13.8	3.3	3.6	0.9	6.2	2.7	3.4	0.8
Furniture	–	0.7	0.0	1.0	1.8	3.8	–	0.8	–	2.0	0.1	0.9	0.1
Pulp-paper	0.5	4.2	0.1	5.0	3.2	2.6	1.2	4.1	0.3	3.3	1.3	3.9	0.3
Publishing	0.3	2.9	0.1	5.0	3.9	3.7	0.2	3.0	0.1	4.3	0.2	2.5	0.1
Chemicals	5.2	10.5	0.5	12.0	7.8	3.3	5.3	10.4	0.5	6.7	6.8	8.8	0.8
Petroleum-coal	0.7	2.0	0.4	1.6	0.6	0.4	0.5	2.0	0.3	0.5	0.4	2.4	0.2
Rubber	0.6	1.6	0.4	1.9	1.6	0.5	0.9	1.4	0.6	1.6	2.6	1.5	1.7
Leather	0.2	0.5	0.4	0.5	0.5	0.8	0.4	0.5	0.8	0.6	0.1	0.5	0.2
Ceramics	5.7	3.6	1.6	5.5	5.3	6.6	6.1	3.3	1.8	5.3	4.4	3.4	1.3
Iron-steel	20.7	11.2	1.8	7.6	6.5	2.3	8.9	11.6	0.8	5.5	9.6	10.8	0.9
Nonferrous metals	3.8	4.6	0.8	3.5	2.0	0.9	2.0	4.9	0.4	2.0	0.6	4.4	0.1
Fabricated metals	3.2	2.7	1.2	3.1	3.8	5.6	2.6	3.3	0.8	4.8	3.8	3.6	1.1
Machinery	4.8	5.2	0.9	7.6	8.0	6.7	4.7	5.6	0.8	8.1	6.0	7.6	0.8
Electric machinery	1.5	3.7	0.4	5.6	4.6	2.3	2.0	4.6	0.4	5.6	6.8	8.4	0.8
Transport equipment	2.8	5.9	0.5	7.3	6.7	2.7	12.7	6.9	1.8	6.4	10.4	8.9	1.2
Measuring instruments	1.3	0.7	1.9	1.1	1.4	1.2	1.8	0.9	2.0	1.6	2.5	1.1	2.3
Ordnance	–	–	–	–	–	–	–	–	–	–	–	–	–
Miscellaneous	3.5	1.3	2.7	1.7	2.9	4.8	4.8	1.8	2.7	3.5	6.1	2.5	2.4
Total Manufacturing	98.1	100.0	100.0	100.0	100.0	100.0	97.4	100.0	100.0	100.0	98.5	100.0	100.0

226

Table 6 (continued)

Industry	1964 share of				1968 share of			1970 share of					
	Exports	Shipments	Intensity[a]	Employment	Exports	Shipments	Intensity[a]	Exports	Shipments	Intensity[a]	Value added	Employment	Firms
Food	4.7	11.9	0.4	10.4	3.3	11.3	0.3	3.3	10.3	0.3	7.9	9.5	13.5
Textiles	14.7	9.0	1.6	12.4	9.7	7.1	1.4	7.5	6.3	1.2	5.9	10.2	13.0
Apparel	4.2	1.4	3.0	3.0	2.8	1.4	2.0	2.2	1.4	1.6	1.5	3.5	5.2
Lumber-wood	1.4	3.5	0.4	5.2	1.3	3.5	0.4	0.8	3.2	0.3	2.8	4.5	8.0
Furniture	0.2	1.2	0.2	2.2	0.2	1.4	0.1	0.2	1.4	0.1	1.6	2.4	4.5
Pulp-paper	1.0	4.6	0.2	3.4	0.9	3.4	0.3	0.9	3.3	0.3	3.0	2.9	3.0
Publishing	0.2	3.9	0.1	4.4	0.3	3.0	0.1	0.2	2.9	0.1	4.3	4.0	5.3
Chemicals	8.6	10.8	0.8	5.0	9.1	8.4	1.1	7.7	8.1	0.9	10.2	4.4	1.3
Petroleum-coal	0.3	2.5	0.1	0.4	0.2	2.7	0.1	0.2	2.6	0.1	1.1	0.3	0.2
Rubber	2.5	1.4	1.8	1.7	2.1	1.2	1.8	1.8	1.1	1.6	1.3	1.5	1.0
Leather	0.3	0.6	0.5	0.7	0.3	0.5	0.6	0.3	0.5	0.6	0.5	0.7	1.3
Ceramics	3.7	3.6	1.0	4.9	2.6	3.7	0.7	2.0	3.6	0.6	4.8	5.0	5.3
Iron-steel	13.5	9.7	1.4	5.2	13.2	8.9	1.5	14.7	9.6	1.5	7.0	4.9	1.6
Nonferrous metals	0.9	3.9	0.2	1.9	1.2	4.2	0.3	1.3	4.5	0.3	2.7	1.9	1.0
Fabricated metals	3.5	4.6	0.8	6.4	3.6	4.8	0.8	3.7	5.4	0.7	6.4	7.1	10.7
Machinery	7.2	8.2	0.9	9.6	9.0	8.8	1.0	10.4	9.9	1.1	11.9	10.3	8.3
Electric machinery	10.8	8.5	1.3	9.4	14.2	9.6	1.5	15.1	10.7	1.4	12.0	11.9	5.0
Transport equipment	12.1	9.3	1.3	6.7	17.2	11.2	1.5	17.8	10.6	1.7	9.6	7.8	3.1
Measuring instruments	2.9	1.2	2.4	1.9	3.6	1.3	2.8	3.5	1.3	2.7	1.6	2.1	1.6
Ordnance	–	–	–	–	–	–	–	–	–	–	–	–	–
Miscellaneous	5.1	3.1	1.6	4.6	4.3	3.5	1.2	3.6	3.5	1.0	3.8	4.9	7.1
Total Manufacturing	97.8	100.0	100.0	100.0	99.2	100.0	100.0	97.2	100.0	100.0	100.0	100.0	100.0

Sources: Tsūsanshō Daijin Kambō 1961 and Census by Industry, 1964 and 1970 editions; Ōkurashō Nihon Boeki, various annual editions.

[a]Export intensity is defined in Table 2. In 1970 firms with fewer than four employes account for 37.9 percent of the firms but only 4.4 percent of employment and 1.0 percent of total shipments. Thus for the purposes of this paper, no generality is lost by using figures for firms greater than three. Indeed, these numbers tend to understate the case, as these small firms are concentrated in areas of declining comparative advantage or little export importance. Examples include food, lumber, furniture, leather, publishing, textiles, apparel, ceramics, and miscellaneous manufactures, which account for 76 percent of firms of fewer than four employes.

Table 7
Weight of Large and Small Firms in Industrial Structure 1952-1970
(in percent)

| | 1952 | | | | | | | | 1956 | | | |
| | Small firms' share | | | | Large firms' share | | | | Small firms' share | | Large firms' share | |
Industry	Firms	Employment	Shipments	Value added	Firms	Employment	Shipments	Value added	Employment	Value added	Employment	Value added
Food	96.3	70.6	45.2	46.3	0.1	5.5	10.4	10.1	67.3	46.4	4.1	8.4
Textiles	91.3	38.0	25.2	23.1	0.7	27.0	39.6	42.7	40.4	25.4	23.1	38.9
Apparel	93.8	65.5	55.3	52.1	0.1	4.8	7.7	13.9	54.5	57.2	–	–
Lumber-wood	97.9	88.5	80.3	80.5	–	–	–	–	82.8	77.8	1.2	1.7
Furniture	97.4	81.2	74.6	75.7	–	–	–	–	80.4	75.5	–	–
Pulp-paper	91.3	38.1	16.5	13.9	0.8	26.2	46.0	55.2	38.7	15.9	24.2	47.3
Publishing	92.0	48.2	34.5	26.1	0.5	19.6	34.7	37.6	49.4	25.7	19.6	42.0
Chemicals	95.8	18.2	13.6	11.8	1.9	51.9	49.0	52.2	15.3	8.9	53.5	59.8
Petroleum-coal	87.6	36.6	9.7	10.3	1.2	25.1	50.9	56.7	35.2	12.7	30.4	63.0
Rubber	67.3	14.6	8.6	8.1	1.8	26.9	38.0	40.8	26.7	20.2	38.9	52.6
Leather	94.7	65.4	58.4	55.2	–	–	–	–	68.0	59.8	–	–
Ceramics	93.3	50.2	24.0	22.1	0.3	13.2	33.3	34.9	45.7	19.7	13.6	39.4
Iron-steel	85.6	19.0	9.1	12.5	1.9	58.6	70.1	66.2	19.8	10.2	54.0	65.4
Nonferrous metals	86.1	22.6	12.4	11.2	2.0	48.6	56.2	53.9	20.7	10.7	49.6	60.7
Fabricated metals	95.0	66.7	44.4	49.1	0.1	2.8	2.4	2.3	60.1	48.1	4.8	7.2
Machinery	89.0	39.9	26.3	27.5	0.7	22.3	32.5	32.5	39.2	27.8	19.9	28.2
Electric machinery	85.4	25.1	14.8	13.3	1.7	42.7	54.0	55.7	22.1	12.8	46.8	59.8
Transport equipment	86.3	20.0	10.4	11.3	1.8	57.7	71.6	68.8	18.2	10.3	56.5	66.7
Measuring instruments	90.1	41.0	34.3	31.0	0.6	19.4	23.0	29.9	38.7	28.2	22.8	31.1
Ordnance[a]	–	–	–	–	–	–	–	–	–	–	–	–
Miscellaneous	95.8	69.3	59.4	53.5	0.04	2.4	3.5	5.4	61.8	49.6	3.4	4.7

Table 7 (continued)

Sources: Tsūsanshō Daijin Kambō 1961, and Tsūsanshō, Kōgyō.

aOrdnance manufactures numbered thirty-five in 1970, all with fewer than 500 employes. Exports were minimal, and shipments only ¥3.5 billion.

Small firms are those with fewer than 50 employes but greater than 3; large firms have 500 employes or more.

	1970							
	Small firms' share				Large firms' share			
Industry	Firms	Employment	Shipments	Value added	Firms	Employment	Shipments	Value added
Food	93.2	49.9	28.8	32.2	0.2	8.3	14.4	13.2
Textiles	93.2	43.0	33.8	40.1	0.6	21.5	26.4	21.7
Apparel	92.3	57.0	53.5	57.1	0.1	2.8	4.6	4.2
Lumber-wood	96.1	70.8	61.3	62.9	0.1	3.8	5.9	6.6
Furniture	95.3	63.2	50.7	53.4	0.1	2.6	4.2	4.5
Pulp-paper	90.1	40.6	22.4	24.8	0.6	19.0	32.6	32.3
Publishing	93.9	50.5	30.9	32.6	0.3	20.0	33.8	33.7
Chemicals	70.6	11.7	7.4	6.0	3.9	49.3	55.1	59.4
Petroleum-coal	80.8	20.8	4.7	10.5	3.3	40.3	62.6	66.0
Rubber	89.5	26.7	20.4	20.2	1.3	42.7	54.3	53.1
Leather	95.7	63.0	65.1	66.1	0.2	10.2	5.8	6.8
Ceramics	90.4	43.0	34.6	30.4	0.4	15.4	21.4	25.2
Iron-steel	79.8	16.0	8.6	11.2	2.2	55.9	67.2	63.3
Nonferrous metals	85.1	19.6	10.7	13.2	2.4	48.5	59.3	60.4
Fabricated metals	94.7	57.2	45.2	49.1	0.2	7.8	12.0	11.3
Machinery	88.8	32.1	20.0	23.8	0.8	30.8	45.1	41.9
Electric machinery	80.4	17.8	9.7	10.6	2.0	47.6	64.1	65.1
Transport equipment	84.6	15.5	6.1	8.9	2.0	58.9	76.8	73.7
Measuring instruments	88.7	30.3	22.3	25.9	1.1	33.2	43.6	39.1
Ordnance^a	–	–	–	–	–	–	–	–
Miscellaneous	93.7	52.4	38.6	41.8	0.2	9.7	14.3	13.4

dominate those industries, particularly those industries' exports.[22] As one can see in Table 8, among the two hundred leading exporters there are no producers of apparel, lumber and wood products, furniture, leather, fabricated metal, or ordnance. These leading export producers are concentrated in only fifteen of the twenty-two major industry categories, accounting for 36.9 percent of total shipments and 64.8 percent of total exports in these industries. In textiles, chemicals, petroleum, rubber, iron and steel, nonferrous metals, electric machinery, transportation equipment, and precision instruments, dominance of export markets is especially marked. In these nine categories, 165 firms account for 70.7 percent of all these industries' exports.[23]

Expanding the analysis to all large firms, Table 9 shows that 2164 firms, or all firms over three hundred employes which are exporting, account for about 74 percent of total exports. This means about 0.3 percent of all firms account for more than 75 percent of total processed exports. In terms of firms over five hundred employes, about 1333 firms accounted for an estimated 68 percent of exports. However, as the leading two hundred sold some 81.4 percent of all large firms' (over three hundred employes) exports, their influence on the export market would appear substantial, particularly in the nine industries noted here. Thus, it seems reasonable to conclude that large firms currently have a dominant position in exports.

Concurrently, those capital- or technology-intensive industries which have exported an increasing share of production between 1952 and 1970—chemicals, rubber, machinery, electric machinery, transportation equipment, and measuring equipment—have had a rising share of shipments by large firms. Conversely, iron and steel experienced a slight decline in large firms' share of total shipments corresponding to a slight decrease in exports as a percentage of output. For some reason petroleum and nonferrous metals do not follow this pattern, perhaps because both export only a small percentage of production. Petroleum has never been export competitive and nonferrous metals were only competitive during the Korean War. Therefore, among major export industries there is a fairly consistent pattern indicating the predominance of large firms in exports and a structural shift toward industries in which this predominance is quite marked.

This in turn raises an interesting issue. At a minimum it is clear product cycle evolution and changing comparative advantage have favored industries which are relatively concentrated, thus increasing export concentration. But

[22]In 1970, there were 2009 firms with over five hundred employes, including all two hundred companies on the leading-exporter list. The leading-exporter subgroup accounted for 61 percent of total shipments and 90 percent of estimated exports for the whole group. These two hundred made 34 percent of Japan's total manufactured shipments and 60 percent of total exports.

[23]These firms are taken directly from *President Directory* and do not take account of corporate control such as Sony's ownership of Aiwa, Matsushita's of Kyūshū Matsushita, and so forth, which would reduce the number of firms cited.

additionally one could argue that concentration may also be favoring the increased export competitiveness of these industries. As described earlier, a primary reason for changing comparative advantage is changing factor costs and demand for more sophisticated products. Though considerably more research needs to be done in addressing this question, it is an important hypothesis emerging from the interaction of Japan's industrial development, changing comparative advantage, and increasing export concentration. A contributing and supportive factor in the mutual interaction of changing comparative advantage and firm size is the effect of larger marketing areas on increased productivity as noted by Pryor.

This conclusion concerning increased domestic concentration and increased export specialization by large firms is strongly supported by data in the *President Directory* (1965-73 annual issues) on the two hundred leading manufacturers of exports as well as material presented in the *Kōgyō Jittai Kihon Chōsa* (Tsūsanshō 1973). In reviewing these data, as presented in Tables 8 and 9, one sees that in all industries the share of industry exports for the two hundred leading export firms substantially exceeds their share of shipments. These large firms are export intensive relative to their industry as a whole, with export shares ranging from 1.2 to 3.5 times their share of industry output. In addition, the highest degree of concentration on both an export and sales basis is in those industries where Japan's comparative advantage has been developing: chemicals (including textile fibers), petrochemicals, rubber, iron and steel, electric machinery, transportation equipment, and measuring devices.

Conversely, in Table 9, which is estimated using enterprise data combined with export sales share data, one sees that apparel, miscellaneous manufactures, and fabricated metal have little concentration, while large firms' share of total exports is less than their share of total shipments.[24] Thus industries with declining comparative advantage reflect an opposite concentration trend compared to the new industries. During the 1960s these labor intensive industries not only lost comparative advantage to other Japanese industries but to the LDCs as well (Table 10).

Examination of the data presented in Tables 8 and 9 also raises serious doubts about the reliability of government figures published on the export production share of small- and medium-sized firms; they appear to be overestimates. Though there is no survey data comparable to the *President*'s poll of the largest firms, the Osaka Government Economic Research Institute has estimated the value of small firm exports by multiplying small- and

[24]Tsūsanshō (1973) gives the percentage of firms exporting by firm size categories for 1971 and the range of export sales as a percentage of sales for those firms exporting. These data were used to compute a weighted average percentage of sales for each enterprise category. As examination of earlier reports showed not much change in these percentages for given industries over time, I applied them to the 1968 census data to get a rough estimate of probable exports. A similar calculation was made for 1970. In both cases, exports by firms of over three hundred employes were about 74 percent of total exports.

Table 8
Export and Production Composition by Major Industry Groupings 1970
(in billion yen)

Industry	Total		By 200 leading manufacturing exporters				
	Shipments	Manufactured exports	Number of firms[a]	Sales	Percentage total	Exports	Percentage total
Food related	7150.6	229.1	6	543.0	7.6	60.5	26.4
Textile mill[b]	5170.1	703.5	26	2144.8	41.5	514.2	73.1
Apparel-other	956.7	154.7	–	–	–	–	–
Lumber-wood	2331.9	52.8	–	–	–	–	–
Furniture	1009.1	10.8	–	–	–	–	–
Pulp-paper	2269.6	65.7	3	281.7	12.4	10.6	16.1
Publishing	1999.6	15.3	1	104.0	5.2	3.0	19.6
Chemicals[b]	4803.7	358.6	31	2168.9	45.2	237.6	70.9
Petroleum-coal	1791.1	16.3	3	820.2	45.8	28.2	70.9
Rubber	766.9	125.8	5	292.2	38.1	55.7	44.3
Leather	342.8	22.9	–	–	–	–	–
Ceramics	2469.7	138.1	6	341.0	13.8	35.9	26.0
Iron-steel	6564.8	1023.8	23	4102.7	62.5	902.8	88.2
Nonferrous metals	3054.7	89.3	11	1268.5	41.5	74.7	83.7

Table 8 (continued)

Industry	Total		By 200 leading manufacturing exporters				
	Shipments	Manufactured exports	Number of firms[a]	Sales	Percentage total	Exports	Percentage total
Fabricated metals	3727.7	258.2	–	–	–	–	–
Machinery	6802.8	722.6	17	978.9	14.4	159.7	22.1
Electric machinery	7330.5	1048.3	35	4405.6	60.1	793.6	75.7
Transport equipment	7275.8	1239.4	20	4469.8	61.4	1043.6	84.2
Measuring instruments	891.7	243.3	11	341.7	38.3	126.1	51.8
Ordnance	3.5	–	–	–	–	–	–
Miscellaneous	2465.0	248.8	2	114.1	4.6	14.8	5.9
Total	69,034.8	6767.3	200	22,377.1	32.4	4061.0	60.0

Sources: *President Directory*, 1972 edition; Tsūsanshō, *Kogyo*, 1970 edition; Okurashō, *Nihon Boeki*, 1970 edition.

[a] Number of firms in industry that are among the 200 leading manufacturing exporters.

[b] As large textile exporters produce the bulk of synthetic fiber (¥179.0 billion), for the purposes of this table only such fiber and yarn has been included in textiles rather than chemicals.

Table 9

Export and Production Composition by Major Industry Groupings 1968

(in billion yen)

Industry	All enterprises		Enterprises over 300 employes			
	Shipments	Manufactured exports	Shipments	Shipment Percentage[a]	Exports	Export Percentage[b]
Food related	5490.6	152.0	2547.3	56.4	123.0	80.9
Textile mill	3579.6	451.4	1554.7	43.5	241.0	53.6
Apparel-other	687.7	132.8	89.7	13.1	6.4	8.0
Lumber-wood	1696.3	58.4	212.8	12.6	5.8	10.0
Furniture	436.6	7.8	126.7	29.0	7.4	94.9
Pulp-paper	1637.7	40.0	894.0	54.6	36.4	90.1
Publishing	1470.2	12.1	643.0	43.8	17.8[c]	(100.0)[c]
Chemicals	3983.0	427.2	3047.7	76.5	346.2	81.0
Petroleum-coal	1216.4	10.9	1048.3	86.2	36.0[c]	(100.0)[c]
Rubber	591.8	96.5	406.8	68.8	74.6	70.9
Leather	234.9	13.4	26.3	11.2	1.7	12.7
Ceramics	1765.5	122.1	782.8	44.4	62.6	51.3
Iron-steel	4378.0	616.5	3446.6	78.8	654.5[c]	(100.0)[c]
Nonferrous metals	1964.6	58.2	1574.1	80.1	92.4[c]	(100.0)[c]
Fabricated metals	2287.0	171.1	583.1	25.5	41.9	24.5

Table 9 (continued)

	All enterprises		Enterprises over 300 employes			
Machinery	3757.9	420.4	1677.8	47.4	226.9	54.0
Electric machinery	4792.1	663.4	3722.3	77.7	640.9	96.6
Transport equipment	5679.2	804.8	4868.2	85.8	800.3	99.4
Measuring instruments	602.2	168.5	319.9	53.1	84.5	49.6
Ordnance	6.1	–	–	–	–	–
Miscellaneous	1663.0	204.1	506.2	39.9	59.5	29.2
Total	48,278.5	4631.6	28,178.3	58.4	3451.8	74.5
Total leading 200 exporters			15,012.5	31.1	2634.7	57.0
Total for enterprises with over 300 employes as estimated by Tsūsanshō, Chūshō Kigyō-chō			--		2740.0	59.3

Sources: Tsūsanshō, Census by Enterprise, 1968 edition, and Tsūsanshō, Chūshō Kigyō-chō.
aEnterprises with over 300 employes' share of all manufactured shipments.
bEnterprises with over 300 employes' share of all manufactured exports.
cThe method used to estimate the value of large enterprises' (over 300 employes) exports, when applied to the data in the Chūshō Kigyō Hakusho, yields values larger than the total reported exports for all firms, and thus export shares exceeding 100 percent. In part this is due to overestimation of the large enterprises' exports. The most important reason, however, is that these firms export products other than those defined as their basic output in the trade (export) figures used to estimate industry exports.

Table 10
Loss of Comparative Advantage by Small and Medium Industry:
Changes in Export Share to the United States between Japan and Less
Developed Countries, 1960 and 1967
(in percent, except change in percentage points)

| | 1960 | | 1967 | | Change | |
	Japan	LDCs	Japan	LDCs	Japan	LDCs
Cotton goods	25.2	36.8	26.9	50.2	+ 1.7	+13.4
Plywood	50.4	18.8	33.4	54.1	−17.0	+35.3
Silk goods	73.6	2.5	41.4	5.9	−32.2	+ 2.4
Carpets, etc.	43.0	14.5	42.1	34.1	− 0.9	+19.6
Toys, dolls	76.0	8.2	45.5	27.3	−30.5	+19.1
Scarves, handkerchiefs	38.3	37.3	49.3	25.4	+11.0	−11.9
Dry-cell batteries	44.2	11.8	50.8	43.9	+ 6.6	+32.1
Umbrellas	87.9	2.8	61.5	33.9	−26.4	+31.1
Forks	80.7	0.6	71.9	11.1	− 8.8	+10.5
Spoons	79.7	0.5	72.7	11.7	− 7.0	+11.2
Transistor radios	97.6	0.5	77.7	19.7	−19.9	+19.4
Christmas decorations	99.1	0.7	84.4	14.9	−14.7	+14.2
Binoculars	97.6	0.0	92.6	4.5	− 5.0	+ 4.5

Source: Keizai Kikaku-chō 1969, p. 154.
Note: Prepared on the basis of U.S. Department of Commerce, "U.S. Imports of Merchandise for Consumption." LDCs are other than OECD countries, Finland, Australia, New Zealand, South Africa, and Communist countries.

medium-sized firm production share times the value of each commodity exported. In other words, they make the crucial assumption exports are neutral to firm size. The estimates are more detailed than the two-digit industrial classification generally used in this paper. The results are given in Table 11.

In many cases, these figures correspond to those computed at the two-digit level for the top two hundred large diversified exporters as well as the more detailed estimates for firms of over three hundred employes given in Table 9. The export share of small firms in chemicals, rubber, iron and steel, nonferrous metals, electric machinery, and transportation equipment is low, though sometimes somewhat higher than the limits indicated by the leading two hundred exporters and the data in Table 9. Also, as expected, apparel, lumber and wood products, leather, ceramics, fabricated metal products, and miscellaneous goods show high shares for small- and medium-sized firms. However, using their approach, textile exports by small firms are much too high, even if one allows for the fact that much of large firms' production is synthetic fiber and yarn, normally classified as chemicals. In addition their shares for food, furniture, pulp and paper products, and publishing (printing) seem way out of line, even allowing for some slippage in the estimation procedure used to arrive at the export shares presented in Table 9.

The problem, of course, is that the assumption on which these data were compiled for small- and medium-sized industries is incorrect. Evidence

Table 11
Estimated Export Share of Small Firms in Manufactured Exports
(in percent, except change in percentage points)

Industry	Change 1956-1970	1956	1961	1964	1968	1970
Food related	-18.5	76.5	76.3	55.4	57.2	58.0
Textile mill	- 8.9	79.8	79.9	84.6	88.7	88.7
Apparel-other	-14.0	95.5	97.3	80.8	78.2	81.5
Lumber-wood	- 4.0	82.4	79.7	98.7	77.3	78.4
Furniture	- 7.1	97.9	94.3	100.0	100.0	90.8
Pulp-paper	- 7.3	45.5	41.7	46.8	49.8	52.8
Publishing	-13.2	69.9	77.9	73.3	72.8	56.7
Chemicals	-16.3	44.9	35.4	26.8	23.8	28.6
Petroleum-coal	-53.6	-	10.9	23.9	46.3	53.6
Rubber	- 2.3	27.8	30.5	25.1	40.6	30.1
Leather (shoes)	- 3.4	96.6	97.7	100.0	100.0	100.0
Ceramics	- 0.0	51.7	49.8	45.2	51.1	51.7
Iron-steel	- 0.4	19.3	20.4	19.7	19.9	19.7
Nonferrous metals	- 6.7	32.9	34.8	53.3	41.3	39.6
Fabricated metals	-12.5	95.1	92.5	76.3	85.4	82.6
Machinery	-17.0	53.6	54.0	49.9	46.1	36.6
Electric machinery	-30.1	52.4	25.2	21.9	23.6	22.3
Transport equipment	4.1	8.7	12.0	11.9	10.2	12.8
Measuring instruments	-24.0	66.7	62.2	54.8	50.9	42.7
Ordnance	--	--	--	--	--	--
Miscellaneous	- 8.0	95.9	89.0	96.3	83.9	87.9
Total	-22.7	59.4	55.2	45.5	41.0	36.7

Source: Tsūsanshō, Chūshō Kigyō-chō, 1956 to 1973 editions.
Note: Based on four-digit industry-classification weighting of shipments by small and medium firms; small firms have fewer than 300 employes or capital less than 50 million yen.

available for several prewar industries as well as the more complete data available for the postwar period confirms that for many industries, large firms have a greater proportion of exports than they do of domestic shipments.[25] Therefore small- and medium-sized firms cannot have the same percentage. In fact, if one revises the small- and medium-sized industry weightings to conform to the survey data compiled by *President*, the share of small- and medium-sized firms in total exports will drop to around 30 percent for 1970.[26] The same procedure used in Table 9 for 1970 data indicates that about 26 percent of exports are produced by firms with fewer than three hundred employes, which is about the same as for 1968. Instead of small- and medium-sized firms having 41.0 percent and 36.7 percent of exports in 1968

[25]Examination of Tsūsanshō 1959, which is a survey for 1957, shows basically the same results as the 1971 survey (Tsūsanshō 1973), with the percentage of exporting firms rising steadily from 2.0 percent for firms with one to three employes to 81.3 percent for firms with over one thousand.

[26]Similar results are evident for 1957 from Tsūsanshō 1959.

and 1970 respectively as reported in the *White Paper* and Table 11 (Tsūsanshō, *Hakusho*), they have around 26 percent.

Therefore, it seems that official government export figures for small- and medium-sized firms, which have been used by various scholars and newspapers to demonstrate the importance of small industries in Japan's export development, cannot be accepted. They overstate the case for the importance of exports to small firms and of small firms in total exports. In fact, the share of small firms in exports is smaller than their production weight. To the extent the government thinks differently and makes policy on the basis of misleading information, the consequences could be serious. MITI's Small and Medium Enterprise Agency would do well to revise its estimates on the basis of its own survey data and more appropriate assumptions. In addition, on the basis of MITI's original figures, one can see that only 31.5 percent of exports by small- and medium-sized firms were accounted for by "specialty producers" (for examples, makers of umbrellas, spectacles, sewn products, cutlery), whose exports may have accounted for as much as 42 percent of their total sales. This 42 percent compares with at most only 8 percent of sales for small- and medium-sized firms as a whole and 5 percent for nonspecialty producers. As in 1970 manufacture exports accounted for 9.8 percent of total shipments, export sales were thus more important to larger firms as a whole than to small- and medium-sized firms, particularly the nonspecialty firms. Therefore, in any discussion of Japan's small- and medium-sized producers' dependence on exports, what is really being described is a special group of firms in a limited number of industries: 62 percent of their exports are textiles and apparel, 18 percent sundry goods, and 7 percent fabricated metal products.

During 1971, specialty exports fell 5 percent in value, whereas exports as a whole grew 21 percent. Specialty exporters' dependence on the United States market (around 50 percent) plus greater competition from the LDCs accentuated the problem. It is primarily their relatively slower growth and resulting decline in comparative advantage, as resources have shifted to newer products, that has accounted for their declining export importance. This applies to small firms generally. In the postwar period the increase in the export weight of iron and steel, chemicals, petroleum, nonferrous metals, electric machinery, and transportation equipment—that is, the capital- and technology-intensive industries (in 1952, 35.3 percent of exports, and in 1970, 58.4 percent) characterized by large firms, has meant a decline in small firms' share of exports. This shifting pattern of industrialization, and subsequently of comparative advantage, explains large firms' increasing export visibility, and current export dominance, despite the historical importance of small firms' exports.

CURRENT SITUATION

Large firms are not necessarily more export specialized than smaller firms. Examination of the *President Directory* and the *Chūshō Kōgyō Jittai Kihon*

(Tsūsanshō, 1959 and 1973) shows that though larger firms are more likely to export, and export quantitatively more than small firms, they are not as dependent as smaller exporters. In fact, it is the greater number of large firms exporting that make large firms as a group appear somewhat more export specialized. Thus, whereas in 1971, 76.5 percent of all firms with more than one thousand employes exported, only 2.4 percent of firms with three employes or fewer exported and only 6.8 percent of all Japanese firms exported. The *Dai Yonkai Chūshō Kōgyō Jittai Kihon* (Tsūsanshō 1973) demonstrates conclusively that the percentage of firms exporting is a systematically increasing function of firm size for both industry as a whole and individual industries. The only exceptions are apparel and lumber, where I have already noted the greater export competitiveness of smaller production units, and even here the difference is only among firms with more than three hundred employes; smaller firms still are less likely to be exporting.

Also, in 1972, the three leading exporters are the three top manufacturing firms in Japan, and twelve of the sixteen largest exporters are among the sixteen largest manufacturing firms in terms of sales. In addition, examination by industry for the two hundred leading exporters shows that the two largest electric producers are also the two top electrical exporters, and similarly for the two top auto producers, the leading rubber company, the leading petroleum company, the five top steel companies, the two major shipbuilders, and the seven top textile producers (*President Directory* 1973).

But whereas size and export sales or the likelihood of exports are positively correlated, size and export specialization are not. The *Dai Yonkai Chūshō Kōgyō Jittai Kihon* shows that among firms that are exporting, the smallest are usually the most export specialized. Thus in 1971, among exporting firms, the category with the greatest percentage of firms with export sales above 90 percent of their total sales were firms with 1 to 3 employes. Conversely, those firms with export sales less than 10 percent of their sales were highest among firms with 500 to 999 employes, followed closely by those with over 1000. In fact, the percentage of exporting firms with greater than 90 percent export sales is a systematically decreasing function of firm size, while the percentage of firms with less than 10 percent export sales is a systematically increasing function.

In addition these results appear to hold even among large firms that are exporting. According to *President*'s 1970 survey, the seven leading electrical goods producers in terms of export intensity ranked respectively eleventh, sixteenth, fourteenth, eighteenth, twelve, twenty-first, and twenty-fourth out of the top thirty-five firms in terms of total export sales within the industry. That is, only one of the top ten electrical producers in terms of export volume was ranked in the first seven in terms of export specialization. In terms of total sales, their rankings were even lower. Similarly, the most export-intensive textile producer relative to other textile producers was ranked twenty-sixth out of twenty-six in terms of export sales; the three most export-specialized steel companies were nineteen and fifteen respectively out of twenty-three in terms of export sales. Thus, the results we first saw indicated for pre-World War I in cotton spinning do not appear to be an isolated case. In these other industries, too, export specialization appears a fesible way of competing against larger firms.[27]

Though export specialization appears to be generally correlated with smaller firm size, this is not true in all cases. Fuji Film had 97.5 percent of all film exports in 1971; Nissan and Toyota had 82 percent of all passenger car exports. In both cases, their export share exceeded their domestic market share. No other large producers were as export intensive. Although the reasons for such differences in industries are not clear, they probably relate to technology and minimum efficient plant size as well as returns to scale. Electronic appliances, wire drawing, and shipbuilding all require relatively small plants or a single efficient facility. After a certain size is reached, additional production returns to increased volume may decrease or level off. In more capital-intensive operations or where marketing or after-sales service are important, size and scale probably give a distinct export advantage.

There is also the issue of market and/or product segmentation. In those industries where the small producer can effectively segment a particular overseas market for a certain product, he can compete. Where such segmentation is not possible, difficulties will emerge. This is clearly indicated by noting that among the industry groups into which the two hundred leading exporters are divided there are distinct subgroups. Transportation equipment can be separated into producers of passenger cars, minivehicles, trucks, motorcycles, superships, and ordinary vessels. Though there is some overlap, in fact each company is only competing directly with two or three other producers, often of similar size. Thus, the twenty producers are not a cohesive competitive group. Similarly, electrical equipment might be divided into heavy equipment manufacturers, high quality hi-fi components and consumer durables, or steel into integrated and specialty producers. The degree of export and production specialization and concentration by product and market is much greater than at first might seem apparent. This situation is of course intensified by subsidiary relationships within the top two hundred exporting firms. Thus, the ability of the relatively small exporter to survive may also be a function of being a big firm in a small market (finding a niche) or of attaching oneself to a large producer or marketer.

TRADING COMPANIES AND SUBCONTRACTING

It is often argued that the importance of small firms in Japanese exports at least historically has been supported by the role of the trading company as a "putter-out" of export work and by their subcontracting relations with larger firms. Though space does not permit detailed examination of these questions,

[27]Similar results are apparent using data for other years, including 1972. The data here are from *President Directory* 1974 edition covering 1972, but similar conclusions are reached examining data for 1967-71.

it should be noted the arguments basically support the proposition that size, at least marketing and financial size, is important for export sales. Thus in terms of export control and competitiveness, size is a crucial factor, which has been already shown in this paper. Still, I will briefly examine the relation of trading companies to large and small exporters as well as the possible importance of subcontracting relations.

Research by Kozo Yamamura, Fujii, and others indicates small producers usually use small trading companies and large producers, large trading companies (Fujii 1960 and 1971; Ajia Kyōkai 1957). This is logical when one recognizes the large trading firms began as either zaibatsu sales and purchasing companies, raw cotton suppliers and yarn exporters, or ore and coal buyers and later exporters for large steel producers. The big *sōgō shōsha* (Mitsubishi, Mitsui, Itoh, Marubeni, Tōmen, Ataka, Nisshō, and so forth) all fall into these three categories. Their growth and development thus depended on their relationships with large producers.

In 1970, all trading firms (about five thousand) accounted for 69 percent of exports, down from 80 percent in 1960. Their share of imports remained fairly stable: 84 versus 81 percent. The decline in export share is due almost solely to the increased importance of various machinery and equipment exports. Trading companies' share of these exports is low (53 percent), as many machinery and equipment producers (shipbuilders, auto companies, and electrical equipment manufacturers) export directly. But the trading companies generally have maintained their export share of certain commodities, particularly textiles, steel, chemicals, and nonferrous metals (Table 12). In effect, trading companies, particularly large trading companies, usually export items requiring little marketing or after-sales service. This is what they do well both in importing and exporting.[28]

In 1970, there were only twenty-eight trading companies with over ¥100 billion in sales, but they accounted for 68 percent of trading company exports and 47 percent of total Japanese exports. As most of these exports were probably produced by large firms (compare Table 12 and Table 9), as were the direct machinery exports that accounted for the bulk of nontrading company sales, small producers and trading companies exported about 20 to 25 percent of total Japanese exports, reconfirming the figure computed earlier.[29]

The current dominant role of large exporters, whether trading company or producer, seems well established. Historically, the role of the large producer vis-à-vis the trading company has probably been understated. Changes in

[28]Before the war the nine leading trading companies had 50 percent of total exports and imports, about equivalent to their share after the war. But prewar direct exports were smaller. Under these circumstances the 45 percent figure hypothesized for prewar exports by large producers seems reasonable.

[29]As in 1970 the 200 leading exporters represented 60.0 percent of total exports but only 32.4 percent of shipments, it seems reasonable that the other 1133 exporting firms with over five hundred employes, which

Table 12
Exports Handled by Trading Companies
(in percent)

Commodity	1960 exports	1965 exports	1970 exports
Foodstuff, tobacco	84.5	83.3	76.8
Textiles	92.3	87.8	85.5
Lumber, pulp, paper	92.8	85.6	79.7
Petroleum, fats, oil	47.6	54.0	38.9
Chemicals	80.8	83.8	81.9
Iron-Steel	94.8	91.4	90.2
Nonferrous metals	74.7	71.9	73.2
Machinery	52.6	54.3	53.9
Total	80.2	74.9	69.2

Source: Tsūsanshō 1971.

comparative advantage associated with Japan's industrialization have made the large producers' current role both more obvious and more important.

Subcontracting relations in Japan are particularly complex, but as the main thrust of this chapter is in terms of export sales by large firms, the importance of subcontracting to the chapter's main hypotheses and inquiry is minor. Nevertheless, as subcontracting has aroused much discussion in Japan, I will briefly examine its importance with respect to the relative roles of small and large firms in exports.

First, one must recognize that the subcontracting phenomena varies by industry and by the stage of industrial production where exports take place. In the case of such products as food, synthetic yarn and fibers, nonferrous metals, steel, chemicals, paper and pulp, petroleum products, rubber tires, glass, and cement, the output of large firms for domestic and export use is at the initial production stage, and subcontracting is basically a finishing process. Thus, in these industries small firms are likely to export through trading companies, and their production has little to do with the export production of large firms. Further, their share of total output is generally small. Data provided in Table 13 show how many small firms export directly, through trading companies, or through other makers. These data confirm that exports through other makers are most important in the assembly industries. Thus, the importance of small firms in large firms' export

accounted for 12.8 percent of industry shipments, might have produced as much as 13 percent of exports. Certainly for the other 1964 exporting firms with over three hundred employes, which shipped 16 percent of total output, one should be able to assume exports at least somewhat less than output share. This makes the figure for exports by small firms (under three hundred employes) about 24 percent. The official government figure of 36 percent again seems unreasonable, and the estimate of 75 percent or more for large firms appears appropriate.

Table 13
Percentage of Small Firms Exporting Directly, through Trading Companies,
and through Other Manufacturers, and Percentage
that Were Subcontractors in 1971

Industry	Direct	Trading company	Other	Subcontractors
Food	13.7	81.8	4.4	30.2
Textile	0.9	74.0	25.1	75.4
Apparel	4.0	70.7	25.3	71.7
Lumber	3.2	44.1	52.7	43.7
Furniture	17.3	65.0	17.7	49.7
Pulp-paper	3.6	60.9	35.6	43.8
Printing	21.9	41.6	36.5	51.0
Chemicals	14.9	74.8	10.3	38.4
Petroleum	21.1	71.1	7.9	29.5
Rubber	3.6	63.8	32.6	53.4
Leather	4.1	62.2	33.7	64.5
Ceramics	3.7	66.6	29.7	33.7
Iron-steel	5.2	58.2	36.7	65.0
Nonferrous metals	4.3	63.3	32.4	69.2
Fabricated metals	3.8	51.2	45.0	71.5
Machinery	6.6	57.8	35.6	75.5
Electric machinery	9.2	40.4	50.4	78.9
Transport equipment.	5.7	37.6	56.7	77.2
Precision equipment	10.4	51.0	38.6	70.5
Miscellaneous	4.6	70.9	24.5	57.8
Total	5.0	62.9	32.2	57.9

Source: Tsūsanshō, 1973.

production is essentially confined to the assembly industries such as machinery, metal fabrication, transportation equipment, electrical equipment, and precision equipment. The subcontracting relation is not a general phenomenon with respect to large firm export production.

In addition, according to MITI's Small and Medium Enterprise Agency, even within the assembly industries, the small firm role is indirect. The largest companies, who in fact assemble and market, are supplied by large contractors who in turn are supplied by smaller companies, and so forth. Therefore any management influence by small firms on export strategy and marketing or on overseas investment is minimal at best. It is hardly surprising that the percentage of firms exporting directly increases with firm size, whereas the percentage exporting through other firms declines (Table 14). These data of course support the basic arguments that large firms have some advantage in export sales. In summary then, though the number of subcontracting firms is large, about 350,000 or 58 percent of all small- and medium-sized firms, the production importance of subcontractors varies by industry, particularly their importance to large firms and large firm exports.

Table 14

1971 Percentage of Firms Exporting Directly, through Trading
Companies, and through Other Manufacturers, by Firm Size

Firm size (employes)	Direct	Trading companies	Other manufacturing firms
1-3	1.1	54.7	44.2
4-9	2.3	64.2	33.4
10-19	3.6	62.8	33.6
20-29	5.4	63.0	31.7
30-49	5.8	64.6	29.5
50-99	9.7	65.8	24.5
100-199	12.0	66.0	22.0
200-299	16.0	65.6	18.5
300-499	20.8	63.7	15.6
500-999	24.0	65.6	10.4
Over 1000	26.2	67.8	6.0
Total	5.0	62.9	32.2

Source: Same as Table 13.

But most important, their decision-making influence on resource allocations
by large firms in terms of overseas marketing is small.

SUMMARY AND CONCLUSIONS

This chapter has examined the interaction over time of changes in Japan's
industrial structure, her changing comparative advantage, and the size of
export producers. Particularly it has addressed the issue of whether in the
early stages of development export advantage lends itself to small labor-
intensive firms, or whether in certain industries even then economies of scale
and technological sophistication give a clear export advantage to larger
manufacturers.

Unfortunately, the available data from Meiji until the early 1960s are
neither complete nor totally conclusive. The analysis, based on available
information, strongly suggests, however, that the export role of large
producers has exceeded their role in domestic production for both individual
industries and for manufacturing as a whole. Further, the more comprehensive data that exists for the late 1960s and early 70s confirm this fact
conclusively for the current period, and demonstrate that shifts in industrial
structure and comparative advantage have amplified the importance of this
greater export role over time. Indeed, the shift in industrial structure and thus
comparative advantage is shown as the prime factor in increasing the export
role of large firms from 20 to 25 percent of exports in 1909 to roughly 75
percent in 1970.

In assessing this development, I analyzed increasing export concentration
and its consequences as part of an ongoing historical trend which is presently

being accelerated by rising wages, a leveling birth rate, increased education, overseas political pressures, and revaluation. During the Meiji period, export production concentration generally was not important. However, since Meiji there has been a significant alteration in Japan's industrial structure; in turn exports have changed from processed primary products and light industrial goods to the output of more capital- and technology-intensive industries subject to economies of scale and marketing. Because the production, export, quality requirements, and marketing costs of traditional industries differ from those for steel, autos, electric appliances, or film, the larger companies in these new fields have obtained a greater participation in export markets. At the same time, the optimally efficient plant size may have increased more sharply for these new industries than the older ones, increasing both domestic and export concentration.

The extent to which these various factors explain the historical change in Japan's export supply structure represents the major inquiry of this paper. However, the paper also explores the role of size in Japan's export development and whether a change in export concentration was a definite aspect of Japan's modernization and industrialization as incomes grew. It appears reasonable that in simple labor-intensive industries where economies of scale, after-sales service, and brand name (advertising costs) are unimportant and entry is easy, there should not be much concentration. When production sophistication, research, after-sales service, or brand become more important, this situation changes. Competition abroad by large foreign firms further magnifies the problem. That is, Japan's recent export success is primarily the result of the competitiveness of a few large firms in a limited number of industries rather than dependence on a multitude of small producers, though this was not always the case.

The benefits of concentrating greater economic power, particularly export power, in a few production units is not clear-cut. If gains in increased productivity are not shared in price declines or income increases, or if largeness reflects abuses of monopoly power rather than greater efficiency, the alleged benefits may be lost. Therefore, though a continued restructuring of the economy may seem logical or even inevitable, the political and welfare consequences of this are not completely beneficial. But in any case, the emerging pattern of Japanese export competition is somewhat different than it was in the past: a few large export firms are now competing in a limited number of industries and products with other large multinational firms. Japan's reliance on small export production units is passing.[30]

[30]A concurrent development of the greater capital and technical intensity favoring a greater export role for large firms has been the higher value added per worker, per unit of output, and thus per yen of export in these newer industries. Capital-intensive industries with export intensity greater than 0.5 accounted for 52 percent of total manufactured value added compared to 50.0 percent of shipments and 40.8 percent of employment. Thus, shifts in comparative advantage contributed to higher net foreign exchange earnings as well.

In addition the paper reached some definite conclusions regarding the relation of export structure and firm size:

1. Larger Japanese firms are significantly more likely to export than smaller firms.

2. However, among firms that are exporting, smaller firms are likely to be more export specialized. This is true even among large export producers.

3. Nevertheless, the greater sales volume of large firms combined with the larger percentage of firms exporting means that, as a group, large firms export relatively more than small firms as a percentage of total sales. Further, in those cases where large firms as a group have a large share of output, they export absolutely more as well.[31]

4. As the trend of product cycle development has been toward industries with increasing concentration and more large firms exporting, the export role of large firms increased both relatively and absolutely over time. The primary agent in this process has been the changing industrial structure.

A possible explanation for these results has been argued elsewhere (Abegglen and Rapp 1972). It appears due to differences in economic efficiency resulting from intense competition within the Japanese context and reflecting economies of scale in production, research, marketing, and overseas operations. In most Japanese industries profit margins on sales are closely related to firm size. The larger producer appears more price, resource, and factor competitive. In addition, these advantages can only be offset by concentrating scale, research, marketing, and overseas operations in an export market, that is, export specialization.

Given this kind of export structure, several scenarios can be put forward for the immediate future if currency unrest and industrial development both continue. A likely one may be further consolidation of export production into a few major industries including steel, transportation equipment, electric machinery, machinery, precision equipment, rubber, and chemicals, thus narrowing Japan's export structure further and continuing past trends. The large companies in these industries have the market investment, resources, and commitment to maintain export sales and/or invest abroad. Further, some smaller producers will find it difficult to compete despite export specialization. Under both these conditions, a smaller number of firms should account for an increasing share of exports.

In the much longer run, Japan may shift its economic structure toward less capital-intensive industries, a so-called postindustrial structure. Under these conditions more foreign exchange earnings could come from overseas manufacturing investments and services. The role of large Japanese multi-national firms could loom even larger in this scenario, especially if services are

[31]The industries where more than 75 percent of firms of one thousand or more employes export are chemicals, rubber, steel, nonferrous metals, machinery, electrical equipment, transport equipment, measuring equipment, miscellaneous manufactures, and furniture. These are generally the capital/technology-intensive industries dominated by a relatively small number of large producers.

primarily banking and insurance and investments are by current major exporters.

In conclusion, I want to emphasize that no value judgment with respect to an optimal industrial structure by firm size for export performance is intended. Oligopoly may not encourage exports, though it seems apparent that in more capital- and technology-intensive industries larger firms are better able to compete internationally, perhaps because competitors are similar in size. Further, the increasing role of large firms in exports is due primarily to a shift in comparative advantage toward heavy industries as a result of changing production structure over time. Historically an innate ability of large firms to compete abroad is a minor and secondary explanatory factor.

However, shifting comparative advantage and increasing or decreasing exports do increase or decrease the role of large firms in an industry as a whole. Conversely, when there are few exports, as in the case of the printing industry, there is little change in industry structure over time.

Nevertheless, this development may well have important implications by indicating that as economies grow and change their structure, one natural consequence is the emergence of large exporters who in turn become large foreign investors and large multinational companies. This subsequently has a long-term impact on a country's balance of payments and the government's control over international economic activity. In addition, once such corporate institutions emerge, they tend to perpetuate themselves despite continued structural shifts, by introducing and marketing new products.[32] The outlook for Japan would thus seem to be for greater export concentration in the future as the economy continues to grow and develop.

[32]Tilton's study (1971) of the semiconductor industry demonstrates large Japanese companies have an ability to respond to major changes in product and technology (for example, out of vacuum tubes into transistors).

REFERENCES

Abegglen, James C., and William V. Rapp. 1972. "Competative Impact of Japan's Growth." In *Pacific Partnership: United States-Japan Trade*, edited by James Cohen. Heath.

Ajia Kyōkai. 1957. *The Smaller Industry in Japan*. Ajia Kyōkai.

Akamatsu, Kamae. 1962. "An Historical Pattern of Economic Growth in Developing Countries." *The Developing Economies*, preliminary issue no. 1 (March-Aug. 1962).

Fujii, Shigeru. 1960. "Recovery and Development of Foreign Trade Firms in Kobe after the War." In *Small Business in Japan*, edited by Tokutarō Yamanaka. Japan Times.

———. 1971. "Japan's Small Enterprises and Export Trade." In *Small Business in Japan's Economic Progress*, edited by Tokutarō Yamanaka. Asahi Shinpōsha.

JERC [Japan Economic Research Center]. 1972. *Japan's Economy in 1980 in the Global Context*. JERC.

Keizai Kikaku-chō [Economic Planning Agency]. 1969. *Keizai Hakusho*, 1968 edition.

———. 1970. *New Economic and Social Development Plan, 1970-1975*.

Kojima, Kiyoshi. 1973. "Reorganization of North-South Trade: Japan's Foreign Economic Policy for the 1970s." *Hitotsubashi Journal of Economics*, Feb. 1973.

Melvin, James R., and Robert D. Warne. 1973. "Monopoly and the Theory of International Trade." *Journal of International Economics*, May 1973.

Nihon Ginkō, Tōkei-kyoku [Bank of Japan, Statistics Bureau]. 1966. *Hundred-Year Statistics of the Japanese Economy*. 3 vols. including 2 vols. of English translation of the notes.

Okurashō [Ministry of Finance]. *Nihon Bōeki Geppō*. Published monthly with Dec. issue giving annual figures. The 1937, 1952, 1956, 1960, 1964, 1968, and 1970 Dec. editions have been used, each published in year following cover date.

Oriental Economist. 1935. *Foreign Trade of Japan Statistical Survey*.

President Directory. Published annually by Diamond-Time.

Pryor, Frederic L. 1972. "The Size of Production Establishments in Manufacturing." *Economic Journal*, June 1972.

Pursell, G., and R. H. Snape. 1973. "Economics of Scale, Price Discrimination, and Exporting." *Journal of International Economics*, Feb. 1973.

Rapp, William V. 1967*a*. "A Theory of Changing Trade Patterns under Economic Growth Tested for Japan." *Yale Economic Essays*, fall 1967.

———. 1967*b*. "A Theory of Changing Trade Patterns under Economic Growth Tested for Japan." Ph.D. dissertation. University Microfilms.

Takahashi, Kamekichi. 1935. "Superiority of Small Industries and Special Character of Japanese Economy." *Shakai Seisaku Joho*, April 1935.

Tilton, John. 1971. *International Diffusion of Technology*. Brookings.

Tsūsanshō (Tsūshōsangyōshō) [Ministry of International Trade and Industry]. 1959. *Dai Ikkai Chūshō Kōgyō Jittai Kihon Chōsa*. Covers 1957. (The *Chūshō* is published every four years.)

———. *Kōgyō Tōkei-hyō*. "Report by Industry" and "Report by Enterprise," 1964 and 1970 annual editions, published in 1966 and 1972.

———. 1971. *Bōeki Gyōtai Tōkei*.

———. 1973. *Dai Yonkai Chūshō Kōgyō Jittai Kihon Chōsa*. Covers 1971.

———. Chūshō Kigyō-Chō [Small and Medium Enterprise Agency]. *Chūshō Kigyō Hakusho*. Published annually.

———. Daijin Kambō, Chōsa Tōkei-bu [Research and Statistics Division]. 1961. *Kōgyō Tōkei Gojūnenshi*. 3 vols.

Uyeda, Teijiro. 1938. *The Small Industries of Japan*. Oxford University Press.

The Evolution of
Dualistic Wage Structure

Yasukichi Yasuba

Much fuss has been made about the so-called dualistic structure in postwar Japan, with endless talk about the difference in wages, productivity, and technology between big and small businesses, between traditional and modern sectors, or between agriculture and industry. Some of the differences, however, are not very interesting from an economist's point of view. For example, different industries may use different technologies, including different capital-labor ratios, with the so-called modern industries usually adopting more capital-intensive technologies than traditional industries. The coexistence of steel mills, cement factories, and power plants with barbershops, gardeners, and grocery stores can be found in any industrialized country. Disparity in the average labor productivity of different industries is also a common phenomenon, but a large part of this disparity should be explained by the difference in capital intensity.

The dualistic structure, or dualism, becomes an interesting phenomenon only when there is a long-lasting disparity which is expected to be wiped out if the society consists of economically rational men and if market forces are at work. For example, in the celebrated models of Lewis and of Fei and Ranis, marginal productivity of labor is continually higher in the capitalistic sector than in the traditional sector (until the turning-point is reached),

I am indebted to Mataji Miyamoto, Yasuzō Horie, Henry Rosovsky, Robert Cole, Koji Taira, and particularly Hugh Patrick and Ryūtarō Komiya for helpful comments and suggestions. I am also grateful to the Kansai Economic Research Center for financial support and to Tōyō Keizai Shimposha for granting access to the original returns of *Moderu Chingin Chōsa* for 1958 and 1968. The present paper is partially based on an earlier paper ("Emergence of Dualism in Japan's Wage Structures") presented to the Far Eastern Meetings of the Econometric Society and the Rokkō Conference in 1967. Kōnosuke Odaka's comments on the paper at the Econometric Society meetings were most helpful.

presumably because, although the ethos of capitalism is dominant in the former, the rule of the extended family is at work in the latter.[1]

The wide wage differential by size of an establishment or a firm seems to be another case of dualism which calls for further examination.[2] Hiromi Arisawa is believed to have been the first to use the term *nijū-kōzō* (dual structure) to describe this phenomenon. That was in 1957, but the fact itself had been known for quite some time. For example, the 1953 *Rōdō Hakusho* called attention to the fact that "wage differentials by the size of an establishment had been widening after the Korean War" and called this phenomenon "a characteristic of the labor economy of this country."

Statistics supporting such an inference for this period were usually average wages by size of establishment, based on the *Maigetsu Kinrō Tokei Chōsa* or the *Shitsugyō Hokenryō Shinkoku*. Figure 1 shows the disparity in average wages based on the former. Its magnitude, particularly before 1960, may look extremely large compared to that of other industrialized countries where the disparity, if any, is on order of 10 to 20 percent at most.

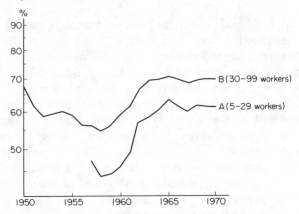

Figure 1. Wage differentials in manufacturing industries (average wages at small establishments as a percentage of those at large establishments).

Source: Maigetsu Kinrō-tōkei Chōsa Sōgō Hōkokusho.

Note: A: 5-29 workers. *B:* 30-99 workers. Wages include bonuses and all other monetary remunerations.

[1]Lewis (1954) is not so restrictive in his assumption at least in the original presentation, but we should not get involved here in hairsplitting details.

[2]An "establishment" is a specific place of work or business, such as a factory, office, or store. A firm, such as a proprietor, partner, or incorporated enterprise, comprises one or more establishments. Hence data by establishment size may understate the size of firms. A large establishment means a large firm, but a small establishment does not necessarily connote a small firm, though that usually is the case. In general, small firms have one establishment, whereas larger firms have several or many. Data collected in a census of manufactures, in Japan as well as the United States, are typically reported by size of establishment rather than firm; this is particularly true for the prewar period.

As Sumiya (1961) pointed out, the divergence is somewhat exaggerated and the trend is quite misleading because of the crucial way in which the changing age composition of labor was involved. In the early 1950s, large establishments (or firms) employed disproportionately large numbers of older (high-wage) workers and small establishments (firms) employed disproportionately large numbers of younger workers, as shown in Table 1. As a result, the disparity in average wages appeared more pronounced than the disparity in wages of comparable groups of workers.

For some time, the age composition of workers employed by large establishments became still older with the result that the disparity in average wages became even more pronounced. In fact, the distortion was such that while the wage differentials for comparable groups of workers tended to narrow from the mid-1950s, differentials in average wages continued to widen almost throughout the 1950s. The distortion became less pronounced in the 1960s, and its direction has been reversed recently as the age composition of workers in larger establishments has become younger than that of workers in small establishments.

If our interest centers on obtaining some idea about the reality of differentials among firm sizes for comparable groups of workers, it is sufficient to look, as Sumiya did, at figures for wages of workers classified by education, sex, white collar-blue collar status, and age.[3] In order to present a summary picture, however, it is necessary to use, as Blumenthal (1966) did, an analysis of variance, or to standardize, as Ono (1973) did, using the composition of the labor force as a weight in computing the averages. Figure 2 shows ratios for selected years of the standardized average wages of workers in small establishments to those of workers in large establishments, computed by

Table 1
Age Composition of Labor, Male, Manufacturing Industries
(in percent)

Size	Age	1954	1959	1965	1970
Firms employing more than 1000 workers	Younger than 30	49.1	42.4	50.8	50.8
	30 and older	50.9	57.6	49.2	49.2
Firms employing 10 to 99 workers	Younger than 30	56.3	62.6	50.5	39.6
	30 and older	43.7	37.4	49.5	60.4

Sources: 1954 and 1959: Sumiya 1961, 1965 and 1970: Rōdōshō, Chingin Kōzō Kihon Chōsa.

[3]Such statistics were collected and compiled by Rōdōshō (Ministry of Labor) in the Chingin Kōzō Kihonchōsa (1958-) and its predecessors such as Shokushubetsutō Chingin Chōsa (1954-57), and also by various Moderu Chingin Chōsa. The results of various model wage surveys are summarized in Tōyō Keizai Shimpōsha's annual Chingin Sōran (1968-). Other surveys are given under Rōdōshō in the reference list.

applying correction factors obtained from Ono's book. It may be observed
that differentials in the standardized wages are considerably smaller than
those in the nonstandardized wages. Yet substantial differentials still remain
even in 1966 and presumably in the 1970s as well. Particularly when it is
remembered that fringe benefits, excluded from Figure 2, favored workers in
large-scale establishments even more than wages did, it is undeniable that a
considerable size-oriented differential in material welfare appears to have
been an important feature of the postwar years.[4]

Various hypotheses have been presented to explain this peculiar phenomenon. Most economists believed the segmented labor market for large-scale

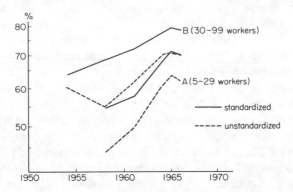

**Figure 2. Wage differentials in manufacturing
industries (average wages in small establishments as a percentage of those in large establishments, standardized and unstandardized).**

Sources: Correction factors for standardization are
from Ono 1973, p. 173. In this source, size refers to
average number of workers per firm, rather than per
establishment. Wage data are from *Maigetsu Kinrō-
tōkei Chōsa Sōgō Hōkokusho,* and Ono 1973, p. 173.

Notes: The labor force has been standardized with
respect to sex, status, and age. Large establishments
are those employing 500 or more workers. *A:* establishments with 5-29 workers. *B:* establishments with
30-99 workers.

[4]In recent articles (1973*a* and 1973*b*), Stoikov contends "there is no
evidence that larger firms pay higher wages than smaller ones for the same
quality of labor input, as measured by an array of human capital components
(1973*a*, p. 1103). This contention is hardly warranted. First, though he pays
lip service to the role of bonuses, Stoikov in his formal analysis neglects them,
as well as omitting workers with thirty or more years of experience. The
exclusions are serious because these are the two most important components
causing size-oriented wage-differentials in recent years. The second and more
serious error is his interpretation of the length of service as representing the
amount of on-the-job training. The lack of correlation, beyond certain years,
between these two variables in large-scale firms is exactly what Japanese
economists have been trying to explain. Stoikov simply formulated his
analysis in such a way as to let all these problems disappear.

firms with the system of lifetime commitment and seniority-determined wages was responsible. A number of economists further believed the system had its origin in Japanese tradition. For example, Sasaki and Magota (1956) thought it unrealistic to ascribe the wage differentials of various groups to differentials in their members' average capabilities. They suggest wage differentials should not be understood as mere divergences from equilibrium but rather as problems deep-rooted in Japan's economic structure and social structure. This theme was accepted widely in Japan among observers of the postwar scene and was publicized in the Western world by Abegglen (1958).

Most economists also mentioned higher unionization ratios of workers in large firms as another factor making wages in large firms higher than in small firms. Thus, Shinohara (1959, p. 105) stated that "the enterprise unions which tended to be stronger in large firms further intensified the segmentation of the labor market there."

Students, then, have tried to explain why large-scale firms have been able to continue to pay higher wages to workers, particularly to workers with a lifetime commitment. Shinohara (1959 and 1961, ch. 5) detected two characteristics of large firms that made this possible: price-controlling power in the product market and credit rationing in the capital market. The first point was also emphasized by Komiya (1961 and 1962), who found that the advantages associated with large firms were absorbed in higher wages rather than monopolistic profits.

Shinohara particularly emphasized the second point. He had in mind the zaibatsu of the prewar years and what was called *kinyū keiretsu* (groups of firms organized around large commercial and development banks). The keiretsu were further analyzed by Miyazaki (1962), who discovered a "one-set principle" operating within each group.[5] Miyazawa (1961) also shed new light on the capital market side of dualism by uncovering size-oriented differentials in interest rates, with large firms borrowing at lower rates than small firms.

While these discussions were going on among observers of the current scene, labor economists have been aware of the exaggeration in claims that lifetime commitment and age-determined wages in large firms, as well as the dualistic wage structure, were deep-rooted in Japanese tradition. Umemura (1955) noted that significant differentials in average wages did not exist in 1909 or in 1914. Labor historians including Sumiya (1955, 1963, 1967), Fujita (1961), and Hyōdō (1971), and sociologists such as Hazama (1964) have suggested the system of lifetime commitment and age-determined wages emerged largely in this century.[6]

---

[5] The "one-set principle" states that each group tries to have an affiliated firm in every field, with the result that no group has price-controlling power in more than a few product markets. Accordingly, what is called "excessive competition" between a few large corporations becomes the order of the day.

[6] See particularly Sumiya, et al. (1967) or the English version (Sumiya 1963). Also, Shōwadōjinkai (1960), Tsuda (1968), and Horie (1972).

Lifetime commitment and seniority-determined wages did not exist for blue-collar workers in most modern factories in the mid-Meiji period. It is the opinion of these history-oriented scholars that the so-called Japanese system of labor relations was basically a response on the part of the management to changes in technical requirements and to the emerging threat of the labor movement. To quote Ōkōchi (1959), the transition to the new system was a response to "the need for retaining new types of skilled workers" and also "an act of defense by individual firms to cope with the development and radicalization of labor union movement." Some modern economists such as Odaka (1970) and Taira (1970) have taken similar views, interpreting the evolution of the dualistic wage structure in more or less neoclassical terms, with some time-lag allowed.

However, it may be doubted that the continuation of such extreme wage differentials by firm size for almost half a century can be explained as a matter of time-lag. Or, if it has to be accounted for as such, the unusual length of the lag will have to be explained. Moreover, a number of labor economists, including Fujita and Ōkōchi, and sociologists such as Hazama admit the peculiarly Japanese tradition played an important part in the evolution of the system of labor management. Thus, there is still much room for further study. As the first step, the next section places postwar wage differentials in proper historical perspective.

EMERGENCE OF DUALISM IN PREWAR JAPAN

The only known source which gives a general picture of industrial wages by size of establishment for the early Meiji period is the table on factories for 1885 presented in the second *Nōshōmu Tōkei-hyō* [Statistics on Agricultural and Commercial Affairs]. This unique table shows *for each factory* the number of man-days worked by operatives classified according to sex and age (fifteen and younger and sixteen and older), the total amount of wages paid to different classes of workers, average operating hours per day, days of operation per year, and a host of other information. Although only seventeen prefectures submitted reports and there were apparent omissions even from them,[7] the table gives some idea of the general state of affairs, for such then-important industrial prefectures as Osaka, Fukuoka, Nagasaki, Hiroshima, Gifu, Fukushima, and Yamanashi are represented. Factories were classified by size, by the type of motive power (steam engine, water power, or none), and by industry, to see whether any systematic pattern appeared in the average wages of male workers age sixteen or older, in the average wages of female workers in the same age class, or in average operating hours per day.

[7]All the factories with steam engines were tabulated. Among factories without steam engines, every one except those engaged in silk reeling was tabulated; only one in five silk-reeling factories in this category were tabulated, to save time and labor.

Table 2
Average Wages and Operating Hours for Factories, 1885

Size (operatives per factory)	Average daily wages[a] Male, age 16 and up	Female, age 16 and up	Average operating hours
1-9	16.4 sen	12.9 sen	11.4 hours
10-29	15.8	8.8	11.6
30-49	13.9	7.7	11.8
50-99	17.5	8.4	12.1
100 and up	14.9	8.2	12.8
Average[b]	15.7	9.2	12.0
Type of motive power			
Steam engine	20.0	9.8	12.8
Water power	13.5	8.8	11.8
No power	15.0	10.3	10.9

Source: Nōshōmu Tōkei-hyō.
[a]Unweighted by hours worked.
[b]Average of column entries weighted by the number of establishments.

Average wages differed from one industry to another with grain-and-flour milling, spinning, shipbuilding, and printing paying relatively high wages and silk reeling (particularly male), cloth, and matches paying relatively low wages. When it comes to size-oriented differentials, however, as Table 2 shows, no systematic pattern appears within industries or for the entire manufacturing sector. Factories with steam engines paid considerably higher wages to male operators than other types of factories did, but they paid only average wages to females.

If any systematic pattern is to be found, it is in average operating hours per day. Larger factories operated longer hours than smaller ones, with factories with one hundred and more workers operating 12.8 hours in contrast to 11.5 hours for factories with fewer than ten workers. Operating hours were also associated with power-intensity. Factories with steam power operated, on an average, 12.8 hours. Those using water power operated 11.8 hours, and those without any power operated only 10.9 hours. The tendency for larger and more power-intensive factories to operate longer hours apparently reflected the emergence of two-shift operations within these factories.

For 1909, 1914, and 1932/33, we have more comprehensive data that have been analyzed by Umemura (1955). Among other things he found (1) there were only small differentials in wages associated with the size of the establishment in manufacturing industries before World War I, (2) the size-oriented differentials became extremely wide by 1932 or 1933, and (3) differentials of similar magnitude existed in 1951. The changing pattern of the size-oriented wage differentials Umemura found is reproduced in Tables 3 and 4.

Table 3

Average Wages of Operatives in Manufacturing Industries
by Size of Establishment, 1909, 1914, and 1951

| Size (Operatives per establishment)[a] | 1909 (Sen per day) | | | 1914 (Sen per day) | | | 1951[c] (¥100 per year) |
	Weighted average	Male	Female	Weighted average	Male	Female	Male and female
5-9	34	43	20	39	47	22	594[b]
10-19	33	46	21	37	50	23	641
20-29							699
30-49	32	48	23	35	52	25	760
50-99	32	49	25	36	54	27	842
100-199	33	50	26	36	55	27	968
200-499							1130
500-999	32	49	26	39	57	31	1332
1000 and up	34	54	24	43	66	31	1502

Source: Computed by Unemura 1955, 2:257, from Kōjō Tōkei-hyō for 1909 and 1914 and from Kōgyō Tōkei-hyō for 1951.
Notes: Simple averages of each operative's wage regardless of hours worked.
[a]"Operatives" are defined as shokkō in 1909 and 1914, and rōmusha in 1951.
[b]Size strata for 1951 represent employes per establishment and Stratum I reads "4-9."
[c]Wages in 1951 include money wages only.

Table 4

Average Wages of Employes in Manufacturing Industries
by Size of Establishment in Major Industrial Centers, 1932/33

Size (Average capital per establishment in thousand yen)[b]	Average number of employes per establishment[a]	Average annual wage (in yen)
5-10	6.7	363
10-50	14.5	453
50-100	29.3	524
100-500	67.9	566
500 and up	409.8	671

Source: Computed by Umemura 1955, 2:258, from Kōgyō Chōsasho for the cities of Tokyo, Yokohama, Nagoya, Kobe, and Osaka, and for Osaka prefecture (other than Osaka city). Data for small establishments with capitalization of less than 5000 yen are not shown, as the average number of employes at these establishments is too few to be included in the census data for 1909 and 1914 as shown in Tables 3 and 5.
[a]Employes include engineers and white-collar workers as well as factory operatives.
[b]Capital is the total value of assets. Size 5-10 means five or more but less than 10,000 yen; the same applies to other sizes.

The lack of significant size-oriented differentials in *average* wages in the first two years in Table 3 is misleading. For both male and female, wages were higher in larger establishments, particularly in 1914. This does not show up in averages mostly because large factories in these years were predominantly in textile industries where female workers (with wages lower than those for males) were employed extensively. If we standardize the composition of labor, the average wages, of course, reveal size-oriented differentials of some magnitude. Table 5 shows such standardized average wages for each year.

By the mid-1930s the importance of large-scale plants in the male-dominant heavy industries had become much larger, so that size-oriented differentials showed up even on the basis of simple weighted averages. When the composition of labor is standardized, measured differentials in average wages (hereafter referred to as standardized wages) actually become smaller for these years mainly because two additional operations have been performed. First, the original yearly wages have been converted into daily wages using the average figures of operating days per year by the size of the establishment in 1914. This reduces differentials somewhat, for there tended to be more operating days per year in large-scale than in small-scale plants. Second, average wages for operatives rather than for all employes have been estimated. This again lessened the differentials, because larger establishments tended to employ a greater proportion of high-wage white-collar workers and engineers. For 1951 direct data to estimate daily wages for different sizes are not available and use of the figures for prewar operating days does not seem warranted, so original yearly wages have been converted into monthly averages using the figures for the average number of workers per month available for this year.

Because the largest size stratum in the 1932/33 data is broader than in other years, representing establishments with 327 operatives on average, one more operation is needed to make 1932/33 comparable with other years. Size strata for establishments with 100 operatives or more in 1909, 1914, and 1951 have been merged into one stratum, with an average 355, 338, and 334 operatives for 1909, 1914, and 1951, respectively. This makes the new largest stratum roughly comparable for all years. Finally, wages are expressed in the form of two series of index numbers, one with wages for the original largest stratum as 100 (Table 5, column 4) and the other wages for the new largest stratum as 100 (column 5).

Now the results of the entire operation can be summarized. Wage differentials associated with the size of the establishment, on the order of 20 percent, already existed in 1909 (column 4). The differentials widened between 1909 and 1914 and continued to widen thereafter. By 1932/33, the magnitude of differentials became very large, almost comparable with those in 1951 (column 5). The differentials between the largest and smallest strata were about 40 percent in 1932/33 and more than 50 percent in 1951. However, the average number of operatives for the smallest size stratum was smaller in 1951 than in 1932/33 and, moreover, wages in kind such as room, board, and clothing were included in 1932/33 and excluded in 1951. Thus, the difference in the 1932/33 and 1951 differentials should be discounted.

That 1909, 1914, 1951, and particularly 1932/33 were all close to the bottom of a business cycle must have had some influence on the magnitude of differentials. However, the general trend is unmistakable; the wage differentials began to form between 1885 and 1909 and widened thereafter until they became almost comparable with the postwar differentials.

Table 5
Standardized Wages of Operatives in Manufacturing by Size
of Establishment 1909, 1914, 1932/33, and 1951

1909

(1) Size (operatives per establishment)	(2) Average number of operatives per establishment	(3) Standardized average wages (sen per day)	(4) Index[a]	(5) Index[a]
5-9	6.5	32.6	80.7	82.3.
10-29	15.8	34.7	85.9	37.6
30-49	37.4	36.7	90.8	92.7
50-99	67.1	38.2	94.5	96.5
100-499	184.5	39.1	96.8	--
500-999	680.7	38.6	95.5	--
1000 and up	2772.1	40.4	100.0	--
100 and up	(354.8)	(39.6)	--	100.0

1914

5-9	6.4	35.7	71.3	78.5
10-29	16.0	37.8	75.4	83.1
30-49	37.5	39.8	79.4	87.5
50-99	66.9	41.8	83.4	91.9
100-499	188.1	42.3	84.4	--
500-999	667.5	45.2	90.2	--
1000 and up	1891.6	50.1	100.0	--
100 and up	(337.8)	(45.5)	--	100.0

1932/33[b]

(1) Size (capital per establishment)[d] (in thousand yen)	(2) Average number of operatives per establishment[c]	(3) Standardized average wages for operatives[c] (sen per day)	(4) Index[a]
5-10	6.3	119.6	61.2
10-50	13.1	144.6	74.0
50-100	25.6	158.4	81.1
100-500	58.2	174.2	89.2
500 and up	326.7	195.3	100.0

1951

(1) Size (persons engaged per establishment)	(2) Average number of operatives per establishment	(3) Standardized average money wages for operatives (yen per month)	(4) Index[a]	(5) Index[a]
4-9	4.3	4894	41.7	47.1
10-19	10.6	5399	46.0	52.0
20-29	19.4	6870	50.0	56.5
30-49	31.2	6392	54.4	61.5
50-99	56.6	7081	60.3	68.2
100-199	114.6	8040	68.5	--
200-499	250.6	9417	80.2	--
500-999	571.1	10,785	91.8	--
1000 and up	1866.8	11,741	100.0	--
100 and up	(334.0)	(10,389)	--	100.0

Sources: Computed from Tables 3 and 4 and their sources.
Notes: See Appendix 1.
[a]Standardized average wage (col. 3) for each size as a percentage of the largest size.
[b]Only for the cities of Tokyo, Tokohama, Nagoya, and Osaka, and for Osaka prefecture (other than Osaka city).
[c]Average number and average wages are for operatives only. Job titles included are *shokko, totei,* and *sonota jūgyōsha.* Note that in Table 4 data for this year are for all employes.
[d]Capital is the total value of assets. Size 5-10, for example, means 5000 or larger but less than 10,000 yen. The same applies to other sizes.

Unfortunately statistics available prior to 1932/33, and particularly before 1909, the formative period of dualism, are fragmentary. Nevertheless, some inference may be drawn about what probably happened by examining wage differentials within specific industries. Intraindustry analysis is also preferred because it permits further standardization of the quality of labor being compared.[8] Statistics for 1909, 1914, 1932/33, and 1951 have been examined by industry. The data are the same as used in Table 5, that is, the *Kōjō Tōkeihyō* for 1909 and 1914, the *Kōgyō Chōsasho* for industrial centers either for 1932 or 1933, and the *Kōgyō Tōkeihyō* for 1951.[9]

Industries have been selected by the following criteria: (1) each was roughly comparable for 1914, 1932/33, and 1951, and (2) it was an important industry in the sense of employing more than five thousand operatives in 1914, although a few more which gained importance later have been added. Some of the twenty-three industries thus selected (paper, cars, and carriages, and cement and its products, for example) are composite in nature. They were retained because otherwise there are too few comparable important industries. For 1909 and 1914, composite industries are subdivided where possible, and a few more added to make the total number of industries thirty-five.

Adjustments have been made for sex composition, operating days (for 1909, 1914, and 1932/33), white collar-blue collar ratio (for 1932/33), and age composition (for 1909 and 1914) to arrive at standardized average wages. They represent the average daily (monthly in 1951) wages of operatives weighted by the sex (and age when applicable) composition of operatives in that industry in the given year. The sources and method of estimation for standardized average wages are shown in Appendix 1.

To summarize wage differentials, two measures are adopted. One is the coefficient of variation in wages, which shows the extent of disparity. To avoid the disturbance resulting from changes in the method of forming size strata in different years and to best emphasize the size distribution of income, we have chosen a coefficient of variation in average wages weighted by the number of operatives included in each stratum.

The second measure, size elasticity of wages, tells how closely the differentials are associated with the size of an establishment or, in other words, whether there is a distinct tendency for larger establishments to pay

[8]Odaka (1968) has compared the wages paid at a few large factories, mostly in heavy industries, and those for workers of traditional trade engaged in similar work in the same localities. Odaka (1969 and 1970) and Minami (1970) also examined wage differentials between minifactories employing less than five persons and other factories employing five or more persons in the city of Tokyo. They both found a number of industries had a significant widening of differentials in the 1920s.

[9]The data for Yokohama and the City of Tokyo in 1932, and those from Nagoya, the City of Osaka, and Osaka Prefecture other than the City of Osaka in 1933 are used in the analysis. Reports from Kobe cannot be incorporated due to the inadequacy of industrial classification.

higher wages. Again in an effort to make the measure as independent as possible from the arbitrary and changing method of grouping of data, the coefficient for the independent variable, size of the establishment, was read directly from a log-linear regression equation in which each observation was weighted by the average of two shares, one in terms of the number of establishments and another in terms of the number of operatives.[10]

The results of the computation are shown in Figures 3 through 7. Two diagrams are used for 1914, 1914A comparable with 1909 and 1914B comparable with later years. (See Appendix Tables 1 and 2.) Each dot in the diagram represents the coefficient of variation (measured on the horizontal axis) and the size elasticity of wages (measured on the vertical axis) for a particular industry. Cases where the size elasticity is positive and significantly different from zero at the 5 percent level are represented by a star.

When intraindustrial wage differentials are small in all industries, the dots tend to gather near the vertical axis and usually near the origin. If many industries are characterized by large wage differentials, the cluster of dots moves to the right. Where wages of the large-differential industries are also positively correlated with the size of the establishment, satisfying the def-

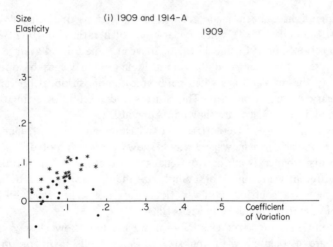

Figure 3. Measures of variation in standardized wages—1909.

Note: 1914*a* consists of thirty-five industries comparable to 1909.

[10]The weighting stems partly from the wish to avoid the problem of heteroscedasticity. Without knowing the effects of the number of establishments and of the number of operatives on standard errors, we simply decided to use an average. Thus, the size elasticity, β, is obtained when

$$\Sigma_i \; \tfrac{1}{2}\left(\frac{L_i}{\Sigma L_i} + \frac{F_i}{\Sigma F_i}\right)\left((\log \alpha + \beta \; \log S_i) - \log w_i\right)^2$$

is minimized; where L_i is the number of operatives, F_i the number of establishments, S_i the average size of establishments, and w_i the average wage for size stratum i; and α and β are the coefficients to be estimated.

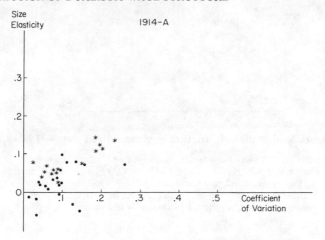

Figure 4. Measures of variation in standardized wages—1914a.
Note: 1914a consists of thirty-five industries comparable to 1909.

inition of dualistic structure, the points will be stars rather than dots, and the more they reflect size differentials the farther they are from the horizontal axis.

In 1909 (Figure 3), the dots and stars form a fairly tight cluster not far from the origin, but a surprisingly large proportion (more than half) of all the industries are represented by stars. By 1914 (Figures 4 and 5), the cluster moves somewhat upward and considerably to the right, but in general is still rather close to the origin. By 1932/33 (Figure 6), the cluster moves farther from the origin to the northeast. The number of stars is somewhat less than before, but this may be ascribed to the smallness of samples and the inadequate grouping of establishments for these years. A similar pattern can be observed for 1951, except by that time most points are stars rather than dots.

The conclusion drawn from Table 5 is confirmed and extended. Namely, dualism in the sense of size-oriented wage differentials already existed in 1909, and the degree of duality was considerable; the differentials widened until 1932/33, when a pattern similar to that in a postwar year could be observed.[11]

[11]Actually the differentials are believed to have narrowed during the war and then to have been widened after the war, but here, being interested only in the long-term movement, I shall neglect these fluctuations.

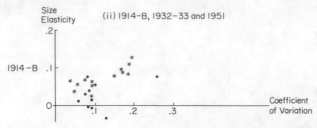

Figure 5. Measures of variation in standardized wages—1914*b*.

Notes: 1914*b* consists of twenty-three industries roughly comparable with 1932/33 and 1951. 1932/33 and 1951 consist of the same number of industries, and 1932/33 represents establishments only in those size strata in which the average number of operatives per establishment is five or more.

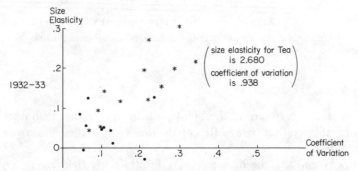

Figure 6. Measures of variation in standardized wages—1932/33.

Notes: 1914*b* consists of twenty-three industries roughly comparable with 1932/33 and 1951. 1932/33 and 1951 consist of the same number of industries, and 1932/33 represents establishments only in those size strata in which the average number of operatives per establishment is five or more.

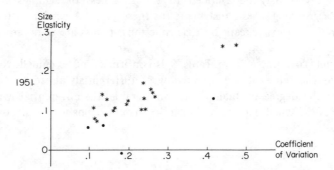

Figure 7. Measures of variation in standardized wages—1951.

Notes: 1914*b* consists of twenty-three industries roughly comparable with 1932/33 and 1951. 1932/33 and 1951 consist of the same number of industries, and 1932/33 represents establishments only in those size strata in which the average number of operatives per establishment is five or more.

INDUSTRIAL PATTERNS OF DIFFERENTIALS IN 1909 AND 1914

Let us now turn to an examination of the industrial patterns of wage differentials. Figure 8 shows the ranges for standardized average wages in 1909 and 1914. To facilitate comparison among different industries, the composition of labor used for the computation of average wages in this figure was standardized to that for the entire manufacturing industry in each year. For the benefit of intertemporal comparison, all the wages are expressed in 1914 prices and shown on a semilog scale.[12] The degree of size orientation— the extent to which larger establishments paid higher wages—is illustrated by the shading of the bars, corresponding to the stars in Figures 3-7. If a bar is shaded, there is significant positive association between wages and the size of the establishment in that industry. Thus, when a conspicuous dualistic structure exists in an industry, it is represented by a long shaded bar. However, if a wide differential occurs in an erratic fashion or in a perverse way (smaller establishments paying higher wages) the bar is left unshaded.[13]

Looking at Figure 8, it is clear that for these early years the long shaded bars are concentrated in textile and other light industries, and that most of the heavy and chemical industries are represented by unshaded and/or short bars. There is another distinct group of industries represented by unshaded and/or short bars. They are the traditional industries, such as pottery, Japanese paper, sake, and soy sauce, which had not yet been much affected by foreign technology.

Now I define a dualistic industry as one satisfying the following two conditions: (1) wage differentials within the industry are so wide as to include it in the upper half of industries ranked by coefficient of variation in wages, and (2) such a significant tendency for the larger establishments to pay higher wages that the industry is in the highest quintile of industries ranked by size elasticity.[14] Let us also define a homogeneous industry as one in which wages were so uniform that the industry is in the lowest quintile in terms of the coefficient of variation.

[12]LTES (8:246) presents a series of daily wages in manufacturing industries for the period 1899-1964, expecting a few years between 1944 and 1946. This series is used to make the wages for different years comparable with each other. An adjustment has been made to average wages in each size in different industries, so the overall average wages for the entire manufacturing industries coincide with LTES's average wages in the same year. Then, the results have been converted into real wages using the LTES (8:135-137) consumers' price index for urban families (all items). As we are interested particularly in the early years, the base-year for the price index was shifted to 1914. The two largest size strata have been merged as in Table 6.

[13]This latter case is rare. It occurred only for "batteries and electric appliances" in 1909 and for "sake" and "beer" in 1914*a*.

[14]In some cases an industry which satisfied the second condition has been disqualified because it did not meet the first condition. In each such case the industry next in line in terms of size elasticity has been included.

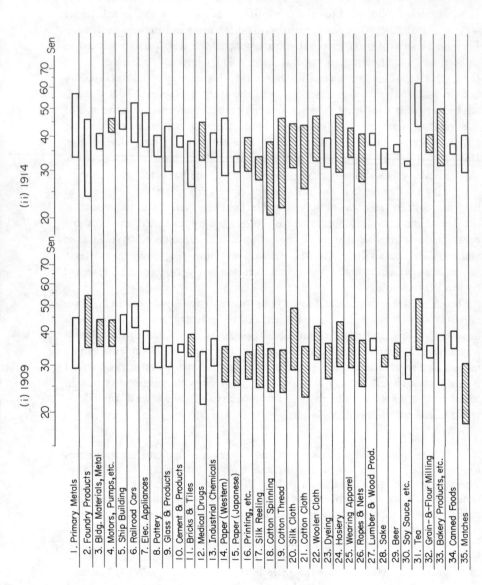

Figure 8. Ranges for standardized average wages in real terms for different industries, 1909 and 1914.
Source: See Appendix 1.

Table 6 shows the standardized average wages of dualistic and homogeneous industries in 1909 and 1914. Hosiery, ropes and nets, cotton thread, and cotton cloth were dualistic in both these years. Dyeing, silk reeling, and tea in 1909 and bakery products, medicines, and printing in 1914 round out the list. Matches in 1909 and grain and flour milling in 1914 are two industries disqualified as dualistic mainly because of the concentration of workers in factories of particular sizes. It may be noted that six of the dualistic industries are textile or textile related.

Virtually all of the dualistic industries had borrowed foreign technology during their early years. Most became established industries at an early stage using imported technologies modified and acclimatized in different degrees, so it might be proper to call them older modern industries. It is easy to imagine a productivity gap would appear when the larger and more modern branches of these industries happened to be very advanced in technology from the outset, or when sufficient time had elapsed to allow for the maturing of indigenous managers or engineers working in larger factories, or when indigenous entrepreneurs and engineers had developed superior acclimatized technologies suitable for medium- and large-scale operation, while smaller establishments continued to use more traditional technologies.[15]

It is worth noting in Table 6 that most of the dualistic industries in 1909 and 1914 were paying only average wages in the large-size factories and lower than average wages in the small establishments. When productivity became higher in the more modern branches, flooding the market with cheaper commodities, incomes in the small establishments were pushed lower. Given the paternalistic and personalistic labor-management relations particularly strong in small establishments, it is not surprising workers there accepted lower wages.

The quarter-century preceding the beginning of World War I represented a period of rapid technical progress in many branches of the textile industry as well as in some other light industries such as tea and matches. Prices of the products of some older modern industries declined considerably relative to other industrial prices before World War I, corroborating the conjecture presented here.

In cases where the technological gap was too great from the outset or in cases where the pace of improvement was too rapid in the modern branches, traditional branches had no other alternative but to disappear. This is apparently what happened in cotton spinning and indigo production.

For cotton spinning, where the emergence and virtual disappearance of dualism proceeded with unusual rapidity, it is possible to trace the factory statistics back to at least 1894, fifteen years before the first census of factories. Of course, most of the process of displacing the indigenous

[15]Ono (1968) examined the process of acclimatization and hybridization of imported technology with respect to silk reeling and concluded various technologies representing different capital-intensities were developed.

Table 6
Standardized Average Wages of Dualistic and Homogeneous Industries, 1909 and 1914
(wages in sen per day)

A. Dualistic industries

1909 (1) Size (persons per establishment)	(2) Hosiery	(3) Dyeing	(4) Silk reeling	(5) Ropes and nets	(6) Tea	(7) Cotton thread	(8) Cotton cloth	(9) Average for dualistic industries	(10) Over-all average	(11) Ratio of (9) to (10)
5-9	28.4	25.7	23.9	24.3	32.8	23.0	22.1	25.7	28.8	0.892
10-29	31.9	29.2	25.0	27.7	34.8	24.0	27.7	28.6	30.6	0.935
30-49	31.9	33.0	27.5	28.0	44.5	25.7	27.2	28.6	32.6	0.877
50-99	36.4	35.0	30.7	35.7	50.6	29.0	27.1	34.9	34.2	1.020
100-499	42.1	33.5	31.7	31.3	40.1	33.0	31.3	34.7	35.2	0.986
500 and up	–	–	34.8	–	–	33.0	34.3	34.0	35.3	0.964

1914 (A)	(2) Ropes and nets	(3) Cotton thread	(4) Bakery products	(5) Cotton cloth	(6) Hosiery	(7) Medicines	(8) Printing	(9) Average for dualistic industries	(10) Over-all average	(11) Ratio of (9) to (10)
5-9	28.2	21.6	30.2	25.5	29.2	32.0	29.3	28.0	32.1	0.875
10-29	26.9	24.0	34.3	27.8	29.0	32.9	33.0	29.7	33.9	0.876
30-49	29.8	32.9	35.8	31.6	34.9	34.5	31.8	33.0	35.9	0.919
50-99	40.1	45.9	35.9	32.6	36.5	33.0	35.0	37.0	37.9	0.976
100-499	39.3	43.9	–	34.2	38.0	44.7	37.6	39.6	38.3	1.034
500 and up	–	41.8	49.9	43.2	47.4	–	39.4	44.3	43.9	1.009

Table 6 (continued)

B. Homogeneous industries

1909 (1) Size (persons per establishment)	(2) Beer	(3) Railroad cars	(4) Electric appliances	(5) Cotton spinning	(6) Grain and flour milling	(7) Sake	(8) Lumber and wood products	(9) Average for homogeneous industries	(10) Over-all average	(11) Ratio of (9) to (10)
5-9	–	40.0	37.3	23.3	30.6	28.4	32.9	35.4	28.8	1.229
10-29	30.9	49.6	39.1	24.2	31.7	30.6	33.5	34.2	30.6	1.118
30-49	–	–	36.2	28.4	33.2	31.1	36.2	33.0	32.6	1.012
50-99	–	44.9	35.8	25.7	34.2	31.5	32.9	34.2	34.2	1.000
100-499	34.8	40.6	33.4	33.3	31.6	31.1	35.9	34.4	35.2	0.977
500 and up	33.1	–	–	33.0	–	–	–	33.1	35.3	0.938

1914 (A) (1) Size	(2) Sake	(3) Cotton spinning	(4) Canned foods	(5) Beer	(6) Soy sauce, etc.	(7) Paper (Japanese)	(8) Lumber and wood products	(9) Average for homogeneous industries	(10) Over-all average	(11) Ratio of (9) to (10)
5-9	32.4	20.3	36.0	–	31.6	29.4	36.4	31.0	32.1	0.966
10-29	32.7	24.3	35.5	–	31.9	30.3	36.7	31.9	33.9	0.941
30-49	34.2	27.6	36.7	–	30.9	33.6	38.3	33.6	35.9	0.936
50-99	35.5	29.4	34.4	36.9	32.0	31.0	40.4	34.2	37.9	0.902
100-499	29.8	38.0	33.8	34.2	30.4	30.7	40.5	33.9	38.3	0.885
500 and up	–	37.2	–	34.4	–	–	–	35.8	43.9	0.815

Notes: Dualistic industries are those in the highest quintile of size elasticities on the condition their coefficients of variation are larger than the median. In case the latter condition is not satisfied, the industry next in line with respect to size elasticity is used.

Homogeneous industries are those whose coefficients of variation are in the lowest quintile. Cotton spinning is homogeneous because almost all its workers were in large establishments by 1914, as is discussed in the text.

Averages in column 9 are simple arithmetic averages.

Weights are those for all industries in a particular year.

branches and their improved version, *garabō*, had already been completed by
1894. Yet, even among the "factories" which existed then or appeared later,
the phenomenon of transient dualism can be observed between 1894 and
1909. In 1894, when Sanji Mutō took over the management of the Hyōgo
branch of Kanebō, the average wages of the largest factories (1000+ workers)
were considerably higher than in other factories. The improvement in
productivity and growth in output in the ensuing years caused the notorious
scouting wars for operatives at the turn of the century. This resulted in the
rapid rise of wages in factories of almost all sizes and particularly in
medium-sized factories, which had hitherto been rather slow in adjusting
wages. Most of the small-scale operators, who numbered twenty-nine in 1899,
disappeared after the boom. By 1909, when the first census of factories was
taken, operatives employed by factories of fewer than one hundred operatives
became such an insignificant portion (0.3 percent) of the total number of
operatives that dualism as a social problem all but disappeared despite the low
wages still paid by small factories.

Beer, cotton spinning, sake, and lumber and its products appear in the list
of homogeneous industries both in 1909 and 1914. Other homogeneous
industries were railroad cars, electric appliances, grain and flour milling,
canned food, soy sauce, and Japanese paper. Here, three different groups of
industries can be noted. The first are the indigenous industries which had not
been affected much by foreign technology, such as sake, soy sauce, and
Japanese paper. Lumber and its products, although using some imported
technology, may be deemed as basically similar to the first group because
foreign technology did not, at this stage, call for significant reorganization of
the industry. The second group—beer, railroad cars, electric appliances, and
canned foods—consists of imported modern industries which did not have
indigenous branches to compete with. It is only natural that significant differentials did not appear in these newer modern industries at this stage. For the
first two in particular, it is difficult to conceive of heterogeneous branches
appearing later. Cotton spinning constitutes a third group. As described in the
preceding paragraph, it is a former dualistic industry from which the
indigenous portion had disappeared and which came to resemble a purely
modern industry; it had the largest concentration of workers in large-size
factories of any industry.[16]

As homogeneous industries consist of several groups with distinct characteristics, the overall average of the average wages for different sizes depends a
great deal on the proportion of industries of different groups included.
Generally, the average tends to be higher when more newer-modern industries
are involved, as in 1909, and the relatively high average wages in small-scale
establishments are conspicuous. The contrary situation occurs in 1914 when

---

[16]Note that a weighed regression and a weighted coefficient of variation are
used to determine whether an industry is dualistic or homogeneous. Cotton
spinning was counted as homogeneous due to this procedure despite the
existence of a considerable wage gap.

three purely indigenous industries are involved, with the result the average wages in large-scale factories are much lower than the overall average.

My conjecture about technical changes and the formation of dualism may be tested by the examination of horsepower-intensity, or the number of horsepower per operative used for driving machines.[17] It may be presumed that in dualistic industries, modernization in larger factories was so much more pronounced than in smaller factories that both horsepower-intensity and productivity were high enough to permit payment of higher wages. To test this hypothesis for different industries, horsepower-intensity has been regressed log-linearly on factory size, and the average wage has been regressed log-linearly on horsepower-intensity for each industry (see footnote 10; the same weights are used here). For the hypothesis not to be negated, dualistic industries ought to show positive associations in both of these relations. Conversely, it is expected homogeneous industries will be characterized by lack of positive association at least in one of them.

Table 7, which shows the values and significance of coefficients for independent variables, reveals that the attempt proved to be a moderate success. In most dualistic industries, larger factories tended to use more power per operative. More intensive use of power in larger factories also tended to be associated with higher wages, presumably via higher productivity. This hypothesis is supported (not negated, to be more precise) for hosiery, ropes and nets, and cotton cloth in both years, for dyeing and tea in 1909, and printing in 1914.

In contrast, the hypothesis is negated by all but one homogeneous industry, cotton spinning in 1909. It may be remembered this was a former dualistic industry, simply included among homogeneous industries in 1909 and 1914 because, by then, most workers were concentrated in large factories. For other homogeneous industries, as expected, the hypothesis did not hold, even though in some, particularly newer modern industries, larger establishments tended to use more power per operative.

CHANGING PATTERNS OF DIFFERENTIALS IN LATER YEARS

Moving to 1932/33 and 1951, the picture is quite different. In Figure 9, the ranges for standardized average wages per day in 1914 prices are shown for different industries in 1914, 1932/33, and 1951. For the benefit of intertemporal comparisons, the 1951 wages are expressed in daily terms in this figure.[18] For both 1932/33 and 1951, bars tend to be longer, and in 1951

[17]Defined as the total horsepower of steam engines and turbines, gas and oil motors, electric motors and water wheels, per operative.

[18]The same procedures as in Figure 8 have been applied. As the explanation in footnote 12 shows, the 1951 figures are simply converted into daily figures in such a way as to make the average real wage computed equal to Ohkawa's figure. As no adjustment for probable differences in the average operating days per month was made, the 1951 daily wages should be treated cautiously. For 1932/33, strata expressed in terms of capital were merged to make them

Table 7

Explanation of Wages for Dualistic and Homogeneous Industries 1909 and 1914

1909

	Sample size	Independent variable: Size of establishment / Dependent variable: Horse-power, β	Independent variable: Horse-power / Dependent variable: Average wages, β
Dualistic industries			
Hosiery	5	0.926*	0.118*
Dyeing	5	1.140*	0.077*
Silk reeling	7	0.066	0.058
Ropes and nets	5	3.040*	1.032*
Tea	5	2.409*	0.037*
Cotton thread	6	0.219	0.208*
Cotton cloth	7	0.572*	0.141*
Homogeneous industries			
Railroad cars	4	0.430*	0.034
Electrical appliances	5	0.353*	-0.130
Cotton spinning[a]	7	0.084*	0.545*
Grain and flour milling	5	0.007	-0.007
Sake[a]	5	-0.421	-0.010
Lumber and wood products	5	-0.008	0.020
Shipbuilding[b]	7	0.441*	-0.020

1914

	Sample size	Independent variable: Size of establishment / Dependent variable: Horse-power, β	Independent variable: Horse-power / Dependent variable: Average wages, β
Dualistic industries			
Ropes and nets	5	1.095*	0.133*
Cotton thread	7	0.135	0.299
Bakery products	5	0.244*	0.296
Cotton cloth	7	0.522*	0.186*
Hosiery	6	0.515*	0.187*
Medicines	5	-0.037	-0.220
Printing	7	0.236*	0.212*
Homogeneous industries			
Sake	5	-0.068	0.079
Cotton spinning[a]	7	0.189	0.061
Canned foods	5	-0.263	0.079*
Soy sauce	5	0.588*	0.046
Paper (Japanese)	5	0.328*	0.064
Lumber and wood products[a]	5	-0.171	-0.129
Silk reeling[a, b]	7	-0.193	-0.166

β is the coefficient for the independent variable in a log-linear regression equation.

*β is positive and significant at the 5 percent level.

[a] "Homogeneous" industries characterized by significant positive association between the size of the establishment and wages.

[b] Beer, for which the sample size was only three in both years, has been replaced by shipbuilding and silk reeling in the list of "homogeneous" industries.

there are more shaded bars than in 1914. (As explained in the first paragraph of the previous section, shading means the existence of a significant positive association between size and wages.) The concentration of dualistic industries in textiles and other older-modern industries in 1914 is not seen in later years. Indeed, in 1932/33 a number of industries in this group, such as spinning, thread, and wearing apparel, have differentials which become erratic or perverse (indicated by unshaded bars). There are even cases, such as cloth, thread, and paper in 1932/33 or wearing apparel and hosiery in 1951, where differentials narrow in the face of a general widening of differentials.

Dualistic industries included bricks and tiles, hosiery, primary metals, printing, and grain and flour milling in 1932/33, and cement and its products, paper, medicines, grain and flour milling, and ceramics in 1951. It appears that, as in the early years, a dualistic wage structure tended to develop in those industries a part of which had experienced, or was experiencing, rapid technical progress. Iron and steel, fire bricks, printing, and flour milling all experienced rapid technical progress after World War I. Somewhat later, the same may be said for cement, Western paper, Western medicines, and a part of the ceramics industry (exported chinaware and electric insulators).[19] An upward polarization, or conspicuous increase in the share of labor at large establishments at the expense of medium-size ones, in primary metals and grain and flour milling prior to 1933[20] or in medicines and paper prior to 1951 (see Table 8) may have been caused by such underlying forces.

The period after 1920 is one in which small-scale businesses increased rapidly in a number of industries, developing acclimatized technologies dependent on cheap labor and newly available electric motors (see Minami's essay in this volume), and often organized on a subcontract basis by big firms. In all of the dualistic industries, by 1932/33 the share of workers at establishments with fewer than ten operatives (fewer than thirty operatives in the case of primary metals) had increased much more rapidly than in other industries.

Homogeneous industries consist of spinning, silk reeling, paper, cloth, and bakery products in 1932/33, and matches, tea, hosiery, wearing apparel, and

---

comparable with those in other years. The two largest strata in 1914 and the three largest strata in 1951 were also merged. As before, the average labor composition for the entire manufacturing industry was used for standardization of wages.

[19]Sasaki (1960) found wage differentials expanded greatly between 1914 and 1954 in such modern industries as sugar refining, pulp, medicine, and mineral oil, while no conspicuous differentials developed in traditional industries. A similar finding led Watanabe (1968 and 1970) to the hypothesis of "induced dualism" based on borrowed technology.

[20]Figures for 1933 were taken from *Kōjō Tōkei-hyō* rather than from *Kōgyō Chōsasho* because of the incomparability of size classes in the latter with those in other years.

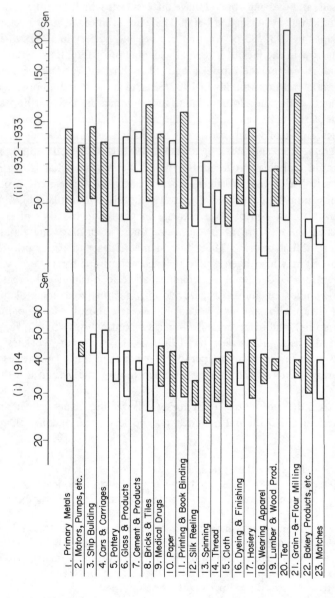

Figure 9. Ranges for standardized average wages in real terms for different industries, 1914, 1932/33, and 1951.

Source: See Appendix 1.

(iii) 1951

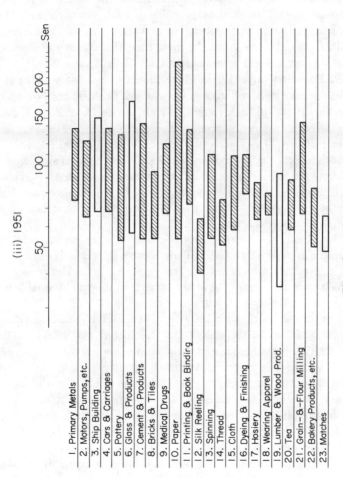

Figure 9 (continued)

273

silk reeling in 1951. Virtually all of these may be considered to have been older-modern industries with considerable polarization in the composition of operatives by factory size. From fairly early on, the process of concentration of operatives in a few size strata has been underway in most of these industries. For example, tea had about 12 percent of operatives working in large factories employing one hundred workers or more in 1933. By 1951 no factory in this industry employed one hundred or more workers. More than 80 percent of operatives were working for small establishments employing fewer than thirty workers. At the other end of the spectrum is spinning, which moved toward concentration in large sizes. As early as 1914, 91 percent of operatives in this industry were working for establishments with five hundred operatives or more. In most other industries the direction of concentration was toward intermediate sizes. This is clearly true of paper (before 1933), hosiery (after 1933), silk reeling, matches, and wearing apparel.

Table 9 shows the standardized average wages of dualistic and homogeneous industries for 1914, 1932/33, and 1951. In 1932/33 and 1951 dualistic industries were no longer generally characterized by low wages paid by small-scale factories. There were some industries which still followed this pattern, such as printing and hosiery in 1932/33 or ceramics and cement and its products in 1951. However, there were more dualistic industries distinguished by higher than average wages paid by large-scale establishments. A change in the opposite direction had taken place in most homogeneous industries. With the exception of paper and silk reeling in 1932/33, large factories in all of these homogeneous industries were paying much lower wages than the average for factories of comparable sizes in other industries. In contrast, small-scale establishments in homogeneous industries tended to pay wages which were on average about the same as those paid by establishments of comparable sizes in other industries.

An analysis similar to that for 1909 and 1914, on the relationship between size, wages, and capital intensity, was conducted for 1932/33. Power-intensity in earlier years was translated into capital-intensity for 1932/33, and a similar hypothesis was tested for each industry, using the weighting techniques described in footnote 10. Only the results for the extremes, namely, dualistic and homogeneous industries, are shown in Table 10. This time, the hypothesis is negated for none of the dualistic industries. Neither is it negated for two of the homogeneous industries, paper and cloth, but it should be remembered the latter is characterized by a significant size elasticity despite its low status in terms of the coefficient of variation in wages.

A standard procedure for further analysis is to see whether average labor productivity was higher in the larger establishments using more capital-intensive technology. As shown in Table 11, columns 1 and 3, it was, particularly for dualistic industries, both for 1932/33 and 1951.[21] Then, it

[21]The elasticity (coefficient) for ceramics in 1951 was not significant, but the T-value was fairly high (1.560).

Table 8
Distribution of Operatives in Different Size Strata, Dualistic and Homogeneous Industries, 1914, 1933, and 1951
(in percent)

Dualistic industries in 1932/33

Size (persons per establishment)	Bricks and tiles 1914	1933	Hosiery 1914	1933	Primary metals 1914	1933	Printing 1914	1933	Grain and flour milling 1914	1933
5-9	26.5	42.2	18.9	26.1	2.1	2.4	12.6	20.7	21.9	31.3
10-29	30.4	18.6	35.0	25.6	6.1	8.9	26.2	25.3	40.8	21.6
30-49	9.5	9.9	11.1	13.1	4.1	5.1	13.7	12.7	13.0	17.6
50-99	12.5	15.2	11.1	10.9	9.8	5.8	18.2	12.5	19.9	17.3
100-499	21.2	14.1	14.1	24.3	47.8	23.5	20.4	21.2	4.5	12.2
500 and up	--	--	9.8	--	30.0	54.4	8.9	7.7	--	--

Homogeneous industries in 1932/33

Size (persons per establishment)	Spinning 1914	1933	Silk reeling 1914	1933	Paper 1914	1933	Cloth 1914	1933	Bakery products 1914	1933
5-9	0.1	0.4	1.5	0.7	0.7	3.6	11.9	13.9	46.7	27.5
10-29	0.3	0.3	7.5	4.5	1.4	9.9	30.7	22.9	30.9	21.8
30-49	0.1	0.5	10.4	6.5	5.3	10.7	11.9	11.2	6.0	9.0
50-99	0.3	0.6	22.4	15.9	5.9	22.1	11.4	11.8	6.6	13.4
100-499	8.3	9.3	44.1	52.7	59.0	40.7	14.9	18.6	--	17.4
500 and up	91.1	89.3	14.1	19.7	27.8	13.2	19.1	21.7	9.8	10.9

Dualistic industries in 1951

Size (persons per establishment)	Cement and products 1933	1951	Paper 1933	1951	Medicines 1933	1951	Grain and flour milling 1933	1951	Ceramics 1933	1951
4-9	7.4	11.6	3.6	3.6	10.7	3.5	31.3	20.8	15.0	13.4
10-29	8.6	22.0	9.9	8.4	22.0	15.7	21.6	48.0	22.2	26.7
30-49	6.3	10.4	10.7	8.7	12.2	9 1	17.6	14.6	12.6	12.9
50-99	6.5	13.0	22.1	11.9	20.2	13.7	17.3	9.4	9.2	12.0
100-499	53.5	23.0	40.7	32.5	28.3	36.7	12.2	7.3	29.2	21.3
500 and up	17.8	20.0	13.2	34.9	6.6	21.2	--	--	12.1	13.7

Homogeneous industries in 1951

Size (persons per establishment)	Matches 1933	1951	Tea 1933	1951	Hosiery 1933	1951	Wearing apparel 1933	1951	Silk reeling 1933	1951
4-9	2.6	1.0	16.2	36.6	26.1	14.0	21.9	14.1	0.7	1.9
10-29	8.6	13.5	49.3	47.5	25.6	29.9	21.0	29.8	4.5	6.4
30-49	6.6	9.9	15.2	9.8	13.1	14.8	9.0	17.6	6.5	3.4
50-99	14.6	18.8	7.5	6.2	10.9	16.0	10.2	18.5	15.9	5.1
100-499	51.8	56.9	11.7	--	24.3	25.3	20.0	13.8	52.7	83.3
500 and up	15.9	–	--	--	–	--	17.9	6.3	19.7	–

Source: Kōjō Tōkei-hyō and Kōgyō Tōkei-hyō.
Notes: Dualistic industries are those in the highest quintile of size elasticities on the condition their coefficients of variation are larger than the median. In case the latter condition is not satisfied, the industry next in line with respect to size elasticity is used.
Homogeneous industries are those whose coefficients of variation are in the lowest quintile.

Table 9

Standardized Average Wages of Dualistic and Homogeneous Industries, 1914, 1932/33, and 1951
(wages are in sen per day for 1914 and 1932/33, and yen per month for 1951)

A. Dualistic industries

1914 (B)								
(1) Size (persons per establishment)	(2) Bakery products	(3) Hosiery	(4) Cloth	(5) Paper	(6) Thread	(7) Average for dualistic industries	(8) Over-all average	(9) Ratio of (7) to (8)
5-9	30.2	29.2	27.3	29.4	28.0	28.8	32.1	0.897
10-29	34.3	29.0	28.4	30.5	25.1	29.5	33.9	0.870
30-49	35.8	34.9	31.4	34.2	31.1	33.5	35.9	0.933
50-99	35.9	36.5	33.4	31.4	36.9	34.8	37.9	0.918
100-499	–	38.0	35.2	43.1	39.8	39.0	38.3	1.018
500 and up	49.9	47.4	43.3	–	40.7	45.3	43.9	1.032

1932/33								
Size (capital per establishment in thousand yen)	Bricks and tiles	Hosiery	Primary metals	Printing	Grain and flour milling	Average for dualistic industries	Over-all average	Ratio of (7) to (8)
5-10	119.1	118.9	110.8	113.5	–	115.6	119.6	0.967
10-50	175.5	153.5	135.3	138.9	137.7	148.2	144.6	1.025
50-100	148.9	298.7	150.6	196.2	147.3	188.3	158.4	1.189
100-500	205.3	159.0	174.3	195.4	199.5	186.7	174.2	1.072
500 and up	273.4	222.0	220.6	260.5	298.8	255.1	195.8	1.345

Table 9 (continued)

1951 Size (persons per establishment)	Cement and products	Paper	Medicines	Grain and flour milling	Ceramics	(7) Average for homogeneous industries	(8) Over-all average	(9) Ratio of (7) to (8)
4-9	4584	4571	5682	5719	4494	5139	5216	0.985
10-29	4778	5026	6197	5996	6225	5499	5949	0.924
30-49	6672	7086	8103	6402	6537	7066	6813	1.037
50-99	7984	9228	8400	8734	6641	8587	7547	1.138
100-499	12,098	11,061	10,076	12,485	7411	11,430	9407	1.215
500 and up	15,768	20,368	12,731	--	11,023	16,239	12,257	1.325

B. Homogeneous industries

1914 (B) (1) Size (persons per establishment)	(2) Spinning	(3) Lumber and products	(4) Silk reeling	(5) Ship building	(6) Cars and carriages	(7) Average for homogeneous industries	(8) Over-all average	(9) Ratio of (7) to (8)
5-9	23.8	36.4	27.3	44.0	44.5	35.2	32.1	1.097
10-29	28.0	36.7	29.3	48.3	53.2	39.1	33.9	1.153
30-49	30.2	38.3	31.0	42.2	42.6	36.9	35.9	1.028
50-99	30.0	40.4	32.6	49.7	44.3	39.4	37.9	1.040
100-499	38.6	40.5	32.6	44.8	43.2	39.9	38.3	1.042
500 and up	38.1	--	33.8	45.8	45.5	40.8	43.9	0.929

Table 9 (continued)

1932/33	Size (capital per establishment in thousand yen)	Spinning	Silk reeling	Paper	Cloth	Bakery products			
	5-10	152.4	–	–	91.1	–	121.8	119.6	1.018
	10-50	171.1	–	152.6	117.7	86.9	132.1	144.6	0.914
	50-100	88.8	138.8	199.0	126.6	113.0	133.2	158.4	0.841
	100-500	141.9	88.6	197.7	114.7	101.3	128.8	174.2	0.739
	500 and up	115.8	145.5	192.1	119.4	90.2	132.6	195.8	0.677

1951	Size (persons per establishment)	Matches	Tea	Hosiery	Wearing apparel	Silk reeling			
	4-9	5332	5014	5410	6301	3431	5098	5216	0.977
	10-29	4173	5546	5778	5657	3609	4953	5949	0.833
	30-49	4971	5899	6153	5730	3817	5314	6813	0.780
	50-99	5641	7606	6524	5962	4747	6096	7547	0.808
	100-499	5639	–	7456	6774	5449	5064	9407	0.538
	500 and up	–	–	–	8653	–	–	12,257	0.706

Note: For the definition of dualistic and homogeneous industries, see Table 8. Averages in columns 7 are simple arithmetic averages. Weights are those for all industries in a particular year. Strata for 1932/33 expressed in terms of capital (value of assets) should read, for example in the case of 5-10, "5000 or more but less than 10,000 yen" and so on. Wage figures for strata with fewer than five operatives are not shown even when they are available.

278

Table 10
Explanation of Wages for
Dualistic and Homogeneous Industries
1932/33

Independent variable:		Size of establishment	Capital intensity
Dependent variable:		Capital intensity	Wages
	Sample Size	β	β
Dualistic industries			
Bricks	5	0.768*	0.295*
Hosiery	6	0.594*	0.406*
Primary metals	5	1.033*	0.187*
Printing and bookbinding	5	0.535*	0.386*
Grain and flour milling	4	1.045*	0.289*
Homogeneous industries			
Spinning	6	0.446*	−0.110
Paper	4	0.550*	0.140*
Cloth[a]	7	0.674*	0.064*
Bakery products	4	0.422*	0.123
Dyeing[a, b]	5	0.061	0.124

β is the coefficient for the independent variable in a log-linear regression equation.
*β is positive and significant at the 5 percent level.
[a]Homogeneous industries characterized by significant positive association between the size of the establishment and wages.
[b]Silk reeling, for which the sample size was only three, has been replaced by dyeing in the list of homogeneous industries.

may be asked, were operatives working in larger establishments sharing in a part of the excess profit which accrued to these establishments? In other words, was the rate of return on capital higher for larger establishments in dualistic industries, or at least, was there any significant positive association between the size of the establishment and the rate of return in these industries? The answer is a resounding no, so far as 1932/33 is concerned, as Table 11, column 2 reveals. No industry shows a significant positive association between the size of the establishment and the rate of return. In fact, significant negative association is found for six industries including four dualistic industries.

For computing the rate of return, wages have to be imputed for proprietors and unpaid family workers. Estimates used in this table and also in Table 12, showing the characteristics of the manufacturing industry as a whole, are

Table 11
Size, Productivity, and the Rate of Return on Capital for Dualistic and Homogeneous Industries 1932/33 and 1951

	1932/33				1951	
	(1) Size of establishment		(2) Size of establishment		(3) Size of establishment	
Independent variable:	Average productivity of labor[a]		Rate of return on capital[b]		Average productivity of labor	
Dependent variable:	Sample size	β	β		Sample size	β
Dualistic industries						
Brick and tiles	5	0.404*	0.270	Cement and products	8	0.459*
Hosiery	6	0.233*	−0.279*	Paper	9	0.407*
Primary metals	5	0.522*	−0.414*	Medicines	8	0.264*
Printing and bookbinding	5	0.277*	−0.310*	Grain and flour	7	0.244*
Grain and flour milling	4	0.322*	−0.479*	Ceramics	8	0.068
Homogeneous industries						
Spinning	6	0.003	0.296	Matches	7	0.295
Paper	4	0.418*	−0.231	Tea	5	0.075
Cloth[c]	7	0.243*	−0.298*	Hosiery[c]	7	0.057*
Bakery products	4	0.063	−0.228	Wearing apparel[c]	8	0.134*
Dyeing[c, d]	5	0.127*	−0.341*	Silk reeling[c, d]	7	0.197*

β is the coefficient for the independent variable in a log-linear regression equation.

*β significant at the 5 percent level.

[a]Average value added per operative.

[b]Rate of return on total capital used, inclusive of interest paid but exclusive of depreciation and taxes. Capital is the total value of assets at the factory.

[c]Homogeneous industries characterized by significant positive association between the size of establishment and wages.

[d]Silk reeling, for which the 1932/33 sample size is only three, has been replaced by dyeing.

Table 12

Characteristics of Industrial Establishments in Industrial Centers, 1932/33

Size of the establishment by capital[a] (in thousand yen)	(1) Operatives per establishment	(2) Standardized average wages[b] (sen per day)	(3) Capital intensity (yen per operative)	(4) Rate of interest on debt[c] (in percent)	(5) The ratio of debt to total capital in percent	(6) Rate of return on capital[d] (in percent)
1-2	2.0	85.9	0.674	5.8	12.3	18.0
2-5	3.4	109.0	0.857	7.2	13.0	20.1
5-10	6.3	130.4	1.001	7.5	15.2	25.3
10-50	13.1	157.7	2.854	7.6	16.9	24.1
50-100	25.6	172.7	2.513	8.5	17.2	19.0
100-500	58.2	190.0	3.700	7.4	17.0	16.5
500 and up	331.3	212.9	10.662	8.1	11.7	11.5

Note: See text and Appendixes 1 and 2 for sources and method.

[a]Capital is the total value of assets. Size 1-2 means "1000 or more but less than 2000 yen." The same applies to other sizes.

[b]Average wages based on the all-size standard weight for 1932/33. The two smallest sizes are shown in this table, because in some industries the average number of operatives per establishment is five or more in these size strata.

[c]Nominal interest rate on debt for Tokyo and Yokohama only. No information for interest received or for deposits is available.

[d]Based on the standard assumption on the imputed wages of proprietors and unpaid family workers.

based on the assumption proprietors' imputed hourly wages were one-third less than the *average* wages of operatives *for the industry* and the hourly wages of family workers were the same as the wages of operatives employed by the same establishment.

The assumption strategically affecting the estimated value of the rate of return is the level of imputed wages for proprietors. According to the standard assumption adopted, the rate of return was inversely associated with size, particularly for establishments with capital of ten thousand yen or more. Wages for proprietors were assumed to have been lower than those for operatives, because they must have been getting psychic income from their status. The validity of this assumption may be questioned. In fact, as higher wages are imputed, the inverse association becomes less strong. However, no reasonable assumption can change the inverse association for the four largest size-strata representing, roughly, all factories employing ten or more operatives (see Figure 10). Moreover, the assumption of much higher imputed wages (cases *A* and *B*, for example) produces unbelievable negative rates of return for very small establishments. If wage differentials are allowed for proprietors, the difficulty is somewhat alleviated. Nonetheless, an inverse association between the size of establishment and the rate of return for medium and large size-strata still remains. Hence, it is difficult to escape the inference that the rate of return tended to be higher for smaller establish-

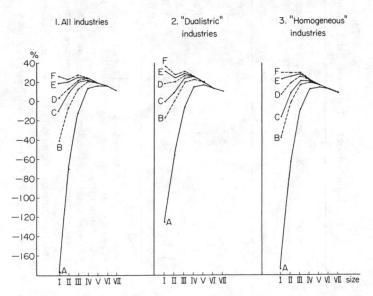

Figure 10. Alternative estimates of the rate of return on capital in industrial centers, 1932/33, by size of establishment.

Source: The same as in Table 11.

Note: Assuming proprietors' wages to be *A*, five times as much as that of operatives; *B*, twice as much as that of operatives; *C*, the same as that of operatives; *D*, two-thirds as much as that of operatives (standard case); *E*, a half as much as that of operatives.

ments both in dualistic and homogeneous industries, at least for establishments with capital of ten thousand yen or more (approximately ten or more employes).

For postwar years (1953-59), Ryūtaro Komiya (1962) uncovered such inverse differentials for manufacturing *firms* using *Hōjin Kigyō Tōkei*. Inverse differentials even more pronounced can be found for later years, particularly for firms with capital of fifty million yen or more (see Figure 11). Although the postwar concept is not directly comparable with the 1932/33 one, the similarity of patterns is striking.

Returning to Figure 10, perhaps even more surprising at first sight may be the similarity between the curves of the rate of return for dualistic and homogeneous industries. Despite much higher wages paid at large factories in dualistic industries, the rate of return there was no higher than in homogeneous industries. Conversely, despite much lower wages paid at small factories in homogeneous industries, the rate of return there was no lower. These findings have also been confirmed for individual dualistic and homogeneous industries, but are not presented here.

All these, however, are not really surprising, for the rate of return at a particular date may have been significantly different from the average of the rates of return for a number of preceding years. The profit level of previous years as well as the current year are relevant in determining wages, so it is better to compare wages at a particular date with profitability for a number of preceding years. Better still one can examine the association between changes in wages and the rate of return over time, as a substantial part of the effect of differences for labor quality can be removed by this method.

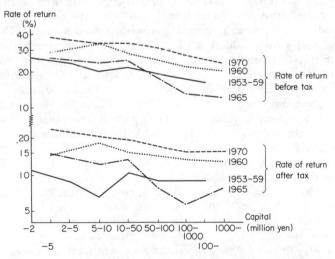

Figure 11. Rate of return on equity capital for industrial firms by size of the firm, 1953-59, 1960, 1965, and 1970.
Source: 1953-59, Komiya 1962, p. 157. Other years, *Hōjin Kigyō Tōkei Nempō.*

Unfortunately, data for prewar years are too fragmentary and inconsistent to make this kind of examination.

A clear-cut test of this kind can be made in the postwar years. One of the best sources of information on this issue is Tōyō Keizai Shimpōsha's *Survey of Model Wages*, because it gives expected average wages for different classes of workers at different ages by firm. The information may be combined with other data in an effort to analyze the effect of different variables on wages. With this objective in mind, wages and other related data for 1958 and 1968 have been examined.

Several pertinent results were obtained from the study. First, the ranking of big firms included in the survey with respect to lifetime income changes drastically between these two dates.[22] The coefficients of rank correlation of firms between lifetime wage income in 1958 and in 1968 are as low as 0.343, 0.429, and 0.600, respectively, for male white-collar, male blue-collar, and female blue-collar workers. Perhaps still more conclusive is the change in the ranking of firms with respect to wages received by the same cohorts of middle-aged workers. The coefficients of rank correlation between wages of workers aged forty in 1958 and wages received by the same cohorts of workers ten years later are only 0.352 for male white-collar and 0.435 for male blue-collar.[23] The drastic changes in a short time span indicated by these low correlation coefficients suggest factors other than the quality of labor have to be introduced to account for these changes.

[22]From the original survey returns covering more than one hundred large firms, we chose only those belonging to manufacturing industries and computed lifetime incomes for each of the three categories of workers: male white-collar workers who graduated from college, male blue-collar workers who graduated from junior high school, and female blue-collar workers who graduated from junior high school. Lifetime income is defined as the present value of wages for the lifetime of a worker. As we are interested only in comparisons, discounted wages at certain ages were simply added. For college graduates, the ages are 25, 30, 35, 40, 45, and 50; and for male junior high school graduates they are 20, 25, 30, 35, 40, 45, and 50; and for female junior high school graduates, they are 15, 20, 25, and 30. Figures unavailable for certain ages were estimated through (log-linear) interpolation when wages for at least three other ages were available (four in the case of male blue-collar workers).

Such lifetime income could be computed for both 1958 and 1968 in at least one of the three categories of workers for twenty-one firms ranging, in terms of the number of workers in 1958, from Miyoshi Yushi with 459 to Tōyō Rayon with 18,949. The stocks of all of these firms were traded on the Tokyo Stock Exchange (first or second section), and virtually all major branches of manufacturing industries are represented.

[23]All coefficients are significant at the 5 percent level. Sample sizes for the first set of correlation analyses are twenty-one for male white-collar, fifteen for male blue-collar, and eleven for female blue-collar. Sample sizes for the latter set are twenty-one for white-collar and twenty-four for blue-collar. A similar test for a cohort could not be applied to female workers due to the scarcity of information on wages of those middle age or older.

Second, lifetime wage income in 1968 is most satisfactorily explained by income in 1958 and the increase between 1958 and 1968 in profit as a proportion of paid-in capital in 1958.

The relationships are shown here: y_{wt}, y_{bt}, and y_{ft} are lifetime incomes for, respectively, male white-collar workers who graduated from college, for male blue-collar workers who graduated from high school, and for female blue-collar workers who graduated from high school in year t ($1 = 1958, 2 = 1968$); $(\frac{\delta P}{K})$ is the increase in profit between 1958 and 1968 as the percentage of capital in 1958.[24]

$$y_{w2} = \underset{(0.2163)}{0.5657y_{w1}} + \underset{(54.1)}{(245.7)(\tfrac{\delta P}{K})} + 128,771 \quad \bar{R}^2 = 0.7129$$

$$y_{b2} = \underset{(0.3183)}{0.8512y_{b1}} + \underset{(34.6)}{(127.6)(\tfrac{\delta P}{K})} + 79,294 \quad \bar{R}^2 = 0.6423$$

$$y_{f2} = \underset{(0.3612)}{1.3008y_{f1}} + \underset{(28.5)}{(76.8)(\tfrac{\delta P}{K})} + 24,653 \quad \bar{R}^2 = 0.8588$$

The numbers in parentheses are the standard errors of the estimated coefficients. All results are significantly different from zero, and the percentage of differentials explained ($\bar{R}^2$) is quite high. The result from such a small sample should be accepted with reservation, but it at least suggests that a part of the wage differentials should be accounted for by some form of profit sharing.

CONCLUDING REMARKS

The dualistic wage structure apparently did not exist widely in Japan's manufacturing industry in the 1880s or probably in the 1890s either. Contemporary literature corroborates this finding. Wages were generally low, workers were highly mobile, and there were numerous labor-management troubles. Apparently, this was a period of trial and error in the labor relations at factories transplanted into a society with a tradition more paternalistic and personalistic than that of the West.

Paternalistic and personalistic human relations characteristic of Tokugawa society could not be abolished by law nor, at least not within a short period of time, by economic forces. They continued to exist in the countryside and also in the commercial sector of the economy. In the latter, most of the ingredients of the labor-management relations of commercial families in the Tokugawa period were kept almost intact, with lifetime employment, loyalty

---

[24]No weighting has been used here. Profits and other relevant statistics were obtained from Nihon Keizai's *Kaisha Nenkan* and Tōyō Keizai's *Tōkei Geppō*. Other independent variables tested are size (both capital and labor), profitability, and capital intensity. Size was irrelevant for this group of firms. Profitability and capital intensity explained wages fairly well. The sample sizes were thirteen for male white-collar, fourteen for male blue-collar, and eight for female blue-collar.

to superiors, paternalistic care of subordinates covering not only work but also daily life.[25]

This kind of human relations continued into the modern period in small businesses, where, with the system of apprenticeship, paternalistic care of the workers and hope for future independence could compensate for low wages. In larger businesses, however, it was becoming increasingly more difficult for employers to keep close informal contact with workers. The hope for future independence was also diminishing. As a result, the old *detchi* (apprentice) system was becoming unpopular in larger businesses even in the Meiji period, as exemplified in a most dramatic way by the strike of workers at Harimaya (Sogō Department Store) demanding the modern salary system (Maruyama and Imamura 1912, p. 89).

Thus, it was natural that larger firms should institutionalize paternalism into seniority-oriented, higher wages and richer fringe benefits. Such evolution apparently can be traced most clearly in modernized commercial family companies including department stores, trading companies, storage companies, and banks. An examination of company histories in these fields and of the remarks by their leading figures, included as an appendix to Maruyama and Imamura's book, reveals the progress of the evolution as early as the mid-Meiji period.[26]

It is true that, in manufacturing, most of the modern enterprises in the mid-Meiji period were not characterized by paternalistic practices. But even in this period it was possible for government-owned factories to adopt paternalistic practices in incipient forms (see Fujita 1961 for some case studies on this). A number of big firms in light industries were also able to pay relatively high wages and offer administrative paternalism of various kinds (see, for example, Hazama 1964). Further study is certainly needed, but the quantitative evidence presented in the section on 1909 and 1914 differentials corroborates such an observation.

There is little doubt that labor-management relations in large firms, including seniority-determined wages which appeared in heavy industries and were reinforced in light industries after World War I, represented rational behavior on the part of management trying to cope with new technical requirements. Managers at mechanized factories adopted these systems resulting in higher wages so that they could retain, so to speak, the fruits of on-the-job training of workers.

[25]Labor-management relations in commercial families during the Tokugawa and Meiji periods are described at great length in Miyamoto (1948). A pioneering work in this field is Kaneda (1927). Harafuji (1960) studies the Meiji period, and Osaka-shi (1928) gives a detailed account of the life and work of employes at dry-goods stores in the 1920s.

[26]Among the company histories in these industries, those of Iwai, Akata Sangyō, Daimaru Sogō, Takeda Yokuhin, and Sumitomo Ginkō are particularly instructive on the evolution of labor-management relations, even though none gives any idea about relative wages.

However, if an economist wants to explain wage differentials from a thoroughly neoclassical viewpoint, he will have difficulty in accounting for inversed differentials in the rate of return on capital by firm size for all manufacturing industries. Neither inverse differentials in the effective rate of interest nor greater risk for smaller establishments, on which he can rest his case, seem to be persuasive. First, as shown in Table 12, the nominal rate of interest was no higher for smaller establishments. Still, it is possible that the effective interest rate was higher for smaller businesses due to higher deposit-to-debt ratios, but in view of the relatively low ratio of debt to total capital in the prewar period, this factor would be able to explain only a small portion of inverse differentials. Nor was it likely that risk for small businesses was so important, and so much more so in Japan than in other countries (Serizawa 1962).

Apparently, if both dualistic differentials in wages and inverse differentials in the rate of return on capital are to be fully explained, other size-related factors such as differences in the degree of paternalistic care of workers, in union pressure (both overt and potential), and in the degree of the separation of management from ownership will also have to be considered. Then, if inverse differentials in the rate of return were peculiar to Japan, as Komiya (1962) shows, peculiarly Japanese features will have to be picked up.

The inverse differential in the rate of return for prewar years is not an established fact. The period 1932/33 may have been an unusual one. Also, there is some question as to the accuracy of some of the data for 1932/33, particularly interest, debt, and transactions between factories and head offices. All that can be proposed at this stage is that the inverse differential is implied by the 1932/33 data, and this fits well with the presumption Japanese society was paternalistic and personalistic. Managers of large factories or firms in such a society must have had to pay higher wages because paternalistic and personalistic compensation could not be easily offered by large organizations. Capital in large factories had to be satisfied with less profit partially in return for greater security but partially for being unable to offer as much paternalism as in small factories.[27] Of course, in thoroughly individualistic societies large firms do not have to pay premiums to workers for the lack of paternalism, for it does not exist in small firms either. In this sense, traditional paternalism may have played a role, albeit a negative one, in the formation of the dualistic wage structure.

It is not possible, however, for this interpretation to explain away the entire phenomenon of dualism even when it is heavily assisted by the assumption of differences in the quality of labor, including different degrees of human capital formation. The resultant markets are supposed to have been in real equilibrium, and workers would not have moved to larger firms (or factories), even if such an option had existed. It is difficult to accept such a situation as

[27]Here the size of a factory rather than a firm ought to be a relevant concept. Technical differences in different jobs and the degree of difficulty in supervising workers are also relevant.

historical fact. It is also difficult to explain the positive association between the rate of return and wages at large firms either through this kind of paternalism or labor quality. Other variables such as institutionalized paternalism, union pressure, and a greater degree of separation of management from ownership in larger firms or factories will have to be introduced as factors responsible for a scheme of profit-sharing which was instrumental in creating a part of the dualism, and particularly interindustry differences in duality.

APPENDIX 1: SOURCES AND METHODS FOR ESTIMATING STANDARDIZED AVERAGE WAGES

Original statistics were taken from *Kōjō Tokei-hyō* for 1909 and 1914; from *Kōgyō Chōsasho* for the cities of Tokyo and Yokohama in 1932 and for the cities of Nagoya and Osaka as well as Osaka Prefecture outside the city of Osaka in 1933; and from *Kōgyō Tōkei-hyō* for 1951. Industrial classifications are largely those used in these *Kōjō Tōkei-hyō*. A few industries, however, had to be combined for 1914 (1914*B*) so that they could be compared with later years. Industrial classifications are shown in Appendix Table 1 in which subindustries included in each major industry are indicated by their names and reference numbers for 1909 and 1914, and by reference letters or numbers for 1933 and 1951.

1914*A* is comparable with 1909, and 1914*B* with later years in industrial classification. For 1933 only those strata were adopted in which the average numbers of operatives per establishment were five or more.

Operatives are *shokkō* for 1909 and 1914, *jyūgyōsha* (exclusive of *kajin*, *jimuin*, and *gijutsusha*) in 1932/33, and *jōyō rōmusha* in 1951.

The daily wages of operatives in 1932/33 were estimated on the following assumptions. (1) The wage ratio for *shokuin* and other *rōmusha* in a given industry was the same as the average ratio for the same industry in 1951. (2) The wage ratio for different sexes in a given industry was the same as the average ratio for the same industry in 1914. (3) Operating days for each stratum in an industry were the same as in the comparable stratum in 1914. Operating days for the manufacturing industries as a whole were computed as weighed averages of operating days for the twenty-three industries chosen for intraindustrial analysis. (4) Except for Table 12 and Figure 11, wages and other indicators are computed only for those strata having an average of five or more operatives per establishment.

The monthly wages of operatives in 1951 were estimated on the following assumptions. (1) The wage ratio for different sexes in a given industry was the same as the average ratio for the same industry in 1914. (2) The ratio of *tsuki-betsu jōyō rōdōsha nobesū* (total by-the-month permanent workers) to *nenmatsu genzai jōyō rōdōsha gōkei* (total year-end permanent workers) was the same for *shokuin* (white collar) and *rōmusha* (operative).

For Table 5, the average of sex ratios (and age ratios when applicable) for the whole industry in 1914 and 1932/33 was used as the standard weight for computing average wages. For Tables 6, 9, 11, and 12 (col. 2), Figures 8 and

Appendix Table 1
Industrial Classification

Industry	Classification Used for 1909 and 1914A 1909 and 1914 Kōjō Tōkei-hyō
1. Primary metals	*Kinzokuseirengyō*
2. Foundry products	*Kinzokuseirengyō-3*
3. Building materials, metal	*Kinzokuhin seizōgyō-9*
4. Motors, pumps, etc.	*Kikai seizōgyō-1*
5. Shipbuilding	*Senpakusharyō seizōgyō-1*
6. Railroad cars	*Senpakusharyō seizōgyō-2*
7. Electric appliances	*Kigu seizōgyō-4*
8. Ceramics	*Yōgyō-1*
9. Glass and products	*Yōgyō-2*
10. Cement and products	*Yōgyō-3*
11. Bricks and tiles	*Yōgyō-4*
12. Medicines	*Seiyakugyō-1*
13. Industrial chemicals	*Seiyakugyō-2*
14. Paper (Western)	*Seishigyō-1*
15. Paper (Japanese)	*Seishigyō-2*
16. Printing and bookbinding	*Insatsu seihongyō*
17. Silk reeling	*Seishigyō*
18. Cotton spinning	*Bōsekigyō-2*
19. Cotton thread	*Yoriitogyō-2*
20. Silk cloth	*Orimonogyō-1*
21. Cotton cloth	*Orimonogyō-2*
22. Woolen cloth	*Orimonogyō-5*
23. Dyeing	*Senshoku seiri-1*
24. Hosiery	*Kumimono, Amimonogyō-1*
25. Wearing apparel	*Zatsugyō-3*
26. Ropes and nets	*Zatsugyō-2*
27. Lumber and wood products	*Ki, Take, Tsuru, Kuki-seihingyō-1*
28. Sake	*Jōzōgyō-1*
29. Beer	*Jōzōgyō-2*
30. Soy sauce, etc.	*Jōzōgyō-3*
31. Tea	*Seichagyō*
32. Grain and flour milling	*Seikoku Seifungyō*
33. Bakery products, etc.	*Kashi Seizōgyō*
34. Canned foods	*Kanzume binzumegyō*
35. Matches	*Hakkabutsu seizōgyō-1*

Appendix Table 1 (continued)

Industry	1914 Kōjō Tōkei-hyō	Osaka city, Osaka pref., and Yokohama	1933 Kōgyō Chōsasho Tokyo	Nagoya	1951 Kōgyō Tōkei-hyō
			Classification Used for 1914B, 1933, and 1951		
1. Primary metals	Kinzokuseirengyō	15	B1	B1	33
2. Motors, pumps, etc.	Kikai seizōgyō-1	21, 22, 24, 39	C3, C4, C6, C21	C3, C4, C6, C20	351, 361-4, 366, 367, 3693-99
3. Shipbuilding	Sempakusharyō seizōgyō-1	55	C37	C36	373
4. Cars and carriages	Sempakusharyō seizōgyō-2, 3	54	C36	C35	371, 372, 374-9
5. Ceramics	Yōgyō-1	64	D1	D1	324, 3294
6. Glass and products	Yōgyō-2	65, 71	D2, D8	D2, D7	321
7. Cement and products	Yōgyō-3	68, 69, 70	D5, D6, D7	D5, D6	322, 327
8. Bricks and tiles	Yōgyō-4	66, 67	D3, D4	D3, D4	323
9. Medicines	Seiyakugyō-1	74	E1	E1	287
10. Paper	Seishigyō	95	F22	F15	2612, 2613

Appendix Table 1 (continued)

	Classification Used for 1914B, 1933, and 1951				
	1914 Kōjō Tōkei-hyō		*1933* Kōgyō Chōsasho	*1951* Kōgyō Tōkei-hyō	
11. Printing and bookbinding	*Insatsu seihongyō*	G	G1, G2	G1, G2	27
12. Silk reeling	*Seishigyō*	1	A1	A1	2211
13. Spinning	*Bōsekigyō*	2	A2	A2	2221-2226
14. Thread	*Yoriitogyō*	3	A3	A3	2227
15. Cloth	*Orimonogyō*	4	A4	A4	223, 224
16. Dyeing and finishing	*Senshoku seiri sonota kakōgyō*	14	A4	A4	226
17. Hosiery	*Kumimono amimonogyō-1*	5	A5	A5	225
18. Wearing apparel	*Zatsugyō-3*	143	J18	J15	23
19. Lumber and wood products	*Ki, Take, Tsuru, Kuki-seihingyō-1*	F	F1, F2	F1, F2	241, 242, 2432-2436
20. Tea	*Seichagyō*	120	H11	H11	2093
21. Grain and flour milling	*Seikoku seijungyō*	113, 114	H4, H5	H4, H5	205, 2094
22. Bakery products, etc.	*Kashi seizōgyō*	116	H7	H7	207
23. Matches	*Hakkabutsu*	148	J23	J20	3983

10, and Appendix Table 2, sex ratios for the whole industry in that year were used as the weight. For other cases sex ratios for each industry were used as the standard weight.

The wage for a particular sex, age, and plant size in an industry in 1909 or 1914, when no such figure existed, was estimated from the wage of the labor of the opposite sex belonging to the same age class, plant size, and industry, applying the ratio of the industrial average wage of the particular class of labor to that of the labor belonging to the same age class and the opposite sex. When this procedure was not feasible, the wage was estimated from the wage of the labor of the same sex and plant size belonging to the different age-class in the same industry, applying the industrial average interage wage ratio for the same sex.

APPENDIX 2: ESTIMATION OF THE RATE OF RETURN ON CAPITAL FOR 1932/33

The rate of return on capital, or more accurately the rate of profit inclusive of interest paid on the book value of total assets at a factory, was estimated on the following assumptions.

Kazoku jūgyōsha are specified in the instructions of the survey to include proprietors and unpaid family workers. The observed male-female ratio for this category of labor is about five to one, strongly suggesting the instructions were closely followed. The application of ratios of male and female proprietors (79.9 and 28.1 percent, respectively) in family labor obtained from the 1940 census (Shōwadōjinkai 1957, p. 44) yielded reasonable estimates of proprietors for different size-strata, namely, about the same as the number of establishments for very small sizes, with a rapid decline in the proportion for larger sizes.

Hourly wage rates for unpaid family workers were assumed to have been the same as those for operatives in the same establishment, and hourly wage rates for proprietors were assumed in the standard case to have been one-third less than the average wage rates for operatives in the same industry. In Figure 11, alternative assumptions were tested. Working hours were estimated from *Shūgyō Kōzō Kihon Chōsa* for 1956 (p. 77). Compared with employes, they are 10.0 and 5.2 percent longer for male proprietors and family workers, whereas they are 19.9 and 9.4 percent shorter for female proprietors and family workers, respectively.

Unreported interest paid was estimated from the average rate of interest in Tokyo and Yokohama (7.84 percent) and the reported debt for other areas. The estimated value of interest was added to the difference between revenue and cost to arrive at an estimate of profit inclusive of interest.

Power plants of the largest size in the City of Osaka were excluded from the calculation of figures for the manufacturing industry as a whole because the profit figure was clearly in error, showing a loss equal to profits in all other industries in the nation. Similarly, Tokyo's spinning factories of 100,000 to 500,000 yen capital were excluded from the calculation for homogeneous industries. Homogeneous industries include dyeing in place of silk reeling.

Appendix Table 2
Characteristics of Various Industries

1909	(1) Estab- lishments	(2) Opera- tives	(3) Average size[a]	(4) Wages[b]	(5) Size elasticity[c]	(6) Coefficient of variation[d]
1. Primary metals	44	1196	27.2	33.8	0.026	0.165
2. Foundry products	89	2062	23.2	36.8	0.075*	0.106
3. Building materials, metal	112	2380	21.3	40.8	0.060*	0.093
4. Motors, pumps, etc.	309	7932	25.7	40.5	0.060*	0.102
5. Shipbuilding	112	17,672	157.8	40.0	-0.007	0.037
6. Railroad cars	16	2346	146.6	41.5	0.022	0.010
7. Electric appliances	86	3199	37.2	35.4	-0.067	0.019
8. Ceramics	676	8897	13.2	31.2	0.005	0.078
9. Glass and products	247	7082	28.7	32.3	0.043	0.072
10. Cement and products	181	7129	39.4	33.4	0.008	0.050
11. Bricks and tiles	798	11,258	14.1	34.6	0.037*	0.051
12. Medicines	89	1833	20.6	26.7	-0.039	0.180
13. Industrial chemicals	49	1743	35.6	32.6	0.020	0.078
14. Paper (Western)	71	5649	79.6	32.7	0.071*	0.073
15. Paper (Japanese)	529	6517	12.3	26.9	0.056*	0.075
16. Printing and bookbinding	962	21,322	22.2	30.6	0.057	0.105
17. Silk reeling	3720	191,561	51.5	30.1	0.103*	0.106
18. Cotton spinning	111	89,781	808.8	32.9	0.058*	0.020
19. Cotton thread	190	3612	19.0	28.4	0.087*	0.172
20. Silk cloth	4193	59,574	14.2	28.5	0.065*	0.095
21. Cotton cloth	3568	71,759	20.1	28.3	0.079*	0.135
22. Woolen cloth	54	13,855	256.6	38.3	0.068*	0.106
23. Dyeing	772	9748	12.6	30.9	0.103*	0.110
24. Hosiery	215	3681	17.1	32.7	0.114*	0.150
25. Wearing apparel	569	8523	15.0	32.7	0.033*	0.098
26. Ropes and nets	154	3459	22.5	31.3	0.100*	0.099
27. Lumber and wood products	1201	14,431	12.0	26.8	-0.001	0.035
28. Sake	2305	27,533	11.9	30.1	0.038*	0.031
29. Beer	7	1477	211.0	34.3	0.028*	0.011
30. Soy sauce, vinegar, etc.	573	7455	13.0	28.2	0.051	0.094
31. Tea	1360	12,422	9.1	35.6	0.090*	0.140
32. Grain and flour milling	456	6139	13.5	31.7	0.006	0.029
33. Bakery products, etc.	484	4170	8.6	29.5	0.109	0.124
34. Canned foods	114	2152	18.9	35.0	0.047	0.063
35. Matches	192	16,802	87.5	28.5	0.082*	0.053
1914A						
1. Primary metals	40	3638	91.0	39.2	0.073	0.261
2. Foundry products	140	4486	31.9	44.2	0.076	0.135
3. Building materials, metal	135	1493	11.1	38.7	0.095	0.098
4. Motors, pumps, etc.	315	19,868	63.1	45.1	0.025*	0.091
5. Shipbuilding	162	24,337	150.2	45.8	0.013	0.059
6. Railroad cars	7	1890	270.0	46.1	-0.050	0.147
7. Electric appliances	164	5606	34.2	42.0	0.005	0.064
8. Ceramics	510	10,201	20.0	35.7	-0.004	0.099
9. Glass and products	293	9104	31.1	36.8	0.055	0.095
10. Cement and products	191	7400	38.7	38.1	0.016	0.092
11. Bricks and tiles	685	9927	14.5	33.8	-0.035	0.126
12. Medicines	109	2537	23.3	35.0	0.074*	0.150
13. Industrial chemicals	73	3598	49.3	37.6	0.024	0.095
14. Paper (Western)	48	6978	145.4	41.4	0.069	0.159
15. Paper (Japanese)	336	7255	21.6	31.1	0.020	0.043
16. Printing and bookbinding	1214	28,069	23.1	35.3	0.060*	0.091
17. Silk reeling	3400	224,287	66.0	32.3	0.052*	0.056
18. Cotton spinning	105	112,858	1074.8	37.1	0.079*	0.022
19. Cotton thread	173	6744	39.0	38.0	0.133*	0.237
20. Silk cloth	2713	45,649	16.8	32.4	0.047*	0.073
21. Cotton cloth	3438	88,662	25.8	32.1	0.113*	0.201

Appendix Table 2 (continued)

1914A	(1) Estab- lishments	(2) Opera- tives	(3) Average size[a]	(4) Wages[b]	(5) Size elasticity[c]	(6) Coefficient of variation[d]
22. Woolen cloth	75	13,597	181.3	41.0	0.053*	0.078
23. Dyeing	755	10,622	14.1	34.7	0.076	0.113
24. Hosiery	419	7302	17.4	33.4	0.106*	0.187
25. Wearing apparel	511	7224	14.1	37.5	0.053*	0.090
26. Ropes and nets	182	5828	32.0	34.3	0.143*	0.185
27. Lumber and wood products	1350	19,013	14.1	38.2	0.037*	0.048
28. Sake	2120	27,099	12.8	33.0	-0.018	0.014
29. Beer	7	1573	224.7	34.4	-0.063	0.033
30. Soy sauce, vinegar, etc.	609	8024	13.2	31.6	0.024	0.041
31. Tea	855	11,583	13.6	45.0	0.032	0.076
32. Grain and flour milling	535	7645	14.3	36.7	0.067*	0.062
33. Bakery products, etc.	564	5594	9.9	34.7	0.123*	0.196
34. Canned foods	124	2572	20.7	35.4	-0.019	0.033
35. Matches	179	17,677	98.8	32.1	0.037	0.085

1914B						
1. Primary metals	40	3638	91.0	39.2	0.073	0.261
2. Motors, pumps, etc.	315	19,868	63.1	45.1	0.025*	0.091
3. Shipbuilding	162	24,337	150.2	45.8	0.013	0.059
4. Cars and carriages	115	4822	41.9	37.5	-0.002	0.075
5. Ceramics	510	10,201	20.0	35.7	-0.004	0.099
6. Glass and products	293	9104	31.1	36.8	0.055	0.095
7. Cement and products	191	7400	38.7	38.1	0.016	0.092
8. Bricks and tiles	685	9927	14.5	33.8	-0.035	0.126
9. Medicines	109	2537	23.3	35.0	0.074*	0.150
10. Paper	384	14,233	37.1	31.0	0.085*	0.172
11. Printing and bookbinding	1214	28,069	23.1	35.3	0.060*	0.091
12. Silk reeling	3400	224,287	66.0	32.3	0.052*	0.056
13. Spinning	133	124,637	937.1	37.3	0.067*	0.034
14. Thread	367	10,947	29.8	35.2	0.080*	0.185
15. Cloth	6769	159,606	23.6	33.5	0.089*	0.168
16. Dyeing and finishing	1135	14,876	13.1	32.5	0.076	0.083
17. Hosiery	419	7302	17.4	33.4	0.106*	0.187
18. Wearing apparel	511	7224	14.1	37.5	0.053*	0.090
19. Lumber and wood products	182	5828	32.0	34.3	0.037*	0.048
20. Tea	1350	19,013	14.1	38.2	0.032	0.076
21. Grain and flour milling	535	7645	14.3	36.7	0.067*	0.075
22. Bakery products, etc.	564	5594	9.9	34.7	0.123*	0.196
23. Matches	179	17,677	98.8	32.1	0.037	0.085

1932/33						
1. Primary metals	493	18,923	38.4	180.6	0.195*	0.216
2. Motors, pumps, etc.	648	16,978	26.2	146.8	0.123*	0.228
3. Shipbuilding	52	7208	138.6	215.4	0.141*	0.112
4. Cars and carriages	897	23,719	26.4	152.3	0.165*	0.260
5. Ceramics	97	6787	70.0	148.2	0.049	0.125
6. Glass and products	681	15,762	23.1	129.1	0.124	0.248
7. Cement and products	46	1863	40.5	186.0	0.009	0.133
8. Bricks and tiles	76	1705	22.4	194.9	0.276*	0.230
9. Medicines	213	6897	32.4	184.0	0.124*	0.156
10. Paper	45	3759	83.5	189.6	0.066	0.061
11. Printing and bookbinding	1587	30,946	19.5	194.2	0.207*	0.290
12. Silk reeling	6	2568	428.0	144.7	0.081	0.046
13. Spinning	106	56,456	532.6	120.5	-0.048	0.052
14. Thread	187	3751	20.1	134.7	0.052	0.107
15. Cloth	1539	62,322	40.5	116.0	0.040*	0.071
16. Dyeing and finishing	857	18,524	21.6	133.5	0.068*	0.103
17. Hosiery	1658	17,494	10.6	153.2	0.220*	0.352

Appendix Table 2 (continued)

1932/33	(1) Estab- lishments	(2) Opera- tives	(3) Average size[a]	(4) Wages[b]	(5) Size elasticity[c]	(6) Coefficient of variation[d]
18. Wearing apparel	998	14,519	14.5	99.8	-0.035	0.215
19. Lumber and wood products	1454	18,302	12.6	139.7	0.094*	0.099
20. Tea	31	185	6.0	134.0	2.680	0.938
21. Grain and flour milling	59	779	13.2	216.4	0.309*	0.319
22. Bakery products, etc.	585	10,801	18.5	97.4	0.058	0.102
23. Matches	13	326	25.1	93.5	0.124	0.073
1951						
1. Primary metals	5176	295,707	57.1	11.93	0.100*	0.160
2. Motors, pumps, etc.	4260	150,454	35.3	8.82	0.116*	0.194
3. Shipbuilding	1387	109,736	79.1	9.58	-0.010	0.177
4. Cars and carriages	3049	122,050	40.0	9.53	0.129*	0.237
5. Ceramics	2640	43,559	16.5	7.19	0.143*	0.260
6. Glass and products	1199	36,114	30.1	9.36	0.127	0.414
7. Cement and products	2030	41,026	20.2	9.91	0.264*	0.475
8. Bricks and tiles	3659	26,851	7.3	5.71	0.134*	0.266
9. Medicines	979	32,423	33.1	9.54	0.168*	0.236
10. Paper	1393	56,480	40.6	13.16	0.260*	0.438
11. Printing and bookbinding	6564	104,976	16.0	8.63	0.104*	0.233
12. Silk reeling	973	69,449	71.4	5.31	0.138*	0.132
13. Spinning	1857	217,062	116.9	9.06	0.126*	0.146
14. Thread	1543	16,389	10.6	5.11	0.088*	0.140
15. Cloth	16,274	353,820	21.7	6.65	0.101*	0.235
16. Dyeing and finishing	2769	57,311	20.7	8.25	0.121*	0.198
17. Hosiery	2478	40,796	16.5	6.29	0.079*	0.112
18. Wearing apparel	5345	85,005	18.0	6.37	0.074*	0.121
19. Lumber and wood products	20,630	204,573	9.9	5.00	0.062	0.134
20. Tea	372	2355	6.3	5.49	0.105*	0.111
21. Grain and flour milling	3479	37,589	10.8	7.11	0.149*	0.259
22. Bakery products, etc.	6660	75,689	11.4	5.31	0.101*	0.164
23. Matches	144	7761	53.9	5.34	0.057	0.094

*The size elasticity is positive and significantly different from zero at the 5 percent level.
[a]Operatives per establishment.
[b]Standardized average wages (in sen per day for 1909, 1914, and 1932/33, and 1000 yen per month for 1951).
[c]Size elasticity of standardized wages.
[d]Coefficient of variation in standardized wages.

REFERENCES

Abegglen, James C. 1958. *The Japanese Factory*. Free Press.

Blumenthal, Tuvia. 1966. "The Effect of Socio-Economic Factors on Wage Differentials in Japanese Manufacturing Industries." *Economic Studies Quarterly* 17 (Sept. 1966).

Fujita, Wakao. 1961. *Nihon Rōdō Kyōyakuron*. Tokyo Daigaku Shuppankai.

Harafuji, Hiroshi. 1960. "Meiji-Zenki no Koyōhō." In *Kanazawa Daigaku Hōbungakubu Ronshū*, Hōkeihen, vol. 8.

Hazama, Hiroshi. 1964. *Nihon Rōmu Kanri-shi Kenkyū*. Daiyamondo.

Horie, Yasuzō. 1972. "Meiji Sanjū-nendai no Shokkō Koyō no Jōtai." *Keizai Keiei Ronsō* 7 (July 1972).

Hyōdō, Tsutomu. 1971. *Nihon ni okeru Rōshikankei no Tenkai*. Tokyo Daigaku Shuppankai.

Kaneda, Heiichirō. 1927. "Tokugawa Jidai ni okeru Koyōhō no Kenkyū." In *Kokka Gakkai Zasshi*, vol. 41, nos. 7-10 (July-Oct.).

Kawaguchi, Hiroshi. 1962. "Futatsu no Nihon Keizai-ron." In *Nihon Keizai no Kōzō*. Shunjūsha.

Komiya, Ryūtarō. 1961. "Dokusen-Shihon to Shotoku Saibumpai-Seisaku." *Sekai*, March 1961.

_____. 1962. "Nihon ni okeru Dokusen to Kigyō Rijun." In *Kigyō Keizai Bunseki*, edited by Tsunejirō Nakamura, Hisao Otsuka, and Kōichiro Suzuki. Tokyo Daigaku Shuppankai.

Lewis, W. Arthur. 1954. "Economic Development with Unlimited Supplies of Labour." *Manchester School of Economic Development and Social Studies* 22 (May 1954).

LTES [Estimates of Long-Term Economic Statistics of Japan]. Series edited by Kazushi Ohkawa, Miyohei Shinohara, and Mataji Umemura. 1965-. 14 vols. Tōyō Keizai Shinpōsha.

_____. Vol. 8. *Prices*. 1967. Kazushi Ohkawa et al.

Maruyama, Kandō, and Nanshi Imamura. 1912. *Detchi Seido no Kenkyū*. Seikōsha.

Minami, Ryōshin. 1970. *Nihon Keizai no Tenkanten*. Sōbunsha.

Miyamoto, Mataji. 1948. *Kinsei Shōgyō Keiei no Kenkyū*. Reprint 1971. Seibundō.

Miyazaki, Yoshikazu. 1962. "Katō Kyōsō no Ronri to Genjitsu." *Ekonomisuto*, autumn special edition.

Miyazawa, Ken'ichi. 1961. "Shihon Shūchū to Nijū Kōzō." In *Shihon Chikuseki to Kinyū Kōzō*, edited by Ichirō Nakayama. Tōyō Keizai Shinpōsha.

Nōshōmushō [Ministry of Agriculture and Commerce]. *Nōshōmu Tōkei-hyō*. Annual, 1884-.

Odaka, Kōnosuke. 1968. "A History of Money Wages in the Northern Kyushu Industrial Area, 1898-1939." *Hitotsubashi Journal of Economics* 8 (Feb. 1968).

_____. 1969. "Chingin Keisha Kōzō no Hassei to Tenkai." In *Nihon Keizai no Kōzō Hendō to Yosoku*, edited by Koichi Emi and Toshiyuki Mizoguchi. Shūnjusha.

_____. 1970. "Chingin Keisha Kōzō no Chōkihendō." *Nihon Rōdō Kyōkai Zasshi*, nos. 7 and 8.

Ōkōchi, Kazuo. 1959. "Nihonteki Rōshi kankei no Tokushitsu to Sono Hensen." *Nihon Rōdōkyōkai Zasshi* 1 (April 1959).
Ono, Akira. 1968. "Gijutsu Shimpō to Borrowed Technology no Ruikei, Seishigyō ni Kansuru Jirei Kenkyū." In *Keizai Seichō Riron no Tembō*, edited by Jinkichi Tsukui and Yasusuke Murakami. Iwanami Shoten.
———. 1973. *Sengo Nihon no Chingin Kettei*. Tōyō Keizai Shimpōsha.
Osaka-shi. 1928. *Honshi ni okeru Gofuku Ten'in no Seikatsu to Rōdō* (no. 72 in Shakaibu Hōkoku series). Kōbundō.
Rōdōshō [Ministry of Labor]. 1954-57 (annual). *Shokushubetsutō Chingin Chōsa*.
———. 1954. *Shokushubetsutō Chingin Chōsa Kojinbetsu Chingin Chōsa Kekka Hōkokusho*.
———. 1955-57 (annual). *Shokushubetsutō Chingin Jittai Chōsa Hōkokusho*.
———. 1958- (annual). *Chingin Kōzō Kihonchōsa*.
———. 1958-60 (annual). *Chingin Kōzō Kihon Chōsa Kekka Hōkokusho*.
———. 1961. *Chingin Jittai Sōgō Chōsa Kekka Hōkokusho*.
———. 1964. *Chingin Kōzō Kihon Tōkei Chōsa Hōkokusho*.
———. 1965- (annual). *Chingin Census*.
———. *Moderu Chingin Chōsa* Published irregularly.
Sasaki, Takao. 1960. "Chingin Kakusa no Hendō." In *Wagakuni Chingin Kōzō no Shiteki Kōsatsu*, edited by Showadōjinkai. Shiseidō.
Sasaki, Takao, and Ryōhei Magota. 1956. "Sangyōbetsu-kibōbetsu Chingin Kakusa." In *Chingin Kihon Chōsa*, edited by Ichirō Nakayama. Tōyō Keizai Shimpōsha.
Serizawa, Hyoe. 1962. "Kōdō seichō-ka ni okeru Kigyō no Shūekisei ni tsuite." In *Kigyō Bunseki*, edited by Tsunejirō Nakamura, Hisao Ōtsuka, and Kōichirō Suzuki. Tokyo Daigaku Shuppankai.
Shinohara, Miyohei. 1959. "Nihon Keizai no Nijū Kōzō." In *Sangyō Kōzō*, edited by Miyohei Shinohara. Shunjusha.
———. 1961. *Nihon Keizai no Seichō to Junkan*. Sōbunsha.
Shōwadojinkai. 1957. *Tōkei kara Mita Koyō to Shitsugyō*. Shōwadōjinkai.
———. 1960. *Wagakuni Chingin Kōzō no Shiteki Kōsatsu*. Shiseidō.
Stoikov, Vladimir. 1973a. "Size of Firm, Worker Earnings, and Human Capital: The case of Japan." *Industrial and Labor Relations Reviews*, vol. 26, no. 4 (July 1973).
———. 1973b. "The Structure of Earnings in Japanese Manufacturing Industries: A Human Capital Approach." *Journal of Political Economy*, vol. 81, no. 2 (March/April 1973).
Sumiya, Mikio. 1955. *Nihon Chinrōdōshi-ron*. Tokyo Daigaku Shippankai.
———. 1961. "Chūshō Kigyō Rōdō Mondai no Honshitsu—Chingin Kakusa wa Sonzai Suru-ka." In *Nihon Rōdō Kyōkai Zasshi*, no. 6.
Sumiya, Mikio, Kenichi Kobayashi, and Tsutomu Hyōdō. 1963. *Social Impact of Industrialization in Japan*. Japanese National Commission for UNESCO.
———. 1967. *Nihon Shihonshugi to Rōdō Mondai*. Tokyo Daigaku Shuppankai.
Taira, Kōji. 1970. *Economic Development and the Labor Market in Japan*. Columbia University Press.
Tōyō Keizai Shimpōsha. 1968-. *Chingin Sōran*.
Tsuda, Masumi. 1968. *Nenkōteki Rōshi Kankeiron*. Minerva Shobo.

Umemura, Mataji. 1955. "Chingin Kakusa to Rōdō Shijō." In *Nihon Keizai no Bunseki*, vol. 2, edited by Shigeto Tsuru and Kazushi Ohkawa. Keisō Shobo.

Watanabe, Tsunehiko. 1968. "Industrialization, Technological Progress, and Dual Structure." In *Economic Growth: The Japanese Experience since the Meiji Era*, edited by Lawrence Klein and Kazushi Ohkawa. Irwin.

The Introduction of Electric Power and Its Impact on the Manufacturing Industries: With Special Reference to Smaller Scale Plants

Ryoshin Minami

The history of energy utilization constitutes an important part of the history of economy, society, and culture. One of its most important aspects is the transformation of motive power, which is closely associated with improvements in production machinery and has contributed to the rapid development of manufacturing industries.[1] This was the case in the so-called Industrial Revolution which began with improvements in spinning machinery during the 1760s in England.[2] Waterframe spinning machinery invented by Richard

The writer is very much indebted to Kazushi Ohkawa, Professor Emeritus of Hitotsubashi University, for his encouragement in this study. Great thanks are also due to Mataji Umemura also of Hitotsubashi, and to Richard F. Kosobud of the University of Illinois and Hugh Patrick of Yale University for their help in finding relevant literature. Greateful acknowledgement is also made to Yukihiko Kiyokawa of Hitotsubashi for his many comments and to Susumu Suzuki of the Hitachi Company Ltd. for guidance to a history of the electric machinery industry. Finally, thanks are due to Paul Zimmer for an initial English editing.

[1]*Motive power* stands for the work done by prime movers which converts the energy of nature directly into the energy of motion. Strictly speaking, electric motors are not prime movers in that they consume electricity generated by other prime movers. In this study, however, they are included as prime movers, because from the standpoint of the user that is what they are (see Fenichel 1966, p. 443).

[2]On the transformation of motive power during and after the Industrial Revolution in Western countries, see Landes (1966). For a history of the introduction of steam engines and electric motors, see Temin (1966) and DuBoff (1967).

Arkwright (1766) led to substitution of water power for human power. The further development of spinning machinery demanded new engines, powerful and independent of water streams. This demand was met by the appearance of the steam engine.

Improvements by James Watt during the 1770s and the following decade permitted steam engines to be used for the first time for industrial purposes. Because of subsequent increases in speed and decreases in price, steam engines began to be employed to a greater extent in industry, notably in spinning factories equipped with waterframes and mules. Steam engines were continuously improved in response to various demands: large capacity, low fuel consumption, high speed, small size, light weight, and so forth. During the late nineteenth century, however, these technical improvements reached a plateau. Steam engines were gradually replaced by steam turbines having large capacity and high speeds, and internal combustion engines, small in size and light in weight. Furthermore, electric motors began to be used in a wide range of factories after the invention of the alternating current motor (1885-90) and eventually displaced the steam engine. This transformation from steam engines to electric motors—electrification—was really the most sweeping and complex technological change in manufacturing industries.

This paper aims at a quantitative study of electrification and its impact on smaller scale manufacturers in Japan. Emphasis is placed on the smaller plants because of the economic significance of electrification to them. By way of introduction, however, I will discuss the whole motive-power transformation process including electrification in larger manufacturing plants. In the first section the process of transformation will be surveyed for the manufacturing sector as a whole and then by the scale of plants in this sector. In the last part of the section factors responsible for electrification will be reviewed. A section is devoted to an examination of the impact of electrification on smaller plants. The hypothesis that persistent growth of these plants was dependent largely on the introduction of motive power through electrification will be tested. That is, the relationship between electrification and the introduction of motive power is examined, and the effects of motive power on productivity increases will be clarified for two industries, match-making and weaving, as examples typical of smaller scale factories. Finally, conclusions from the first two sections will be summarized and their implications discussed. Further, another form of electrification, the use of electric lighting, and its significance will be taken up.

THE HOW AND WHY OF ELECTRIFICATION
IN MANUFACTURING INDUSTRIES

Prior to the age of electric motors, water wheels and steam engines were used by Japanese manufacturers. Water wheels were dominant from the end of the Tokugawa era until about 1890 in industries such as silk reeling and cotton spinning. Yamaguchi's compilation from the *Prefectural Statistical Tables* (*Fuken Tōkei-hyō*) shows that around 1884, 47.3 percent of factories were

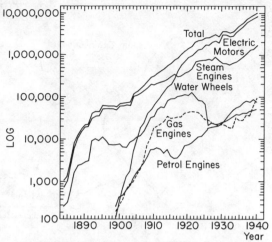

Figure 1. Horsepower of prime movers by type in manufacturing industries.

Source: LTES 12:223.

Note: Excludes gas and electric utilities. Figures for 1884-1918 are for establishments with ten or more production workers, figures for 1919-40 are for establishments with five or more production workers.

equipped with water wheels whereas only 3.6 percent had steam engines, 44.2 percent had no motive power, and 4.9 percent were unaccounted for (Yamaguchi 1956, p. 96).

The introduction of steam engines dates from the 1860s. In 1861 the Nagasaki Iron Mill began to use steam power. Shimazu Hisamitsu of the Satsuma clan, who imported cotton-spinning machinery from England in 1866, completed a spinning plant equipped with a steam engine the next year. In 1871, the Tomioka Silk-Reeling Plant, a government enterprise, began to operate steam-powered machinery imported from France. The Takashima Colliery Company ran shaft transporters powered by a steam engine. Thereafter steam engines diffused rapidly, especially in the 1890s. Yamaguchi's statistics show factories equipped with water wheels decreased to 19.9 percent around 1892, whereas factories using steam power increased to 25.3 percent (1956, p. 111). A rapid rise in steam power since 1884 can be seen in Figure 1, which shows horsepower of prime movers by type. Horsepower supplied by steam engines (including steam turbines), shown in Figure 2, already exceeded 85 percent in 1889. In contrast, water wheels (hydro turbines, Pelton, and Japanese type) continuously decreased, amounting to less than 10 percent at the turn of the century.

During the phase of steam power diffusion, introduction of techniques for generating, transmitting, and using electric light and power was already in progress.[3] The first actual use of electric light in Japan was at the Sangenya

[3] For a history of electric generation in Japan, see Kurihara (1964) and Arisawa (1960a).

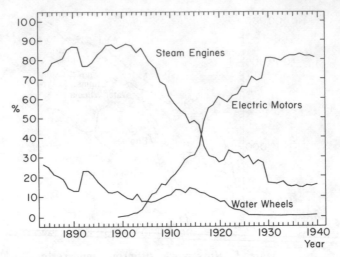

Figure 2. Composition of prime movers in terms of horsepower.

Source: Same as Figure 1.

Plant of the Osaka Spinning Company in 1886, from electricity generated within the plant. The supply of electric lighting for public use was begun by the Tokyo Electric Light Company in 1887. In both cases power was obtained by thermal generation. Hydro generation dates from 1890. In this year two companies, Shimotsuke Jute Yarn Spinning and the Ashio Copper Mine, commenced hydroelectric generation for their own use. In 1892 Kyoto City set up a water plant, the Keage Power Plant, and began to supply electricity for public use. Thereafter, numerous hydro plants were established in various regions, and a remarkable rise in generating capacity occurred.

Statistics for generating capacity are available from 1903, and for electricity generated and consumed, from 1907. They are given in Table 1, columns 2, 3 and 4, respectively, for every fifth year. The number of electric bulbs installed, shown in column 1, suggests use spread rapidly after 1890.

During the late 19th century and the beginning of this century, electric power generation by firms for their own use was much greater than that by electric utilities. Statistics for 1907 show the latter was only 39 percent of total power generated. However, owing to a rapid increase in output by utilities, this increased to over 50 percent in 1913. The predominance of the utilities was made possible by their rapid progress in transmission techniques. A representative example is the completion of a power transmission line by the Tokyo Electric Light Company in 1914, which enabled the long distance (228 kilometers, third longest line in the world at that time) and high voltage (115,000 volt) transmission of 37,500 kilowatts from the Inawashiro Hydro Plant to the Tokyo district.

In the course of the development of electric generation, electric motors came to be widely used. Figure 1 shows horsepower of electric motors

Table 1
Number of Electric Bulbs Installed, Electric Generating Capacity, Electricity Generated and Consumed

	Number of electric bulbs installed (1)	Electric generating capacity (2)	Electricity				Capacity-output ratio (5)
			Generated (3)		Consumed (4)		
	(1000)	(1000 kw)	(million kwh)		(million kwh)		(1/1000 hours)
1890	21						
1895	89						
1900	217						
1905	464	39					
1910	1949	161	427	(621)	329	(523)	377
1915	7538	569	1811	(2217)	1396	(1802)	314
1920	16,138	951	2815	(4669)	2941	(3795)	249
1925	27,321	2167	7735	(9093)	5964	(7322)	280
1930	36,840	3961	14,034	(15,773)	10,878	(12,618)	282
1935	43,231	5137	22,155	(24,698)	17,389	(19,932)	232
1940	54,083	7881	30,603	(34,566)	24,614	(28,576)	258

Source: LTES 8: col. 1 from p. 69; col. 2, p. 206; col. 3, p. 196; col. 4, p. 198.
Note: Smaller figures are for electric utilities only. Figures including industrial plants are shown in parentheses. Col. 5 = col. 2 ÷ col. 3.

increased remarkably after 1899.[4] In 1905 it exceeded the horsepower of water wheels, and in 1917 it exceeded that of steam engines. Figure 2 shows a rapid decrease in the percentage of steam power, which signifies a sweeping substitution of electric power for steam. The relative decrease in steam power and the increase in electric power, however, stopped around 1930, implying electrification in factories was actually completed about that time.

In summary, the substitution of steam engines for water whells took place in 1890-1905. The substitution of electric motors for steam engines, beginning in the 1890s, occurred from 1905 to 1930. It appears that these two substitutions occurred in a much shorter time than was the case in the other industrialized countries.

Examination by Scale of Factory

Power statistics by scale of factory are available from the Kōjō Tōkei-hyō beginning with 1909, though on an annual basis only from 1930. From these data, percentages of various prime movers in terms of horsepower are calculated and shown by scale of factory for six years from 1909 to 1940 in Table 2. In 1909 steam engines constituted about half of available horse-power in even the smallest plants, increasing to four-fifths for those with more than five hundred production workers. The share of water wheels was somewhat greater for smaller firms. However, the data for water wheel usage

[4]Continuous statistics for horsepower of electric motors are not available prior to 1898. Kanbayashi et al. (1943, p. 300) state the introduction of electric motors began in the mid-1880s.

Table 2
Composition of Prime Movers by Type and by Scale of Factory
in Terms of Horsepower
(in percent)

Factory size (persons)	Electric motors (β)	Steam engines	Gas engines	Petrol engines	Water wheels
1909					
Total	13.0	70.0	3.7	2.5	10.7
5-9	10.6	49.6	6.7	12.5	20.6
10-29	9.8	59.7	7.8	9.6	13.2
30-49	7.0	63.4	6.0	5.4	18.2
50-99	9.8	76.0	4.2	3.1	6.9
100-499	13.2	64.5	4.0	0.7	17.7
500-999	9.7	83.7	1.5	0.0	5.0
1000-	18.3	78.2	1.4	0.0	2.2
1914					
Total	30.1	46.8	6.0	1.0	16.0
5-9	27.4	41.8	10.6	6.9	13.2
10-29	26.1	46.3	15.4	4.9	7.2
30-49	20.5	47.2	11.8	1.2	19.3
50-99	23.7	40.0	8.1	1.0	27.2
100-499	26.1	47.2	7.7	0.2	18.8
500-999	33.7	32.8	0.6	0.1	32.9
1000-	36.7	60.1	2.9	0.0	0.2
1919					
Total	58.5	28.0	4.3	0.5	8.6
5-9	56.9	19.7	6.4	4.4	12.6
10-29	58.7	24.3	9.1	2.6	5.3
30-49	55.1	34.0	7.3	0.7	3.0
50-99	59.8	30.7	5.2	0.6	3.8
100-499	59.3	27.9	3.4	0.1	9.2
500-999	69.1	29.3	0.8	0.1	0.8
1000-	55.7	28.0	4.0	0.1	12.1
1930					
Total	86.7	11.4	0.6	0.6	0.7
5-9	84.4	6.4	2.1	3.3	3.8
10-29	86.3	9.3	0.8	1.7	2.0
30-49	82.9	13.8	0.7	2.2	0.4
50-99	88.0	9.8	0.4	1.0	0.8
100-499	87.2	11.2	1.0	0.2	0.4
500-999	95.8	3.9	0.0	0.1	0.2
1000-	80.4	18.5	0.1	0.3	0.7

Table 2 (continued)

Factory size (persons)	Electric motors (β)	Steam engines	Gas engines	Petrol engines	Water wheels
1935					
Total	82.2	15.3	0.7	1.2	0.5
5-9	85.5	4.2	2.5	5.0	2.8
10-29	87.8	6.3	1.3	3.5	1.0
30-49	87.8	6.9	0.9	3.9	0.6
50-99	90.9	5.6	0.2	3.1	0.3
100-499	80.4	18.1	0.0	0.9	0.6
500-999	90.3	8.5	0.0	1.1	0.1
1000-	78.6	19.7	1.2	0.2	0.4
1940					
Total	81.5	16.4	0.5	0.7	0.9
5-9	89.3	1.0	2.1	4.8	2.8
10-29	92.4	2.7	1.1	2.8	1.0
30-49	93.5	3.3	0.6	2.3	0.3
50-99	94.9	3.3	0.2	1.4	0.2
100-499	84.8	14.0	0.1	0.7	0.3
500-999	86.2	12.1	0.1	0.2	1.4
1000-	74.8	23.6	0.6	0.1	0.9

Source: LTES 12:232-245.
Note: Excluding gas and electric utilities. Steam engines in this table include steam turbines. Water wheels are composed of hydro turbines, Pelton water wheels, and Japanese-type water wheels. Factory (establishment) size is measured in number of production workers.

by large firms are so erratic for 1909-19 that problems of sampling and reporting may be significant. Plants with over a thousand workers relied relatively somewhat more on electric motors, but up to that level there was no significant scale pattern.

By 1930 composition of prime movers by type and by scale of establishment had changed substantially. The percentages of water wheels and of steam engines decreased sharply from 1909 to 1930. By 1930 the share of water wheels was almost zero in all scales except the smallest. Steam engines amounted to only 4 to 14 percent in the under 999 group and 19 percent for plants over 1000 persons. The percentage of electric motors (β) increased rapidly in all scales, reaching 80 to 95 percent in 1930. That is, the completion of electrification at all scales had occurred by around 1930. Another index of electrification, γ, the percentage of electric motors to total prime movers, is calculated in Table 3 by scale of plant for the same six

Table 3
Percentage of Electric Motors (γ)
by Scale of Establishment
(in percent)

Factory size	1909	1914	1919	1930	1935	1940
Total	19.7	50.8	74.7	94.1	97.8	98.9
5-9	17.2	52.1	71.7	91.5	93.8	95.2
10-29	15.2	44.8	69.9	92.4	95.2	97.2
30-49	10.7	33.3	63.3	91.6	95.7	98.0
50-99	13.4	34.8	61.8	90.6	95.9	98.5
100-499	26.2	49.5	73.5	94.6	97.4	98.9
500-999	42.3	70.3	87.7	97.0	98.7	99.6
1000-	63.6	89.3	94.5	98.6	99.7	99.8

Source: *Kōjō Tōkei-hyō.*
γ = (number of electric motors/total number of prime movers)
× 100.

years.[5] Electric motors were only one-fifth of total prime movers on average in 1909, less for smaller plants and substantially greater for large factories; by 1930 electric motors were the predominant prime mover in all factories. With this index the more rapid electrification in the smaller plants and the completion of electrification around 1930 in all scales can be observed again.[6] And as is discussed later (see Table 8), the percentage of factories with prime movers, always high for the largest scale factories, increased from low to high rates for small factories as well.

Reasons for Electrification

The major factors responsible for the rapid substitution of electric power for steam power were the advantages electric motors have over steam engines and developments in the electric utilities and electric machine industry. Even though electric motors were advantageous compared with other prime movers, without cheap electric motors rapid introduction of electric power would not necessarily have occurred.

Merits of electric motors. Electric motors differ from steam engines in ease of operation and efficiency of small units of operation. Table 4, panels *A* and *B*, show average capacity (horsepower) of prime movers by type: electric

[5]The differential in the level of γ among factories by size in 1909 is large compared with the differential in β. This is because the average horsepower of an electric motor is much smaller than that of a steam engine. (Refer to Table 4.)

[6]An examination of electrification by industry group appears worthy of further study. A brief reference to this is found in LTES 12:74-76.

Table 4
Horsepower per Prime Mover

Average of establishments	Electric motors	Steam engines	Steam turbines	Gas engines	Petrol engines	Water wheels
1909	15	35	46	13	5	12
1914	14	41	84	19	5	35
1919	19	42	134	28	6	36
1930	22	44	844	38	14	15
1935	9	41	1965	76	21	16
1940	8	64	3888	70	14	41
By scale of establishments (1940), number of persons						
5-9	4	17	9	21	8	7
10-29	5	30	5	27	11	11
30-49	7	35	150	42	17	16
50-99	8	26	313	39	20	21
100-499	11	31	2435	60	36	165
500-999	10	34	2949	94	35	3700
1000-	7	297	5456	1777	66	2512

Source: *Kojo Tokei-hyo.*

motors, steam engines, steam turbines, gas engines, petrol engines, and water wheels. Panel *A* gives figures for all scales of factories by year and shows all other engines with the exception of petrol engines had greater average capacity than electric motors. The average capacity of steam turbines increased remarkably, to 3900 horsepower in 1940. Panel *B* gives figures by scale of factory for 1940 and indicates little difference in the average capacity among scales in the case of electric motors, whereas in the other engines (for example, steam engines and turbines) an increasing trend can be seen in the average capacity as scale increases.

The significance of introducing small-capacity electric motors into smaller factories and into larger ones will be considered separately. Because small plants could not be equipped with large-capacity steam engines, tools and machinery continued to be operated by human power for a long time. The appearance of electric power had a revolutionary effect on these plants by enabling the replacement of human power, in many cases merely by extending an electric wire to an ordinary house and installing one small electric motor within the house (Hoshino 1956, p. 181). On the other hand, in larger plants, a comparison of economic efficiency between steam engines and electric motors was crucial.

The use of steam power necessitated group drive arrangements, where power of one or more steam engines was transmitted to machinery by means of big shafts and long belts. The introduction of electric motors gave rise to unit drive arrangements, where electric motors directly operated each tool and machine. This new system has many merits. One was greater flexibility of factory layout and design, because the limitations entailed by big shafts were eliminated. Capital cost was reduced through reductions in floor space and in building construction; heavy, multistoried structures with reinforced floors capable of supporting reciprocating steam engines were not needed. Loss of energy was reduced because individual parts of the production process could be stopped independently.[7] This system was widely introduced in various industries during World War I and after, when small induction motors began to be produced in Japan. In the spinning industry, for example, the unit drive system was employed extensively from about 1932.[8] In two plants constructed in that year, the Inami Plant of the Kureha Spinning Company and the Sasazu Plant of the Tenman Weaving Company, all processes through spinning utilized unit drive arrangements. In the Sekigahara Plant of the Dai Nippon Spinning Company, completed in 1934, the new arrangements were introduced in all processes (Moriya 1948, p. 181).

Electric utilities. Prior to 1932 electric light and power rates were not under government control but were determined by generating costs and supply-demand conditions. Table 5, columns 1 and 2, shows the average rates of electric light and power, respectively.[9] During 1907-15 the average rate for electric light (used mainly for household consumption) showed a decrease,

[7]The impact of introducing electric motors in large manufacturing plants was different between the two periods. In the first phase, when electric power was mostly supplied by the manufacturing factories themselves, a substitution of electric motors for steam engines did not necessarily mean a saving in capital costs, because these factories needed large plants for electric power generation. Savings occurred only in fuel consumption, because of the greater efficiency of electric motors compared to steam engines. According to DuBoff, citing estimates by engineers for 1895-97 in the United States, loss of power was cut by 20 to 70 percent in various circumstances. In the second phase, cheap electric power was available from electric utilities. Elimination of the need for generation plants in large factories greatly saved capital costs. An estimate by another engineer shows that by dismantling steam engines and purchasing electric power a firm might cut power costs by 70 to 83 percent, taking into account expenses for fuel, labor, and above all capital (DuBoff 1967, pp. 510-512).

[8]Merits of the unit drive arrangements in the spinning industry have been mentioned by many authors such as Arisawa (1960c, 7:59), Moriya (1948, pp. 80-81), Iijima (1949, pp. 201-202), and Nippon Sen-i (1958, p. 788).

[9]Indexes of electric light and power estimated from electric rates tables of individual electric utilities are conceptually superior to these average-rates estimates. However, the reason for not using the former is that in the period of oversupply after World War I, electric power was sold at much lower rates than those indicated in the rate tables, so indexes based on them would probably substantially overestimate the actual rates during this period.

Household and industrial use are fairly clearly separated. Different wires were used to deliver electric light and electric power, so even small-scale factories were using service provided under the electric power rate schedules.

Table 5
Average Electric Light and Power Rates
and Coal Price Index

| | Average rate of | | |
	Electric light (1)	Electric power (2)	Wholesale price index of coal (3)
	(yen/1000 kwh)		(1934-36 = 1)
1900			0.34
1905	85.1[a]	20.2[a]	0.42
1910	69.4	30.0	0.42
1915	50.5	30.0	0.44
1920	72.4	66.3	1.40
1925	88.9	55.6	1.00
1930	98.8	38.0	0.86
1935	105.9	29.4	1.00
1940	112.4	37.6	1.48

Sources: Columns 1 and 2 from LTES 12:222. Column 3 from Arisawa 1960a: appendix tables, pp. 10-11.
[a]Data for 1907.

whereas that for power (used mainly for industrial purposes) showed an increase. The increase in power rates is a superficial trend resulting from statistical and methodological problems in estimation. In reality, the rate for electric power also seems to have declined during this period.[10] This was the result of a decrease in generating costs coming from the introduction of hydro generation and, after the Russo-Japanese War, the success of high voltage transmission. In 1908 the Tokyo Electric Light Company cut light and power rates by 12 percent and 22 percent, respectively, because of a sharp drop in generating costs due to the completion of the Komabashi Power Plant in 1907 (Nitta 1936, pp. 99-100). Aggressive competition among utilities accelerated this declining trend. In Tokyo, for instance, overlapping supply of light and power began around 1907 among three sources: the Tokyo Electric Light Company, Tokyo City government, and the Tokyo Electric Railway Company (Arisawa 1960a, 3:114).

The Tokyo Electric Light Company reduced rates when the Yatsuzawa Power Plant started to operate in 1912 (Nitta 1936, p. 107). After a trough in 1915 (at which time the average electric power rate was 30 yen per 1000 kwh), rates began to rise because of a big increase in demand caused by the economic boom during and after World War I. The upward trend during these inflation years (1915-19) was much larger for the power rate than for the

[10]The index for electric power rates estimated by Fujino (1956, pp. 66-67, and 1965, Statistical Note IV) did show a decline during this period.

Table 6
Ratios of Electric Lighting Rate
to Consumer Price Index and of Electric Power
Rate to Manufacturing Output Price Index

	Ratio of electric lighting rate[a]	Ratio of electric power rate[b]
1907	1.30	0.83
1910	1.14	1.33
1915	0.82	1.23
1920	0.47	1.13
1925	0.64	1.27
1930	0.90	1.30
1935	1.00	1.00
1940	0.83[c]	0.77

Sources: Electricity rates: Table 5. Consumer price index: LTES 8:135-136. Manufacturing output price index: LTES 8:192-193.
[a]Average electric lighting rate/consumer price index.
[b]Average electric power rate/manufacturing output price index.
[c]1938 data.

lighting rate. Because of this, as shown in Table 6, the ratio of the electric power rate to the manufacturing output price index (column 2) was almost constant, whereas the ratio of the lighting rate to the consumer price index (column 1) decreased for 1915-20.

During the recession years after the war boom the lighting and power rates showed different patterns of change. The lighting rate continued to rise during this period. It was 72 yen in 1920 and 99 yen in 1930 per 1000 kwh. Consequently the ratio of this rate to the consumer price index increased. On the other hand, the power rate began to decline from a peak in 1923 (69 yen per 1000 kwh) and returned to the 1916 level in 1932. This decline was caused by aggressive price cutting among electric utilities resulting from excess supply.[11]

There were two reasons for this oversupply. The first is a technical one: hydro plants at that time did not have dams and thus could not control seasonal variations in water flow. Consequently, the need to have sufficient generation capacity to meet peak loads in periods of water shortage necessarily gave rise to oversupply under normal conditions. The second

[11]Severe competition among electric suppliers was also found in Nagoya. Thus, electric rates were much cheaper in Tokyo and Nagoya than in other areas. This may explain a predominance of small-scale enterprises in these cities, as pointed out by Tsunehiko Watanabe at the conference, and leads to a hypothesis that geographical differences in the price of electricity were related to the geographical distribution of small firms. This hypothesis merits empirical testing.

reason is a decrease in the growth of the demand for industrial use during the depression of the 1920s and early 30s. The low prices resulting from oversupply of electric power, however, created new sources of demand: smaller factories in manufacturing and electrochemical industries such as ammonium sulphate and electrolysis.[12] The appearance of these new users lessened the financial difficulties of the electric utilities (Fujino 1965, pp. 444-449; Kurihara 1964, pp. 256-261).

Differences in changes between the lighting rate and the power rate are explained by differences in their price elasticities of demand. Electric lighting consumption, with a much lower elasticity, does not decrease much in response to a rise in its rate. This is not the case for the more elastic electric power consumption. Therefore the utilities intended to stimulate demand for electric power by reducing its price while increasing the lighting rate to compensate for the lower profits from power rates. In this way a large difference between the two rates appeared in this particular period.[13]

Since 1932, the year the electric power cartel was established, rates have been under government control. Owing to this control, rates for electric light and power could not increase rapidly compared with other price indexes: the ratio in column 1 of Table 6 decreased from 1935 to 1938, and the ratio in column 2 declined from 1930 to 1940.

As for substitution of electric power for steam, changes in the price of coal must also be considered.[14] The coal price index in Table 5, column 3, shows a sharp increase after 1915. Consequently, the ratio of the electric power rate to the coal price, shown in Table 7, column 1, began to decline remarkably in the early 1920s. One of the basic causes of this decline seems to be that technological progress was much faster in the electric utilities than in coal

---

[12]Of these two oversupply factors, the first seemed to have been much more influential. Electric light and power generated, shown in Table 1, column 3, continued to increase during the years after the war boom. On the other hand, electric generating capacity, shown in column 2, increased even faster. Consequently, column 5, the ratio of column 2 to column 3 and hence a proxy for the capital-output ratio in the electric utilities, increased from 1920 to 1930. This ratio changed with changes in economic activity. A study on the capital-output ratio in the electric utilities has been made in LTES 12:81-82.

[13]It should be emphasized that this difference continues even to the present day. There are several factors for this. The first is a difference in transmission cost coming from a difference in voltage. (Large users take high voltages and are often closer to the thermal power stations.) The second is that large companies often consume most of their electricity late at night. The third, and most important, lies in the intention of the government to stimulate industrial development. Such an energy policy is possible basically because of the difference in the price elasticity between the electric light and power (see Hoshino et al. 1964, pp. 338-339).

[14]For an estimate of the substitution of electric power for coal, see Fujino (1956).

Table 7
Price Ratio of Electric Power to Coal and Labor,
and the Productivity Ratio of Electric Utilities
to Coal Mining

	Price ratio[a]	Productivity ratio[b]
	(1934-36 = 1)	
1907	1.56	
1910	2.43	0.22
1915	2.32	0.40
1920	1.61	0.71
1925	1.89	0.76
1930	1.50	0.96
1935	1.00	1.00
1940	0.86	1.33

Sources: Electric power rate: Table 5. Electric power
generated per employe: LTES 12:207. Number of employes in coal mining and coal output: Arisawa 1960*a*:
appendix tables, pp. 10-11.
[a]Average electric power rate/wholesale price index
of coal.
[b]Electric power generated per employe/coal produced per employe.

mining: relative labor productivity calculated in Table 7, column 2, shows an
increasing trend for the entire period. In short, the difference in the rate of
technological progress between electric utilities and coal mining accelerated
the substitution of electric power for steam power.[15]

Electric machine industry. A wide range of electric machinery and
appliances was imported, mainly from the United States, in the Meiji era. The
Miyoshi Electric Plant, the first manufacturer of electric machinery, began to
operate in 1884. In the 1890s the Ishikawajima Shipbuilding Yard, the Tokyo
Shibaura Electric Company, and others appeared. However, production
techniques in these plants were poor, and products were merely an imitation
of the imports. Furthermore, technological progress was too slow to keep
pace with the rapid development in the electric utilities. They produced
mainly small capacity, low voltage machinery. With an increase in demand for
electric machinery, the number of manufacturers increased from the late
Meiji period. Because of progress in production techniques and the
interruption of imports during World War I, production of previously
imported large capacity, high voltage machinery began in the mid-Taishō
period. By the early 1930s, demand was almost entirely met domestically. In

[15]The substitution of electric power for steam power does not necessarily
mean a substitution for coal, if thermal generation depending on coal was
dominant. Such a transformation in energy sources is worth further study.

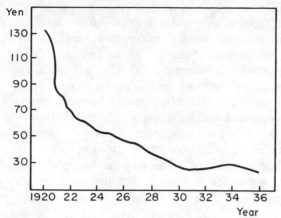

Figure 3. Price of one-horsepower electric motors.
Source: Hitachi 1949, 2:118.

this process borrowed technology was predominant. This is easily understood, for almost all the major electric manufacturers had technological tie-ups with foreign manufacturers.[16]

This was the case for production of electric motors. The first domestically produced motor was a 25 horsepower two-phase induction motor manufactured by Tokyo Shibaura in 1895 (Meiji 1928, p. 401). Thereafter production was carried on by several manufacturers mainly for small capacity motors. Mass production of standard small capacity motors began in 1918 when Hitachi began to produce this type of motor at its Kameido Plant. A history of this company tells us this caused the price to go down and quality to improve.[17] Figure 3 shows a sharp decline in the price of electric motors of one horsepower after 1920. This decline seems to have made electric power more accessible to smaller plants (see Chūshō 1960, p. 21).

IMPACT ON SMALLER SCALE PLANTS OF INTRODUCING ELECTRIC POWER

The impact of the introduction of electric power on the growth of smaller enterprises deserves special attention, because the introduction of motive power occurred directly with electric motors. This change seems to have contributed to a rise in labor productivity.

According to a series based on the *Nōshōmu Tōkei-hyō* for establishments with ten or more production workers, only about 30 percent of factories were equipped with prime movers at the end of the nineteenth century. This

[16]The first cooperation began in 1909 between the Tokyo Shibaura Electric and General Electric of the United States; it continues to the present.

[17]Hitachi 1949, 2:118. The Tokyo Shibaura Electric Company, as well, began to produce standard electric motors in 1919 (Tōkyō 1963, p. 651).

increased steadily thereafter and reached 70 percent in 1918. Table 8 shows the ratio (α) of factories equipped with prime movers to total factories for all scales of manufacturing factories as a whole, based on data from *Kōjō Tōkei-hyō* for establishments with five or more persons. This ratio rose from 28 percent in 1909 to 93 percent in 1930. That is to say, the introduction of power was almost completed by the latter year. In comparison with Table 2 and Figure 2, one may see the introduction of power during the end of the nineteenth century and the beginning of the twentieth was accomplished mainly by the installation of steam power, whereas the introduction of power thereafter came from the utilization of electric motors.

I shall now elaborate on the relationship between power introduction and the electrification by scale of factory. The percentage by scale of powered factories α appears in Table 8 and of electric motors β (in horsepower) and γ (in numbers) in Tables 2 and 3, respectively.[18] Figure 4 depicts changes over time in the percentages α, β, and γ for factories employing five to nine persons and for one thousand persons or more. For the very small plants α, β, and γ show conspicuously increasing trends for 1909-30. However, α was already 100 for the largest factories in 1909 and thereafter did not show any relationship with electrification. The contrast between these two factory sizes is much clearer in Figure 5, which shows the relationship of α to β and γ.

Table 8
Percentage of Powered Factories (α) by Scale of Establishment

Number of production workers (persons)	1909	1914	1919	1930	1935	1940
Total	28.2	45.6	61.1	82.5	86.0	84.1
5-9	14.4	28.5	46.0	76.6	80.4	78.5
10-29	30.1	48.8	65.0	87.2	90.5	88.4
30-49	63.7	75.9	85.7	93.8	95.5	95.8
50-99	78.0	87.7	92.8	97.3	98.0	98.2
100-499	87.1	92.8	97.2	99.1	99.7	99.6
500-999	95.1	96.8	100.0	100.0	99.7	100.0
1000-	100.0	97.6	99.4	100.0	100.0	100.0

Source: LTES 12:228-231 and *Kojo Tokei-hyo*.
α = (number of factories with prime movers/total number of factories) × 100.

[18]Data for firms with fewer than five production workers are not provided in the *Kōjō Tōkei-hyō*. A survey in Tokyo city in 1934, however, gives some information for this scale. Most of the factories not covered in the *Kōjō Tōkei-hyō* were not equipped with any prime movers. For small factories with fewer than five employes having prime movers, the percentages of electric motors β and γ were near 100 (*Tōkyō-shi* 1934, pp. 86-88 and 94-95).

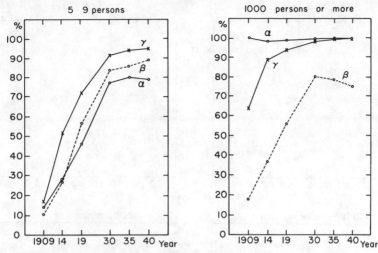

Figure 4. Percentage of powered factories (α) and percentages of electric motors (β,γ) for the two extreme scales.

Source: Tables 2, 3, 8.

High correlations are found for the small plants, whereas no correlations are found for the large ones. In other words, small firms relied much more than large on electrification for the introduction of power, with electricity supplied by public utilities. Large firms were able to introduce other power sources directly and hence earlier, and could also generate their own electricity.

Introduction of Motive Power and Technological Progress

The impact of motive power on technological progress in smaller factories will be demonstrated for two industries: match-making and weaving. This selection is for two reasons: the production processes are relatively easy to understand, and they are characterized by small factories.

Match-making industry. Production of matches consists of producing matchsticks and boxes, spreading chemicals on the sticks, and putting the sticks into boxes.[19] With the exception of large manufacturers who carried out all of these processes within their plants, firms purchased matchsticks and boxes from special producers. Therefore, match-making in Japan usually signified only the second and the third steps, with the arraying of matchsticks for spreading chemicals the most important process. This production requirement regulated the introduction of machinery and motive power.

There were three stages in the development of this procedure.

1. In the beginning boys and girls arrayed matchsticks by hand. This system was employed from about 1880 until 1905.

[19]For information on the match-making industry, this study relies heavily on Komiyama (1941).

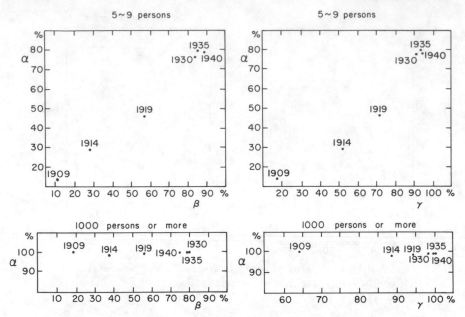

Figure 5. Relationship between percentage of powered factories (α) and percentages of electric motors (β,γ) for two representative scales.
Source: Tables 2, 3, 8.

2. Treadle machines were introduced after 1895, operated by female adult workers.

3. Finally, the German-type machinery, made of iron and run mostly by electric motors, was used. This machinery, called *doitsu* (the Japanese word for *German*), was already known in early Meiji and came into wide use in late Meiji when Japanese matches began to be exported. Usually male adult workers operated this machinery. The productivity of labor was several times greater than for those using treadle machines.

The shift from treadle to German-type machinery was uniquely dependent on the introduction of prime movers. In 1906 the total capacity of prime movers used in the industry was 80 horsepower. More than half of this was produced by steam engines; gas and petrol engines were used to a lesser extent. By 1914 the total capacity had risen to 335 horsepower, with 116 from steam engines. Thereafter, as shown in Table 9, β, 76 percent, and γ, 35 percent, in 1914, increased to 90 and 67 percent, respectively, in 1919 and to 97 and 81 percent in 1930. Owing to this rapid introduction of electric motors, the percentage of powered factories α, only 26 in 1914, increased to 49 in 1919 and to 86 in 1930.

Let us examine the same thing by scale of factory. In 1914 all the largest factories (500 to 999 persons) were equipped with prime movers. On the other hand, none of the smallest factories (5 to 9 persons) had prime movers, and only 6 percent of the second smallest (10 to 29 persons) were so

Table 9

Percentage of Powered Factories (α) and Percentages of Electric Motors among All Prime Movers (β, γ) in the Match-Making Industry by Scale of Establishment

Number of production workers (persons)	1914			1919			1930		
	α	β	γ	α	β	γ	α	β	γ
Total	37.5	54.6	29.9	53.2	77.9	64.9	90.4	96.4	81.9
5-9	17.2	69.9	52.2	33.4	81.8	64.7	87.1	96.0	93.5
10-29	43.1	49.1	27.6	58.5	73.1	51.9	93.1	96.0	94.5
30-49	71.9	42.2	24.9	85.7	70.2	57.0	95.7	96.9	93.5
50-99	81.8	50.8	30.2	92.6	66.4	54.6	98.8	96.4	94.8
100-499	90.8	53.5	27.9	87.8	69.0	51.3	99.5	94.3	82.2
500-999	100.0	56.7	32.4	100.0	97.0	66.0	100.0	98.3	91.9
1000-	100.0	83.3	31.3	100.0	97.7	78.6	100.0	99.2	66.0

Source: Kojo Tokei-hyo.

equipped. In these small factories the level increased to about 80 percent in 1930 through the introduction of electric motors. If these factories had run one or two German-type machines (about 2 horsepower) with steam engines, they probably could not have survived the heavy burden of capital and operating costs. The Sweden Match Trust, established in 1921, drove Japanese matches out of foreign markets. Moreover, it intended to dominate the market in Japan by founding two companies, Daido Match and Asahi Match. Ths plan was not completely successful, in part because of the existence of a number of small-scale factories (Komiyama 1941, p. 198), whose survival was supported by a decline in nominal wages during the depression years of the 1920s and by the mechanization of production processes during and after World War I.

Weaving industry. Japanese weavers were classified into two groups. The first group consisted of companies which produced foreign (double) width cotton cloth, that is, the weaving section of cotton-spinning companies and a small number of companies belonging to the All Japan Cotton-Spinner's Association. The second group consisted of small-scale factories which produced domestic (single) width cloth and silk fabrics. Between these two groups there was a difference of timing in the introduction of power looms: whereas they were already in use by 1887 in the first group, in the second group they were employed only experimentally after 1897 and only after World War I were they used extensively. The diffusion of power looms was made possible by electrification. As seen in Table 10, the percentage of powered factories, α, jumped from 38 percent in 1914 to 90 percent in 1930, and the use of electric motors increased similarly. Examination by scale of factory shows the diffusion of motive power based on electrification went on at a higher speed in the smaller scale factories belonging to the second group.

   The electrification of smaller scale weavers was possible because of the commencement of service by electric utilities. Three examples of the relationship between the start of electric utilities and the introduction of power looms in these factories are given from Sanpei (1961, p. 408).

   1. In the case of the weaving industry of Tokamachi, Niigata prefecture, electric motors and power looms were introduced in 1924. This is attributable to the foundation of the Uonuma Electric Company in 1911.

   2. The introduction of power looms in the Kiryu and Ashikaga districts was dependent on the supply of electric power by the Watarase Electric Company established in 1908.[20]

   3. Weavers in Ichinomiya, Aichi prefecture, introduced power looms relying on cheap electric power purchased from the Ichinomiya Electric Company founded in 1923.

---

[20]In the Ashikaga district electric power was introduced during and after World War I into small-scale home plants. These plants were called thereafter *dōryoku-ya*, which signified weaving plants with power looms run by electric motors (Sanpei 1961, p. 426).

Table 10
Percentage of Powered Factories (α) and Percentages of Electric Motors among Prime Movers (β, γ) in the Weaving Industry by Scale of Establishment

Number of production workers (persons)	1914			1919			1930		
	α	β	γ	α	β	γ	α	β	γ
Total	37.5	54.6	29.9	53.2	77.9	64.9	90.4	96.4	81.9
5-9	17.2	69.9	52.2	33.4	81.8	64.7	87.1	96.0	93.5
10-29	43.1	49.1	27.6	58.5	73.1	51.9	93.1	96.0	94.5
30-49	71.9	42.2	24.9	85.7	70.2	57.0	95.7	96.9	93.5
50-99	81.8	50.8	30.2	92.6	66.4	54.6	98.8	96.4	94.8
100-499	90.8	53.5	27.9	87.8	69.0	51.3	99.5	94.3	82.2
500-999	100.0	56.7	32.4	100.0	97.0	66.0	100.0	98.3	91.9
1000-	100.0	83.3	31.3	100.0	97.7	78.6	100.0	99.2	66.0

Source: Kōjo Tōkei-hyō.

The transition from hand and treadle looms to power looms seems to have stimulated labor productivity. Quantitative evidence for this relation is found in the *Niigata-ken Minami Kanbara Gunze* in 1920. This survey shows that around 1916 daily production of striped cotton cloth per worker amounted to only one *tan* (about twelve yards) for hand looms and three *tan* for treadle looms, whereas it was nine *tan* in the case of power looms (Sanpei 1961, p. 407). Another survey (Tōyō 1950, 2:225) shows whereas one worker operated only one hand loom or treadle loom, he could run four to twelve power looms or forty to sixty automatic looms, clearly displaying the increase in labor productivity from the transformation of looms.

A time-series test for the relationship between the introduction of power looms and technical progress is made for the cotton-weaving industry. Data are available from the *Shōkōshō Tōkei-hyō* for 1922-38. Denoting the volume of production in physical terms (in foreign width cloth equivalent) per production worker, the number of looms per worker, and the percentage of power looms by p, k and α, respectively, the following model is set forth:

$$ln\ p_t = a_0 + a_1\alpha_t + a_2 ln\ k_t + u_t, \quad a_1 > 0, \quad a_2 > 0,$$

where ln signifies the natural log of a variable, and u_t is the error term. In the case where the number of looms was a good index of capital stock and the ratio of value added to gross output was constant, parameter a_2 can be taken as the output (value added) elasticity of capital. Special attention must be paid to the second term, $a_1\alpha_t$, which corresponds to an increase in labor productivity stemming from technological progress (defined as a shift in the production function). This formulation comes from my basic hypothesis that technological progress in this industry was dependent largely on the diffusion of power looms.

The results of estimation of this equation are given in the upper part of Table 11. Data for 1938 were omitted because p showed an unreasonable drop, due perhaps to the dislocation of wartime industrial adjustment. The

Table 11
Estimates of Production Function and Annual Rate of Growth
of Productivity by Components in Cotton-Weaving Industry:
1922-37

Estimates of production function[a]

| | Parameters | | | |
a_0	a_1	a_2	R^2	d
−1.274	0.046	0.457	0.990	0.82
(5.4)	(10.5)	(1.6)		

Annual rate of growth of output and its components (in percent)

$G(p)$	$a_1\Delta\alpha$	$a_2G(k)$	Error
10.50	9.81	1.31	−0.62
(100)	(93)	(13)	(−6)

Source: Data underlying Figure 6.
[a]The model for estimation is $ln\ p_t = a_0 + a_1\ \alpha_t + a_2\ ln\ k_t + u_t$. R^2 and d
stand for the determination coefficient and Durbin-Watson statistic, respectively. Statistics in parenthesis under parameters signify student t-value of
the respective parameters.
[b]$G(\ )$ stands for the exponential rate of growth of the variable in
parentheses.

high determination coefficient suggests the model is appropriate for this
industry, though there is some serial correlation. Parameter a_1, significant at
the conventional significance level, shows high sensitivity of labor productivity to the diffusion of power looms. Parameter a_2 suggests the output
elasticity of capital was on the order of 0.4 to 0.5.[21] In the lower part of the
table, one may see that of the 10.50 percent annual rate of increase in labor
output, 9.8 percentage points was attributable to technological progress based
on the introduction of power looms, and only 1.31 percentage points to the
increase in the number of looms per worker.

ELECTRIC LIGHTING

Another aspect of electrification, the diffusion of electric lighting, has not
been discussed in this paper. In factories, as has already been mentioned,
electric lighting was introduced much more rapidly than electric power. This
introduction contributed to the reduction of production costs by promoting
night shifts. Before the introduction of electric light, petrol lamps were used.
Because of the danger of fire from using these lamps, however, there was a
movement for the abolition of night shifts (Arisawa 1959, 1:67). Electrification eliminated this and permitted the widespread use of the system. (This

[21]Kiyokawa (1973) estimates the output elasticity of capital as 0.391 in the
weaving sector of the cotton-spinning companies for 1919-24. My result is
close to his estimation.

gave rise to the widely known tragedy of young female workers detailed in *Jokō Aishi*.

The rapid diffusion of electric lighting for home use is indicated by the number of electric bulbs installed shown in Table 1, column 1. During Meiji, traditional lamps such as *tōmyō* (tapers), *andon* (paper-covered lamps), and Japanese candles were gradually being replaced by modern lamps using petrol, gas, and so forth. Gas lamps were dominant until the late Meiji era, but then, owing to a decline in electric lighting rates and the appearance of tungsten bulbs, the use of electric lights increased remarkably. Consequently, the number of gas lamps began to decrease after a peak in 1917. The substitution of modern lamps for traditional lamps and the transition among modern lamps (from petrol to gas to electric bulbs) may be explained by differences in economic efficiency. Table 12 gives mean candle power, cost per hour, and hourly cost per candle power, respectively, in columns 1, 2, and 3, for various lamps. Mean candle power is very small in the traditional lamps: only 0.25 for tōmyō, 0.2 for andon, and 0.5 for a Japanese candle. It is large in the modern lamps: 3.2 for petrol, 20.0 for gas, and 18.0 to 30.0 for electric bulbs. Hourly cost per candlepower is larger in the traditional, and smaller in the modern lamps. Among modern lamps, hourly cost per candlepower is lowest in electric bulbs (0.021 to 0.025) and highest in petrol bulbs (0.12). Thus, diffusion of electric lighting seems to have had a significant influence on the daily life of the people.

Table 12
Mean Candlepower, Cost per Hour,
and Hourly Cost per Candlepower of Various Lamps

	Mean candle-power (1)	Hourly cost (2)	Hourly cost per candlepower (3)=(2)/(1)
		(sen)	*(sen)*
Traditional			
Tōmyō	0.25	0.5	2.0
Andon	0.2	0.5	2.5
Japanese candle	0.5	2.5	3.1
Modern			
Western candle	0.9	0.9	1.0
Lantern (with Western candle)	0.6	0.9	1.5
Petrol lamp (15 mm wick)	3.2	0.38	0.12
Acetylene lamp	16.0	1.5	0.093
Gas lamp (rated 20 candlepower)	20.0	0.6	0.03
Carbon electric bulb (rated 10 candlepower)	8.5	0.57	0.067
Tungsten electric bulb (rated 24 candlepower)	18.0	0.45	0.025
Gas filled electric bulb (40 W)	30.0	0.65	0.021

Sources: Estimates by Seki Shigehiro, in Kurihara 1964, p. 65.
Note: Figures in 1926 prices.

CONCLUSIONS AND SOME IMPLICATIONS

There are five main conclusions from this analysis.

1. A distinctive characteristic of the revolution in motive power in Japan lay in its high speed compared with countries which had developed earlier.[22] During the late 1880s when horsepower of water wheels increased rapidly, horsepower of steam engines also showed a big increase. Furthermore, even during the golden age of steam engines, up until the beginning of the twentieth century, the introduction of electric motors made rapid progress. Consequently, the capacity of electric motors surpassed steam engines in 1917, and electrification was eventually completed around 1930. In the case of smaller factories, the introduction of electric motors proceeded during and after World War I and was almost completed by 1930.

2. One of the factors responsible for electrification is this form of motive power's divisibility into small units. It was due to this characteristic that unit drive arrangements replaced group drive arrangements in large-scale factories, saving production costs. In smaller factories the initial introduction of motive power consisted of installing small capacity electric motors. Another factor in electrification was the externalities from developments in electric utilities and in the electrical machine industry.

3. The introduction of motive power through the electrification of smaller factories enabled labor productivity to increase and gave rise to a persistent growth in these factories. As an example, in the match-making industry, where smaller factories were dominant, the substitution of the German-type machinery for treadle machines was facilitated by the introduction of electric motors. This substitution, which raised labor productivity, was considered to be one of the main reasons why the smaller plants did not disappear in the wake of the invasion of the Japanese market by the Swedish Match Trust. A second example is the weaving industry. A shift from hand and treadle looms to power looms relied on electrification and, again, increased labor productivity.

4. The more rapid displacement of steam power by electric power than in the case of countries which had developed earlier was largely due to the rapid progress of electric utilities. For example, the first supply of electricity for public use by the Tokyo Electric Light Company in 1887 lagged by only five years the establishment of a distribution station in New York by the Edison Electric Company. At the beginning of hydro generation, a ten-year lag existed between the United States and Japan: 1882 for the hydro plant in Appleton, Wisconsin, and 1892 for the Keage Hydro Plant in Kyoto.

---

[22]This is stressed by Kanbayashi et al. (1943, p. 300). For instance, a peak in the percentage of steam engines in the total horsepower in manufacturing was reached during almost the same period in both Japan and the United States. In Japan, it was in 1890-1905 (Figure 2) and in the United States, at the turn of the century (Fenichel 1966, p. 425).

The rapid progress of electric utilities in Japan was entirely dependent on borrowed technology. Generation and transmission techniques were introduced from abroad, and tools and machinery were all imported. Let us take two plants of the Tokyo Electric Light as examples. For the Komabashi Power Plant completed in 1907, water wheels, generators, and transformers and distributing boards were imported from Switzerland, Germany, and the United States, respectively (Arisawa 1960b, 6:24-25). Even the Inawashiro Hydro Plant in 1914 was equipped almost entirely with imports: water wheels from Germany, generators from England, and transformers, transmission towers, and insulators from the United States. Electric wires were the only exception. Thus development of electric utilities was independent of a domestic electric machine industry for a long time. The history of electrification in Japan provides a good example of a characteristic inherent in the concept of borrowed technology: various kinds of techniques tend to be introduced into less developed countries with shorter intervals between techniques relative to the countries developing these techniques.

5. Without the introduction of motive power, many of the smaller plants would have disappeared during the 1920s, which were depression years in Japan. Large factories made some attempts to prevent declining profits by introducing new technologies, discharging unskilled workers, and so forth. On the other hand, smaller plants could introduce motive power and raise profitability because of the diffusion of cheap electric motors and the big decline in the cost of electric power. Smaller enterprises, like agriculture, have been taken as a pool of disguised unemployment. Large numbers of workers discharged from large enterprises during the 1920s were absorbed in these enterprises. It appears this absorption would not have been possible without an improvement in technology in the smaller enterprises.

These suppositions lead to another hypothesis: if the era of steam engines had continued for as long as in the earlier developed countries, smaller establishments would have been swept away by larger enterprises equipped with steam engines.[23] That is, the survival of smaller establishments in Japan seems to have been in some part due to the earlier start of the age of electric power. The existence of surplus labor has usually been pointed out as a basic reason for the dual structure of the economy or the coexistence of small-scale and large-scale enterprises.[24] As an additional factor, in the writer's opinion, the very rapid transformation of motive power in Japan has to be taken into due consideration.

[23]The impact of electrification on Japan's persistent growth has not been properly appreciated, as can be seen from the lack of literature on it. (See Suzuki 1936, p. 92.) The fact that the introduction of electric motors increased labor productivity can be seen in other countries. According to DuBoff (1967, p. 516), for instance, printing and publishing, one of the first major industries to be electrified in the United States, was also a leader in productivity increases.

[24]See the survey on studies of small-scale enterprises by Shinohara (1968).

REFERENCES

Arisawa, Hiromi, ed. 1959. *Kindai Sangyō no Hatten. Gendai Nippon Sangyō Kōza*, vol. 1. Iwanami Shoten.

. 1960a. *Enerugi Sangyō. Gendai Nippon Sangyō Kōza*, vol. 3. Iwanami Shoten.

. 1960b. *Kikai Kōgyō. Gendai Nippon Sangyō Kōza*, vol. 6. Iwanami Shoten.

. 1960c. *Seni-i Sangyō. Gendai Nippon Sangyō Kōza*, vol. 7. Iwanami Shoten.

Chūshō Kigyō Chōsa Kai [Research Association on Medium and Small Enterprises], ed. 1960. *Chūshō Kigyō no Tōkei-teki Bunseki*. Tōyō Keizai Shimpōsha.

DuBoff, Richard B. 1967. "The Introduction of Electric Power in American Manufacturing." *Economic History Review*, second series, vol. 20 (Dec. 1967).

Fenichel, Allen H. 1966. "Growth and Diffusion of Power in Manufacturing, 1838-1919." In *Output, Employment, and Productivity in the United States after 1800, Studies in Income and Wealth*, vol. 30, edited by the National Bureau of Economic Research. Columbia University Press.

Fujino, Shozaburō. 1956. "Senzen ni okeru Denryoku Juyō ni tsuite." In *Denki Ryōkin ni kansuru Rironteki narabini Jisshōteki Kenkyū* by Denryoku Keizai Kenkyū-jo [Central Research Institute of the Electric Power Industry]. Kenkyū Hōkoku: Keizai 5601, no. 4. Keisō Shobū.

. 1965. *Nippon no Keiki Junkan*.

Hitachi Seisaku-Jo [Hitachi Co., Ltd.]. ed. 1949, rev. 1960. *Hitachi Seisaku-Jo Shi*, vols. 1 and 2.

Hoshino, Akira, et al. 1964. *Nippon no Enerugi Mondai*. Diamond Sha.

Hoshino, Yoshirō. 1956. *Gendai Nippon Gijitsu Shi Gaisetsu*. Dai Nippon Tosho.

Iijima, Hanji. 1949. *Nippon Bōseki Shi*. Sōbun Sha.

Kanbayashi, Teijiro. 1948. *Nippon Kōgyō Hattatsu Shi-ron*. Gakusei Shobō.

Kanbayashi, Teijiro, et al. 1943. "Nippon Kōgyō Denka Hattatsu Shi." In *Nippon Sangyō Kikō Kenkyū*. Itō Shoten.

Kiyokawa, Yukihiko. 1973. "Menkōgyō Gijitsu no Teichaku to Kokusan-Ka ni Tsuite." *Keizai Kenkyū* 24 (April 1973).

Komiyama, Takuji. 1941. *Nippon Chūshō Kōgyō Kenkyū, Dai San Bu*. Chūō Kōron Sha.

Kurihara, Toyo, ed. 1964. "Denryoku." *Gendai Nippon Sangyō Hattatsu Shi*, vol. 3. Kojunsha.

Landes, David S. 1966. "Technological Change and Development in Western Europe, 1750-1914." In *The Cambridge Economic History of Europe*, vol. 6: *The Industrial Revolution and After: Incomes, Population, and Technological Change (I)*, edited by H. J. Habakkuk and M. Postan. Cambridge University Press.

LTES [Estimates of Long-Term Economic Statistics of Japan]. Series edited by Kazushi Ohkawa, Miyohei Shinohara, and Mataji Umemura. 1965-. 14 vols. Tōyō Keizai Shinpōsha.

. Vol. 8. *Prices*. 1967. Kazushi Ohkawa et al.

. Vol. 12. *Railroads and Electric Utilities*. 1965. Ryōshin Minami.

Meiji Kōgyō Shi Hensan Iinkai [Committee for Editing the History of Manufacturing Industries in the Meiji Era]. 1928. *Meiji Kōgyō Shi: Denki Hen.* Kōgaku-kai.

Minami, Ryōshin. 1973. *The Turning Point in Economic Development: Japan's Experience.* Kinokuniya.

Moriya, Fumio. 1948. *Bōseki Seisanhi Bunseki.* Nippon Hyōron Sha.

Nippon Sen-i Kyōgigai [Japanese Association of Textiles]. 1958. *Nippon Sen-i Kyōgigai, Sōron Hen.* Sen-i Nenhan Kankō Kai.

Nitta, Muneo, ed. 1936. *Tōkyō Dentō Kabushiki Kaisha Kaigyō 50-Nen Shi.* Tokyo Electric Light Company.

Sanpei, Takako. 1961. *Nippon Kigyō Shi.* Yūsan Kaku.

Shinohara, Miyohei. 1968. "A Survey of the Japanese Literature on Small Industry." In *The Role of Small Industry in the Process of Economic Growth,* edited by Bert F. Hoselitz. Mouton.

Suzuki, Taira. 1936. "Denki Kōgyō no Jūyōsei to Sono Kakuritsu." In *Kōgyō Chōsa Ihō,* vol. 14, no. 3, edited by Shōkōshō Kōmu-kyoku [Ministry of Commerce and Industry, Bureau of Industrial Affairs]. Kōgyō Chōsa Kyōkai.

Temin, Peter. 1966. "Steam and Waterpower in the Early Nineteenth Century." *Journal of Economic History,* second series, vol. 26 (June 1966).

Tōkyō-shi. 1934. *Tōkyō-shi, Kōgyō Chōsasho.*

Tōkyō Shibaura Denki Kabushiki Kaisha [Tokyo Shibaura Electric Company]. 1963. *Tōkyō Shibaura Denki KK 85-nen Shi.*

Tōyō Keizai Shinpō Sha, ed. 1950. *Shōwa Sangyō Shi,* vol. 2. Tōyō Keizai Shinpō Sha.

Yamaguchi, Kazuo. 1956. *Meiji Zenki Keizai no Bunseki.* Tōdai Shuppan Kai.

PART THREE

Some Social Consequences

Demographic Transition

in the

Process of Japanese Industrialization

Hiroshi Ohbuchi

The most remarkable population phenomena found in the industrialization of developed countries were demographic transition and urbanization. The focus of this paper is the socioeconomic analysis of demographic transition in Japan: how the vital events, in particular fertility, have changed since the beginning of the Meiji era.

There are many problems, both theoretical and practical, in the process of demographic transition. The experience of Japan may provide valuable materials for investigating such problems. Although many studies have achieved useful results, greater efforts must be made in the socioeconomic analysis of fertility changes. Still lacking is any definite information about the transition in Japan, even as regards changes in the various rates, let alone clarification of the causes. Before the first population census was taken in 1920, the official Japanese demographic statistics, both static and vital, are not reliable. To correct probable faults, some estimates have been attempted by demographers, statisticians, and others. I will examine these estimates by various criteria to decide which is the most plausible one.

Since 1920, there are few problems with the data on vital statistics. There are still problems, however, in examining the course of population changes. It is not known exactly when birth rates began to decline. Birth rates continuously declined slowly throughout the twenty years of the prewar period. After World War II, Japan experienced a rapid drop in birth rates, the pace of which was unprecedented, in comparison to the European decline. Is this radical decline the recovery movement toward the secular trend of the

I benefited greatly from critical comments and suggestions made by James I. Nakamura, Yasukichi Yasuba, Gary Saxonhouse, Susan B. Hanley, Ryōshin Minami, and others for the first version of this paper. Great thanks are due to Mr. Kozo Ueda for a preliminary editing of my English. However, I alone am responsible for the contents of this paper.

prewar period? Or is it a change in trend from prewar? Opinions vary on these points.

The demographic transition in Japan arouses not only an intellectual interest, but also involves practical political implications. Decreasing fertility is considered one of the most important strategies for economic development in the less developed and densely populated countries, and especially Asians have expected the experience in Japan to be the most instructive model for them. Unless the mechanisms of declining fertility are understood, however, the value as a model will be reduced.

POPULATION DYNAMICS BEFORE 1920

Demographic Statistics prior to 1920

A modern population census in Japan was taken for the first time in 1920. Nationwide enumerations were made more than ten times between 1721 and 1868, but samurai, some women and children, outcasts, and the like were excluded or underreported, often by large margins. After the Meiji Restoration, a registration law was enacted (1871), and *honseki* (legal domicile) population and two kinds of *genjū* (present residence) populations were enumerated. It is generally believed, however, that almost all the data derived from the registrations are of doubtful completeness and accuracy. On the other hand, vital statistics have been published since 1900, though many errors probably exist, particularly for the earlier years (Morita 1944, pp. 373-374).

Many attempts have been made to correct the deficiencies in the pre-1920 data. The principal estimates are compared in Table 1 for total population

Table 1
Various estimates of Japanese Population, 1865-1920
(thousands)

Year	Honseki	Official	Okazaki	Akasaka	Yasukawa
1865	--	--	--	--	34,505
1870	--	--	36,288	--	35,384
1872	33,111	34,806	--	34,234	--
1875	33,997	35,316	37,198	34,757	36,528
1880	35,929	36,649	38,166	36,130	38,174
1885	37,869	38,313	39,245	37,844	39,634
1890	40,072	39,902	40,353	39,487	41,020
1895	41,813	41,557	41,789	41,188	42,472
1900	44,270	43,847	43,785	43,521	44,393
1905	47,220	46,620	46,257	46,343	46,825
1910	50,254	49,184	49,066	48,851	49,637
1915	54,142	52,752	52,500	52,389	52,949
1920	57,234	55,473	55,450	55,033	56,139

Sources: Honseki: Morita 1944; official: Naikaku Tōkei-kyoku 1930; Okazaki: Okazaki 1962; Akasaka: Akasaka 1964; Yasukawa: Yasukawa and Hirooka 1972.

and in Tables 2 and 3 for vital rates. The methods used roughly divide into two types: one based on the existing official statistics, and the other using the reverse survival method. Representative of the former is the Naikaku Tōkei-kyoku (Cabinet Statistical Office) estimate (Naikaku 1930), which I will term the "official" estimate, and which is still generally utilized. The Akasaka estimate (Akasaka 1960 and 1964) is similar to the official one in method. The second method includes the Okazaki estimate (Okazaki 1962), the Yasukawa estimate (Yasukawa and Hirooka 1972), and the Morita

Table 2
Comparisons of Estimated Birth Rates, 1865-1920
(per thousand)

Year	Official	Morita	Okazaki	Yasukawa
1865	--	--	--	31.28
1870	--	--	--	30.85
1875	25.4	31.1	36.3	34.37
1880	26.0	32.1	36.4	33.89
1885	29.0	30.5	33.9	32.17
1890	30.4	29.2	33.7	32.16
1895	30.7	29.7	34.3	33.84
1900	34.1	32.6	36.3	35.60
1905	33.1	32.2	35.2	34.32
1910	36.2	35.0	37.0	36.81
1915	35.4	34.9	35.6	35.36
1920	35.7	34.6	33.2	38.19

Sources: See Table 1.

Table 3
Comparisons of Estimated Death Rates, 1865-1920
(per thousand)

Year	Official	Morita	Okazaki	Yasukawa
1865	--	--	--	25.45
1870	--	--	--	25.78
1875	18.5	23.6	31.3	26.11
1880	18.1	23.7	31.3	26.64
1885	21.0	23.3	28.3	25.86
1890	20.9	22.8	28.1	25.26
1895	21.5	22.7	27.3	24.90
1900	21.2	23.1	27.0	24.99
1905	21.4	23.0	24.2	24.84
1910	21.5	23.1	25.3	24.17
1915	21.4	22.9	22.1	23.35
1920	24.5	22.6	22.3	21.81

Sources: See Table 1.

estimate (Morita 1944, pp. 373-374), which is the pioneering attempt of this type. The estimation methods of Morita, Okazaki, and Yasukawa are summarized as follows.

Morita uses as the base the honseki population by sex and age at the end of 1886. He applied the probability of surviving fifteen years obtained from the First Complete Life Table (1891-98) to the base population, and estimated the age composition of population at the beginning of 1872. From this population for 1872, he estimated the population by age, birth rates, and death rates every five years from 1872-76 to 1917-21, using the assumed number of births and the probability of dying (one minus the probability of surviving given in the First Life Table). The number of births prior to 1891 was estimated by tracing the honseki population at the end of the 1891 back to the beginning of the Meiji era. After 1891 the registered number of births was used as given.

Okazaki uses as the base the census population by sex and age on October 1, 1920, but to eliminate the influence of influenza in 1918 and 1920, he estimated the population by sex and age on January 1, 1918, by using registered vital statistics and applying the reverse survival method to it. Thus, the population and vital rates in 1870-1920 were estimated. The probability of surviving was estimated from the extrapolation backward of the linear trend of the probability of dying derived from the eight life-table estimates between 1891-98 and 1947.

Yasukawa also uses as the base the census population of 1920. He multiplied the base population by sex and age by the reciprocals of the stationary population in the Model Life Tables of Japan, which he had earlier constructed (Yasukawa 1971), and estimated the population size, birth rates, and death rates for 1865-1920. In order to determine the levels of life expectancy at birth, $\dot{e}_0$, in the Model Life Tables, he applied Gompertz curves to the values of $\dot{e}_0$ in the existing life tables. By these procedures, the levels of $\dot{e}_0$ prior to the First Life Table were estimated, and the corresponding probabilities of dying and stationary populations were determined. Then, taking account of some degree of age concentration in the census population and the extraordinary increase in deaths from influenza in 1918 and 1920, he revised those results.

I first examine differences in estimated vital rates. Birth rates in the official estimate rise almost constantly from the early years of the Meiji era, and death rates also have a rising trend. Estimates by the reverse survival method are considerably different from one another, though all have a similar overall pattern. The initial level of death rates is the highest in the Okazaki estimate, and the lowest in the Morita estimate. As the levels of death rates in 1920 are not much different, the degree of decline is the highest in the Okazaki estimate and is nearly flat in the Morita estimate. Birth rates fluctuate more widely than death rates, and it is noticeable that their levels rise uniformly from the 1880s through about 1900. Again, the level of the Okazaki estimate is the highest, and the Morita estimate is the lowest.

Thus, the two major types of estimates of vital trends imply rather different courses of demographic transition in Japan. Above all, as seen in Figure 1, the official estimate shows a pattern sharply contrasted to that of Okazaki's. Naturally the choice of estimates gives completely different pictures of the process of demographic transition. The former shows the main cause of the rising rate of population growth during Meiji to have been a rise in fertility, and the latter explains it by a decline in mortality.

It is possible the main difference between these two types is attributable to the method of estimates. Although both have flaws, there is a reason to believe the reverse survival method is technically better. This method includes some arbitrary assumptions about mortality, so the estimates are partly a predetermined result of the working hypotheses. According to the well-known theory of stable population, however, the principal factor which determines the age composition of a population is fertility. Therefore, if one neglects the effect of international migration, which was small, the level and structure of fertility causing the age composition of the 1920 census population may be similar to that of earlier periods, even though assumptions about mortality are somewhat different. This provides a strong basis for the reverse survival method.

Examination by the Rate of Population Growth

The rates of population growth implied by the different estimates are shown in Table 4. In every estimate the rate rose from 0.5 percent per annum about 1870 to the 1 percent level around 1900. However, the paths of rise are different from one another. Further, greater differences appear in the growth rates between 1852 (when the last population enumeration of the Tokugawa era was made) and the first year of each estimate (Table 5). To the enumerated population of 27.2 million in 1852, 3 to 5 million is added for probable omissions (Sekiyama 1959, pp. 63-66). According to recent

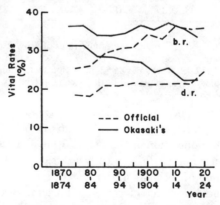

Figure 1. Comparison of vital rates prior to 1920.

Source: Same as Table 1.

Table 4
Comparisons of the Estimated Rates
of Population Growth, 1865-1920
(percent)

Period	Official	Okazaki	Akasaka	Yasukawa
1865-1870	--	--	--	0.50
1870-1875	0.49[1]	0.50	0.51[2]	0.61
1875-1880	0.74	0.52	0.78	0.89
1880-1885	0.89	0.56	0.93	0.76
1885-1890	0.82	0.56	0.85	0.69
1890-1895	0.82	0.70	0.85	0.70
1895-1900	1.08	0.91	1.11	0.89
1900-1905	1.23	1.10	1.26	1.07
1905-1910	1.08	1.19	1.06	1.17
1910-1915	1.41	1.36	1.41	1.30
1915-1920	1.01	1.10	0.99	1.18

Sources: Calculated from Table 1.
Note: [1]1872-1875. [2]All rates are annual average compound rates of growth.

Table 5
Rates of Population Growth before and after the Meiji
Restoration for Different Assumed 1852 Populations
(percent)

Population (in thousands)	Official	Okazaki	Akasaka	Yasukawa
30,000	0.75	1.06	0.66	1.08
32,000	0.42*	0.70	0.34*	0.58
33,000	0.27*	0.53	0.18*	0.34*

Note: The average annual compound rates of growth refer to
the following period: official, 1852-72; Okazaki, 1852-70;
Akasaka, 1852-72; Yasukawa 1852-65. Values with asterisk are
the plausible ones, as explained in the text.

research, it is possible the omitted population gradually increased in each successive Tokugawa census (Hayami 1971, pp. 67-68).

If one assumes the population in 1852 to be 30 million, the growth rate for every estimate is higher than for the early years of the Meiji era. However, assuming a population of 32 million, the growth rates of the official and the Akasaka estimates are below the 0.5 percent annual increase of early Meiji. At 33 million, the Yasukawa estimate is also included in this group, and only the Okazaki estimate gives a slightly higher rate. There is no evidence, of course, that the population increased by less than 0.5 percent per annum between 1852 and 1868. But the enumerated population in 1721-1852 was nearly

constant, and political confusion and economic instability were relatively
great in the last days of the shogunate, so one can hardly imagine the rate of
population growth was higher than after the Meiji Restoration. Accordingly,
it is possible the population in early Meiji is overestimated by Okazaki. The
five cases with asterisks in Table 5 are considered the probable range. If the
population in 1852 is assumed to have been 33 million, the underenumera-
tion was nearly 6 million; this is higher than the generally accepted view, so
Yasukawa's estimate is also on the high side. It should be noted that my
analysis in the following sections depends in part on my assumptions about
the population at the end of the Tokugawa, a problem beyond the scope of
this paper.

Socioeconomic Change and Vital Rates

Another means of checking the plausibility of various estimates is to
investigate the relevance to social and economic change in the corresponding
period. To begin, I examine social and economic conditions in the Meiji era in
terms of per capita product, and the extent of industrialization and or
urbanization.

It is generally considered the Japanese economy succeeded in "taking off"
during the 1880s and 90s, whether it is called industrial revolution or not.
For example, Figure 2 shows per capita product abruptly spurted in 1886-99;
it was stagnant in 1900-04, but afterward rose sharply again. These specific
results are based on the Yasukawa population estimates, but the same general
patterns emerge regardless of the population series used. The economic
takeoff was attained by industrialization. The degree of industrialization can
be shown by various indexes. The one I use here is the ratio of nonprimary

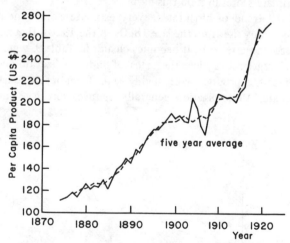

Figure 2. Annual growth of per capita product,
1874-1922.

Sources: GNP: LTES, various volumes and unpuslished
worksheets of the authors. Population: Yasukawa and
Hirooka 1972.

employment to the total, which I term the level of industrialization. Figure 3 shows industrialization went on steadily throughout the period.

Industrialization in Japan has been accompanied, as in Western countries, by the rapid migratory movement of population from agriculture to nonagriculture, and from rural to urban areas. Various indexes of urbanization are given in Table 6. It is obvious that urbanization went on steadily, but Japan actually retained her rural features in many respects until 1920 and later.

Attempts to correlate the estimates of death rates in Table 3 with the rate of industrialization, the rate of urbanization, and per capita product give varying results depending on which death rate estimate is used, as shown in Table 7. The official estimate is positively correlated with these three indexes, whereas the other estimates are negatively correlated. The Morita estimate provides less good correlation, whereas the Okazaki and Yasukawa estimates are fairly well fitted.

The early stage of industrialization in Western Europe had rising mortality, but it was a temporary and transitional phenomenon. In the long run, social and economic development has reduced mortality in every country. Thus, it is reasonable to think that, throughout the process of industrialization in the Meiji era, mortality tended to decline, even if it temporarily rose. By this criterion, the official estimate is doubtful.

Because such a strong relationship of time-series data might be obtained by mere coincidence of trend, Table 8 presents the correlation of the variations from the trend path of death rates with the rate of industrialization and the per capita product. It is noteworthy that the negative correlations in the Yasukawa estimate are statistically significant. The other results are not significant, and the positive correlation is different than expected. The Yasukawa estimate scores best on this basis.

As regards the trend of birth rates, every estimate except the official one shows a conspicuous rise from the late 1880s to the 1910s, that is, the period of so-called economic takeoff. It becomes clearer in Table 9, where estimated birth rates are regressed against the rates of industrialization and urbanization, and per capita product, with highly significant results except for the Okazaki estimate. Modernization generally reduces fertility, but economic

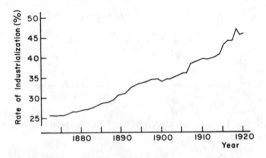

Figure 3. The rate of industrialization, 1872-1920.
Source: Minami 1973, pp. 312-313, Table *A*-11, for underlying data.

Table 6
Indicators of Urbanization, 1885-1920
(percent)

Year	Ub	Uc	Ud
1885	19.5	--	--
1888	--	12.9	7.4
1890	18.4	--	--
1893	--	16.0	7.9
1895	18.6	--	--
1898	--	17.7	9.4
1900	19.5	--	--
1903	--	20.7	11.4
1905	20.5	--	--
1908	--	24.6	13.0
1910	21.7	--	--
1913	--	27.7	14.2
1915	21.5	--	--
1918	--	31.9	16.5
1920	24.0	32.2	15.8

Sources: *Ub*: Minami 1973, p. 25. *Uc* and *Ud*: Odabashi 1937, p. 506.
Note: Odabashi used Honseki population figures to obtain these ratios. He did not estimate population himself.

Ub is the ratio of population in the prefectures containing the six largest cities to the total. *Uc* is the ratio of population in shi (cities), machi (towns), and mura (villages) with ten thousand or more inhabitants to the total. *Ud* is the ratio of population in shi, machi, and mura with fifty thousand or more inhabitants to the total.

Table 7
Correlation Coefficients between Crude
Death Rates and Some Socioeconomic Variables

Estimated crude death rates	Rate of industrialization	Per capita product	Rate of urbanization
official	0.842**	0.888**	0.818**
Morita	−0.731*	−0.748**	−0.264
Okazaki	−0.931**	−0.883**	−0.897**
Yasukawa	−0.963**	−0.969**	−0.901**

*Significant at 0.05 level.
**Significant at 0.01 level.
These are the results of a simple correlation between the vital rates and the three socioeconomic indicators.

Table 8

Correlation Coefficients between Variations from Trend in
Crude Death Rates, the Rate of Industrialization,
and Per Capita Product

Estimated crude death rates	Rate of industrialization	Per capita product
official	0.078	0.455
Morita	−0.036	0.112
Okazaki	0.128	−0.238
Yasukawa	−0.720*	−0.638*

*Significant at 0.05 level.
Data on urbanization are insufficient to compute coefficients.

Table 9

Correlation Coefficients between Crude
Birth Rates and Some Socioeconomic Variables

Estimated crude birth rates	Rate of industrialization	Per capita product	Rate of urbanization
official	0.964**	0.962**	0.814**
Morita	0.920**	0.940**	0.952**
Okazaki	0.909*	0.881*	0.725
Yasukawa	0.890**	0.931**	0.853**

Note: See Table 7.

takeoff is accompanied by increasing demand for labor and rising levels of living, which may raise the birth rate through a fall in the age of marriage and a rise of nuptial rates. In this respect, the official estimate, which recorded a continuous rise before takeoff, is doubtful and the estimates by the reverse survival method are more strongly justified.

The Japanese economy grew relatively well after takeoff, but experienced a temporary setback at the beginning of the twentieth century, including great fluctuation at the time of the Russo-Japanese War (1904-05). These economic changes were perhaps reflected in the fall and recovery of birth rates during that period. Further, since 1915, per capita product grew more rapidly than in the period of takeoff, and the birth rates rose with a few years' time lag.

A regression analysis of the relationships between variations from trend in birth rates and such economic changes and birth rates did not yield statistically significant results, even if lagged five or ten years. The results in general are similar to those in the case of death rates, and the Yasukawa estimate provides comparatively good results. In particular, for the period 1875-1905 the correlation coefficient with per capita product in the Yasukawa estimate rises considerably, to 0.800, a significant result. For the other cases the coefficients also rise, but not sufficiently to be significant. The official estimate shows relationships which are contrary to what is expected and is rejected.

General Appraisal of Various Estimates

One should not jump from the preceding analysis to definitive conclusions, but one may recognize several points. The vital rates estimated by using the elaborated methodology of formal demography are neither mere fiction nor predetermined results of the working hypothesis; they pass some tests checking the relationship with actual economic changes. The official estimate meets the test of the rate of population growth, but it is disqualified with reference to economic fluctuation. I conclude that the reverse survival method is the better method of estimation. Nevertheless, among the estimates by that method I can also find various deficiencies. Regarding the Okazaki estimate, I have judged that the rate of population increase before the Meiji Restoration was too high, suggesting the population at the beginning of Meiji may be overestimated by Okazaki. The Morita estimate has little relation to socioeconomic factors, though more so than the official estimate. The Yasukawa estimate has no gross fault, and fits well for trend and cyclical variation of per capita product as well as the rate of industrialization. Therefore, I can tentatively conclude that the Yasukawa estimate is the most plausible for vital rates prior to 1920.

POPULATION CHANGE IN THE INTERWAR PERIOD, 1920-1943

The Beginning of Fertility Decline

During the Meiji era, overpopulation is often given as the reason for the failure of living standards to improve substantially despite the period's economic growth. Population pressure was used by some groups to promote expansion of Japanese territorial control (Yoshida 1944, chapter 3). Although many considered a large population part of being a strong nation, there was no pronatal program. Indeed, the government had no real population policy—there was very little understanding of demography anywhere in the early twentieth century.

The rice riots (Kome Sōdō) in various parts of Japan in the summer of 1918 are considered to have first awakened people to a population problem (Jinkō Mondai 1959, pp. 3-4). When the actual nature of the population was made clear as a result of the first census in 1920, the necessity of birth control as a measure to meet overpopulation was argued by socialists and others (Abe 1927 and Yamamoto 1929). Just at this time signs of fertility decline began to appear.

However, the exact time when the birth rate began to fall is not known, because of unreliable data before 1920. According to the official data, 36.3 births per thousand in 1920 was the peak, and afterward the rates tended to fall, though undulating. On the whole, post-1920 data are reliable, so the question is whether the decline began earlier. As shown previously, Yasukawa's population estimates are the most plausible prior to 1920. His data show birth rates rose continuously, from about 1890, attaining 38.2 per thousand in 1920. This is higher than the official figure by about two births per thousand; if Yasukawa is right, it may be necessary to reevaluate the official figures since 1920. Be that as it may, both put the peak in 1920. Moreover, data on the population by single years of age in the quinquennial census since 1920 show the birth cohort of 1920 was much larger than that of adjacent years. This confirms a peak in the birth rate in 1920. The level of the peak itself still remains a question.

In the eighteen years after 1920, the number of births fluctuated around 2 million annually, with a relatively narrow range between 1.97 million in 1922 and 2.19 million in 1935. Meanwhile, the total population was increasing from about 55 to 70 million, so the birth rate was falling gradually, going below 30 in 1934. In 1935-37, the rate recovered but dropped to 26.6 in 1939, the lowest in the prewar period. Although it surged with the outbreak of World War II, it seems the general drift was downward.

Demographic Factors of Declining Fertility

The demographic factors determining the crude birth rate are the age composition of female population, the ratio of married to total number of women, and the marital fertility rate.[1] The age-specific fertility rate of the female population is a good index of fertility. Even though it is the same in two populations, crude birth rates may vary because of differences in the age composition and marital status of the female population. Only when these influences are removed can the fertility of one population with another be compared directly, and for this purpose standardized birth rates are calculated.

Crude birth rates (cbr) and two kinds of standardized birth rates (sbr), A and B, for the period 1920-40 are compared in Table 10. Sbr$A$ refers to females of all marital statuses, and sbr$B$ to presently married females. The rates of decline from 1920 to 1940 were 19.0 percent for cbr, 23.0 percent for sbr$A$, and 8.8 percent for sbr$B$. These percentages show the prewar decline in birth rates was mainly due to changes in the marital status of the population: the ratio of married females fell sharply throughout the twenty prewar years, despite a decline in husband's mortality. This trend was mainly attributed to the fall in rates of marriage and the rise of age of marriage. This point is important, because it suggests the prewar decline was due to what A. J. Coale called Malthusian, rather than neo-Malthusian low fertility. In other words, the pure decline in fertility, after adjusting for marital status, was small during this period (Tsubouchi 1970).

Much research has been done on the relationship between marriage and birth rates, as most births are within wedlock. In fact, both rates in Japan

[1]This disregards children born out of wedlock, which is a generally safe omission for Japan.

Table 10
Crude and Standardized Birth Rates, 1920-1940

| Year | cbr | sbr | |
		A	B
1920	36.32	36.18	34.87
1921	35.23	35.21	--
1922	34.38	34.44	--
1923	35.26	35.31	--
1924	34.03	34.21	--
1925	35.00	35.26	33.82
1926	34.72	35.10	--
1927	33.49	33.77	--
1928	34.19	34.37	--
1929	32.78	32.82	--
1930	32.42	32.35	32.35
1931	32.19	32.01	--
1932	32.92	32.57	--
1933	31.51	31.07	--
1934	29.95	29.40	--
1935	31.67	30.94	32.66
1936	30.01	29.17	--
1937	30.91	29.82	--
1938	27.14	26.07	--
1939	26.63	25.45	--
1940	29.43	27.85	31.79

Sources: Jinkō Mondai Shingi Kai 1959. Kōseishō Jinkō 1963.
Note: Includes Ryūkyū Islands.
Standard population is the whole Japan population for 1930.

kept pace closely with each other, and the correlation coefficient between them for 1920-34 is -0.879. After 1935, their close relationship began to break down. It is apparent that this was partly due to stronger controls on marital fertility.

The age of marriage rose steadily after 1925, so that the ratio of married females fell considerably, in particular at ages under twenty-five. In the 1930s the ratio for twenty-five years old and over fell a little. As the greater part of births were by mothers under thirty years of age, the reduction in the ratio of married females of these ages makes a great contribution to declining fertility. For ages thirty years or more, the ratio of married females ought to rise at least superficially in accordance with decline of mortality among their husbands, unless there is a fundamental change in nuptiality at these ages. It is worthy of note, however, that the ratio actually recorded a slight decrease during this period, as shown in Table 11.

Table 11
The Ratio of Married to Total Women
by Five-Year Age Groups, 1920-1940
(percent)

Age	1920	1925	1930	1935	1940
All ages	68.3	68.0	65.8	64.1	61.4
15-19	16.6	13.2	10.3	7.2	4.2
20-24	64.9	67.1	60.1	53.3	45.2
25-29	85.8	87.7	87.6	85.0	82.8
30-34	89.5	90.5	90.8	90.2	88.8
35-39	88.2	89.0	89.3	89.3	88.5
40-44	84.6	85.0	85.5	85.6	85.5
45-49	79.1	79.0	79.3	79.7	79.9

Sources: Sōrifu Tōkei-kyoku 1970.

Industrialization and Fertility

Why was marriage delayed during this period? Why did fewer women get married? Research on these questions is still limited, but it is generally recognized these changes in social patterns were closely connected with industrialization and urbanization (Taeuber 1958, p. 245).

First, I will consider the relation between industrialization and fertility. The rate of industrialization tended to rise during 1920-40, while the birth rates declined. This inverse relation is the opposite of the situation before 1920. The correlation coefficient is −0.903. However, the short-term variations of both suggest parallel movement in the first half of this period, with the change to the inverse relation coming in the 1930s. The correlation coefficient is +0.453 for 1920-31, and for 1932-40 is −0.401, but both are statistically insignificant.

According to cross-sectional data from all forty-six prefectures, the relationships between industrialization and fertility were already inverse in 1920. Fertility in typical industrial and agricultural prefectures are compared in Table 12. Data on fertility represented by gross reproduction rates (GRR) by prefecture were prepared by Taeuber (1958, p. 244); all figures in Table 12 are averages weighted by the population of each prefecture. Fertility in agricultural prefectures was distinctly higher than in industrial ones, and the speed of decline in the former was also smaller than in the latter.

Table 13 shows the correlations between GRR and the rate of industrialization for all prefectures. There are fairly clear inverse correlations throughout the interwar period. The correlations were so strong that the effect of industrialization on the declining fertility may be confirmed, at least during this period.[2]

[2]The following data show the average number of children born alive per married couple by occupation of husband in 1940. These data are derived from the First Fertility Survey conducted by the Institute of Population Problems, Ministry of Health and Welfare. The fertility of primary workers

Table 12
Comparison of Gross Reproduction Rates between
Industrial and Agricultural Prefectures, 1920-1940

	Gross reproduction rates	
	---	---
Year	Industrial prefectures	Agricultural prefectures
1920	2.36	2.89
1930	2.02	2.69
1940	1.74	2.25

Note: Industrial and agricultural prefectures are divided by the rate of industrialization, that is, the percentage of persons employed in the nonprimary sector, as follows:

Prefecture is:	if the percentage having industrial jobs is, in		
	1920	1930	1940
industrial	over 50%	over 60%	over 70%
agricultural	below 30%	below 35%	below 40%

Correlations by age groups are given in Table 14. Calculations are possible only for 1925 and 1930 because of data limitations. All of the coefficients are negative, and are significant at the one percent level, except for the forty-five to forty-nine age group. The coefficient is the highest for women between twenty-five and twenty-nine, and is lower in the younger and older ages. This is the usual phenomenon at a time when high fertility is prevailing and implies fertility differences by district appear more clearly in the age group with a higher reproductive capability.

From 1920 to 1940, it seems fertility differences by district widened, and then narrowed. As shown in Table 12, the ratio of GRR in industrial to agricultural prefectures was 1:1.22 in 1920, but increased to 1:1.33 in 1930 and declined a little to 1:1.29 in 1940 (Taeuber 1958, pp. 246-247). These changes are attributed to the spread of industrialization to rural districts.

The level of per capita product fluctuated but did not significantly change between 1920 and 1931, due to recurrent slumps after World War I (Nakamura 1971, p. 136). After 1931 Japan emerged from depression as

was high, and that of nonprimary workers was low. (Source: Aoki and Nakano 1967.)

Occupation of husband	Number of couples	Number of children ever born alive per married couple
Farmers, lumbermen, and fishermen	24,344	4.20
Manual laborers	18,553	2.94
Nonprimary employers	8,513	3.29
Nonmanual laborers	15,415	2.53
Others	2,580	4.43
All occupations	71,606	3.39

Table 13
Gross Reproduction Rates and the
Rate of Industrialization, 1920-1940

Year	Simple correlation coefficients
1920	-0.592**
1925	-0.637**
1930	-0.705**
1935	-0.724**
1940	-0.638**

Note: See Table 7.

Table 14
Age-specific Birth Rates and
the Rate of Industrialization

Age group	Simple correlation coefficients	
	1925	1930
15-19	-0.415**	-0.421**
20-24	-0.640**	-0.622**
25-29	-0.674**	-0.718**
30-34	-0.570**	-0.671**
35-39	-0.492**	-0.609**
40-44	-0.395**	-0.533**
45-49	-0.264	-0.278

Note: See Table 7.

expansion of production resumed, and per capita product increased rapidly.

The decline in birth rates was relatively small in the 1920s when per capita product was stagnant, and it was large in the later period of rising per capita product; the relationship between both variables was inverse. However, using deviations from trends, one finds another picture of the situation. In Figure 4, with birth rates lagged two years, both cyclical variations roughly coincide, with a significant correlation of +0.563. This finding is interesting, because it is consistent with the view that change in income has a positive effect on fertility with some time lag.

Urbanization and Fertility

What is industrial is not identical with what is urban, in particular when a region is subdivided. Nevertheless, both industrialization and urbanization have moved in the same direction as a whole, and have a similar effect on fertility.

Although the percentage of population of a *shi* (urban area) to the total, an adequate indicator of urbanization, is not available prior to 1920, one may say extensive urbanization began from about that time. The percentage of

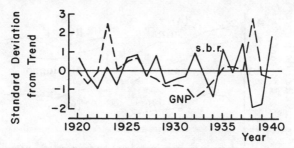

Figure 4. Cyclical variations from trend in
standardized birth rates and in per capita GNP,
1920-1940.
Source: Ohbuchi 1974, p. 90 (figures 2-15).

population in all shi was only 18 percent in 1920. It rose to 24 percent in
1930, and 38 percent in 1940. The number of persons residing in shi areas
was 10 million in 1920, over 15 million in 1930, and in 1940 it swelled to
27.5 million, nearly three times as many as in 1920.

"Urbanization had a dual influence on national fertility," said Taeuber
(1958, p. 256). One was the decline over time in fertility of urban residents,
and the other was the increase of urban areas, which have rates of fertility
lower than rural areas. In the period prior to the China War (1937), the major
influence of urbanization on fertility occurred through the latter rather than
the former. Indeed, declining fertility went on together with urbanization in
1920-40. Unfortunately, however, there is no evidence on the processes
whereby persons who moved from rural to urban areas changed their old
reproductive behavior into urban patterns of behavior.

There are suitable data showing the difference in fertility between urban
and rural residents. They are the standardized birth rates by shi and *gun*
(county, typically a rural area), prepared by the Jinko Mondai Kenkyūjo. The
data are standardized for both age structure and marital status of the female
population (Kōseishō 1968). Figure 5 shows those transitions from 1920 to
1940. It is noteworthy that the birth rates of all shi were always markedly
lower than those of all gun, and had already fallen to the 25 per thousand
level in 1920. In prewar Japan as a whole, as urbanization was not advanced,
the national birth rates kept pace with that of all gun. The standardized rates
based on age structure and fertility of women of all marital statuses dropped
substantially, whereas those based on presently married women fell only a
very little. Thus the national pattern (as shown in Table 10) was found
equally both in shi and gun.

Wartime Population Policy

Worldwide depression in the 1930s also had a serious influence on the Japanese economy. Consciousness of overpopulation became strong within the
country, and many economists debated the population question (Minami
1936). The urgent problem of overpopulation in Japan drew much attention
from foreign countries, in part out of fear it might lead to war (Thompson

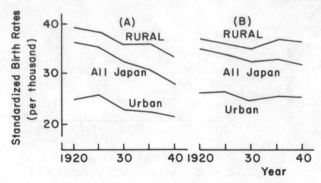

Figure 5. Standardized birth rates by urban and rural
areas, 1920-1940.
Source: Kōseishō Jinkō Mondai Kenkyūsho 1968.

1929). A birth control movement appeared, but government and military
authorities, as well as industrialists, stood against and suppressed it, for they
regarded population as an important source of military strength and labor
force in the midst of expansionism. After the Manchurian Incident,
population increase was more and more glorified, so knowledge and
techniques of birth control could not be spread to the public at large (Jinkō
Mondai 1959, pp. 82-83).

The "Jinkō Seisaku Kakuritsu Yōkō" [Outline for the Establishment of
Population Policy], decided on by the cabinet on January 22, 1941, spelled
out the objective of population increase for the first time as a national policy.
Various measures to promote marriage and large families were taken.
Examples are a system of marriage loans, restraint of gainful employment
among women over age twenty, a tax on single persons, family allowances,
and the prohibition of birth control and abortion (Kōseishō 1941, pp.
183-186, and Taeuber 1958, pp. 367-368). Although the government had
virtually suppressed the practice of birth control since the Meiji Era, this was
the first official expression of the policy.

The effects of the wartime population policy were considerable. Marriage
rates jumped to 11 per thousand, and crude birth rates, down to 26.6 in
1939, rose over 30 for the three years 1941-43. As fertility itself originally
had not fallen very much, it is natural that the birth rates rose with the
marriage rate increase.

POSTWAR DECLINE IN FERTILITY, 1947-70

Rapid Decline in Fertility after the Baby Boom

After World War II, a baby boom occurred, with fertility rising unusually in
1947-49. For each of these three years, the number of births was nearly 2.7
million, the largest in the history of Japan. The birth rates of 33 to 34 were
the highest since the mid-1920s. This upsurge was a transitional phenomenon

due to the accumulation of postponed marriages and births caused by the war. This is an almost universal postwar phenomenon.

Thereafter birth rates dropped suddenly and precipitously, something not experienced in Europe and America. The rate, 33.0 in 1949, declined to 28.1 in 1950. Subsequently it declined by nearly two per year; in 1955, it broke the 20 level and hit the bottom at 17.2 in 1957. Superstition concerning *hi-no-e-uma* (the year of fire and horse) in 1966 greatly confused the trend of fertility in Japan, but crude birth rates have been stable at 17 to 19.[3] The annual number of births fell below 2 million in 1953, and dropped to about 1.6 million in 1956. In the 1970s it is again approaching 2 million. Thus, the postwar decline in fertility occurred in only a few years before leveling off; no other international experience can compare with it in rapidity of decline.

The change in age structure was so drastic that it is necessary to investigate the process by using age-specific fertility. Figure 6 compares the crude birth rates (cbr) with the two kinds of standardized birth rates (sbr); all indexes fell rapidly during the 1950s. If one compares the extent of decline in birth rates for the period 1950 through 1960, the largest decrease is for sbr*A* (standardized for age structure only), which recorded a drop of 42.3 percent. The cbr declined 38.8 percent in this period. The smallest decrease, 31.5 percent, was for the sbr*B* (standardized for both age structure and marital status). This means the decline in marital fertility played a decisive part in the process of declining fertility in postwar Japan, as did the decline in the ratio of married females (Yamaguchi 1967, pp. 69-70). The change of age structure had the effect of raising the apparent birth rates.

Figure 7, the transition of age-specific fertility per woman, shows that the rapid decline of the 1950s occurred in all age groups. The width and duration of decline varied with age. For those in their twenties the decline was about 40 percent and was reversed slightly in the mid-1950s; the reduction for age groups fifteen to nineteen and above age thirty, particularly above age forty, was to levels below one-twentieth their 1947 peaks, and the levels have remained low.

Character of the Declining Trend

Should the steep postwar decline of fertility be regarded as the recovery movement toward a long-term trend of the prewar period? If not, is it a different tendency from the prewar trend? These are perhaps the key questions for analyzing the factors of declining fertility. In Figure 8, two

[3]Hi-no-e-uma is the name of a particular year in the sixty-year Sino-Japanese calendar cycle. According to this superstition, a woman born in the year hi-no-e-uma is strong willed, will kill seven husbands, and dissipate her family's fortune. This superstition was introduced from China in ancient times, and apparently still has a strong influence. Since the Meiji Restoration, it has occurred in 1906 and 1966. In both years, the number of births greatly decreased compared to the preceding and following years. The number of births registered in 1966 was 1.36 million, even less than the 1.39 million in 1906, and the lowest on record.

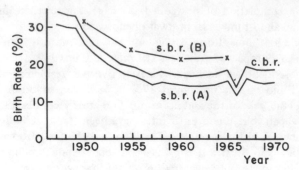

Figure 6. Crude and standardized birth rates, 1947-1970.

Source: Kōseishō Jinkō Mondai Kenkyūsho 1967 and other unpublished material.

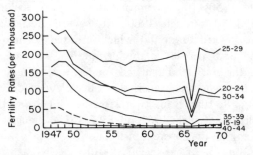

Figure 7. Age-specific fertility rates, 1947-1970.

Source: Kōseishō Daijin 1972.

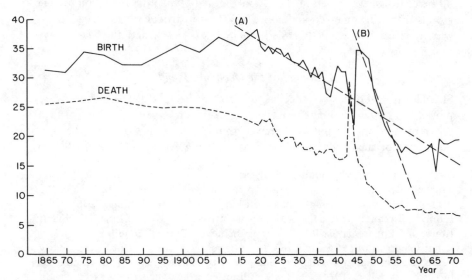

Figure 8. Demographic transition in Japan.

Sources: Yasukawa and Hirooka 1972; Jinkō Mondai 1959; Kōseishō Daijin, *Jinkō*, various issues.

linear trends are depicted, prewar *A* and postwar *B*. Trends *A* and *B* intersect around 1953, but the actual birth rate dropped sharply for a few years after that. Although trend *A* again crosses the actual rate in the middle of the 1960s, it is not reasonable to consider this a return to the prewar trend. Instead, the movement since the mid-1950s is a new trend.

The percentage of the work force outside the primary sector is plotted against the sbr*A* in Figure 9. This figure suggests the prewar trend of fertility was quite different from the postwar one with reference to this socioeconomic index, and the level of fertility has little changed from 1955 to the present in spite of considerable change of this index. When sbr*A* is related to the rate of urbanization and per capita product, the same results are obtained. Consequently, one can conclude industrialization and related changes have had a different effect on fertility in the postwar period compared to the prewar period.

Socioeconomic Background of Declining Fertility

The Japanese economy received a heavy blow in World War II. The gross national product was reduced to about 60 percent and industrial production to 25 percent of the prewar level. Despite the large number of deaths caused by the war, the population increased rapidly because of repatriation and the baby boom. Up to September 1950, the number of repatriates numbered 6.25 million (Jinkō Mondai 1959, p. 6). Population problems in the double sense of shortages of both food and jobs were imminent (Minami 1955, chapters 2 and 3). Consciousness of the situation led to arguments to restrict population and control births.

In the late 1940s, limiting the number of children as a means to maintain or raise a family's living standard became an increasingly accepted idea. When the ban on contraceptives was removed in May 1949 and the amendment of the Eugenic Protection Law the next month permitted abortion for purely

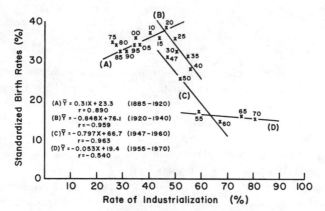

Figure 9. Relationship between standardized birth rates and the percentage of work force in nonprimary sectors.

Source: Ohbuchi 1974, p. 100 (figures 3-4).

economic reasons, the effect of birth control appeared at once, and the birth rate fell off sharply.

The Japanese economy recovered swiftly with special procurement for the Korean War as a springboard, while the birth rate continued to decline. The living standard did not rise in proportion to the growth of the national economy, and there were feelings of relative poverty. Although the problem of food shortage disappeared relatively early, problems of unemployment and housing shortages, worsened by the continuous drift of people toward metropolitan areas, were not so easily settled. Indeed, the serious shortage of land and living quarters has become progressively worse. These conditions are not at all conducive to a high level of fertility in Japan.

The sudden change in values accompanying the defeat in World War II had important effects; above all one can find a great change in ways of thinking about family and children. In the prewar period, most persons thought children should provide for their retired parents, succeed to the family business, and maintain the lineage of the family. This way of thinking was firmly supported by the paternal family system, yet the collapse of this system, guaranteed by the amendment of civil law after World War II, tended to sweep away much of such traditional thinking in a stroke. Moreover, the progress of industrialization and urbanization lowered the proportion of population in rural districts, where tradition was strongest. The development of mass communications, centering on television, was also important as a medium of change.

Thus, the demographic transition in Japan was completed, at least in form. As everyone knows, the declining fertility in Japan was actually attained by induced abortion, not by preventing conception, which is what most people think of as birth control (Aoki 1967). However, the means of fertility control is not the point. Attention is first directed to the motivation. Generally, declining fertility is not due to the availability of contraceptives or the easy access to induced abortion but to the social and economic change which motivates couples to limit their number of children (Hashimoto 1974, pp. 170-194).

The Econometric Model

The socioeconomic mechanism is now analyzed by using an econometric model. As there are ample data in the postwar period, other explanatory factors will be added to those of industrialization, urbanization, and level of income already related to fertility. The additional factors are the standard of education, mortality, and housing conditions. These are embodied in a series of regression models using cross-section data mainly from the census for all forty-six prefectures for every five years from 1950 through 1970.

The focus of the analysis is the response of fertility to changes in social and economic factors, and the changes of response over time. Age-specific fertility rates of the female population are the dependent variables in the regression model. They are used as the index of fertility to eliminate the variations in birth rates attributable to purely demographic reasons. Ages are divided into seven five-year groups from fifteen to nineteen through forty-five to forty-nine. Therefore, the total is thirty-five regression equations for the entire period 1950-70.

The independent variables selected to explain the variance of fertility are the following five factors: (1) the ratio of nonprimary to total employment, (2) monthly total cash earnings per regular employe, (3) infant mortality, (4) the ratio of students continuing on to senior high school to total graduates of junior high school, and (5) extent of living space or population pressure.

For each year, the regression equations to be estimated are of the following form:

$$\log b_i = a_{0i} + a_{1i} \log I + a_{2i} \log W + a_{3i} \log M + a_{4i} \log E + a_{5i} \log T$$

where b equals number of live births per 1000 females in the ith age group.

I equals level of industrialization.

W equals wage level.

M equals infant mortality.

E equals standard of education.

T equals number of tatami per person.

As all the variables are expressed in logarithms, the partial regression coefficients a_{ji} ($j = 1, 2, \ldots 5$) measure the elasticities of fertility in the ith age group with respect to the jth variable.

Table 15 shows the conditions of sign expected a priori for all variables in the model. A plus means that an increase in the variable enhances fertility, and a minus indicates a suppressing effect.

Analysis of Regression Results

The results of each year derived from the regression model are summarized in Tables 16 to 20. The upper entry of each age group in these tables is an unbiased estimate of the regression coefficient a_{ji}, and in parentheses below the corresponding coefficients the standard error of these estimates is given. C is the constant term, and S is the standard error for each respective regression surface. R^2 is the coefficient of determination, indicating the percentage of the change in fertility attributable to the explanatory variables used. $\bar{R}^2$ is the R^2 adjusted for the degrees of freedom.

According to these tables, the regression models account for 50 to 70 percent of differential fertility by region for 1950-60, and roughly 20 to 60

Table 15
Conditions of Sign Expected a priori

	Variable	Expected sign
I	rate of industrialization	−
W	wage level	+
M	infant mortality	+
E	standard of education	−
T	number of tatami per person	−

Table 16
Summary of Regressions (1), 1950

Age	Regression coefficient					C	S	R^2	$\bar{R}^2$
	I	W	M	E	T				
15-19	-0.502†	1.082*	1.942*	0.220	-0.379	-6.053	0.140	0.587*	0.546
	(0.274)	(0.271)	(0.392)	(0.356)	(0.387)				
20-24	-0.293*	0.343*	0.723*	-0.005	-0.122	2.733	0.140	0.591*	0.552
	(0.116)	(0.115)	(0.166)	(0.151)	(0.164)				
25-29	-0.198*	0.018	-0.045	-0.187*	-0.111	7.240	0.071	0.551*	0.506
	(0.059)	(0.058)	(0.084)	(0.076)	(0.083)				
30-34	-0.227*	0.065	-0.206	-0.378*	-0.118	8.326	0.119	0.436*	0.387
	(0.098)	(0.097)	(0.140)	(0.128)	(0.139)				
35-39	-0.346*	0.227	-0.226	-0.607*	-0.233	9.024	0.175	0.480*	0.429
	(0.145)	(0.143)	(0.207)	(0.188)	(0.204)				
40-44	-0.678*	0.338†	-0.363	-0.792*	-0.441	10.522	0.241	0.555*	0.511
	(0.199)	(0.197)	(0.284)	(0.258)	(0.281)				
45-49	-0.890*	0.441	-0.491	-0.980*	-1.029*	10.258	0.329	0.569*	0.524
	(0.273)	(0.269)	(0.389)	(0.354)	(0.385)				

*Significant at 0.05 level.
†Significant at 0.10 level.
Unless otherwise indicated, all values are not statistically significant.

Table 17
Summary of Regressions (2), 1955

Age	Regression coefficient					C	S	R^2	$\bar{R}^2$
	I	W	M	E	T				
15-19	-0.638† (0.352)	1.128† (0.601)	1.431* (0.421)	0.027 (0.539)	-0.805 (0.485)	-3.166	0.405	0.430*	0.359
20-24	-0.345* (0.151)	0.399 (0.258)	0.744* (0.181)	-0.098 (0.231)	-0.117 (0.208)	2.795	0.174	0.551*	0.495
25-29	-0.316* (0.069)	0.086 (0.117)	-0.138† (0.082)	-0.323* (0.105)	-0.096 (0.095)	8.129	0.079	0.637*	0.592
30-34	-0.546* (0.121)	0.178 (0.207)	-0.417* (0.145)	-0.617* (0.186)	-0.239 (0.167)	10.663	0.140	0.634*	0.588
35-39	-0.801* (0.180)	0.628* (0.307)	-0.513* (0.215)	-0.969* (0.275)	-0.417 (0.248)	11.545	0.207	0.641*	0.597
40-44	-0.956* (0.222)	1.311* (0.379)	-0.345 (0.265)	-1.474* (0.340)	-0.824* (0.306)	10.715	0.256	0.715*	0.679
45-49	-1.473* (0.307)	1.156* (0.524)	-0.328 (0.367)	-0.853† (0.469)	-1.573* (0.423)	8.818	0.353	0.658*	0.615

Note: See Table 16.

353

Table 18
Summary of Regressions (3), 1960

| Age | Regression coefficient | | | | | C | S | R^2 | R^2 |
	I	W	M	E	T				
15-19	0.054	1.352*	1.874*	-0.659	-0.910*	-5.455	0.306	0.641*	0.596
	(0.387)	(0.489)	(0.385)	(0.472)	(0.344)				
20-24	0.029	0.367	0.895*	-0.208	0.119	1.023	0.179	0.495*	0.432
	(0.226)	(0.286)	(0.225)	(0.276)	(0.201)				
25-29	0.144†	-0.015	-0.223*	-0.334*	-0.045	8.032	0.064	0.468*	0.401
	(0.080)	(0.102)	(0.080)	(0.098)	(0.072)				
30-34	-0.421†	0.101	-0.776*	-0.726†	-0.377†	11.927	0.173	0.445*	0.376
	(0.219)	(0.277)	(0.218)	(0.267)	(0.195)				
35-39	-0.856*	0.430	-0.655*	-0.958*	-0.919*	12.780	0.247	0.557*	0.501
	(0.311)	(0.394)	(0.310)	(0.380)	(0.277)				
40-44	-1.217*	0.773	-0.505	-1.176*	-1.391*	12.676	0.302	0.637*	0.592
	(0.382)	(0.483)	(0.380)	(0.466)	(0.340)				
45-49	-1.522*	1.679*	-0.510	-1.000	-1.338*	7.604	0.418	0.523*	0.463
	(0.528)	(0.668)	(0.526)	(0.645)	(0.470)				

Note: See Table 16.

Table 19

Summary of Regressions (4), 1965

Age	Regression coefficient						C	S	R^2	R^2
	I	W	M	E	T					
15-19	0.135	1.907*	0.901*	−1.294*	−0.940*	−1.906	0.234	0.651*	0.607
	(0.437)	(0.536)	(0.359)	(0.568)	(0.271)				
20-24	0.305	0.400	0.582*	−0.700†	0.336†	2.735	0.158	0.406*	0.331
	(0.295)	(0.362)	(0.242)	(0.383)	(0.183)				
25-29	0.162	−0.431*	−0.119	−0.248†	−0.109	7.755	0.058	0.270*	0.178
	(0.109)	(0.133)	(0.089)	(0.141)	(0.067)				
30-34	0.201	−0.601	−0.305	−0.494	−0.661*	9.800	0.176	0.304*	0.216
	(0.330)	(0.404)	(0.270)	(0.428)	(0.204)				
35-39	0.239	−0.210	−0.117	−0.749	−1.129*	7.995	0.253	0.385*	0.308
	(0.473)	(0.580)	(0.388)	(0.615)	(0.293)				
40-44	−0.607	0.186	−0.133	−1.117	−1.785*	10.987	0.281	0.586*	0.534
	(0.527)	(0.646)	(0.432)	(0.684)	(0.326)				
45-49	−1.683†	1.041	0.419	0.173	−2.511*	3.649	0.530	0.421*	0.349
	(0.991)	(1.215)	(0.813)	(1.287)	(0.614)				

Note: See Table 16.

Table 20

Summary of Regressions (5), 1970

Age	Regression coefficient					C	S	R^2	$\bar{R}^2$
	I	W	M	E	T				
15-19	1.596†	0.836	0.517	-3.070*	-0.684*	6.541	0.271	0.404*	0.397
	(0.806)	(0.655)	(0.482)	(0.854)	(0.333)				
20-24	0.870†	-0.276	0.504†	-1.148*	0.497*	4.828	0.163	0.301*	0.213
	(0.482)	(0.392)	(0.288)	(0.511)	(0.199)				
25-29	0.053	-0.034	-0.045	-0.060	-0.007	5.661	0.070	0.012	0.0
	(0.208)	(0.169)	(0.125)	(0.221)	(0.086)				
30-34	-0.235	0.159	-0.147	0.098	-0.703*	5.983	0.168	0.293*	0.205
	(0.499)	(0.406)	(0.299)	(0.529)	(0.206)				
35-39	-0.154	0.618	-0.073	-0.366	-1.193*	4.942	0.210	0.509*	0.447
	(0.622)	(0.505)	(0.372)	(0.659)	(0.257)				
40-44	0.084	0.799	0.414	-0.902	-1.616*	3.010	0.245	0.589*	0.537
	(0.725)	(0.590)	(0.434)	(0.769)	(0.300)				
45-49	-0.381	1.280	0.944	-0.370	-1.765*	-1.022	0.630	0.207	0.107
	(1.867)	(1.518)	(1.117)	(1.979)	(0.772)				

Note: See Table 16.

percent for 1965-70. All the coefficients of determination over age twenty-five rise between 1950 and 1955, and most of them decline between 1955 and 1970. Perhaps this is not a mere coincidence. It may be that regional differentials were large when fertility was declining rapidly in the early 1950s, so that the explanatory power is great. However, once the changes spread over the whole country and the process of adjustment to low levels of fertility comes to an end, the factors bringing about the remaining differentials become obscure, so that the explanatory power declines. It well reflects the fact that the conspicuous decline in fertility had finished by 1960, and thereafter fertility leveled off. Nevertheless, the patterns of the fifteen to nineteen age group are somewhat different. This group was more affected by the decline in the ratio of the married females than by marital fertility, and it seems to show a pattern of behavior different from that of ages over twenty-five. The pattern of the twenty to twenty-four age group is more or less similar to that of the fifteen to nineteen age group.

Demarcation of the same kind by age is found in the specific parameter values. This is particularly clear for infant mortality (M). In age group fifteen to twenty-four, the elasticities of M are very high, and their plus signs coincide with my prior expectations. However, from age twenty-five onward, the signs change to minus, and elasticities become smaller. As it appears for almost all years, it is not merely an accidental phenomenon. My interpretation is as follows: if infant mortality is assumed to parallel the mortality of the whole population, high mortality curtails the duration of marriage by raising the ratio of separation by death in married couples, and consequently reduces the completed fertility of families.

In general, I obtained expected results for variables other than M. Most of the parameters of the rate of industrialization, I, have minus signs and are highly stable. However, for young women (under thirty), their signs have changed to plus since 1960, and in 1970 their elasticities are high, though statistical significance is less than for earlier years. These results can be regarded as reflecting the fact that Japan's high rate of economic growth mainly has been from the rapid advance in the heavy and chemical industries since the late 1950s, with the consequent concentration in urban areas of many young people moving from rural areas. This group's fertility has ceased to decline further at a relatively early stage. Further, one must not forget that the development of mass communications has increased similarities in both rural and urban areas. But over the age of forty, the elasticities of variable I also have minus signs and are significantly high until 1965, implying the more the area was urbanized, the earlier women tended to complete their childbearing. In 1970, the elasticities decline and the estimates generally are not statistically significant, reinforcing the view that differences in behavior between farmers and others are disappearing.

Such tendencies are also demonstrated in Table 21, showing the simple correlation coefficients between the level of industrialization and the age-specific and total fertility rates. The minus and stable coefficients were maintained until 1960, but in 1965 they fell, and in 1970 the signs changed

Table 21
Simple Correlation Coefficients between the Rate of Industrialization and the Age-Specific and Total Fertility Rates, 1950-1970

Age groups	1950	1955	1960	1965	1970
All ages	−0.616**	−0.724**	−0.650**	−0.271	0.107
15-19	−0.301*	−0.355*	−0.359*	−0.061	0.118
20-24	−0.489**	−0.537**	−0.463**	−0.368*	−0.307*
25-29	−0.653**	−0.694**	−0.459**	−0.041	0.079
30-34	−0.484**	−0.609**	−0.220	0.114	0.202
35-39	−0.452**	−0.558**	−0.399**	0.107	0.294*
40-44	−0.532**	−0.491**	−0.460**	−0.200	0.191
45-49	−0.459**	−0.482**	−0.358*	−0.222	0.057

Note: See Table 16.

to plus, though not significantly. Moreover, the statistical significance of even these direct correlation coefficients disappears from 1965. This suggests the major urban concentrations are becoming greater contributors to the fertility of Japan as a whole.

The effect of rising wages (W) to encourage births and of the spread of education (E) to restrict them are almost perfectly demonstrated. Parameters of both variables have a peak in 1960, except E in the younger age groups. The significance is high in 1950-1960, and thereafter becomes low. As the regional differentials of wage and education have diminished gradually, their influence might become smaller (Hashimoto 1974, pp. 12-15).

The number of tatami per person, T, has come to display a major influence since 1960. In particular for age thirty-five and over, the elasticities are greater than unity. Moreover, they are stable. The interpretation of this variable involves some difficult problems. One possibility is that when the parameter has a minus sign, couples make an effort to increase their living space by forgoing a baby. Another interpretation, which I feel is less important, is that a minus sign for T means the existing living space is decreased by the increasing number of children, and consequently the dependent variable is actually the independent one. At any rate, it is necessary to make more empirical tests of this variable.

As I have suggested, the impact of each variable on fertility shows a fairly distinct pattern of variation with age. In every year, parameters of almost all variables are high among younger persons, declining through the twenty-five to twenty-nine age group, then rising again from age thirty until reaching the highest level after age forty. This is a U-shaped pattern. Adelman (1963, pp. 321-322) has shown this pattern for the income effect on fertility. In my regression models, I find it for every variable, though it often has an incomplete shape. It means the timing effect of socioeconomic factors on childbearing is strong, particularly in the younger and older age groups, and fertility is almost completely controlled.

Between the 1965 and 1970 censuses the *U*-shaped pattern of parameters was considerably disturbed, including some change of signs. Furthermore, the elasticities became smaller on the whole, and the coefficients of determination declined greatly. A series of such changes suggests a situation different from the 1950s in these years. The influence of the hi-no-e-uma superstition may be responsible, although I cannot prove this directly. I can conjecture, for instance, that the mild rise in birth rates in 1965 was due to an acceleration of the timing of fertility in order not to have babies in 1966. Even so, taking account of various materials, one may infer that the thoughts and behavior of the Japanese regarding reproduction began to change from about the middle of the 1960s (Mainichi 1970). At the least, it becomes clear from these regressions that the response of fertility to changes in social and economic factors after 1960 came to differ greatly from previous experience.

SUMMARY AND CONCLUSIONS

During the past century, the Japanese economy has made rapid progress, and at the same time population in Japan has been observed as an unprecedented experience in history. Above all, the great change of vital rates called the demographic transition has provided various interesting observations on the social consequences of industrialization.

With the progress of analytical techniques, the incomplete materials on population prior to 1920 have been corrected by many students. As a result of various tests, I tentatively conclude the Yasukawa estimate is the most plausible to date. It shows birth rates rose with some fluctuations from the late 1880s through 1920. This change appears to correspond with the economic takeoff, and thereby I infer the birth rate most likely rose for a time in the early stage of industrialization. Death rates began to decline slowly from about 1880, and steadily accelerated their speed of decrease.

In and after 1920, the modern decline in birth rates started. It was primarily due to the fall in the ratio of married females to the total, and the decline in pure fertility was rather small. The response of fertility to the progress of industrialization and urbanization, however, came to be gradually reversed, and to show a different tendency from that in the period of economic takeoff. Although in the early 1940s the birth rates reversed their course, moving upward because of wartime population policy, they otherwise seem to have had a continuous tendency to decline on the whole.

After the postwar baby boom, birth rates dropped at a surprising rate. This was an actual decline in maternal fertility, and no return to the prewar declining trend. Looking into the relationships between social and economic factors and fertility, this judgment is adequately justified. This view was confirmed by the regression analysis of fertility for 1950-70.

The regression models of the age-specific fertility rates provide a great deal of explanatory power in the period of fertility change, 1950-60, though this power fell considerably in 1965-70 when fertility leveled off and displayed less regional variation. A clearly discernible *U*-shaped pattern of parameters was found, and I confirmed the timing effect of childbearing was strong in younger and older age groups. The restraining effect of education and the promoting effect of rising wages were quite clear. Interestingly, industrialization lowered fertility at first, but after 1960 it had a raising effect in the younger age groups.

Compared with the Western countries, the fertility decline in Japan was accomplished in a relatively short time. This is almost assuredly the result of rapid industrialization after the takeoff. In other ways too, the process of the demographic transition in Japan was different from that of Western countries, particularly in respect to the means of fertility control and the form of transition. But substantively, both Japanese and Western experiences have a similar character. For example, the rising standard of education reduced fertility in Japan as in Europe, whereas it is not likely to have such a direct effect in currently less developed countries. Generally, demographic transition in Japan and Europe are in the same category.

REFERENCES

Abe, Isoo. 1927. *Jinkō Mondai to Sanji Seigen*. Nōson Mondai Sōsho Kankōkai.

Adelman, Irma. 1963. "An Econometric Analysis of Population Growth." *American Economic Review* 53 (June 1963).

Akasaka, Keiko. 1960. *Meiji 31 nen - Taishō 8 nen, Danjo Nenrei betsu Kakusai betsu Jinkō no Suikei*. Hitotsubashi Daigaku Keizai Kenkyūjo, Kokumin Shotoku Kenkyūkai Shiryō (unpublished).

———. 1964. *Danjo Nenrei betsu Jinkō no Suikei, 1872-1898*. Hitotsubashi Daigaku Keizai Kenkyūjo, Kokumin Shotoku Kenkyūkai Shiryō (unpublished).

Aoki, Hisao. 1967. *Shusshō Yokusei ni Kansuru Tōkei Shiryō*. Institute of Population Problems, Research Series no. 181 (Dec. 1967).

Aoki, Hisao, and Nakano Eiko. 1967. *Dai 1-4 Ji Shussan Ryoku Chōsa Kekka no Yōyaku*. Institute of Population Problems, Research Series no. 177 (July 1967).

Crocker, W. R. 1931. The *Japanese Population Problem: The Coming Crisis*. Allen and Unwin.

Hashimoto, Masanori. 1973. "Economics of Postwar Fertility in Japan: Differentials and Trends." *Journal of Political Economy* 82 (March/April 1974), supp., pp. 170-194.

Hayami, Akira. 1973. "Tokugawa Kōki Jinkō Hendō no Chiiki-teki Tokusei." *Mita Gakkai Zasshi* 64 (Aug. 1971).

Jinkō Mondai Shingi Kai, ed. 1959. *Jinkō Hakusho: Tenkanki Nihon no Jinkō Mondai*.

Kōseishō Daijin Kanbō Tōkei Chōsa-bu [Health and Welfare Statistics Division, Minister's Secretariat, Ministry of Health and Welfare]. 1972. *Shōwa 45-nen Jinkō Dōtai Tōkei*.

Kōseishō Jinkō Mondai Kenkyūjo [Ministry of Health and Welfare, Institute of Population Problems]. 1941. *Jinkō Seisaku no Shiori.*

. 1963. *Waga Kuni no Nenjibetsu Hyōjunka Jinkō Dōtai Ritsu.* Research Series no. 155 (Aug. 1963).

. 1967. *Zenkoku Jinkō no Saiseisan ni kansuru Shihyō.* Research Series no. 178 (Oct. 1967).

. 1968. *Zenkoku Shibu Gunbu Betsu Hyōjunka Jinkō Dōtai Ritsu.* Research Series no. 186 (Oct. 1968).

Mainichi Shinbunsha Jinkō Mondai Chōsa Kai, ed. 1970. *Nihon no Jinkō Kakumei.* Mainichi Shinbunsha.

Minami, Ryōshin. 1973. *The Turning Point in Economic Development: Japan's Experience.* Kinokuniya.

Minami, Ryōzaburō. 1936. *Jinkō Ron Hatten Shi.* Sanseidō.

. 1955. *Meian no Nihon Jinkō.* Dōbun Kan.

Morita, Yūzō. 1944. *Jinkō Zōka no Bunseki.* Nihon Hyōron Sha.

Naikaku Tōkei-kyoku [Cabinet Statistical Bureau]. 1930. *Meiji Gonen Ikō Waga Kuni no Jinkō.*

Nakamura, Takafusa. 1971. *Senzenki Nihon Keizai Seichō no Bunseki.* Iwanami Shoten.

Odabashi, Sadatoshi. 1937. "Waga Kuni Jinkō no Chihō-teki Bunpu to sono Idō." In *Nihon Jinkō Mondai Kenkyū*, vol. 3, edited by Ueda Teijiro. Kyōchōkai.

Okazaki, Yōichi. 1962. *Meiji Shonen Ikō Taishō 9-nen ni itaru Danjo Nenrei betsu Jinkō Suikei ni tsuite.* Institute of Population Problems, Research Series no. 145 (Feb. 1962).

Sekiyama, Naotarō. 1959. *Nihon no Jinkō.* Shinbundō.

Sōrifu Tōkei-kyoku [Bureau of Statistics, Office of the Prime Minister]. 1970. *Nihon no Jinkō.* Abridged report series 1, part 1.

Taeuber, Irene. 1958. *The Population of Japan.* Princeton University Press.

Thompson, Warren. 1929. *Danger Spots in World Population.* Knopf.

Tsubouchi, Yoshihiro. 1970. "Changes in Fertility in Japan by Region: 1920-1965." *Demography* 7 (May 1970).

Yamaguchi, Kiichi. 1967. "Kekkon oyobi Haigū Kankei Kōzō no Hendō to Shusshō Ryoku." In *Nihon Jinkō no Kōzō to Hendō*, edited by Kōseishō Jinkō Mondai Kenkyūjo.

Yamamoto, Senji. 1929. *Sanji Chōsetsu Ron.* Rogosu Shoin.

Yasukawa, Masaaki. 1971. "Nihon no Moderu Seimeihyo." *Mita Gakkai Zasshi* 64 (May 1971).

Yasukawa, Masaaki, and Keijirō Hirooka. 1972. "Meiji-Taishō Nenkan no Jinkō Suikei to Jinkō Dōtai." *Mita Gakkai Zasshi* 65 (Feb./March 1972).

Yoshida, Hideo. 1944. *Nihon Jinkō Ron no Shiteki Kenkyū.* Kawade Shobō.

Changes in Income Inequality
in the Japanese Economy

Akira Ono and Tsunehiko Watanabe

Long-run trends of income distribution including some explanation of the changes in income inequality are the topics of this essay. The main emphasis is on the changes in income distribution that have occurred in the past century of modern economic development, rather than the determinants of the structure of income distribution at the beginning of the period. It is appropriate, at the outset, to point out a few difficulties and obstacles.

1. As might be expected, no reliable data on size distribution of income are available for the prewar period. The prewar trends of income inequality given in this paper are, therefore, estimates based on changes in certain related variables such as differentials in per capita income between rural and urban sectors, income (or wage) differentials, and relative factor shares of income within respective sectors, and so forth.

2. As is suggested by the title, attention is focused on the distribution of income, as distinguished from assets. The concept of income in this analysis is the same as is used in income statistics, which covers incomes from work and returns from assets, but excludes capital gains due to a rise in asset prices. Rapid price increases of land and stocks in the 1960s yielded huge capital gains to asset holders, so inclusion of capital gains would give a quite different picture of income inequality, at least for the postwar years. It is impossible, however, to obtain long-run data on capital gains.

3. The division of the economy into rural and urban sectors introduces another factor closely related to income differentials. Especially in the early stages of economic development, the absence of a nationwide market gives rise to significantly different prices for the same commodity between sectors. These sectoral differences in consumer prices must be considered in comparing per capita incomes, say, between farm households and urban employe households. Otherwise, income inequality is sure to be over-estimated.

4. In an analysis of income inequality, income data should be defined on a per capita basis rather than a per household basis. Income data classifying

persons by household income per family member must be used, for data on a per household basis exaggerate income inequality when higher income groups support more family members than lower income groups. However, sometimes data limitations force use of income per household in parts of the discussion.

In the next section, intersectoral differential in per capita incomes, one of the determinants of the historical pattern of income inequality, is discussed. Then other factors are considered, for the purpose of estimating income inequality in the prewar economy. The following section deals with the post-World War II economy, for which considerable data are available. Long-run changes in inequality are then discussed, and the last section is devoted to a summary of the findings.

THE TREND OF INCOME DIFFERENTIALS BETWEEN SECTORS

The first task is to develop a measure of the inequality of income distribution. For this we use the coefficient of variation; the smaller its value the greater the equality of income distribution.

Let y_{ij} be per capita (or per household) income in the jth income class in the ith sector, N_{ij} the population (or the number of households), and y_i the average per capita (or per household) income in the ith sector (that is, $y_i = \sum_i N_{ij} y_{ij} / \sum_j N_{ij}$). Then the coefficient of variation in the ith sector, C_i, which indicates the intrasectoral income inequality, is defined by Equation 1.

$$C_i = \frac{\sqrt{\sum_j N_{ij} (y_{ij} - y_i)^2 / \sum_j N_{ij}}}{y_i} \tag{1}$$

If we express that fraction of the total population (or of all households) located in the ith sector by W_i, and the per capita income differential between the sectors by λ, the coefficients of variation for the economy as a whole, C, can be given by Equation 2.

$$C = \frac{\sqrt{W_r C_r^2 + W_u C_u^2 \lambda^2 + W_r W_u (\lambda - 1)^2}}{W_r + W_u \lambda} \tag{2}$$

where r and u stand for rural and urban areas respectively, and λ is defined as y_u / y_r.[1]

[1]This equation was derived by Swamy (1965). There are several measures of income inequality, such as the concentration ratio, coefficient of variation, standard deviation of the logarithms of income, Pareto's coefficient, and so on, of which Morgan (1962) gave the highest priority to the first. The international comparison of income inequalities by Kravis (1960) shows the concentration ratio moves in approximately the same direction as the coefficient of variation. In this paper we use the coefficient of variation for the sake of computational convenience, particularly given the nature of the prewar data.

Equation 2 shows income inequality, measured by the coefficient of variation (C), depends on intrasectoral income inequalities (C_r, C_u), the average per capita income differential (λ), and the proportion of urban population (W_u). The equation serves to identify the causes which bring about changes in income inequality; and it also serves as a tool for estimating the behavior of income inequality from changes in the variables involved in Equation 2, or in their approximate substitutes, where, as in the case of prewar Japan, reliable data on size distribution of income are not available.

The Bureau of Statistics conducted household consumption surveys several times after 1926, and compiled data on income distribution. These data, however, may not be used for the purpose of measuring inequality, because the surveys were based on biased samples. Income tax data also are available from about the middle of Meiji, but they exclude low-income groups exempt from the tax. Therefore, the changes in income inequality before World War II can be compiled only by indirect estimation from related data.

In this section, the differential in per capita incomes between urban employe households and farm households is taken into consideration as a proxy of income differential between the sectors (λ). From Equation 2, we get $\frac{\partial C}{\partial \lambda} > 0$ if $\lambda > 1$ and $C_u > C_r$. $\lambda > 1$ means per capita income in the urban areas (y_u) is higher than in the rural areas (y_r); $C_u > C_r$ means incomes are more unequally distributed in the urban areas than in the rural areas. These two conditions are satisfied for most years in the postwar period, as is shown in the following paragraphs. If they hold true for the entire period under observation, a wider average per capita income differential between the sectors will generally signify a more unequal size distribution of income.

Figure 1 depicts two kinds of per capita rural-urban income differentials: nominal and real obtained by deflating nominal incomes by the consumer price indexes constructed for rural and urban areas, respectively. (The estimating procedures are given in the statistical appendix.) For the pre-World War II years, large differences can be found between the nominal income

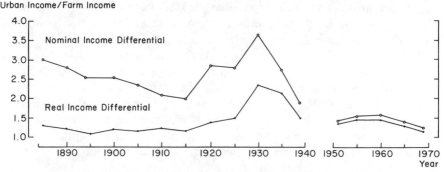

Figure 1. Differentials in per capita household income between urban-employe households and farm households.

Source: The estimating procedures are given in the statistical appendix.

Note: Income differentials in 1886, 1939, 1951, and 1969 are three-year averages, and others are five-year averages.

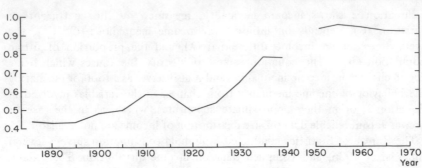

Figure 2. Ratios of consumer prices in rural areas to those in urban areas (urban prices in 1934-36 = 1).

Source: The estimating procedure is given in the third section of the statistical appendix.

Note: Relative prices in 1886, 1939, 1951, and 1969 are three-year averages, and others are five-year averages.

differential and the real income differential. Especially in the 1880s, the nominal income differential between rural and urban areas was about three, whereas the real income differential was not greater than 1.3. Since the railway between Tokyo and Yokohama opened in 1872, a unified domestic market has gradually developed. But in Meiji, before railway networks had fully developed, there existed wide differences in consumer prices between areas.

Figure 2 shows the changes in relative prices, that is, ratios between consumer prices in rural areas and those in urban areas. In the years before the turn of the century, relative prices were less than half, so that the great differential in nominal incomes between rural and urban areas served mainly to compensate for regional price differences. As the railways developed, differences in prices between areas became smaller, and the nominal income differential narrowed from three in the 1880s to two in 1915.[2] The real income differential between the areas consistently showed very small deviations from unity in the years 1887-1915. These small deviations in per capita real incomes may be interpreted as the minimum costs needed to make farm population leave their lands for urban areas, that is, the cost of migration, the compensation for the psychological cost of city life, and so on.

The trend of narrowing regional price differences was delayed by a sharp increase in consumer prices in the urban areas during the boom years after the outbreak of World War I, which include the 1918 rice riots. Part of the increase in the rural-urban nominal income differential in 1920 can be explained by a decrease in relative prices. It should be noted, however, that the real income differential also started to become wider during the period from 1915 to 1930. A marked widening in the real income differential for the

[2]Taira (1970, p. 16) found a rapid narrowing in regional wage differentials from the 1880s to the 1920s. This is also attributable to the changes in price differences by region.

years 1925-30 is partly attributable to the short-run downward rigidity of money wages during the depression in the early 1930s. This explanation may be a reasonable conjecture, judging from the narrowing differential in the subsequent boom period. However, this is not the end of the story. According to Ohkawa and Rosovsky's (1962) periodization, 1919 and 1938 are peak years in the long swings, so taking these two years or the years around them for the sake of comparison should allow observation of a trend excluding short-run fluctuations. The years 1920 and 1938 in Figure 1 show a widening in the real income differential. Thus, the typical movement of the real income differential for the prewar period is a constancy up to 1915 and a subsequent widening.

There is some further evidence supporting this conclusion. First are the changes in the labor productivity differential. Ohkawa and Rosovsky estimated the ratio of real output per worker in the agricultural sector to that in the manufacturing sector, and found this ratio started to decline steeply in the 1920s.[3]

This same trend also can be found in Ohkawa's comparison of per capita real farm and nonfarm consumption expenditures. The ratio of urban to rural per capita consumption was almost stable between 1.3 and 1.4 until the time of World War I, and then it increased sharply to 2.07 in 1930 and 1.65 in 1938 (Ohkawa 1973). Note that Ohkawa compares per capita consumption, whereas per capita *incomes* are compared in Figure 1. Further, Figure 1 compares per capita incomes between *farm* households and *urban employe* households, whereas Ohkawa deals with a wider scope of comparison, namely, between *farm* and *nonfarm* consumption. The important fact common to both Ohkawa's estimate and Figure 1, however, is that, although the estimates were made independently of each other, there exists a similarity of intersectoral differentials with respect to levels and behavior over a period of time.

According to Equation 2, a widening in intersectoral income differential will, other things constant, make size distribution of income more unequal. Our findings for the prewar years suggest income distribution measured by the coefficient of variation may have been stable until 1915 and then become unequal. The validity of this statement is, however, dependent on the assumption of *ceteris paribus*, which will be examined in the next section. Another point to emphasize is the large differences between nominal income and real income differentials, especially in the Meiji era. This warns of possible overestimating of income inequality in the early stages of economic development if coefficients of variation are calculated using nominal incomes.

The per capita real income differential at the beginning of the postwar period is slightly narrower than that at the end of the prewar period. The same fact shown also by the ratio of real output per worker in agriculture to

[3]Ohkawa and Rosovsky 1968. Ratios of agricultural labor productivity to manufacturing productivity in the peak years of their long swings were 43.8 percent in 1898, 44.8 percent in 1919, and 22.8 percent in 1938.

that in manufacturing (Ohkawa and Rosovsky 1968). The change in relative output prices due to food shortages immediately after World War II improved the per capita income of farm households relative to that of urban employe households. The rate of increase in total productivity in the agricultural sector is higher in the postwar period than in the prewar period (Yamada and Hayami 1973). The proportion of nonfarm income in total farm household income also has increased remarkably. These factors, together with the government's price support policy for agricultural products, had a favorable effect on farm household incomes. Figure 1 shows that the rural-urban income differential narrowed after about 1960, and was not far from unity around 1970.

OTHER VARIABLES FOR ESTIMATING INCOME INEQUALITY IN THE PREWAR PERIOD

In this section, other variables in Equation 2 are taken into consideration: the proportion of urban population (W_u) and factor shares and income (or wage) differentials as proxies for intrasectoral income inequality (C_r, C_u).

Proportion of Urban Population

Wu is defined as the ratio of nonfarm population to total population. It increased gradually from about 30 percent at the end of the last century to 44 percent around 1940 (Ohkawa 1973, Table 5). Table 1 shows the coefficients of variation C calculated by substituting hypothetical values into Equation 2. In this table the values of C_r and C_u in case B are approximately equal to the postwar averages of the coefficients of variation, as discussed in the following section, and the range of λ is based on the real income differentials shown in Figure 1.

Table 1
Coefficients of Variation in Hypothetical Cases

Case		W_u =	$\lambda = 1.5$	2.0	2.5	3.0
A	$C_r = 0.6$ $C_u = 0.7$	0.3	0.693	0.788	0.844	0.971
		0.5	0.713	0.791	0.862	0.920
		0.7	0.715	0.765	0.805	0.837
B	$C_r = 0.7$ $C_u = 0.8$	0.3	0.790	0.884	0.979	1.066
		0.5	0.810	0.888	0.957	1.016
		0.7	0.814	0.862	0.902	0.933
C	$C_r = 0.8$ $C_u = 0.9$	0.3	0.890	0.982	1.077	1.165
		0.5	0.910	0.986	1.055	1.114
		0.7	0.913	0.961	1.000	1.032

Note: Figures are calculated by substituting values indicated for C_r, C_u, λ, and W_u into Equation 2.

The effect of an increase in W_u on income inequality as measured by C is not consistent, but depends on intersectoral income differentials, and seems to be smaller than the effects of other factors such as C_r, C_u, and λ. If we confine W_u to between 0.3 and 0.5 in accordance with prewar data on the rate of urbanization, the effect of urbanization becomes even smaller. Therefore, in the prewar period, per capita income differentials between the sectors (λ) and intrasector income inequalities (C_r, C_u) have more important effects on size distribution of income in the economy as a whole than the shift of farm population to urban areas.[4]

Proxies for Intrasector Income Inequality

Agricultural sector. Relative income shares of land, labor, and capital in agricultural income are presented in Table 2. An increase in the relative share of land means a larger part of the agricultural income produced by tenant farmers accrues to landowners, so it may be regarded as a sign of widening inequality in agriculture. According to Table 2, column 1, the relative share of land decreased temporarily in the years 1925 and 1930, but was almost constant over the entire period under observation.

Table 2

Factor Shares of Income in the Agricultural Sector
(in percent)

	Land (1)	Labor (2)	Capital (3)
1885	30.5	57.1	12.4
1890	32.8	54.3	12.9
1895	34.1	53.9	12.0
1900	33.0	55.9	11.1
1905	33.3	55.5	11.2
1910	33.1	55.8	11.1
1915	33.1	55.0	11.9
1920	33.5	54.8	11.7
1925	28.9	58.9	12.2
1930	26.7	61.0	12.3
1935	32.1	54.7	13.2

Source: Yamada and Hayami 1973.
Note: Figures for 1885 are 1885-89 averages. The others are five-year averages. The relative share of capital is derived by subtracting the other two relative shares from 100.

[4]Urbanization is accompanied by an increase in employes, which mitigates income inequality in the nonagricultural sector. Notice the explanation in the text assumes income distribution in the nonagricultural sector is independent of the rate of urbanization.

Another proxy for estimating income inequality within the agricultural sector is the ratio of the income differential between tenant and owner farmers. In most cases landowners rented out agricultural equipment together with land (Kajinishi 1969, p. 269), so the numerator of labor's relative share is equal to the income per tenant farmer. On the other hand, if we assume equality of labor productivities between the owner farmer and the tenant farmer, the denominator of the relative share is the total income per worker which the owner-farmer produces, using all factors of production. Therefore, labor's relative share can be interpreted as being the ratio of the per capita income of tenant farmers to that of owner-farmers. We owe this interpretation to Umemura (1961, p. 86). Table 2 shows these income differentials were fairly stable.

Other evidence is available to reinforce these conclusions. The survey of farm households conducted by Saito Mankichi for the years 1890-1920 provides supporting evidence on the behavior of labor's income share. Table 3 compares consumption expenditures per household of tenant and owner-farmers. This comparison also indicates the differential of consumption was fairly stable at a level of about 55 percent except in 1908. The reason for this exception is not yet understood.

On this basis, there appears to have been long-run stability of income inequality within the prewar agricultural sector, in spite of the temporary narrowing of the differential in 1925 and 1930.

Nonagricultural sector. Two proxies are adopted for estimating income inequality within the nonagricultural sector: labor's relative share, and wage differential by scale. As nonwage incomes are distributed more to higher income households, a decrease in labor's relative share may be assumed to increase the inequality of income distribution. This assumption is reinforced by the fact the differential of rates of capital return is larger than that of

Table 3
Differences in Consumption per Household
between Owner-Farmers and Tenant Farmers

	Owner-farmers (1)	Tenant farmers (2)	Ratio (3) = (2)/(1)
1890	196 yen	107 yen	54.6%
1899	306	180	58.8
1908	406	253	62.3
1911	555	311	56.0
1912	634	357	56.3
1920	1227	645	52.6

Source: Figures are from Mankichi Saito's research cited in Shinohara 1967, p. 25.

Table 4
Labor's Relative Share in the Nonprimary Sector
(in percent)

1885	80.3[a]	1915	57.3
1890	77.2	1920	66.6
1895	73.6	1925	67.2
1900	68.6	1930	64.3
1905	65.4	1935	61.5
1910	65.3	1940	58.3[b]

Source: Minami and Ono, unpublished.
[a]Average of 1885-87.
[b]Average of 1938-40.

wages. Watanabe (1970) has confirmed this fact by using cross-sectional data by industry. Table 4 reveals labor's relative share decreased during the periods 1885-1905 and 1930-40. Labor's relative share before 1905 is preliminary, so we cannot put much emphasis on the decrease in labor's relative share in 1885-1905.

Wage differentials are a proxy for income inequality of urban employe households. Wage differential by scale of firm is used because income inequality in the nonagricultural sector can be assumed to be closely related to the coexistence of small and big businesses. Often quoted data on scale-oriented wage differentials for the prewar period are (1) manufacturing wages by the number of operatives, available for the years 1909 and 1914 from the Kōjō Tōkei-hyō, and (2) wages by the amount of capital per firm, which are available for several cities in 1932 from the Kōgyō Chōsasho.[5] Recently, Yasuba found data on wages by scale for 1885 in the second Nōshōmu Tōkeihyō and analyzes them in his essay in this volume.

They showed no systematic pattern in wage differentials by scale in 1885, but slightly scale-oriented wage differentials could be perceived in the 1909 and 1914 data, and in 1932 wage differentials by scale became wider than in the previous years. It could be said that in the early Meiji years, old established firms hiring skilled workers were rather small, whereas new expanding firms were large-scale businesses employing young unskilled workers. Therefore, if wages were standardized with respect to skill as well as sex, wage differentials by scale could be shown to exist in 1885 to the same extent as in 1909 and 1914.[6] If so, it is still possible to maintain the opinion commonly held by Japanese economists, that wage differentials appeared

[5]Umemura (1955 and 1961) was the first person to analyze these data. Yasuba (1967) has intensively analyzed the prewar wage differentials by scale.

[6]There was no trend, either widening or narrowing, in occupational wage differentials for the years 1885-1912. Coefficients of variation calculated from the data for seventeen occupations were 29.9 percent in 1885-87, 27.2 percent in 1892, 27.1 percent in 1894-97, 27.8 percent in 1898-1902, 29.4

some time between about 1910 and the mid-1920s. Research by Minami (1973) and Odaka (1967 and 1970) clarify the emergence of scale-oriented wage differentials in the early half of the 1920s. Thus, in the 1920s there occurred some changes exerting unequalizing effects on the size distribution of income for urban employe households.

The Estimation of C in the Prewar Economy

Of the four variables in Equation 2, λ, W_u, C_u, and C_r, the last two are not directly available. However, by combining direct observation of λ and W_u with indirect observation of C_u and C_r, it is possible to trace the movement of income inequality for the prewar period, although it is inevitably incomplete. One noteworthy feature of the observed movements of income distribution is the widening in income inequality that seems to have occurred in the 1920s. As wage differentials by scale widened in the 1920s and labor's relative share declined in the 1930s, it is possible that income distribution in the nonprimary sector (C_u) became more unequal in the years after about 1920. In the agricultural sector, however, the decreasing relative share of land and the narrowing income differentials between tenants and owner-farmers during the period 1925-30 might have lessened C_r. It is difficult to evaluate quantitatively the net effect of these offsetting changes. But assuming for the sake of simplicity that the effects of changes in C_u and C_r were negligible in the economy as a whole, then, as the effect of urbanization was also rather small, a depiction of income inequality (C) can be obtained mainly from the intersectoral real income differential (λ) depicted in Figure 1. Indeed, in view of the widening differential in the years 1920-38, income inequality also started to increase in the same period.

In the years prior to 1920, the intersectoral real income differential, the relative share of land, the income differential between tenants and owner-farmers, and the wage differentials in the nonprimary sector were fairly stable over the long term. Therefore, reflecting the downward trend in labor's relative share in the nonprimary sector suggested by the preliminary estimates, income inequality in the economy as a whole may have widened slightly in the years 1885-1905—slightly, because the nonprimary sector loses its relative importance as we go back to earlier years.

In Meiji, there were changes in ownership of land from small owner-farmers to wealthy persons including large landowners, merchants, and usurers. Land of small farmers unable to pay the land tax was foreclosed by the government, put up for auction, and purchased by the rich (Yamaguchi 1968, p. 150). This leads to the inference income inequality increased at that time. Some fragmentary data on per capita consumption differentials are available

---

percent in 1903-07, and 30.9 percent in 1908-12 (Rōdō Undō Shiryō Iinkai 1959, 10:270-273). A similar trend was noticed by Taira (1970, p. 16) in wage differentials by industry in the manufacturing sector. Wage differentials by age and those by industry in the nonprimary sector, if available, would also help us infer the changes in urban income differentials.

Table 5
Differences in Per Capita Consumption Expenditures between Lower and Upper Classes in Tochigi and Shizuoka Prefectures in the Early Meiji Period
(lower as percentage of upper classes)

| Period | Tochigi prefecture | | | Shizuoka prefecture | |
	Agriculture	Industry	Commerce	Year	Total
1868-72	46.8	55.7	45.8	1868	36.3
1873-77	45.3	54.0	44.9	1872	38.1
1878-82	43.8	56.6	42.3	1877	43.3
1883-87	42.8	55.9	40.7	1882	49.2
1888-90	42.8	57.6	42.7	1887	36.2
1891-93	42.7	59.2	43.1	1892	37.6

Source: Figures are from *Kaheiseido Chōsakai Hōkoku*, cited in Shinohara 1967, p. 24.

to help verify this. According to Table 5, in the agricultural sector in Tochigi prefecture, the ratio of per capita consumption of the lower class to that of the upper class decreased from 1868-72 to 1883-87. Judging from the importance of agriculture, in this prefecture as a whole per capita consumption differentials most likely widened, and therefore income distribution also became more unequal during this period. In Shizuoka prefecture, however, per capita consumption differentials narrowed during the years 1868-82. The existence of these contradictory examples suggests the effect on income distribution of the concentration of land should not be exaggerated.

Some drawbacks exist concerning the income tax data. The coverage for the prewar period is restricted to high-income groups, and is affected by changes in the tax system. Nonetheless, Pareto's coefficients calculated from the income tax data, shown in Table 6, indicate a change in equality similar to that estimated from the related variables and proxies mentioned previously.[7] The coefficients began to decrease in 1915, indicating an increase in income inequality. The decrease in Pareto's coefficient for 1915 was caused by an abnormal increase in the share of nonwage incomes during the boom years of World War I.[8] Excluding those boom years (1917-19) in order to observe the long-run trend, Pareto's coefficient starts to decline from about 1920.

[7]The income tax statistics classify incomes into three categories: corporate income, interest from various kinds of bonds, and all other kinds of personal income. Pareto's coefficients in the text are for incomes of the third category. The coefficients are obtainable for the years prior to 1900, but the income tax statistics before that time differ from subsequent statistics because the three categories are combined, and the data show the number of taxpayers (rather than households) for each income class. Due to these differences in data, Pareto's coefficients in the years before 1900 are omitted. Kokumin Seikatsu Kenkyū-jo (1965), Shiomi et al. (1933), and Takahashi (1955) should be referred to for analyses using these income tax data.

[8]This same short-run increase in nonwage incomes can also be found in the

INCOME INEQUALITY IN THE POST-WORLD WAR II PERIOD

The size distribution of income in the post-World War II years seems to be more nearly equal than prewar. Data on income distribution supplïed by the United States Department of State for 1930 (Lockwood 1968, p. 272) yield a far higher coefficient of variation (202.8 percent) than those calculated from the *Employment Status Survey* for the postwar period, which are less than 90 percent. The reason for the great magnitude of the 1930 coefficient is that income differentials were very wide that year. The income tax data are also available. Comparison of Lorenz curves between 1939 and 1955 shows a narrowing of income inequality in the postwar years (Hitotsubashi 1951, pp. 10-11).

The Bureau of Statistics *Employment Status Survey* (Sōrifu, *Shūgyō*), covering about one percent of all households and conducted every three years since 1956, provides data on average income per household and number of households for each income class both by major industrial group and by employment status.[9] Figure 3 shows coefficients of variation obtained from this source. The surveys for 1968 and 1971 do not contain average income data for respective income classes; therefore these two years are omitted from

Table 6
Pareto's Coefficient

1905	1.87	
1910	1.90	
1915	1.81	$(1.87)^a$
1920	1.70	$(1.78)^b$
1925	1.72	
1930	1.66	
1935	1.65	
1940	1.57^c	

Source: Calculated from the data in Shiomi et al. 1933 and Taka-hashi 1955.
[a]1913-16 average.
[b]1920-22 average.
[c]1938-39 average.

---

sharp decrease in labor's relative share in the nonprimary sector in 1915 as shown in Table 4.

[9]In the *Employment Status Survey* (Sōrifu, *Shūgyō*) households are classified into income classes by income per household. The number of income classes differs from year to year: eleven in 1956, thirteen in 1959, twelve in 1962, thirteen in 1965, and ten in 1968 and in 1971. The occupation of the head of the household is used to classify the household by industry and employment status. The head of the household is defined as the person who assumes responsibility for the income of the family.

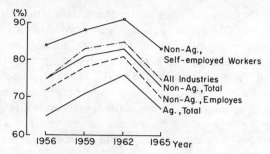

Figure 3. Coefficients of variation by industry and employment status.

Source: Sōrifu, *Shūgyō.*

Notes: Ag. means agriculture and forestry, and *nonag.* means all other industries. Figures in 1965 are for ordinary households; others are for all households (ordinary households plus one-person households). Households whose heads are without jobs are excluded.

Table 7
Coefficients of Quartile Deviation by Industry and Employment Status
(in percent)

	1956	1959	1962	1968	1971
All industries	45.0	48.5	46.2	43.4	42.9
Agriculture	44.4	46.1	44.5	43.0	45.5
Nonagriculture	44.2	46.6	45.3	43.9	42.6
Self-employed	55.5	48.9	48.1	48.9	48.0
Employe	43.1	45.7	44.4	42.6	41.3

Source: Sōrifu, *Shugyo.*

Note: Agriculture means agriculture and forestry, and *non-agriculture* means all industries other than agriculture.

Figures are for all households (ordinary households plus one-person households), but households whose heads are without jobs are excluded. The concept of income for the 1956-62 surveys differs from that for the 1968-71 surveys, as mentioned in the text.

Figure 3. To include data for these years, Table 7 gives coefficients of quartile deviation calculated from the same source.[10]

There is a difference in the concept of income between the surveys until 1965 and those from 1968. Before the 1968 survey, household income included not only income from work but also returns from assets (such as rent, dividends, and interest, but excluding capital gains) and social security

[10]Let Q_1, Q_3, and Me be the first quartile, the third quartile and the median, respectively. Then the coefficient of quartile deviation is defined as $1/2 (Q_3 - Q_1)/Me$.

benefits, whereas from the 1968 survey it excludes returns from assets and social security benefits. However, this change may have only a minor effect on statistics of income distribution. The reason for this conjecture is that asset income and social security benefits as percentages of household income are very small, being 2.1 percent and 1.2 percent, respectively, for all households in 1965. In addition, these two income components offset each other. Exclusion of returns from assets narrows measured income inequality, because most are received by higher income groups. (For all industries in 1965, asset income as a share of household income was 1.9 percent for the less-than-¥200,000 income class, and 7.9 percent for the more-than-¥2,000,000 income class.) On the other hand, excluding social security benefits widens measured inequality, because they go mostly to lower income groups. (The proportions of social security benefits were 12.8 percent and 0.2 percent, respectively, for the previously cited income classes.)

Observations from the surveys follow:

1. Coefficients of variation for the economy as a whole are 75 percent for 1956, 83 percent for 1959, 85 percent for 1962, and 75 percent for 1965. As is shown in the note to Figure 3, data in 1965 do not include one-person households, which are mostly in lower income groups. It is certain exclusion of one-person households has exaggerated to some extent the reduction in income inequality for the years from 1962 to 1965. However, the same pattern of changes can be found in the data for ordinary households. Corresponding coefficients of variation calculated from data which exclude one-person households are 73 percent for 1956, 80 percent for 1959, 82 percent for 1962, and 77 percent for 1965. The difference between 75 percent and 77 percent in 1965 comes from the inclusion of household heads without jobs. Coefficients of quartile deviation given in Table 7 show similar movements of income inequality, that is, an increase until about 1960 and then a decrease.

2. Coefficients of quartile deviation in the agricultural sector increased from 43.0 percent in 1968 to 45.5 percent in 1971. The increase in coefficients between these two years obscures the trend for the postwar period. However, according to the Ministry of Agriculture and Forestry (Nōrinshō, *Nōka Seikeihi*), coefficients of variations are 47.1 percent for 1955-57, 46.8 percent for 1959-62,[11] 45.1 percent for 1963-67, and 44.7 percent for 1968-70, showing decreasing income inequality in recent years, which is consistent with the recent remarkable narrowing in differentials in farm household incomes by land area cultivated, as will be discussed here.

Figure 3 and Table 7 make clear that income inequality is higher in the nonagricultural sector than in the agricultural sector for most years. This is due to greater diversity of occupations in urban areas and the existence of farm workers willing to accept urban occupations at low wage rates (Gannagé 1968; Kravis 1960). To these factors we can add the *nenkō joretsu chingin*

[11]The data in 1953, 1954, and 1958 are not available. Therefore five-year averages centering on 1955 and 1960 cannot be obtained.

(seniority wage system), one of the main determinants of wage differentials by scale, prevailing in the nonagricultural sector. This is the system whereby young workers hired by urban industries start at a low wage and gradually obtain higher wages as they get older. Therefore, income distribution is more unequal than if such a wide range of wage differentials by age did not exist.

3. As for inequality among self-employed worker households in the nonagricultural sector, there are some differences between Figure 3 and Table 7. Coefficients of quartile deviation in Table 7 move in a direction opposite to coefficients of variation in Figure 3 for the years 1956-62, and do not show any systematic tendency after 1959. Therefore, the narrowing of income inequality in the nonagricultural sector as a whole reflects changes in income inequality of employe households in this sector. This is reasonable, for employe households occupy the majority of nonagricultural households: 71 percent in 1956 and 82 percent in 1971. Coefficients of quartile deviation calculated for employe households from the *Employment Status Survey* began to narrow after about 1960. The same tendency can be observed in the coefficients of variation for urban employe households calculated from the Bureau of Statistics' *Annual Report on the Family Income and Expenditure Survey* (Sōrifu, *Kakei*). They were 50.9 percent in 1953-57, 51.3 percent in 1958-62, 45.6 percent in 1963-67, and 40.7 percent in 1968-70.

Income distribution in the nonagricultural sector is more unequal for self-employed worker households than for employe households, as self-employed worker households are distributed over a wider range, from proprietors of very small firms who barely earn their daily livelihood to successful owners who run fairly large companies.

4. Table 8 shows the differentials of income per household between agricultural and nonagricultural sectors (λ in Equation 2), and the proportion

Table 8
Intersectoral Income Differentials and
Proportions of Nonagricultural Households

Year	Income per nonagricultural household divided by income per agricultural household (λ)	Proportion of nonagricultural households (W_u)
1956	1.39	0.710
1959	1.57	0.738
1962	1.53	0.791
1965	1.41	0.820
1968	1.29	0.850
1971	1.19	0.884

Source: Sōrifu, *Shūgyo*.
Note: Figures are for all households (ordinary and one-person households).

of nonagricultural households in all households (W_u). In order to identify the effect of those two factors on C (income inequality in the economy as a whole), we have only to change λ and W_u, keeping other variables such as C_u and C_r constant at their values in (say) 1956. This computation yields changes in income inequality similar to actual values. Computation results show 75 percent for 1956, 77 percent for 1959, 76 percent for 1962, 76 percent for 1965, 75 percent for 1968, and 74 percent for 1971. These changes are, however, very small compared to the actual changes, suggesting that change in intrasectoral income inequality, expressed by C_u and C_r, is the main factor determining the movements of income distribution in the postwar period.

There is a marked difference in consumption patterns between low- and high-income groups. Expenditure on foodstuffs as a share of total consumption is larger in low-income groups, and miscellaneous expenses such as education, reading and recreation, and social expenses are larger in high-income groups. It follows that a relative rise in food prices, other things constant, makes the distribution of real income more unequal.

The Bureau of Statistics (Sōrifu, *Kakei*) provides data on income distribution by quintile group which serve to illustrate the effect of price increases on income inequality.[12] For each quintile group we can construct consumer price indexes with 1965 = 1, and thereby obtain real incomes by quintile group.[13] Coefficients of variation in terms of real incomes for urban employe households are shown with an index of 1965 = 100 in the upper part of Figure 4, and in the lower part the ratios of the coefficients of variation of real incomes to those of nominal incomes are depicted. According to this figure, there are no significant differences between the distributions of real income and of nominal income, a finding also obtained by Niida et al. (1972). This means prices are increasing in miscellaneous expenses as well as in foodstuffs, and in fact, price indexes of both have been rising at almost the same rate since 1955.

Figure 4 also shows that income inequality remained almost stable up to 1960, and then began to narrow rapidly. This is for urban employe households, but a similar result is obtained for all households in the nonagricultural sector from the Sōrifu's *Kakei* in the years 1964 to 1970.

If higher income groups support more family members than lower income groups, the coefficient of variation calculated from data for income classes by household income will overstate income inequality. To examine this problem,

---

[12]The *Annual Report on the Family Income and Expenditure Survey* covers about 4200 households in twenty-eight cities up to 1962, and thereafter about 8000 households in all of Japan. Households are confined to the nonprimary sector. Household income includes income from work, returns from assets, social security benefits, and so forth. (Sōrifu, *Kakei*).

[13]These indexes are constructed by weighting consumer price indexes of five major expenditure items with the consumption expenditures for respective income quintile groups.

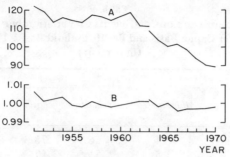

Figure 4. Coefficients of variations of
real incomes: urban-employe households.

Source: Sōrifu, Kakei.

Note: A = index of coefficient of variation of
real incomes (1965 = 100). B = ratio of
coefficient of variation of real incomes to that
of nominal incomes. Gaps in 1963 are due to a
change in income concept and enlargement of
coverage.

we need data on income distribution on a per capita basis. Such data,
however, are not available. Therefore, the average number of family members
in each income class is used as a rough adjustment. Coefficients of variation
calculated from these adjusted data are shown in Table 9, together with
coefficients based on household income. Because there is a positive
correlation between the average number of family members and income per
household, the distribution on a per capita income basis is more equal than
on a household income basis.[14]

Coefficients of variation shown in Figure 3 are affected by various kinds of
social security payments. The survey gives data on social security benefits for
each income class. From this, coefficients of variation of incomes exclusive of
such benefits can be calculated.[15] As can be seen in Table 10, the resulting
distribution is more unequal than that of incomes including benefits.
However, the difference in coefficients of variation between these two cases is
small, because the range of adjustment has not been extended to all benefits
in kind provided by the government nor to direct and indirect taxes.

[14]Strictly, we should use some adult equivalent base instead of a mere
average number of family members. Kuznets (1963, pp. 31-33) discovered a
correlation of household size and income exists for some countries in his
international comparison of income inequalities, but at the same time added
that, when we can distinguish subgroups by number of persons within each
income class, the shift from a per household basis to a per capita basis makes
income distribution more unequal.

[15]The subtraction of social security benefits from income does not mean
the complete exclusion of their effects on income distribution. Old-age
pensions, for instance, create separate households of aged people with
incomes too low to live without benefits, and thus widen inequality of
income excluding benefits. This effect cannot be eliminated by a mere adjustment of income with respect to benefits from social security.

Table 9
Comparison of Coefficients of Variation between
Per Capita Basis and Per Household Basis: 1965
(in percent)

	All industries	Agriculture	Nonagriculture		
			Total	Self-employed worker	Employe
Per household basis	75.1	66.9	73.3	83.1	70.1
Per capita basis	61.5	51.5	57.2	69.9	52.3

Source: Sōrifu, Shūgyo.
Note: Figures are for ordinary households. Households whose heads are without jobs are excluded.

Table 10
Effect of Social Security Benefits
on Coefficients of Variation
(in percent)

	1956	1959	1962	1965
(1) Income including benefits	73.0	79.5	82.1	76.8
(2) Income excluding benefits	74.1	81.4	83.2	77.7
(3) Ratio (1)/(2)	98.5	97.7	98.7	98.8

Source: Sōrifu, Shūgyo.
Note: Figures are for ordinary households. Households whose heads are without jobs are included.

EXPLANATION OF THE CHANGES IN INCOME INEQUALITY

The analysis in the previous sections reveals the long-run changes in income distribution that occurred in the Japanese economy. The reduction in inequality from the prewar to the postwar periods can be attributed to several factors. Trade unions organized mainly in large establishments may have widened wage differentials by scale in the postwar period. However, it also may be true that the effect of widening wage differentials on income distribution was smothered by the following factors: (1) labor's relative share in the nonprimary sector was higher in the postwar period than in the 1930s;[16] (2) land reform removed a major cause of unequal distribution in agriculture through a drastic reduction in the number of tenant farmers; and (3) the rural-urban real income differential was narrower in the postwar years than at the end of the prewar period.

[16]It was 75 percent in 1955 and 70 percent in 1960, because of the increase in the supply price of labor caused by the postwar land reform.

Particularly of note in the long-term movement in income distribution is the widening of inequality in the 1920s and the tendency toward equality which occurred in the postwar period. As emphasized before, this had to do with the development of wage differentials by factory size.

The explanation for the emergence of scale-oriented wage differentials in the 1920s is as follows. During the boom period after the outbreak of World War I, a group of modern industries developed rapidly and many firms encountered a shortage of skilled workers. Especially in industries where advanced technologies imported from abroad required new types of skilled workers, entrepreneurs had to train them within their own firms. As an example, demand for skilled workers such as lathe operators, assemblers, and finishers was newly created by the introduction of advanced technology from abroad (Nōshōmushō 1903, 2:97). Introduction of new technology was mainly confined to big firms. They paid higher wages, even in the slump after World War I, in order to keep scarce, skilled workers. Wages of unskilled workers, however, went down during the slump. Wide wage differentials by skill also played a role in isolating workers from the labor movement, which was becoming more radical at that time. Wage differentials by skill have a similarity to those by age, which promise higher wages to older men, and hence stimulate workers' loyalty to their company (Nakamura 1961, pp. 52-53; Sumiya 1967, pp. 20 and 188).

Large firms could pay higher wages to skilled workers because of the higher labor productivity possible using imported technology.[17] Moreover, capital equipment which embodies new technological knowledge necessitates a large investment, and the allocation of investment funds was favorable to big firms. Besides the government policy of promoting so-called modern industries (industries which included most of the big enterprises), the bankruptcy and amalgamation of small banks in the 1920s accelerated concentration of investment funds in zaibatsu companies.[18] Thus, the concentration of funds and the advanced technologies imported gave rise to wide differences in capital intensities by firm size, hence in labor productivity, which in turn made it feasible for big firms to pay higher wages to skilled workers. Whether scale is used as a proxy for skill or as important for other reasons, the net effect is a significant difference in incomes for workers in large and in small firms. In addition, the slowing of labor migration from the countryside to the cities in the 1920s depressed labor productivity in agriculture and widened the rural-urban income differential. These are the main facts explaining rising income inequality in the 1920s.

The agricultural sector is the chief source of unskilled workers, whose supply price depends on technological conditions in this sector, the natural rate of increase in the farm population, and the growth rate of the

[17]Watanabe (1970) and Yasuba (1967 and in his essay in this volume) also emphasize the importance of imported technology as a determinant of scale-oriented wage differentials.

[18]This hypothesis has been proposed by Shinohara (1961).

Table 11
Differentials in Per Capita Farm Household Income by Land Area Cultivated
(per capita income as a percentage of per capita income
of households cultivating 2.0 or more hectares)

	0.3-0.4	0.5-0.9	1.0-1.4	1.5-1.9	2.0-
1955	69.8	70.1	80.3	90.3	100.0
1960	75.2	70.6	76.6	85.2	100.0
1965	86.9	81.1	83.0	88.0	100.0
1970	110.2	98.8	95.1	91.3	100.0

Source: Nōrinshō, Nōkai Keizai.
Note: Farm household income is composed of income from farm and nonfarm sources.
A hectare is about 2.5 acres.

nonprimary sector. In contrast to the 1920s, rapid growth in the nonprimary
sector in postwar Japan caused a drastic reduction in the farm population,
steeply raising the wages of unskilled workers. Competition for unskilled
workers makes the labor market more mobile and more national in scope, and
tends to narrow various kinds of wage differentials such as those by region,
by scale of establishment, and by age of worker.[19] It also encourages some
small-scale firms heavily dependent on unskilled workers to become more
capital intensive. The same holds true in agriculture. Growth in the
nonprimary sector offers farm households opportunities for side occupations
outside the agricultural sector, which helps narrow the per capita income
differential within the sector (as is shown in Table 11) as well as between
sectors.

The effects of the rapid economic growth of postwar Japan on income
distribution can be summarized as follows:

1. Narrowing wage differentials reduced income inequality for urban
employe households. Changes in income distribution for all households in the
nonagricultural sector were similar to those for employe households in this
sector, as is clear from the coefficients of quartile deviation shown in Table 7.
This means the decreasing inequality in the nonagricultural sector has been
determined mainly by the narrowing wage differentials.

2. Rapid expansion of the nonagricultural sector increased labor migration
away from agriculture. The decrease of farm households, especially among
small-scale farms, tended to equalize income distribution in the agricultural
sector. More abundant opportunities for side occupations also gave rise to
narrower income inequality within the agricultural sector, because it was
easier for small farmers to supplement their income by earnings outside
agriculture.

3. The narrowing in per capita real income differentials between urban
employe households and farm households is attributable to the increase in

[19] Some of these wage differentials are intensively analyzed by Ono (1973).

nonfarm income within farm household income. If nonfarm income had been excluded from farm household income, the rural-urban income differential would have continued to widen for the entire postwar period; the ratios of per capita real income of urban employe households to that of farm households would have been 2.29 in 1950-52, 2.56 in 1953-57, 2.85 in 1958-62, 2.88 in 1963-67, and 2.97 in 1968-70. Thus, growth of the nonagricultural sector certainly made income distribution more equal through the decrease in the rural-urban income differential.

Kuznets (1955, p. 18) assumed a long swing in equality as characterizing the secular income structure: widening in the early phases of economic growth, becoming stabilized for a while, and then narrowing in the later phases. Our findings seem compatible with his assumption, although some reservations should be made: (1) prewar changes in income inequality are estimated from indirect observations; (2) it may be a little too early to regard the narrowing income inequality in recent years as the start of a long-run trend; and (3) there might be quite a different picture of inequality, especially in recent years, if income is defined as including capital gains.

Long-run changes in income distribution have been accompanied by a rising trend of per capita real income. Per capita incomes are depicted in Figure 5 for farm and urban employe households. The increase in per capita real income can be found not only for urban employe households but also for farm households. Farm household income is composed of farm income and nonfarm income. The former is determined by output per worker in the agricultural sector, and the latter by employment opportunities and the level of earnings, both of which are offered by the nonagricultural sector.

Figure 5 reveals a rapid increase in the per capita income of farm households after World War II, which owes much to the increase in nonfarm income. Nonfarm income as a percentage of farm household income rose from about 40 percent in 1950 to 65 percent in 1970. A high proportion of nonfarm income has an important effect on income distribution, as previously discussed. In an international comparison of the income inequalities

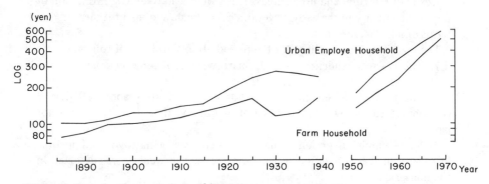

Figure 5. Trends of per capita real incomes.

Source: The estimating procedures are given in the statistical appendix.
Note: Per capita incomes in 1886, 1939, 1951, and 1969 are three-year averages, and others are five-year averages.

in five countries (Ceylon, Malaya, Japan, the Philippines, and the United States), Oshima (1962) found the lowest inequality in Japan. He suggested the explanation lay in Japan's high percentage of nonfarm income earned by farm households, a point consistent with our analysis.

CONCLUDING REMARKS

This final section is devoted to a summary of the previous discussion. For the prewar period, reliable data are not available. Therefore, long-run changes in income distribution were estimated on the basis of certain data connected with income distribution. Allowing for unavoidable shortcomings in the data, our conclusions are as follows.

1. Income inequality expressed by the coefficient of variation depends on the rural-urban per capita real income differential, the proportion of urban population, and income inequality within rural and urban areas.

2. The differential of per capita real income between rural and urban areas was almost stable before 1915, and then increased sharply.

3. The effect of urbanization on income inequality was negligible.

4. Certain data compiled for agricultural and nonagricultural sectors suggest income inequality in the agricultural sector decreased, and in the nonagricultural sector increased, after about 1920.

5. On the assumption that the effects of changes in income inequality within the urban and rural sectors canceled out in the economy as a whole, we submit that changes in the rural-urban income differential caused the changes in income distribution in prewar Japan. Our estimates of intersectoral income differentials suggest an increase in income inequality in the 1920s. This is in accordance with the changes in Pareto's coefficients calculated from income tax data.

6. Unlike per capita *real* incomes, there were large differentials in per capita *nominal* incomes between farm households and urban employe households in the Meiji era. This was due to wide differences in consumer prices between rural and urban areas. This would lead to an overestimation of income inequality in the early stages of economic development if measured in terms of nominal incomes.

The main empirical findings for the period after World War II follow.

7. There was a tendency toward a narrowing of income inequality in the economy as a whole after about 1960.

8. The rural-urban income differential decreased after about 1960, and contributed to the overall narrowing of inequality, though its effect was not large.

9. Some empirical evidence indicates there was a narrowing of income inequality in the agricultural sector. A decreasing inequality was detected in the nonagricultural sector also.

On the basis of the preceding, several remarks can be made for the entire observation period.

10. Income inequality in Japan increased in the 1920s, was less in the early postwar period than prewar, and started to decrease about 1960.

11. This finding is compatible with Kuznets's hypothesis, though a quite different picture of inequality in recent years might emerge if capital gains are taken into consideration.

STATISTICAL APPENDIX

Estimation of Farm Household Income

Farm household income is composed of income from farm and nonfarm sources. The Umemura data on net value added give fairly reliable information about farm income, but not about nonfarm income. Therefore, the latter, or the sum of both incomes, must be estimated to obtain farm household income.

Farm household income, Y, is estimated as

$$Y = V \cdot \frac{Y'}{V'} \cdot \mu \qquad (1)$$

where variables, all on a per household basis, are defined as

Y: Farm household income, composed of both farm income and nonfarm income.

V: Net value added in agriculture, available from LTES 9 for every year before World War II and from Keizai Kikakuchō, *Kokumin Shotoku*, for the postwar years.

Y': Farm household income. Data are available for every year in the postwar period, but only for occasional years in the prewar period. See Inaba (1952) for the prewar period, and Nōrinshō, *Nōka Keizai*, for the postwar period.

V': Net value added in agriculture, from Nōrinshō, *Nōka Keizai*. As in the case of Y', V' is available only for occasional years in the prewar period.

μ: Coefficient for adjusting the ratio (Y'/V') for the upward bias of the figures from Nōrinsho, *Noka Keizai*. In order to obtain this coefficient, we estimated the equation

$$Y' = \alpha (V')^{\beta} \qquad (2)$$

by using the cross-sectional data by scale of farm compiled in *Nōka Keizai*. Suppose that the equation can be applied to the relation between Y and V. Then we have

$$Y = \alpha (V)^{\beta} \qquad (3)$$

By taking the ratio of Y to Y', we get

$$\frac{Y}{Y'} = \left(\frac{V}{V'}\right)^{\beta}$$

or

$$Y = V \cdot \left(\frac{Y'}{V'}\right) \cdot \left(\frac{V}{V'}\right)^{\beta-1} \qquad (4)$$

In the preceding equation, V/V' is a measure of the upward bias of Nōrinshō,

Nōka Keizai, and $\left(\frac{V}{V'}\right)^{\beta-1}$ is equal to the adjusting coefficient μ. Due to the availability of data, the 1951 *Nōka Keizai* was used for estimating the parameter β, which was then used for all the prewar years. For the postwar years β was estimated using data for 1962, which is about the center of the postwar observation period.

Y'/V' and V/V' are available for years when the *Survey of Farm Household Economy* was conducted, and the ratios for other years are estimated by linear interpolation. Thus we have year-to-year data on Y'/V' and μ. By substituting them, together with V, into Equation 1 in this appendix, we get the values of Y. By dividing Y by the average number of persons in farm households, the series of per capita incomes of farm households is obtained.

Estimation of Income of Urban Employe Households

For the prewar period, data on per capita incomes is available for 1921-22 from Kyōchō-kai (1925), and for 1926-27 and after 1931-32 from the Naikaku Tōkei-kyoku. Per capita incomes for the years when these surveys were not conducted were estimated by linking with the average wages in the nonprimary sector. For every year after World War II, per capita incomes are available from Sōrifu (*Kakei*).

In estimating per capita income of urban employe households for the prewar period, the income data available from Kyōchō-kai and Naikaku Tōkei-kyoku were used without any modification. However, they are not based on random sampling, so representativeness of the data required checking. One of the methods used for checking was to compare the ratios of per capita income of urban employe households to wage income per employe between prewar and postwar years. The table shows this.

According to the upper part of the table, the prewar ratios are higher than the postwar one. However, these differences can be accounted for mainly by the differences in the average number of workers per household. For example, the estimated income ratio for 1922 is 2.40, if we use postwar figures and the number of workers per household in 1920. (That is, 2.15 ÷

Appendix table 1

	1922	1932	1960
Household income/Wage income per employe	2.50	2.40	2.15

	1920	1930	1960
Average number of workers per household in five urbanized prefectures	2.20	2.12	1.97

Source: Average number of workers is from Sōrifu, *Nippon*.
Note: The five urbanized prefectures are Tokyo, Aichi, Osaka, Hyōgo, and Fukuoka.

1.97 = $x \div 2.20$. Hence, $x = 2.40$.) In the same way, the ratio for 1932 is estimated at 2.31. Both are only slightly below the respective values appearing in the table. It follows that per capita income of urban employe households in the prewar period may be overestimated, but only to a slight extent.

Estimation of Difference in Consumer Prices between Rural and Urban Areas

To begin, we prepared consumer price indexes with 1934-36 = 1 for rural and urban areas, respectively. The price index in the urban areas, P_u, is available from LTES 8 and Sōrifu (*Kakei*). The consumer price index in the rural areas, P_r, is found in LTES 8 and Nōrinshō (*Nōson Shōhisha*). The price index for rural areas for the prewar years, however, does not fully reflect regional differences in consumer prices. Therefore, we estimated it by using

$$P = \gamma P_r + (1 - \gamma) P_u \qquad (5)$$

where P is the implicit price deflator for consumption expenditures, available from Ohkawa's worksheet, and γ is the fraction of rural consumption expenditures estimated by the same method adopted in estimating farm household income. In Equation 1 in this appendix, we had only to substitute farm household consumption (C') for Y', and make the required changes in the adjusting coefficient.

The difference in consumer prices between rural and urban areas in the base year (1934-36) was obtained by using the price levels of sixty commodities commonly available for respective areas from the statistical appendix of Ohkawa (1953). From the regional differences in prices in the base year and the price indexes for rural and urban areas, we estimated the relative prices between the areas, that is, the ratios of the consumer prices in the rural areas to those in the urban areas for the entire period under observation.

According to our estimating procedure, the relative price in 1960 was 0.94. This figure is very close to the relative price estimated for the same year by the Ministry of Agriculture and Forestry, which was 0.98 (see Nōrinshō 1961).

REFERENCES

Gannagé, Elias. 1968. "The Distribution of Income in Underdeveloped Countries." In *The Distribution of National Income*, edited by J. Marchall and Bernard Ducros. Macmillan.

Hitotsubashi Daigaku Keizai Kenkyū-jo [Institute of Economic Research, Hitotsubashi University]. 1961. *Kaisetsu Nippon Keizai Tōkei*. Iwanami Shoten.

Inaba, Taizo, ed. 1952. *Fukkoku-ban Nōka Keizai Chōsa Hōkoku*. Nōrin-shō Nōgyō Sōgō Kenkyū-jo.

Kajinishi, Mitsuhaya. 1969. *Nippon Shihonshugi Hattatsu Shi*, rev. ed. Yūhikaku.

Keizai Kikaku-chō [Economic Planning Agency]. *Kokumin Shotoku Tōkei Nenpō.*

Kokumin Seikatsu Kenkyū-jo [Social and Economic Affairs Research Institute]. 1965. *Shotoku Bunpu no Jittai oyobi Setai Kōzō Henka ni kansuru Kenkyū.*

Kravis, Irving B. 1960. "International Differences in the Distribution of Income." *Review of Economics and Statistics*, Nov. 1960.

Kuznets, Simon. 1955. "Economic Growth and Income Inequality." *American Economic Review*, March 1955.

———. 1963. "Quantitative Aspects of the Economic Growth of Nations: VIII. Distribution of Income by Size." *Economic Development and Cultural Change*, Jan. 1963.

Kyōchō-kai [Association of Cooperation]. 1925. *Hōkyū Seikatsu Sha Shokkō Sei Kei Chōsa Hōkoku.*

Lockwood, William W. 1968. *The Economic Development of Japan.* Princeton University Press.

LTES [Estimates of Long-Term Economic Statistics of Japan]. Series edited by Kazushi Ohkawa, Miyohei Shinohara, and Mataji Umemura. 1965-. 14 vols. Tōyō Keizai Shinpōsha.

———. Vol. 8. *Prices.* 1967. Kazushi Ohkawa et al.

———. Vol. 9. *Agriculture and Foestry.* Mataji Umemura et al.

Minami, Ryōshin. 1973. *The Turning Point in Economic Development: Japan's Experience.* Kinokuniya Bookstore.

Minami, Ryōshin, and Akira Ono. Unpublished. "Factor Prices and Relative Shares."

Morgan, James. 1962. "The Anatomy of Income Distribution." *Review of Economics and Statistics*, Aug. 1962.

Naikaku Tōkei-kyoku [Cabinet Statistics Bureau]. *Kakei Chōsa Hōkoku.*

Nakamura, Takafusa. 1961. "Kigyō Kibōbetsu Chingin Kakusa ni tsuite no Futatsu no Shiten." In *Nippon Gata Chingin Kōzō no Kenkyū*, edited by Miyohei Shinohara and Hisamichi Funabashi. Rōdō Hōgaku Kenkyū-jo.

Niida, Hiroshi, et al. 1972. "Infurēshon to Shotoku Saibunpai." *Keizai Bunseki* 39 (April 1972).

Nōrinshō [Ministry of Agriculture and Forestry]. *Nōka Keizai Chōsa Hōkoku.*

———. *Nōka Seikeihi Tōkei.*

———. *Nōson Shōhisha Bukka Chōsa.*

———. 1961. "Nōson to Toshi no Bukka-sa Santei ni tsuite." Mimeo.

Nōshōmushō [Ministry of Agriculture and Commerce]. 1903. *Shokkō Jijō.*

Odaka, Konosuke. 1967. "Kita Kyūshū ni okeru Kahei Chingin no Hendō." *Keizai Kenkyū*, July 1967.

———. 1970. "Chingin Keisha Kōzō no Chōki Hendō." *Nippon Rōdō Kyōkai Zasshi*, July and Aug. 1970.

Ohkawa, Kazushi. 1953. *Seikatsu Suijun no Sokutei.* Iwanami Shoten.

———. 1973. "Personal Consumption in Dualistic Growth." In *Economic Growth: The Japanese Experience since the Meiji Era*, vol. 2, edited by Kazushi Ohkawa and Yujirō Hayami. Japan Economic Research Center.

Ohkawa, Kazushi, and Henry Rosovsky. 1962. "Economic Fluctuations in Prewar Japan: A Preliminary Analysis of Cycles and Long Swings," *Hitotsubashi Journal of Economics*, Oct. 1962.

. 1968. "Postwar Japanese Economic Growth in Historical Perspective: A Second Look." In *Economic Growth: The Japanese Experience since the Meiji Era*, edited by Lawrence R. Klein and Kazushi Ohkawa. Irwin.

Ono, Akira. 1973. *Sengo Nihon no Chingin Kettei*. Tōyō Keizai Shinpō Sha.

Oshima, Harry T. 1962. "The International Comparison of Size Distribution of Family Incomes with Special Reference to Asia." *Review of Economics and Statistics*, Nov. 1962.

Rōdō Undō Shiryō Iinkai [Committee of Historical Statistics of Industrial Relations]. 1959. *Nippon Rōdō Undō Shiryō*, vol. 10: *Statistics*.

Shinohara, Miyohei. 1961. "Shihon Shūchū to Chingin Kōzō." In *Nippon Gata Chingin Kōzō no Kenkyū*, edited by Miyohei Shinohara and Hisamichi Funabashi. Rōdō Hōgaku Kenkyū-jo.

. 1967. *Kojin Shōhi Shishutsu*. Tōyō Keizai Shinpōsha.

Shiomi, Saburo, et al. 1933. *Kokumin Shotoku no Bunpai*. Yūhikaku.

Sōrifu, Tōkei-kyoku [Office of the Prime Minister, Statistics Bureau]. *Kakei Chōsa Nenpō*.

. *Nippon no Jinkō*.

. *Shūgyō Kōzō Kihon Chōsa*.

Sumiya, Mikio. 1967. *Nippon no Rōdō Mondai*. Tokyo Daigaku Shuppan Kai.

Swamy, Subramanian. 1965. "Pattern of Income Distribution in an Under-developed Economy: A Case Study of India: Comment." *American Economic Review*, Dec. 1965.

Taira, Koji. 1970. *Economic Development and the Labor Market in Japan*. Columbia University Press.

Takahashi, Chotaro. 1955. *Shotoku Bunpu no Hendō Yoshiki*. Iwanami Shoten.

Umemura, Mataji. 1955. "Chingin Kakusa to Rōdō Shijō." In *Nippon Keizai no Bunseki*, vol. 2, edited by Shigeto Tsuru and Kazushi Ohkawa. Keisō Shobō.

. 1961. *Chingin, Koyō, Nōgyō*. Taimeidō.

Watanabe, Tsunehiko. 1970. *Sūryō Keizai Bunseki*. Sōbun Sha.

Yamada, Saburo, and Yūjiro Hayami. 1973. "Agriculture." In *Economic Growth: The Japanese Experience since the Meiji Era*, vol. 1, edited by Kazushi Ohkawa and Yūjiro Hayami. Japanese Economic Research Center.

Yamaguchi, Kazuo. 1968. *Nihon Keizai-shi*. Chikuma Shobō.

Yasuba, Yasukichi. 1967. "Emergence of 'Dualism' in Japan's Wage Structure." In "Dai-5-kai, Kenkyū-kai Gijiroku," mimeo, edited by Keiryō Keizai Gaku Kenkyū-kai.

Poverty in Modern Japan: Perceptions and Realities

Masayoshi Chūbachi and Koji Taira

THE FRAME OF REFERENCE

Evolving perceptions and the realities of poverty in the course of Japan's economic development and modernization since the Meiji Restoration of 1868 are this paper's concern. Whom the Japanese public has considered "poor" at various times, how awareness of their condition has improved over the years, how those conditions have changed with time, and how the number of poor has varied in relation to the total population are all explored.

We must confess at the outset that poverty is an annoyingly unclear subject for tidy discussion and a discouragingly murky area for technical research. However, as Japan is a society where equality of opportunity for upward mobility through individual effort is considered a basic part of the socioeconomic process, attitudes toward poverty are a mirror image of those toward wealth. This means poverty in Japan can be meaningfully discussed using a bundle of theories on relative poverty associated with such names as Veblen (1899), Duesenberry (1949), Galbraith (1958), Harrington (1962), Townsend (1962), Abel-Smith (1966), Lewis (1965), Ornati (1966), and Scitovsky (1973). Common to these authors is the notion poverty involves not only material deprivation, but also a life style distinctly different from the generally prevailing one.

Poverty is relative to time and place, because it is relative to the average standard and style of living in each society. Moreover, the average residents of a community consider the poor not only different, but indecent. Galbraith notes, "People are poverty-stricken when their income, even if adequate for survival, falls markedly behind that of the community. Then they cannot have what the larger community regards as the minimum necessary for decency; and they cannot wholly escape, therefore, the judgment of the larger community that they are indecent. They are degraded for, in the literal sense, they live outside the grades or categories which the community regards as acceptable" (Galbraith 1958, p. 261).

391

Standards of living thus have social dimensions such as decency and acceptability, which define the standing of an individual in society. The subjective implication of the average is the cozy feeling of full membership in society, and all kinds of human values and emotions take part in defining this. Socialization, assimilation, and acculturation in any ongoing social system ensure members have the faculty for discerning class status. These processes also bring about a high degree of congruence between the class one perceives as one's own and the class society assigns one to.

This essay is an overview of the history of poverty in Japan, subject to qualifications in the first section on the place of poverty in the Japanese world view. To a large extent, this is a generalized form of historical ethnography of the urban poor trapped in *hinmin-kutsu* ("Grottos of the poor," ghettos, or slums). The topics covered include the habitats, incomes, jobs, and life styles of the poor. Using data on the size distribution of income, we end with a discussion of the extent of poverty in Japan, and the progress that has been made toward its abolition.

POVERTY IN THE JAPANESE WORLD VIEW

Initial Stratification by Income

In the early 1880s, Masana Maeda, author of *Kōgyō Iken*, classified the population by living conditions. There were three grades: *jōtō*, *chūtō*, and *katō* (superior, intermediate, and inferior). The first step in the grading was the assumption, "It is customarily believed that the common people of the inferior grade devote one half of the total cost of living to the expenditure on rice." Maeda then assumed the per capita rice requirement was 1.8 koku a year, which at that time (January 1884) cost ¥5.597 a koku (1971, 1:40-42). Thus the per capita cost of living for the inferior grade comprising the expenditure on 1.8 koku of rice and the same amount on nonrice foods, clothing, shelter, and other necessities equaled ¥20.15 per annum. Maeda assumed the cost of living for the superior grade required at least ten times, and for the intermediate grade at least five times, the annual rice requirement of the low grade. These assumptions resulted in the distribution of the population as superior, 13.3 percent; intermediate, 29.2; and inferior, 57.5.

It may be noted, however, the consumption of rice alone at the annual rate of 1.8 koku per person is a rather generous estimate for a grade of living considered "inferior." Maeda also assumed rice consumption was the same for all grades (an assumption of zero income elasticity of demand for rice, which would invite instant objections from modern economists). From the Meiji period until the 1930s, the standard of public relief for aged adults was the cash equivalent of 1.8 koku of rice, exactly one-half the cost of living for Maeda's "inferior" grade. Further, it is not clear whether Maeda's figures meant a minimum or average cost of living for each grade. This important point is fortunately clarified by contemporary official data.

Several prefectures reported to the Ministry of Agriculture and Commerce on the living conditions of ex-samurai using a variant of Maeda's three-grade classification and specifying a *minimum* income for each grade. The data for Gifu prefecture (date not specified, but considered to be 1883) list four grades: superior, intermediate, inferior, and *mutō* (no grade). Minimum stable annual incomes (with emphasis on stable) are specified for the superior and intermediate grades. On a per capita basis, the minima can be calculated for the superior and intermediate grades as ¥46 and ¥23 per annum, respectively.[1] It is striking that the superior grade is exactly twice as high as the intermediate grade, as in the case of Maeda.

No figures are specified for the inferior grade and the no grade on the grounds persons in these grades are without "stable annual incomes" that can be counted on. Whatever the sources of income, the inferior grade of living must afford a bare minimum of "routine living with household maintained intact" (*kyoka nichijō no seikei*). This is an illuminating description of living conditions. It defines the bare minimum of living at which persons are just acceptable as social beings. Thus, no grade can be seen as households failing to live a routine normal life with families intact. These are (1) single-person households with no resources, (2) large households suffering from a scarcity of resources, (3) households with human resources (*rōryoku no shihon*) but without ways to make use of them, and (4) households which have "no will to utilize their own human resources and have fallen into indolence and poverty."[2] Note poverty is paired with indolence, and a productive use of labor is viewed as a matter of will and wit on the part of individual households. These official definitions of the inferior grade and the no grade indicate the Japan of the 1880s was more Protestant in certain values than the Protestants.

If we apply Masana Maeda's consumption gradient to the intermediate and inferior grades of the Gifu ex-samurai, the *minimum* per capita consumption of the inferior grade, which could be considered the poverty line of the 1880s, would have been ¥9.2 (that is, ¥23 divided by 2.5). This may be compared with Miyohei Shinohara's latest estimate of per capita consumption

[1]Maeda 1971, 1:14-18. The income appropriate to a grade varies according to the household size. We turned the household income into a per capita amount by dividing it by the number of persons in the household. For the intermediate grade, for example, the annual household income is given as follows:

For a household of:	6	4 or 5	3 or fewer
At least:	¥150	¥120	¥70

The figures result in wild variations in the per capita income. But if we take the three income figures and divide them by six, five, and three persons, respectively, we get reasonably close figures: 25 yen, 24 yen, and 23.2 yen. Hence we consider 23 yen to be the annual minimum per capita income for the intermediate grade.

[2]Maeda 1971, 1:17. The poor have "no grade." It is striking that in the 1880s the Japanese already had the Galbraithian notion the poor are degraded and outside the regular grades of the community.

expenditure which puts the 1883 and 1884 values at ¥18 for all of Japan.[3] The public relief standard of 1.8 koku of rice, multiplied by the price used by Maeda, amounts to ¥10.1. There is thus a high degree of consistency in the relationships of various levels of income and living standards that together define poverty. Japan in the 1880s was a well-structured society with widely shared criteria or feelings about what was meant by poverty.

Mikio Sumiya, writing in the "Impoverishment of the Inferior-Grade Society" (katō shakai no kyūbō), presents an elaborate table showing the worsening of living conditions in Yamanashi prefecture from 1883 to 1885.[4] During these years, the Matsukata deflation, which halved the price level between 1881 and 1886, was in full swing. The poor (hinmin) increased from 47,024 persons in 1883 to 78,547 in 1885 in Yamanashi, nearly one-fifth the total population of about 400,000 in 1885. Sumiya notes the data are good enough to be considered indicative of the nationwide tendency toward general impoverishment. Further, the Yamanashi data indicate one-fifth of the "poor" were "extremely poor" and the rest, if not deserving of this designation, were still deficient in food and clothing. Putting together the Maeda grades and the findings by Sumiya and others, we may visualize the income-grade structure of the Japanese population around 1887 as follows:

Percent:	10-15	25-30	40-45	15-20
Grade:	Superior	Intermediate	Inferior	Poor

Changing Views of Stratification

Throughout modern history, income as a base for status has had to contend with other criteria. In Japan, the legitimacy of income as a yardstick for grading persons was weaker during the Meiji period than it is today. Even Maeda thought differently of "poor" ex-samurai and "poor" peasants or artisans. Several views of social stratification have come and gone in the last hundred years. The feudal stratification was a sort of caste system which determined status by birth. There were four regular castes (shi-nō-kō-shō or samurai-peasant-artisan-merchant) and several outcaste groups (eta and hinin, the former untranslatable and the latter literally "nonpersons"). This system, which shaped attitudes toward life and conditioned social behavior during the two hundred fifty years of the Pax Tokugawa, had quickly diminished as a relevant structure of society after the Meiji reforms simplified it into shi (ex-samurai) and heimin (commoner) and declared all people equal despite remaining nominal distinctions. But a consciously reactionary contrivance

[3]LTES 6:12. It may also be recalled the minimum per capita income for the intermediate grade (by definition, the maximum for the inferior grade) was 23 yen. With savings subtracted from this, consumption expenditure may very well have been close to Shinohara's 18 yen. For a further check on the consistency of figures, see Chūbachi (1971a, 7:3-39).

[4]Sumiya 1955, pp. 94-98. Partial data are available for a number of prefectures, but not in a form that allows aggregating and averaging. For an enumeration of these data, see Nihon Shakai (1960, pp. 10-23).

was made at the top, while criminal negligence was perpetuated at the bottom of the new social order.

At the top, the *Tennō* was transformed from a traditional guardian of ancient tribal gods and medieval culture as a heavenly king into a direct ruler of the realm as Emperor and Supreme Commander of all armed forces. Furthermore, a new nobility (*kazoku*, literally, a flower race) was created out of former court nobles and feudal lords as an entourage of the Emperor.[5] At the bottom of the social order, there was ignobility as a counterpoint to nobility. The logic that created the Meiji nobility also created a modern pariah, the people of Buraku, out of the feudal outcastes (eta and hinin).[6] "That all people are now free and equal" did not apply to either extreme of the social structure. One was more equal, and the other less equal, than the bulk of the population.

Among the ordinary Japanese (former shi-nō-kō-shō), there was a great confusion of language. Old caste-based symbols were fast fading out as regulatory devices for social relations. New expressions were needed to fix a coherent image of social order. Indeed, with the influx of Western civilization, the need for verbal innovations was endless. Maeda's three-grade classification, using somewhat awkward and hence less durable expressions, for a time represented the most popular conceptual innovation about the structure of the emerging Japanese society. Eventually, orators and journalists, some time in the middle of the 1890s, hit upon a more expressive form of social stratification which was to shape the Japanese perception of their own society until the 1930s. These were (1) *jōryū shakai* (upstream society, or high society, indicating noble birth, elegance of demeanor, fashionableness, a touch of quaintness, and a natural claim to the adulation of the masses), (2) *chūsan kaikyū* (middle propertied class, or simply middle class, with emphasis on property ownership in a reasonable amount, an expression connoting sturdy character, hard work, stubborn determination, and a will to a material success above all), and finally (3) *kasō shakai* (lower class society, with all the flavors of condescension and contempt). In terms of this stratification, Japan's subsequent social progress coupled with economic development meant status migrations of people from kasō shakai into chūsan kaikyū.

The kasō shakai did not talk about themselves. Those who talked about them were members of the smaller segment of Japan (public officials, police, teachers, intellectuals, and so forth) who were a few flights above the lower

---

[5]The creation of *kazoku* was derided by Gen'nosuke Yokoyama, who will figure prominently in the subsequent pages of this essay. *Kà* (*hua* in Chinese) is a pleasant-looking Chinese letter, and the Chinese also use it as their own identity, calling themselves *huà-rén* (flower people). Self-flattery is a way of life in China and Japan. *Kazoku* was created by a Ministerial Decree of 1869. See Kasumi Kaikan (1966, p. 82).

[6]This paraphrases what Ji'ichiro Matsumoto, a great leader of Buraku origin said: *Kizoku areba senmin ari* (If there is a nobility, there is an ignobility), quoted in Inoue (1959, p. 14). Throughout, Inoue also harps upon this Matsumoto theme.

class society. The relationships between observers and observed were therefore stratified from the beginning. The remnants of Confucian ethics gave a distinctive orientation to early discussions of lower class society. The Confucian concept of *min* (or *tami* in poetic Japanese) implying people as a collective mass, rather than as individuals, was used without reservation about its implications. Prior to the conceptual innovation that produced kasō shakai (*shakai*, usually translated "society," has a particularly modern flavor), observers more arrogantly spoke about the residents of this society as *kasō-min*, which conjures up an image of a big dirty blur, or of something unworthy of serious attention. *Kasō-min* often meant "lowly people."

However, the "lowly people" were also differentiated by moral quality and level of living in the view of their observers. Most of the kasō-min were *saimin* (lean people, petty folk, connoting weakness, powerlessness, and dependency). They could be lovable too; indeed, great rulers in the history of Confucian states such as China, Korea, and Japan have bled their hearts endlessly on the lot of the petty folk. Confucian scholars, too, often heard the Voice of Heaven among the petty folk on earth. Meiji bureaucrats who in due course wanted to know more about the people and to whom the novelty of kasō shakai with its implied criticism of social order was anathema, glowed in the romantic use of saimin.

Below saimin, there were hinmin (poor people) to whom traditional rulers always delivered stern admonitions for greater moral and physical efforts. Attitudes toward hinmin contained elements of deprecation, rejection, and discipline, moderated occasionally by some grudging understanding as to why some otherwise worthy people could fall into poverty. Places where hinmin lived were called hinmin-kutsu, a term evoking horror more than anything else. (We will look into hinmin-kutsu in the next section.) No normal residential area, however homogeneous internally and however sharply differentiated it may be from its surroundings, would ever be suffixed by *kutsu*. Monstrous gangs of criminals were believed to have their *sōkutsu* (nesting grottos), and in the rhetorical trappings of a stratified society this often was interchangeable with hinmin-kutsu.

Those at the end of the rope or at their wits' end were called *kyūmin*. *Kyū* puts emphasis on the "end" of all hopes—a state of extreme deprivation. To kyūmin pushed to the wall with nowhere to turn, Japanese society traditionally showed a certain humaneness. Of course, as in any society, temporary deprivations caused by earthquakes, storms, epidemics, famines, or large-scale disasters, if manmade in origin (such as wars, rebellions, or fires) were accorded priorities for relief and assistance at public expense. But some of the deprived, initially due to these causes, would join the ranks of the poor by losing the capability to bound back. Because of these cases, the question of who deserved help and who did not was a permanent source of unresolved controversy.

At this point, it may be well to illustrate the extent of the saimin population in Japan. Partly in response to a depression after the Sino-Japanese War (1894-95), there was a movement to reform and expand the existing public relief system under the authority of the relief regulations enacted in 1874. Therefore data on the extent of hardships in Japan were needed. The Home Ministry ordered reports from prefectural governors. Some of the reports were published in the official gazette and recently have been studied by Kunijirō Tashiro.[7] Most of the reports are only descriptive of hardships suffered by saimin. However, one report, from Hyōgo prefecture, where Kobe is located, offered a reasonably comprehensive statistical estimate of saimin and their impoverishment for each city and county in the entire prefecture in 1897 and 1898. Saimin were estimated to be 22.7 percent of the total prefectural population. Those suffering from hardships were put at 8.7 percent of total population, indicating nearly one-third of Hyōgo saimin were in difficulties. The governor considered small tenant farmers, fishermen, petty merchants, small-scale factory workers, day laborers, doers of odd jobs, unemployed, and underemployed to be saimin. They were described as highly vulnerable not only to economic fluctuations but also to weather conditions. A majority of them could be called "poor," with nearly a third of them in dire difficulties.

As Hyogo illustrates, saimin were almost the same as the "poor." Toward the end of Meiji, saimin was definitely used in place of hinmin in the Home Ministry's surveys of the poor (Naimushō 1914). The popularity of the word saimin continued in official circles until about 1930. By then new ways of looking at social stratification had emerged. Radical intellectuals and workers took "proletariat" as their collective identity in the 1920s and set themselves against the "bourgeoisie." With "proletariat" arose "lumpen proletariat" (Japanized as "rumpen"). Both were part of the active Japanese vocabulary in the early 1930s (Miyade 1950, p. 18). Poverty ceased to be considered a well-deserved attribute of the lowly, as during Meiji, and instead was viewed as an unjustified threat to the modern proletariat. Those frightened by the revolutionary view of society as a structure of antagonistic classes seriously thought of rhetorical escape, harking back to a dream world of classless antiquity and integrating all Japanese into an undifferentiated mass called "children of the emperor" (tennō no sekishi).

Emperor-worship, with its ironical twist in favor of plebian equality for all, became the official ideology of the leadership to save Japan from Marxism and communism. As the events of the 1930s and 40s show, the "children of the emperor" selflessly gave up everything for the Father Emperor's "Holy War" (seisen). In this way, everyone became poor, with no need for a separate place for the poor. From the general and absolute poverty of 1945-46, postwar Japan has staged a comeback as a democratic monarchy with emphasis on economic growth, producing nearly thirty years of economic miracle, only recently punctured by environmental concerns and the petroleum crisis. Today, saimin and hinmin are dead letters. Kasō shakai lives only in nostalgia. In Japan of the 1970s, there are no longer people who are called poor.

[7]Tashiro 1965. Data quoted on Hyōgo are from pp. 200-205.

Japan's Minority Groups

There are still social anomalies in today's otherwise classless, povertyless Japan. These are the disadvantaged groups not fully sharing in Japan's hard-earned prosperity. A hundred years after the Meiji Restoration, inhabitants of Buraku and certain "foreigners" still suffer from inequities in income and status because of their group identities. Equality of opportunity and freedom of occupational choice have not fully reached these groups. Buraku-min in 1971 numbered about 1,200,000 in more than 4000 *dōwa-chiku* (areas to be integrated) (Buraku Kaihō 1971; DeVos and Wagatsuma 1967, chap. 5). The disadvantaged foreigners are Asians (mostly Koreans and Korean-Japanese), Ainu, who are believed to be racially different from the Japanese, and Okinawans, who became Japanese with the annexation of the Ryukyus in 1879 and who from the end of the Second World War to May 1972 were only "latently" Japanese due to their being under the United States' administration. There are various historical reasons for the disadvantaged status of these "foreigners." Asians (roughly 700,000 persons of whom 600,000 are of Korean origin) and Okinawans (about 1,200,000, of which somewhat more than 900,000 live in Okinawa prefecture) are legacies of the empire. The Ainu (conservatively put at 60,000, of which about 20,000 are in Hokkaido) are original occupants of the Japanese islands who have been "chased" north by ordinary Japanese. Their ethnic brethren are scattered over Japan, the Kurils, and Sakhalin. The aspiration for a Greater Ainu Republic entertained by the Ainu-Japanese, even if it is a mere state of mind, indicates their profound dissatisfaction with Japan.[8] Ordinary Japanese hardly consider the Ainu-Japanese on an equal footing with themselves.

The Problem Defined

It is clear the existence of minority groups (accounting for a not negligible 3.5 percent of the Japanese population) splits Japan into two, mainstream Japan and the "other Japan." For reasons of expositional feasibility within the space limitations of this essay, we concentrate on poverty in mainstream Japan. Poverty in the other Japan is a substantial issue in its own right, inescapably tangled up with such *mondai* (problems) as Ainu-mondai, Buraku-mondai, Chōsen-mondai (problems of Koreans), and Okinawa-mondai. Volumes have been written on each of these.

[8]There is no Japanese counterpart of an expression like Ainu-Japanese. The Ainu-Japanese are at best Japanese Ainu. Likewise, there are no Korean-Japanese, they are always Koreans-in-Japan (*zainichi chōsenjin*). Interestingly, during the United States occupation of Okinawa, the "real" Japanese who happened to be there referred to Okinawans as Okinawan-Japanese when they spoke to Americans about the people of Okinawa. By the same token, the "real" Japanese may now be speaking to foreigners about the Ainu as Ainu-Japanese or about Koreans-in-Japan as Korean-Japanese. This practice would constitute a minor innovation in perception. See Sarashina (1970) and, especially Tokukei (1973).

There is some geographical separability between mainstream Japan and the other Japan, but it is not watertight. Residential and geographical mobility is legally free throughout Japan, so some members of disadvantaged groups have moved into areas of mainstream Japan and vice versa. Thus, the poor in mainstream Japan must by definition include those of minority origins. This is especially the case with the people of Buraku, where urban growth has made former Buraku areas ghettos of mainstream Japan. Still, as only a small fraction of ghettos owe their origin to Buraku, it is possible to discuss urban poverty without reference to Buraku. Two foci emerge here. One is poverty in Japan (with no differentiation between the two Japans). Another is urban poverty in Japan. In organizing the discussion of poverty in Japanese history, we will follow the historical growth path of perception or awareness of poverty as a social problem on the part of the general public. This path starts with the discovery of urban ghettos—hinmin-kutsu.

HINMIN-KUTSU STUDIES, 1886-1926

In a well-defined community (city, town, or village), social consensus exists as to who is poor and where the poor live. A popular image of what poverty means is formed by impressions of how the poor live in the areas considered slum, ghettos, or (in Japan) hinmin-kutsu. But whether information on the ghetto poor goes beyond the diffuse stereotypes, largely derogatory and often incorrect, shared by the mainstream majority of the community is another matter. The demand for information on the poor can be safely assumed to be rather low in any place and any age. Those who write about the poor, out of necessity to overcome reader apathy, are often forced to picture life in the ghettos as something unbelievable, "out of this world." Earlier materials on hinmin-kutsu read like adventure stories in faraway lands (Sumiya 1972, 1:648). But over time, interest in hinmin-kutsu and concern over the poor has increased.

In this section, we describe how the Japanese discovered hinmin-kutsu in Tokyo, Osaka, Kobe, and other cities, what the studies of hinmin-kutsu can tell us about the extent of urban poverty, and how interest in the poor gave way to interest in housing standards with emphasis on the physical structure and appearance of a city. From the 1920s on, a ghettto was perceived as an area of substandard housing rather than as a habitat of the poor. At the same time, the rise of social work and the expansion of public assistance resulted in a new approach to poverty which absorbed the ghetto poor into a broader framework including the nonghetto poor.

Tokyo

The Matsukata deflation (1881-86) wrought uneven hardships. Municipalities were preparing for a modern system of cities, towns, and villages (promulgated in 1888) and a system of prefectures and counties (promulgated in 1890). Areas aspiring to be "cities" were concerned with the standards to be met in terms of population, occupational structure, and urban amenities. Everything damaging the chances for meeting these standards was to be brought under control. Because the economic hardships of the mid-1880s increased the incidence of beggary, vagrancy, delinquency, and crime in Japanese cities, the poor and criminals were the first to receive intensive official attention.

Newspapers caught the straw in the wind and initiated explorations of hinmin-kutsu. A classic compendium of reports on life in hinmin-kutsu, now widely regarded as the first landmark in the history of poverty research in Japan, appeared in the *Chōya Shimbun* in 1886 (Nishida 1970, 2:53-63). Reporters were sent out to all parts of Tokyo to locate the poor and to describe their living conditions, jobs, and customs. One result of these earlier explorations was the discovery of Tokyo's "three great grottos of the poor" (*san dai-hinmin-kutsu*): Yotsuya Samegabashi to the west of the Imperial Palace, Shiba Shin'amichō to the south, and Shitaya Mannenchō to the east. These were visited and studied by many other individuals at different times. The same reporters, for their newspapers or on their own, also covered other urban centers such as Osaka and Kobe.

The most durable work from these early attempts to collect, examine, and analyze data on the poor is Yokoyama's *Nihon no Kasō Shakai* (1898), which set the usage of kasō shakai for many years to come.[9] In this book, the number of households (H) and of residents (R) in the Three Greats are given as follows: Samegabashi: H, 1365; R, 4964, Shin'amichō: H, 532; R 3221, and Mannenchō: H, 865; R, 3849. It is to these figures other writers referred when illustrating how good or bad the particular ghetto they discovered was. Samegabashi was for a long time the standard by which other ghettos were evaluated.

Hinmin-kutsu first hit the eyes of an observer as an area dominated by bad housing. Although clustering of poor houses does not necessarily imply all the residents there are poor, housing poverty often means poverty on other counts such as income and culture, and thus such areas offer society at large easy initial contact with the world of the poor.[10] Popular prejudices against the poor often involved seeing the surface (poor housing) and jumping to the conclusion the inhabitants (the poor) were deficient in moral qualities.

In the study of poverty, who is concerned about the poor and why anyone is interested in them are questions as important as who is poor. The Meiji discoverers of the urban poor were men of good will. They were able to separate means from ends and contributed enormously to the awakening of the general public about some of the profound human consequences of poverty. Their technique was to visit various sections of a city to look into the living conditions of areas which appeared particularly hideous. Their impressions were naturally greater in areas especially unusual in terms of

[9]Reprinted by Iwanami in 1949. References to *Nihon No Kasō-Shakai* are to the reprint edition. Data quoted are from pp. 23-25.

[10]This is of course implied in the logic of the Engel Coefficient. What is interesting is that while scholars have emphasized the Engel Coefficient for food, popular prejudices related to poverty have been based on shelter.

housing quality, population density, manners and dress of the people, and the "sound and smell of life" in general. In other words, Meiji journalism's discovery of poverty was largely synonymous with discovery of the worst ghettos. Keen eyes, a sensitive nose, a warm and impressionable heart, plain unassuming demeanor so as not to arouse suspicion, a pair of sturdy legs to withstand hours and miles of walking every day, and a talent for writing were some of the essential qualifications of Meiji social reporters. Yokoyama Gen'nousuke (1871-1915) was exemplary in these respects. It is no wonder he has since become one of the most respected models for social researchers, as well as for members of his profession interested in the problems of life at the bottom.

Soon the ghetto poor won official attention. Toward the end of Meiji, in 1911 and 1912, the Home Ministry conducted surveys of the poor in certain sections of Tokyo. The City of Tokyo undertook a similar survey in 1920, and the Home Ministry studied the household budgets of the poor in 1921 (Naimushō 1912, 1914, and 1922 editions; Tōkyō-shi 1921). After these surveys, official attitudes toward the grottos of the poor were increasingly dominated by interest in the face-lifting of Tokyo as a modern city.

However, data generated via ghetto explorations are inadequate for questions such as how many persons in a given city are actually poor, although they offer useful hints. Neither Yokoyama in 1898 nor the Home Ministry in 1911-12 intended to be comprehensive in coverage and enumeration; their interests were in understanding how the poor lived rather than how many poor there were. In order to help the poor, interest in a full enumeration was expressed by the City of Tokyo in its 1920 survey, but how successful implementation was remains a question.

Ghettos are also subject to considerable locational shifts and qualitative changes over time, and only with vigorous and sustained attention to all aspects of city life can one hope to minimize oversight. The 1920 Tokyo city survey put ghettoized poor households at 18,351, with 74,493 residents, which was 3.4 percent of the city's population.[11] The same survey also identified 16,640 "transient" poor, mostly migrant unskilled laborers who stayed in cheap inns. The addition of this number to the ghettoized poor raises the percentage of the Tokyo city poor to 4.2 percent for 1920. If a similar percentage is assumed for the nonghetto poor, Tokyo's poor would rise to 8 or 9 percent of the city's population for 1920. This is a conceivable

[11]Tōkyō-shi 1921, p. 5. In addition to curiosity about life in hinmin-kutsu, interest in the real extent of poverty rose around 1910. Kagawa was most insistent on the need for knowledge about the overall extent of poverty. Kagawa (1915, p. 87) quotes a 1911 study by the City of Tokyo which puts the Tokyo poor at 205,026 persons. Later, Isomura (1959, p. 184) quotes this figure and observes that the poor in Tokyo were 11 percent of the total city population in 1911. However, Tokyo city reports (1921, p. 6) mention there were no studies telling anything about the total magnitude of poverty in the city. Nevertheless, 11 percent as a proportion of Tokyo residents being poor is a highly plausible figure.

extent of poverty for Tokyo in 1920, but the city specifically disclaimed the possibility of ascertaining the number of dispersed (nonghetto) poor.[12] The 1920 survey was undertaken as a preliminary step in Tokyo's program to build "social work facilities." Clearly, knowledge of the ghetto poor alone would not lead to an optimal program of this nature.

By 1920, a division of labor had occurred in public policy toward the ghetto. Poverty of the residents became a problem for social work and public assistance. Dilapidated housing structures became targets for clearance under the urban planning law enacted in 1919. The national government subsidized face-lifting programs in major cities, but neglected legislative or administrative efforts to help the poor. Under the circumstances, one suspects urban renewal amounted to resettlement.

Even without urban renewal, the poor were constantly chased out of the city limits by a combination of diverse factors. Fire hazards in the ghetto and higher rents on new apartments after each fire were the principal forces which chased the poor out and brought about face-lifting of ghetto areas. In this respect, the Great Earthquake of 1923 was a godsend for Tokyo's urban renewal policy. The poor were burned out of their ghettos, and it required no genius to see considerable improvement in Tokyo's urban scenery could result simply by preventing the poor from returning. Of course, postearthquake reconstruction and renewal policy accomplished more than that. In 1926, a survey by the city identified only thirteen poverty enclaves containing 1100 households, far fewer than once contained in the three greatest ghettos of the Meiji era. These lingering eyesores lay farther toward the city limits than the earlier ghettos. However, just outside the city limits, there were sixty-four poverty enclaves containing 6258 households and 22,074 persons.[13] The total number of the ghetto households in the city and adjacent areas in 1926 was 40 percent of the city's ghetto poor of 1920. With ghettos diminishing or moving out of sight, poverty in Tokyo became less visible than before and needed more the specialized attention of welfare authorities and social workers.

[12]In his useful historical review of Tokyo ghettos, Kusama (1930, 3:370) identifies the poor, whom he calls saimin, in 1926 as follows:

1. Ghetto and nonghetto poor,
   inside the city   more than 100,000 persons
   in adjacent areas   about   200,000
   sub-total   more than 300,000
2. *Doya* and other inns   about   15,000
3. Squatters and campers
   (*saburi*)   about   150
4. Hobos (*okan* or *nojuku*)   about   700

   Total   more than 316,000 persons
   As a percentage of greater Tokyo population: 6 percent

[13]We owe the postearthquake description of Tokyo ghettos to Kusama (1930: figures on the intracity ghettos, p. 380; ghettos in adjacent areas,

Osaka

The interactions among poverty, ghettoization, and urbanization are not identical in all cities, but the processes do seem broadly similar. As in the case of Tokyo, ghettos moved out of the central city area of Osaka, and those trapped inside the expanding city limits were brought under control by planners intent on the improvement and beautification of the city. The City of Osaka for many years after the Meiji Restoration remained a small area well within the bounds of the present-day National Railway Loop (*Osaka kanjō-sen*). In 1888, Osaka became a modern "city" under new legislation. In order to reach "city standards" in housing, slum clearance was actively pursued. Osaka expanded in 1897 by taking in some areas both inside and outside the loop. At this time, Osaka, previously an inland town, reached the sea. The city expanded again in 1925 to roughly the same area as the present-day city, incorporating many outlying towns and villages. Many Buraku came within the jurisdiction of the city at that time.

At the beginning of modern Japan, about one-sixth of the Osaka population was said to be "destitute" (Osaka-fu, p. 183). Osaka also enjoyed dubious fame for having the worst slum in all of Japan, commonly known as Nagomachi, a corruption of Nagomachi of the Tokugawa period. Today, this area is fashionable Nihonbashi-suji, running south from the well-known Dōtonbori area to the Ten'oji Park. The earliest surviving account of Nagomachi is Umeshiro Suzuki's reportage for the *Jiji Shimpō* in 1888, when the Osaka police started a slum clearance program in earnest (Suzuki 1970, 2:123-152). Suzuki pointed out the three great ghettos of Tokyo, though not the best habitats for the poor, nevertheless paled in comparison with this largest and most hideous ghetto. In 1888, there were 2255 households with 8532 persons in Nagomachi, almost twice as many in the largest of Tokyo's ghettos.

However, when Yokoyama Gen'nosuke visited the Nagomachi area in 1897, the renowned ghetto had largely disappeared. Osaka city officials explained that life in Nagomachi began to improve when match factories were opened in its vicinity in the early 1880s, and the situation improved markedly after the police began a program of stiff supervision of public sanitation in the area in 1888, expelling the worst offenders. Yokoyama was positive Nagomachi was no longer a hinmin-kutsu by the standards of the Tokyo ghettos. But astute Yokoyama did not miss the fact that although ghettos were largely

---

p. 378). A note in this source indicates some oversights in spotting and counting the ghettos (p. 380). The 22,074 ghetto poor, when compared with Kusama's figure on all poor in areas adjacent to the city, account for only 11 percent of all poor. One has to allow for imperfections in the counting of ghetto residents. This at least indicates far more nonghetto ("dispersed") poor than ghetto poor, suggesting further that the elimination of ghettos would not mean the elimination of poverty. For a brief post-1926 history of Tokyo ghettos as substandard housing areas rather than as habitats of the poor, see Taira (1969, pp. 159-160).

absent within the city limits, some of the adjacent towns and villages were hideously ghettoized. Pockets of poverty and clusters of day laborers' cheap inns (*doya*) ringed Osaka, to the north, east, and south. (The city opens to Osaka Bay on the west.) Yokoyama, however, laid special emphasis on the southern part of Nishinari-gun, south of the city. In the Tennoji-son and Imamiya-son parts of this area, "countless deaf, crippled, limbless, and pygmies, all wrapped up in worst rags, are wiggling like worms with griefs filling the air" (Yokoyama 1949, pp. 25-27). A great historical development was thus in store, for this is the area which later became Japan's most celebrated urban problem area, commonly known as Kamagasaki.

By the First World War, Osaka had succeeded in clearing most of its worst housing clusters. At the end of Meiji, Toyohiko Kagawa, the internationally known Kobe-based evangelist and social reformer, pointed out there were no hinmin-kutsu in Osaka. There were small clusters which, in comparison with their surroundings, did look like slums, but Kagawa thought that it was totally inappropriate by Tokyo standards to call them hinmin-kutsu (1915, pp. 89-92). But Kagawa's "fortunate" Osaka evidently acquired more poor people during the First World War. In 1919, Teizo Inoue looked around in the Nihonbashi-suji area. Within four hundred yards on either side of Nihonbashi Avenue, Inoue (1923, pp. 49-73) identified twenty large and small pockets of poor people, comprising 1561 households with 6118 persons. The rather strict building code of Osaka made the structures two-storied and decent in appearance, but some of these buildings were in appalling condition inside, and crowded. Rooms were occupied by more than one person per tatami. The incongruity between appearance and substance in these areas was a consequence of Osaka's urban face-lifting policy. In view of the extensive poverty of the adjacent areas, the expansion of the city in 1925 amounted to slum acquisition in contrast to the slum clearance pursued with a measure of success within the old city limits. The subsequent ghetto history of Osaka is the story of growth of one area, Kamagasaki, as a comprehensive ghetto which has attracted the poor of all kinds.

Kobe

Kobe offers a typical example of the ghettoization of Buraku when trapped in the sprawling urbanization of a mainstream Japanese city. Kobe is only twenty miles west of Osaka along the coast of the Inland Sea. Unlike Tokyo or Osaka, which were sizable cities before Meiji, the area which grew to be Kobe was only a few scattered fishing villages before being designated an international port in the mid-nineteenth century. When Kobe was incorporated as a city in 1888, its population was only 35,000 in an area one-twentieth its present size.

Gen'nosuke Yokoyama visited Kobe in 1897, when it had a population close to 200,000. He saw in Kobe what he did not see in Osaka: abject ghetto poverty within the city limits. Eleven years later, Toyohiko Kagawa moved into one of the Kobe slums for his missionary work. In 1919, Teizo Inoue visited Kagawa and reported on the ghettos and minority groups of Kobe

(Inoue 1923, pp. 74-80). In the twenty-odd years covered by these sources, Kobe's city limits and population both expanded threefold. Also during this period, three Buraku turned into urban ghettos by absorbing non-Buraku poor, while non-Buraku ghettos of earlier years disappeared. The small pockets of poverty Yokoyama saw in 1897 were mostly non-Buraku, while the Buraku he saw were not particularly poverty-stricken by the standards of his day. These non-Buraku poverty pockets had disappeared by the time Kagawa took up residence in Kobe eleven years later. When Inoue wrote about Kobe in 1920, he did not mention any non-Buraku ghettos.

In 1897, an unusually high proportion of the Kobe residents were poor. The previously cited report of Hyōgo prefecture to the Home Ministry noted the following figures for the City of Kobe (Tashiro 1965, p. 200).

Total	193,000 persons	100.0 percent
Saimin	67,450 persons	34.9 percent
of which:		
Poor	28,730 persons	14.8 percent

Yokoyama's rather imprecise figures total, at most, 920 to 940 households in the ghettos he saw in Kobe. At an assumed rate of four persons per household, the ghetto poor would number fewer than 4000 persons, one-seventh of all poor.[14] Thus, the concentrated poverty Yokoyama saw was only a small fraction of total poverty in Kobe. This is a useful piece of information on the relative magnitudes of ghetto poor and all poor. Although this particular example is perhaps atypical, it at least suggests there were far more dispersed poor than ghetto poor in a city.

The largest poverty pocket (with 300 households) in Yokoyama's notes was non-Buraku. Yokoyama observed that even compared to Tokyo's Samega-bashi, living conditions in this spot were unbelievably hideous. He did mention two of the three Buraku (Ujigawa and Fukiai-Arakawa) which were to become, ten years later, the worst slums in all of Japan in Kagawa's account. However, Yokoyama passed them over rather light-heartedly, saying their problems were "social" handicaps rather than "economic" difficulties. He missed the third Buraku completely, perhaps because it (Nagata-mura) was then a small village outside the city limits. The rather remarkable absence of indignation on the part of Yokoyama about the "social" handicaps of the Buraku people was one of the weaknesses of Tokyo-based social observers who lacked a direct personal experience in relation to Buraku.[15]

[14]Sumiya 1972, 1:500. Considering the ghetto/nonghetto population ratio among the Tokyo poor, Yokoyama's coverage of the Kobe ghettos seems rather thorough.

[15]Tokyo intellectuals' view of poverty was already reasonably modern. In the forward to Yokoyama's Nihon no Kasō-Shakai, Shimada Saburō, president of Mainichi Shimbun and Yokoyama's employer, attributed the origin of poverty in modern society to technological progress, accumulation of capital, and free competition resulting in the defeat of the weak and the slow (p. 3).

Kobe-based Kagawa was different. He went to the other extreme, maintaining all urban poor could be traced to a Buraku origin. To support this rather absurd claim, he pointed out the poor would never talk about their homes and birthplaces and inferred it was because they were from the Buraku (Kagawa 1915, pp. 85-86). Kagawa's uncompromising Buraku-determinism for Japan's urban poverty, which he defended vehemently at the expense of the character and reputation of the people of Buraku, is an unfortunate scar in his otherwise praiseworthy career as a social reformer. As for Kobe, Kagawa identified four major Buraku ghettos (with fewer than 6000 persons). Compared with the Kobe city population of about 400,000 at the time, the total ghetto population in Kagawa's estimate was more than 6 percent. At the same time, the Kobe police were using a figure one-half of his (Kagawa 1915, p. 93). At the time of the rice riots in 1918, the police paid special attention to the three Buraku whose combined population, according to the police, was about 13,000 persons (Inoue and Watanabe 1960, 3:46). (One of the Buraku, Arata, mentioned by Kagawa was not on the police list; nor was it on Inoue's.) Inoue's total for the three came to more than 24,000, 4 percent of the Kobe city population of 1920 (Inoue 1923, pp. 74-76). By Inoue's time, however, the largest of the Buraku, Fukiai-Arakawa, where Kagawa lived, had been overwhelmed by non-Buraku poor. This may be seen by comparing the number of "pure" Buraku people the police counted in 1918, about 4000 persons, with Inoue's 1920 figure of the 19,000 total poor in the same area. The loss of the Buraku identity in this way probably happened to many other urban Buraku. Under the urban planning law Kobe, like other cities, upgraded housing standards in the ghetto areas during the interwar period.

Other Cities

Yokoyama wrote about poverty in small provincial cities in Toyama prefecture and observed that in 1896 one-sixth of all households in these cities were exempt from any tax payments for reasons of poverty (Tashiro 1965, 1:463-481). Kagawa, the missionary, had something specific to say on nearly thirty cities, specifically noting eleven had no ghettos. He observed poorer regions such as Tōhoku did not necessarily have urban hinmin-kutsu (Kagawa 1915, p. 81). General poverty of a region does not promote urbanization, and the poor are principally scattered peasants. Ghettoization is a much more complex process than what is implied by the statement some people in a city are poor.

Inoue was specifically interested in the six major cities of Japan (Tokyo, Yokohama, Nagoya, Kyoto, Osaka, and Kobe). In Yokohama, port city for Tokyo, Inoue saw a number of rather bad ghettos but no Buraku. In Nagoya in central Japan, ghettos were developing in and around former Buraku. In Kyoto, there were several Buraku, but they were not poor enough to be considered hinmin-kutsu by Inoue's standards based on his Tokyo experience (Inoue 1923, pp. 47-49).

In concluding this section, it may be reemphasized that the merit of ghetto studies was not in producing accurate estimates of the extent of poverty for a city or for a nation, but in promoting an understanding of living conditions in the ghetto. A widely quoted figure on the extent of poverty in all of Japan in the 1910s and 20s (the Taishō era) was 10 percent (*ichi-wari*, more a magical expression than a number). After considering criteria and figures at some length, Kagawa himself concluded (1915, p. 81) the poor in Japan could "easily" reach one-tenth of the total population. A Home Ministry publication of 1922 mentioned that by the most conservative estimate, the poor could rise to ichi-wari of the total population and the extremely poor, those not able to meet the minimum requirements of life, could be ichi-wari of the poor, or one percent of the total population (Naimushō 1922, p. 203). The round figures do not inspire confidence, for they sound more rhetorical than quantitative, but there is no doubt this was the way Japanese in the Taishō era looked at poverty.

INCOMES AND JOBS OF THE POOR

Incomes

A major hypothesis in the discussion of incomes of the poor uses the concept of relative poverty: in a dynamic economy, real incomes of all groups including the poor increase in absolute amounts over time, but the poor remain poor relative to the rising contemporary standards of income and living. There are two kinds of income involved in the discussion of poverty. One is the poverty line, a normative standard, which has to be exceeded for a person or a household to be considered nonpoor. It is based on the cost of the basic, irreducible necessities of life. The other kind has to do with the actual incomes of people considered poor by social consensus. In the previous section, we discussed whom society considered "poor"—the ghetto residents. The average actual income of the poor may therefore be obtained from the incomes of the ghetto residents. It is this kind of average income that we shall discuss in the following paragraphs. It is well to remember, however, that not every ghetto dweller is income-poor. There are fabled misers who, feigning poverty, have chosen to live in a ghetto. Their numerical unimportance does not pull up the average ghetto income much.

Available sources of ghetto incomes in Tokyo are more fully discussed elsewhere (Taira 1969), so only a brief summary is necessary here. A year-to-year time series of the average ghetto income is impossible to construct. In fact, the sources are available for only nine isolated points in time scattered over a long period. In 1934-36 constant prices, these are:[16]

Year:	1886	1898	1912	1920	1926	1929	1934	1957
Yen:	42	65	78	124	121	128	92	174

Real income of the poor increased over time, but they still lived in ghettos

[16]The same sources as in Taira (1969, p. 161), with additions for 1920 and 1934, have been reappraised. The figures here are different from those cited in Taira for two reasons: (1) revision of the current figures, and (2) the use of the latest price index estimate in LTES, vol. 8. The additional sources are for 1920, Tōkyō-shi (1921), and for 1934, Tōkyō-shi (1936).

and were looked down on by the general public. The relativity of poverty
with respect to time is quite clear.

Another way of showing income change is conversion of money income
into the amount of rice it can buy. The average ghetto income was equivalent
to 1.5 koku of medium-grade rice at retail in 1886. It increased to more than
4 koku in 1929. Typical ghetto incomes in 1886 and 1898 were even lower
than the relief standard of 1.8 koku. Indeed, for the ghetto families of the
1880s and 90s, medium-grade rice was a great luxury. Many of the poor did
not even eat freshly cooked low-grade rice. They bought leftover food
obtained from such places as military mess-halls and restaurants of the gay
quarters, something that ordinarily would go to pigs.[17] Society therefore
considered ghetto residents not quite human. By the end of Meiji, ghetto
income had risen to par with Maeda's minimum. At this level, freshly cooked
rice should have been possible in most ghetto households. Three meals with
the best available rice was a widely shared ideal in prewar Japan, particularly
among poor and low-income groups who had known meals without rice. By
1930, in terms of rice and its quality, the average poor were absolutely much
better off than the poor of a generation before, though remaining poor
relative to contemporary standards.

Jobs

Implicit in the discussion of industrialization's impact on employment is the
hypothesis that the poor, initially constituting an "unlimited supply of
labor," are gradually drawn into the capitalist sector (especially factory jobs)
in some orderly fashion. The examination of the jobs of the poor should
indicate to what extent the poor have been involved in factory employment
or capitalist enterprises in general. The diversity and irregularity of jobs
available to the poor, as well as multiple job-holding common among them,
make it extremely difficult to summarize the employment characteristics of
the poor. Statistical neatness would perhaps conceal more than it would
reveal. Some aggregation is unavoidable, but it is useful to know first how
diverse the jobs of the poor are.

Among the activities of Tokyo poor during Meiji were carrying, common
labor, and scavenging. Representative carrying jobs were rickshaw-pulling and
hand-carting. Rickshaw-pulling was the best occupation. *Okakae* (rickshaw-
pullers working exclusively for one wealthy family) were evidently several
flights above the poverty line. Operators of taxi rickshaws (particularly those
working in evenings, called *mōrō*) were the least well off subgroup. Ranking
in terms of income slightly below carriers were those hiring themselves out by
day for odd jobs and ubiquitous roving venders of all kinds. The handling of
mud, sand, and pebbles (for building roads, for example) was as unskilled as
any odd job but enjoyed an air of respectability because of its occupational
title, *dokata*.[18]

[17]Yokoyama 1949, pp. 45-47. For a fuller discussion see Gonda 1926, and
Tōkyō-shi 1921, p. 74.
[18]*Dokata* were also rather well organized in the fictitious kin-group

A predominant form of scavenging was the collection of waste paper in the streets. This was largely monopolized by men called *bataya*. Women scavengers went from house to house asking for broken glassware and other discards. Street scavenging was the least remunerative activity; begging was often preferable insofar as cash earnings were concerned. But begging was not an easy occupation to step into even for the poor so long as there still remained any sense of personal worth. Therefore, a division of labor developed with begging assigned to children. Vagrant orphans were often organized by beggar-entrepreneurs on a considerable scale. Physically handicapped adults showed up in the streets as beggars, but even they preferred to work through children who may not have been their kin but were attracted by mutual pity. Ranking with beggars and scavengers at the bottom of lower class society were migrant entertainers (*geinin*), and prayer-offerers and soothsayers clad in a variety of religious attire asking for money in exchange for a few lines from the sutras.

This would be the hierarchy of earnings by occupation among the slum dwellers of nineteenth-century Japan: rickshawmen at the top (around the poverty line); unskilled day laborers in the middle; roving venders, scavengers, entertainers, prayer-offerers; and finally at the bottom, beggers not yet caught or barely tolerated by the police. Wives and children of the poor at home also did piece work such as covering bamboo fan frames with paper, finishing match boxes, and so forth.

Given these initial slum occupations, the question is how economic development affected the activities of the poor. In 1890, an observer of the ghettos compiled a list of sixty-two poverty-linked occupations. His survey also showed 70 to 80 percent of the poor engaged in rickshaw-pulling and scavenging. How general this survey was is unknown. None of these sixty-two occupations seemed related to modern methods of production. In 1902, another author gave the following percentage distribution by type of work for adult males of Yotsuya Samegabashi (one of the three great Meiji ghettos): rickshawmen 20 percent, mud-handlers 15 percent, operatives (*shokkō*) 16 percent, day laborers (*dekasegi*) 12 percent, miscellaneous activities 25 percent, waste collectors 10 percent, and unemployed 2 percent.[19] It is not clear what "operatives" covers, but some of them (though undoubtedly not all) were in fact factory workers. This is significant in historical perspective, for it indicates that in the middle years of Meiji, demand for labor in modern production had finally reached the Tokyo ghettos. The tie was closer between Osaka and Kobe ghettos and factories. According to the 1911 Home Ministry survey of the poor, in four downtown

---

oyakata-kokata relationships. The structured and disciplined human relations within their groups afforded the dokata a measure of pride and dignity despite their low income and status. It is when this subculture broke down that the dokata fell into the amorphous world of poverty characterized by demoralization and degradation (Yokoyama 1949, p. 29). The novelist Shin Hasegawa left masterpieces dealing with the world of dokata which are valuable as sources of information on this subculture.

[19]The two studies are cited in Tsuda 1972, p. 59 and pp. 62-63.

wards of Tokyo, 26 percent of the heads of poor households were engaged in manufacturing (*kōgyō*). How many were in factories is unknown, however. One suspects many might have been workers in subfactory, back-alley workshops employing five or fewer workers. In the same statistics, the old standby of poverty-linked occupations such as rickshaw-pulling and scavenging were down to 14 and 2 percent, respectively. Those engaged in unspecified day labor were 9 percent. Occupations of the poor had changed considerably by the end of the Meiji era.

Occupations became further diversified as time passed. The 1920 Tokyo city survey enumerates 204 occupations for male heads of poor households (Tōkyō-shi 1921, pp. 42-49). Twenty-seven of them are considered principal occupations, accounting for 62 percent of all households identified in the surveyed ghettos. (An occupation was labeled "principal" when it engaged at least ten households.) The remaining 38 percent of households are scattered over some 177 occupations. In addition, there are nearly 50 gainful activities available to women and the aged to supplement the earnings of their household heads. Waste collection or scavenging now belongs to one of those 177 less important activities of the poor. The 1920 distribution of the principal 1902 occupations was rickshawmen 6.8 percent, mud-handlers 0.6, operatives 9.8, day laborers 19.4, miscellaneous 2, waste collectors were negligible, and unemployed were not observed. Day laborers, operatives, and rickshawmen remain most numerous among ghetto residents of 1920, although their weights (except day laborers) are less than in 1902. The fourth most important poverty-linked job of 1920 is handcarting, accounting for 4.1 percent of all households. Thus, about 40 percent of heads of household were concentrated in these four occupations. The rise in importance of day labor is quite plausible, for carriers disappeared under the impact of competition from automobiles and trucks and factory workers gradually moved above poverty.

The 6096 household heads in the ghettos of newly incorporated areas of Tokyo city in 1934 were engaged in more than six hundred occupations (Tōkyō-shi 1936, pp. 333-339). The method of enumeration had improved considerably by this time. There are ten major divisions by industry; finally, workers in each of the intermediate groups are distinguished by job title. Evidently, the surveyors adopted the job titles verbatim as mentioned to them by the workers. The result was a proliferation of job titles despite many apparent overlaps of job content. The most frequently mentioned categories are unskilled day laborers (1260 persons, 20.7 percent of the total); operatives, presumably employes (900, 14.8 percent); craftsmen, presumably self-employed (650, 10.7 percent); waste collectors, buyers as well as pickers (490, 8.1 percent); and persons not occupied (493, 8.1 percent). These account for 62.4 percent of the identified household heads. If we add the 5.9 percent classed as mud-handlers (dokata and dokō), unskilled workers in day-to-day unstable employment rise to more than 26 percent. Reflecting the suburban nature of the areas covered, rickshawmen number only 19 (0.3 percent). But there are twenty-one automobile drivers and six assistants to drivers; the motor age had appeared in peripheral areas of Tokyo by 1934.

Handcarting is not among the job titles mentioned in this survey, but it may have been subsumed under the day-labor category in transportation. The foregoing shows a general pattern of unstable, unskilled day labor had emerged.

Turning to the postwar period, data for 1957 use the less detailed occupational classification which became standard after the war. The groups are self-employed 29.6 percent, clerical and technical 25.3, common labor 22.5, miscellaneous 12.7, unemployed 7.9, and not known 2.0 (Tōkyō-to 1965, pp. 290-291). In 1961, the Tokyo metropolitan government made an intensive study in four "representative" slum areas. Jobs of household heads are enumerated in somewhat greater detail than in the 1957 report on the poor. By regrouping and aggregating where necessary, ·the occupational breakdown of the 408 heads of household covered is self-employed, 17.0 percent; family workers, 0.6; managerial, professional, technical, and clerical, 20.0; common labor, 48.5; students and others, 3.6; unemployed, 5.9; and no response, 4.4. Common laborers included waste pickers (*bataya*), temporary workers, day laborers, mud-handlers (dokō), and certain other low-level construction jobs (Tōkyō-to 1962, pp. 28-29). No explanation is given for the rather substantial group of managers and so forth, but they were probably not associated with established firms. Scavengers were rather numerous among postwar slum dwellers. Areas predominantly inhabited by them bore their occupational category as their community name (*bataya buraku* or, more politely, *bataya machi*—"town"), accounting for 11 percent of all the ghetto areas identified in the 1957 survey (Tōkyō-to 1965, p. 290).

The Poor and the Japanese Employment System

No simple generalizations are possible about the characteristics of the jobs of the poor, though at least one clear negative conclusion does emerge. The jobs of the poor are outside the regular Japanese employment system with its emphasis on stable, long-term (almost lifetime) employment relationships.[20]

The poor tend to describe their gainful activities by what they do, that is, their job titles, in sharp contrast to the well-known enterprise consciousness of employes of large, established firms. As the smug middle class of Japan often say, the poor are more "Western" in their attitudes toward jobs and living. Coming from a class to which most Western things command a premium, this remark is a curious twist that may sound contradictory. But Japanese writings about the poor, ever since the days of the Meiji reporters of ghetto life, abound with remarks likening the loosely structured social relations and high mobility of lower class Japanese to Western behavioral patterns. Hardly taking their alleged "Westernness" with pride, Japanese poor have only felt miserable for being different from the mainstream Japanese citizenry.

Unlike mainstream Japanese, the poor are compelled to live with their dubious privileges of individualism and freedom. They change jobs and employers almost daily. What counts is what they can perform, not whom

[20]One of the most recent contributions on the sociology of the regular employment system is Dore (1973).

they work for. Eiichi Isomura, doyen of Japanese ghetto researchers, calls the ghetto poor *shigoto zoku* (job-doer race). He notes six features of their jobs: (1) irregular manual work, (2) at the mercy of weather, (3) requiring frequent moving, (4) often indirectly employed for fees (the real employer unknown), (5) involving no discretion or decision (doing things as told from moment to moment), and (6) having no future, sometimes verging on illegality from momentary gains (Isomura 1959, pp. 80-82).

THE LIFE STYLE AND LIFE CHANCES OF THE POOR

The Meiji Poor

Historically, hinmin-kutsu tended to develop at physically disagreeable sites such as marshland or other lowland areas with poor drainage, a dry riverbed with risks of floods, a rugged hillside with no transportation facilities, or a deep valley between hills literally looked down on by general society.[21] The physical environment of the ghetto is almost by definition deficient of requisites for a minimal standard of health. Man-made deficiencies compound the natural. The ghetto is crowded and its houses are decrepit, with little protection against the elements. Rain leaks through the roof, and wind blows in through cracks in the wall. Ill-fit doors rattle most of the time and form no barriers against theft, prowling, or other attacks. Traditionally the standard living space of a ghetto family has been 9-*shaku* by 2-*ken* (roughly 9 by 12 feet, equivalent to 6 tatami) within a cheap multiplex called a *nagaya* (long house).[22] Despite the limited space, it was common in Meiji ghettos to take in a boarder or two, so that fewer than one tatami per person was usual.

Although arranged marriages were the norm for the whole country, family formation on the basis of "love" was the rule rather than an exception in

---

[21]In this paragraph, we attempt a summary of the rich descriptions of physical and social aspects of ghetto life Yokoyama, Kagawa, Inoue, and others have left behind. What is summarized here is a sort of central tendency—some ghettos were better, and others worse. Readers may also sense a touch of Oscar Lewis's concept of a "culture of poverty." Whether this applies to Japanese ghetto life requires careful examination, but the conditions Lewis considers prerequisite existed in broad outline in prewar Japan. These conditions are "(1) a cash economy, wage labor, and production for profit; (2) a persistently high rate of unemployment and underemployment for unskilled labor; (3) low wages; (4) the failure to provide social, political, and economic organization, either on a voluntary basis or by government imposition, for the low-income population; (5) the existence of a bilateral kinship system rather than a unilateral one; and finally, (6) the existence of a set of values in the dominant class which stresses the accumulation of wealth and property, the possibility of upward mobility and thrift, and explains low economic status as the result of personal inadequacy or inferiority" (Lewis 1965, pp. *xliii-xliv*).

[22]Nagaya originated during the Edo period as temporary accommodations for migrant, usually construction, workers. They became permanent homes when poor persons cut their ties with their original homes (see Yanagida 1903).

ghettos—a fact disgusting Meiji ghetto-watchers and leading them to liken ghetto life to Western patterns and impute the ghetto residents' origins to some remote foreign races. Family quarrels were frequent, and mutual spite between man and wife often led to the man's sabotage of his day's work. While children cried at home for food, the man was out borrowing for his drinks. It would be lucky for the family if the wife turned up something to pawn.

There were no schools in the neighborhood, but charitable persons from general society occasionally appeared to instruct ghetto children in the three R's. Legal registrations of marriages, births, and deaths were shunned. Many children thus grew up illegitimate, a social handicap in later life. Speech habits were plebeian, conspicuously lacking the respect words the middle class considered essential minimum decency. Humanity was not lost entirely, however; death in the neighborhood elicited widespread sympathy, and the funeral was a kind of communal enterprise, though unstructured. A measure of solidarity against the outside world was present, too, especially against the police, who ran into a wall of silence or a barrier of equivocation among ghetto residents when they looked for offenders. The ghetto was disorganized, free, and anonymous, distinctly different from the rest of the community.

In this setting, where any kind of planning by the inhabitants seems impossible, quantitative indicators nonetheless show regularities expected from the general theory of consumption patterns. However, these regularities differ from those in working-class household budgets even where the level of income was similar. In the rest of this section, we interpret illustrative materials using a hypothesis suggested by Tsuda that the poor and workers belonged to two distinctively different social groups (*ishitsu no shūdan*).[23] Table 1 presents two kinds of household income and expenditure. One is for the household of a rickshawman living in a ghetto. The other, for which three examples are shown, refers to the households of skilled factory workers in Tokyo receiving above average pay for factory workers.[24]

[23]Tsuda 1972, p. 142. Although Tsuda clearly suggests this hypothesis and even illustrates it with data which in part are similar to ours, its importance is virtually obliterated by other conflicting hypotheses he advances at the same time. We alone are therefore responsible for according central importance to this hypothesis. For an examination of ambiguities or ambivalences in Tsuda's discussion of poverty groups as against workers, see the review of his work by Chūbachi (1973).

[24]The national averages were much lower than the earnings of the rickshawmen and factory workers shown in Table 1. LTES (8:243-245) gives these daily wage rates for factory workers: male, 36 sen; female, 20 sen (100 sen = 1 yen). Founders and blacksmiths were paid at 43 sen and 41 sen, respectively. Construction wages were higher. The simple average for Tokyo of all entries for nonagricultural daily wage rates by occupation in the *Nippon Teikoku Tōkei Nenkan* is 60 sen for "superior grade" wages in these occupations. Superior wages were 50 to 60 percent higher than "inferior grade" wages.

Table 1
Monthly Incomes and Expenditures of Meiji Workers' Households, 1898

	I	II	IIb	IIc
Head of household[a]	Rickshawman	Lathe operator (36)	Finishing worker (24)	Metalworker in rifle manufacturing (38)
Dependents[a]	Head's mother, 2 children	Wife (28), 1 child	Wife (20), 1 child (2), head's father (67), head's mother (64)	Wife (33), 1 child
Daily earnings	¥0.500	¥0.65	¥0.63	¥0.85
Monthly household income	*n.a.* 13.00	16.25	16.38	25.96
Expenditure, total	[0.459] 13.77	23.54	19.60	17.60
Food and drink	[0.356] 10.68	12.20	13.71	9.90
Rice	[0.286] 8.58	7.60	7.00	6.50
Others	[0.070] 2.10	4.60	6.71	3.40

Table 1 (continued)

	I	II	IIb	IIc
Fuel (firewood, chemical, kerosene)	[0.063] 1.89	2.69	1.68	1.30
Rent[b]	[0.040] 1.20	4.00	1.65	1.75
Others:	?	4.65	3.98	4.65
Barber		0.35	0.38	0.35
Bath		0.30	1.00	0.80
Children's allowance		1.00	0.30	1.00
Miscellaneous (including clothing)		3.00	2.30	2.50
Surplus (+) or deficit (−)	?	− 7.29	− 3.22	+8.36
Engel coefficient	77.6%	51.8%	69.9%	56.3%

Source: Yokoyama 1949, p. 42 and pp. 227–230 (see text for discussion of data).

Note: The figures in brackets for the rickshawman are the daily earnings given in the data's source. The daily rate has been multiplied by 26, an assumed number of working days per month, for comparison with the other workers' incomes, which are given in the source on a monthly basis.

[a]Figures in parentheses are age.

[b]IIa has a three-room dwelling, IIb and IIc each have two rooms totaling 8 mats (a mat is about 18 square feet).

How data for Table 1 were generated indicates certain fundamental differences between ghetto poor and factory workers. Information on the rickshawman was based on Yokoyama's own observations, whereas that on workers was taken from more than seventy returns to a newspaper questionnaire. Yokoyama did not fully analyze these returns; nor is it known whether they were published in full or have survived to the present. The point deserving emphasis is that so many factory workers were educated enough to fill out this type of questionnaire, at a time Japan's adult literacy was probably no higher than 50 to 60 percent (Taira 1971). It is possible these factory workers came from better educated parts of the population by contemporary standards. Furthermore, respondents were giving monthly averages of normal year-round incomes and expenditures. This kind of time horizon was lacking on the part of ghetto rickshawmen, who lived from hand to mouth and day to day.[25]

In Table 1, the rickshawman's family was incomplete, the wife being absent despite two children, in contrast to the workers' families, one of which was "extended" to include the man's parents. Broken families are characteristic of ghetto society in any country. In the rickshawman's expenditures, there is no entry for "others." Yokoyama wondered about this absence, suggesting expenses other than for bare necessities may not have occurred in the households of the ghetto poor, at least as regular outlays worth mentioning. (For example, how could any Japanese avoid going to the community bath house?) The rickshawman's Engel coefficient (outlay on food as percentage of total consumption expenditure) is 77 percent. With the retail price of medium-quality rice at ¥0.187 per sho (100 sho = 1 koku), the outlay on rice could have bought 5.6 koku over a year, or 1.4 koku per person. This was certainly a reasonable rice consumption, and if the rickshawman and his family wanted to cut down the food bill, they could settle for lower grade rice or other kinds of cereal. The fact this family was in a position to afford medium-quality rice indicates they were probably better off than other poor.

Data on factory workers' households in Table 1 are full of interesting implications. IIa and IIc are nuclear families. IIa lives a somewhat fancier life than ordinary factory workers. His rent, ¥4.00 per month for three rooms, is high for his household size. Another household in Yokoyama's book, not shown in Table 1 because it was definitely atypical, rented a dwelling of three rooms (a total of fifteen tatami) for ¥3.70. Perhaps IIa upgraded his life style somewhat too fast, living beyond his means, as shown by a considerable deficit. Yokoyama, too, considered IIa out of line, tilting to the luxurious side for a factory worker. The household of IIc lives in two rooms (with eight tatami) for ¥1.75. For its economy-mindedness, this household is in sharp contrast to IIa's. Despite the higher earnings of the head, further augmented modestly by the wife's earnings, IIc's expenditure is nearly 25 percent below IIa's.

[25]It is remarkable workers in Meiji Japan had such a long time horizon, for their wages were "daily" rates, though in most cases paid only once a month.

II*b* is a young man of twenty-four, married only a few years earlier. This is the type of household Meiji Japan considered a fine example of wholesome living. He supports two aged parents, and from the presence of medicinal items in "miscellaneous," one of the parents might be ill. This family (again from the items under "miscellaneous") reads newspapers, uses writing paper, and pays dues to at least one organization. These cultural expenses constitute a factor which improve the man's future earning capability and life chances. He thus evokes the feeling of an exemplary young adult befitting an ideal personality encouraged by the Imperial Rescript on Education. Even the expenditure on sake and tobacco may not be for the young household head himself but his venerable old father. The dwelling unit is rather small for a household of this size, but there are at least two rooms, affording one for the man's parents and another for the rest of the family. The man may be poor now in material respects, but he is young and constantly improving himself. He is already rich as a moral being. Of course, what has been said about II*b* in this paragraph is fiction, except the figures cited. This is only to illustrate that the life pattern of this kind was perhaps close to the requirements of minimum economic and moral standards shared by the general public of Meiji Japan.[26]

It may also be noted that the incomes of II*a* and II*b* do not cover their living expenses. However, this was not unusual in the Meiji era. Of more than seventy returns to the questionnaire mentioned earlier, only ten or so indicated any possible savings. The great majority were running into debt. Yokoyama observed, "Where a worker earns less ¥0.70 a day and has no supplementary income while supporting his parents and his children, his living is generally extremely strained. The ability to live at a minimum standard requires wages higher than ¥0.70, or remaining single, or having parents who can supplement the household income. Yet, how many workers today have the luck of being paid more than ¥0.70 a day?" (Yokoyama 1949, p. 232). The answer is, of course, very few indeed. Yokoyama then goes on to chide the moralists of Japan who exalt the work ethic, pointing to the irony of

---

[26]This model fits rather well with the ideal type of worker households inferred from data on life cycle that became available in the 1920s. For example, a worker joins the labor force at the end of six to eight years of primary school as an apprentice earning his keep only. In his twenties, his earnings increase to a man's level, and he plans a family of his own. If he is the first son, he continues to live with his parents, meshing the two families (as done by II*b* in Table 1). In his thirties, death usually removes his parents, and the family becomes nuclear until his first son grows up and starts earning a man's wages. He and his wife then become dependents of their son's family and in due course pass on while the grandchildren are still going to school, giving their son the chance for a nuclear family. See, for example, Kyochō-kai 1930, pp. 182-183, and Gonda 1926, 7:131-132.

The life-cycle model is a durable ideal. The best-selling book by Prime Minister Tanaka (1973) has this variation of the theme: "Housing policy must

Japan where the dignity of work is already debased by wages too low to support a family.[27]

Toward the end of the Meiji era, interest in the living conditions of wage-earners' households arose among officials and intellectuals. Oka Minoru, then with the Ministry of Agriculture and Commerce, reported the findings of his investigation into the incomes and expenditures of workers' households at an annual convention of the Japanese Association for Social Policy (an organization inspired by Germany's Verein fur Sozialpolitik, so social policy must be interpreted within this special context) (Oka 1912, pp. 51-84). The investigation was made in March, April, and May 1912. Household income and expenditure were given for "typical" workers in "typical" factories engaged in textiles, printing, and the manufacture of paper. These typical workers were in the middle range of the pay scale (about ¥0.70 a day) in the factories observed. The household consisted of four persons: man, wife, and two children (or the man's father or mother in lieu of a child). Total monthly income of the household was ¥21.00, of which ¥3.00 was from the wife's work, and the outlay on food was 59 percent of consumption expenditure. There were no savings.

It is remarkable ¥21.00 was the monthly income of the typical worker's household in 1912, when the Home Ministry was using ¥20.00 per month as the poverty line. Unskilled day laborers (janitors, dock workers, and the like) and their families were well below the poverty line. Oka cites an unskilled worker's household of five persons (man, wife, and three children) with a total household income of ¥17.00 per month. Data from three factories covering 3804 workers altogether showed, adjusted for household size, all had household incomes well above the poverty line. Perhaps these workers were employed by some of the high-wage employers of the time, although Oka does not specify. This at least indicates a considerable number of male factory workers were already beyond poverty in 1912.

After the First World War

A perceptible differentiation in life style between the poor and factory workers occurred during and after the First World War, suggesting that in terms of attitudes and values, workers were improving their psychic resources

---

be in harmony with the people's 'life cycle' and the different style of living each phase of this cycle typically represents. For example, young people often like to live in apartments separate from their parents. . . . In their forties and fifties, these same people, now more affluent than before, will chose to build their own homes in the suburbs . . . where they may take care of their aged parents" (pp. 199-200). As for the prewar period, given a life expectancy of less than fifty years, workers' households experienced years of nuclear status even without asking for it. See Morioka 1967 and, for a recent study of life cycles, Chūbachi 1971*b*.

[27]One may summarize the poverty research of Meiji journalists, which culminated in Yokoyama's classic, by noting three levels of poverty for a

to take advantange of expanding opportunities for higher earnings, whereas
the poor were lagging further behind the requirements of a dynamic
economy. The Home Ministry study of factory workers' household budgets in
1919, the Tokyo city survey of the ghettoized poor in 1920, and the Home
Ministry inquiry into the household budgets of the Tokyo poor offer an
opportunity for the observation of this differentiation (Tsuda 1972, pp.
139-144). Table 2 summarizes the relevant information from these sources.
The data on factory workers purport to show monthly averages of yearly
totals; the 1920 data on the poor are impressionistic and for 1921 are for the
month of November. Factory workers were asked to keep daily records of
household incomes and expenses for one year, but the actual time varied.
There were forty satisfactory returns covering a total of 183 months. The
data therefore refer to monthly averages of these 183 household-months.
How accurately these reflect true monthly averages of annual totals per
household cannot be determined precisely.

The 1920 data on the poor were generated by direct interviews.
Unfortunately, the sample of 1690 households providing income data was
different from the sample of 612 households giving expenditure data. Income
and expenditure in the "average" column for 1920 are thus based on these
different samples. The column for the "richer" poor is based on still another
set of data about 93 households of four persons. The "richer" poor are about
12 to 15 percent above the poverty line for 1920.

The 1921 data, limited to the month of November, are not adjusted for
seasonality or other factors that must be considered if implications are to be
drawn for the whole year. The two columns refer to averages of those on the
lower and the higher sides of the ¥70 average of 497 households keeping
daily records.

1. The average worker and the average poor. Table 2 shows the 1919
"average" household income of factory workers is 40 percent above the 1920
"average" household income of the poor. However, as money wages increased
by at least 30 percent between 1919 and 1920, the same factory workers
should have earned more in 1920 than in 1919, making the 1920 income
differential even larger. The text of the data source observes the average poor
did not save (although this cannot be clear from Table 2), whereas there was
obviously some saving in the "average" household of workers. This difference
in the behavior of saving is not surprising, because the saving ratio decreases
as income decreases where the marginal propensity to consume is less than
unity.

———————

household of four persons as of 1898. The daily figures are meant to be daily
earnings, and the monthly figures are based on the assumption of twenty-six
working days in a month.

	Per day	Month	Year
Break-even point	¥0.70	¥18.20	¥218
Poverty line	0.50	13.00	156
Average poor	0.30	7.80	94

Table 2

Monthly Household Incomes and Expenditures: Factory Workers and the Poor Compared, 1919, 1920, 1921

Items	Factory workers (1919)		The poor (1920)		The poor (1921)	
	Average	"Poorer"	Average	"Richer"	¥60-70	¥70-80
Household size (persons)	4.2	4.0	4.2	4.0	4.3	4.5
Head's earnings	¥63.27	¥56.90	n.a.	n.a.	¥52.33	¥57.10
Household income	72.50	61.27	¥51.40	¥62.00	57.93	66.38
Household expenditures	69.76	62.73	n.a.	n.a.	56.66	61.08
1. Food and drink	35.09	30.45	38.17	40.30	34.84	36.14
Rice and cereal	18.74	n.a.	20.34	n.a.	16.95	17.40
Other	16.25	n.a.	17.83	n.a.	17.89	18.74
2. Shelter	7.19	7.02	n.a.	n.a.	4.48	4.68
Rent	6.52	n.a.	4.12	3.77	n.a.	n.a.
Other	0.67	n.a.	n.a.	n.a.	n.a.	n.a.
3. Fuel and lighting	4.33	3.85	n.a.	n.a.	4.30	4.68
4. Clothing	6.77	5.70	n.a.	n.a.	3.60	4.82
5. Other expenditures	16.38	15.71	n.a.	n.a.	9.44	10.76
6. Not elsewhere specified	--	--	(5.25)	(8.12)	--	--
Surplus or deficit	+2.74	-1.46	n.a.	n.a.	+1.27	+5.30
Engel coefficient	50.3%	48.5%	74.3%	65.0%	61.5%	59.2%

Sources: 1919: *Kakei Chōsa* 1971, pp. 105-150. 1920: Tōkyō-shi 1922, 10:540-542. 1921: Naimushō 1921, p. 63 and pp. 76-82.

Note: Engel's coefficient, normally defined as the ratio of food in total expenditures, has income as its denominator for 1920.

Interesting differences are observed in the structure of household expenditures. Despite lower income for the same household size, the poor spent a larger *absolute* amount of money on food than workers. (A higher relative outlay on food is expected.) This larger outlay on food and drink by the poor in 1920 than by workers in 1919 is an enigma because the price of medium-grade rice hardly changed, whereas that of low-grade rice fell 36 percent.[28] Further, the Tokyo city report subsumes the outlay on sake and tobacco by the poor under *shikōhin*—"discretionary and recreational expenses" (entered as "not elsewhere specified"), and these items were the bulk of such expenditures. Usually, they are put in the food and drink category. The Engel coefficient for the poor is high, 74 percent. The "truer" coefficient, with the addition of sake and tobacco to the food and drink category, would raise it to 80 percent. This suggests the life of the average poor was dominated by the sheer necessity (or joy?) of eating and drinking at the expense of everything else. Emphasis on eating is due in part to high residential mobility, which precludes thinking of living on the basis of a stable community life requiring other forms of cultural or social expenses.

2. "Poorer" workers and "richer" poor. To be more positive about life-style differences between factory workers and the poor, it is desirable to standardize income and household size. If there remain noticeable differences in the expenditure pattern between worker and poor households, the life styles of the two groups can be said to be different. (The question may be raised as to which life style is "desirable" or "acceptable" from the point of view of middle-class criteria for allocating honor and stigma to various population groups.) The data in Table 2 make possible a direct comparison between poorer workers in 1919 and richer poor in 1920, for households were the same average size and average incomes were about the same.

Table 2 suggests that despite the same level of income, the richer poor of 1920 spent 30 percent more on food than the poorer workers of 1919. (The consumer price index with respect to food rose 4 percent between 1919 and 1920.) If their sake and tobacco consumption were transferred from "not elsewhere specified" to the "food" category, the expenditure on food by the poor would easily rise to 50 percent above that by workers. Despite their ability to pay, the richer poor paid less for rent than the poorer workers, indicating the inferior housing conditions the poor, however rich, would tolerate. As the poor moved frequently, their reasoning may well have been "why pay more for housing than necessary until the next move?"

The incomplete itemization of the poor households' accounts in Table 2 affords only broad observations. The expenses to be met by the poor after food, sake, and tobacco covered such items as fuel and lighting, clothing, health and sanitation, education, and others which were enumerated in greater detail in the workers' household accounts. For convenience of identification, we may call these "status-demonstrating" expenses. Even if the

---

[28]For the price of medium-grade rice, see LTES 8:153. For the price of low-grade rice, see Tōkyō-shi 1921, p. 85.

richer poor devoted to status-demonstrating expenses everything left after meeting expenses for food, rent, sake, and tobacco, this would still amount to only 16 percent of household income or expenditure. In the poorer workers' households, the status expenses (everything other than food and shelter) amounted to about 40 percent of total consumption expenditure. Further, the Tokyo city survey, the source of the data for Table 2, suggests a possibility of saving in households of four persons with incomes exceeding ¥60 a month. The richer poor in Table 2, with an income of ¥62 a month should therefore at least have balanced income and expenditure. For the same level of income, however, the "poorer" workers were consuming more than their incomes.

3. The poor in 1921. This contrast between workers and poor is further supported by the survey into incomes and expenditures of the poor, based on households keeping daily accounts for the month of November 1921. The "income" bracket was constructed on the basis of total income for the reference month, which therefore included such "extraordinary" items as cash carried over from the previous month, money borrowed during the month, and dissaving. However, the income shown in the third row of Table 2 is net of these extraordinary items.

The 1921 figure for food and drink includes expenditure on sake and tobacco, so coverage is directly comparable to this category of workers' household accounts for 1919. There was a 7 percent fall in the price level between 1920 and 1921, contrasting with the 4 percent rise between 1919 and 1920. The 1921 income of ¥57.93 thus is equivalent to ¥61.80 in 1920 prices, a figure close to the 1920 household income of the richer poor and the poorer workers. Food prices fell more drastically between 1920 and 1921 than other prices. The 1921 expenditure of ¥34.84 on food and drink was equivalent to ¥43.00 in 1920 prices and ¥41.00 in 1919 prices.[29] Thus, for the same level of real income, the 1921 outlay on food and drink by the poor was little different from the 1920 outlay of the same category by the richer poor and much higher than that by the poorer workers. The poor in 1921 were eating and drinking more than workers of the same income level. Differences in life style are thus obvious between workers and the poor. The poor seem to be culture-poor compared with workers equally poor in terms of income.

Because the status-demonstrating expenses mentioned previously have to do with fairly visible aspects of life style, the relative enormity of these expenses in workers' households around 1920 indicates the workers' subculture already had its own demonstration effect similar to that of the middle class, a shared urge for upward mobility in terms of income, job, and status. Workers' aspirations and efforts also should have produced beneficial externalities by contributing toward neighborhood face-lifting. Through their life style, workers should have transmitted their aspirations and motivations to their

[29]The comparison is based on the Consumer's Price Index for food in LTES 8:135.

children, who in their turn would be impelled to carry them further. From this point of view, sociocultural components of household expenditure may well be regarded as an investment in the quality of the next generation. One may therefore say that around 1920 workers were already fairly well integrated into the process of Japanese society's structural evolution, whereas the poor probably had weaker linkages with this process and were, for this reason, more alienated from society at large.

Origins of the Poor

It becomes increasingly clear that by "poor" we are speaking of persons incapable of moving out of poverty on their own. The ghetto was the final destination after a series of straight or zigzag movements down the socioeconomic scale. High residential mobility among the poor can be inferred from various sources.[30] Among the household heads in the Tokyo surveys of 1911 and 1912, more than two-thirds had originated in prefectures outside Tokyo. The 1920 Tokyo survey points out school transfers among poor children were fifteen times higher than among ordinary households. The 1934 survey of the poor in newly incorporated areas of Tokyo for the first time showed data on the distribution of poor households by length of residence in the surveyed areas. About 11 percent had resided for less than one year and 46.3 percent less than five years. But an amazingly high proportion, 23.1 percent, had lived in the areas more than ten years. Presumably, therefore, there was some sort of hard-core poor. More than twenty years earlier, the 1912 survey classified the poor into two groups: those born poor and those becoming poor in their own lifetime. The first group contained 28 percent of the poor. What degree of importance to give this information is not clear. The reasons given for being poor by those surveyed in Tokyo in 1911, 1912 (only those becoming poor in their own lifetime), and 1920 are economic failure, 30 percent; poor health, aging, and death in the family, 20 percent; certain personal deficiencies, 20 percent; and the rest, natural calamities and miscellaneous causes.[31] The personal deficiencies include lack of skills and education, low native ability, sloth, debauchery, drinking, gambling, indebtedness, and family breakup.

In short, the ghetto poor lack the requisite economic and psychic resources to overcome poverty. When the dynamics of a growing economy push upward, with higher and higher standards of skill, education, discipline, health, and sociability, the dynamics of life for the poor push downward. Their hand-to-mouth living and unhealthy environment render them vulnerable to increasingly frequent illnesses, which bring about larger deficits in their household budgets; their ability to work becomes more irregular, resulting

[30]See Tsuda 1972, pp. 102-106; Tōkyō-shi 1921, pp. 93-94 and 165, 1936, pp. 49-50; and Naimushō 1914.

[31]For a more detailed distribution of the poor by cause, limited to 1911, see Taira 1969, p. 166.

in even lower earnings and lower level jobs. Paying rent becomes more difficult, necessitating moving to inferior housing; family cohesion is threatened; and finally, personality breakdowns seal off many in permanent poverty.[32] Possibly, long before this final stage is reached, and while some physical strength is left, some individuals might try to claim a share in society's resources by unlawful means. By resorting to this course of action, they would usually find themselves not in ghettos but in penal institutions.[33]

When we consider the divergent process in which society goes up and the poor go down, we suspect there is a dividing line, however difficult to define, below which families or individuals simply cannot help but be sucked down into deeper poverty. At this level, the poor need outside help. This rather obvious conclusion was the hard-earned lesson of more than thirty years of private and public ghetto-watching in Japan between the 1880s and the 1920s. Thus, public assistance and social work became serious topics for debate and policy in the 1920s.

Public Assistance to the Poor

A brief summary of the long history of public assistance in Japan seems appropriate here.[34] In December 1874, the Meiji government issued a relief regulation consolidating the diverse, customary practices of the Tokugawa period. Assistance was to be given at public expense to persons thirteen years of age or younger, chronically ill, or seventy years or older. However, even this stringent scheme suffered setbacks in the late years of Meiji. One special category of poor could not be disregarded: disabled veterans, their families, and the bereaved families of the war dead. The Veterans Assistance Law was put into effect in 1917. Prefectural and local governments then had to provide the general assistance, and in their hands considerable institutional and conceptual progress was made. In May 1917, Okayama prefecture introduced a social innovation in dealing with the problems of the poor: utilizing the voluntary services of eminent local citizens as welfare counselors, each looking after one welfare district. By 1928, all the prefectures and more than twenty municipalities had welfare commissions, and the number of welfare counselors or commissioners in all Japan exceeded 15,000.

Of these prefectural systems, Osaka's was the most elaborate and pur-

---

[32]Hard data to support this downward process are not available for earlier years. However, generalizations similar to it, with supporting data from life histories of poor and welfare recipients, are available for recent years. See Kagoyama 1970, especially chap. 5, and Tsuda 1972, pp. 250-275.

[33]At the risk of sounding facetious, it may be pointed out the cost of maintaining prison inmates has traditionally been regarded as equivalent to the subsistence cost of the poor. One often hears, however, that life in jail is better than life outside for the poor. The resort to petty offenses for a brief vacation in prison is a serious proposition among the poor.

[34]For more detail, see Taira 1967.

poseful. The important factor in this case was the rice riots, which raged in Osaka 11-19 August 1918. The rice riots began in Toyama on 23 July and spread throughout Japan, the last reported incidence being in Fukuoka on 17 September. A rice riot (*kome sōdō*) is a somewhat derogatory expression for a consumer protest of sudden sharp increases in the retail price of rice (for example, by 50 percent in two weeks in Osaka in August 1918), which often involved assaults on rice merchants and looting of rice stores (Inoue and Watanabe 1960, 1:72-104). By the nature of the event, the 1918 protesters were predominantly those with no reserve of rice or money to tide them over the period between the price increases and the adjustments of income to prices.

The Japanese government put down the riots by a combination of ruthless use of police power and large-scale handouts of rice to the eligible poor. The authorities learned one lesson, however: the poor had the capability to rise up and disrupt law and order when their living was suddenly threatened by a massive decline in their real income. The authorities therefore sought methods for the early detection of discontent, so unrest could be dealt with before developing into a major disturbance. The Okayama welfare commission system looked ideal for the purpose. The Osaka prefectural government was particularly perceptive of the value of the system for surveillance of the poor.[35] Thus an ignominious marriage of authoritarian government and the charitable spirit of local leaders was effected. The prefectural government deployed the police in collaboration with welfare commissioners. Each commissioner maintained a card file recording living conditions of the poor in his district. Thus a new euphemism for the poor arose: card class (*kādo kaikyu*). The commissioners obtained public assistance for the worst cases under their charge.

Further progress was made during the interwar period. An improved relief and protection law passed the Diet in 1929 and was put into effect in 1932. The system was further modernized and expanded by the Occupation after the Second World War. Under the postwar Livelihood Protection Law, subject to a means test, anyone whose standard of living fell below a certain official minimum was entitled to assistance up to that minimum, regardless of what brought about the need for assistance.

This law was to implement Article 25 of the new constitution, which guarantees every Japanese national at least a "healthy and cultured minimum standard of living." Literally interpreted, this means anyone unable to attain a "healthy and cultured minimum" is entitled (as a matter of right) to assistance from the state in the amount and manner enabling reaching that minimum with dignity. The sum of one's own income (which may be zero) and public assistance would equal the minimum standard. Thus, the life style of the income-poor would no longer be sharply differentiated from that of ordinary citizens and would be free of the charge that the poor are indecent.

[35] A viewpoint expressed in Naimushō 1971.

Poverty as defined in the conceptual framework for this article would be eliminated from Japan.

However, the implementation of this constitutional provision has been full of practical difficulties. Until 1955, the majority of Japanese had not even recovered the level of income considered normal before the war (the level that prevailed in 1934-36). Further, one was not sure whether the prewar norm itself met the standards of health and culture appropriate to the 1950s, for aspirations for a better living had risen in the meantime.[36] Under the circumstances, it was impossible to determine the monetary value of the minimum standard required by the constitution. Thus, the system was forced to operate by a series of improvisations.

In determining the guarantee level, the government initially used a market basket of specific items considered necessities for a certain level of living (but hardly a healthy and cultured minimum). Beginning in 1961, the formula was simplified by use of the concept of the Engel coefficient, while retaining the estimate of food requirements through a method essentially similar to the former market basket formula. The required food expenditure was divided by a certain Engel coefficient to obtain the total level of assistance.[37] The use of the Engel coefficient method formally recognized freedom of consumer choice for the nonfood portion of the welfare household's budget. Actually, the welfare recipients were always free in the use of the assistance money, because checks on the life style of the recipients were not so rigorous as to make the actual expenditures identical to the items in the official market basket.

[36]The standard of living and its structural characteristics with respect to nonpoor households have given rise to a lively field of research and discussion called *seikatsu-kōzō-ron* (approximately translated as "structure of living conditions"). See Chūbachi 1971c and 1972; and Chūbachi and Eguchi 1972.

[37]For the theoretical and empirical justifications of the use of the Engel Coefficient, see Chūbachi 1961. To illustrate, the first step is to estimate the Engel Coefficient corresponding to a level of living that allows for an expenditure on food capable of providing 1885 calories per day per person. An empirical cross-section function, $Y = f(X)$, is fitted on data from four-member household budgets, where Y is the Engel Coefficient and X, the expenditure on food. Substituting a family's minimum necessary food expenditure for X yields the requisite Engel Coefficient, and the total minimum expenditure for a family is X/Y. Assistance standards for shelter, medical care, and children's education are separately determined, and there are limits on retained earnings. After adjustments for these separate items, the remaining amount is termed the "standard for livelihood assistance" (*seikatsu fujo kijun*). After the schedule of assistance by kind and family size is drawn up, the maximum a family can expect is the sum of assistances for livelihood, shelter, children's education, and medical care plus the maximum retained earnings. The full package constitutes the "guaranteed minimum level of living" (*saitei seikatsu hoshō suijun*). For practical examples, see Kagoyama 1970, pp. 29-33.

In 1965 the Engel coefficient formula was replaced by a method designed to keep welfare household budgets abreast of increases in consumption expenditures of the lowest decile of all households (Shakai Hoshō 1973). It was recognized that during the 1960s the degree of inequality in income distribution by size was decreasing perceptibly, resulting from faster increases in incomes at the lower end of the distribution than in other parts. Because the new method brings about a narrowing of the differential between the level of living of welfare households and ordinary households, it is called the differential-narrowing method (*kakusa shukushō hōshiki*). In 1970, the actual consumption expenditures of welfare households stood at 51.3 percent of those of the ordinary households in Tokyo. The Ministry of Welfare is discreetly silent as to how much the differential should be allowed to narrow. It is obvious the ministry has created formidable conceptual and operational problems for itself. If, for example, the public perceives that assistance guarantees a level of living no different from that of the average household, there are likely to be enormous political repercussions, for welfare money eventually comes from the taxes paid by the ordinary households.[38] What is important from the point of view of this paper is that the Japanese have finally struck on the method of eliminating relative poverty, for the indignity and degradation of the poor are the function of a drastic deviation of their life style from the community standards.

Toward an Abolition of Poverty

Data on the size distribution of income enable us to ascertain the extent of income-poverty in a society. Characteristics of the Japanese size distribution of income are discussed by Ono and Watanabe in their essay in this volume. We limit our attention to 1930 and 1968, to illustrate the changing nature of Masana Maeda's income grade structure composed of poor, inferior, intermediate, and superior grades. The relevance of this set of expressions has long since vanished, but as Maeda's classification is based on numerical coefficients, it is of interest to see if their application to later size distributions of income produces income grade structures similar to Maeda's observations for the 1880s. The 1930 size distribution of income is the only suitable one available for the prewar period. A variety of data on the size distribution of income is available for a number of postwar years, making it possible to observe trends and fluctuations.[39] Among these, the 1968 data adequately illustrate whether or not income poverty is disappearing from Japan.

1. 1930. The results of applying Maeda's classification to the 1930 size distribution of income are shown in Table 3. There are considerable similarities between Table 3 and its 1880s counterpart presented earlier. The previous tabulation referred to *population* and the present one to *households*.

[38]Some writers are aware of these difficulties. See Kagoyama 1970, pp. 37-38.

[39]See Yamamura 1967, pp. 170-172; Keizai Kikaku-chō; Kokumin 1965, chap. 4.

Table 3
The Income-Grade Structure of Japan, 1930

Grade	Income bracket (yen)	Households (in percent)	Income share (in percent)	Income per household (yen)
Superior	Over 1000	10.6	47.1	3100
Intermediate	500 ~ 1000	24.6	24.6	670
Inferior	200 ~ 500	47.1	25.5	360
Poor	~ 200	17.7	3.8	150
Total		100.0	100.0	694

Source: Computed from Lockwood 1954, p. 272 (table 23). Data referring to the ¥0-200 bracket are reproduced from Lockwood's table. Other income brackets have required numerical adaptations. For example, the ¥200-500 bracket is obtained by splitting Lockwood's ¥400-800 bracket into ¥400-500 and ¥500-800, and adding the first part to Lockwood's ¥200-400 bracket. Likewise, the intermediate grade is constructed from the ¥500-800 bracket obtained previously and the ¥800-1000 bracket split from Lockwood's ¥800-1200. All other upper-income brackets are drawn into the superior grade of this table.

The average household size in 1930 was 5.1 persons. As the poor and the inferior-grade households were smaller in size than the national average, restating the income-grade structure in terms of population raises the proportion of superior grade, and lowers the proportions of inferior grade and of the poor. For example, allocating the total population on the basis of 4 persons for poor and 6.9 persons for superior-grade households, the proportion of the poor in terms of population is reduced to 14.7 percent and that of the superior grade raised to 14.2 percent. Compared with the 1880s, the superior grade rises close to the upper limit of the range hypothesized for it (15 percent), while the poor fall just below the lower limit of the range for them (15 percent). However, these differences cannot be taken as a serious indicator of substantial differences between the income-grade structures of the two periods.

The choice of ¥200 as the 1930 poverty line on which to erect Maeda's income-grade structure is primarily for convenience, because it is the upper limit of the lowest income bracket in Lockwood's tabulation. For example, the 1930 poverty line used by the Tokyo welfare commissioners for maintaining the card class files mentioned earlier was ¥55 per month for a family of three and ¥65 for a family of four, which on an annual basis is ¥660, and ¥780 (Tōkyō-shi 1932 and Isomura 1959). For all of Japan, one can hardly use the Tokyo poverty line, because for a household of five it rose to ¥840 a year, which is higher than the ¥694 average household income calculated from Lockwood's income distribution. Tokyo's poverty line makes 85 percent of all Japanese income-poor in 1930! This only indicates the enormity of interregional income differentials in 1930. Although the standard of living in Tokyo may well have been two or three times as high as in the rest of the country, ¥200 nonetheless seems low as a national average poverty line.

Another test of ¥200 as a possible poverty line is to compare it to the ruling public assistance standard. In 1930, the relief standard of 1874 was still in effect. It allowed 1.8 koku of rice a year to the aged and 0.7 koku to the young. The standard of living of a family of four (two adults and two children) on the basis of the relief standard is 5.0 koku per annum, which at Tokyo's retail price of medium-grade rice (¥0.34 per sho) amounted to ¥170, or 15 percent lower than ¥200. Because the poverty line as an expression of some morally tolerable level of living is usually higher than the rock bottom of administratively feasible relief standards, ¥200 again appears to have been a conservative level. But a higher poverty line would make the proportion of households in the poor category rise above 20 percent. Therefore, ¥200 seems acceptable as the poverty line for 1930.

2. 1968. Better calculations can be made for 1968 than for 1930 with respect to the income-grade structure of both households and population. Data on the size distribution of household income are available in the Employment Status Survey undertaken every three years by the prime minister's office (Sōrifu). "Income" in the 1968 survey means earnings through personal participation in production, that is, wages, salaries, fees, and profits, without including returns to assets, remittances, or transfer payments. With respect to households, two types are distinguished, single person and multiple person (ordinary family). To this size distribution of household income by type of household, we apply Maeda's coefficients built on a poverty line equal to the Welfare Ministry's "guaranteed minimum level of living" (saitei seikatsu hoshō suijun) by household type. The 1968 median guaranteed minimum (there are four standards because of geographical differences in the cost of living) is ¥350,400 per annum for a family of four.[40] The minimum is subject to a scale of marginal adjustments for larger or smaller households. The minimum for a single-person household is slightly less than one-half of the four-person household norm. The adjustment scale is actually fairly complicated due to further adjustments for variations in age and sex. For simplicity, though without any loss of generality or plausibility, we have assumed the single-person household minimum is exactly one-half the four-person household norm. On this basis, the application of Maeda's income-grade coefficients to the 1968 size distribution of household income is presented in Table 4.

Nearly 15 percent of all households have earnings below the officially guaranteed minimum. But this discouraging picture is due mainly to the heavy concentration of single-person households in the poor and inferior-grade categories. Among multiple-person households, the poor are fewer than 10 percent. On the basis of population, the proportion is even smaller, less than 9 percent for the entire population and about 7 percent for the population attached to ordinary households. Thus, compared with 1930, the

[40]See Kōseishō 1968. Geographical differentials in the assistance standards are as follows:

Class:	I	II	III	IV
Percentage:	100	91	82	73

Table 4
The Income-Grade Structure of Japan, 1968
(numbers in thousands, percentage in parentheses)

Grade	Income bracket index	Households			Persons		
		Ordinary	Single-person	Total	Ordinary households	Single-person households	Total
Superior	500 and over	847	290	1137	4400	290	4696
		(4.0)	(5.3)	(4.1)	(4.6)	(5.3)	(4.6)
Intermediate	250 ~ 500	9614	1308	10,922	42,765	1308	44,073
		(41.8)	(23.4)	(38.2)	(44.7)	(23.4)	(43.6)
Inferior	100 ~ 250	10,327	2022	12,349	41,539	2022	43,561
		(44.9)	(36.3)	(43.2)	(43.5)	(36.3)	(43.1)
Poor	0 ~ 100	2162	1949	4111	6826	1949	8775
		(9.3)	(35.0)	(14.5)	(7.2)	(35.0)	(8.7)
Total		22,950	5569	28,519	95,530	5569	101,099
		(100.0)	(100.0)	(100.0)	(100.0)	(100.0)	(100.0)

Source: Sōrifu, Employment 1968, p. 300.

Note: The income-grade structure is separately estimated for ordinary households and single-person households by applying to the respective size distributions of household income the income brackets scaled by Masana Maeda's coefficients with the "poverty line" = 100. The "poverty line" for the ordinary households of four persons is ¥350,400, while that for single persons is ¥175,200. In the case of the ordinary households, the household size varies from one income bracket to another in the source data. In order to adjust for differences in household size, the lower and upper limits of each income bracket are divided by the number of persons per household for that bracket to obtain per capita income brackets. For example, the original bracket, ¥300 to ¥390 thousand is associated with an average household size of 3.6 persons. On a per capita basis, this bracket becomes ¥83 to 109 thousand. This is compared with the per capita "poverty line" of ¥87,600 (= ¥350,400 divided by 4). These per capita income brackets are regrouped to obtain Maeda's income grades on the basis of the per capita "poverty line" for the household of four. The same operation, without the complication of adjustment for the household size, is undertaken for reorganizing the original distribution of single-person households by income bracket into Maeda's income grades. The intervals of the new income grades do not coincide with simple combinations of the original brackets. Therefore, Table 3's method is used for splitting up the number of households in an original bracket for allocation to one or the other of the neighboring income grades.

"poor" were relatively fewer in 1968. Because these figures are based on earnings before taxes or transfers, if all income flows into households such as remittances, transfers, returns to assets, gifts, and so on are taken into account, the proportion of the poor should be smaller, given the same guaranteed minimum. Furthermore, the poverty line for 1968 as a percentage of the 1968 average household earnings is higher than in 1930 as a percentage of the 1930 average household income (44.5 percent as compared to 28.8 percent).[41]

A more spectacular difference between 1930 and 1968, however, is the reduction in the weight of the superior grade. Compared to 1930, the 1968 income-grade structure represents a considerable income democratization of households, although this observation must be qualified to some extent if account is taken on all kinds of income, especially property income, which may increase the number in the superior grade. It should also be noted 1968 income democracy was a product of equalization of income distribution during the 1960s, which may be seen in proper perspective in the essay by Ono and Watanabe in this volume. Based on different sources of data and by a different method of estimation, the Economic Planning Agency has also ascertained a decreasing trend in the extent of poverty in recent years. In 1960, 15.6 percent of all households in Japan were "poor," but only 6.3 percent were "poor" by the same criteria in 1967. Thus, the Economic Planning Agency's *White Paper* in 1970 proudly proclaimed a "dissolution of poverty" (*mazushisa no kaishō*) was taking place in Japan (Keizai Kikaku-chō 1970, pp. 192-193).

3. Status equalization. On the basis of income statistics alone, there is no doubt income poverty has greatly diminished in recent years. We now examine how these objective conditions relate to various individuals' perceptions of their own standing in society. For some time, the Japanese public has been conditioned by repeated opinion polls to visualize social stratification in terms of upstream, midstream, and downstream (*jōryū, chūryu*, and *karyū*).[42] The typical poll question is, "Suppose Japanese society is composed of five levels such as upstream, upper midstream, lower midstream, upper downstream, and lower downstream. Where do you think you belong?" For convenience, these strata may be abbreviated as *U, UM, IM, UD*, and *LD*. In 1955 and 1961, Tokyo residents answered as follows (in

[41]Calculated from sources for Tables 3 and 4.

	A : "poverty line"	*B*: average household income	*A/B*
1930	¥ 200	¥ 694	28.8
1968	¥787,000	¥350,400	44.5

[42]Compare the modern "stream" analogy with Maeda's straightforward "grade." The hierarchical adjectives are the same: *jō-chū-ge*. The last Chinese ideograph, can also be read *ka*, thus *katō* (downgrade, inferior) or *karyū* (downstream). Idiomatically, *ge* for "down" is pejorative. One of the worst things a man can be called is *gesu*, "lowly official," but usually connoting a

percentages, the first figure refers to 1955 and the second to 1961): U (0, 1); UM (10, 10); LM (38, 40); UD (39, 33); and LD (12, 7).[43]

The rather high "no response" rate for 1961 (9 percent) is troublesome. It is possible the nonrespondents found their status too unsatisfactory to admit. If so, these statuses generally are downstream, which raises the total percentage of UD and LD to 49 percent, only two percentage points lower than the total of UD and LD for 1955. Under this assumption, one can only say there was some, though not very spectacular, upward drift in self-perceived status among Tokyoites between 1955 and 1961. On the other hand, "no response" may indicate status anxiety—a lack of confidence in where to locate oneself in the rapidly changing sociopolitical milieu of 1960-61.[44] In this case, the "real" (corrected for anxiety) upward status mobility between 1955 and 1961 is much greater than these figures imply.

To ascertain expectations, pollsters asked: "Where do you think you will belong in the future?" In 1961, Tokyoites on the whole perceived moving *at least* one step upward: 23 percent of present UM to U, 43 percent of present LM to UM, 1 percent of present LM to U (two steps up), 47 percent of present UD to LM, 22 percent of present UD to UM (two steps up), 3 percent of present UD to U (indomitable optimists), 22 percent of present LD to UD, 25 percent of present LD to LM (two steps up), and astonishingly, 3 percent of present LD all the way up into U. Naturally, the upstream denizens foresaw no floating down. If status mobility continued in this way, all Japanese would eventually gain the upstream status. Furthermore, as the parents' achieved status is likely to be transmitted to their offspring at least as a state of mind, high-status feelings would permeate the entire society. Everybody would be jōryū! Thus, social stratification would disappear, with everyone leveled up to the upstream status and with no one below. The society would be a democracy of aristocracy.

However, the dynamics of status mobility has not worked itself out yet, or modesty has constrained many to be content with midstream status. Public opinion polls by the prime minister's office on the basis of a slightly different wording of stratification in 1959 and 1969 showed a strong convergence of self-perceptions in the middle of the midstream as follows (in percentages, the first figure refers to 1959 and the second to 1969): U (0, 1); UM (3, 7); MM—middle midstream—(37, 52); LM (32, 30); D—no differentiation—(17, 8); and not clear (11, 3). Nearly 90 percent of the Japanese were chūryū in 1969 (Keizai Kikaku-chō 1970, pp. 5-6).

---

devious rascal. *Katō* is also a derogatory expression not unlike "down and out." On the other hand, *karyū* is only an analogy; no one need be upset over its meaning or sound.

[43]Nishihara 1963. The shortfall of the figures from 100 percent is due to "no response."

[44]In 1960-1961, the stormy Ampō struggles were just giving way to the flamboyant *shotoku-baizō* (income doubling) plan, creating a general mood of expectation mixed with a sense of uncertainty.

The question eliciting these results is interesting: "Given these statuses, where do you think the general public puts you?" In other words, "self" was used as an agent for the public and these "selves" put nearly 90 percent of themselves in the middle of the midstream. Of further interest is that the breakdown of status perceptions mentioned here closely conforms to the income-grade structure of Table 4, if we liken poor to downstream, inferior and intermediate to midstream, and superior to upstream. Evidently, when the income structure has reached a substantial degree of equality, as represented by the 1968 structure, such glaringly stratified expressions as those used for Maeda's income grades have no valid descriptive value. After a point, quantitative change is accompanied by qualitative change. Japan has finally left Meiji far behind. Thus, there is a high degree of congruence between the objective conditions of income distribution and the subjective feelings of status belonging. As with income poverty, both kinds are disappearing from Japan. Japan is as solidly a middle-class society today as any country in the world.

CONCLUSION

To write about the Japanese poor in English is an anomaly in itself, because whatever stands for "poor" in the Japanese language has its unique flavor within the Japanese sociocultural context, lost when rendered into English. In this essay, in order to minimize this anomaly, we have consciously tried to weave a number of different threads into a small fabric. The loom on which this is done is the historical flow of some central tendency in society's shared awareness of inequities in income, status, and power among its members. Although this historical flow is captured only for the segment stretching from the early 1880s to the present, poverty is not an invention of this period. It existed before that. Therefore, the popular notion of social stratification modern Japan inherited from its preceding era, with subsequent adaptations, became the initial framework that gave meaning to the station of the poor in Japanese society.

But the history of awareness of poverty had its new, if rude, beginning at the time of Japan's initiation into modern economic growth in the 1880s. This was the discovery of hinmin-kutsu (grottos of the poor) by the molders of public sentiment—political leaders, administrators, and intellectuals. Due largely to the intensity of human misery in hinmin-kutsu and to the difficulties of understanding the factors responsible for this state of affairs, the magical hold of hinmin-kutsu on the public's mind lasted a long time, roughly until 1920, by which time it had become reasonably clear not all the poor were in hinmin-kutsu. It was also realized poverty was a ubiquitous risk for anyone in a dynamic society, requiring the understanding of the total socioeconomic processes through new approaches. In fact, by 1920, efforts for reducing this risk had already begun for society in general, especially for the working class, under the movement for *shakai seisaku* (social policy), which is not discussed here.

Concern over the problems of the poor branched into *shakai jigyō* (social work) and public assistance. Thus the central tendency of awareness of the poor after 1920 has revolved around the meaning and method of social services to the poor. In the meantime, modern economic growth continued at an accelerated rate, though it was temporarily reduced to a shambles during and after the Second World War. The war initiated radical changes in many aspects of Japanese life, including attitudes toward poverty, methods of dealing with the problems of the poor, and even the language used for thinking about poverty and the poor. Postwar economic growth and new approaches to income distribution and poverty had positive effects by 1970, when opinion leaders were finally able to say poverty (now politely called *mazushisa*, a poetic expression with a touch of heart-squeezing sentimentality) was being "dissolved" in Japan.

However, the problems of the "other Japan," the minority groups, still exist. There are also problems of unusual population density in places such as Tokyo's Sanya and Osaka's Kamagasaki districts, mentioned but not discussed in this article. The relationships between general society and Sanya or Kamagasaki may require analytical attention of the kind appropriate to the "other Japan." Today, neither Sanya nor Kamagasaki is a ghetto or slum in the conventional sense, let alone a hinmin-kutsu. But the number of low-income, low-skilled, single male workers is large in these areas and creates special problems for law and order (Caldarola 1968-69).

In addition to whatever may be usefully covered by the notion of the "other Japan," the mainstream itself faces a number of problems threatening the quality of life. These come under the umbrella of externalities of economic growth. As discussed in Prime Minister Tanaka's tract (1973) on a remodeling of Japan, they affect all Japanese roughly equally, requiring thorough changes in all aspects of Japanese life—a century of revolution to correct the ills of the previous century. One therefore finds that, despite their high *level of living* (*seikatsu suijun*), the affluent of today's povertyless Japan claim they are worse off than before relative to the *standard of life* (*seikatsu hyōjun*) their productivity should bring about. Mainstream Japan, where nearly everyone is equally "middle class," is "immiserated" in a new sense.[45] Further investigation is needed into this "new poverty," known by the catchy phrase, *atarashii hinkon*.

[45] For a theoretical discussion of this issue, see Scitovsky 1973.

REFERENCES

Abel-Smith, Brian. 1966. "The United Kingdom." In *Low-Income Groups and Methods of Dealing with Their Problems*, edited by the Organization for Economic Cooperation and Development.

Buraku Kaihō Dōmei, ed. 1971. *'71 Buraku Kaihō Undō*.

Caldarola, Carlo. 1968-1969. "The Doya-Gai: A Japanese Version of Skid Row." *Pacific Affairs* 41.

Chūbachi, Masayoshi. 1961. *Teishotoku-kaiso ni okeru Teishotoku no Genkai no Settei ni Kansuru Kenkyū*. Social Welfare Association.

——, ed. 1971a. *Kakei-chōsa to Seikatsu-kenkyū*, vol. 7 of *Seikatsu Koten Sōsho*. Kōseikan.

——, ed. 1971b. *Kazoku-shūki to Kakei-kōzō*. Shiseidō.

——. 1971c. "Seikatsu-kōzō-ron Oboegaki." *Mita Gakkai Zasshi* 64.

——. 1972. "Seikatsu-kōzō Henka no Gendaiteki Kadai." *Mita Gakkai Zasshi* 65.

——. 1973. Book Review of Masumi Tsuda: *Nihon no Toshi Kaso Shakai* in *Nihon Rōdō Kyōkai Zasshi*, Jan. 1973, pp. 1-3.

Chūbachi, Masayoshi, and Eiichi Eguchi, eds. 1972. *Shakai-fushi to Seikatsu-kōzō*. Koseikan.

Chuma, Teruhisa, ed. (This name may also be read as Nakama.) 1931. *Nihon Chiri Fūzoku Taikei*, vol. 9. Shinkōsha.

DeVos, George, and Hiroshi Wagatsuma, eds. 1967. *Japan's Invisible Race*. University of California Press.

Dore, Ronald. 1973. *British Factory-Japanese Factory*. University of California Press.

Duesenberry, James S. 1949. *Income, Saving, and the Theory of Consumer Behavior*. Harvard University Press.

Galbraith, John K. 1958. *The Affluent Society*. Penguin.

Gonda, Yasunosuke. 1926. "Rōdōsha oyobi Shōgaku-hōkyū Seikatsu-sha no Kakei-jōtai Hihaku." Reprinted in *Seikatsu Koten Sōsho*, vol. 7, edited by Masayoshi Chūbachi. Kōseikan. 1971.

Harrington, Michael. 1962. *The Other America*. Macmillan.

Inoue, Kiyoshi. 1959. *Buraku Mondai no Kenkyū*. Buraku Monkai Kenkyūjo.

Inoue, Kiyoshi, and Tōru Watanabe, eds. 1960. *Kome-sōdō no Kenkyū*. Yūhikaku.

Inoue, Teizo. 1923. *Hinmin-kutsu to Shōsu-dōbō*. Ganshobō.

Isomura, Eiichi. 1959. *Suramu*. Kōdansha.

Kagawa, Toyohiko. 1915. *Hinmin Shinri no Kenkyū*. Keisei-sha.

Kagoyama, Takashi. 1970. *Teishotoku-sō to Hihogo-sō*. Minerva.

Kasumi Kaikan. 1966. *Kazoku Kaikan Shi*.

Keizai Kikaku-chō [Economic Planning Agency]. 1970. *Kaizai Hakusho*.

——. *Kokumin Seikatsu Hakusho*. Annual.

Kerr, George. 1958. *Okinawa*. Tuttle.

Kokumin Seikatsu Kenkyūjo [National Life Research Institute]. 1965. *Shotoku Bunpu no Jittai oyobi Shotai-kōzō-henka ni Kansuru Kenkyū*.

Kōseishō [Welfare Ministry]. 1968. *Kōsei Hakusho*.

Kusama, Yaso'o. 1930. "Dai Tōkyō no Saimingai to Seikatsu no Taiyō." *Nihon Chiri Taikei*, vol. 3, edited by Teruhisa Chuma. (The editor's name may also be read Nakama.) Shinkō-sha.

Kyōchō-kai. 1930. *Saikin no Shakai-undō*.

Lewis, Oscar. 1965. *La Vida*. Random House.

Lockwood, William W. 1954. *The Economic Development of Japan*. Princeton University Press.

LTES [Estimates of Long-Term Economic Statistics of Japan]. Series edited

by Kazushi Ohkawa, Miyohei Shinohara, and Mataji Umemura. 1965-. 14 vols. Tōyō Keizai Shinpōsha.
. Vol. 6. *Personal Consumption Expenditures.* 1967. Miyohei Shinohara.
. Vol. 8. *Prices.* 1967. Kazushi Ohkawa et al.
Maeda, Masana. 1971. *Kōgyō Iken.* Reprinted in *Seikatsu Koten Sōsho,* vol. 1, edited with a contribution by Yoshio Ando and Hirobumi Yamamoto. Kōseikan.
Miyade, Hideo. 1950. *Rumpen Shakai no Kenkyū.* Kaizō-sha.
Morioka, Kiyomi. 1967. "Shūki-ron kara Mita Gendai Kazoku no Dōtai." *Hōritsu Jihō,* Nov. 1967.
Naimushō [Ministry of the Interior]. 1912, 1914, and 1922. *Saimin Chōsa Tōkei-hyō.* (The 1922 report was reprinted in 1959 in *Nihon Rōdō Undō Shiryō* 10:540-542, edited by Rōdō Undō Shiryō Iinkai. Page references are to the reprint edition.)
. 1971. "A Study by the Home Ministry Council on Health and Sanitation, 1918-19." Reprinted as part of Yasunosuke Gonda, "Tōkyō-shi ni okeru Rōdōsha Kakei no Ichi-mokei," 1923, in *Seikatsu Koten Sōsho* 7:105-113, edited by Masayoshi Chūbachi. Kōseikan.
Narita, Tokuhei. 1973. "Ainu toshite no Watakushi-no On'nen." *Chūō Kōron.*
Nihon Shakai Jigyō Daigaku [College of Social Work]. 1960. *Nihon no Kyūhin Seido.*
Nippon Teikoku Tōkei Nenkan [Statistical Yearbook of the Empire of Japan].
Nishida, Taketoshi. 1970. "Meiji-zenki no Toshi Kasō-Shakai." *Seikatsu Koten Sōsho,* vol. 2, edited by Taketoshi Nishida. Kōseikan.
Nishihara, Shigeki. 1963. *Nihonjin no Iken.* Seishin Shobō.
Oh, Lim-Jung. 1972. *Chōsenjin no Hikari to Kage.* Gōdō Shuppan.
Oka, Minoru. 1912. "Shokkō no Seikei Jōtai." Reprinted in *Seikatsu Koten Sōsho* 7:53-84, edited by Masayoshi Chūbachi. Kōseikan. 1971.
Ornati, Oscar. 1966. *Poverty Amid Affluence.* Twentieth Century Fund.
Osaka-fu Shakai Jigyō Shi. Reprinted in Nihon Shakai Jigyō Daigaku, *Nihon no Kyūhin-Seido.*
Sarashina, Genzō. 1970. *Ainu to Nihonjin.* NHK Books.
Scitovsky, Tibor. 1973. "The Place of Economic Welfare in Human Welfare." *Quarterly Review of Economics and Business,* autumn 1973.
Shakai Hoshō Kenkyūjo [Social Development Research Institute]. 1973. *Shakai Hoshō Suijun Kiso-tōkei.*
Sōrifu [Office of the Prime Minister]. 1969. *1968 Employment Status Survey: All Japan.*
Sumiya, Mikio. 1955. *Nihon Chinrōdō Shi-ron.* Tokyo University Press.
. ed. 1972. *Yokoyama Gen'nosuke Zenshu.* Meiji Bunken.
Suzuki, Umeshiro. 1970. "Osaka Nago-machi Hinmin-kutsu Shisatsu-ki." In *Seikatsu Koten Sōsho,* vol. 2, edited by Taketoshi Nishida. Kōseikan.
Taira, Koji. 1967. "Public Assistance in Japan: Development and Trends." *Journal of Asian Studies* 27 (Nov. 1967).
. 1969. "Urban Poverty, Ragpickers, and the 'Ants' Villa' in Tokyo." *Economic Development and Cultural Change,* Jan. 1969.
. 1971. "Education and Literacy in Meiji Japan: An Interpretation." *Explorations in Economic History* 8 (July 1971).

Tanaka, Kakuei. 1973. *Building a New Japan*. Simul Press.

Tashiro, Kunijirō, ed. 1965. *Nihon Shakai Fukushi no Kisoteki Kenkyū*. Dōshin-sha.

Tōkyō-shi. 1921. "Tōkyō-shi ni Okeru Rōdōsha Kakei no Ichi-mokei." Reprinted in *Seikatsu Koten Sōsho*, vol. 7, edited by Masayoshi Chūbachi. Kōseikan. 1971.

. 1932. *Tōkyō-shi Yōhogo-shotai Seikei Chōsa*.

. 1936. *Tōkyō-shi Shin-shi'iki Furyō-jūtaku-chiku Chōsa*.

Tōkyō-to. 1962. *Tōkyō-to ni okeru Suramu-shakai Keisei ni Kansuru Kenkyū*.

. 1965. *Tōmin no Seikatsu*.

Townsend, Peter. 1962. "The Meaning of Poverty." *British Journal of Sociology*, Nov. 1962.

Tsuda, Masumi. 1972. *Nihon no Toshi Kasō-shakai*. Minerva.

Veblen, Thorstein. 1899. *The Theory of the Leisure Class*. Macmillan.

Yamamura, Kozo. 1967. *Economic Policy in Postwar Japan*. University of California Press.

Yanagida, Kunio. 1931. *Meiji-Taishō Shi: Sesō-hen*.

Yokoyama, Gen'nosuke. 1898, reprinted in 1949. *Nihon no Kasō Shakai*. Reprinted by Iwanami. Page references to 1949 reprint.

Industrialization and Social Deprivation:

Welfare, Environment, and the

Postindustrial Society in Japan

John W. Bennett and Solomon B. Levine

This essay deals with the consequences of industrialization and economic growth for the environment and social welfare in Japan, especially since the end of the Pacific War. The first part defines industrialization as a process which generates social deprivation as well as gratification; the second part describes the major deprivations, absolute and relative, created by industrialization in Japanese society; and the last part summarizes the public and organizational responses to these deprivations and their long-range political significance, for which we use the catch-phrase postindustrial society. Our approach is interdisciplinary in the sense that we review the influence of industrialization on physical, institutional, political, cultural, and psychological phenomena. Our data for this review are drawn primarily from Japanese sources; evidence for the "deprivations" of industrialization has been supplied by Japanese economists, sociologists, labor specialists, and survey researchers. We have not been able to go into detail on these effects, for each constitutes a specialized inquiry in its own right. Our aim is an overview of social aspects of the process of industrialization in Japan and not an exhaustive analysis of its consequences.

The authors wish to acknowledge the assistance of Sukehiro Hasegawa of the United Nations Development Programme and Washington University; Haruo Shimada of Keio University; and Joe B. Moore, University of Wisconsin, in the preparation of this paper. We are grateful to Herbert Passin, of Columbia University, for a critical reading of the final draft. After finishing our paper, we became aware of an early essay by Passin which forecast the discontents associated with economic growth (Passin 1962). We are also indebted to the Social Science Research Council for a grant-in-aid for research assistance and travel in Japan and the United States to gather materials.

In our analysis, we are not concerned with how Japanese traditional social organization may be compatible with the structure and process of industrial production. We assume industrialization can be initiated in a variety of social systems, so long as sufficient motivation exists and agreement on the essential means and ends can be obtained. We assume further that all industrial societies, whatever the adaptations and modifications visible in the process as seen from the standpoint of a particular model, will eventually pass through similar broad experiences. We do not focus on the many details of difference between the Japanese and any other national experience, but on the general similarities.

INDUSTRIALIZATION AS AN ADAPTIVE SYSTEM

Rewards and Deprivations

As a general system, industrialization is a process of energy transformation which requires both material and social inputs; possesses systemic components which are not necessarily synchronized with others; contains feedbacks, many of which are unpredictable, as they are governed by human whim or ideology; and exhibits a tendency to accumulate strain in the system which is relieved suddenly when a certain threshold is reached.[1] In this process, industrialization, in addition to increased per capita output, generates dislocations requiring continuous adaptive responses on the part of members of society. When industrialization is expanding, it requires ever-larger amounts of energy and therefore exerts increasing pressure on the physical environment. Eventually the point is reached when these pressures are interpreted by the members of society as deprivations. Industrialization also generates feelings of want, as its growing use and output of energy contains promises, stated or unstated, for the better life. The promises engender demands for equity as well as for increasing individual shares in the system, or for more and even-better products at ever-lower costs. All available evidence indicates by 1972 Japan had reached this stage of contradiction and tension as a consequence of rapid economic growth in the 1950s and 60s.

As there is no finite limit to human wants, and as industrial systems seem to require continual growth, wants and their fulfillments eventually become embedded in the political process; that is, the operation of the economy becomes an essential part of the maintenance of public order. This process is usually accompanied by increasing literacy, which encourages the appearance of spokesmen who can articulate the wants and needs of the people and make comparisons with other nations, putting further pressure on the managers of the industrial system to perform at a high rate of efficiency or output. The idea of a social minimum, but one that constantly rises, becomes an essential accompaniment of industrialization, especially in those countries where there are no enforced restrictions on consumption. However, because the system

---

[1]This is called "step function" in systems theory.

inevitably generates conflict and contradiction, the public increasingly tends to perceive deprivation, even in the midst of (actually, because of) rising levels of consumption or political participation.

These accumulating deprivations must be managed in some fashion. Of course, some of the demands might have been met early in the game, by investing sufficiently in social welfare at the outset of industrialization. But this is no certain way of avoiding the problem, as the demand for equity seems to emerge even when the distribution of rewards is relatively equal. If grievances accumulate to the point of social unrest, measures need to be swift and effective; they can be ameliorative, cooptative, repressive, or some mixture of these. Measures will be more or less effective depending on the ability of the elite to perceive what is really wrong and to make fundamental changes. However, such understanding may not help if the nation is highly literate and in close contact with other countries going through similar processes. In other words, the perception of deprivation, absolute or relative, comes to be a worldwide process.

The accumulation of grievances also seems to proceed at a roughly exponential rate, although the rate over short periods varies from country to country, and from time to time in the same country. The ideologies associated with industrialization seem to resist acceptance of this fact: there is often a conspicuous lag on the part of the elite to anticipate accumulating tension. Similarly, *overt* public protest does not usually emerge in strict proportion to the increase in feelings of deprivation. There may be, for long periods, a considerable disparity, with sudden outbreaks when the inconsistency becomes marked. These long periods of relative quiescence give the elite an opportunity to delay reform under the illusion that people really accept the status quo. Or, when ameliorative measures or cooptation seem to allay protest, thoroughgoing reform is postponed under the belief that all is well once again.

In the post-Pacific War period in Japan, industrialization has succeeded in satisfying a number of important demands. Most obvious among these is personal consumption. Second, risks associated with health and unemployment have been reduced: medical care, public and private, has been extended to most of the population, and a combination of governmental supports and enterprise-provided welfare has reduced the rate of unemployment to a low level. Third, reforms generated in the Occupation have led to greater equality of opportunity and political participation: the labor movement and opposition political parties are more effective than before World War II, and freedom of expression has developed rapidly. These changes have materially altered the social atmosphere; the opportunity for government to revive the extensive manipulative and cooptative strategies of the prewar years is greatly reduced, and most observers seem to agree Japan cannot revert to her folk totalitarianism.

As the Japanese public has been prepared for self-expression, and encouraged to form interest groups and participate in the national political process, it has become increasingly aware of the costs of a rising standard of living and a more literate and sophisticated existence. Wherever the economic gains of the post-Pacific War period have failed to measure up to expectations, or where serious inequities and deprivations remain or have emerged, there is articulate discontent and protest, including such areas as the physical and social environments, housing, leisure activities, increasing urbanization and population density, and the relative position of certain age and skill groups in the working population. These topics are reviewed in the second part of the paper.

"Production First" and "Social Quiescence"

Although industrialization as a system generates social deprivation and protest along with the manifest rewards of higher consumption and a more secure life, these are all variables subject to changing attitudes and values. The specific circumstances of accumulating grievances, and the timing of protest, will vary with the social and political institutions of the society in question. For example, the context of grievance and protest in a capitalist nation will differ generally from that in a socialist, although industrialization, however organized, eventually generates the kinds of deprivation which concern us here. The main issue is not the deprivation, but how society manages it.

For our purposes, we view Japan as a member of a particular class of nations, mostly capitalist but including a number of socialist countries as well, which chose a pathway toward economic growth described by the phrase (currently a pejorative term in Japan) "production first." This refers to a decision to permit the social system to bear the costs of readjustments to the new order with minimal help from the state, based on the theory all capital has to be plowed back into production in order to achieve a high level of economic growth.

The policy of production-first among the capitalist nations also assumes that ideally the free market will make up for social deficiencies, absolutely or relatively perceived, which may accumulate in the system, as such a market is supposed to function to provide the greatest good for the greatest number. Although economists and planners know there is no such thing as an ideal free market, the concept has influenced the general decision to allocate minimal amounts of economic resources to social needs, especially in the early stages of industrialization. In contrast to these assumptions, the decision to save on social expenditures seems only to lead to an accumulation of grievances which then cost much more to alleviate at some future date.

The Japanese followed a production-first policy from the initial decision to industrialize in the Meiji era. The general course of Japan's industrialization did not differ in terms of our definition of the process from nearly all other nations beginning industrialization in the 19th century. Only one European country, Germany, followed a somewhat different course. Under Bismarck, the Germans instituted social welfare and employment security schemes from the outset, which created a tradition of support that has given the worker an enviable position compared to other countries. Although the Japanese were impressed with many features of Bismarck's policies, they did not adopt his social welfare schemes.

Perhaps the most general reason for this is that the Japanese leaders were keenly aware of the reservoir of discipline and conformity in the existing social system, which had been projected into the modern era largely without change—at least in the basic microstructure of social relations, with its well-worn pathways of hierarchal authority. This has been viewed by many scholars as Japan's historic advantage over other nations entering the industrialization process at a relatively late date; it meant the Japanese elite could do what they wanted and at the same time be able to count on a docile and hard-working population.

However, this view does not really answer all the questions. It is not sufficient to explain why the Japanese population remained relatively quiescent for such a long time, permitting itself, for example, to be a participant in several wars with their privations and dislocations; or why the rise of industrial structures such as labor organizations did not produce conflict on a scale comparable to that of most Western countries; or why, in the face of obvious differentials of prestige, power, and income, a sharper sense of social class did not emerge. This relative quiescence of the Japanese population in the face of sweeping changes in the national structure has been a persisting problem in the study of Japanese industrialization and modernization.

Attempts to explain this quiescence have often resorted to an analysis of the peculiarities of Japanese culture. For example, Maruyama (1963) expounded a theory that responsible political decisions were impossible because there was no "free, objective awareness." Leaders were part of some homogeneous entity; they passed on messages "from above," which automatically became decisions. As it was believed that these messages went all the way down the family line of the national population, the entire public was implicated in the decisions (and any subsequent guilt). Thus, equilibrium was maintained and protests against decisions had little chance of success.

Another name for this type of system is communal society, used by Tsurumi (1970). She proposes Japanese society has changed, since the defeat, from a "communal-totalitarian" to a "communal-mass" type. The communal element in these concepts is the familiar notion of a society in which all groups are bound together by a single ideology: the primary-group principle of the family-nation, with the emperor as Great Father. Hence, "any change in the state initiates an identical pattern of change in both intermediate and primary groups" (Tsurumi 1970, p. 206). The totalitarian factor refers, however, to manipulations of this system by the militarist government of the 1930-45 period, and the institution of certain formal controls to guarantee loyalty and conformity. Tsurumi also contrasts Japan to both "pluralist" and "mass" societies. The former is, of course, the American system of interest groups expected to compete and bargain democratically for shares in the national wealth and prestige, supervised by a hopefully impartial government. "Mass" refers to societies in which reasonable conformity is ensured by propaganda and distractions contributed by the media and consumerism—a society with the forms of democracy but not the substance. Tsurumi's proposal is an interesting one, although unfortunately it was made just before the Japanese public blossomed with pluralist citizen protest and interest groups in the early 1970s.

Theories of Japan as a kind of folk-totalitarianism contain part of the explanation of quiescence in the face of rapid change. It is true Japan has displayed characteristics of a monoethnic society with extensive social networks and complex hierarchies and reciprocities, and it is true there has been a strong sense of shared national purpose which cannot be explained entirely by propaganda alone. And it is true Japan's leaders in the modern era seemingly were under a cultural compulsion to avoid or minimize outright repression and the use of force.

However, these theories cannot possibly explain the whole phenomenon, nor do they tell us whether or not, or to what degree, quiescence was really characteristic of Japanese society during its development periods. Granting the absence of outright revolt, Japan's history is replete with incidents of protest, riot, and combinations against authority, which at least testify to feelings of deprivation.[2] If one looks for them, the familiar signs of social strain accompanying modernization are visible, always acknowledging the possibility they were milder than in some other countries. But for some reason scholars have tended to play these down, just as Japan's elite has also managed to hold them in check and often deny their very existence.

In the face of at least contradictory evidence on the relative quiescence of Japanese society, one is inclined to suspect a high quotient of manipulation and cooptation of the population on the part of the political leadership—a conclusion which fits that part of the communal theory calling attention to paternalism. Although studies of this institution have been made for particular sectors of the Japanese economy and formal organizations, very little research has been done on the application of paternalistic methods to the society as a whole, as a national political strategy, along the lines, say, of Lerner's study (1958) of comparable phenomena in the Middle East. However, information exists if one looks for it. An example is a recent study by Pyle (1973) on the Local Improvement Movement (*Chihō Kairyō Undō*), inaugurated by the Taishō government. This movement saw the government-sponsored inauguration of youth organizations, agricultural cooperatives, public education, soldiers' organizations, and rural leadership training programs. Although this comprehensive program to gain control of the society, to establish channels of direct communication between social groups and the government, and to develop new, more responsive and controllable organizations was not a complete success, it did achieve its basic aims and consolidated a tradition of meticulous government supervision.

Other examples of the repressive, cooptative, and paternalistic styles of Japanese prewar governments can be observed in the history of the labor movement. In its early stages, toward the end of the 19th century, the

[2]For compilations of these incidents in earlier Japanese history, see Aoki 1967, 1968, and 1971.

governmental response was one of drastic and effective repression. Labor leaders then turned to more subtle techniques designed to develop gradual acceptance of unionism in the established political system: the Yūaikai during World War I and the 1920s was the result. In the early 1920s a more radical union movement attempted to capture the organization, and the oligarchy responded with a variety of techniques: the creation of the Kyōchōkai was an outright gesture at promoting establishment-controlled unions; paternalistic institutions in industry were encouraged in order to promote a familial atmosphere; and repressive techniques were directed toward the most radical unions with the public police law of 1926. Following the militarist ascendancy in the 1930s, the cooptative strategy blossomed with the founding of the Sampō under government sponsorship, a more effectively controlled body than the Kyōchōkai, and a device with some of the trappings of unionism but really a means to control labor for national purposes.[3]

The description of conscious policies leading toward a consensus-style society could be prolonged indefinitely. Our purpose is not to document this system, but only to point out that explanations of the relative passivity of the Japanese population in the course of industrialization and modernization must take account of these strategies, in addition to pointing to various traditional, preindustrial features of the social organization the leadership was able to use and rely on. Clearly, if care was taken to create formal institutions for the keeping of order and the buying of allegiance, there is the suggestion the population was potentially less passive than has been assumed, and there must have existed accumulating tensions, conflicts, and deprivations, of which at least some of the elite, or the police, were aware.

We suggest, therefore, because of Japan's late entry into the modern world, and because this was done with the values of a feudal hierarchical society intact, there existed impressive opportunities for a prescient leadership to manipulate this system to gain the time, the relative internal tranquility, and—whether economically justifiable or not—the capital to complete the task. That this objective also accumulated its own exploitative and gain-oriented goals there is no doubt, and of course this fed the tendency to maintain the status quo and to require society to bear the social costs of industrialization without substantial help from the wealthy sectors. The techniques were expertly conceived; they included symbolic concessions to both tradition and modernity; and they utilized cooptation and incremental rewards when tension increased.

The elite were, on the whole, careful to avoid overly authoritarian behavior, resorting to open repression only when the dangers, in their eyes, were clear. We suggest on the whole this process was not unique to Japan, although it had distinctive Japanese cultural symbolic trimmings as well as features

[3]For studies of the labor movement and its control by government, see Levine 1958; Okochi, Karsh, and Levine 1973. Other analyses are found in Silberman and Harootunian 1974.

traceable to the surviving traditional social systems. After all, most nations in the industrial era, whatever their political systems, have tried to avoid or reduce conflict and have resorted to manipulation of various kinds to keep the peace.[4]

As this process of social control matures, the industrial order in all highly developed countries probably makes its transition into postindustrial society. In our definition of this term, the political manipulations which have served to allocate resources in a particular way, usually unequally, become less effective. The accumulation of wants leads to greater diversity of interests, demands, and grievances, not to mention greater diversity of problems and contradictions. The strategy of production-first becomes less and less possible, and the system changes toward a mass society with guarantees of a basic level of living and with considerable political awareness. Welfare, however defined, becomes the major goal of society, rather than production. Japan has been described as one of the first postindustrial societies (Morley 1974); if she is, then it may be testimony to the intensity of the deprivations generated by production first.

The Concept of Social Cost

Many of the phenomena to be described have been referred to by such terms as social costs, external diseconomies, or relative deprivations, the choice depending on the disciplinary provenance of the analyst. Our use of these terms is purely heuristic; we do not intend to make calculations of costs and benefits, or to measure the strength of deprivation attitudes, other than to cite survey data on specific issues. Nevertheless, a few comments on the meanings of these terms are desirable.

In its broadest sense social cost refers to anything considered to be a loss borne by third persons resulting from productive activities—that is, not borne, directly at least, by the producers themselves. Deprivations considered to be a result of a production-first policy can be defined as social costs. Since social costs are dependent on someone perceiving them, the concept implies a sense of value, or social goals. As the only goal in growth-oriented economic

---

[4]Edelman (1964) develops a theory which helps us to understand this process. He bases his approach on the fact most modern social systems are quiet most of the time; social upheavals are comparatively rare events, and people seem to put up with a lot before they protest openly. Moreover, he observes all political elites are continuously engaged in symbol manipulation and institution modification in order to maintain these attitudes, whether they are expressed consciously as the willingness to accept sacrifice or simply are ignorant of the real conditions. He notes, "To quiet resentments and doubts about particular political acts, reaffirm belief in the fundamental political rationality and democratic character of the system, and thus fix conforming habits of future behavior is demonstrably a key function of our persisting political institutions. . . . Policies severely denying resources to large numbers of people can be pursued indefinitely without serious controversy" (p. 17). Edelman is referring to the United States.

policies is growth, or production itself, consideration of these social problems and objectives has been technically ruled out of economic analysis.

Nevertheless, the increasing awareness of accumulating costs has required the development of a new technical concept: external diseconomy. This is defined as something added that was not originally included in the cost calculations by the producers; that is, something external to the actual material costs of production, like the damage to the environment, or the sanity of the workers. The term thus highlights a defect in microeconomic theory: the tendency of the theory to assume that which it ought to be studying. The existence of an external diseconomy (or social cost) means the producers have had the power to drive ahead with their activities at the expense of something or someone. When this power is prolonged, diseconomies accumulate and create social tensions. The production process and the market are in reality very complex sociopolitical processes, including many different agents, types of bargaining, manipulation, secret dealing and so on, with resulting unforeseen consequences of great complexity. Standard microeconomic theory is simply powerless to explain this kind of process; thus it has difficulty with the incorporation of social cost and diseconomy variables, based as they are on social attitudes and goals. In recent years economists have made an effort to search for methods of creating quantitative measures of social costs and benefits (Staaf and Tannian 1973). Japanese economists have been as active as any, and the Keizai Shingikai (Economic Council), a quasi-government agency, published in 1973 an experimental attempt to reduce the diseconomies of the current industrial system in Japan to a measuring scheme entitled Net National Welfare (NNW). Essentially this scheme consists of inserting into the national income accounts for 1955 to 1970 a series of welfare indicators which permit a recalculation of income, the GNP, or any other such addititive measure based on gross accumulative growth. This recalculation involves subtractions or additions of welfare factors. For example, a monetary conversion of hours spent on commuting in cities in excess of a standard amount is subtracted. The results of the study show both GNP and NNW in Japan rising more or less consistently from 1955 to 1968, with NNW slightly above GNP. After 1968 the rate of increase of NNW drops, and NNW declines below GNP, which continues to grow at a rapid pace (Keizai Shingikai 1973).

Relative deprivation, a sociopsychological concept, depends on what one was habituated to in the past; if these habituated gratifications are abridged in some fashion, a feeling of loss is experienced.[5] It also concerns promises

---

[5]Relative deprivation has a special poignancy in Japan because of the tendency to consider disbenefits to the person as grounds for serious embarrassment to the group—especially the family. For example, a recent study of Japanese welfare and cultural life, in an analysis of health and accident trends, and attitudes toward these, makes the point that the two most important reasons given by respondents on a national survey for being concerned over health was "decline of income" and "embarrassment to the family" (Keizai Kikakuchō 1972b, p. 25).

made to people or aspirations acquired which are not met by the time implied or guaranteed. This type becomes particularly important in industrializing societies as educational and literacy levels increase (Hirschman and Rothschild 1973). Thus, as political sophistication and general awareness increase, so does the incidence of felt deprivation.

In order to list and describe the current diseconomies and social costs, we take our cure from the presence of articulated deprivation in the population. For example, we consider both the loss of time spent on commuting and the general frustration engendered by crowds as costs arising out of urbanization and industrialization, although from the standpoint of a narrow economic definition, the commutation-time factor would be the only proper social cost. Expressed attitudes of discontent, which narrowly conceived are sociopsychological epiphenomena subject to random variation, we consider to be prima facie evidence of deprivation and of a historical problem that must be solved.

THE DEPRIVATIONS OF INDUSTRIALISM

The Welfare Gap

Despite the impressive gains after the mid-1950s, by the late 1960s the growing disparity between economic growth and social welfare had gained wide recognition by both liberal and conservative elements of Japanese society. The concept of a welfare gap (*fukushi gappu*) was explained officially in the 1971-1972 *Economic Survey of Japan* (Keizai Kikakuchō and *Japan Times* 1972) as the consequence of largely unrestricted growth, mainly through reliance on the market system. As a result, the report noted, persons affected by the gap had become increasingly articulate and inclined to engage in protests and legal action.

The welfare gap appears to be a mixture of both *absolute* and *relative* deprivations, felt or perceived by large and growing segments of the Japanese population. It involves one or more of the following: (a) losses from previously attained welfare levels or styles of life; (b) failures in attaining minimum expectations or rewards; (c) issues of equity among individuals and groups or of expectations of gaining equal rewards or benefits; and (d) failures to experience steady advances in life styles or welfare. The first is clearly an absolute deprivation; the latter three, relative. Examples of absolute deprivation include deterioration of the physical environment; reduction of income as the result of involuntary unemployment or retirement; increased congestion in living space; reduced opportunity for the pursuit of leisure; or increased commuting time. While these may also involve degrees of relative deprivation, the latter includes innumerable situations in which individuals make conscious comparisons with other individuals or groups either within a given society or across international boundaries.

Recent annual economic reports and other publications of the Economic Planning Agency (Keizai Kikakuchō 1971, 1972*a*, 1973*a*) and the Keizai

Shingikai (1972) further identify the following as the principal phenomena of the gap:

1. The consequences of urban density are high prices for both necessities and luxuries, difficulties in obtaining suitable housing, discomfort and time wasted in overcrowded commutation facilities, and general deterioration of the social environment.

2. The cost of social overhead capital has been increasing rapidly. Solutions to some of the problems in the preceding paragraph are to be found in larger investments in housing, transportation, parks, and the like, but as density has increased prices of land and all other facilities, it becomes increasingly difficult to supply the needs or solve the problems.

3. Although income equalization in general has made progress in Japan, notably in the wage sector, certain groups in the population have lost ground relative to the active labor force as a whole. These are, in particular, most older people, fatherless families, the handicapped, and chronically ill persons. Moreover, tax favors for property holders have contributed to income inequalities.

4. Although the Japanese social security system has increased in comprehensiveness and coverage greatly since the end of the Pacific War, the ratio of transfer income to the national income remains small compared with other highly developed countries. The immaturity of the retirement pension system is adduced as a principal cause. However, all categories of public investment in welfare as a percent of GNP are low in Japan when compared to other industrial countries.

Government expenditures on social welfare have become a major part of the national debate about the welfare gap; and by 1972 and 1973 plans emerged for wholesale restructuring and improving the social security system. As shown in Table 1, Japan's level of social welfare expenditures in various categories has been comparable to North American and Western European countries only in the field of health and medical care. The low figures shown in Table 1 for the United States and Japan describe societies in which private individuals or organizations to a large extent provide for protection against health, unemployment, and old age hazards through their own savings and social resources such as the family or voluntary group association. In Japan, the lack of government-provided security programs has necessitated a very high rate of savings on the average by the individual household and enterprise compared to other countries, despite low levels of unemployment. The so-called frugality or austerity of the Japanese may be as much the result of financial insecurity as any devotion to a cultural work ethic or desire to retain austere traditional life styles.[6]

[6]In a survey reported by Keizai Kikakuchō (1972c, the Japanese edition of 1972b) made on a national sample of respondents, the marginal rate of savings was higher than that of the increase in income. Although the ratios fluctuated to some extent from year to year, the pattern was consistent for

Table 1
Social Welfare Expenditures by Government in Various Countries
as a Percent of GNP (1970)

	Japan	West Germany	Italy	France	United States
Health and medical care	2.86	3.90	3.25	4.54	1.03
Income and employment security	2.59	16.02	11.78	14.68	6.58
Social security and retirement	5.45	19.92	15.03	19.22	5.45

Source: Nihon Ginkō 1971.

However that may be, the family, once a convenient source of security, no longer functions adequately because its strength lay in the solidarity of extended kin groups, now greatly attenuated as a result of industrialization and its individualized wage-work system. In other words, industrialization has been threatening one of the major supports for privatized security in society; but one of the most effective substitutes, socialized welfare, has not yet fully taken its place. As noted, private savings, inadequately and unequally distributed through the population, has become the principal substitute.

There is, of course, an argument here. It can be asked whether public supports in the welfare field are superior to a system in which the individual and his family service their own needs, thereby avoiding some of the unpleasant aspects of the welfare state—its alleged contribution to alienation, restlessness, and the feeling society owes me a living. This argument has been used in all the production-first countries including Japan, but in the stage Japan has now entered, where the family is reduced to a nuclear core, mobility is increasing, the economy is increasingly complex, and inflation prevents adequate self-insurance, public guarantees become a necessity.

Another measure of the gap may be found in the proportion of personal property and entrepreneurial income in the net national income. Data for various countries from the United Nations (1973) include the following proportions: Japan 42 percent, Italy 36, United States 20, and Germany 29. Japan's proportion is higher than those of the industrial countries of Western

---

the period 1964 through 1971. For example, in 1965 there was an increase of 20.8 percent in savings over the previous year and a 14.3 percent increase in personal income, yielding an overall savings to income ratio of 17.4 percent. In 1971 the figure was 14, 13.5, and 20.5 percent. This included all forms of savings, from cash to securities as well as real assets. In surveys taken in 1966 and 1971 by Keizai Kikakuchō (1972d), respondents with savings went from 90 to 96 percent of the sample total. Types of savings changed: in 1966 the dominant form was stocks and bonds; in 1971 savings deposits had increased at the expense of securities.

Europe and North America and is reflected in the high rate of reinvestment in production facilities on the part of Japanese business and industry, and the correspondingly lower percentages allocated to the population in the form of wages, social services, and other government-overhead investments. It is recognized, of course, that Japanese percentages may be somewhat higher because of comparatively larger agricultural and self-employment sectors.

Some reports also define the welfare gap in Japan in terms of the ratio of governmental to private contributions to the gross national expenditures (GNE). They note the private sector has dominated the GNE (United Nations 1973). In figures reported to the United Nations (1971, table 2*a*) government contributions to the gross domestic product (GDP) were 8 percent of the total, with private contributions 51 percent. This compares with 20 and 63 percent for the United States, and 19 and 57 percent for Canada. It means that, although the tax burden of the Japanese was relatively small as compared with that of other countries where the ratio followed the United States-Canada pattern, many services provided by government in these countries were lacking or poorly developed in Japan. In recognition of this deficiency, the Japanese reports have long insisted on the necessity of increasing government expenditures for social welfare, the environment, and social security.

Some additional data on international comparisons should be provided at this point, although neither definitions nor measurements of social welfare are easy to make on a cross-national basis due to differing cultural patterns and life styles. This has been particularly important in the case of Japan due to the persistence of standards in domestic living arrangements which have been generally lower than those of other developed countries. Until recently, much of the discussion of Japan's response to industrialization stressed the existence of a pattern of aesthetically defined austerity which, along with the rapid rise of incomes, permitted massive personal savings. This pattern, if it really existed, began to change in the 1960s with the rise of the consumer economy (Bennett 1967). The development of rising standards of consumption was inevitable, especially given Japanese desires to equal or outdo social gains in other industrial and industrializing countries. International comparisons of Japan's position with respect to various indexes of level of living and well-being, as well as with production, have been intensively publicized in the 1960s and 70s, with a rising sense of lag or inadequacy in the former.[7]

Per capita disposable income in real terms rose steadily in Japan from $421 in 1960 to $1676 in 1970. During the same period West Germany went from $1176 to $2657; the United States from $2546 to $4262; Italy from $913 (1963) to $1592; and Mexico from $316 to over $500. These figures put Japan ahead in rate of increase, but alongside Italy in absolute terms as of

[7]One of the first systematic reports on this subject was published by the Keizai Kikakuchō (1972*c*). We also are indebted to Walter Galenson and Konosuke Odaka for calling attention to many of these comparisons in their ongoing study of Japanese labor markets.

1970. West Germany, with a generally similar emphasis on productivity, working hours, and exports, nevertheless provided its population on the average a larger share of the proceeds (United Nations 1971, table 185).

In food consumption alone, Japan has shown, at least through 1970, one of the lowest average daily calorie intakes, and the smallest percentages of calories derived from animal sources (United Nations 1971, table 160). In 1970 food intake as measured by calories stood at 2450 daily on the average—the lowest among the industrial countries of France, Germany, Italy, the United Kingdom, and the United States. Daily protein intake for the same year was 75 grams, also the lowest in this group (United Nations 1971, table 160). And Kōseishō (1971) noted that for 1968, calorie and protein intake for working-class household adults was still about 85 percent and 92 percent of the nutritional levels considered necessary for fueling the actual labor output. (These standards are somewhat suspect, however, for the Japanese sources appear to have been using American standards. But the actual calorie intake is not the main issue here: equally important is the sense of relative deprivation.)

In 1971, expenditures in working-class households for food constituted 34 percent of the total (Sōrifu 1971). Japanese reports on the dietary situation conclude that although the worker is eating much better than he did a decade ago, he is still marginally nourished as compared with the working population of other industrial nations. This has been a matter of increasing concern for industrial medicine because of its implications for labor efficiency, and to labor unions because of its implications of differential rewards. (The averaged national figures, of course, disguise differences by income, age, and other groups; meat protein sources, for example, are more evident in the middle- and upper-income groups than in the lower, and lowest of all in families with aging worker heads.)

Data on housing facilities reflect similar lags. Among the North American and European industrial countries, Japan stands lowest with regard to the percentage of dwellings equipped with flush toilets: 17.1 percent against 28.9 for Italy (the next lowest), 83.3 for West Germany and 89.7 for the United States. Japan and Italy have the largest number of persons per room of dwelling houses (both with 1.1) against the United States 0.7, Germany 0.9, United Kingdom 0.6 (United Nations 1971). Moreover, space per room in Japan is the smallest. Residential construction in Japan has been increasing; it is 6.5 percent of GNP, equaled only by France. This in part merely reflects public housing and government-subsidized housing programs stepped-up from a very low level in recent years.

Housing for workers remains a problem, probably with even less of the relative gain shown for consumption items (and much less so than for middle-to-upper income Japanese). The percentage of income required for housing has been reported as relatively low: for households in which the head is twenty-nine or under, about 12 percent (Sōrifu 1971), dropping to 9 percent for older heads. However, as an analyst in the *Japan Labor Bulletin* (Umetani 1973, pp. 5-6) notes: "Although the relative cost of housing . . .

may seem rather low, such an interpretation must be modified by three considerations. First, the quality of housing is rather low. ... The average space of houses rented from private owners is approximately half that of owned houses. A second problem is the time required for commuting. ... The average time spent for commuting was 80-90 minutes per day for those living in Tokyo itself and even more for those living in the surrounding suburbs. A third problem is the fact that the ... statistics do not include payments for debts on housing or savings for the purpose of purchasing a house." In other reports the extremely high, and continually rising, prices for land are cited as making it increasingly difficult for workers to buy housing, which throws them back into the rental market.

With regard to private motor transportation, Japan had 85 passenger cars per 1000 persons in 1971, against 187 for Italy, 237 for Germany, and 432 for the United States. In contrast, in the same year, the number of television sets per 1000 inhabitants was 215, more than Italy (181) and France (201), although less than West Germany (272) and the United States (412). The number of telephones had a similar distribution (United Nations 1971). By 1970, 98 percent of all employe households in Japan owned a washing machine; 95 percent a gas or electric refrigerator; 80 percent a vacuum cleaner; 67 to 70 percent a television set; 77 percent a camera. Over 60 percent of all households had a telephone and 10 percent a piano. Air conditioning was enjoyed by 12 percent, but only 0.6 percent had central heating (Umetani 1973, pp. 5-6). The profile is similar to that for the United States working population about 1955: ownership of the basic convenience durables, such as televisions and refrigerators, but with the comfort or luxury items, such as air conditioning, still to come (although specific items defined as basic or luxury will vary in the two countries).

In the social field, Japan has boasted a well-developed public education system throughout her modern period, and it is no surprise to find that in 1970 she ranked with Italy and France and surpassed West Germany, although well under the United States and Canada, in terms of the amount spent on education as a percentage of GNP: 4.5 percent for Japan, 3.6 for West Germany, 4.3 for Italy, 4.5 for France, 13.5 for Mexico, 6.3 for the United States, and 8.9 percent for Canada. (The Mexico figure reflects a special push toward education in an emerging country with a relatively modest national income.) In educational expenditures as a percentage of all public expenditures, Japan was high—20.4 percent—with Italy 19.2 percent, France 22.3, Germany only 11.2 (United Nations 1971; OECD, appendix). However, although the annual educational budget in Japan, both at the national and local levels, has increased, its percentage of the total national government expenditures for social and welfare purposes has fallen slowly— from nearly 54 percent in 1955 to about 50 percent in 1968 (Mombushō 1971). With respect to other educational indicators, Japan also ranks high. Attendance at senior secondary school and college is exceeded only by the United States. However, the teacher-pupil ratio in all public schools is higher than that of any of the other countries (Mombushō 1971 and OECD 1972).

The proportion of all students enrolled in two- or four-year colleges in Japan is 16 percent, higher than in any other of the industrial countries except the United States, with 34 percent (*Japan Report*, March 1972). Yet some of these indicators imply serious problems. The high teacher-pupil ratio means serious crowding in many schools, and the large number of applicants per opening makes for severe and debilitating competition for college entrance. (Changes in the grade sequence introduced during the occupation period also created many new problems, including what may be an overemphasis on college and the production of highly educated, underemployed people.)

Medical care in Japan is statistically comparable to other countries, except for one factor: population per physician, which in 1971 was 898 as compared to the United States's 669, Germany's 568, Italy's 553, France's 747, Mexico's 1846. In other respects, Japan's medical care was equal or superior to other countries: population per hospital bed was 79, against the United States's 123, Germany's 87, Italy's 99, France's 113, Mexico's 549 (United Nations 1971). Although the earliest law concerning health insurance dates only from 1922, in the post-Pacific War period Japan developed a maze of public health insurance schemes, so that if the worker successfully negotiated maximum protection for himself and family, he could by the mid-1960s expect nearly 100 percent coverage on all expenses (*Japan Labor Bulletin*, April 1965, p. 4). Also health insurance has received priority in national planning over other forms of social security and compensation, and has continued to exceed unemployment insurance and retirement pensions in adequacy of coverage. Actually, deficiencies in Japanese medical care may emerge more clearly in the quality of hospital and physician services, rather than in absolute quantity of and access to facilities. For example, the favorable population per hospital bed figure reflects the existence of hundreds of small private doctors' clinics and hospitals with varying standards of care and treatment.

Although we deal with the problem of recreation and leisure in greater detail later, data on the area of urban parks show Japan has the smallest figure, 0.9 percent, among industrialized nations. France, the next lowest, has 5.8 percent; Italy, 10.4; Germany, 14; and the United States, 19 (Zen Nihon Rōdō Sōdōmei 1972, p. 20).

Japan's general welfare position emerges fairly clearly from these comparisons. In most respects, Japan is in the category of the developed, rather than emerging nations. But for key indexes the rank is lower than for other industrial societies. The similarities to Italy are striking, but the advantages over Mexico equally so. Residues of the older, austere patterns remain in housing facilities, certain consumption items, and in aspects of medical care. The most significant feature is the amount spent for welfare facilities as compared with expenditures for industrial plant: public investment in Japan, although increasing, has not maintained its percentage of the national income. It is this disparity which is viewed by the experts as the root of the welfare gap, and their concern seems to be shared by the public.

The background of public thinking on the welfare situation is presented by Tatsuzo Suzuki (1970, 1974), who analyzed the results of a series of surveys on social attitudes and cultural patterns from the late 1950s to the early 1970s. The results indicated the respondents had moved away from a series of important traditional patterns toward new ones associated with urbanization and industrialization. The most important items reflect the change from extended familism toward a nuclear, short-term family; from a life guided by moral objectives to one guided by personal interests; from a faith in leaders to a feeling leaders often cannot be trusted; from feelings of kinship with nature toward conquest of nature in order to satisfy human goals. However, the survey data also show increases in the belief science may destroy human feelings, paternalism and other traditional social relations may be superior to the new rational forms, the Japanese are superior to Western peoples, and a feeling of pride in economic accomplishment. In other words, a mixture of confidence in the new Japan and anxiety over the loss of traditional cultural qualities.

Survey data on satisfaction and dissatisfaction with living conditions (*kurashimuki*) for the same period show the basic trend is a decline in the number who feel living conditions are getting better, and a rise in the proportion who believe they are getting worse. In surveys made in 1962, 1966, and 1971, the Kokumin Seikatsu Kenkyujo (1971), a survey research institution comparable to the National Opinion Research Center in the United States, asked the same question of its respondents on a national sample: "Do you think general living conditions are improved; unchanged; worsened; can't say (choose answer)?" Between 1962 and 1966 the respondents who chose "worsened" increased by about 10 percentage points; those who felt things had improved decreased by about 8 points. About 30 percent of the total answers were in the worsened category. By 1971, the worsened category rose to 33 percent, and the improved answers dropped another two percentage points. Between 1962 and 1971, the proportion answering unchanged rose from about 32 to 49 percent, which is interpreted by the report as meaning many respondents felt things were not good in 1962 and 1966 and had not changed for the better despite the rise in real incomes and the virtual disappearance of economic poverty. Breakdowns by income and age on these surveys revealed the higher the income, the greater the satisfaction with living conditions; the lower the income, the greater the dissatisfaction.

The surveys also tested the degree of optimism or pessimism about changes in living conditions in the future. The higher income respondents were more likely to feel conditions would improve; the lower were steadily more pessimistic from 1962 to 1971; the proportion believing "no change" would take place fluctuated, but began to decline in 1971. The older informants were more pessimistic than the younger, except for a peak of pessimism in the twenty to thirty group.

The surveys also reveal attitudes on specific dissatisfactions. When income is specified as the issue, a tendency toward increasing satisfaction with present income emerges in the late 1960s and early 70s. Blue-collar respondents and younger people show the least such increase. Older people, in a finding which clashed with the previous data on attitudes toward living conditions, show an increase in satisfaction. Respondents also show a change in specific concerns from the 1960s into the 70s. In the earlier period, prices, taxes, social security, and physical facilities in the smaller towns and villages are the main issues. In the 1970s, the emphasis shifts to environmental questions, working conditions, and the welfare of particularly disadvantaged groups in the population.

Environmental Disruption

Analysis of damage to the environment—kōgai mondai (public hazard problems)—begins with the growth and concentration of industrial activities and the output of polluting or disrupting substances by these activities.[8] Economic growth had by 1970 made Japan's GNP third in the world, next to the United States and the Soviet Union—a remarkable feat for a country no larger than Montana or California and largely without mineral resources. The rapid increase was achieved by concentrating industrial activities on a very small land area: in the beginning, the Tokyo-Yokohama region, and by the 1970s, the entire Tokaido strip (Tokyo to Kobe), northern Kyushu, and major portions of the level land area of the entire archipelago (level land, mostly on the seacoast, occupies less than 15 percent of the total surface). Japan's GNP per square kilometer in 1970 was more than four times that of the United States. Whereas the GNP of the United States (excluding Alaska) was about $65,000 per square kilometer in 1960, Japan's was $116,000. By 1970, the GNP per square kilometer increased to $124,000 for the United States, but the increase for Japan was more dramatic: to $533,000. If geographical concentration is expressed in terms of *level* land, the concentration for Japan is even higher. In 1970, the GNP per hectare of level land was close to $18,000 for Japan, and only about $1500 for the United States (Kankyōchō, 1972b, p. 26). Although GNP expressed this way is not necessarily directly related to many economic and social factors, and also reflects physical arrangements, it is a rough indicator of the intensive impact industrialization could be expected to have on a country with limited space.

Comparisons of manufacturing activities in the two countries further reveal the high concentration of industry. In the United States industrial production has been increasing at the rate of 7 or 8 percent per annum. The value of total output of manufacturing in 1969 was $658 billion, or $84,000 per square kilometer. In Japan manufacturing has been increasing at the rate of 14 to 16 percent per annum, and total production reached about $136 billion in 1969, or $367,000 per square kilometer. Economic expansion also required a more rapid rate of increase of the consumption of energy and minerals needed for industry than in any other industrial country. Energy consumption increased gradually by only about 50 percent in the five-year period, 1954-59. In 1960, the total consumption amounted to the equivalent of 109 million tons of

---

[8]The term kōgai mondai has the same generalized and evocative meaning that "ecology" has in public American English: it is a symbol of man's inhumaneness to the environment, and it includes social dangers and discomforts derived from damage to nature.

coal. It then rose rapidly, tripling during the next decade, reaching 289 million tons by 1969. Energy consumption per square kilometer increased from 293 in 1960 to 782 tons in 1969. Although the absolute level of energy consumption was greater in the United States than in Japan, the quantity per square kilometer increased much more gradually over the decade in the United States (Sōrifu Tōkei-kyoku 1971, p. 652).

From the environmental perspective, the crucial aspect of Japan's energy consumption is that since 1961 almost all of the increase in the energy supply has been in fuel oil. In 1954, 51 percent of the energy supply came from coal, and hydroelectric power and fuel oil supplied, respectively, 21 and 19 percent in the same year. By the end of the 1950s, coal declined to 42 percent and oil increased by more than 30 percent. Although hydroelectric power production increased by more than 30 percent, its share of the energy supply remained about the same. During the next ten years, energy supplied by fuel oil increased more than seven times, and its share climbed to 68 percent of the total. Consumption of fuel oil has been increasing at an annual rate of 15 to 20 percent during the last two decades. In the eight years 1964-71 it tripled (Kankyōchō 1972a, p. 5). The concentration of oil consumed in Japan per square kilometer was 8.7 times that of the United States. The environmental impact in terms of hydrocarbon effluents and other forms of pollution from oil has been massive. Mineral usage concentrations have similar proportions. Among the minerals known to have heavy environmental impact, the amount of copper per square kilometer consumed in Japan was 9.6 times that for the United States; lead, 8.6 times; aluminum, 3.9; zinc 8.6 (Keizai Shingikai 1969, pp. 15, 19, 22, 28, 36).

Japan has no shortage of water, but the increase in use of water for industrial purposes has been dramatic. For the period 1962-68, the consumption of industrial water increased from 27 to 36 million tons per day, a 30 percent rise. The major portion of this increase resulted from the use of water for treatment of paper, chemicals, and allied products, and cooling or heating in chemical and metals industries (Kankyōchō 1972d, p. 2; Sōrifu Tōkei-kyoku 1971, p. 238). Particularly significant for environmental impact was the rapid increase in water use by the industries with serious pollution potential: paper and pulp, chemical, and food processing (particularly fish). The share of these industries in total water consumption by manufacturing rose to 61.3 percent in 1968 from about 20 percent in 1962. The proportion of fresh surface water in Japan now containing industrial effluents of some kind is nearly 100 percent.

The effects of this intense geographical concentration of industry, and its concomitant processes like automobile transport, can be summarized briefly.

The most visible impact on water resources occurs in the several major rivers flowing through metropolitan areas of Tokyo, Osaka, Fukuoka, and Nagoya. About 54 percent of the population of Japan and 74 percent of all industrial shipments are concentrated along these rivers, meaning both human and industrial wastes accumulate in them. In 1970 all contained contamination levels, as measured by biological oxygen demand, averaging three times the minimal standards set by the government. Although no better or no worse than pollution levels found in some rivers in American industrial cities, contamination in Japan has a more massive potential impact because of the extremely high population concentration in river valleys.

Eutrophication—overfertilization by nutritive chemicals—of fresh-water supplies has become acute in several regions. Japan has relatively few large lakes, and the two largest, Kasumiga Ura, near Tokyo, and Biwa, near Kyoto, have both become famous in recent years for the high concentrations of eutrophying chemicals.

Polluting conditions also are becoming acute in several coastal ocean districts. Tokyo Bay, Ise Bay, and the Inland Sea have all displayed serious contamination from industrial wastes and sewage, and in the Inland Sea overfertilization of the waters has contributed to the red tides of algal growths which have seriously injured the fishing industry, leading to mass protests by fishermen. A report issued by the Ministry of Agriculture and Forestry notes 52 percent of Japanese protein intake consists of ocean products. However, shrinkage of near-shore fisheries and seaweed plantations due to pollution and land reclamation has led to a decline in most of the important items in the annual seafood harvest since the 1960s. Strict pollution control measures have been proposed along with the construction of artificial reefs and other habitats for fish culture (Nōrinshō 1972).

Sewage is also a problem. In 1972 only about 23 percent of the urban land area in Japan had sewer systems, compared to 90 percent in the United States (Kankyōchō 1972e). That year the national government spent 2.6 trillion yen on sewage systems, with the goal of increasing coverage to 38 percent by the end of 1975. Entry of untreated or inadequately treated human wastes into ground sumps and waterways remains a typical feature of Japanese communities, and has got much worse since the cessation of the use of night soil as agricultural fertilizer during the 1950s.

Atmospheric pollution has received far more vigorous public attention in Japan than water, for it is experienced by a larger number of people. Contamination from industrial and thermal power plant smoke and soot was the first serious pollutant to be reduced to tolerable levels, in the early 1960s—as it has been in almost all large cities in Europe and the United States. Sulfur oxides, nitrogen oxides, and other invisible pollutants increased rapidly into the 1970s, reaching, by 1971, levels considered dangerous to human health. Since then, a slight decline has been reported in government reports (Kankyōchō 1972b, pp. 137-140). Similar small declines are reported for the nitrogen series, and the government believes modifications in production methods and installation of antipolluting devices have begun to be effective. However, although these substances may be in check, their spread across Japan has continued. In 1955, sulfur dioxide reached levels of more than 1000 kilograms per square kilometer in the four or five major industrial centers in the Kantō, Kinki, and northern Kyushu areas, but by 1970 similar levels were detectable in every part of the archipelago except Hokkaido (Kankyōchō 1972b, p. 30, and annex, p. 4; Keizai Kikakuchō and *Japan Times* 1972, p. 128).

Carbon monoxide and constitutents of photochemical smog produced by automobile emission became increasingly evident in the Tokyo and Osaka metropolitan areas between 1964 and 1971. The average yearly concentrations fluctuated between 4 and 5 particles per million, and failed to show the slight decline sulfur and nitrogen oxides did over the same period (Kankyōchō 1972b). No government-inspired attempts to limit or control traffic have yet been put into effect for these urban areas, but reports of smog conditions have increased in urban areas in the years 1972 and 1973: 176 public warnings in 1972 against 7 in 1970 (Asahi, 22 April 1973).

Emissions and effluents contaminating the urban environment do not exhaust the list of environmental problems related to industrialization and urbanization. Land subsidence, due to withdrawal of fresh water; soil erosion, due to cultivation of submarginal slope areas; siltation of waterways and coastal areas; overcutting of forests; and many other consequences not classifiable as ordinary pollution have been some of the environmental costs of Japan's intensive economic and urban growth. The summary of effects presented thus far are sufficient to indicate the pattern, and we may turn now to the consequences for health and food supply.

The most extensively publicized consequences for health are the Minamata and *itai-itai* diseases. The former involves methyl mercury poisoning of residents of Minamata village, Niigata city, and possibly other communities, from eating fish contaminated by the substance discharged by a chemical plant. Itai-itai is caused by eating rice grown in water polluted with cadmium. Minamata disease symptoms are those of classic mercuric poisoning: death or comatose states at termination, and crippling, loss of speech, and other sensory-motor disturbances of varying degrees of severity. Itai-itai victims have been mainly females who suffer from bone pains and convulsion of the femoral abductor muscles. The number of victims was officially reported as 282 Minamata cases, with sixty deaths as of March 1972, and 123 itai-itai cases, with thirty-four deaths, as of February 1972[9] (Kankyōchō 1972c). Another well-publicized case involving chemical poisoning is the Kanemi rice bran incident of 1972—the first reported case in the world of PCB ingestion (polychlorinated byphenyl—a chemical extensively used in plastics manufacture and extremely resistant to degradation in the environment). The 1081 Fukuoka victims ate edible oils contaminated with the substance, with some sixteen deaths.

Respiratory diseases with pollution-related causes are asthma and particular forms of bronchitis and emphysema. The Yokkaichi case is the most publicized. It is difficult to establish medically the contribution of polluting substances to the incidence of these diseases, especially in individual cases, because of the large numbers of substances mixed together, and because of other contributing causes of the symptoms. Sufferers from such illnesses officially certifiable as due largely to atmospheric pollution are mainly the

[9]As of March 1974, just in Kumamoto prefecture, the number of certified Minamata disease victims has risen to 584 (Thurston 1974, p. 26).

oldest and youngest groups in the population. As of March 1972 a total of 6376 patients were so certified and were eligible for financial aid provided by a recent compensation law. Over 30 percent were under four years of age; 19 percent between five and nine; and 21 percent were over sixty. Most of the deaths attributed to air pollution are among persons over sixty. A conspicuous case given maximum publicity in Tokyo involved forty girl students hospitalized with acute respiratory symptoms in July 1970. There has been at least one such multiple incident due to some form of environmental contamination each year in the 1970s (Kankyōchō 1972b, p. 178).

Damage to agriculture, forestry, and fisheries by pollution has been extensive, but often difficult to prove and harder to quantify, as much of the damage may be slow-acting. Reports cite damage to plants by sulfur dioxide, hydrogen flouride, chlorine, and soot and dust in various parts of Japan—particularly level land areas adjacent to metropolitan districts. Water pollution of various kinds, including eutrophication, is reported to have damaged some 194,000 hectares of agricultural land in 1970, a 50 percent increase over 1965 (Kankyōchō 1972b, p. 145). Fish crop damage also has been increasing: 147 cases were reported in 1970, not including the red tide conditions in the Inland Sea, mentioned previously. Kankyōchō (1972b, p. 163) estimates fisheries damage in 1970 as about $48 million.

One other monetary measure of environmental disruption: settlements of claims cases brought against polluters by individuals and groups of victims of water and air pollution totaled, from late 1969 to early 1973, some $4 million. This figure can be expected to rise, as Japanese courts have shown an increasing willingness to find judgments in favor of plaintiffs.[10]

Summing up, environmental problems in Japan are characterized by a rapidly increasing impact due to the very small land areas involved for concentrating industrial activity. High industrial growth rates therefore have had a more massive impact in many respects than in the United States. This puts Japan in a class with Italy and other smaller European nations. There have so far been no cases in the United States so clearly damaging to the health of a community as the Minamata and other disasters; only the Donora, Pennsylvania incident, involving a number of deaths from smoke contamination in the 1940s, can be compared. The environmental problems traceable to

---

[10]The consequences of industrialization in a heavily populated country also have been observed in the deterioration of recreational areas—a peculiarly important issue in Japan, which has always been a nation of internal tourists. Damage to the gardens, temples, historic buildings and their environs, parks, national forests, and the like has been severe, and a source of considerable public discussion. Overpricing of land available for badly needed recreational and park areas also has been cited by government reports as one of the serious kōgai mondai. Perhaps these matters are better classified as problems of the welfare gap, rather than of the environment, but in any case they constitute a mounting social cost of increased density and valuation of public goods.

industry and technology also are accentuated in the Japanese case by the existing large urban population (regardless of low population increase rates) and the greater affluence, which has increased pressure on all environmental and social facilities.

All industrial countries have been moving through various stages of public awareness and concern over environmental problems in the past decade, as the problem of disruption has become increasingly severe. Levels of awareness vary to some extent by particular patterns of communication and social structure—citizen noise generally has been louder, and occurred sooner, in the democratic countries than in those with tighter public controls. But aside from such differences in timing, the level of articulate concern is roughly proportional to the amount of objective danger or damage. Japan, with a relatively late start for its environmental movement, has since developed one of the most vigorous citizen environmental movements among the industrial countries. The rise of action groups of all kinds has implications beyond the problem of environmental disruption, because it also constitutes an example of the change from a closed society, where grievances are resolved in private bargaining, to a more open system of public opposition and advocacy (Gallagher 1973).

Students of the environmental movement in Japan trace the origins of active public concern to the Minamata cases and the other instances of health damage noted previously. The earliest reports of Minamata did not arouse widespread insterest, although a small group of Japanese scientists and medical men did attempt to publicize the cases, in the face of official apathy and opposition from industry. When scientific reports on the disease were published in 1964, revealing mercury poisoning traceable to a nearby chemical plant operated by Shōwa Denkō was the cause, public interest erupted. Coincident with the publication of these official reports on the Minamata disaster, various types of air and water pollution had been spreading rapidly across Japan and had begun to bring environmental problems closer to more people. During this same late 1960s period other disadvantages and deprivations associated with economic growth had begun to attract attention: pollution problems began to merge with the others— urban crowding, health and welfare deficiencies, inflation, housing, and others—the set which by 1971 had acquired the label "welfare gap."

A dramatic and broadly representative case has been Fuji, a city of 170,000 south of Tokyo, where pollution problems have existed since the early 1900s. From an agrarian and fishing area, it developed over the years into a manufacturing and chemical industrial center, in which paper and pulp production predominated. The first known protest actually occurred in 1889 where, as in the case of Ashio twenty years later, peasants complained bitterly about waste drainage into their fields. Although the polluter, the Fuji Paper Manufacturing Company, compensated the villagers and actually built drainage ditches, these protests continued. By 1910 the company could ignore the local inhabitants, as the proportion of peasants in the nearby population dwindled and industrialization of the area increased. It is significant that in 1934, the mayor of Fuji paid 8000 yen from the municipality's treasury to the head of the local fishing association with the stipulation: "No complaints or objections shall hereafter be raised from the association as to the drainage and/or filthy water from the paperworks of this area." Little protest occurred again until 1957. By this time Fuji was caught up in the mushrooming industrial effort and the about-to-be-launched income doubling plan. The farmers of the area protested and demanded compensation for damage to crops, but were quieted with a small cash offer. Fishermen also protested, received compensation, and eventually ended fishing activity by 1969. From 1966, however, Fuji city residents took up the cudgels of protest and over the next six years built up an organization that launched demonstrations, undertook research, engaged in bargaining, and in the process extracted antipollution agreements from the local companies, instituted damage suits in courts, succeeded in excluding new industry and plants from the area, and brought pressure on the Diet, the cabinet, and prefectural government for pollution prevention (Okamoto 1972, pp. 4-8).

Various public opinion polls taken between 1959 and 1973 indicate a steeply rising curve of national concern over environmental problems. For example, in 1959 and 1970 the Sōrifu survey group asked a national sample of informants, "What things would you be most interested in having the government do for the country?" In 1959, the list of items was dominated by better housing, lower prices, social security, lower taxes, better facilities in small towns and villages, and issues of then-current concern such as clean politics (Sōrifu 1961, p. 41). In 1970, many of these same issues were present, but the highest percentage—over 60 percent—of responses advocated the elimination of kōgai mondai (Kōseisho 1972). As the concept of kōgai mondai has absorbed some of the welfare issues, the difference is not clear-cut, but the general trend of opinion seems plain enough: environmental disruption and pollution became major public issues in the early 1970s.

The media show similar concerns. During 1971 and 1972, environmental matters constituted the second or third most common topic in newspaper discussion of national issues, resembling the situation in United States media in 1968 and 1969. One difference in the discussion in the two countries was the greater willingness of the Japanese governmental and business leaders to face the basic question of priorities and national goals; that is, to elevate the environmental dialogue above the level of counterculture faddism, which so strongly marked its American manifestation, to a serious debate over the direction of Japan's economic and social development.

This national debate resulted in a series of development plans published in the early 1970s (Keizai Kikakuchō 1971, 1972a, 1973a). These plans have been referred to as the welfare-environment policy, which combine the familiar welfare-gap issues of social security, treatment of the aged, reduced working hours, and the like, with changes in industrial priorities in order to clean up pollution and redistribute population. Prominent in these documents, and in the national debate, have been references to the information society or postindustrial society, meaning a relatively affluent economy based on clean industries such as computers, operated by a highly educated labor force accepting a comfortable but perhaps less luxurious level of living (Hayashi 1970). However, few serious analyses have yet been published indicating just how Japan could support even a modest scale of affluence without foreign exchange earned from exports of chemicals, steel, machinery, automobiles, and other products of high-polluting processes. Indeed, the highest industrial growth rates in post-Pacific War Japan have been in industries consuming large amounts of raw materials, involving the discharge of polluting substances.

The national discussion of kōgai mondai was fueled by a number of private voluntary organizations representing Japan's version of the environmental movement. One such group is the Jishu Kōza, a union of scientists and citizens interested in fact-gathering and research on environmental issues. Jishu Kōza and others like it have issued a series of reports and white papers dealing with environmental questions and sought to mobilize public opinion, particularly in cases of danger to human health, such as the Minamata incident (Ui 1972). Other groups have organized around esthetic issues, such as the Right-to-Sunshine League, a group of householders opposing the construction of large highrise apartments which block light and views. These groups have won a number of court suits.

Such local citizen groups (called *shimin undō* or *jūmin undō*) and others have opposed industrial expansion and land use for other than customary pursuits. A new international airport at Narita, northeast of Tokyo, was virtually completed in 1970, but by court actions protesting the disruption of agriculture and the dangers created by aviation fuel pipelines in a region especially prone to earthquake damage, local farmers and residents of Chiba city have thus far prevented use of the facility. Fishermen's protests delayed, up to mid-1974, use of the nuclear-powered freighter, *Mutsu*. Local citizens' groups have also forced the down-scaling of ambitious plans for the construction of a vast industrial park near Tomakomai in Hokkaido on the grounds of its possible pollution potential and destruction of recreational areas.

Nature conservation groups also have become active. The one that may have the largest membership, the National Nature Protection League (somewhat comparable to the Sierra Club) sued the governor of Ehime prefecture in an effort to stop construction of a special scenic highway to attract tourists, claiming the highway defaced the natural beauty of the region. The suit was eventually lost, but the action delayed construction of the road and forced changes in its location and engineering.

Like its analog in other countries, the Japanese labor movement has been in a difficult position on environmental questions, due to the fact jobs may depend on current levels and types of production, and also because environmental cleanup frequently is aimed at specific factories and unions in Japan are enterprise-based. Despite such obvious conflicts of interest, some have joined antipollution campaigns in cooperation with local citizen groups. In several cases the unions have joined in protesting pollution in their own enterprises, but the more common pattern has been for unions to initiate discussion meetings with industry management over pollution questions. The Socialist, Communist, and Kōmeitō parties also have been important forces in bringing unions into the environmental movement. One observer notes the decisive movement of public opinion against the big polluters has been a major force in arousing union conscience, despite the serious conflict of interest involved. In some cases, however, citizen groups have accused unions of siding with business in opposing cleanup measures (Koshiro 1973).

Between June 1971 and April 1973, four major court cases involving corporate responsibility for pollution endangering life and health were decided in favor of the plaintiffs, subjecting the companies to heavy damages. These cases include the Minamata mercuric poisoning involving Shōwa Denkō and the Chisso Corporation; the itai-itai cadmium and other poisons involving the Mitsui Mining Company; and the asthma air pollution cases in Yokkaichi city, involving several factories of major firms. Also influential has been the recent tendency of the Ministry of International Trade and Industry to deny polluting firms the protection or defense they are accustomed to on other issues. Newspaper accounts describe the feelings of "embarrassment" or "shame" exhibited by executives of companies involved in pollution—a typical gesture in Japanese public life which nonetheless is evidence of a change in attitude. A number of influential groups of businessmen have begun doing research and issuing reports on environmental problems. One of these, the Sangyō Keikaku Konwakai (1973) took a strong stand against further development of types of industries responsible for pollution.

Legislation dealing with environmental matters in Japan is well advanced, with laws similar to, or more far-reaching than, comparable American measures. It is too early to tell how effective these laws may be in controlling pollution, but there have been a few factory closures and well-publicized, tough investigations of accused polluters by both national and prefectural governments. Laws specifically permit prefectural governors to modify national government standards of emission and effluent if the evidence indicates these standards are inadequate in specific communities. Other provisions, especially for water, require immediate penalties for violations without the necessity of proving exact effect. In several recent instances, local communities have set environmental quality standards higher than those established by the national government. In some cases such actions have been caused by reformist political groups and parties acting in concert with labor unions, including successful electoral campaigns with pollution clean-up as a major objective. Mayors representing the Socialist and Communist parties have been elected in recent years in five major cities, including Tokyo. Negotiations between the urban and prefectural governments and particular industries have led to agreements to cease contamination procedures, as in the case of the Nihon Kokan Steel Company and Kanagawa prefecture

(Yokohama and Kawasaki cities). The company agreed to reduce sulfur dioxide and other sulfuric discharges (Koshiro 1973).[11]

Although this list of accomplishments gives the impression the Japanese are actively engaged in solving their environmental problems, the decisive changes in disruptive procedures have been few. Like the United States, reform proceeds slowly, controlled by the reluctance of government and industry to find economic and political alternatives. As in the United States, business resists every attempt to require it to change its ways, and government is reluctant to enforce its laws too vigorously. Environmental groups in Japan consider substantial changes in national priorities, although more openly discussed in Japan than in the United States, are as far off as they are in America, and it may take economic recession and shortages to bring about relief.

Population Density and Urbanization

The decision of the Japanese to move in the direction of the modern industrial state was accompanied—as it has been everywhere—by an initial spurt of population growth, thus reversing a long period of informal demographic control followed in the last half of the Tokugawa period. The motives favoring population growth were a response to economic and ideological forces: economic in that a youthful, expanding labor and military force was desirable for industrial development and expansion; ideological in that a large population was part of the image of a strong, vigorous modern nation. The demographic outcome is fully dealt with by Ohbuchi in this volume, but it should be noted here that there emerged a population problem at the end of the Pacific War, with repatriation and the postwar baby boom. However, as Ohbuchi shows, soon thereafter Japan had reached a very low-growth population (a rate of 1.1 per thousand in the period 1963-70; the United States had 1.2 per thousand for the same period). The population problem resulting from industrialization now had shifted from overall growth to concentration in urban areas.

As late as 1920, when the population was about 56 million, Japan still retained many of the demographic characteristics of an agrarian, partly urbanized, semi-industrialized society: most people lived in the country or in

[11]If a new plan for compensating pollution victims proposed by the government in October 1973 is translated into law and implemented, Japan will have the most advanced program of its kind. In the existing law, victims can acquire some compensation only for medical care. In the proposed system, much more will be available, including bereavement compensation for families of victims, childrens' allowances, and funeral expenses. The system will be funded by a tax based on the amount of pollution emitted. This tax will be collected by a special Public Nuisance Prevention Corporation and distributed to medical services, where it will become available to the patient after approval of his application by a screening board (*Japan Report*, 1 Nov. 1973).

small towns and villages; high-density urban conditions existed only in the Tokyo and Osaka areas; the average number of persons in the household was five—a high figure associated with agrarian conditions elsewhere in the world.

By 1970 the picture was very different. Measured in square kilometers, population density had risen rapidly to 191 in 1950, and 280 in 1970. As Table 2 shows, by 1970 over half of the total population lived in urban centers with more than 100,000 population, in contrast to 1920 when only 12 percent were in such centers. The proportion of population in densely inhabited urban centers rose gradually up to the war. In 1950 there was a slight loss, due to wartime damage of urban housing, then a dramatic rise to 1970 as the large centers drew population from smaller towns and rural areas, and as some small centers became large ones. The 1920 distribution between large and small centers is thus nearly reversed by 1970.

These increasing densities have occurred despite decreasing numbers of children per couple and decreasing numbers of persons per household (*Japan Report*, 16 Oct. 1973). By 1972 the number of persons in the average household had declined to 3.7. The 1970 census reported that 63 percent of all families were of the nuclear type, reflecting the great increase in the urban wage-earning family, and the decline in the two- and three-generation families of rural areas. The average number of children per couple in 1940 was 3.39; by 1972 it was 1.92. The census also reported that 64 percent of wives between 35 and 39 years of age were earning wages. Only 18.4 percent of all wives consider children to be a means of support in their old age—an index of nuclearization (*Japan Report*, 16 Oct. 1973).[12]

Even more important, also shown in Table 2, was the massive movement of the population into densely inhabited centers, that is, the growth of cities. In 1970 Japan had 103 cities and metropolitan areas of over 100,000 population; 87 of these cities were in seven urbanized prefectures. (There are forty-seven prefectures, fifteen classed as urbanized.) Of these 103 cities, 44 had populations over 200,000, and 8 had more than 1,000,000—metropolitan Tokyo was above 11,400,000. In 1920, only two urbanized prefectures— Tokyo-to and Osaka-fu—had more than 50 percent of their population

[12]It should be noted that a controversy exists among Japanese sociologists over the extent of the nuclearization process. The traditional familial kinship unit in Japan is the three-generation household, consisting of an older couple, one or more of their sons, with their wives and children. One group of sociologists (for example, Morioka 1973) regards any sign of contraction of this unit as evidence of nuclearization (that is, census or survey data which show fewer sons remaining with parents). Another group views current data showing contraction as a temporary phase due to economic conditions or as a misunderstanding of the concept of nuclear family (for example, Oikawa 1973). This argument seems of little significance to the present paper, for whatever the typological issues may be, the size of the household kinship unit *has* been dropping in Japan, and this reflects known changes in the national social structure and economy.

Table 2
Distribution of Population by Size of City, Town, or Village 1920-1970
(in thousands)

	100,000 and over	Percentage of total population	10,000-99,999	Percentage of total population	Under 10,000	Percentage of total population	Total population	Population per square kilometer
1920	6753	12	10,918	20	37,719	68	55,963	147
1940	21,291	29	15,249	21	35,998	50	74,114	191
1950	21,326	26	23,581	28	38,293	46	83,200	226
1960	37,802	40	45,917	50	9700	10	93,419	253
1970	53,527	52	40,563	39	9630	9	103,720	280

Source: Sōrifu, *Japan Statistical Yearbook*, 1966 and 1971.
Note: In 1955 the number of villages and towns was sharply reduced by law, resulting in mergers of towns and villages and establishment of new cities. This led to a sizable shift of population from the "under 10,000" category to the "10,000-99,999" and "100,000 and over" categories.

residing in cities; this urbanization increased to five prefectures by 1940; to thirteen by 1960; and by 1970, fourteen. Only one urbanized prefecture, Ibaraki, near Tokyo, still had less than 50 percent of its population living in the urban sector. Compared to the national average of 280 persons per square kilometer, in 1970 the density of Tokyo proper was 15,322; Osaka proper, 14,463; Kyoto proper, 2326; and Kitakyushu City, 2236 (Sorifu Tōkei-kyoku 1971). This movement of the population into cities, moreover, has been accompanied by a proportional loss of the population in the rural areas.[13]

More graphically, a virtually continuous urbanized strip along the coast from the Tokyo area on the east through Nagoya and Osaka to Kobe on the west, sometimes called the Tokaido Megalopolis, has emerged. Urban density in the Tokaido area, northern Kyushu, and the whole Kinki region of central Japan (including Kyoto, Osaka, Kobe) has assumed megalopolitan proportions, constituting one of the most impressive settlements of this type in the world. Some 6 percent or more of former agricultural land in the coastal and level areas has been lost to this urban sprawl.

Meier and Hoshino (1967) compared the Tokaido strip with the United States East Coast megalopolitan corridor (Boston-Washington, D.C.), finding close similarities and some superior efficiencies for the Japanese version, although their study was done before a full consciousness of the social and environmental costs of these massive concentrations had emerged. The populations of the two megalopoles are approximately equal (about 30 million), and the corridor lengths similar (500 km. for the Japan strip; 750 for the United States). The Japanese are able to move many more commuter bodies per day than the Americans, largely due to the greater efficiency of high-speed trains. Telephonic and other communications seem comparable, although large-scale data needed for comparisons are often hard to find. Educational facilities needed to sustain the technical operations of a megalopolis were not fully adequate for Japan in the mid-1960s, as Meier noted; but by the 1970s, the Japanese had caught up in most respects. The authors were concerned with facilities for providing a food supply adequate

[13]The Japan census includes a concept, depopulated areas, defined as any community where the population as of February 1973 declined by 10 percent or more during the period 1960-65, and where the ratio of local tax revenue and other forms of local financing avéraged less than 0.4 percent of the total revenue in the period 1966-68. Such areas accounted for 41.7 percent of total land area, 32.4 percent of all cities, towns, and villages, and 8.6 percent of the total population. The average density of such areas was 58 persons per square kilometer, as compared to 438 for nondepopulated areas, and 280 for Japan as a whole. The population of gainfully employed persons in the depopulated areas shrank by a fifth from 1960 to 1970, although there were some gains in certain classes of employment. These depopulated areas constitute a cost of space problem for Japan somewhat comparable to the western United States where low. densities result in substandard social services (*Japan Report*, 1 Jan. 1964).

for the massive population concentration, finding this is difficult without substantial reliance on imports from abroad. However, as they felt Japan's favorable trade situation would provide the resources for food imports, they accepted these growing dependencies of the megalopolis on exogenous supports: "a megalopolis draws upon many territories and can substitute the products of one for those of another when shortages appear," and also noted, "the most important feature of the megalopolis, however, is its enhanced capacity to innovate, improvise, and organize" (Meier 1967, p. 304). In the colder light of the 1970s, with their shortages and international political changes, these capacities, so impressive and seemingly flexible to scholars of the 1960s, appear to be subject to unpredictable rigidities and hence may constitute major social costs for the future.

What we are witnessing is nothing uniquely Japanese, for the same processes are under way in every highly industrialized society. The concentration of population in cities, the complex interlinking of functions between communities, and the accumulation of industrial and economic power go hand in hand. The industrialized system, with its drive toward economies of scale, is responsible for this build-up in population and function. Conventional methods of cost accounting have ignored the human costs of density, and only recently have the actual economic disadvantages of increasing density and size begun to make themselves felt. The increasing costs of land and all public facilities in the central areas are borne by business only in part, and until these externalities are charged to the cost of operations, density of population and function can be expected to increase, though a slowdown can occur when human discomfort becomes acute—as it has in Tokyo since about 1967.

Progress in calculating the cost of social overhead of urban density is conspicuous in Japanese government research organizations, and there is no shortage of information on this point (Keizai Kikakuchō 1972b and with Japan Times 1972, Kokumin Seikatsu Shingikai 1969). A summary of available data shows the most conspicuous cost increase is in land acquisition. In 1971, land in the central Tokyo area had reached 120,000 yen per square meter, and was rising at a rate of about 20,000 yen annually. As land was selling for about 17,000 yen per square meter in suburban areas, the location of businesses in the outlying areas was proceeding rapidly, thereby enlarging the sprawl zone, with underutilized land between held for speculative purposes, and increasing costs for transportation and other services. Another rapidly increasing cost factor is construction. Much construction work in densely populated areas of big cities has been carried on at night—no doubt as a way to save capital costs but with a 20 percent higher net cost due to overtime wages and lighting. For example, the cost of subway construction in Tokyo increased to 9 billion yen per kilometer by 1972, compared to around 3 billion in 1960, largely because of added precautions to avoid noise and vibration in the densely built city. A third cost increase has been in delivery charges for basic necessities. The cost of water mains and services in Tokyo went up 2.7 times in ten years—this due largely to the need to find adequate supplies at greater distances from the users. Even the cost of disposing of excess dirt from construction sites had doubled in the same period, due to the need to carry it farther away. It is possible, of course, that these costs could slow down concentration, but perhaps with the consequence of accentuating urban sprawl.

Economic reports issued by the Japanese government and private sources in the early 1970s also were concerned by the amount of time spent in commuting to work because of the concentration of economic activity (Keizai Kikakuchō 1972b). The Japan Travel Bureau, the railroads serving Tokyo and Osaka, and the Sōrifu's survey agency have made studies of the commuter services and patronage in large cities, with reference to the possible effect these might have on work efficiency. Between 1960 and 1970, the number of persons required to commute from outlying areas into the central Tokyo business and industrial districts doubled. This is interpreted by Japanese sources as meaning the increasing density of the city, and increasing location of businesses in the central portions, resulted in pushing worker residences into outlying areas. Actual average time spent commuting in 1960 was 19.3 minutes; by 1970, 49.3.

Urban density of this magnitude is the consequence of powerful forces, and there is little doubt the major factor in Japan's case is the growth and concentration of industry—especially in the post-Pacific War period. The increases in urban population and function were accomplished in large part by the rapid migration of rural residents to the city to obtain employment in Japan's new industries and businesses. Such concentrations of population in a relatively small geographical space mean devotion of an entire country to tasks best performed in densely populated centers for reasons of efficiency and cost. The structural consequences of this change are indicated by our figures on the drop in household and family size and the social overhead costs; the cultural changes, whether good or bad, are indicated by consumerism and the general shift of cultural standards away from a kind of refined, rustic estheticism to the mechanical imagery of the city and its industrial technology. Although Japan continues to purvey her traditional culture as a facet of tourism and international imagery, her population has left it behind in its adaptation to the industrial system.

Both Western and Japanese sociologists have made a number of studies of the consequences for social relationships and behavior of this population movement. The middle-class salarymen and their families studied by Vogel (1963) stated they were no longer inclined to rely on their relatives for help in emergencies, nor were they inclined to offer such help. The increased isolation and alienation of urban life has been considered as a major reason for the emergence of the new religions, such as Soka Gakkai (White 1970). White (1972) described the felt need for clubs and social circles among these new urbanites, and Ishida (1966) noted the difficulty of obtaining true participation in group activities by these lonely people, who join such groups largely to feel wanted and not to pursue definite goals.

Some of these findings seem quixotic: the emergence of new cults and clubs, and the increase in their membership, also can be viewed as an adaptive response, not necessarily as evidence of social pathology. Tsurumi (1970), in her study of housewives, found some of these new organizations were meeting social and psychological needs of the new woman quite well, and the widespread habit of writing biographical documents as social circle activity constitute an effective defense against alienation. Indeed, the conventional interpretation of Japanese urban social organization, from Dore's classic study (1958) to more recent work by Yazaki (1968), Suzuki (1957), Vogel (1963), Ishida (1966), and others emphasizes that, despite the problems of city life, the social structure contains numerous highly organized cells displaying the integrity and responsibility of village life. That is, there has been a tendency for the urban mass to break down into *gemeinschaft* units which satisfy the needs of their members to an extent greater than in the more atomistic cities of the West, particularly North America.

However, these generalized interpretations of urban social organization, mostly based on observations made before the emergence of the exceedingly dense conditions in the 1960s, are not necessarily indicative of some permanent quality of city life in the largest centers. There remains the possibility that like other social relationships, those in the urban society can be influenced by changing density and population magnitudes, and especially by the increasing inconveniences associated with crowds, transportation difficulties, atmospheric pollution, and the like. People who may feel a sense of social identity due to their associational life in the city nevertheless reach the breaking point over increasing difficulties in commuting—as apparently Tokyo suburbanites did in 1972 and 1973, when some of them responded by rioting in the train stations, their frustrations heightened by a railway strike.

White (1972), in a preliminary report on a study made in a new industrial city in the late 1960s, found the relatively high level of satisfaction and emotional health among the migrants was due to the recency of the migration, and the fact that in this first generation nearly everyone found better jobs and incomes after the move to the city. In other words, there is a suggestion that the achievement of the goals sought in the initial cityward move, plus the cushioning effect of the cellular organizational structure of city life and its projections out of village or kinship structures, has tended to make city populations in Japan relatively tolerant of conditions which might, under other circumstances, result in widespread demoralization and disturbance. The adaptive pattern thus may be historical; there is no guarantee it is a permanent condition.

Our data suggest that conditions are changing. If newspaper accounts are any measure, the risks and hazards of city life became major news in the Japanese press between 1970 and 1973. The topics dealt with repeatedly, in a rough order of frequency, were environmental pollution, especially traffic smog and industrial fumes; commuting time and discomfort, both on trains and for automobiles and roads; housing problems; deterioration of public facilities due to crowding and overuse; and evidence of human exasperation and anxiety resulting from density. Many of the newspaper reports describe the activities of citizens' protest and reform groups attempting to cope with problems of density; the word *dense* (*chūmitsu*) has become a symbol of much that is felt to be wrong and uncomfortable in Japanese life.

Efforts were under way in the early 1970s to alleviate transportation difficulties due to the increasing number of automobiles on the limited road and street network characteristic of Japanese cities—which until the mid-1950s had not changed much beyond the level reached around 1920. Fatalities from traffic accidents constituted the single largest cause of deaths in Japan for a number of years in the 1960s and 70s. In 1970 the number was approximately 20,000 (as compared with about 55,000 in the United States). In 1968, Japan was second in the world in terms of the number of pedestrians killed per number of persons per 10,000 automobiles, about 3.7 compared to West Germany's 4.4; however, Japan had about eight persons per car while West Germany had almost five (Keizai Kikakuchō 1972b). This high accident rate was caused to a large extent by the inadequate street facilities. Until recently, streets in Tokyo stood at about 9 percent of the total land area, compared to about 35 percent for New York and 23 percent for London. Intensive efforts in the late 1960s and early 1970s resulted in an increase to about 12 percent in Tokyo, and several major intercity expressways also had been constructed. With respect to the latter, there has been an intense public debate among environmentalists and growth-minded industrial spokesmen over the advisability of committing Japan, with its superb rail network, to the automobile age—a debate which took on new meaning in late 1973, with its looming petroleum shortages.

Other investments for public protection from automobile hazards included the construction of pedestrian bridges (the number in 1970 was twenty times that in 1965); sidewalks had increased by six times over the 1965 level (pedestrians walking in traffic arteries is an especially common cause of fatalities in the outlying areas of large cities, and in all small towns and villages); and traffic signals had increased over three times (Keizai Kikakuchō 1972b, pp. 170-172). These figures represent a substantial public investment, and apparently did slow down the rate of traffic accidents.

Along less tangible but perhaps sociologically significant directions, signs of unease in the cities also were developing in the sphere of the social community. There has been much discussion in Japan in recent years about the loss of community—a word as often quoted directly from English as translated into one of several available Japanese equivalents (Kokumin Seikatsu Shingikai Chōsakai 1969). A Keizai Kikakuchō survey (1972b) of social trends explored what is called the increasing "hollowness" of the urban community. By this is meant the rupture of continuous network relationships among neighbors characteristic of Japanese city life until the current trend toward separating home and workplace became endemic. Similar developments are found in the country with the great increase in part-time farming (some 65 percent of all farm families have one or more resident member commuting to other places for wage work). Surveys like one conducted by the Ministry of Education in 1974 indicated this was a source of considerable unease: 24 percent of all respondents in this national survey felt "bonds among neighbors are being weakened." About 30 percent felt "people are becoming self-centered," and 18 percent considered community problems have increased with greater job availability and prosperity (Keizai Kikakuchō 1972*b*, p. 127). These attitudes have been translated in recent years into much more active protest behavior in the form of frequent public demonstrations against road building and high-rise construction and protests against factory location, commuter services, traffic accidents, and the ever-present fear of atmosphere pollution. Participation in these movements, however, appears to cut across community groups and, hence, should not necessarily be seen as an expression of strong communal ties in the traditional sense.

Sociological surveys confirm the loss of community and neighborhood ties. These include the many civic associations characteristic of Japanese city neighborhoods and are fully reported on in Dore's study (1958) of a Tokyo ward in the early 1950s: volunteer fire service, night watches, collection activities for charities and neighborhood services, funeral clubs, care for the aged and nurseries for children, shrine organizations, and many other organizations. However, surveys conducted by the Tokyo Municipality Research Association in 1971 in several Tokyo wards and in one other city show these organizations have lost ground in recent years, becoming fewer in number and membership. Residents display a desire to have the services provided by these organizations become official government activities; that is, they are no longer so willing to devote their free time to them (Keizai Kikakuchō 1972*b*, pp. 131-137).

Labor and Leisure

Although Japan entered the ranks of the industrialized countries by the end of World War I (when, for the first time, more than half of the labor force was engaged in nonagricultural work), it was not until about 1960 that wage and salary employes in industry began to outnumber farm workers, self-employed, and family workers taken together. By 1973, nonagricultural wage and salary employes comprised two-thirds of the labor force. The drastic decline of farm employment (from 12.7 million in 1960 to 6.6 million in 1973), family workers, and self-employed, and rapid expansion of the wage and salary employes (from 22.8 million in 1960 to 35.6 million in 1973) accounted for this marked change in labor force structure (*Japan Labor Bulletin*, May 1974).

In all likelihood, these structural changes alone account for the emergence of occupational consciousness and identification in Japan, as Cole and Tominaga point out in their chapter in this volume. Today, a much larger sector of the Japanese population is directly concerned with the conditions and problems of wage- and salary-earners than ever before. Increasing attention, as a result, has been given to the adequacy of public policy and legislation regarding union-management relations, labor standards, and worker welfare, especially as employment has become depersonalized and working rules bureaucratized. In 1971 more than one-third of nonagricultural employes worked in public or private enterprises with at least 1000 employes each (*Japan Labor Bulletin*, Oct. 1974, p. 5).

Even with the upsurge of the wage and salary sector and the resulting shortages of labor in Japan, labor's proportional share in national income showed no marked increase in the 1960s. In 1970, the share for labor in fact stood at 57.2 percent, which despite the rise in the proportion of wage- and salary-earners in the total labor force was still no more than in 1955. According to the Keizai Kikakuchō, this compared to 77.5 percent for Great Britain, 71.6 percent for the United States, 64.5 percent for Germany, and 62.5 percent for France. Although the lower figure for Japan reflects a smaller proportion of wage- and salary-earners in the Japanese labor force than in the other advanced countries, it was probably due also to such factors as the *nenkō* wage systems and large percentages of newly recruited young and female employes who were paid at relatively low levels (*Japan Report*, 1 Feb. 1974). Although total monthly earnings of urban employe households advanced 60 percent in real terms from 1960 to 1970 despite a nominal rise of 284 percent (Umetani 1973, p. 4), apparently wage-earners were not keeping pace with the expansion of the real GNP. From 1965 to 1970, for example, real hourly earnings, adjusted for bonus and other incremental payments, climbed at an average annual rate of 9.2 percent, but this was only about three-fourths of the annual increase in GNP for those years. In contrast, real hourly earnings in West Germany, which rose in the same period by 4.6 percent annually, kept slightly ahead of the annual GNP increases.[14] One of the reasons for the failure of Japanese wages to rise along with the increase in GNP has been the steady inflation of consumer prices.

To be sure, since the mid-1950s, the wage-earner has enjoyed a high degree of employment security. Throughout the 1960s the unemployment rate has rarely exceeded 1.5 percent (and from 1965 until 1974 it has usually been close to 1 percent), and the ratio of claimants to eligible employes for unemployment insurance has been no more than about 3 percent (*Japan Labor Bulletin*, 1 May 1974). Involuntary separation (discharge to reduce excess labor) in all industries except construction between 1966 and 1970 averaged less than 9 percent per year (Rōdōshō 1970). This stability of employment is responsible in large part for the stability of income for most workers in Japan who are regular or permanent employes up to the age of retirement. It also accounts to a considerable extent for the disappearance of poverty, as Taira and Chubachi point out in their chapter in this volume.

[14]In both Italy and the United Kingdom, however, the ratio of the rise in real hourly earnings to rise in GNP for these years was 0.88 (OECD, appendix).

However, the stability of employment and income during these productive years is not matched by a corresponding stability and security of income in the older age ranges (*Japan Labor Bulletin*, Jan. 1973). A combination of factors has brought this about: the quite young mandatory retirement age, fifty-five to sixty for most industries; relatively low retirement payments; low social security benefits (a worker can expect at most $65 a month if he has contributed for twenty years); the abolition of the Old Civil Code in 1945 (requiring older sons to support their parents), which promoted the nuclearization of families; and the increasing longevity of the population. These plus the difficulty of finding a good job after retirement and insufficient cash savings have made the plight of the older worker a serious one.

A high percentage of retirees actually have remained in the labor force. The ILO reports the Japanese figure for labor-force participation of persons sixty-five and older is 34.4 percent as against 19 percent for the United States and 14.2 percent for West Germany. At the same time, the social security investments of these countries expressed as a percentage of the GNP shows Japan with only 5.8 percent, the United States with 7.2, and West Germany with 16.8 (International Labor Organization 1971). As Fisher (1973, p. 9) points out: "It is generally agreed that Japanese retirement benefits are so low as to compel the beneficiaries to continue work as long as possible."

Although the government instituted legally required pensions in 1959, and the picture has steadily improved, the value of the payments has consistently fallen behind due to the factors summarized here plus inflation. The inadequacy of benefits in the statuatory pensions and social security schemes has no doubt encouraged the system of lump-sum retirement allowances in private industry, which have only gradually been converted to pensions. These systems, however, usually exist only among the larger firms. In 1967, fewer than half of the firms with thirty to ninety-nine employes had a retirement payment scheme (*Japan Labor Bulletin*, Oct. 1967). Presumably the percentage of those with fewer than thirty was even less. Therefore, the spread of uniform retirement pay systems into small and medium firms has been relatively recent, and the sums provided are far short of needs for minimum living standards. Retired workers seeking employment tend to be in the unemployed and underemployed ranks for long periods of time and therefore may comprise the bulk of the statistically unemployed. If reemployed, the retired worker is likely to be a temporary or casual employe, at a wage far below what he had received before retirement.

Actual working hours (exclusive of commuting) in industrial and business establishments averaged, from 1923 to the end of the Pacific War, 250 to 260 hours per month, the highest among all industrial nations during that period. In 1945 the Labor Standards Law officially reduced workers hours to 48 per week, or 192 per month, beyond which overtime pay is required. This law was widely ignored during the period of industrial expansion in the 1950s and 1960s, especially by small-scale firms. Hard work was urged as a national duty. Labor began showing discontent over hours in the mid-1960s, and this, plus labor competition among major industries and demands from younger workers, led to a tendency toward reduction in working hours. By 1970, monthly hours averaged around 185, and the forty-hour or five-day week became a topic of widespread discussion, research, and in an increasing number of cases, actual practice (Keizai Kikakuchō 1972*b*, p. 82, Keizai Kikakuchō 1972*c*, pp. 170-171, 397).

Accident insurance for workers goes back to 1875, though no reasonably adequate program was enacted before the Factory Law of 1912. Most of these early plans were not really insurance, but lump-sum awards paid out of a fund and adjusted to the needs of the particular worker. True premium insurance, with uniform coverage, did not begin until a 1947 law established a national insurance scheme. Merit-ratings were adopted in 1951, and sliding payment scales in 1953. Pensions based on permanent disability came in 1965, and long-term sickness payment in 1969. By 1969, coverage in some form or another was universal for all workers, bringing Japan into conformity with ILO standards adopted in 1952. The law, however, is not portal-to-portal; that is, it does not cover accidents occurring while commuting. Such accidents constituted about 20 percent of all industrial accidents in 1970 (*Japan Labor Bulletin*, June 1971). Between 1955 and 1970, deaths from industrial accidents of all types increased, but injuries have slightly decreased (Rōdōshō 1971). The number of accidents has remained constant, despite intensive safety campaigns. Moreover, worker compensation statistics show a steady rise in the number of certified and paid claims, suggesting the accident rate may be higher than the figures reported by industries.

If there is discontent with wages, benefits, and working hours, there are similar complaints about leisure or discretionary time. In recent years, principally because of the six-day week, workers have averaged only about 70 days off annually—compared to 130 in the United States and 120 in Germany (*Japan Labor Bulletin*, Oct. 1971). In small firms the number was much less, probably about 50, which reverses the situation in most countries, where workers in small companies usually have much more time off than in large (*Japan Labor Bulletin*, Dec. 1972). Annual paid leave in Japan was about 6.5 days, against 14 in the United States and 15 in West Germany (Keizai Kikakuchō 1972*b*, p. 107). Although through the 1960s there was a trend toward shorter working hours and more holidays and leave with pay, the Japanese worker was still far short of the standards in most Western industrial countries, and also of some of the European Communist-bloc countries.

Although these facts provide an objective basis for complaints of insufficient discretionary time in an age of supposed affluence, surveys of leisure activities and attitudes have shown only one-fifth of all Japanese workers actually took their paid vacations: 61 percent stated they felt they "did not really need it," and the remainder divided between persons who did not wish to take a vacation while their colleagues had to stay on the job, and those, a minority, who actually did take them; 23 percent used the time for

necessary family purposes, such as illness or weddings, or for personal
business and education (Keizai Kikakuchō 1972b, p. 88). In another survey,
over 50 percent of the respondents stated they used their discretionary time
mainly for "self-improvement"—and the majority of these also emphasized
their desire to find a job with similar self-improvement opportunities, so they
might move to a better position with more leisure potential (Kokumin
Seikatsu Kenkyūjo 1971, p. 227). In other words, the demand for more
leisure time is qualified, for many workers, with a desire for improved
working conditions and wages, which in turn would provide the kind of
discretionary time they seek.

In still other surveys, in which the relative deprivation theme was not
explored, leisure time received low priorities when the informant was asked
to compare it with family needs. For example, less than 10 percent of
summer bonuses was spent on leisure. Respondents emphasized the need to
save money for essential family expenses, such as education and marriage,
retirement, or paying off debts (*Japan Labor Bulletin*, Oct. 1971). These
findings should be considered in the context of the data summarized earlier
concerning low social security and pension payments.

However, some leisure activities reflect the changing patterns of an
industrial society. Traditional pursuits, such as shrine pilgrimages, have been
giving way to more individualized or familial activities involving automobiles,
media, sports, weekend travel, concerts, and the like (Keizai Kikakuchō
1972b, p. 104). Studies of travel and recreation made by the Japan Travel
Bureau also show these trends: the increases between 1964 and 1970 were in
relatively passive pursuits, such as casual driving on weekends and simple
sightseeing in nearby localities. Pursuits requiring more careful planning, such
as long-distance travel or formalized sports, either declined or did not
increase. The pattern suggests a turn toward less expensive activities as well as
the use of family cars (Kankyōchō 1972b).

Even more striking is the fact 42 percent of all leisure time in Japan is spent
watching television (against 25 percent in the United States and 17 percent in
West Germany) (*Japan Labor Bulletin*, Nov. 1971). Despite a good deal of
traveling and its consequent pressure on public facilities, most leisure time is
spent at home. The expression *mai hōmu shugi* (my-homeism), although
usually referring to giving priority to family recreation over work, also
includes this type of passive leisure. These constrained patterns are
explainable in part by shortages of facilities: Tokyo has only 0.89 square
meters of park space per capita, against 19 in the four largest United States
cities, and 14.4 in West Berlin. Of a total of 18,563 gymnasiums in Japan,
only 357 were open to the public in 1971, and 80 percent of all sports clubs
outside schools were located in company offices or factories. Of 8897
swimming pools, only 729 were public; there are only 7771 public libraries
(one for every 125,230 persons), 237 cultural halls, and 123 art museums.
These restricted facilities help explain the popularity of such pastimes as
pachinko and mahjong. The *Japan Labor Bulletin* (Nov. 1971) saw this as a

"poverty of leisure"—the mark of "an administered society overly committed to industrialism and the market economy."[15]

Summarizing the relative gains and deprivations of industrial labor, the following can be said: 1. The consumption position of the employed worker has shown steady gains since the late 1950s, but in comparison with other industrial countries, especially the North American and Western European, is still behind. 2. Financial security remains a major problem, due to inflation, inadequate savings, early retirement, and weak social security. This is reflected both in households where illness or accident has incapacitated the breadwinner, and in retirement. Great differences in these respects exist between employes of large and small companies. 3. Working hours, while shortening, are still long in comparison with those of other countries. The general living environment, especially in the large cities, has continued to deteriorate; difficulties in housing, commuting, and related problems have been a source of increasing concern. 4. Demand for leisure is on the rise, although constrained by social pressures and financial needs. What there is, moreover, tends to be unsatisfying because of lack of facilities. The worker's position relative to that in other advanced economies, and the fact that the GNP per capita exceeds that of several European countries, are widely disseminated facts in Japan.

We turn now to the question of how the employed sector of the Japanese population views its relative position in the nation. Is the industrial labor force still willing to accept modest rewards for hard work in the cause of Japan's economic greatness? Or put another way, what are the expressed attitudes toward deprivation?

We shall consider the problem in two ways: first, as a matter of changing attitudes of satisfaction and dissatisfaction with working conditions and the general level of living; and second, as a possible change in the values embodied in the phrase "work ethic," and in concepts of leisure. Discussion of the work ethic has been ubiquitous in the media and professional circles. Some observers allege the miracle of growth at all stages of Japan's industrialization

---

[15]Women's leisure activities in Japan have diverged increasingly from men's. Surveys show women depend more on each other to help them spend their time; are more likely to engage in spectator sports than men; are more concerned than men with the self-improvement concept still important in Japanese leisure, despite changes away from it in recent years; are more inclined to develop circles of like-minded women to engage in activities in homes (flower arrangement and language learning are very popular); and are more inclined to "worry about something else" while engaged in leisure activities (*Keizai Kikakuchō* 1971a, p. 225). Tsurumi (1970) interprets such develops in female society in part as stimulated by back-flowing socialization from children educated in modern schools. The influence is felt principally by mothers, as they spend far more time than fathers with the children and remain primarily agents of child socialization. Tsurumi states also that in some respects, especially in white-collar and blue-collar wage-earning families, women may be more aware of social problems and issues than their husbands.

was made possible by an obedient, hard-working labor force, willing to work for delayed gains and to suffer private costs in order to advance Japan's international prestige and power. The possibility this ethic is changing alarms those who have believed Japan's economic success rests fundamentally on a homogeneous social structure.

To examine the problem, we have available attitude surveys on the same topics made at regular intervals, sometimes by the same agency with the same questions and sampling techniques. Perhaps the most generalized indication of rising expectations in an industrializing society, with high levels of education and increasing sophistication, is the individual's perception of his class position. The Japanese population displays a pattern common to all developed nations: a steady increase in the perception of membership in the middle segment of the society. In a survey taken in 1958, and again in 1969, in which respondents were asked what class they considered themselves belonging to, the percentages saying middle class moved from 72 percent in 1958 to 89 percent in 1969 (Kokumin Seikatsu Shingikai 1970). Breakdowns by income and education yielded the expected results: the percentage of middle class has increased in the lower income group as education has moved upward through the population, making part of the difference in the two surveys attributable to actual changes in life chances.

Also to be considered is the general level of satisfaction with present conditions of life among employed persons. A national sample survey of managerial, white-collar, and blue-collar workers made in 1971 showed blue-collar workers were the least satisfied of all employes—the order was the same as the listing of types of workers, with the white-collar group in the middle of all opinion distributions (very satisfied, satisfied, unsatisfied, very unsatisfied). The percentage of blue-collar workers who were unsatisfied was double that of managerial. At the same time, the percentages of very satisfied and very unsatisfied were quite small in all categories of workers, although with the same pattern of rise and fall from managerial to blue collar (Sōrifu, p. 133; Kokumin Seikatsu Kenkyūjo 1970, pp. 154, 307-308).

Turning to satisfaction-dissatisfaction with present job, the data show comparable results: as in the case of current income the most dissatisfied are the young manual wage-workers; the white-collar segment shows considerable dissatisfaction but less so; and the managerial and executive groups are the most satisfied. In one survey, the same agency asked what kind of jobs they would prefer, if they could choose: 44 percent of all respondents selected jobs "suited to their personality," and another 25 percent opted for an "interesting" job. In another survey taken in 1969 which asked respondents for the major causes of their dissatisfaction with life, wages, and the nature of the job ranked highest (32 and 30 percent, respectively), with "too long" hours and "unsatisfactory" human relationships on the job each yielding 19 percent (Sōrifu 1970a, p. 162).

Putting various findings together, we note the group in Japan least articulately satisfied with present income and job is the young industrial wage-workers. The older people, who have been seriously disadvantaged by the pattern of industrial growth and who are an increasing proportion of the population, show, at least in surveys, less dissatisfaction than might be predicted on the basis of their real-wage position, although their dissatisfaction did begin to increase in the early 1970s. This group, it should be noted, was socialized in the loyalty-consensus atmosphere and school system of prewar Japan and are less inclined to make their feelings of dissatisfaction, if they have them, public. Also, as is well known everywhere, the gap between aspiration and achievement tends to decline with age; Japan does not appear to be an exception.

The next problem is to see if these changing attitudes toward income and the job situation have been accompanied or caused also by a change in the concept of work. The standard hypothesis is that as industrialization becomes a completed and institutionalized system, and a new generation of workers moves into job markets, the classical loyalty and dedication of the Japanese wage-worker—and in many respects, his salaried white-collar cousin—will give way to an allegedly common Western attitude: work is something you have to do, but should not interfere with the fulfillment of personal goals. This hypothesis has been widely accepted already by various spokesmen for Japanese business and industry.[16] There is a note of regret in this type of literature for the good old days when labor was presumably willing to put in long hours for small rewards. However, the question of whether labor is willing to work hard, and the question of the rewards they might demand, are to some extent separate issues.

The results of several surveys showed an increasing number of respondents from the late 1960s to the early 1970s felt they were working too many hours, or not getting enough leisure—this was also the most common complaint about living conditions in general. In one survey, a plurality of over 30 percent felt they were not getting enough money to do what they wanted (Sōrifu, 1970a, p. 162). In earlier years the balance was tipped toward money rather than working hours. In 1966 and 1968 surveys showed about 30 percent were still willing to reduce their leisure time and work longer in order to get more money. (This appears to be confirmed in labor statistics by relatively large amounts of overtime.) However, by 1968 this percentage had become smaller, suggesting the balance began shifting toward leisure. People were willing to accept their present income if an increase required longer working hours.

A related issue concerns what people do with their wages, in particular, incentive, overtime, or bonus pay increments which constitute from 3 to 23 percent of the total wage in Japan (as against 1 to 3 percent in the United States). Recent surveys found around 30 percent of the respondents spent their bonus money, usually on leisure and consumer goods, and over 50 percent put the money into savings. However, the age differential was once more apparent: around 40 percent of the spenders were in their twenties (Kokumin Seikatsu Kenkyūjo 1971, p. 157).

[16]See, for example, an address of the president of Nissan Motors (*Japan Report*, 1 Apr. 1973).

The survey data show no evidence Japanese workers were alienated from work as such. There is no reason to believe the decline of the traditional work ethic, if it ever existed, means a loss of willingness to work, or the emergence of the attitude that society owes me a living. However, there is evidence workers want to exercise more choice over their job; are more concerned over wages, hours, and working conditions; and want jobs offering more self-fulfilling experiences. This suggests they are inclined to see work less as a responsibility or patriotic duty, and more as a pragmatic undertaking required for survival, and for getting the things they want in life. The attitudes summarized are more prominent in the younger employe population—those in their late teens and twenties, the MacArthur generation come of age. In general, work attitudes no longer appear to differ substantially from those of other industrialized nations.

The study of national social trends also confirms the Japanese are not inclined to consider leisure as a way of escaping from work, but rather as an overdue reward for a quarter-century of hard work and as a means of enjoying their increasing wages. The results display a seemingly contradictory pattern: many persons do not take all the vacation time available to them, while they also express sentiments favorable to increased free time to do the things they wish. They are under social pressure to work hard and not disgrace their teammates, family, or employer, while at the same time they want to obtain more of the benefits of the affluent society (Keizai Kikakuchō 1972b).

The same report also reviews data showing the chief problem in the leisure sphere is not the relative scarity of facilities or money (increasingly available as wages have risen) but time: "This creates a vicious cycle: people tend to work longer for more money or for promotion in order to get higher salary, reducing their leisure time, thus they must rush into leisure activities in a short time, pushing the cost of leisure higher" (Keizai Kikakuchō, 1972b, p. 106).

INSTITUTIONAL CHANGE IN POSTINDUSTRIAL JAPAN

Consequences of industrialization in present-day Japan associated with the welfare gap, environmental pollution, population density and urbanization, and conditions of work and leisure raise an important issue: has the emergence of deprivations cutting through sections of the population changed Japan irrevocably? Is this a temporary rise in public dissatisfaction, or a fundamental change in the national polity?

Our position is that the developments of the late 1960s and early 1970s signify a fundamental social change. The policy of unrestricted economic growth followed for the past century is terminating, and the next quarter century will find Japan—like other hyperdeveloped industrial nations—seeking ways to shift priorities. The Japanese leaders say to themselves more definitely than the American, though whether they mean it is another question. But the message seems clear enough: the welfare society and social justice are to replace high economic growth as the primary national goal.

Japan industrialized rapidly, with limited resources and land area. An ambitious and fertile population has pressed continually against these sparse resources, setting the stage for rationalization of overseas adventures as well as intensive domestic economic growth. A high level of literacy furnished the public with abundant information on Japan's relative position among the nations; the competitive spirit this fostered, or simply reinforced, has been another spur toward rapid and decisive industrialization. All of these processes have been under way in the past century; all of them reached unprecedented levels in the post-Pacific War period. In a period of approximately thirty years, the Japanese moved from an oligarchic, semitotalitarian, and militarist society, with sharply unequal levels of living, to a society with many of the "open" characteristics of Euro-American countries: flourishing interest and protest groups; strong mass cultural standards of consumption; and increasing demands for social welfare. This transition has come so rapidly that most social scientists, Japanese and Western, have been caught largely unaware, or at least unprepared.

However, this transition may have been more gradual than it seems. The tendencies toward a consumer-oriented and pluralistic system were visible by the 1920s, and although the militarist regime managed to control most of these, the society had begun to make the accommodation that was then resumed in the Occupation and during the 1950s. Preoccupied with the exotic social microstructure, and with the issue (received from Weberian and Parsonian sociology) of whether or not a non-Western nation could industrialize along Western lines, social scientists failed, in large part, to perceive Japan was taking the same course every other industrial society had taken. For example, the growth of the labor movement tended to be discounted: the focus of attention was on the fact that labor organization was different from that of the West. But it turns out the difference was due in large part to government policy, or to the adaptive skills of labor itself, which was willing to roll with the constraints and bide its time. And of course the Occupation was a cataclysmic event.

We have engaged this process of rapid economic and social change at a particular level: the emergence of public grievances associated with economic growth, which can be considered the consequences of industrial and urban transformation with social costs unaccounted for. These grievances, or deprivations as we have called them, have a distinctive meaning in Japan as in other countries, for they tend to cut across groupings and strata, however defined. Although some are confined to particular groups in the population, most of the others are transgroup; and even the former tend to reflect probably temporary confinement to special segments. For example, although the aged in the labor force have probably fared worse than other age groups, a turn of the wheel might shift the deprivation toward others in a short time. The rapidly accumulating and shifting deprivations we have described are, on the whole, a new phenomenon in history insofar as they affect larger numbers and involve grievances other than, or in addition to, the old issues of class exploitation. Perhaps environmental disruption is the most typical example.

These issues have another general characteristic: they have tended to represent bearable costs in all industrial countries until quite recently. Although they were felt by the public throughout the industrial revolution since the late 18th century; and although overt protest, revolt, and subsequent amelioration and reform proceeded at intervals in all industrializing societies, on the whole the public has been willing to put up with discomforts and insecurities for long periods because the promised rewards seemed to outweigh the punishments. Various countries have of course shown different degrees of tolerance: it is quite possible in many respects the Japanese, for example, are more tolerant of urban congestion than others, due to certain features of the social microstructure. But it is now clear even the Japanese have their limits. Or it may be simply that ideological and value changes have shortened the reaction time to perceived discomforts: if world opinion says we are crowded, then we shall feel crowded. Such effects simply cannot be discounted; they are an inherent and vital part of the process we have proposed and described.

The public response to these problems has been interpreted by social historians influenced by the Marxist tradition as class struggle—in extreme cases, revolution, or in very general terms as the interplay between left and right. These interpretations persist in scholarly work as well as the communication media of all industrial countries, and of course they contain an element of truth. However, while acknowledging this historic class division of industrial society, and also the meaningfulness of left-right ideological division, we nevertheless are inclined to see the emergence of the welfare gap and associated problems in Japan, as elsewhere, as the dawn of a new political era. This has been widely interpreted as the postindustrial society.

The characteristics of the postindustrial society, as we define it, are as follows: (1) the cross-social-group nature of many deprivations; (2) loss of faith in the doctrine of progress and in the automatic benefits of industrialization and urbanization generally, but desire to maintain a high level of living nevertheless; (3) increased tendencies for citizens to form combinations along special-interest lines which also cut across old class divisions and traditional community entities; (4) the increase in public protest and citizen action against perceived threats and deprivations, especially those associated with growth, inflation, and the like; (5) increased resort to the courts and the legal system to make wants and demands effective; and (6) a decline of interest in the standard democratic political apparatus of parties and elections.

The changed climate of opinion has another distinctive trait: although the sense of deprivation is sharp, at the same time there is no strong evidence of a desire to relinquish the gains already made. Several examples of this mood were alluded to in our review of the data. One concerns the automobile: while the Japanese city-dweller is concerned about the air pollution caused by the internal combustion engine, there is at the same time a demand for the automobile as a symbol of the social minimum—that basic consumption level considered a right and necessity. A second example is more complex and concerns the demand for leisure. We noted the demand for leisure increases the prices of limited leisure facilities. As these prices rise, the worker demands higher wages, which until recently has meant working long hours, which in turn cuts into leisure time, or forces people to indulge en masse in recreation on weekends, further straining the facilities and driving prices upward. Thus, while the citizen wants more leisure and complains of its scarcity, his very demands create the conditions which tend to deny it to him. And of course although the urban environment generally, despite its dense crowds and inaccessibility to facilities, seems to be responsible for mounting frustration, the amusements and excitement of city life continue to attract large numbers of country and small-town people. Congestion of population and housing shortages are still other examples of the huge demands on limited resources. The deprivations are not industrialism and urbanism in toto, but certain conditions they have created. What is significant here are not the contradictions of the attitudes and behavior, but that deprivations have become part of a political climate: elections can be fought on these issues, and politicians must declare themselves.

Yet these issues, and the politicians who must deal with them, are themselves part of an even larger contradiction: increasing political participation on the one hand, and the decline of party identification and loyalty on the other. The situation closely resembles that in the United States: evidence of mounting government and business corruption, or at least increasing awareness of such corruption, coupled with growing doubts of the virtues of the industrial system, have led to intensified political activity on the part of citizens, and also a widespread desertion of the regular parties. In Japan, the deserters are called *datsu seitō* (party leavers); in 1973 they accounted for over one-third of the electorate. The largest proportions of these were concentrated in the cities, where the effects of industrialization and population density have been the most severe (*Asahi*, 26 June 1971; 8 and 9 Dec. 1972). Analyses of electoral data seem to show the party-leaver vote consists of opposition to the regular parties, their platforms, and candidates who seem not to grasp the significance of the new national issues.

Tsurutani (1972) attributes the victory of a progressive candidate, supported by the Communists, Socialists, and independents, in the 1972 Tokyo gubernatorial election to this phenomenon. He also points out not even the countryside is safe for the parties: both the Liberal Democratic Party and the left-wing parties have lost ground in rural areas; and although the datsu seitō have been fewer in the country than in the cities, they are still nearly a third of the electorate there. He interprets the phenomenon largely as the consequence of urban sprawl: industrial and transportation complexes are spreading into the country along with air and water pollution.

The other side of the political profile is the citizen action groups we described, especially in the environmental field. These movements seem motivated by the distrust of the orthodox parties already noted, plus frustration at the mounting issues for which the politicians and business spokesmen often seem to have little more than rhetorical awareness, shown in the case of Fuji city. As in the United States in the late 1960s and early 1970s, such groups have formed around particular irritating issues—air pollution, right to sunshine, new construction, traffic hazards, food labeling, consumer gouging, dangers to children—and usually consist of residents of a particular community, neighborhood, or adjoining country hamlets, not necessarily friends or relatives (*Asahi*, 23 May 1973; Tsurutani 1972). These groups constitute a new element in Japanese social structure which has little in common with the traditional networks beloved of anthropologists.

Although it is too early to be able to say whether new class alignments may be emerging, there is little doubt of the resentments felt by the masses for the business and government elite who upheld the production-first policy without calculating its social effects. The failure of the standard left-wing parties to reap all the benefits of this disaffection testifies to the nature of the dissatisfaction: both the right and the left are seen as agents of industrialization, both agreeing on the basic goals of economic growth, regardless of any disagreement on means. This helps to define the basic nature of the new deprivations: they lead to alienation from the familiar institutions and organizations. The majority of citizens, or at any rate very large pluralities, gradually feel detached from power groups of all ideological colorings, and in various ways and degrees seek to create new forms of political and social participation.

The activities of the citizens' groups are not confined to public demonstrations; they move on into the courts. The increasing use of the legal system for the redress of public grievances in Japan probably relates to two things: the precedents for court action introduced by changes in labor-management relations; and the assumption of judgeships by younger men who were involved in, or sympathetic observers of, student activities in the 1950s. Increased confrontation between labor and management in the 1950s and 1960s caused an array of conciliation machinery to be developed. Designed to supplement union-employer collective bargaining on the traditional model of corporatism at the company level, the hope was to reinforce the enterprise union system and its various cooperative devices. However, the governmental source of these new measures introduced a large public element in the disputes: the third-party intervention principle, with its implication that grievances have a national scope and public legitimacy rather than being merely localized affairs of particular managements and their own employes.

However, these measures did not handle all problems, and labor and management have increasingly resorted to the courts in a general tendency to shift labor-management relations onto a legal plane (Matsuda 1973). A marked step-up in the use of the courts for the resolution of labor-management conflict became noticeable in the mid-1960s, setting the stage for similar use of legal apparatus in litigation of issues concerning pollution and other problems engendered by industry, urbanization, and transportation. The tendency to conceive of grievances as public, national, and adjudicable, and as something not to be borne as the citizen's duty or fate, has been stimulated by many factors. Among these are increasing education and awareness of life styles, and the movement of all life styles toward a new generalized type or social minimum (called, by Hazama in his paper in this volume, the enterprise type).

If the legal system is becoming the bearer of issues which until recently have been thought to belong to the private sphere—from the right to sunshine to labor disputes—then they will have to deal with these in the context of constitutional questions. In simplest terms, the concept of absolute right to this or that, or not to have to be subjected to this or that, underlies most of the deprivation issues—it is this new concept of "right" rather than reciprocal duties and obligations at the personal level that is now spread over the legal scene.

The traditional means of conflict resolution concerning transfers of social costs were particularistic and private, and in labor-management relations the enterprise union was their symbol and embodiment. The system persisted for a long time because it provided cheap social security for some. At least in many large companies, adoption of corporatist welfare devices was a relatively late and conscious event (Sumiya 1963 and Taira 1970). Many of the ideas may have been influenced by experiments with corporate paternalism during the 1920s in the United States (called the American Plan in international management circles). Lacking government-guaranteed security something had to serve the need, and the government's constant propagandizing for the unique Japanese way of doing things, allegedly so superior to the Western in many respects, managed to convince a population, still largely rural in orientation, and with many close ties to the family and village, that these were the only efficient methods.

From a sociological standpoint these changes mean alterations of that segment of the Japanese social structure traditionally concerned with security and life chances. The changes have been a conscious policy as well as the result of powerful economic and ideological forces. Since the end of the Pacific War, the rhetoric of modernization has included the elimination of undemocratic or feudal institutions associated with the recent past and especially the militarist era. The formal step on this road was the revision of the Family Code during the Occupation to eliminate the principle of extended kinship and duty to relatives from the legal system. The acceptance of the United States and high-development national models generally was believed contingent on the elimination of these traditional social features. Although there has been recurrent doubt among Japanese leaders and intellectuals concerning this policy, it has had its effects on the family, the worker-employer relationship, and the structure of the community.

The aggressive development of an urban wage-earning population, and the flight of country people to the city, has helped to further loosen the bonds of extended kinship which were still widespread at the beginning of the Occupation despite slow attenuation under the impact of modernization beginning in the late 19th century. The system of relying on relatives and community networks for security and protection served the Japanese well during the bombing and fires of the wartime period, just as it gave employment to permanent workers and security for the aged in a population unprotected by government or private pensions during an era of production-first economic growth policy. Such privatized systems of security have their defects, but they also have advantages: they make do with a very small overhead investment for social security; and the system operates on the basis of favorable sentiments and thereby makes allowances for privation and uncertainty.

Two questions arise. If Japan had to pass through another period of either war or economic depression, one wonders if the withering of these privatized security systems would be viewed as a good thing. The second question concerns their relative effectiveness in an age of high industrialization. We have already offered conclusions on the second point: although they were maintained intact down to the Pacific War, in the period of intense economic growth after the war they failed at an accelerating rate to meet a number of adverse consequences of industrialization, leaving large segments of the labor force poorly protected against unemployment, retirement, health hazards, congestion, and poor housing. The sheer number of persons involved in industry, and the disruption of kin and community ties resulting from migration and urbanization—not to mention changed beliefs and expectations—put a severe strain on the traditional system.

Therefore, government has had to step in, and as it has done so the fate of the old system has become doubtful. But if the attenuation or elimination of privatized social security or particularistic worker-employer relations should leave Japan in serious straits at some future date, the change can be considered one of the major social consequences of Japanese-style production-first industrialization because of the failure to develop adequate alternatives to replace them.

The orientation of most writings on Japanese social change in the modern era has been toward the order, stability, and conformity of the population in the face of rapid transformation of the economy and formal structure of the society that we called quiescence. The accepted explanations of this phenomenon have featured interpretations of the microsocial structure of cooperation based on a hierarchal social structure, and a consensus between the establishment and the masses: an agreement to accept differential status as a duty; a basic level of living in return for loyalty; and an obedient political posture on the part of the population allowing the oligarchy to proceed with its plans of economic development and overseas expansion.

In the economic sphere, a major symbol of consensus was the persistence of dualism (see Yasuba's chapter in this volume) or differential structure. This much-debated arrangement concerns the division of the production function in a modernizing society into a high-technology, high-production sector and a personalized, family-controlled, low-technology sphere of small shops and craft industries. The former requires social organization of the Western type, emphasizing rationality and universalism; the latter operates with the patterns of a preindustrial or status-oriented social system. This implies income inequality between the two sectors and therefore the problem in dualistic economic theory is basically sociopsychological or political: when will the members of the traditional sector begin to feel they are receiving less than their labor is worth, or that the social-emotional rewards of working at home for modest returns are no longer a good trade-off for higher wages and the anonymity of the factory?

However, the distinctive feature of dualism in Japan, as compared with other modernizing countries, was the growing and considerable integration between the two sectors. The traditional sector performed many economic subcontracting and assembly tasks for the advanced industrial sector, and the small retail and wholesale businesses became thoroughly adapted to the distributional needs of an urbanized society—as, indeed, they already had been in the preindustrial but still relatively urbanized Japan. In contrast to most other developing countries, Japan managed to maintain economic (as well as social welfare) institutions of a traditional origin which would guarantee a basic level of security in the midst of transformation of the rest of the system. One of the cultural values assisting in this process was the famous Japanese esthetic austerity pattern, which defined simple living as appropriate and good. There is no doubt this concept, and its propagandistic support, helped suppress a consciousness of poverty in various groups and therefore helped delay the development of high expectations and consequent deprivation.

Here, again, one can raise questions about the disappearance of useful arts. The tension between a cautious, conservative, pragmatic approach to modernization and a liberal, equity-oriented view is clear: the former is inclined to say the Japanese have lost a useful facility in their ability to accept less and like it; whereas the liberal critic says that as the old institutions are no longer effective, the government must step in and create a welfare state on the ruins of the communal society, and the consequences must be borne. Whatever the answer, the observer must record that social change has left Japan without certain social devices she possessed in the past, and this adaptive step will surely have its consequences for future problems and decisions. Such is the nature of growth and change: present solutions beget future problems.

And so back to the concept of rights. Are the Japanese replacing the duty-obligation configuration which served them well during the transition to modernism with a different conception of the role of the citizen and government? We believe this is the case, granting a degree of confusion and certainly contrasting evidence at different levels in the social structure. We leave that to the specialists; for our purposes it is clear enough Japanese citizens are beginning to claim things because they think it is their right to have them. In our view Japan's feudal-like system is in its final stages of liquidation and change. The microsocial level, which survived the Meiji Restoration largely intact because the elite used it as an instrument of adaptation, now has begun to wither under the impact of rising levels of education, economic growth, spreading felt deprivation, the emergence of a consciousness of individual rights, and the notion industrial society must provide the citizen with basic security.

REFERENCES

Aoki, Kōji. 1967. *Meiji Nōmin Sōjō no Nenjiteki Kenkyū*. Shineisha.
          . 1968. *Nihon Rōdō Undōshi Nenpyō Dai 1-kan, Meiji Taishō Hen*. Shinseisha.
          . 1971. *Hyakusho Ikki Sōgo Nenpyō*. Sanichi Shobo.
Asahi Shimbun. 26 June 1971. 8 Dec. 1972. 9 Dec. 1972. 22 April 1973. 23 May 1973.
Bennett, John W. 1967. "Japanese Economic Growth: Background for Social Change." In *Aspects of Social Change in Modern Japan*, edited by Ronald P. Dore. Princeton University Press.
Dore, Ronald P. 1958. *City Life in Japan: A Study of a Tokyo Ward*. University of California Press.
Edelman, Murray. 1964. *The Symbolic Uses of Politics*. University of Illinois Press.
Eto, Jun. 1965. "Old America and New Japan." *Journal of Social and Political Ideas in Japan*, vol. 3, no. 2 (Aug. 1965), pp. 72-74.
Fisher, Paul. 1973. "Major Social Security Issues: Japan, 1972." *Social Security Bulletin*, vol. 36, no. 3 (March 1973), pp. 26-38.
Gallagher, Charles F. 1973. *The Environment in Japan*. American Universities Field Staff. Asia Series, vol. 20, no. 2.
Government of Japan. 1971. *Problems of the Human Environment in Japan*.
Hanayama, Yuzuro. 1972. "Urban Land Prices and the Housing Problem." *The Developing Economies* 10 (Dec. 1972):468-478.
Hayashi, Yujiro. 1970. *Perspectives on Post-Industrial Society*. University of Tokyo Press.
Hazama, Hiroshi. 1960. "Keiei Kazokushugi no Ronri to Sono Keisei Katei." *Shakai Gaku Hyōron* 2 (July 1960).
Hirschman, Albert O., and Michael Rothschild. 1973. "The Changing Tolerance for Income Inequality in the Course of Economic Development." *The Quarterly Journal of Economics* 87 (Nov. 1973).
ILO [International Labour Organization]. 1971. *Yearbook of Labor Statistics*.
          . 1972. *The Cost of Social Security*.
Ishida, Takeshi. 1966. "Nihon ni Okeru Toshika to Seiji." *Shisō* 510 (Dec. 1966).
Japan Labor Bulletin. Japan Institute of Labor. April 1965, Oct. 1967, June 1971, Oct. 1971, Nov. 1971, Nov. 1972, Dec. 1972, Jan. 1973, Aug. 1973, May 1974.
Japan Report. Japan Information Service, Consulate General of New York. 1 April 1973; 1 Nov. 1973; 1 Jan. 1974; 1 Feb. 1974.
Kankyōchō [Environment Agency]. 1971. *White Paper on Pollution in Japan*.

. 1972a. Air Pollution Control in Japan.
. 1972b. Kankyō Hakusho: 1972. (1972 White paper on the Environment.)
. 1972c. Pollution-Related Diseases and Their Control in Japan.
. 1972d. Water Pollution Control in Japan.
. 1972e. Quality of the Environment in Japan.
Keizai Kikaku-chō [Economic Planning Agency]. 1971, 1972a, 1973. Keizai Shakai Kihon Keikaku. (Basin Plan for Social and Economic Development.)
. 1971a. Kokumin Seikatsu Hakusho 1971. (White Paper on National Livelihood.)
. 1972b. The Japanese and Their Society. Part 2 of the Report on National Life 1972. (English version of Kokumin Seikatsu Hakusho below.)
. 1972c. Kokumin Seikatsu Hakusho 1972.
. 1972d. Shōhi To Chochiku no Dōkō.
Keizai Kikaku-chō and the Japan Times, Ltd. 1972e. Economic Survey of Japan: 1971-1972.
Keizai Shingikai, Shigen Kenkyū Iinkai [Economic Council, Committee on Resources Research]. 1969. Kokusai Jidai no Shigen Mondai.
Keizai Shingikai, NNW Kaihatsu Iinkai [Economic Council, NNW Measurement Committee]. 1973. Atarashii Fukushi Shihyō: NNW. [Translated into English in 1974 as Measuring Net National Welfare.]
Kokumin Seikatsu Kenkyūjo [Institute for the Study of National Life]. 1971. Nihonjin no Seikatsu Ishiki.
Kokumin Seikatsu Shingikai [Deliberation Committee on National Life]. 1969. Shōrai no Kokumin Seikatsu Zō.
. 1970. Ningen Kankyō Seibi e no Shishin.
Kokumin Seikatsu Shingikai Chōsakai [Deliberation Committee of the Survey Agency for National Life]. 1969. Komunite: Seikatsu no Ba ni Akeru: Ningensei no Kaifuka.
Kōseishō [Ministry of Welfare]. 1971. Current Level of Nutrition for the Japanese People. Daiichi Shuppan.
. 1972. Kōsei Hakusho 1972.
Koshiro, Kazutoshi. 1973. Trade Unions and Industrial Pollution in Japan. Japan Labor Bulletin, vol. 12, no. 8 (Aug. 1973), pp. 5-8.
Lerner, Daniel. 1958. The Passing of Traditional Society: Modernizing the Middle East. Free Press.
Levine, Solomon B. 1958. Industrial Relations in Postwar Japan. University of Illinois Press.
Maruyama, Masao. 1963. Thought and Behavior in Modern Japanese Politics. Oxford University Press.
Matsuda, Yasuhiko. 1973. "Judicial Procedure in Labor Disputes in Japan." Japan Labor Bulletin 12, May 1973, pp. 4-8, and June 1973, pp. 5-8.
Meier, Richard (with Ikumi Hoshino). 1967. "Notes on the Creation of an Efficient Megalopolis." Ekistics 23:294-307.
Mita, Munesuke. 1967. Patterns of Alientation in Contemporary Japan. Journal of Social and Political Ideas in Japan 5 (Dec. 1967):139-178.
Mombushō [Ministry of Education]. 1971. Education in Japan.
Morioka, Kiyomi. 1973. "Kazokushugi Ron Kara Mita Rōjin." In Rōjin to Kazoku no Shakaigaku, edited by Sōichi Nasu and Kōkichi Masuda. Kakiuchi Shuppan.

Morley, James, ed. 1974. *Prologue to the Future: United States and Japan in the Post-Industrial Age*. Lexington.

Nagai, Michio. 1964. *Nihon no Daigaku*. Chūōkōronsha.

Nakamura, Hajime. 1966. "Modern Trend in Religious Thoughts." In *The Modernization of Japan*, edited by Seiichi Tohata. Maruzen.

Nakanishi, Hideo, and Tsutomu Yamaguchi. 1974. "Pollution." *Japanese Economic Studies*, vol. 2, no. 4 (summer 1974), pp. 62-91.

Nihon Ginkō [Bank of Japan]. 1971. *Kokusai Hikaku Tōkei*.

Nōrinshō [Ministry of Agriculture and Forestry]. 1972. *White Paper on Fisheries*.

OECD [Organization for Economic Cooperation and Development]. 1972. *1972 OECD Economic Surveys: Japan*.

Oikawa, Hiroshi. 1973. "Kakukazoku Gainen to Shūsei Gainen." *Meiji Gakuin Ronsō* 211.

Okamoto, Hideaki. 1972. "Industrialization: Environment and Anti-Pollution Movements: A Case." *Japan Labor Bulletin*, vol. 11, no. 7 (Nov. 1972), pp. 4-12.

Okochi, Kazuo, Bernard Karsh, and Solomon B. Levine, eds. 1973. *Workers and Employers in Japan: The Japanese Employment Relations System*. Princeton University Press.

Passin, Herbert. 1962. "The New Japan: Prospects and Promise." Paper delivered at the fifty-first meeting of the Princeton University Conference. Litho.

Pyle, Kenneth D. 1973. "The Technology of Japanese Nationalism: The Local Improvement Movement: 1900-1918." *Journal of Asian Studies* 33 (Nov. 1973):51-66.

Rōdōshō [Ministry of Labor]. 1970. *Survey of Employment Trends*.

——. 1971. *Annual Report on Worker Injuries and Deaths, 1955-1970*.

Sangyō Keikaku Konwakai [Industry Planning Discussion Group]. 1973. "Teigen: Sangyō Kōzō no Kaikaku-Kōgai to Shigen wo Chūshin ni." *Ekonomisuto*, April 1973, pp. 105-122.

Silberman, Bernard S., and Harry D. Harootunian, eds. 1974. *Japan in Crisis: Essays on Taishō Democracy*. Princeton University Press.

Sōrifu [Office of the Prime Minister]. 1961. *Public Opinion Surveys in Japan, 1959-1960*.

——. 1970*a*. *Seishōnen Hakusho*.

Sōrifu, Tōkei-kyoku (Statistics Bureau). 1971. *Annual Report on the Family Income and Expenditure Survey, 1960-70*.

——. *Japan Statistical Yearbook*. Annual issues for 1949, 1950, 1961, 1966, 1971.

Staaf, Robert, and Francis X. Tannian. 1973. *Externalities: Theoretical Dimensions of Political Economy*. Dunellen Publishing and Kennikut Press.

Sumiya, Mikio. 1963. *Social Impact of Industrialization in Japan*. Japanese National Commission for UNESCO.

Suzuki, Eitaro. 1957. *Toshi Shakaigaku Genri*. Yuhikaku.

Suzuki, Shigenobu. 1965. "Education in Japan: A Disregard for Tradition and Human Nature." *Journal of Social and Political Ideas in Japan*, vol. 3, no. 2 (Aug. 1965), pp. 83-85.

Suzuki, Tatsuzo. 1970. "A Study of the National Japanese Character."

Annals of the Institute of Statistical Mathematics. Part 4, Fourth Nation-wide Survey, supplement 6.

———. 1974. "Changing Japanese Values: An Analysis of National Surveys." In *Prologue to the Future: United States and Japan in the Post-Industrial Age*, edited by James Morley. Lexington.

Taira, Koji. 1970. *Economic Development and the Labor Market in Japan.* Columbia University Press.

Thurston, Donald R. 1974. "Aftermath in Minamata." In *The Japan Interpreter*, vol. 9, no. 1 (spring 1974), pp. 25-42.

Tominaga, Ken'ichi. 1974. "An Approach to the Measurement of the Levels of Welfare in Tokyo." In *Prologue to the Future: United States and Japan in the Post-Industrial Age*, edited by James W. Morley. Lexington.

Tsuru, Shigeto. 1970. "Environment Disruption." In *Asahi Evening News*.

Tsurumi, Kazuko. 1970. *Social Change and the Individual: Japan before and after Defeat in World War II.* Princeton University Press.

Tsurutani, Taketsugu. 1972. "A New Era of Japanese Politics: Tokyo's Gubernatorial Election." *Asian Survey* 12 (May 1972):429-443.

Tsūsanshō, Yoka Kaihatsu Sangyō Shitsu [Ministry of International Trade and Industry, Office for the Leisure Development Industry]. 1973. *Waga Kuni Yoka no Genjō to Yoka e no Tembō.*

Umetani, Shunichiro. 1973. "The Life of the Japanese Worker." In *Japan Labor Bulletin*, vol. 12, no. 1 (Jan. 1973), pp. 5-6.

Uni, Jun, ed. 1972. *Polluted Japan: Reports by Members of the Jishu-Kōza Citizen's Movement.* Jishu-Kōza.

United Nations. 1971. *United Nations Statistical Yearbook*, vol. 3.

———. 1973. *Yearbook of National Account Statistics.*

Uzawa, Hirofumi. 1974. "The Transition to a Welfare Economy in Japan." *Prologue to the Future: United States and Japan in the Post-Industrial Age*, edited by James W. Morley. Lexington.

Vogel, Ezra. 1963. *Japan's New Middle Class.* University of California Press.

White, James. 1970. *Sōka Gakkai and the Mass Society.* Stanford University Press.

———. 1972. "Political Implications of Cityward Migration in Japan." Mimeo. Department of Political Science, University of North Carolina, Chapel Hill.

Yazaki, Takeo. 1968. *Social Change and the City in Japan.* Japan Publications.

Zen Nihon Rōdō Sōdōmei (Dōmei) [Japanese Confederation of Labor]. 1972. *Welfare Indicators of Workers.*

Index

Note: This index includes all information
contained in figures and tables as well as
textual references.

493